# FAMILY LIFE
# IN THE
# SEVENTEENTH CENTURY

# FAMILY LIFE IN THE SEVENTEENTH CENTURY

## The Verneys of Claydon House

Miriam Slater

ROUTLEDGE & KEGAN PAUL
London, Boston, Melbourne and Henley

*First published in 1984*
*by Routledge & Kegan Paul plc*
*39 Store Street, London WC1E 7DD, England*
*9 Park Street, Boston, Mass. 02108, USA*
*464 St Kilda Road,*
*Melbourne, Victoria 3004, Australia*
*Broadway House, Newtown Road,*
*Henley-on-Thames, Oxon RG9 1EN, England*
*Printed in Great Britain by St Edmundsbury Press, Suffolk*


*Library of Congress Cataloging in Publication Data*

*Slater, Miriam, 1931–*
*Family life in the seventeenth century.*
*Bibliography: p.*
*Includes index.*
*1. Verney family. 2. Family–England–History–17th century–Case studies. 3. Marriage–England–History–17th century–Case studies. I. Title. II. Title: Family life in the 17th century.*
*HQ615.S55 1983 306.8'5'0942 83–11181*

*ISBN 0–7100–9477–9*

This book is dedicated to Professor Margaret A. Judson
with gratitude and affection for first introducing me
to the study of history

# CONTENTS

# ACKNOWLEDGMENTS

The process of researching and writing a book is never completed without a good deal of assistance from others, and in this case it would be impossible to list them all or adequately describe my gratitude for their help and support.

I would like to thank the Woodrow Wilson Foundation and especially Dr Hans Rosenhaupt for the financial support which I received at a time when it was not yet fashionable to encourage the scholarly pursuits of married women with children. In addition, I am indebted to Mr Gilbert Verney of New Hampshire, and to Princeton University for their financial assistance; to Major Ralph Verney and Sir Harry Verney of Middle Claydon, England, for the privilege of examining the original letters of the Verney correspondence in their possession.

I am grateful to Professor Marion Levy, Jr, for reading a draft of Chapter 2 and offering many valuable suggestions for its improvement; to Professor T. K. Rabb for his helpful advice and ideas particularly concerning marriage; to my friend and colleague Professor Penina Glazer for reading the chapter on children. I wish also to thank Barbara Rosenau for her valued assistance in preparing the manuscript. I am, of course, responsible for any deficiencies which remain.

Among those who have been most helpful, I would especially like to thank my husband who (in addition to his many other remarkable qualities) was always gracious about the fact of having to live with me as well as all the seventeenth century Verneys during the several years which it took to complete this work. Although one's parents are not normally cited in these acknowledgments, I wish to depart from the usual practice in the special case of my guardians Mr and Mrs Herbert S. Hartzman, to thank them for their encouragement and generosity during my work on this project, and much else besides, since I was 11 years old.

I am most indebted and very grateful to Professor Lawrence Stone, not only for his valuable advice and assistance at every stage of this project, but for his extraordinary generosity, kindness and encouragement, which transformed what might have been a difficult process into an experience of great satisfaction – a kind of sympathetic magic which I hope I bring to my students.

M.S.

# Introduction

# THE VERNEY FAMILY CORRESPONDENCE

The social historian writing on the landed society of seventeenth century England understandably looks with covetous eyes on the informative and significant anthropological studies of the type which Oscar Lewis pioneered. Professor Lewis struck a particularly sympathetic chord when he observed that 'through the intensive analysis of specific families we learn what institutions mean to individuals. It helps us get beyond form and structure to the realities of human life.'[1] More recent studies of family life by behavioral scientists have made it increasingly apparent that the study of individual families can render special insights that otherwise escape us.[2] Professor Habbakkuk, some time ago, made a strong case for a similar approach with the observation that 'The proper unit of study is the individual family; it must be seen from the inside; and the most fruitful path in this field is the detailed study of particular cases, based upon the family documents.'[3]

Moreover, when one casts the questions to include the attitudes and values of the people being studied, then the detailed investigation of specific families becomes an attractive methodology. This approach can provide the historian, as it has the anthropologist, with a manageable unit of study for the researching of this type of question. It can also provide a more intimate knowledge of the mechanisms of social behavior and social change as well as a better understanding of the ways in which the family influences, and is influenced by, the other institutions and forces in the society.

But with what degree of success can this approach be transferred to the study of a family at more than three hundred years remove? In her fondest dreams, the historian imagines the possibility of obtaining the type of evidence which participant observation and the taped interview provide for the anthropologist. In the waking state, however, the open-ended possibilities inherent in these methods are forever closed to the historian. The latter must work with a given body of evidence, which survives into the present more often than not through fortuitous circumstance. This being the case, the evidence available has fixed limitations both in the amount of information which is available to us and the type of question which can reasonably be asked of it.

There is, however, one type of source material which can approximate the fundamental contribution which the taped interview makes to the contemporary family study. A body of private correspondence which is intimate, ample, consecutive, and continuous through several generations could be made to serve the same purposes. If, in addition, the correspondents included members of the conjugal family, a wide variety of other kin, as well as significant members of the whole social scene, this would be a source of insights and information which would come as close as the historian is likely to get to the taped interview.

The Verney Family Papers fulfill these conditions to a degree that may well be without parallel in the early modern period. The complete collection covers a period of several centuries and includes twelve generations of the Verney family in a body of documents that runs to well over 30,000 items.[4] The letters are particularly voluminous and complete for the seventeenth century, and so far as is known, they are the fullest and most continuous collection of this kind of material for seventeenth century England and perhaps in the western world. As such they constitute an extraordinarily valuable source for an intensive study of family life at this time; this case study is based almost exclusively on them.

The sheer volume and range of this remarkable collection might tempt one to ignore the inherent limitations of this type of source. However, the Verney correspondence, like similar collections of documents, though not to the same degree, presents two basic problems to the researcher. The first and most obvious one is that the survival of a body of personal documents depends on a number of factors which are totally unrelated to the interests and requirements of the investigator. Not only has there been random loss by fire, rats, moisture, etc., but the writers also tended not to commit certain types of information to paper. For example, the Verney letters tell little about sexual matters, and rather less than would be desirable about child rearing practices.

The second problem, which is partially related to the first, is that the evidence about family life which the letters do record suffers from a particular type of distortion. It is not so much the case that the life there revealed is seen as through a glass darkly. The more appropriate metaphor which illustrates the historian's difficulty in using private correspondence is that of a person watching a baseball game through a knot-hole in the fence; some of the play can be seen very clearly indeed, but the players on the periphery of one's vision will only be glimpsed and the activities of still others must be guessed at according to the reactions of those who are within the field of vision.

Fortunately, however, the accuracy of the information and the validity of the conclusions which may be drawn from source material suffering from this type of distortion can be considerably improved in a number of ways. Genealogical information can be very useful for ascertaining formal kin relationships, the ages and numbers of children, affine connections, and social status. Biographical dictionaries and college registers, wills and trusts can also provide important checks on internal evidence. Furthermore, where there are a large number of correspondents, as in the case of the Verney letters, the same situation or event or person can be seen in the round from different points of view. This is extremely helpful in establishing the objective facts in cases where interpretations conflict, in improving perspective on the interpersonal relationships within the family, as well as in determining the beliefs and attitudes of its members.

Armed with these correctives, the Verney correspondence can provide an excellent source for an in-depth study of the family. Moreover, the historian using letters as a major source has one unique advantage. The family can be studied in the very process of living and can therefore provide a reconstruction of that life with the dynamic and complex human relationships appropriate to it which are often lacking in the statistical analyses which can be constructed from tax lists, probate records, inventories, and the like.

This study focuses on only three generations of the Verney

family, covering a period of little less than half a century, while the bulk of the evidence used is still further restricted to about twenty years. It therefore cannot, and is not intended to, throw light upon possible secular changes in the family as an institution. Valid generalizations of that kind require, at a minimum, a much greater time span and a larger sample of families. However, the relatively narrow scope of the present work is especially appropriate to the detailed examination of a different set of problems. A lens of higher intensity on a more limited area allows a sharper focus on interpersonal relationships, values, and attitudes, and permits an examination of the specific ways in which various social arrangements dovetail and reinforce each other. It also provides that sense of immediacy which moves us closer to the intimate understanding of the family which is the primary goal of the study in depth.

I

# A HISTORY OF THE FAMILY IN THE SEVENTEENTH CENTURY

The major thrust of the present study is analytical rather than chronological, but it is necessary to set the stage by first giving a short sketch of the family and its members in the period under consideration. The purpose of this chapter is, therefore, not to offer a complete history of the family but merely to identify the actors and explain their relationships, before proceeding to a more detailed analysis of specific problems.

From what their letters tell us about them we know that the Verneys during the seventeenth century were an upper-gentry family belonging to the county elite of Buckinghamshire. In lifestyle, career patterns, educational practices, and social relationships, the Verneys appear to be typical of the upper-gentry in so far as the defining characteristics of this group have thus far been established.

/ Like other country houses owned by the upper classes, Claydon, the family home in central Buckinghamshire, was more than a residence; it was a visible symbol of status and social prominence which provided the family with a sense of identity and permanence.[1] / Although much of what the present-day visitor sees are eighteenth and nineteenth century additions, it is clear that the seventeenth century version of Claydon House was imposing by contemporary standards. It was a large house which could easily accommodate Sir Edmund Verney, his wife, and their twelve children,[2] as well as the many cousins and other relatives who came to visit the family for various lengths of time. Claydon was only four miles away from Hillesden, which was the ancestral home of Sir Edmund's wife's family, the Dentons,[3] and there was much visiting back and forth between the two houses. Although their ties with the socially prominent Dentons[4] were particularly close, the Verneys exchanged visits and letters with many other relatives, especially with that large group related by blood and marriage which made up the cousinhood.

In the years before the war, Sir Edmund Verney, his wife and the older children usually spent part of the year in London in the family's rented house in Covent Garden.[5] These visits to London were a common upper-gentry practice which afforded a change of pace from the rather monotonous routine of country life. During these visits the head of the family could meet with his influential business and political connections, and since London was already the center of the marriage market it was also the ideal place to find suitable marriage partners for one's children of marriageable age.[6]

As members of the upper-gentry, the Verneys belonged to that roughly 5 per cent of the population which formed the upper classes; above them were the nobility, directly below them the plain gentlemen or mere gentry. They were also one of the estimated 500 upper-gentry families in the England of this period whose politically influential members served as MPs when parliament was in session and frequently held appointments as sheriffs, deputy lieutenants, and JPs. They could be found occupying various posts at court, and competed with the nobility for Crown patronage. They sent their sons as gentleman commoners to the universities and the Inns of Court. While they were eager to find matrimonial prospects for their children among the noble families, they readily accepted matches within their own group, and, at a pinch, they would not exclude the mere gentry as possibilities. Like the nobility they derived most of their income from rents. In terms of wealth, the richest of the upper-gentry were wealthier than the poorest peers, but the nobility in its middle and upper ranges had greater incomes and more lavish spending habits than most of the upper-gentry. In the power structure the upper-gentry were clients of the great noble and in turn served as patrons to the rest of the gentry below them on the social scale.[7]

In the distribution of life chances the members of the upper-gentry were, with the aristocracy, the fortunate group in seventeenth century society. Inasmuch as family connections and influence were the most important variables in determining access to opportunities, whether business or marital, those born into the upper classes enjoyed, by mere inheritance, enormously favorable life chances in the competition for scarce jobs, mates, and wealth. Although influence of this sort is not unknown in modern society, there has occurred a decisive shift in institutional arrangements and social values which has resulted in the triumph of the ideal of professionalism, i.e., careers open to talent and achievement without reference to birth, an ideal which in the seventeenth century took second place to a respect for family ties, social status, and political influence. The social mechanisms of the earlier period can hardly be understood without a clear recognition of the fact that the *douceur* and the bribe, the outright purchase of the college degree as well as office, the initiation of friendships for the purpose of self aggrandizement (while still present in various forms in our own society) were reiterated norms in the seventeenth century while they are not in ours. In order to appreciate the extreme importance of the family in such a society, it is necessary to think oneself back to a period in which the individual was circumscribed by severely limited career and marriage options. The relatively few acceptable options that were available were rarely accessible without the active support and approval of the family, particularly the head of the household.

If the upper-gentry family of this period was patriarchal and autocratic, this was the social reality which made such a family structure viable. It was the father of the family who controlled the patrimony, and it was this control which provided him with the economic power and social prestige to maintain his authority over the other members. As such, he was not only the dispenser of financial support but also the source of family influence which he could give or withdraw as he saw fit.

Sir Edmund Verney (1590–1642), who was the head of the family in the first half of the seventeenth century, was in many ways a typical upper-gentry father. Sir Edmund was the issue of his father's third marriage and the only surviving heir.[8] In 1612, when he was 22 he married Margaret Denton, the eldest daughter of a large and politically powerful Buckinghamshire gentry family.[9] According to the standards of the time, Sir Edmund's 18-year-old bride was a better than average choice, and it is probably fair to say that the groom married upward in this case. He had been born in London[10] and was the first of his line to live in Claydon Manor,[11] whereas the Dentons were an old established county family. As their oldest daughter, Margaret probably received a larger marriage portion or dowry than her younger sisters. Moreover, before the year was out she had given birth to a male heir, which was considered to be the most important contribution (after her dowry) that a wife could make to the marriage. During the twenty-nine years of their marriage, Margaret bore, at about two-year intervals, eleven more children, which was not too unusual for a young woman who survived the first few years of childbearing. What was truly remarkable about the Verney children was not their number but their durability: ten of the twelve survived to adulthood.

This meant that Sir Edmund not only shared with his contemporaries the typical upper-gentry concerns of providing education, marriage portions, annuities, etc., for his children, but that these problems were apt to be more acute and pressing in the Verney household. The male heir was a desirable addition to the family, who would under the rules of primogeniture inherit the lion's share of the estate, whereas his brothers and sisters, whatever their number, had to share what was left. The high death rate among young children ordinarily ensured that only a few siblings would live to adulthood and their share of the family patrimony would then be sufficient to enable them to maintain the life-style appropriate to their gentry status. In Sir Edmund's case, however, the necessity of providing for nine younger children forced him to explore to the fullest extent those institutional arrangements and economic opportunities which society offered to him, in order to fulfill his familial obligations to his children as well as to other members among the kin who had claims on his estate. We can therefore expect to find Sir Edmund adopting all the tactics and strategies to place his children that were open to an upper-gentry father in his position.

Since Sir Edmund held his estate as 'tenant for life,' he was severely circumscribed in his ability to sell off lands if he were in need of money.[12] In order to increase his income, he therefore had to employ other means than land sales (which were considered, in any case, a measure of last resort even by those who were legally free to do so). Inasmuch as most of this income was derived from rent, careful estate management was a high priority. Estimating the quality of an individual's estate management practices is a difficult and complicated matter, but all the evidence indicates that Sir Edmund was an improving landlord who attempted to use modern agricultural methods and who personally decided all matters concerning leasing, enclosure, fines, etc.[13]

Another possibility for increasing one's fortune was to serve the Crown. On the one hand such service contained the possibility of exploiting some lucrative office as well as providing useful contacts with men of power and influence. On the other hand attendance at court was expensive, it made efficient control of one's estates more difficult because of the necessity of being away from home for long periods, and it required a good measure of luck as well as skill in order to be a gainer rather than a loser in the service of a king who was seldom solvent and who was often less than scrupulous in his financial dealings.

Despite these dangers, the financial rewards, when they were forthcoming, could be considerable. For example, it was undoubtedly through his office as knight marshall (which paid a salary of something above £180 p.a.)[14] that Sir Edmund obtained leases on the Marshalsea prison.[15] It was also through his court connections that the knight marshall obtained a patent for the licensing of hackney coaches. This, however, was a somewhat uncertain venture because Parliament had become increasingly vociferous in denouncing and increasingly successful in revoking such patents.[16] In addition to the hackney coaches, Sir Edmund is known to have been involved in tobacoo and wool projects of the same nature and to have tried to make a profit in Irish land investments.[17]

What probably seemed like the best opportunity to profit from Crown service was Sir Edmund's investment in the alnage. The latter was ostensibly an attempt by the government to maintain the quality of cloth manufacture. The administrators of the alnage were supposed to affix a seal to cloths that met specified standards. Since the beginning of the seventeenth century, however, it was well known that the seals were bought openly by the clothiers and that there was no attempt to enforce quality control.[18]

It was, none the less, a lucrative office for those who shared in the profits. Sir Edmund previously had been given two Crown pensions from each of which he was supposed to receive £200 p.a. The king also owed him £1,500 for a personal loan 'that the king . . . had often promised to pay him.' Since his pension payments came out of the general exchequer funds, which were as often as not unpaid, and his loan to the king was unlikely to fare much better, he wisely shifted his pensions and the king's debt to the alnage farm by surrendering both to the Crown in exchange for £400 p.a. for twenty-one years out of the alnage. This was a much safer investment because the claims on the alnage were paid out before the farmers turned their receipts over to the exchequer.[19] Sir Edmund also arranged that the annual income from the alnage be turned over to feoffees in trust for reinvestment in order to raise money for dowries for his daughters and for an annuity for his son Edmund. Any interest which accrued from the feoffees' investments was to be used for the payment of annuities for his children's maintenance.[20]

Although the large number of children to be provided for put a strain on the family finances, in normal times Sir Edmund probably would have succeeded in getting sufficient revenue to serve his needs, by careful husbanding of the family estates, by the profits from his court connected activities, as well as by gifts and loans from the kin. Even his frequent and prolonged absences from home because of his duties at court did not have very serious consequences. In the first place, his wife took an active part in managing the family. It was she, for example, who negotiated the arrangements involved in sending their 19-year old second son (and problem child), Thomas, to Virginia.[21] Secondly, their eldest son Ralph acted as surrogate head of the household under his father's directions, when the knight marshall was absent on court business.[22]

In the event, it was neither the difficulties imposed on the family by Sir Edmund's absences at court nor the birth of numerous long-lived progeny which determined the fortunes of the Verney family. The gravest threat to the family's financial security as well as to its solidarity was the advent of the Civil War and the problems deriving from it. The war years affected the Verneys in three fundamental ways; the family had to cope with serious financial difficulties in part caused by Sir Edmund's untimely death, its cohesiveness was threatened by ideological differences, and its members were geographically separated during a period of family crisis.

Sir Edmund, not unnaturally, opted for the Royalist side. His connection with the court dated back to the previous reign when he was a young man in his early twenties. In view of the nature of his financial involvements and his court ambitions, self-interest alone might have explained his allegiance to the Royalist party in the Civil War. In addition, there is reason to think that he had some personal attachment for King Charles, whom he had served for some years before the latter ascended the throne in 1625.[23] When the king required his services in the war against the Scots (1639), he went north with the English forces despite his son Ralph's pleas to the contrary. Even Ralph's reminder to his father that 'your years, your charge, your distracted fortunes, your former life, were privilege enough to keep you back without the least stain to your reputation' was unavailing.[24] Ralph had good cause to worry. In the first place, by the late 1630s, Sir Edmund had accumulated many debts, and Ralph expressed concern that the interest payments would 'ruin his [his father's] fortune,'[25] and if Sir Edmund died before he settled his debts, his son would be responsible for paying them. Secondly, Ralph's affection for his father did not blind him to the fact that the latter was obsessed with the maintenance of his honor to the point of taking foolhardy risks in battle. As Ralph prophetically put it to his uncle, 'If my father goes to the border, I know his courage will be his destruction.'[26] Under the circumstances, even Sir Edmund's assurance that he would 'not willfully thrust [himself] in danger'[27] could have given little reassurance to his son.

When the Civil War began, Ralph's fears were confirmed. Sir Edmund, the king's standard bearer, was killed in the battle of Edgehill in 1642. According to an eye-witness report, he killed two of the enemy 'with his own hands' but 'he would neither put on arms or buff coat the day of the battle the reason I know not.'[28]

There are some indications that Sir Edmund's apparent contempt for his own safety might have been motivated by other considerations besides that of military glory. There certainly would have been no taint on his honor if he had gone into battle properly armed. We know that in the fall of 1638 he had promised his son that he would settle his debts,[29] which from a financial point of view would have made his death less of a disaster for Ralph. But when he died four years later, Sir Edmund was still heavily indebted,[30] and the war made these debts more burdensome than they would have been in peacetime when normal returns on investments and income from rents could be counted on, as they could not during the war.[31]

Moreover, before his death Sir Edmund had quarreled with Ralph because the latter supported the Parliamentarians. The political division between father and son grieved the father personally and must have made his position in the Royalist camp somewhat suspect.[32] In addition, Sir Edmund's wife's death in the previous year[33] must have taken its toll on him. In a letter to Ralph written two months before his father's death, the Countess of Sussex observed that Sir Edmund was 'infinitely melancholy, for many other things I believe, besides the difference betwixt you.'[34]

Whether Sir Edmund's death was due to an inordinately courageous nature, fulfillment of a suicidal wish induced by financial difficulties and grief, just a piece of bad luck on the battlefield, or some combination of all three will never be known. But from that day the leadership of the family fell to his eldest son, Ralph Verney, who held that position of power and responsibility for more than half a century till his death in 1696.

By training and temperament Sir Ralph was extremely well suited to carry on in his father's place. He was intelligent, articulate, ambitious, and tireless in his efforts to preserve and improve his patrimony. Incapable of great depth of feeling for any but a few intimates, he was sufficiently perceptive about other men's weaknesses to make him a formidable business adversary. Totally humorless, he was not without sufficient tact to appear almost charming when charm was necessary to get what he wanted. Wholly lacking in spontaneity, he was careful, even calculating in his dealings with family and friends, though he prided himself on his scrupulousness. He was blessed with the extraordinary physical and emotional endurance often possessed by the exquisitely patient. Sir Ralph was the sort of man whom older relatives have difficulty remembering as a child.[35] In short, he was the very antithesis of that nightmare of the propertied classes, the profligate heir.

Fortunately for the historian, he was also an assiduous letter writer who seems to have been temperamentally incapable of discarding even the most trivial of his personal papers. If a letter was considered particularly important, he took notes on it and saved those too, and he also preserved the drafts of most of his answers.

As head of the household most letters were directed to him, and the collection, for this period, is largely his correspondence.

Not much is known about his childhood, but Sir Ralph's life after his marriage at the age of 16 in 1629[36] is fairly well documented. His bride, Mary, was the daughter and heiress of John Blacknall of Abingdon, Bucks. Mary's father had practiced law, but his main income came from his estate. She had lost both father and mother in the plague of 1625 when she was 9 years old. As an orphaned heiress, Mary and her estate fell under the jurisdiction of the Court of Wards, and Sir Edmund purchased her from the court as a prospective bride for his eldest son when she was 13.[37]

In order to effect his match, Sir Edmund had to fight off the claims of four of Mary's relatives. After her parents' death, these relatives had leased her lands and gained custody of her by payment of £1,000 to the Crown and giving bond to pay a similar amount in the future. One of these guardians had tried unsuccessfully to marry her to one of his sons when she was only 11. However, Sir Edmund, with the assistance of one of the guardians, persuaded the court to sell the wardship to him for £1,000, in 1629, and she and Ralph were married in the same year.[38] The competition for control of the wardship may have had something to do with the fact that the marriage ceremony was 'privately done,' and not even the Denton grandparents from nearby Hillesden were invited.[39]

Mary's marriage to Ralph was fortunate for both of them. Wealthy orphans whose estates were controlled by the Court of Wards were often sold to the highest bidder and subsequently forced into loveless and sometimes disastrous marriages.[40] There is no evidence that Mary regretted, either at that time or any other, the choice which was made for her by Sir Edmund. Ralph and she were well suited and their relationship grew into one of genuine affection.

Mary was intelligent, tactful, and entirely conformist. She seems to have been quite certain of what was expected of her, and temperamentally capable of complying with those demands.[41] In the early years of their marriage, the couple lived with the groom's parents at Claydon. Since she was an orphan, Mary had few competing demands on her affections and loyalties, and she was easily assimilated into her husband's family. Moreover, as the wife of the Verney heir, her high status within the family undoubtedly protected her from having to bear too much in the way of overt hostility from Ralph's many younger sisters and brothers.

It is likely that at the beginning her relationship with Sir Ralph was more in the nature of a courtship than a marriage. Sir Ralph continued his studies at Magdalen Hall, Oxford, the college which his father and his uncle, William Denton, had attended before him.[42] Residence requirements at the universities were much less rigid at that time, and Ralph undoubtedly had opportunities to visit with his wife during the year. She gave birth to their first child three years after their marriage. This child (who died in infancy) was the first of six that she and Ralph had during the next fifteen years. Only two of them, Edmund and John, survived to adulthood, which was more typical of seventeenth century infant mortality patterns than Ralph's generation had been.

For most of the decade of the 1630s, Sir Ralph and his wife lived at Claydon with his parents. Ralph helped his father with the management of the estate and took on increasing responsibility for his younger sisters and brothers.[43] One of the reasons why Ralph moved so easily into his father's place as head of the family after the latter's death was that the other children had become accustomed to viewing him as a surrogate father. Since his mother predeceased her husband by one year, Ralph had no competition in the parental role. Of equal importance were the legal and financial arrangements which buttressed his position as family patriarch. He controlled the family patrimony, he was the executor of his father's will, and he was also one of the feoffees charged with the administration of the alnage settlement.[44]

It was also in keeping with Ralph's social position and the pattern of upper-gentry life that he was elected to represent Aylesbury when the Long Parliament was called. Until 1643, Ralph Verney was a determined adherent of Parliament, although his father and brothers, as well as most of the family and kin, were Royalists.[45] In that year, Ralph became disenchanted with the aims of the revolution, and for reasons of conscience refused to sign the Covenant.[46] All members who refused to swear to this document were ousted from the Commons. The loss of his seat in the House meant that he also lost his privilege of immunity from suit for debt. The combined difficulties of his political apostasy and threat of imprisonment for debt made the expense and hazard of a removal to France preferable to remaining in England. In the latter part of that year he made the necessary preparations, and by the beginning of 1644 he was resident in France under the assumed name of Ralph Smith.[47] Ralph was accompanied by his wife and two of their three children. The younger son, 3-year-old John, was left at Claydon in the care of servants and the company of Ralph's younger sisters.[48]

Ralph's physical separation from the rest of the family had significant consequences for all the members, particularly for his sisters and brothers. At that distance his authority and control over the others was attenuated. Geographical separation and financial embarrassment often forced him to rely on the voluntary cooperation and/or successful exploitation of the self-interest of the other members in order to maintain his paramount position in the family hierarchy. Consequently, the letters which were written during Ralph's ten-year exile are particularly important for a study of family relationships as well as for an increased understanding of the values and attitudes on which those relationships were based; many revealing exchanges that would have been voiced in face-to-face contact if Ralph had remained at home were instead committed to paper and preserved,

In this regard it should be noted that the problems deriving from the Civil War placed unusual stresses on family relationships, but this does not diminish the value of the letters of this period for assessing beliefs and attitudes. The functions of the family and many of the problems which its members dealt with were basically the same as those which occupied them in times of peace, e.g., choosing of suitable marriage partners, family financing, etc. Moreover, a crisis situation serves to heighten and illuminate beliefs and values rather than to distort them.

During Sir Ralph's long exile, he remained in name and in fact the head of the family. Custom, previously established habits of obedience to him, and institutional arrangements reinforced his position as patriarch. As long as he controlled the family patrimony, his influence and authority over the other members could not be successfully challenged. His primary concern during this period, therefore, was to protect his inheritance from demands made on it by financially hard-pressed relatives as well as by government sequestrators. His estate was encumbered by the debts which his father had left at the time of his death, in addition to the annuities and marriage portions which Ralph was legally bound to meet. At the time of his removal to France only one of his six sisters was married, and he was responsible for the support of the others, two of whom were still young children. In addition, arrangements had to be made and expenses met to care for his youngest son, who did not rejoin the family in France until the beginning of 1648.[49]

In order to perform his familial obligations from that distance, Ralph had to rely on help from a variety of persons. In his absence, and under Ralph's directions, the estate was managed by his hard-working steward, Will Roads.[50] Roads's position was not an enviable one. The financial squeeze sometimes made it necessary to reduce or delay payments on annuities, and also inclined him to refuse advances on allowances. As a result he was obliged to cope with the truculent, or more often desperate, pleadings of Ralph's dependents. Brother Thomas, who was incapable of living within his means even in the best of times, sent an angry and threatening letter to Roads when the latter offered Thomas only £5 instead of the £10 which he had requested. Thomas hotly suggested that the 'five pounds which you send me word I shall have very speedily I pray keep it a[nd] wipe your ass with it.'[51] Thomas later threatened to send his 'company' of soldiers to Claydon to collect the full amount, and tried to frighten Roads into giving way with the suggestion that the soldiers would reward themselves for their efforts by what they would carry away in the process.[52]

Although few members of the family were willing to go to such lengths to squeeze what they needed out of Roads (and even Thomas ordinarily couched his requests in the form of entreaties), the steward was involved in disputes about money with most members of the family and kin.[53] His only defense against the constant barrage of supplications was to plead with Sir Ralph to convince them all that there was simply not enough revenue to supply all their needs and that neither ominous gesturings nor tearful supplications would increase Roads's capacity to oblige them.[54] The fact that there was not enough to go around on the one hand increased their need for Ralph's favor in order to obtain what was available, and on the other hand strained familial relationships when their requests were put off or denied.

The variety and complexity of family and estate problems in many cases went beyond the capacities and responsibilities of the estate steward. For example, the sequestration of the estate became an increasing possibility after 1643, and Roads's contribution to the solution of that problem was necessarily limited. An ordinance to that effect was passed in 1644, but action was not taken on it by Parliament until two years later.[55] To handle this problem Ralph needed the help of friends and relatives to obtain the necessary legal advice, political influence, and labyrinthine property settlements which would bring the desired result of a minimal fine for compounding to recover his property.

One friend who had earlier shown his willingness to help Ralph was Sir Roger Burgoyne. The latter was a member of the House of Commons who retained his seat until 1648, when he became alienated from the party then in power and was 'secluded.'[56] Burgoyne was especially active in helping his friend during the first difficult years of Ralph's exile. It was he who had made the necessary arrangements for Ralph's departure from England, and kept him informed of political developments after he went abroad. He was one of the first to warn Ralph of Parliament's intention to institute the sequestration and helped his friend when it became a reality.[57] Burgoyne assisted Lady Verney when she returned temporarily to England to solicit help in getting the sequestration removed.[58] In view of his loyalty to them it was fitting that Sir Ralph's code name for Sir Roger in his confidential letters was 'Mr Good.'[59]

Another friend, who was not as steadfast as Sir Roger but who ultimately served the Verneys' interest, was the Countess of Sussex. She had been Ralph's patron before the war and was godmother to one of his children.[60] She was a vain, petulant and grasping woman who had reached the top rungs of the social ladder through successive marriages to wealthy old men.[61] As her client, Ralph had performed a variety of favors and services for her, from purchasing carpets and pictures to acting as adviser in her business dealings. On one occasion Ralph was required to request that Van Dyck alter his portrait of her so that the finished product would be more flattering, because as she complained to Ralph 'truly it was too fat.'[62]

However, when Ralph was no longer on hand to serve her, she proved reluctant to reciprocate previous favors. Ralph wanted her to put pressure on her latest husband, the Earl of Warwick, to exercise his influence on the Committee for Compounding so that the Verneys would get a favorable verdict. Lady Verney, who had been sent to England to effect this and similar missions, found the countess polite but willing to offer 'nothing at all of courtesy' that would help them. She therefore did not give the countess the gift of a watch which Lady Verney had intended to offer to their patron if the latter had proved cooperative, and instead took 'it away again as not thinking it fit to bestow there.'[63] Similarly, a guitar, which was also intended to effect the same purpose, was not presented to the countess because she continued to show no interest in favoring the Verneys with her influence.[64] However, as the time for the committee ruling approached, Lady Verney stepped up the pressure on the countess, visiting her '4 or 5 times' in a single week, and was ultimately successful in getting her to persuade the Earl of Warwick to help them.[65]

The one person who never showed any reluctance to assist Ralph with the sequestration proceedings and other business dealings, as well as a whole range of personal and family problems, was his uncle, William Denton. The latter was a younger son of the Denton family who had been a physician to Charles I before the war. During the 1640s he carried on a private practice, took an active part in administering the estate of his deceased elder brother, and also took on increasing responsibilities for the exiled Ralph.[66] It was typical of his good-natured way of dealing with others that he made light of his many contributions to his own family and the Verneys with the remark that family business came to him from all directions because he was the only 'leisure man of the family.' Dr Denton also possessed a good sense of humor, in sharp contrast to Ralph whose rare attempts at the humorous never advanced beyond the coy salaciousness of the locker-room joke.[67]

'Uncle Doctor,' as the Verneys referred to him, was not only kind to Ralph, but to his other nieces and nephews as well. He provided medical care for Ralph's sisters and brothers, acted as peacemaker in family squabbles, and tactfully reminded Ralph of the latter's responsibility for his younger siblings.[68] In addition, he was active in promoting their interests, as a petitioner to Parliament on the matter of the alnage office. Both families, the Dentons and the Verneys, had investments in that office, and during the war Parliament refused to honor claims on it.[69] Inasmuch as the income from this office was the chief source for the funding of annuities and marriage portions for the younger children, Uncle Doctor's efforts in this matter were important to both families.

Unfortunately, their uncle's efforts were not successful, and the Verneys were still involved in litigation on this matter at the end of the decade.[70] Four of Ralph's six sisters, Susan, Penelope, Mary and Elizabeth, were supposed to receive their dowries from the alnage. Susan and Penelope were already of marriageable age when Ralph left England, and Mary grew to maturity during his lengthy absence. The financial and political upheavals of the 1640s made that a most unpromising decade in which to find a suitable husband. However, the sisters could not wait indefinitely upon the questionable outcome of their petitions or the settling of the family estate, for they would have passed the optimum age for marriage. Similarly, sister Margaret, whose marriage portion had been provided by a Denton aunt, was unable to collect it at the time of her marriage in 1646. The three oldest, Susan, Penelope and Margaret, did marry during the mid-1640s, but the poor quality of their marriages reflected the makeshift financial arrangements which were substituted for dowry payments, and Mary was not married off until the following decade.[71]

Cary, the only sister who had been married before Ralph's departure, was widowed two years later when her husband was killed in the war. His death left her a pregnant widow living with in-laws who considered her a disagreeable burden.[72] Their niggardly treatment of their daughter-in-law became apparent to the Verneys when, after the birth of her child, it was reported that 'the unhappy widow [Cary] . . . hath a girl which she nurses herself,' a maternal function that an upper-class woman of means normally hired a servant to perform.[73] In the two years that elapsed between the death of her first husband and her remarriage she was unable to stay out of debt and found it increasingly difficult to provide for her sickly child, which undoubtedly explains why she eagerly accepted the proposal of a man of lesser quality who at least offered her security.[74]

The two youngest sisters, Mary and Elizabeth, were only 13 and 10 respectively in 1643. Arrangements had been made for them to reside at Claydon, but as they matured it became necessary to provide them with the kind of education considered appropriate for young ladies of their station. In their case it was primarily Uncle Doctor and another of the Dentons, Aunt Isham, who were the prime movers in getting Ralph to give the youngsters as much as he could be persuaded to offer.[75] Ralph did not want to take his sisters to live with him in France, not was he willing to spend any more on Mary and Elizabeth than was necessary to quiet the criticism of his relatives about his neglect of them.[76]

Since Mary was easy-going and tractable, he boarded her with any of the relatives who would take her and finally promised to pay for two months of dancing lessons.[77] Elizabeth, the youngest, was a moody and unhappy child whom none of the relatives wished to take, so Ralph had her sent away to school.[78] Although Elizabeth had been unhappy with Ralph's attempts to place her with the relatives, she was so distraught by the prospect of boarding school that, according to Uncle Doctor who made the arrangements, she 'doth not stick to threaten her own death by her own hands.'[79] However, in time she adjusted to staying at school, and as a reward Uncle Doctor promised to take her to his home for the Christmas holidays. This meant an added expense for Ralph, but the uncle believed that it would be preferable to leaving the young girl virtually by herself during the vacation when most of the other students would be gone.[80]

If Ralph's sisters' experiences during this period read like a long jeremiad, their misfortunes cannot be entirely explained in terms of the special problems caused by the war, although the uncertainties and upheavals of wartime conditions exacerbated their difficulties. Many of the Verney sisters' problems had as much to do with their sex, ages and numbers as with the special circumstances of the war. They were far more dependent in every area of their lives, enjoyed fewer options, and were less able to escape from patriarchal domination than their brothers. For example, there were no careers open to them which would provide a source of income to alleviate their financial difficulties, and the decisions concerning where they should live, when and whom they might marry, the nature and extent of the education of the younger girls, were all matters which in the last analysis were controlled by Ralph, and were contingent on his willingness and ability to help or deprive them. Their subordinate position in the family was not a function of the war.

Ralph's three younger brothers, Thomas, Edmund and Henry, enjoyed a more advantageous position within the family and the wider society by virtue of their sex. That advantage, though genuine, should not be exaggerated because it had distinct limitations in a patronage society committed to primogenitural inheritance. Younger sons as compared to daughters could evade the authority of the head of the family partly because they could obtain some degree of financial independence through the pursuit of a successful career and partly because the double sexual standard permitted them greater freedom in their social contacts. However, in a patronage society, success in a career was to a large extent dependent on family and kin influence and generosity – a fact which tied younger sons to the need to cultivate the family patriarch and any of the kin that might prove useful in promoting their careers. Their dependence in this regard was alleviated but not eliminated by the small annuities which they received.

All of the younger sons had been launched on careers before the war started. Thomas, who was only two years younger than Ralph and next in line, was the least successful in his career and personal life. For a time he was only a heartbeat away from the inheritance, but he was destined to remain a younger son whose small annuity and limited prospects condemned him to mere gentry status, a social reality which was contradicted by his self-image and predispositions which were entirely aristocratic. The birth and survival of Ralph's male children blocked the possibility of Thomas's succeeding to the estate, but not the frustration which their unchallengeable claims to the family patrimony must have generated in someone of Thomas's temperament. He often tended to be imperious, but his arrogance stemmed from anxiety rather than achievement. He was totally lacking in scruples, and incapable of assessing his continual failures in any terms that went beyond a paranoiac insistence on the deficiencies of others. He was extremely articulate in mouthing ideals to which he had not the slightest commitment. He was despised by the family and kin, whose opinions and treatment of Thomas were uncomplicated by the kind of strained compassion which can be derived from modern psychological insights. Even Uncle Doctor, who was the most charitable member on such matters, ultimately concluded that Thomas was incorrigible.[81] In so far as he was successful in manipulating others this was due to his equal readiness to play any role from the victimized innocent to the groveling penitent depending on which pose would serve his needs.[82] While it is true that these chameleon-like performances reached a level of perfection in Thomas which was never attained by the other brothers, as younger sons they also lacked the independence which would have made such behavior unnecessary for them.

Thomas was always in debt and borrowed from anyone who would lend him money.[83] His pre-war colonial ventures were a failure, and his career as a soldier was short-lived and did nothing to improve his prospects.[84] His unreliability decreased his sources of credit, and in order to make ends meet he resorted to a variety of unsavory dealings, including selling the furniture from his eldest brother's London house (when the latter was in France), and on a later occasion forging some deeds.[85] Since the latter offense would lead to imprisonment if he were caught, he decided to escape prosecution by a hasty departure for France. Thomas persuaded his brother-in-law, Elmes, to come with him, undoubtedly because he viewed the latter as a potential source of financial support. He subsequently accumulated a number of gambling debts and attempted to pay them off by forging Elmes's name to some bills of exchange. Since this was a capital offense in France, he soon returned to the relative safety of England.[86] He did rather well there for a short time as a professional informer, but he was unable to stay out of debt, and by the end of 1649 was planning to leave the country again.[87] However, early in the following year he was still in England, sick, penniless, and begging Uncle Doctor for help.[88]

Edmund, or 'Mun' as the family called him, was the next youngest brother, and Sir Edmund's favorite of the three younger sons. Mun had been an indifferent scholar when he attended Oxford before the war, and his father decided that he should become a professional soldier.[89] Unlike Thomas, Mun made a genuine attempt to succeed in his career and become financially independent, but throughout his short life that goal eluded him. In the late 1630s he served on the Continent and after a brief return to England in the early part of 1642, he shipped to Ireland.[90] Although he had gone to Ireland 'to make [his] fortune, not to starve,'[91] it was some time before he enjoyed even temporary success as a soldier. By 1645 he had been made a colonel, but two years later he was considering selling part of his annuity because he was hard pressed for money. Earlier he and Ralph had argued over their political differences but by this time they had made it up, and Ralph offered him some money to tide him over.[92]

Mun had been a staunch supporter of the king's side from the beginning. In one of the few letters in which he showed any animosity toward Ralph, written in 1642, he berated his brother for siding with the Parliamentarians because 'majesty is sacred, God sayest touch not my annointed,'[93] and he never changed his mind on this issue.[94] Moreover, his Royalist sympathies coincided with his personal interest. As late as 1648 he was still hopeful 'that the tide will turn and that we shall get it [the alnage money] from the King.'[95] In the meantime Edmund had to continue with his career, and in hopes of furthering that aim he attached himself to the Earl of Ormonde. Edmund followed his patron to France and subsequently served under him in Ireland.[96] However, the Earl proved fickle and Mun was soon out of favor with him and again in trouble financially.[97] He was killed at Drogheda in 1649 and died in debt.[98]

The youngest son, Henry, was also supposed to live by his sword, but he disliked soldiering and would have preferred 'to follow the court.'[99] None the less, it was his father's wish that he remain with the military, and he continued in that profession with little success for six years. In 1643 he was captured and subsequently had to be ransomed with Ralph's help.[100] After his release he gave up army life because he saw no future in it. Since he was fundamentally apolitical, his lack of ideological enthusiasm made that an easy decision, and he let it be known that he was politically 'neuter.'[101]

During the mid-1640s he managed to scrape by with the help of various relatives. He cheated one of his aunts out of some money, and offered his dubious assistance to another, his recently war-widowed Aunt Eure, in exchange for a place in her household.[102] He subsequently obtained a lodge through the influence of a cousin, and bragged to Ralph (who had been instrumental in making this favorable connection) that 'I intend to feast it and to keep fires knowes [i.e., nose] high.'[103] A lodge, such as Henry obtained, was a typical younger son sinecure that not all of them were fortunate enough to acquire. It says something of the mean existence of a younger son that the prospect of enough to eat and a good fire was cause for exultation. Since the revenue from such an office was usually rather meager, Henry made every effort to offer his services to Ralph in the hope of getting some additional income out of him. The two brothers quarreled, however, when Ralph refused to give him an additional annuity at a favorable rate of interest in exchange for some money which Henry had laid out for the eldest brother, and Ralph was cool to Henry for years afterward.[104]

While his younger sisters and brothers did what they could to make their way, with Ralph's often reluctant assistance, the latter as the elder brother concentrated his efforts on securing his patrimony in England and freeing himself from the debts which were the chief obstacles to his return. The sequestration was officially removed in 1648.[105] Although Uncle Doctor observed with atypical disengenuousness when their petition passed in the House that 'there was *digitus Dei* immanently in it,' the successful conclusion of that business had actually required the use of some rather more base instrumentalities.[106] Not only had it been necessary to use the conventional methods of influence and bribery, but also various legal maneuvers, such as conveying titular control of certain properties to persons who were not suspect.[107]

But even after his estate was secured, Ralph decided to remain abroad, partly because of the continuing political uncertainties at home and partly because he needed more time to settle his debts.[108] Lady Verney did what she could to settle her husband's affairs and rejoined him in France in the spring of 1648 accompanied by the young son whom they had previously left at Claydon. Soon after she returned she became seriously ill and died in France in 1650.[109]

Sir Ralph never remarried during the remainder of his long life. He was able to return to England a few years after his wife's death. In 1655 he was briefly imprisoned as a suspected Royalist[110] but thereafter he gradually resumed the position and style of life appropriate to his class. It is indicative of the endurance and tenacity of the upper-gentry that Sir Ralph was returned to Parliament in the 1680s.[111] He died at the age of 85 in 1696 – a lifetime which spanned almost the whole of the seventeenth century.

# 2

# FAMILY RELATIONSHIPS

In one sense the chapters which follow this one, concerning marriage and child rearing, are also discussions of Verney family relationships. But unlike those, this one examines the dynamics of family relations primarily in terms of individual roles, rather than the specific problems of matrimonial selection and financing, or child rearing practices. Relatively little work has been done on the nature of family dynamics, that is, on how family members actually treated each other, particularly of the kind which systematically examines the network of relations within a single family with a view toward assessing the patterns of interaction and their connection to the larger social structure. This is in part due to the lack of evidence which might permit this kind of precision. The Verney correspondence is quite unusual, for the period, in approximating that category of evidence which is analogous to interviews, and from which detailed analysis can be made.

Of course, in real life – that is, in the ongoing everyday process of life as it was actually experienced – the artificial separation between role and response to particular problems did not exist. Instead, an individual's role and personal predispositions combined in any specific social context and affected the person's perceptions and responses. But for the purposes of analysis, family relationships can be examined with an emphasis on the social roles of individual members. Such an approach, while it borrows from the conceptualizations of twentieth century social science, has particular validity in the case of the seventeenth century family where role differentiation, as determined primarily by gender, birth order, and generation, appears to have been a key variable in affecting interpersonal relations. Taken together with the nature of class arrangements, they are central to understanding familial interaction.

The word family, as used in this analysis, refers to the primary kinship unit, parents and their children, although contemporaries used the word to include kin and even servants.[1] Seventeenth century upper-gentry families, just as those of today, had various functions to perform and allocations to make which were required for the continued existence of that kinship unit. Specialists in the period agree that it was also patriarchal, authoritarian, and primogenitural.[2] This type of family unit, because of all that is implied by such a description about distribution of power, responsibility, economic allocations, etc., was conceived by contemporaries to include in its ideal form at least three generations rather than the two generations of the ideal multilineal conjugal family unit.[3] But this ideal conception is more significant for what it says about seventeenth century values than about the actual structure of these families, because the high adult death rates of the period meant that a multigenerational family was in practice quite rare.

As an institution, the family of the seventeenth century was considered to be an instrument of social control, which placed high priority on maintaining the *status quo*. It was an essentially conservative institution which controlled many aspects of the individual's life. Not only were its functions more numerous than they are today, but competing impersonal institutions were significantly weaker. Although the sixteenth century had seen a slow growth of other institutions such as almshouses, orphanages, and asylums, these were mostly intended for the poor, and the upper-class family still assumed responsibility for the poor, insane, orphaned, sick, and anti-social members within its ranks. The only important function it was beginning to surrender was education.

In this matter of education the parents' status and influence were of overriding importance in determining both the extent and application of formal training. In the first place a university degree was not the necessity for a successful career which it has become in post-industrial societies. Many of the sons of the aristocracy did attend the universities but they did not ordinarily receive degrees.[4] Secondly, the universities, like other institutions of the time, were part of the patronage system. This means that tutors at the colleges as well as the masters were more eager to accept the sons of families who would be likely to offer them access to preferment.[5] A student's academic success, certainly at the higher levels, was dependent on his parents' ability and willingness to finance the venture as well as on their patronage potential, rather than on the academic achievements of their son.

Younger children of both sexes could be tutored at home or sent out to one of a number of boarding schools for the purpose of acquiring the necessary social polish and 'breeding' which parents of this class considered important, primarily in order to enhance the child's future value in the marriage market.[6] The direction and extent of formal schooling was, consequently, a matter left to the discretion of the child's parents.

Decisions about education, as well as other aspects of the child's life, such as careers and marriage, were not a matter of parental whim. They were always affected by the child's position in the family hierarchy, a position which was fixed by the accident of birth rather than parental preference. One's role in the kinship structure was determined chiefly by sex, birth order, and generation. For example, if the first born were a daughter she would inherit the family patrimony only in the event that no son born after her survived. The first born son not only inherited the lion's share of the estate but also the greatest allocation of power and responsibility within the family.

If such an arrangement seems peculiar or even repugnant by modern standards, that is partly because we place high priority on kinship relationships based on love and mutual respect. The strength and intensity of family relationships in modern society is presumed to be directly related to personal intimacy, in the sense of direct contact, informality, and overt expression of emotion.[7] It is also assumed that family solidarity is a function of the quality and intensity of the emotional relationships obtaining among the members. Moreover, in Britain and the United States parents are expected, ideally, to provide equal treatment of children without reference to sex or birth order.

Although this was not the case with the seventeenth century English propertied families in general or the Verneys in particular, these families were nevertheless characterized by a very high level of solidarity. This, in part, can be understood by the nature and variety of its functions. In addition to its obvious importance as a nurturing and socializing institution, the family was a vital source of finance and credit. The absence of banks and the scarcity of other agencies for lending and borrowing greatly increased the necessity for maintaining family ties for this purpose. Since family financial arrangements often included the kin, these arrangements strengthened the pre-existent sense of obligation to the family as well as to the kin, and accounts for the extraordinarily close interaction among them. In order to understand more fully the nature of this solidarity it must be examined in some detail, and further definition given to the relational aspects and especially the distribution of power among family members, rather than to the structural aspects of the family which we have been discussing.

For any kinship structure to fulfill its functions there must be some relatively stable set of relationships which permits the undertaking of those functions. This stability is provided by role differentiation of the members and what Professor Levy has termed 'the institutional prescription of the content, strength, and intensity' of those relationships,[8] or in more general terms family solidarity.

In the case of the Verneys, solidarity was dependent on a set of variables which in many respects were quite different from those of present-day families. Firstly, the content of solidarity refers to the general nature of a particular relationship and specifies which members are concerned in it. For example, in the Verney family the parent/child relationship commonly emphasized the necessity for the child's obedience to the parent. Respect and submission to the parent was evoked by fear rather than admiration and affection. Parental attitudes toward and dealings with children were predicated on their role in the kinship structure rather than on emotional response to him or her as an individual or considerations of their needs and aspirations as unique persons.

Indeed, the uniqueness of the individual, and the open-ended possibilities of behavior and achievement stemming from belief in such uniqueness, were actively discouraged rather than stressed. For, while it is true that in modern families individual members play discrete roles, there are also opportunities to operate and function outside such roles. Particularly as one matures, self-directed behavior is not only permitted by many economic and cultural differences, i.e., by structural differences, but is actually encouraged by a belief system which tends to stress the unique and irreplaceable qualities and possibilities of each individual. In so far as such a concept can be said to have existed at all in the Verney family, it was expressed in religious terms and ritualized behavior and was certainly a marginal consideration in personal relations compared with the overwhelming importance of role.

Secondly, the strength of a particular relationship, that is, the precedence of the relationship relative to others,[9] was institutionally prescribed and reinforced by various legal and financial arrangements. For example, the father/eldest son relationship in the Verney family was of greater strength than any other. From the son's point of view it took precedence over any obligations or commitments to other members of the family and kin; from the father's point of view (since his own father was not living), Sir Edmund's relationship with Ralph, the male heir, was stronger than with any other member including his wife.

The third aspect of solidarity, i.e., intensity, is based on two factors: (1) the type of affect involved, described in psychological terms as love, fear, etc., and in social terms as avoidance or intimacy; (2) the degree of this involvement.[10] In modern families it is assumed that love and intimacy are interrelated variables in any relationship and that ideally they are reciprocally experienced to the same degree. Furthermore, such relationships are presumed to flourish because of the unique and desirable qualities of the individuals involved rather than because of the formal kinship relationship existing between them. In the Verney family, by contrast, love and respect were institutionally prescribed even when intimacy was quite lacking, as in the case of the arranged marriage or in the mother/child relationship in which the employment of wet nurses and governesses was the rule. The point here is that solidarity was a striking feature of the Verney family which was hardly diminished even under the stress imposed by civil war and geographical separation.

The remarkable endurance of this family solidarity, despite the low priority placed on feelings of affection, is an intriguing question which becomes explicable when one examines two central features of the family in this period. The first is the fact of the family's importance as a provider of resources, that is as an agent of family strategies for survival rather than as chiefly a provider of affection and love. The second is the distribution of power within the family, both ideally and actually, and the fact of patriarchal control of the other members. In modern British and American families just the reverse is true in regard to its distributive function, and further, patriarchal power has come under increasing attack and disrepute as an ideal. In view of the large and increasing number of impersonal institutions and experts which have taken on many of its functions, the modern family's chief thrust, in terms of what it should provide, has come to be seen as its ability to offer love and affection for its members in an emotionally supportive environment which the family is ideally expected to create.[11]

In families where income is derived from rents, and where decisions concerning its distribution are based on a particular kinship structure (patrilineal rather than multilineal, primogeniture rather than partable inheritance, etc.), the allocation of power and responsibility within the family, as well as the definition of its distributive functions, will vary accordingly. In the case of the Verneys, which was a *rentier* family, the responsibility for maintaining and if possible increasing this income went to the male heir as inheritor of the family estates. This authority over the financial resources of the family also conferred considerable power over the other members and kin.[12] Although the distribution of this income was to some extent institutionally prescribed, through the legal provision of annuities, jointures, dowries, etc., the head of the family still retained important discretionary powers over the other members which affected their relationship with him as well as with each other.[13] In addition, his position was buttressed by a pervasive set of beliefs regarding the legitimacy of patriarchal power and, in England, by the augmentation of paternal control within the family which Protestant practices probably served to enlarge.[14]

The virtually untrammeled authority of the family patriarch rested on the primacy of primogeniture and the consequent control of patrimony which this gave to him. It is this type of patriarchy which is the key to an understanding of the relationships within the Verney family. Its existence permeated all their dealings with each other, and it is the one variable under which all the intricacies of family dynamics can be subsumed. As inheritor of the family patrimony Sir Ralph Verney received not only the greatest part of the family wealth but also the most esteemed, prestigious, and powerful place in the family hierarchy. His inheritance of the family estates provided him with a home, Claydon Manor, and an income in rents sufficiently large to maintain himself and his family in the life-style appropriate to a country gentleman, and relieved him of the necessity of pursuing any other career. By contrast, his younger brothers, who had also been raised to live as gentlemen, were obliged to scrape by on allowances which barely enabled them to maintain their social status. The chief purpose of Sir Ralph's life was to maintain and expand this patrimony, theirs to ward off the threat of social derogation. Their success or failure would depend in large measure on what he was able or willing to do for them.

In a period when family reputation counted far more than individual abilities, Sir Ralph enjoyed the advantage of residing at Claydon, a locus of family influence and power, while their need to pursue some career necessitated a geographic mobility which was not necessarily viewed as an exciting challenge but instead presented the disadvantage of unfamiliar places and people where family influence might not prevail. The younger sons were therefore exposed to a range of social possibilities which Sir Ralph, in normal times, would never experience.

## THE INHERITING SON

Sir Ralph's relationship with his father was also quite different from that of the other children. There is almost no evidence to permit a reconstruction before the 1630s, when Sir Ralph was in his teens. From that point onward, however, the letters become increasingly informative. Because Sir Ralph's father, Sir Edmund, spent a good deal of time following the court, the eldest son took on many of the powers and functions of the head of the family before his father's death. Their relationship with each other was stronger and more intense than with any other member of the family, including their wives. Sir Ralph carried out his father's instructions in matters of estate management, letting of land, conversion of tillage to pasture, etc.,[15] and sometimes supervised the work of the estate steward.[16] When Sir Edmund took the waters at Bath, Sir Ralph accompanied him, leaving his wife and child at home.[17] Further indication of the nature of this father/son relationship, as well as Sir Edmund's order of priorities, can be glimpsed in a letter he wrote to Sir Ralph concerning estate affairs and soil management. After filling more than a page of a two-page letter with detailed directions for spreading dung, Sir Edmund ended with his apologies for not writing to his wife because of lack of time, and asked Sir Ralph to request a favorite cake recipe from her and mail it to him.[18]

In an arranged marriage society where women were considered social and intellectual inferiors, and where primogenitural inheritance gave paramount status to the eldest son, both the value system and legal arrangements tended to make the father/eldest son relationship the strongest and most intense in the family. In the light of the values of the time, Sir Edmund was a good and considerate husband. It was in keeping with those values that he chose to confide his business and personal concerns to his son rather than his wife.[19]

The son, on his part, made obedience to his father's wishes his overriding consideration in his dealings with the rest of the family and kin, even on those occasions when Sir Ralph believed that his actions would threaten his standing with the others. When Sir Edmund instructed Sir Ralph to inform grandmother Denton that she was to give no financial assistance to brother Thomas, whom Sir Edmund wished to punish, Sir Ralph was reluctant to get involved because it left him open to the displeasure of both his grandmother and his brother. Yet he obeyed his father despite the fact that he

> wish[ed] [his] father had made choice of another pen for this employment, but since he commands I must not refuse. I know 'tis my part to obey not to direct, therefore I must submit myself to his pleasure, though it may much disadvantage [me].[20]

When one considers that Sir Ralph was in his mid-twenties and had been married for nine years when he wrote this letter,[21] it becomes apparent that he believed that maturity did not relieve him of the necessity for filial obedience. In its entirety this letter smacks of a certain shrill defensiveness on Sir Ralph's part, but his desire to please his father was quite genuine.

Sir Ralph's conception of his duties and responsibilities as eldest son was learned within the family and reinforced by his educational experiences. His tutor at Oxford, John Crowther, wrote to his 19-year-old charge

> you know what honour to his family, what credit to himself (to let go religious motives) doth a gentleman purchase, who hath not only outward gifts of fortune but is fraught with the diviner perfections of his mind. Make not . . . your natural weakness a fond plea for your future neglect.[22]

When Sir Ralph temporarily left Oxford for a conjugal visit with his bride, the same tutor interrupted Ralph's 'Hymen delights' to remind his pupil to take time out to visit with relatives and keep up with his studies. He also observed that 'pleasures are augmented through their intermissions, and the sweetness of a kiss will relish better after the harshness of a syllogism.'[23] If Crowther was naive about the suitability of a syllogism as preparation for lovemaking, he correctly assessed the conventional wisdom concerning the duties of an inheriting son.

Although Sir Ralph's relationship with his father was primarily based on obedience and respect on the son's part and authority and control on the father's, this did not preclude the development of a certain amount of affection.[24] As in the case of some of the arranged marriages of the period, genuine affection could spring out of an essentially functional relationship.[25] When Sir Edmund wrote from York to assuage Sir Ralph's fears about his safety, he assured his son that he

> never knew so much grief as to part from you, and truly because I saw you equally afflicted with it my sorrow was the greater. But, Ralph, we cannot live always together, it cannot be long . . . by course of nature we must be severed.[26]

Sir Ralph's concern for his father's safety, however, was not unmixed with more practical considerations. At this time Sir Edmund was greatly in debt and Sir Ralph knew the precariousness of his father's financial status.[27] Sir Ralph was very unsettled by the prospect of coming into such a clogged inheritance and wrote to his uncle Dr Denton to plead with Sir Edmund to come home. It was Sir Ralph's opinion that if his father 'goes to the border, he is lost . . . no man did ever so willfully ruin himself and his posterity. God forgive him . . . did he beget us to no other end but to make us the sad spectacles of the world?'[28] The same theme runs through another letter of the same date, in which the son summarized his case by telling his father, 'Sir, you know your years, your charge, your distracted fortune, your former life were privilege enough to keep you back without the least stain to your reputation.'[29] Sir Edmund found nothing offensive in all of this and thanked his son for his 'good advice, it has both expressed your judgement and affection.'[30]

Just as Sir Ralph's relationship with his father was conditioned by his role as eldest son and inheritor of the family patrimony, his dealings with his younger siblings and their responses to him were predicated on their respective positions in the family hierarchy. Sir Ralph's three younger brothers, Thomas, Edmund and Henry, looked to him as surrogate father when Sir Edmund was at court, and continued to do so to varying degrees after their father died. This was even more true for the six younger sisters, who because of their sex had fewer options for escaping from parental control and more need for their brother's good will.

## BROTHERS AND SISTERS

An examination of the sibling relationships illustrates the nature and content of the concept of patriarchy and its importance as the hingepin of family solidarity. Interpersonal relations among the sisters and brothers were marked by a calculated reciprocity which there is no reason to believe was idiosyncratic. Just as psychological needs for affection and emotional gratification were minor considerations in parent/child, husband/wife relationships, siblings' behavior toward one another was unlikely to be predicated on affects of love or affection. From the point of view of any individual member, the family and kin were necessary and useful as a means for getting on in the world; personal success, defined as career advancement for men and marriage for women, was heavily dependent on the willingness and ability of one's relatives, particularly the head of the family, to advance one's prospects.

In this connection, the peculiar use of the word 'friend' by members of the Verney family and other correspondents substantiates this interpretation of family dynamics. In the usage of the period, the word 'friend' meant something quite different from what it usually does today. In the correspondence, 'friend' is repeatedly and almost exclusively used to refer to someone who can be helpful in advancing one's career or prospects, and is never used to describe someone freely chosen on the basis of mutual psychological attraction. A friend was a person who was important to one's interest; he was not necessarily likeable or personally attractive, though he was often related by blood or marriage. As Lady Verney put it accurately if ungrammatically, 'it was friends which did all.'[31]

It would have required a very different social and economic structure for the modern ideal of friendship to have been a common reality. For one thing, an individual's personal options in the matter of friendships were circumscribed by his or her status in the family, and even at the highest rungs of the status ladder a good deal of one's time and energy were spent in cultivating, supplicating, and appeasing the other members. Familial relationships built on the need to avoid disapproval and punishment on the one hand, and to encourage personal advancement on the other, were unlikely to leave the individual with either the emotional currency or the motivation to develop friendships purely on the basis of psychological gratification.

Moreover, the high incidence of the use of the word 'friend' as a synonym for kin designations, particularly when the relative involved was expected to offer a favor or service of some kind,[32] is an important clue to the nature of these relationships. It was with this shared understanding of the word that Sir Ralph's sister Susan wrote to her brother asking for money to conclude her marriage arrangements, and took the opportunity to remind him that 'so nigh a friend as you are will not see me want.'[33] Similarly, when Lady Verney sent one of her children to Misterdon for a visit with an aunt and other relatives staying there, she referred to them collectively as the child's 'friends.'[34] And when brother Thomas (annoyed by his relatives' reluctance to help him out of his financial difficulties) confided to the estate steward that he was 'resolved to perish before any of my kindred (friends I cannot call them) shall know where I am,'[35] he relied on the steward's understanding of the significance of the distinction to justify his hostility toward the family.

From the point of view of any of his brothers and sisters, Sir Ralph was the most important friend to have in the family hierarchy. This was a lesson which they learned as youngsters and which the circumstances of their later life served to reinforce. In their teens the brothers relied on Sir Ralph to intercede for them when they were out of favor with their father.[36] Again, it was Sir Ralph to whom they sent their various requests for a whole range of material necessities, from clothing and books to a new horse.[37] Even in the more serious matter of career choices they recognized that if their own wishes were to prevail with their father they needed Sir Ralph's support for the project. That is why Henry, who wanted to persuade his father to allow him to switch from being a soldier to becoming a courtier, told Sir Ralph that 'I have wrote unto him [father] about it, but I know that a word out of your mouth will do much with him.'[38]

When a younger son failed in the father's expectations of him, he was very much in need of any service which Sir Ralph could do for him. Their father's displeasure was sufficiently feared, even when they reached maturity, to wring the most abject apologies from the offender. The erring Thomas, who was 20 years old at the time, begged Sir Edmund to 'let these lines, dear father, stir you to have pity and compassion upon me, that I may receive but one smiling and merry countenance from you.'[39] Even Sir Ralph's assurances that Thomas had been forgiven his latest transgression (failing to make a success of his military career) was not adequate to erase the fearsome prospect of father's displeasure. Therefore Thomas begged his father a second time 'once again upon my bended knees [to] crave at your merciful hands pardon and forgiveness for that ill misspent life, which I have formerly led.'[40]

The range and duration of the punishments that could be inflicted on a recalcitrant son go far in explaining Thomas's desire to be forgiven. Three years later, after another failure, this time in an overseas project,[41] his father punished Thomas. Sir Edmund sent him to live at Claydon 'like a country fellow'[42] without a change of clothes and even denied him the use of a horse to enable him to ride off the grounds.[43] Thomas, who was virtually imprisoned, appealed to Sir Ralph to deliver him from this 'hellish life' and threatened that before he would 'endure it, I will take a rope and make an end of myself.'[44] It is certain that Thomas did not seriously intend to kill himself, but the humiliation and boredom which gave rise to his threat were real enough. It was more than a month before Sir Ralph arranged to have clothing sent to him,[45] and that comforting gesture was not forthcoming until weeks after Thomas had declared to his father that he would follow any employment which Sir Edmund chose for him 'for I am your son and dispose of me as you shall think best.'[46] When Sir Edmund refused to discuss it with him, Thomas had to appeal to Sir Ralph to tell him their father's plans for his future.[47]

In his dealings with his brothers, Sir Ralph's behavior was largely determined by his father's wishes, but there is nothing to indicate that he disagreed with Sir Edmund's authoritarian treatment of the younger sons. His relationship with his brother Edmund, or 'Mun' as the family referred to him, supports this view of Sir Ralph's attitude. At the beginning of 1636, Sir Ralph was instructed by his father to send Mun to Oxford 'as soon as you can' and to allow him £40 a year 'and a cloth suit' with the warning that Mun was not to exceed this amount 'for more I will not allow him.'[48] In the way of many young gentlemen of that or any period, the 20-year-old Mun spent his time at college in the pursuit of 'company' rather than learning, and by the end of a year he confessed that his 'facile nature which is so apt to be drawn the wrong way' had run him into debt.[49]

When Mun begged to be removed from Oxford and temptation, Sir Ralph admonished him for having 'misspent your fortune and time' and added that he was even 'more sorry to see you continued in your willful unwarranted courses.'[50] Sir Edmund arranged to have Mr Crowther take his 'ill disposed son' into his house for private tutoring, insisting to the minister that 'if he observe not your directions I will never willingly look upon him again.'[51] The penitent Mun was shipped off to Crowther bearing a covering letter which was written by Sir Ralph and which was characterized by the same disapproving and punitive tone revealed in Sir Edmund's note. Sir Ralph informed the minister that 'you will herewithal receive a prodigal young man, ready to sink under the heavy weight of his father's high displeasure. . . . God grant him grace to be guided by your councils,' and made a point of adding, 'but Sir, if he continue refractory give me leave to remember you of the promise . . . to acquaint me with his failings.'[52] Furthermore, it was thoroughly in keeping with Sir Ralph's position and character that he should write on another occasion to Mr Crowther expressing his agreement that Mun needed 'reformation,' and offering his prayers that 'God give a blessing to your labours.'[53]

After the death of their father in 1642, the brothers' relations with Sir Ralph continued to be one of father/son, and their fundamental dependence on him continued well into their mature lives. Some of their supplications were couched in the purple prose affected by Mun, who swore that his respect for Sir Ralph was 'grounded on your worth, honour, and nobleness' and that he had 'not a greater ambition within me then to have it in my power to serve you, O then, how eagerly and fiercely should I pursue so happy an occasion.'[54] Others adopted the more straightforward approach of the then married Thomas, who plainly observed that 'I have not any friend, unless it be yourself, that will lend me sixpence. . . . My livelihood (I acknowledge) is wholly from yourself.'[55] However it was phrased, the need, as Henry put it, to 'reap the fruit of [Sir Ralph's] affection and power'[56] continued undiminished.

If the behavior of his brothers and sisters toward Sir Ralph was dictated by their need for the influence and financial assistance which he could provide for them, his attitude and behavior toward them involved a more complex set of variables. Obviously, his paramount role in the family allowed Sir Ralph greater options in his dealings with them than they had with him. However, he did not have a completely free hand even after he came into his inheritance. In the first place, the minimum that he might do for them in the way of financial support was institutionally prescribed and legally enforced by the terms of his father's will and various trusts and investments.[57] Secondly, he was constrained to observe the reiterated norms in his dealings with them in order to satisfy what was commonly called 'world opinion.' In addition to these general considerations, Sir Ralph's exile on the continent as a political apostate made him especially vulnerable if an offended relative should choose to blackmail him by offering damaging information concerning him to the parties in power.[58] At the very least, their potential usefulness to Sir Ralph as allies in avoiding the worst consequences of sequestration was a consideration which he could not afford to overlook.[59]

The unusual opportunities for revenge or assistance which the political vicissitudes of the war made possible provided at best sporadic and uncertain levers of power. In most cases Sir Ralph's responses to the other members of the family and kin were formulated within that range of options which lay between what he was legally required to perform and what was dictated by the cultural imperatives of 'world opinion.' It was within these limits that Sir Ralph decided when and to whom he would grant or withhold that considerable power, influence, and financial aid which were the birthright of the family patriarch. Underlying any decision of this kind, however, was Sir Ralph's desire to maintain and preserve his estate against the incursions of family and kin.

In order to do this effectively, a propertied gentleman had to be careful about maintaining an unsullied reputation. Since financial arrangements of various kinds formed such a conspicuous part of familial relationships, one's dealings with one's family were used as a barometer of financial reliability in the larger society. In the relatively unsophisticated credit structure in which the propertied classes operated, a good reputation was an important asset. This is what brother Mun meant when he told Sir Ralph that 'a greater curse I know not how to wish myself' than to lose 'all good men's opinion.'[60] Sir Ralph's understandable desire to preserve his reputation also accounts for many of his studied circumlocutions in responding to the requests for his relatives. He did not wish to risk being accused of having broken his word even though some of his 'very good friends . . . condemned and chid [him] for adding so many cautions and conditions to all [his] promises.'[61]

Most of Sir Ralph's 'good friends' were aware of his vulnerability on this score and used Sir Ralph's acknowledged concern for his reputation[62] to advance their own interests. His sister Penelope used this approach when she warned him that if he broke off negotiations in a marriage proposed for her, 'you must look to be censured by the world to be the most unkind and unnatural brother.'[63] Similarly, his Aunt Isham informed Sir Ralph that the niggardly treatment which his sisters received from his estate steward 'should they complain abroad' would mean that 'you would suffer for it in your estate as you did in your credit. Your friends and neighbors wonder you would suffer your sis[ters]' to be treated so badly.[64] His sister Susan employed the same tactic when she was trying to get Sir Ralph to give her some promised clothes for her trousseau by suggesting that his intention of holding back the clothes until the marriage ceremony took place reflected badly on his reputation and hers.[65] Brother Thomas, in whom an endless series of personal and financial disasters had developed a heightened sense of the exploitable in persons and situations, believed that the question, 'what will the world say that such a man's son [i.e., himself] perished in the Gatehouse?'[66] would squeeze the necessary sum out of Sir Ralph.

Obviously this kind of informal and usually unstated pressure was much more effective when combined with other methods of winning approval and reward from Sir Ralph. The three most common approaches to this end were to display real or feigned obedience to his wishes, to offer him some service or favor or to run down the other members and in that way enhance one's prospects of becoming the favorite. Ordinarily, in a large family like the Verneys, ten of whom lived to maturity, a certain amount of backbiting is to be expected, if only as a function of numbers and leisure, and such ephemeral outbursts could not be taken as a valid indication of the real nature of their relationships. However, the kind of backbiting in which the Verneys indulged was more apt to be in the nature of a deliberate shaft rather than a spontaneous slip. Moreover, it was hardly an innocuous method of venting hostility because its intent went beyond that: backbiting was used as a method of achieving, within the limits set by the hierarchy, a redistribution of power and influence at the expense of the other members.

Such designs were unlikely to generate the kind of loyalty which places a high priority on reticence in discussing the faults of others. For example, when sister Margaret argued with their Aunt Eure about some unflattering comments which the former had made concerning the aunt's new husband, sister Susan was not at all reluctant to inform Sir Ralph of the dispute.[67] Inasmuch as similar reports about Margaret's loose tongue had been made to Sir Ralph by other members of the family on previous occasions,[68] Susan's decision to write to Sir Ralph about Margaret's latest transgression was hardly calculated to enhance the latter's standing in the family. Susan's efforts proved unavailing, however, because it was Margaret (perhaps chastened by Sir Ralph's repeated warnings),[69] not Susan, who ultimately received the aunt's 'bounty and goodness' in the form of a generous 'portion.'[70]

In order fully to appreciate how these techniques were used, it is worth examining in detail the relationship between Sir Ralph and his brother Henry. Henry's spotty and unsatisfying career as a professional soldier came to an end in 1643 when he was captured by the Parliamentary forces.[71] He was subsequently ransomed, and shortly after his release he declared himself a political neutral and attached himself to his aunt's household at Misterdon.[72] Although his services for his aunt provided him with a home which was suitable for a gentleman's life-style, his annuity of £40 p.a. was not.[73] He was therefore particularly eager to cultivate Sir Ralph in the expectation that some help might be obtained from his older brother. It is probable that Henry's efforts on this score were encouraged by Sir Ralph's help in obtaining his release.[74] He began by performing small services for his exiled brother such as sending news to Sir Ralph and his wife about their young son whom they had left in England.[75] As Sir Ralph's financial situation became more desperate because of the threat of sequestration, he increasingly relied on Henry for advice and help in preserving his estate.[76] Henry seized on any opportunity to increase Sir Ralph's dependence on him and in that way to cement the growing intimacy between them.[77]

There is nothing to indicate that any of Henry's services for Sir Ralph, or any other member of the family for that matter, were motivated by anything other than self-interest. His seemingly generous offer to prolong a stay in London to attend to his brother's business there was, in reality, a veiled request for Sir Ralph to foot the bill for maintaining Henry in the lively surroundings of the capital since otherwise he would be forced by lack of funds to return to the dull environs of Misterdon. At least this was the construction that Sir Ralph put on the offer when he tactfully refused to have Henry remain in London because he could not afford to support him there.[78] Henry went back into the country to continue in his aunt's service, but not before he took the precaution of assuring Sir Ralph that the latter came 'first' and 'next her.'[79]

Henry was not put off by Sir Ralph's refusal, and offered to negotiate some business for Sir Ralph which involved their cousin Francis Drake. It was Henry who offered himself as the proper instrument to persuade Drake to engage in a legal maneuver which would help preserve Sir Ralph's estate.[80] When the cousin proved reluctant to help, Henry seized this opportunity to denounce the uncharitable behavior of cousin Drake and to offer himself as a more 'resolute' substitute.[81] If Sir Ralph had agreed to do this, it would have meant that Henry's name would appear instead of Drake's as co-owner of a possibly lucrative office. Since Sir Ralph was unwilling to offend Henry and even more unwilling to give him that much claim to any part of his inheritance, he prudently ignored his younger brother's offer. Instead, Sir Ralph counted on Drake's acknowledgment of a few months earlier, that compliance with Sir Ralph's wishes would serve their 'mutual preservation,' to overcome any doubts that the former had concerning the correct course of action.[82] If Henry's meetings with Drake did not serve his purposes in exactly the way he intended, they were not a dead loss either. Henry obtained a lodge at Oatlands through cousin Drake's influence,[83] probably as payment for his part in the negotiations between Sir Ralph and their cousin.[84]

Even Henry's decision to take two of his sisters, Mary and Penelope, to live with him at the lodge was arranged in such a way that it would cost him nothing and would provide him with free household stuff, which he pressured Sir Ralph into giving him.[85] Mary also promised to give him some things which had been left to her.[86] He made a practice of charging all his sisters for mailing their letters to Sir Ralph, and Susan believed that he jacked up the price in order to make a profit.[87] On at least one occasion Henry's services for Sir Ralph were rewarded with a fifty-shilling bonus[88] and on another he received a mare from the older brother.[89]

In addition to any direct rewards that Henry gained out of all this, his services for Sir Ralph required that he write more frequently than he would otherwise have done. This increased correspondence was made to serve the twofold purpose of allowing Henry to dwell at length on the Herculean efforts required of him in order to fulfill Sir Ralph's commands, and at the same time enabling him to suggest, by invidious comparison, the puny response Sir Ralph was likely to get from any of the others. Inasmuch as Henry often served as go-between and informant for Sir Ralph in the latter's dealings with the other sisters and brothers, he was provided with many opportunities for depicting the other siblings in the most unflattering terms, and he had no qualms about employing backbiting as a means of gaining favor with Sir Ralph.

Henry was a practiced hand at this kind of maneuver,[90] but the circumstances of Sir Ralph's removal to France gave increased impetus to his efforts because the stakes were higher. For example, Henry took pains to explain to Sir Ralph, when the latter was accused by Penelope and Thomas of doing less than his best to get the sister married off, that he had tried to prevent 'the sending of those letters to you' and went on to insist that he refused 'to have them enclosed in [his] lines . . . but like a giddyheaded girl, and a shattell cocked fellow, they would prosecute it.' Henry also informed his brother that his defense of Sir Ralph had made the other two so angry that they were sure that Henry was the recipient of 'a yearly stipend for siding' with Sir Ralph.[91] Henry repeated this ugly accusation to Sir Ralph as much to demonstrate his unstinting loyalty to his older brother as to reveal the hostility of their sister and brother. However, the fact that Thomas and Penelope were prepared to believe that such an arrangement was possible is an indication of the bitter rivalry and mercenary considerations which permeated their dealings with one another. Furthermore, in view of Henry's behavior both before and after this incident, it is a moot point whether his indignation stemmed from the suggestion that he was in receipt of such a stipend or from his wish that he was. There is no reason to believe that he would have rejected such an offer had it been made, although he undoubtedly would have preferred to receive such largesse under different conditions.

Certainly his scruples were sufficiently malleable for him to report to his older brother on another occasion that 'the quarrel against you by many of your near kindred is for writing to me so often, and those bear me great malice for it . . . assure yourself they are deadly jealous I am highly in your favour and guide you.' In a particularly revealing piece of imagery he concluded that 'a hard judgement commonly passeth on us, if they could I dare say they would destroy and eat us.'[92] It was also as much in keeping with Henry's perception of the family as with his self-interest that he advised Sir Ralph, in confidence, that Penelope's new groom was actually prepared to settle for half the amount he was asking as a marriage portion, even though he must have realized that a smaller settlement was likely to mean a smaller widow's jointure for his sister.[93] In this case it was clear that Henry was willing to sacrifice his sister's interests for the sake of the possibility of enhancing his own by increasing Sir Ralph's gratitude to him. It was also of a piece with his previous behavior that Henry agreed to help sister Susan with her marriage arrangements only because Sir Ralph asked him to, 'notwithstanding her ill nature.'[94]

Henry acted as agent for Sir Ralph in the marriage negotiations of three of the sisters and on several occasions this obliged him to borrow money in order to complete the transactions. Sir Ralph acknowledged that his brother had helped with the arrangements and promised to pay him back as soon as possible.[95] Although Sir

Ralph increasingly relied on Henry in this as in other of his business affairs, he was very cautious about promising to do very much for the younger brother, and in his letters to Henry he made a point of playing up the financial misfortunes which he had had to endure.[96] In the early part of 1647, after waiting more than a year for repayment, Henry attempted to turn his financial liability into an asset by suggesting to Sir Ralph that the £100 debt which the latter owed to him be converted to a life annuity of twenty pounds per annum – an interest rate of twice the normal 10 per cent.[97] Sir Ralph's reluctance to agree to such an arrangement was shown by the fact that it took several requests on Henry's part in order to get any reply from Sir Ralph on this subject.[98] With a persistence born of desperation Henry repeated his proposition and added that he was even willing to accept Sir Ralph's word on such a deal and to forego the usual legal agreements.[99] When he did answer, Sir Ralph made it clear that he could not afford an additional annuity out of his already strained revenues and that in any case he believed that it was not legally possible for them to enter into such a contract.[100]

Sir Ralph's refusal of the annuity marked the beginning of the decline of his relationship with Henry. Sir Ralph thereafter made increasing use of his uncle Dr Denton and less of Henry in conducting his affairs in England.[101] This switch in allegiance was due, at least in part, to Henry's complaints to others about the unfairness of Sir Ralph having received the whole estate, while he received nothing; this indiscretion was duly circulated back to the older brother.[102] In the vain hope of putting pressure on Sir Ralph to change his mind, Henry attempted to enlist Mun's sympathy for his cause. This move was badly timed because Mun was himself in the process of making it up with Sir Ralph about a previous disagreement between them.[103] After a half-hearted attempt to remain neutral in the dispute between Henry and Sir Ralph,[104] Mun's need to increase his stock with the latter prevailed. He did not content himself merely with siding with Sir Ralph, but by way of added proof of his complete devotion, he turned informer and repeated their younger brother's angry declaration that he never intended to write to the oldest brother again.[105]

Mun was willing, if necessary, to trample on Henry in order to regain his place as the favorite brother, a maneuver which, combined with repeated declarations of his submission and love, was ultimately rewarded with financial assistance and assurances from Sir Ralph.[106] But once he was safely installed in that enviable position, it was Mun who proceeded to help Henry in an attempt at reconciliation with Sir Ralph.[107] Mun's reasons for this about-face were not spelled out. What is certain is that he knew from personal experience the disagreeable condition of a younger brother who was out of favor with the head of the family. One can also fairly conclude that his treatment of Henry in the dispute with Sir Ralph reduces the likelihood that he was motivated by any great love for Henry.

This incident does illustrate, however, the way in which family solidarity was preserved in spite of frequent quarrels among the members. When the chips were down, Mun and Henry both needed Sir Ralph more than they needed each other, and the methods open to them for cultivating Sir Ralph's favor left little room for affectionate and generous behavior. Yet, when Mun was confident that he had regained Sir Ralph's good opinion of him, there was little risk to his own position and probably a certain amount of satisfaction to his own charitable impulses, not to mention the pleasure of exercising his newly regained influence, for him to assist the outcast Henry's tentative gestures for reconciliation. Much as Henry had on occasion requested small favors for the others when he had enjoyed Sir Ralph's confidence,[108] so Mun now came to Henry's aid. It is also necessary to add that in the see-sawing relationships of the sisters and brothers, a younger son could never afford to ignore completely the possibility that at some later date such favors might be reciprocated. Mun's declaration to Sir Ralph that he did 'not at all grudge at the difference and great distance of our powers'[109] was intended to assure Sir Ralph that he, at least, knew his place, but his thorough comprehension of his situation also engaged him to do what he could for the unfortunate Henry.

## UNCLES AND AUNTS

The relationships of the brothers and sisters with members of the wider kinship network were similar in content and function to those which they experienced with each other, and for similar reasons. Properly cultivated, the kin could be of assistance in furthering one's prospects and in serving as an ameliorating influence on the authority and power wielded by the head of the family. With respect to the latter, the kin functioned collectively as the chief formulators of 'world opinion', and in that capacity served as a barrier against the total abuse of power or neglect of responsibilities by the family patriarch. From Sir Ralph's point of view sufficient numbers of the kin were involved in his financial affairs in a ramifying and often reciprocal network of trusts, deeds, and annuities to make it important for him to maintain their good will, or at least to avoid alienating them completely.

In his relations with the kin, as with those of the immediate family, Sir Ralph as the son and heir enjoyed certain advantages over the other siblings. His relationships with the kin were likely to be stronger and more intense, partly because of his financial involvement with them, and partly because these financial arrangements in turn gave rise to a complex variety of reciprocal services. In so far as the brothers and sisters were the recipients of favors from the kin they usually enjoyed those privileges as a sort of secondary patronage allotted to them through their relationship with Sir Ralph.

Among the kin, the Denton family connection (Sir Edmund's wife's family) was the most important. The Dentons of Hillesden were already a power in Buckinghamshire when the Verneys were still newcomers.[110] Lady Susan Denton's family of five sons and five daughters made up that large contingent of Denton aunts and uncles who figure so prominently in the Verneys' affairs.[111] It was one of these, Aunt Eure, who gave her niece Margaret Verney that portion of one thousand pounds. It was a gift of sufficient magnitude to lead Sir Ralph to believe that ''tis impossible that she [Margaret] should ever be able to requite this noble favour,' but he was 'confident upon all occasions she will endeavor to express her real thankfulness . . . and by her future carriage and obedience manifest to all the world that she is wholly yours.'[112] Sir Ralph was doing no more than expressing the accepted values concerning the kind of allegiance which such a gift was expected to evoke in the recipient. In addition to her claim on Margaret's loyalties and to her role as godmother,[113] Aunt Eure had other bonds which linked her to Sir Ralph. In fact this gift of the portion may be viewed as Aunt Eure's *quid pro quo* for previous services performed by Sir Ralph. He had for some years been carrying out a variety of tasks for her, such as collecting her rents and paying her bills.[114] Her gift must also have served to make it much easier for the Verneys to swallow the bitter pill of her having married a Catholic. Despite their expressed and genuine horror at such a choice,[115] Sir Ralph continued to give his assistance to his aunt and her new husband whenever she requested it.[116] The Verneys, with six girls to dower, could not afford to be overly scrupulous about the source of so generous a portion.

The relationship with another Denton aunt, Elizabeth Isham, also illustrates the way in which financial dependency reinforced social relationships between the two families. Following a common practice of the period, Aunt Isham lent money out at interest, and Sir Ralph and some others whom he recommended were the recipients of these loans.[117] During the war years both interest and principal were difficult, if not impossible, to collect. In common with other propertied families, Aunt Isham and her huband suffered from the financial pinch imposed by the war. Rents were slow in coming in, when they were paid at all,[118] and in her case there was the added disaster of having lost most of her 'writings' (the mass of legal documents needed to prove ownership of land)[119] when the Parliamentary forces sacked her ancestral home at Hillesden.[120] Moreover, the dislocations and uncertainties caused by the war made it difficult even to locate other persons necessary to the repayment or collection of debts.[121] For example, Aunt Isham complained to Sir Ralph that she could not collect on the money she lent out through him because the debtors were either dead, imprisoned or had left minor heirs.[122] Her increasing need, and his continued insistence that he could not pay as much as she asked, led to hard words and injured feelings on both sides. After five years of haggling, pleading, and cajoling,[123] Aunt Isham grasped at the last resort of a relative in her situation, and threatened Sir Ralph with a law suit.[124] Sir Ralph attempted to face her down with the deliberately cutting accusation that his most recent offer of land in exchange for the money he owed 'might have satisfied a friend.'[125]

This dispute, and its ultimately amicable settlement, revealed a great deal about the nature of kinship solidarity as well as the values and attitudes of the parties involved. Although the war imposed stresses on their relationship of a kind which would probably not have occurred in normal times, their fundamental need for each other which bound them together in peacetime became greater rather than less during the crisis situation of the war. By her own admission Aunt Isham had no income at this time except what she received from Sir Ralph's estate.[126] He in turn counted on her to inform him of what was happening at Claydon, and especially to keep a watchful eye on his sisters.[127] Since Sir Ralph was also financially entangled with her brother Dr William Denton, and her nephew Francis Drake, he had to satisfy the latter two that his hard bargaining with Aunt Isham was the product of necessity and not of greed.[128] Balanced against this hold she had on Sir Ralph was his position as head of the Verney family. Even if his influence was somewhat weakened by his uncertain financial position, Sir Ralph's reservoir of power had many aspects, of which financial control was only one. For example, at one point in their negotiations, Aunt Isham asked her nephew to pay one of her creditors some money which Sir Ralph had intended to give directly to her as repayment. Her reason for this was that she could only pay half the interest due on this debt, and she believed that this reduction in payment would be more acceptable to her creditor if it came from Sir Ralph's prestigious hand rather than directly from her.[129]

Considerations of this kind, as well as obligations and attachments within her own family, ultimately served to dissuade her from bringing suit. Her brother, Dr Denton, served as mediator, and by means of one of those incredibly complex round-robins typical of family financial arrangements a settlement was finally reached.[130] In the process of bringing this about, the parties in the settlement came to include both Dr Denton and his wife, to whom Sir Ralph also owed substantial amounts.[131] Uncle Doctor cleverly managed it in such a way as to satisfy Sir Ralph and Aunt Isham and at the same time pay off some of his own debts.[132] Nor was this the only benefit which the uncle derived from this dispute between his sister and nephew. During the negotiations he sought Sir Ralph's help in putting pressure on one of his wife's other debtors, who was then living in France.[133] Dr Denton's request for Sir Ralph's cooperation in this undertaking was made at a time when the nephew was apt to be especially responsive to the uncle's needs.

On the whole, however, Sir Ralph's relationship with Uncle Doctor, as compared with any other members of the family and kin, was apt to be less marked by preoccupation with self-interest. This was due to the doctor's family position as well as to his personal qualities. Although he was a younger son, the Dentons were a higher-status family than the Verneys. This, and the fact that he was a successful physician, helped to close the social gap between him and Sir Ralph. Since these were also authoritarian families, the generational difference between them served the same purpose; for if Sir Ralph was paramount in the Verney hierarchy, his uncle belonged to his mother's generation, and the advantage of age (he was Sir Ralph's senior by less than a decade) entitled him to a certain amount of deference from the nephew.

Although Dr Denton was temperamentally quite different from his nephew, the uncle possessed exactly those qualities needed to cement a genuine friendship with someone of Sir Ralph's reserved and often suspicious nature. Dr Denton was easily Sir Ralph's intellectual equal, and was a match for him in being equally hard-headed and serious about business matters. But the uncle generally tended to be optimistic rather than pessimistic, worldly and sophisticated rather than cynical, and he revealed a sense of proportion in adversity which derived from the saving grace of a well-developed sense of humor – a trait totally lacking in the nephew.[134]

While it was true that they were trapped by circumstance and birth into using one another – in the sense that neither was a freely chosen agent – they never pushed their demands to the point of greedy exploitation. This can be explained by their genuine concern and affection for each other, which was something of a triumph in a society whose values and social modes offered barren soil for the blossoming of disinterested giving of any kind. What this society did offer – in fact demanded – from its members was reciprocation in a bewildering variety of forms (gifts, favors, *douceurs*, hospitality, etc.). But sometimes, as in the case of Sir Ralph and his uncle, this reciprocation was not manipulative, but was simply a concerned response to the needs of others.

If the uncle's part in the dispute between Sir Ralph and Aunt Isham ultimately benefited him, there were many other occasions when the doctor's own interests seem to have been a minor consideration to him. He was a key figure in helping to rid the Verney estate of sequestration and in this his assistance to Sir Ralph went beyond judicious advice. He used his influence to make the proper contacts with members of the committee which was to hear Sir Ralph's petition, and he bribed those members who could be bought.[135] He persuaded his wife to undertake the expense and trouble of frequent, sumptuous dinners, to which members of the Parliament were invited 'that they might go along with us to the committee.'[136] The seeming disadvantage of the doctor being a known Royalist (he had been physician to Charles I and would occupy the same office under Charles II)[137] was offset by the fact that his uncle was at this time a leader among the Independents, and he rightly counted on family connection taking a higher priority than ideological commitment.[138] The doctor was no stranger to the techniques one needed to employ in such matters, for he had compounded the previous year for a mere £50.[139]

Sir Ralph's gratitude for Uncle Denton's help in this and other business was understandable and genuine.[140] He instructed his wife, who was then temporarily in England, to give Uncle Doctor £40 as a gift, inasmuch as the nephew suspected that the doctor had probably worn out 'in shoe leather' something approaching that sum in their service.[141] There was nothing extraordinary in Sir Ralph's offer, for he probably would have done the same, under the circumstances, for someone whom he liked less. But it was extraordinary that the doctor refused to take it, and that Lady Verney was made to promise her husband that she would insist on offering it until the doctor accepted.[142]

Dr Denton was unique in other ways. With the exception of Sir Edmund, he was the only correspondent who addressed Sir Ralph by his first name. In a period when salutations were not dead forms, this was further testimony of the closeness of their relationship. And out of thousands of letters written by hundreds of different correspondents, it was entirely in character that it should be one of his to Sir Ralph which contained the postscript 'all our loves (which is better than services) to you and yours.'[143] This postscript reveals his very unusual ability to make the distinction between familial obligation and love, and to see the latter as preferable.

In other ways he was a more typical product of his time. He informed Sir Ralph, without any hint of embarrassment, that he took special care of a patient, one Mr Lisle, primarily because the latter was a member of the committee reviewing claims on the alnage office, in which both the doctor and Sir Ralph had interests.[144] His care of the famous jurist Orlando Bridgeman was offered for similar reasons.[145] This injection of personal self-interest into medical treatment was common in this age since objective standards of professional conduct had not yet been established as taking priority over all other considerations. One of Sir Ralph's acquaintances in France, a Mr Harrison, who wished to get a disinterested diagnosis of his master's illness, asked Sir Ralph to send for Dr Testard (a friend of the Verneys) because the attending physician in the case could not be counted on to do so.[146] It was Doctor Denton who advised Sir Ralph to provide £50 for Bridgeman's son, who was then residing in France and temporarily in need of money, because the jurist's services were needed in some of Sir Ralph's business.[147]

Dr Denton's relations with the Verney nieces and nephews were close and paternal. He was generous and unstinting in his professional services for them,[148] if the barbaric medical treatments of the time can be described in such terms. It was also 'Uncle Doctor' who acted as peacemaker between Mun and Sir Ralph,[149] lent money to Mun, sister Elizabeth, and Lady Verney when they needed it,[150] and defended his unmarried niece Mary against her sister Susan's jealous accusation that the former had made a play for the latter's husband.[151] When Thomas and Susan's husband had a violent argument over some money which Susan had borrowed from Thomas's wife, it was Uncle Doctor who put up £11 of his own money to end the argument.[152] It was Dr Denton who reminded Sir Ralph to write a letter of consolation to his war-widowed sister Cary,[153] and acted for her when she remarried even though he disapproved of the match.[154] Dr Denton's role in the Verney family was accurately reflected in his niece Mary's use of the salutation 'Dear Parent' in her letters to him.[155] It was also appropriate that Lady Verney, who was a keen judge of such matters, should single out Dr Denton as the most trustworthy of all their relatives.[156]

The Verneys' dealings with their Aunt Ursula were more typical of the conventional values and attitudes attending such relationships. When Sir Ralph fell behind in payment of an annuity which she received out of his estate, she put pressure on him by refusing to sign an acquittance for late payment until he agreed to make up the difference for war-incurred taxes.[157] She also reclaimed a cordial (a money gift put aside for future use with right of recall) which she had given to one of Sir Ralph's sisters.[158] When brother Henry quit soldiering she was his first mark, and she rather naively informed Sir Ralph of his younger brother's willingness to serve her.[159] But this was not to last, because Henry took the occasion of her satisfaction with him to cheat her out of £20.[160] Henry, of course, protested his innocence to Sir Ralph and the kin.[161] In the end Sir Ralph paid the £20 which his brother had taken, partly in the hope (as his patron, the Countess of Sussex, suggested) that payment might persuade Aunt Ursula to return the cordial, and probably as a favor to Henry, who was at that time helping Sir Ralph with some business.[162] Perhaps her unpleasant experience with Henry accounted for Aunt Ursula's subsequent refusal to help buy some clothes for Susan. At any rate, Susan reported to Sir Ralph that she found their aunt quite 'backward in all such things.'[163]

## COUSINS

Still another kin group that must be examined in order to understand the nature of upper-gentry family life was that vast network of relatives related by blood and marriage, the cousinhood. In the seventeenth century, this relationship had not yet degenerated to that casual and tenuous alliance described in American and British vernacular as a 'kissing cousin.' It was still a viable and functional relationship, as indicated by the shared values and institutional arrangements which enhanced its intensity and importance. At that time, the act of marriage went beyond alliance to one's spouse to include 'marriage to the whole family.'[164] Moreover, the word 'family' as used by the Verneys and their contemporaries, included the cousins. Francis Drake, Sir Ralph's cousin by marriage, obviously subscribed to this conception of their relationship when he assured him that 'no alteration whatsoever shall deprive me of the remembrances that I am a member of your family, to the upholding whereof I shall while I live . . . contribute my best assistance.'[165]

In this instance the kind of assistance that Sir Ralph required from cousin Drake involved the latter's help in preserving the Verney estate,[166] but the values expressed in the cousin's response predated that crisis. Drake's participation in the Verney's financial affairs had begun before the war.[167] The conflict made family financing much more difficult, and in that way severely tested previously established obligations and values. In Drake's case self-interest coincided neatly with familial loyalties and he ultimately, if reluctantly, gave the needed assistance to Sir Ralph.[168] By 1648, Sir Ralph owed this cousin at least £2,500, a very substantial debt which probably helped to overcome any reservations that Drake may have had about helping Sir Ralph to preserve his estate against the sequestrators.[169]

Sir Ralph's relationships with his other cousins were somewhat different from that with Drake, in that the others were more dependent on Sir Ralph for help than he was on them. His dealings with these other cousins are worth examining as much for what they reveal about the cousinhood as for what they reveal about the ramifying power of patriarchal control over kin outside the conjugal unit. As with the sibling relationships, the cousins' behavior toward each other was not ordinarily dependent upon ties of love or affection. Even when the cousin had been raised in the Verney household, as was the case with Doll Leeke,[170] or when the families had spent extended periods visiting with each other, as was the case with their London cousins Anne and Nat Hobart,[171] the personal intimacy provided by this kind of contact served to increase the demands which they might legitimately make on one another but did not give rise to the kind of loving responses which such familiarity might have been expected to produce.

Doll Leeke was a spinster cousin who received a small legacy from the Verney estate.[172] Using Sir Ralph as her agent, she had put some money out at interest in order to increase her income.[173] When the war came her only source of income was her allowance from Sir Ralph who was frequently behind in payments to her and who claimed that he was unable to pay her in full.[174] She was at that time living as a dependent in the Royalist household of Sir Edward Sydenham and his wife Lady Anne. Doll Leeke shared their politics as well as their hospitality and was critical of Sir Ralph's early alignment with the Parliamentarians.[175] However, Doll was far more concerned with receiving her payments from Sir Ralph than with any political differences that existed between them, and her subsequent dispute with Sir Ralph had more to do with finances than with ideology.[176]

It happened that the Sydenhams owed Sir Ralph money as a result of a deal which he had entered into with them for a lease on the Marshalsea Prison.[177] When they did not pay up, he blamed Doll for not putting pressure on them and did more than hint that if his outstanding debts were paid he could in turn make full payment to her.[178] She defended herself by reminding him that 'I live by them [i.e., the Sydenhams] and know not where to get bread if their charity did not afford it to me.'[179] This reasonable defense of her position did not prevent Sir Ralph's further attempt to rid himself of his debt to her and to recover what was owing to him by suggesting that the Sydenhams pay Doll some of what they owed him.[180] This put Doll in a very difficult position because she was afraid that this added burden on Sir Edward, who was already providing her with free board, might make him 'grow weary of her.'[181] Sir Ralph did not concern himself with the difficulties that such an arrangement would make for his cousin's precarious existence. The final settlement of the 'Prison business' with the Sydenhams tied them to paying Doll the arrears of what was owing to her from cousin Ralph.[182] As confirmation of the nature of patriarchy, it was Doll who wrote to Sir Ralph assuring him of her continued affection,[183] and she even went so far as to apologize to him for removing her money from his control.[184] According to Dr Denton, who was in a position to know, she was in fact quite unhappy about this settlement.[185] Lady Verney, who was on the scene during the negotiations, was unconvinced by Doll's protestations of love, and believed the cousin to be 'rotten at heart.'[186]

On the other hand, there is no reason to doubt the sincerity of Doll's desire to make it up with Sir Ralph and his wife, both of whom were more influential and affluent than she was, even though her declarations of affection were less than believable in the circumstances. In spite of her understandable dissatisfaction with the repayment arrangement, it was prudent, if not just, for her rather than Sir Ralph to have made the first overtures and greatest effort to effect a reconciliation between them.[187] She did succeed in eliciting some friendly replies from Sir Ralph, which were in part the result of Dr Denton's prodding.[188] The social complexities involved in the Marshalsea Prison settlement were further illustrated by Sir Ralph's desire, in this case, to minimize Dr Denton's involvement in the transaction 'lest [the Sydenhams and Doll] suspect him [i.e., Dr Denton] of being too much my friend, and for that cause turn his enemies, which may be much to his prejudice and . . . I am not in a condition to recompense such a loss.'[189]

Sir Ralph's treatment of his cousins, the Hobarts, betrayed nothing of the concern which he showed for the doctor. In their case, neither family alliance nor common engagement in various business undertakings[190] produced any emotional bond other than the calculated network of reciprocal services which formed the major element in most of the kin relationships. When Sir Ralph moved to France he placed many of his estate documents in storage in Holland. Among these 'writings' were a number which were vital to the Hobarts' interests, since without them they could not prove legal ownership of certain properties,[191] collect rents, or use the properties as security for loans.[192] After repeated desperate requests from the Hobarts for the return of their writings, Sir Ralph claimed that he could not afford the expense of getting them out of storage.[193] The Hobarts also canvassed other members of the family and kin in the hope of getting Sir Ralph to comply under pressure.[194] Nat Hobart's offer to lay out £50 to help promote the marriage negotiations of one of Sir Ralph's sisters was probably directed toward the same end.[195] None of this was effective, however, not even Anne Hobart's pathetic letter to Sir Ralph informing him that her husband was then a prisoner and that his very life depended on obtaining those documents,[196] presumably in order to raise the money to ransom him.

Sir Ralph continued to drag his feet on this, partly because of the expense entailed in shipping the documents, and partly because he did not want to risk having anyone mistakenly remove his own writings, which were stored in the same place.[197] His first demurrer was answered by Nat Hobart's assurances that he would pay the costs of shipment;[198] the second was overcome by the fact that it became necessary for Sir Ralph to ship certain of his other writings to England in order to settle the prison deal with the Sydenhams. But this did not occur until 1648, some three years after the Hobarts' first request for their writings.[199]

There would have been an even greater delay if Sir Ralph had taken his wife's advice and 'stopped' the shipment in order to encourage the Hobarts to pay up more quickly.[200] Sir Ralph considered that this would look too 'ugly' and would involve further delay for others, whose documents were included in the same shipment and whom he did not wish to punish in this way.[201] This incident reveals yet another aspect of Sir Ralph's power; his willingness to produce or withhold the legal documents in his possession afforded him a subtle but real advantage in any dealings with the family and kin as well as added incentive for them to maintain his good will.[202]

As far as Anne Hobart was concerned, Sir Ralph's dilatory compliance made her increasingly desperate but not openly hostile. She could not afford to antagonize Sir Ralph because his ability to retaliate was greater than hers. In addition, what is known about her dealings within her own family (the Leekes) does not suggest that she would find Sir Ralph's treatment of her to be especially repugnant. It was she who had written to Sir Ralph in confidence and without her husband's knowledge to ask her cousin if he would help her to get control of a lease which her mother wished to give to one of her other daughters.[203]

There is less evidence for detailed reconstruction of Sir Ralph's relationship with his grandparents because only a relatively small correspondence between Sir Ralph and his maternal grandmother Susan Denton (who died in 1641)[204] is extant. However, what is known of the content of this relationship is similar to that which obtained between Sir Ralph and his father, although it was naturally less strong and less intense.

Sir Ralph signed his letters to grandmother Denton 'Your faithful and obedient son,'[205] which in terms of the obligations they assumed for each other accurately reflected their relationship. Sir Ralph helped her with the administration of her estate.[206] Her confidence in her grandson's sophistication concerning such matters probably accounts for her decision to ask his advice in securing her jointure against the possible future claims of one of her sons.[207] She in turn took Sir Ralph's 2½-year-old son to live with her at Hillesden[208] where, according to Lady Denton, the boy's manners showed a marked improvement.[209] The child stayed at Hillesden for almost a year[210] and the decision to take him back to Claydon was made only after Sir Ralph had quarreled with his grandmother.[211] Sir Ralph claimed that Lady Denton had been unjustifiably angered by some words he had had with her concerning her daughter's (Aunt Eure's) marriage to a Catholic.[212] Sir Ralph protested his innocence to both his grandmother and father and explained to the latter that he 'could not say less, being provoked with as much heat and passion and bitterness as she [Lady Denton] could express.'[213] It had apparently been Sir Ralph's intention further to advertise his indignation by the immediate removal of his son from Hillesden. However, Aunt Eure advised him to wait,[214] presumably because such a move at that time would further antagonize the grandmother. Sir Ralph's irritation with his grandmother was outweighed by his desire to pacify her, for he followed his aunt's suggestion and did not take his son home until several months later.[215] In the interim Sir Ralph continued to perform whatever services his grandmother requested of him.[216]

There is no evidence to indicate that in this dispute the needs of the child were considered at any point. Sir Ralph's son had been sent to his grandmother Denton's home as part of the pattern of familial exchanges that were expected to obtain between his father and grandmother. In the decision to place him there, and even in the timing of his removal, the child was viewed as a piece of currency in a reciprocal exchange between the two adults. It is indicative of the marked reversal of familial values since that time that any anxiety which Sir Ralph expressed in this matter was generated by his concern with the reactions of his grandmother and his father rather than with those of his child. However, if the demands of the family hierarchy required obedience and compliance to those in positions of authority, the same values justified Sir Ralph's treatment of his son.

The patriarchal family which emerges from this study of the Verney family relationships differs in significant ways, not only from that of the present day, but from certain assumptions or generalizations commonly attributed to it by historians. Within the family, patriarchy and patrimony created a system of values and behavior in which the individual's concern for his own welfare came first. In attempting to satisfy the many and sometimes conflicting demands made on the individual by family, kin, the church, county politics or state service, responses were predicated on what the individual conceived to be in keeping with his own advancement. There was, after all, little in the life experience of any of these individuals that would make them give to ideals of selflessness and charity or the duty of patriotism higher priorities than loyalty to one's self, even if they usually justified their motives and behavior in those terms. The singleminded commitment which permits totally disinterested service to the state or church without reference to individual or family needs, responsibilities, and influence requires that the institution in question shall have reached that stage of professionalization which did not as yet exist in seventeenth century England; fully professionalized institutions, by definition, are largely devoid of patronage and have developed beyond the stage of patrimonial bureaucracy, in which recruitment and procedures operate primarily within the control and influence of the family. In the seventeenth century neither service to the state nor to the established church required the subordination of familial and patrimonial considerations to abstract standards of institutional efficiency and loyalty. In fact, just the reverse was true for the upper classes. In the nature of the case the family and the kin were the chief means by which the individual was enabled to offer himself and his talents to other institutions.

Although solidarity was a marked characteristic of family and kin relationships, this cohesiveness was grounded in the very different content of the family's capacity to control and distribute scarce resources and secondarily its ability to provide love and psychological support. This is not to say that such emotions never existed between individual members but that the shared values and possible options experienced by its members tended to make this the exception rather than the rule.

The Verney family correspondence holds many striking examples of the significance of social structures in shaping private attitudes and behavior. Among those which appear to have been particularly decisive, I have emphasized the effects of patriarchal control, the differential treatment of women, the shared agreement on the legitimacy of hierarchy and authoritarianism, and the economic imperatives of *rentier* class status, as a constellation of societal givens which affected the quality of familial interaction irrespective of individual idiosyncrasies. Of course to reiterate the importance of structure and its effect on behavioral possibilities and limits of family members is not the same as insisting that there is always an exact and unfailing correspondence between the two; rather, it is to suggest that much of what we commonly perceive and explain as individual and private psychological preference and behavior is more accurately understood and explained in relation to these wider social phenomena.[217]

The family's responsibilities and functions were more varied and greater than they are today but the process of fulfilling the needs of its members' individual options were, by present-day standards, severely circumscribed. Role assignations, determined by birth order and sex, influenced the nature of personal relations and low priority was placed on individual psychological needs. Adherence to the principle of patriarchy bolstered family and kin solidarity, but not by means of love and sympathy. Nor did patriarchal control preclude frequent and often bitter sibling rivalry. On the contrary, the evidence suggests that the existence of the authoritarian father figure was by no means a guarantee of harmony and good will among the members of the family.

Patriarchy established and sustained a system of social reciprocity, and concomitant (though sometimes forced) communication between the members. The price of keeping these lines of communication open might sometimes require an abject apology or an insincere declaration of devotion and obedience, but these mutually accepted forms involved no uncertainty for the user or the recipient, and were not considered to be incompatible with personal integrity. The ready use and acceptance of such forms, the confidence about the legitimacy of the claims that one member of the hierarchy might make upon another, served to minimize if not eliminate the modern malaise of alienation even in a family where emotional bonds meant little in preserving cohesiveness. Moreover, for members of this class, the family and kin merged imperceptibly into the larger society, as Professor Bailyn has correctly observed,[218] and therefore the trauma of personal adjustment to the outside world was a problem which hardly existed for the Verneys.

Finally, the examination of the relational aspects of family structure suggests that the ideal of friendship as an association freely chosen on the basis of mutual psychological attraction is an historically recent or at least discontinous phenomenon.[219] The place of friends *vis-à-vis* family relationships appears to be contingent on the nature of the family. The use of the word as a substitute for kin designations, and the seventeenth century connotation of friend as someone who will serve one's interests, reveal the importance placed on family and kin in that period.

# 3

# MARRIAGE: THE MALE PERSPECTIVE

The study of matrimonial procedures and attitudes is especially significant in an arranged marriage society, as much for what it can reveal about the specific nature of those practices as for what it can tell us about the institutions and values of the wider society. For example, in order to explain the acceptance and endurance of the practice of arranged marriage among the propertied classes one must analyze its necessary connection with the double sexual standard and the inferior status of women, as well as its enormous influence upon family finances. Moreover, since marriage is the acid test for revealing many of the attitudes and prejudices shared by members of a social class, an examination of their marriage choices and practices can provide an understanding of their value system – that important dimension of individual experience which is so often inaccessible to the historian. Lastly, the study of marriage can point up the way in which various social arrangements dovetail and reinforce each other.

There is an understandable tendency to perceive most readily those aspects of a remote institution or practice which are similar to our own. This is particularly true when the institution being examined is as ostensibly familiar and at the same time as complex as that of marriage, because the latter is both standard and sanction for a whole range of behavior, goals, and values which claim some of our most profound and cherished commitments. However, the historian has an obligation to enlarge our understanding of previous societies by defining and examining those differences which distinguish them from our own.

## THE ARRANGED MARRIAGE

The purposes and procedures of the arranged marriage were in many ways quite different from that of the romantic marriage of the twentieth century. The arranged marriage was, as Professor Stone has concluded 'essentially . . . an institutional device to ensure the perpetuation of the family and its property.'[1] Its primary purpose was therefore quite unlike that of the romantic marriage in which the psychological and physiological needs of the partners are considered to be of paramount importance. Arranged marriages provided a solution to the problem of the preservation of property, but the emotional and physical needs of the couple were peripheral considerations. In so far as the needs of the individuals involved were considered secondary to the rational objectives of preserving property and securing legitimate heirs, the double sexual standard served the function of ameliorating the contradictions which proceeded from that order of priorities; since strict adherence to marital fidelity was incumbent upon women but not upon men, the husband who found himself tied to an incompatible partner could seek relief by recourse to the accepted, if not applauded, alternative of extra-marital affairs.

Moreover, if the arranged marriage sometimes failed to offer very much in the way of personal satisfaction, it was an excellent vehicle for the attainment of certain *social* advantages. In a society in which the marriage ceremony represented more than the alliance of two individuals, because 'the tie of marriage' extended 'to the whole family,'[2] the expansion of social connections through marriage was a benefit which figured prominently in the desire to get a spouse. Because favors of various kinds, even when bestowed upon an individual, were believed to 'oblige the whole family' (including those related by marriage) unmarried adults failed their families in that they did not contribute to the expansion of the social contacts and concomitant services available to them.[3] Since the act of marriage expanded the network of relations upon whom an individual and his family of origin could legitimately make a variety of claims, marriage had a dimension of importance in a patronage society which it seldom has today.

The importance of getting a suitable spouse was also reflected in the fact that helping someone to a good match was considered a great favor[4] and the ability to provide such assistance was used as a lever for obtaining other advantages. When Sir Ralph and Lady Verney cast about for ways of making a 'friend' of the Earl of Warwick, for the purpose of protecting their estate from sequestration, Lady Verney suggested that, in the event that Warwick would be 'useful' to them, she would help the earl's daughter to a good match in return for his assistance.[5]

Since financial considerations loomed so large in the arranged marriage procedure and were of critical importance in determining a woman's marriageability, it is necessary briefly to clarify some of the more significant terms which were used in the negotiations. It was the responsibility of the bride's father to provide her with a sizeable cash sum, which was called a portion, and which was usually paid to the groom's father. The father of the groom was in return expected to provide his daughter-in-law with an annual allowance, or jointure, which was to be paid to her in the event of her husband's death. The widow's jointure might be paid in the form of a fixed annuity or she might be given a specific amount of property of appropriate value. Most of the negotiating prior to the marriage involved arguments over the relative merits of the size of the portion as compared with what the groom's side was willing to offer as a jointure.[6]

If the groom was an eldest son, it was the usual practice to settle the family estates just before he was married. These settlements became increasingly complex and sophisticated in the latter part of the century, but essentially they were designed to preserve the family patrimony intact by limiting the ability of the heir to dispose of his inherited property. He was in effect only a life tenant of the estate and could not legally sell his property outright until his first son came of age. The cash or property set aside for the raising of the portions was frequently conveyed to feoffees in trust. These trustees or feoffees were usually older male members of the family appointed by the girl's father (who was ordinarily one of them) to administer this fund and protect the interests of the young woman.[7]

Sir Ralph's father, Sir Edmund, had made provisions of this kind for his future children at the time of his marriage.[8] Sir

Edmund was 'tenant for life' and the bulk of the estate was to pass to his eldest son.[9] Each daughter was also supposed to receive a marriage portion of £1,000. However, since there were six daughters to provide for, Sir Edmund attempted to minimize the toll on the family finances by investing their portion money in offices. In addition, his younger sons and all the daughters received small annual annuities.[10] However, only the sons received such payments for life; the daughters' annuities ceased when they married.

The double standard also had decided effects on men's decisions whether or not to marry. Bachelorhood did not necessarily consign them either to sexual deprivation or to economic dependency, and they were therefore under considerably less pressure to marry than were their sisters. However, as in all other areas of their lives, younger sons had different needs and choices in regard to marriage than the inheriting son. The arranged marriage, together with most other institutional devices, served the latter's needs better than theirs. Since marriage choices were rarely made on the basis of romantic inclinations, the crucial variable in getting a suitable bride was the ability to maintain her and provide her with a widow's jointure commensurate with her dowry offering, and a propertied heir was in the best position to do this. Marriage was an attractive prospect for him because it was designed to preserve his inheritance and carry on his name, and also offered the opportunity to expand his influence and power through familial connections with the prospective bride's family. Although the compatibility of the couple was barely considered, it was also more probable that he would enjoy at least a workable relationship, since financial problems were less likely to stimulate marital discord. In addition, the wife of the inheriting son, given the prevailing values and the social advantages of her position, was more apt to do what she could to please her husband and keep the marriage going.

In contrast to his younger brothers, Sir Ralph as the eldest son and heir had easier access to a suitable match, and better prospects for enjoying a workable and even affectionate relationship with his bride. In marriage as in much else, the distribution of life chances favored the heir or heiress; the union of the two in matrimony provided excellent chances for a successful alliance. Their combined inheritance would normally protect the marriage from severe financial problems, and their relationship would not be marred by the social and psychological strains of a misalliance. Sir Ralph's marriage to Mary Blacknall, an orphaned heiress, who had been purchased from the Court of Wards for the purpose,[11] was just such a match.

Although the bride chosen by Sir Edmund for Sir Ralph was only 13[12] and the groom a few years older,[13] the extreme youth of the couple did not diminish their chances of establishing a good relationship, in part because neither was expected immediately to take on the full responsibilities of married life. They lived at Claydon with Sir Ralph's parents, and during the early years of the marriage Sir Ralph continued his studies at Oxford.[14] Most of the younger Verneys could not remember a time when Mary was not part of the family, and they probably viewed her as an older sibling rather than as a sister-in-law. That this was likely to be the position of Mary *via-à-vis* the other children is also corroborated by the general practice of making no distinctions in terminology between blood relations and affines: for instance, Mary was referred to as 'sister' by the younger Verneys.[15] And as Sir Ralph's wife she enjoyed the added advantage of occupying the highest status among any of the other children with the obvious exception of Sir Ralph. This diminished the possibility that she would be abused by any of Sir Edmund's natural children, as well as providing early experience for them in the habit of respect for her.

Moreover, she possessed personal qualities of a kind that served to cement the relationship between her and Sir Ralph, a relationship which ultimately grew into one of devotion and love. Her letters reveal her to have been intelligent (they are better phrased and more literate than hundreds written by other women).[16] She was a keen judge of people and knew how to get on with others, which was a valuable asset for a woman in her position, where part of the burden and responsibility for social exchanges as well as the cultivation of important members of the family and kin fell to her.[17] In addition to these accomplishments, she provided the Verneys with a male heir, her second living child (the first baby died in infancy) being a son.

The success of Lady Verney's twenty-one-year marriage to Sir Ralph was also due to the fact that both she and her husband shared similar values and attitudes concerning the conduct and goals of married life. Both of them firmly believed that it was necessary and desirable that Sir Ralph should make all the major (and many minor) decisions concerning the estate, as well as those relating to the maintenance, training, and education of their children. There was, of course, no question of equal sharing of decision-making and authority in any area of their lives; if their marriage revealed great husband/wife solidarity and was not likely to give way under pressure, it was also a marriage ordered and directed along lines prescribed by Sir Ralph, in which his wife looked after the more tedious details. She contributed a certain ease and graciousness to his efforts, but she was not indispensable for their achievement. Her only indispensable contribution to the marriage was her ability to produce heirs. In this connection, it should be noted that Sir Ralph remained a widower for more than forty years after Mary's death, and it is probable that one reason for his decision not to remarry was the fact that at the time of her death two of their sons were half-grown and subsequently lived to adulthood as prospective heirs.[18]

During her lifetime Sir Ralph's behavior toward Mary was that of a loving husband, although his was not the selfless love of the modern romantic ideal, which places the object of one's devotion above all other considerations and solidarities. However, his wife never expected that kind of a relationship. They both viewed his primary responsibility as the conservation of his patrimony, and since she accepted this order of priorities this did nothing to lessen her affection for him. As a woman and his wife, she was prepared to do whatever was required of her in order to help him meet his responsibilities in whatever way he deemed best, and since she also loved him she performed willingly. It was therefore Lady Verney, and not her husband, who was in a position to offer the kind of selfless devotion which came closer to the romantic ideal, the sort of commitment which in the nature of the case he was not required or expected to give.

In the normal course of events it would be difficult to assess the nature of their relationship very accurately, because ordinarily it is a marital breakdown rather than a successful marriage which affords the kind of evidence required for such judgments. The primary evidence of a successful marriage is usually its endurance. However, this is a measurement which provides little information concerning the quality of the relationship between husband and wife except for the certain knowledge that it was made to work in some way, though at whose expense and with what satisfaction for either partner one cannot tell. It is clear, for example, that Sir Ralph and Lady Verney would not have corresponded very much with each other in the normal routine of life, and their relationship with each other would have had to have been extrapolated chiefly from what they chose to confide to other people.

Fortunately for the historian, however, they were separated for more than a year and a half between 1646 and 1648 when Lady Verney was sent back to England from France by her husband in order to help undertake the tedious and prolonged business of settling his estate and other business.[19] During that time they corresponded regularly, and their letters contained not only business matters but the full range of family and personal concerns. Moreover, the contents of these letters were intended to be confidential, because in addition to using code names in referring to other people, Sir Ralph specifically warned his wife against allowing anyone to see them. His concern on this score as well as his attitude toward his wife were revealed when he instructed her to keep his letters in a special place so that no one could read them, and he further warned her that he was going to ask someone to attempt to steal one as a test of her compliance and discretion.[20]

Sir Ralph chose Lady Verney to go to England in his place because he could not go back himself without risking imprisonment for debt.[21] According to Uncle Doctor, the decision to send his wife provided the added advantage of having a woman plead his case before the Committees for Compounding. It was Uncle Doctor's opinion that 'women were never so useful as now' with the committees, 'their sex entitles them to many privileges.'[22] Sir Ralph echoed this point of view when he remarked to Lord Devonshire, whom he was trying to persuade to help him, that 'women are not the worse sollicitors, their sex entitles them to many privileges.'[23] This unusual opportunity for women to prove their usefulness was due to the extraordinary circumstances imposed by the Civil War. But even an upheaval of that magnitude was insufficient to reverse male opinion on the subject of women's innate inferiority or to shake their confidence in the idea that women were largely incapable of dealing with any matter of genuine importance. The husband who chose to send his wife before the Committees for Compounding did so in the belief that the male committee members would be more indulgent with the helpless and incompetent creature before them, and therefore would be more likely to rule in his favor. By this line of reasoning, even if Sir Ralph had been certain that Lady Verney was pregnant at her departure for England,[24] it is doubtful that he would have delayed sending her over.

In spite of Sir Ralph's rather cynical motives for making this decision, he was very unhappy during their separation. His letters to her contained many expressions of his affection and concern for her. He worried about her safe passage to England and confessed that 'the grief of our fatal separation is not to be [i.e., cannot be] expressed.'[25] On another occasion, when he was staying in Caen, he wrote to his wife before leaving for their home at Blois that he hoped to find a letter from her waiting for him there, and continued, 'were I to meet thee there, I should ride night and day: for till now I never knew the sorrow of separation.'[26] Sir Ralph's feelings about his wife were also revealed in his choice of the informal and affectionate salutations of 'Dear Hart' or 'Dear Budd' with which he customarily began his letters.[27] There is no doubt that she was also distressed by their separation. Only weeks after her departure she ended a letter to Sir Ralph

> and now my dear heart I must tell you if I had known what it had been to me to have parted so far from thee I should never had done it. But by the grace of God I will do all that lies in my power for ours and children's good and with all the speed that possible I can. . . .[28]

However, it would not be accurate to see in their shared affection for each other, or in her willingness to make the necessary sacrifices to secure their children's future, any indications that theirs was a relationship in which two equal partners reciprocated love or exercised authority to the same degree. In the first place neither of them believed that she was his equal in any way. In so far as their marriage can be construed as a workable partnership she was definitely the junior partner. His decision to send her to England to act on his behalf was made under duress, and all of her activities there, both social and business, were minutely regulated by detailed instructions from her husband.[29] He not only advised her about which people to cultivate for favors, classifying them according to whether they could be counted on for large or small ones,[30] a matter involving some sophisticated exercise of judgment, but he also instructed her to write to him 'in fine, good paper to save portage, the largeness of it costs nothing.'[31] Nor did he stick at reminding her to make the proper social calls as well as specifying which 'trifles' to give to those who had been helpful.[32]

Secondly, Sir Ralph's attitude toward his wife and her responses to him, reveal a relationship in which she was treated as a child – precocious and lovable but hardly sensible or mature enough to make even the most trivial decisions. Sir Ralph's genuine concern for her welfare, his frequent inquiries about her health, his sensible suggestions about eating the proper diet, his insistence that she be sure to dress herself adequately for the trip back,[33] were all certainly a measure of his love for her, but his concern was always expressed in the manner of a worried parent to a rather frivolous adolescent.

It was also in keeping with this image of her that Sir Ralph reminded his wife – a woman in her mid-thirties – to practice her guitar,[34] keep up with her daily reading of her 'devotions' and to follow that with some reading in French. The latter direction on how to spend her free time productively was presumably sweetened by the observation that ''tis necessary that one of us get the language, and since I cannot you must.'[35] Nor did he hesitate to scold her for not answering his letters in sufficient detail.[36]

Her letters to him, on the other hand, were full of descriptions of her endeavours to bring his business to a successful conclusion,[37] and she took particular care to assure him that she would carry out his instrucrions.[38] Lady Verney never hesitated to express her admiration for and loyalty to her husband. For example, when brother Henry made her angry 'by speaking how little [Sir Ralph] had done for any of them [i.e., the sisters and brothers],' she told her husband that 'believe me, there is nothing puts me in so great a choler as to hear thee taxed that I know are so good and just to all.'[39] On one occasion when she offered Sir Ralph some rather discerning advice on settling the estate (a liberty which she believed might be offensive to him) she was careful to head off any disapproval of her audacity by resorting to the time-honored female device of categorizing her opinions as too uninformed to be worthy of his anger. She told her husband that she was sure he would pardon her if she had offended him because he was aware that she was 'but simple in these matters.'[40]

Thirdly, his love for her was subordinate to his primary responsibility of preserving his patrimony, whereas she loved him unreservedly; for there was no other commitment or person, including her children, that had a greater claim on her concern or love than

Sir Ralph. She proved this when she agreed to sell off part of her own inheritance in order to raise enough money for Sir Ralph to meet his obligations even though she 'should have been very glad to have kept enough of it to have provided well for my two younger boys and my girl, but if that cannot be thou mayest as freely dispose of that as of myself.'[41]

That Sir Ralph's order of priorities in dealing with her was quite different from hers in dealing with him, is also suggested by other evidence. For example, his decision to send her to England to settle his affairs was based on his paramount need to secure his estate. She was the appropriate instrument to employ for this purpose because Sir Ralph knew that he could count on his wife's loyalty as well as on her self-interest to do whatever was necessary, and he was convinced that her sex was an advantage which he was quite willing to exploit for the purpose. But she agreed to go out of love for him, the habit of obedience to his wishes, and their mutual concern with the future welfare of their children.

At another point in the course of their separation, this difference in order of priorities emerged quite clearly. The attempt to clear the estate of sequestration proceedings dragged on longer than either Sir Ralph or his wife anticipated. It was a difficult time for them both and after almost a year had passed without a decision on their petition the frustration and anxiety of waiting made him very depressed.[42] In his agitation he announced to Uncle Doctor that he intended to take a trip through Europe and leave Lady Verney in England, for he could no longer 'endure this place on these solitary terms . . . I may as well (like a mere single man) see what fortune I can find abroad as sit still here [in France] in perpetual expectation.'[43] In another letter announcing similar intentions to make their separation permanent, Sir Ralph made it clear that if he decided to travel he would give his wife 'both her own and mine at home . . . for I confess I love her so well that think all my estate too little for her.'[44]

However, when Lady Verney learned of Sir Ralph's plans, she was hurt and alarmed. She informed her husband that she took his suggestion 'unkindly,' for

> I did believe thou hadest had other thoughts of me than to think I could brook such a proposition; no my heart, you must not whilst I live have any such design without you resolve to

> take me along with you and then live in what part of the world you most fancy; it is not the being entrusted with your estate can give me the least satisfaction. . . . I can be content so I am with you, therefore, I will rely upon His providence and if it be not possible for me to finish your business I will leave it to God's blessing and the honest Dr.s [uncle Denton] care . . . truly this very notion of yours hath gone so near me that I have scarce had one night's rest since I received your letters . . . but my dear heart I'll say no more at this time but that I assure you it cannot be for my good to be here without thee.[45]

Moreover, Lady Verney did not content herself with the hope that Sir Ralph would be persuaded by this declaration of love but went on to assure him that

> I cannot conceive that it can be either for your advantage or our two dear children's to have our small family divided in four several places. I know not what you spend there but I am sure I spend as much here as would keep us all together.

And having dealt with these practical considerations she concluded,

> and beside all this to tell you truth I cannot be any longer from you therefore I am resolved to stand or fall with you and I beg of thee not to let this design any more enter into your thoughts.[46]

In a matter of weeks after this was written, Parliament granted their petition and the sequestration was taken off. Sir Ralph at that point assured his wife that he no longer had any intention of leaving her.[47] It is doubtful that Sir Ralph would have gone through with his departure even if their petition had been denied, because that threat was probably more a symptom of his unhappiness than a genuine statement of his intentions. But the exchanges between his wife and himself on this matter revealed a marked difference in values about the importance of financial security as compared with maintaining their personal union. If it came to a choice, Lady Verney, unlike her husband, was prepared to sacrifice anything rather than lose him.

The kind of relationship which Sir Ralph and his wife shared was perfectly described by Byron more than a century later in the lines, 'Man's love is of man's life a thing apart/'Tis woman's whole existence.'[48] The prevailing economic realities and social values concerning patrimony and the condition of women made it highly unlikely, even in a very successful marriage like the Verneys', that either partner would ever bridge the social distance and discrete obligations which confined them to their separate roles and precluded them from the kind of love which is mutually reciprocated and is based on a husband/wife solidarity which is stronger and more intense than any other relationship. Sir Ralph was a good husband who loved his wife but she was not the chief focus of his life, nor his greatest concern. It was not only that he was temperamentally incapable of the kind of freely invented behavior which would have permitted him to perceive her as a person, as distinct from her role as his wife, but that such behavior would have gone counter to the prevailing value system in which they *both* believed.

Her attitudes about marriage were entirely conventional, and given her advantageous social position she had little incentive to question the prevailing values. When she learned that their cousin Fines and his wife, among others, had separated because the husband in that case did not agree with the wife in matters of 'conscience' (i.e., religion), Lady Verney condemned such wives because she believed that there 'is very little conscience in parting from their husbands.'[49]

Sir Ralph's ideas about the best methods of preserving matrimonial accord were marked by a similar adherence to what passed for acceptable behavior. In discussing his sister Margaret's unhappy marriage, Sir Ralph observed that

> it seems my Brother Elmes [Margaret's husband] desire not that my sister should write to any of her friends, if that would please him she may do well to forbear it in his presence and choose her times when he is in bed or abroad and then he can never know it.[50]

And it must have been Uncle Doctor's knowledge of his nephew's conventional beliefs and values which prompted him to comment to Sir Ralph just before Lady Verney's departure for England that 'if your own engagements hinder you not, I presume that once within these 3 or 4 months you will have as fair an old time of whoring as . . . you are like to have.'[51] Their shared belief in the legitimacy of the double standard must also account for another letter which Uncle Doctor sent to his nephew after Lady Verney's return to France. Shortly after she rejoined her husband she became very ill, and, according to the contents of Uncle Doctor's letter, Sir Ralph had requested his uncle to find and send over a new maid for the Verney household. The doctor told Sir Ralph that the new maid he had chosen had agreed to go

> for £3 per annum. Because you writ me word that you were in love with Dirty Sluts, I took great care to fit you with a Joan that may be as good as my Lady [Sir Ralph's wife] in the dark, and I hope I have fitted you a pennyworth. I will whilst she stays [in England] take her into my house and observe what I can, but Luce [a former servant of the Verneys] is very confident she will match your cock, and she should know for they lived half a year together in one house.[52]

It is just possible that Uncle Doctor was only making a crude joke about the dual services that might be expected from the maid, but there are two reasons for suspecting that his description of what might be required of her in the bedroom as well as in the kitchen was intended to be taken seriously. Firstly, Lady Verney was fatally ill and died within the year,[53] and there is evidence that sexual exploitation of female servants was not an unknown practice of widower/masters in this period.[54] Secondly, Sir Ralph's letter to Uncle Doctor requesting the latter to find him a maid is missing; this is curious, because Sir Ralph was a compulsive collector of letters and his to the doctor on this occasion is one of the few missing drafts.

Whether Sir Ralph actually intended or in fact did use the maid for sexual purposes cannot be known, and is beside the point. What is significant about Uncle Doctor's letter to Sir Ralph is that the uncle, who shared a close and affectionate relationship with both Sir Ralph and Lady Verney, seemed quite confident that his nephew would not find the least offence in his suggestions concerning the maid. Uncle Doctor must have been as aware as some of his contemporaries that a young female servant or 'phillie,'[55] as he referred to them, was an acceptable target for erotic references and fair game for casual sexual encounters.[56]

Moreover, Sir Ralph's father, Sir Edmund, had been accused of attempting a similar arrangement with an innkeeper's daughter. According to the formal statement made by the girl's mother, and dated a year after Sir Edmund's wife's death, one of Sir Edmund's servants had been sent to offer the daughter £5 to fit her for 'lady's service.' The mother construed this proposition to mean that the girl was to serve in a different capacity, for she testified that she would rather her daughter Mary 'should be a poor man's wife than the best man's whore.'[57]

The fact that servant girls did not always accede to the sexual demands of upper-class men does not reduce their importance as possible sexual alternatives for dissatisfied or philandering husbands. The existence of sexual alternatives for the husband, combined with the widespread belief that a wife should turn a blind eye to her husband's extra-marital relations,[58] served to deprive the wife of the personal satisfaction and sense of individual worth which married lovers can derive in a situation of reciprocal fidelity. Upper-class women, once they had provided the necessary heirs, had few vital contributions to make to the marriage. Their contributions as mothers were minimized by the employment of wet nurses, governesses, and tutors. Similarly, their contributions as wife/lover to their husbands could be provided by socially accepted surrogates. The resulting sense of her own insignificance may be one of the factors which explains why even an intelligent and high-status woman like Lady Verney so readily assimilated and expressed negative values about herself and other women, despite the fact that by contemporary standards hers was a very successful marriage.

Any of Sir Ralph's younger brothers would have been very satisfied to have done nearly as well in their matrimonial endeavors. In so far as marriage was one of the chief vehicles of upward mobility or at least offered an opportunity for avoiding social derogation, it was an important possibility in the life choices of all sons. But for younger sons without a substantial inheritance it was likely to prove elusive. In the case of Sir Ralph's three younger brothers only Thomas, the next in line, married. Thomas's marriage was illustrative of the fact that prospective grooms operated in a seller's market and furthermore that the image of the market place is quite appropriate in examining the realities of the arranged marriage. One of the immediate benefits of marriage for a man was the payment to him of his wife's dowry. The anticipation of receiving what was usually a substantial lump sum served as a strong inducement for men in straightened financial circumstances.[59] Thomas married his wife Joyce during a lengthy stay as a prisoner in the Fleet, undoubtedly in order to raise the money for his release.[60] Joyce's reasons for entering into this, as it turned out unfortunate, alliance are not known. However, it is probable that since Thomas was only a heartbeat away from the Verney inheritance (Sir Ralph's sons were children and might not live to adulthood) this consideration was not overlooked. In addition, the attraction of marrying into the prestigious Verney family probably did something to make her consider such a match an attractive one. In the event, Sir Ralph proved quite unwilling to help Joyce when Thomas disappeared shortly after their marriage and left his pregnant wife to beg assistance from the older brother.[61]

Although Thomas later returned to his wife, their relationship was continually plagued by money troubles and even he admitted that he had been 'chargeable to her during my extremities.'[62] That his marital problems were definitely linked to his poverty was further illustrated in a letter which he wrote to Sir Ralph's estate steward, Roads, pleading for a £5 advance on his annuity. Thomas assumed that Roads knew of his wife's 'most ill conditions towards' him and ended his plea with the observation that 'there can be no soul that goes to hell can be more tormented by the devil, than I shall be vexed by a turbulent and most ill-disposed wife' if the steward refused to advance the £5.[63]

Thomas deserted his wife on at least one other occasion. In 1648, some five years after their marriage, he spent the better part of a year living in France.[64] His unsatisfactory relationship with Joyce, whom sister Susan described as 'a very violent woman if she sets of it,'[65] while not the actual precipitant of Thomas's removal to France, undoubtedly heightened his satisfaction in that decision. He was forced to leave England because of some unsavory financial dealings in the course of which it was discovered that he had forged some deeds – a crime punishable in the pillory.[66] His departure for France was made possible by the fact that his brother-in-law Elmes was at that time having great domestic difficulties with Thomas's sister Margaret, and Thomas persuaded the affluent Elmes to finance the trip abroad for both disgruntled husbands.[67]

The two men spent their time at the gambling tables and

Thomas soon found himself in debt beyond what Elmes was willing to provide.[68] In order to meet his debts Thomas forged his brother-in-law's name to some bills of exchange.[69] Although Elmes was angry enough to threaten to 'lay him up'[70] if they met again, he could have been dissuaded from prosecuting Thomas at law, but the merchant who was stuck with the forged bills demanded legal satisfaction.[71] Since in France this was an offence punishable by death, Thomas understandably viewed the lesser risk of the pillory in England as preferable and returned home.[72]

There is reason to believe that he would not have returned to England if his affairs in France had been less than disastrous. During his stay abroad he admitted that he had not heard from his wife and had no idea of the arrangements which had been made to provide for her during his absence.[73] In Thomas's case, he had exploited marriage as but one of a number of devices, legal and otherwise, by which he hoped to avoid social derogation.

Since neither Edmund nor the youngest brother Henry could realistically expect to inherit the estate or persuade a prospective bride of this possibility, the small annuities which they received made it unlikely that they would marry within their own class unless they were fortunate enough to accumulate some wealth by their own efforts. Although neither of them was as irresponsible as Thomas, what is known of their careers would argue that they were financially incapable of making a suitable match.[74]

For this reason it is likely that Edmund would have remained a bachelor, even if his life had not been cut short at 30 as a casualty of the war.[75] Several years before his death, there had been some talk in the family that Edmund was negotiating a match.[76] Sir Ralph commented at the time that he 'should be extremely glad to see him [Edmund] settled with a good rich wife'[77] but apparently was unwilling to offer anything more than that observation in order to promote the negotiations, and it came to nothing.

Despite the fact that he never married, something of Edmund's views on marriage and woman's place in it are known and are in keeping with his entirely conventional values on other matters. He was an ardent Royalist,[78] given to employing the typical 'head and members' metaphor[79] – a choice of imagery much utilized by the political and social conservatives of that time. His attitudes on marriage were of a piece with his general outlook. That is why when Edmund learned that brother-in-law Elmes had left Margaret because the wife refused to live with a husband who had beaten her, Edmund did all he could to effect a reconciliation between them. Moreover, Edmund could say, without a trace of irony, that it was his 'opinion [that Elmes] will never offer to strike her again and some inconveniences were better to be born with than they should live asunder.'[80]

Brother Henry on at least one occasion went 'awooing,' but it was believed to be 'a very inconsiderable match'[81] and in any case his endeavours did not lead to matrimony. The closest that Henry is known to have come to any sort of alliance was his affair with a widow. When that lady appeared in public with 'a great belly' Henry denied that she was pregnant. But whether she was pregnant or not, Henry was in no danger because the 'vox populi,' according to Uncle Doctor, 'fathers it not on Harry but her son-in-law.'[82] When Henry died at the age of 53 he was still a bachelor, and although he never enjoyed the benefits that could be derived from 'a good rich wife,' the double standard made it possible for him now and then to escape the additional burden of sexual deprivation.

In contrast to Sir Ralph's younger brothers, his godson Alexander Denton's marriage serves as a good example of the practices and attitudes attending a successful and acceptable negotiation. Moreover, this match is illustrative of the fact that the arranged marriage of the latter part of the seventeenth century was very similar in procedure and was undertaken with the same motives and values as those which were made before and during the Civil War. There is an exchange of letters, written a decade after the Restoration, between Sir Ralph Verney (long since returned to England) and his godson Alexander Denton, which recapitulate the main outlines of the marriage negotiations of the mid-century. Young Alex informed his godfather that

> when I was in London there was a proposal made to my aunt for me, to one that has six thousand pounds but it 'tis in land, half of it in present and half in reversion. The young lady is Mr [Herman's] daughter of Middleton Stoney. She was 15 years of age last St. James Tide, I suppose my uncle Alexander Denton hath acquainted you with it . . . I am resolved not to do anything without acquainting you with it.[83]

Ralph advised his godson that he had been notified by the uncle of the

> proposal of Mr Herman's daughter and that the Dr. and he and I should consider of it together . . . but it seems the young lady's portion is in land and if that land cannot be sold to secure your two uncles' engagements I doubt they will hardly agree to settle a jointure, and such other settlements as are usual and indeed necessary on such occasion. I pray advise well with your Uncle Woodward of this point, and if he thinks it feasible, so as it may be sold for so much money or near it, I think he and you had best come up to London to confer with your uncles before the term.[84]

When the match had proceeded to the negotiating stage, Sir Ralph composed a list of items which would need to be discussed. Entitled 'Queries at Middleton Stoney,' the list read as follows:

> What money portion and when paid? What land in present during the mother's life? What [separate, crossed through] maintenance for the young lady? Where they shall dwell and at what rate? How the goods, plate and gems shall be secured? What servants she sees fit to keep? What jointure in present, and what when land is settled on him and his heirs? What settlement on heir male or daughters?[85]

The answers to all these questions were apparently satisfactory because a copy of the articles of marriage between Alexander Denton and Hestor Herman dated 7 November 1673 are included among Sir Ralph Verney's papers. One of the items in this document, which deals with the provision of portions for any daughters of this union, names 'Sir Ralph Verney of Middle Claydon' as one of the trustees whose consent must be given in order for the unborn bride to collect her dowry.[86] The control of the current head of the family thus extended far into the future, to affect the lives of children yet unborn.

# 4

# MARRIAGE: THE FEMALE PERSPECTIVE

Married life from the wife's point of view was a significantly different enterprise from that of her husband. Access to matrimony had different requirements for women and at the same time was a more crucial attainment in their lives. Sir Ralph's position as family patriarch as well as the nature of family financial arrangements ensured that his assistance and consent would be sought in the marriages of his younger sisters. In addition, the nature of such arrangements meant that an unmarried woman was seen as a perpetual burden to her family. Until her marriage the head of the family was required, often by legal arrangement and always by 'world opinion,' to provide for her maintenance. Unlike the payment of a dowry which also came out of the family revenues, the annuity paid to a spinster was a sterile investment. By contrast, in exchange for a marriage portion the bride was provided with a husband who relieved the family of the financial burden of maintaining her and promised her continued security in the event of his death.

In addition to these financial considerations, the head of the family, in the case of unmarried females, was responsible for 'disposing' of them into some acceptable and preferably inexpensive situation until such time as a suitable match could be found. In the meantime he had to preserve his own reputation as a sound financial risk as well as to make every possible effort to preserve hers as a virgin commodity.

Since a high premium was placed on female virginity as a factor in determining a lady's marriageability, it was very important that her reputation should be above suspicion. Obviously, if she were actually deflowered before a marriage settlement was concluded she made, as Sir Ralph put it, 'shipwreck of her honour and conscience, both which must be preserved before and above all other things.'[1] The latter calamity also meant that she was 'fit for no other [man].'[2] However, a single woman's reputation could also be sullied and her desirability as a marriage partner consequently decreased in other ways; for, barring direct confession, the condition of a woman's chastity was necessarily extrapolated from other indications.

That is why Sir Ralph was particularly eager to find some permanent place for his sisters Elizabeth and Mary, both of whom were in their teens. He did not want them to be continually shunted about to various relatives like 'vagabonds' and 'beggars' because it would not be to their 'credit.'[3] This consideration undoubtedly influenced Sir Ralph's decision to place the younger Elizabeth in a school when previous attempts to install her with various relatives had proved unsuccessful.[4]

Moreover, Sir Ralph was especially pressed to find some safe place for sister Elizabeth because the latter 'was a very forward young maid and very familiar with all sorts of people.'[5] Elizabeth was relatively unsupervised when she stayed at the family home at Claydon, and Lady Verney had been informed that she was 'very great with [a servant of Uncle John Denton] and they have often found her sitting on his lap.'[6] Such behavior could do almost irreparable damage to a young lady's reputation, and Lady Verney was also concerned that 'if she [Elizabeth] should be so silly as to cast herself away on him it would be a misfortune to all the family.'[7] Aunt Isham believed that despite the 'great charge' to Sir Ralph, the investment in schooling 'may do her [Elizabeth] more good than if you had given her £500 and no breeding.'[8] In Elizabeth's case the boarding school was supposed to provide an acceptable situation where her honor and reputation would be preserved, as well as affording her the kind of training that would enhance her value as a marriage prospect.

The anxiety caused by Elizabeth's behavior as well as the acceptance of Aunt Isham's solution for the problem are symptomatic of the fact that marriage was considered to be the most important endeavor in a woman's life. In the society of the upper-gentry there were few career options for younger sons, but there was only one for daughters. The prospect of marriage was in fact and for good reasons referred to as a woman's 'preferment,' because it was viewed and assiduously sought after as her only possibility for advancement.

In the best of times there was great incentive for a gentlewoman to marry. If anything, the Civil War served to enhance the desire to find a husband, although it made the business of getting one much more difficult. During the war rents were slow in coming in, or were not paid at all, while at the same time taxes rose. The income derived from property was further reduced by the depredations of armies living at free quarter, bribes in money or stock paid out to the military in order to escape even greater losses from pillaging, and outright destruction of property.[9] Not only debts, but annuities, jointures, and marriage portions which had all been calculated and legally contracted for on the basis of the known rhythm and expectations of prewar income had now to be paid from an income that was at best intermittent and unpredictable and at worst unobtainable.[10]

For Sir Ralph's sisters of marriageable age, these wartime conditions made the single life even more unappealing than in normal times. For one thing, as a result of the squeeze on family finances the small annuities which were paid to the sisters were reduced. His sister Penelope complained when her allowance of £50 p.a. was reduced to £40, that she found it hard 'to live like my father's daughter or your sister.'[11] In addition, she had had the misfortune to be staying at her uncle's house at Hillesden when the Parliamentary forces destroyed it. Although Penelope was unharmed, she lost all of her clothes except those she was wearing, and she had to buy new ones out of her reduced allowance.[12]

Brother Thomas was persuaded to appeal to Sir Ralph on behalf of 'Pen' and the other sisters whose difficult existence at Claydon was made more miserable by their being 'subject to the affrights of rude soldiers rushing in at all hours both by day and night and not a man there that dares show himself in their presence.' Thomas believed that the time had come when Sir Ralph should 'strain yourself for their preferment' according to his previous promises.[13] It is also clear that whether the girls continued to reside in their brother's house at Claydon, or moved in with one of the relatives, they were expected to pay for their own food, firewood, medicine, and other expenses, often at inflated prices.[14]

Since several of Sir Ralph's sisters were already in their mid-twenties when he removed to the continent in 1643, they could not afford to put off marrying until his return or wait for better times. For women of their class, the mid-twenties were considered rather late for marriage, and therefore delay could be disastrous.[15] It was also feared that the war was taking its toll of eligible young men. Sir Ralph's Aunt Isham, who frequently came to stay with his sisters, observed in 1644 that 'if these times hold up I think there will be no men left for woman.'[16] The combined factors of their precarious financial situation, their having reached the optimum age for marriage, and the belief that the number of eligible men was declining, all served to make marriage an increasingly attractive alternative to their present situation.

The opportunities for getting a suitable husband, however, were reduced by the unusual circumstances imposed by the war. Sir Ralph, as head of the family, was not on hand to perform his expected role as matchmaker and financial guarantor. Furthermore his sisters' value on the marriage market was greatly deflated owing to the fact that their marriage portions had been wholly or partially dissipated in a credit system suffering from massive default of payment, or by investment in offices that were now defunct. If anything, this increased Sir Ralph's sisters' need for any assistance which he could give them.

There were, in fact, few opportunities for younger siblings of either sex to escape completely from the control of and dependence on the family patriarch even in their mature lives. In the case of men, a successful career would minimize their need to stay in his favor, but in a patronage society that achievement was largely dependent on what kind of influence and financial assistance the head of the family was willing to offer.[17] For a woman, the status of widowhood expanded her options, because the widow's jointure served as a dowry, but with no strings attached, for her next preferment.[18] Obviously there were a variety of social pressures which made it prudent for her to consult her 'friends' among the family and kin. However, if she wished to ignore their advice a widow was at least financially free to make her own choice. If she picked a husband of whom her family and kin did not approve, she could still marry him, especially if he were in a position to offer her the kind of financial resources and influence which could be useful in fending off the subtle tyrannies to which she would then be exposed.

Because the double sexual standard had significant effects on the nature of the marriage negotiations, on the relationship of the marriage partners, and especially on the position of women in the family, it is necessary to examine this phenomenon as it existed in seventeenth century society in more detail. There was a high priority placed on female virginity as a requisite for marriageability. Furthermore, the familial and personal difficulties peculiar to the unmarried woman strongly suggest that, all other things being equal, the father of the prospective bride negotiated under the disadvantages of a buyer's market whereas the father of the prospective groom normally enjoyed the advantages of a seller's market. In this connection, it is possible to view the artificially inflated importance of female virginity as a method of enhancing the value and consequently the marketability of unmarried females.[19]

Sexual discrimination permitted greater sexual freedom for men both before and after marriage.[20] The acceptance of this practice, along with others involving the differential treatment of women, was buttressed by a group of beliefs concerning their innate inferiority. For example, generalizations concerning female behavior were almost always derogatory. Women were described as being talkers rather than doers,[21] it was supposed to be easy for them to 'dissemble,'[22] and they tended to be willful rather than reasonable, for 'their wills, not reason must be satisfied.'[23] Along with papists in general and the 'pagan Irish'[24] and 'prattling' French[25] in particular, women were used as a negative reference group. When Sir Ralph became particularly annoyed with some gentlemen in the course of a business negotiation because the latter refused to settle the deal to his liking, he accused them of being 'women.'[26] Similarly, Dr Denton complained to his nephew about a business deal that was proceeding unsatisfactorily, by saying that it was not concluded because 'the other parties interested bring women' by which he meant his nephew to understand that the gentlemen involved talked and did nothing to effect a conclusion.[27]

Prejudice against women was also revealed by the fact that the announcement of the birth of a male child was always greeted with much greater enthusiasm than the arrival of a girl.[28] The latter misfortune was made somewhat more bearable by the prospect that the girl baby was 'one which in time may bring forth a boy.'[29] However, what has already been described concerning the difficulties involved in maintaining and marrying off daughters gives some rational validity to the preference for male children; for if the social and economic realities of the period were not a sufficient explanation of the causes of prejudice against females, they certainly played a part in the acceptance and expression of such values.

Under certain circumstances the inability to produce the preferred sex could work great hardship on the mother. When brother Henry informed Sir Ralph that their sister Cary had been 'brought to bed of a girl' and added 'to all our griefs'[30] he intended to convey more than a conventional lament about the sex of the baby. Cary's husband had been killed in battle shortly before the birth of her child. If the child had been a son, her in-laws could have been expected to do much more for the young widow. As it turned out, Cary even had difficulty in collecting her widow's jointure.[31] This apparently was the kind of reaction which Henry anticipated from Cary's in-laws, and explains why he believed that the announcement of the birth of Cary's daughter required the dolorous comment which he added in his letter to Sir Ralph.

Just as in the case of the preference for male children, there was enough evidence in objective reality to support most of the negative attitudes and beliefs about women in general. They were less educated and less accomplished in intellectual matters than men. Legal and institutional arrangements ordinarily precluded them from activity in either the professional or business world and they were therefore apt to be economically and psychologically dependent on men. The patriarchal and authoritarian nature of the family consigned them to an inferior position within that institution as well. If one of the partners had to be sexually deprived or constrained for the arranged marriage to function effectively, such demands could be made and enforced on women more successfully because the latter by a combination of dependency and powerlessness were largely incapable of doing anything about it. In addition, the evidence indicates (as will be discussed in more detail below) that some women had internalized the values regarding their inferiority and on the whole accepted the prevailing assessment of their roles and needs.

## SPINSTERHOOD

If marriage was considered to be a woman's preferment, continued spinsterhood was viewed as a form of social derogation. Spinsterhood condemned one to a lifetime of peripheral existence; it was a functionless role played out at the margins of other people's lives without even that minimal *raison d'être* – the possibility of bearing children – which was supposed to comfort and sustain the married woman. For a woman, the single life was hardly an alternative life-style to marriage but rather a despised condition which both the woman and her family sought to avoid. A single woman was ordinarily dependent on the head of the family for assistance and guidance in choosing a husband. Moreover, the necessary of maintaining a good reputation in order to insure her eligibility for marriage increased the single woman's need to conform to parental wishes in a wide variety of matters such as deportment, choice of residence, etc.

Until she married the best that she could hope for was to attach herself to a prominent household, but even in that case an unmarried woman was dependent on the benevolence and generosity of her patron. Sir Ralph's cousin Magdaline Faulkner was a case in point. She had a place with the Countess of Barrymore, but she wanted to marry because 'service is no certainty, and I have tried the utmost of it. There is little to be gotten in it.'[32] She viewed the proposal of a widower with three children and church 'livings [of] two hundred pounds a year' as a stroke of good luck, for she believed that 'God hath provided well for me, if it may be accomplished to come to such a fortune and a honest man.'[33]

The pressure to marry must also have been considerable not only because of the many advantages that marriage provided for the woman and her family, but because the conditions of the single life were such that even a poor match was preferable to having no husband at all. In order to understand what life was like for an unmarried upper-class woman it is worth examining in more detail the existence of Sir Ralph's sister Mary when she was in her late teens and early twenties. As a single woman Mary was subject to the authority of the head of the family, and as Sir Ralph said, while she 'is at my allowance' he was to be kept informed and had to approve of decisions concerning her.[34] Not that she would have been relieved of such control if she had married, for then her husband would have exercised that kind of authority over her. However, as a married woman she and her children would have become her husband's prime responsibilities, whereas in the Verney hierarchy Mary's needs and welfare were secondary to Sir Ralph's concern with his own estate and immediate family.[35] Since the large number of sisters and brothers to be provided for constituted a substantial drain on Sir Ralph's income, his primary concern in decisions about the best way 'to dispose [of] her' was to 'order it for matter of charge.'[36]

Although Mary was undoubtedly exaggerating when she told the estate steward in a two-page plea for money that 'if you do not supply my want and send me some money suddenly, I may go naked,' there is little doubt that her allowance was inadequate for one of her station.[37] The level of poverty at which one feels its pinch is relative, and Mary's views on such matters were suggested by her condescending comment that her brother-in-law Stewkeley's estate was not worth 'above 6 hundred pound a year at the most.'[38] She was continually short of money for clothes, and when she was staying with the Stewkeleys, who entertained a great deal, she asked Sir Ralph for money above her allowance to get some new dresses 'or I shall not be fit to be seen.'[39] Her lack, of what were for her necessities, was not due to her frivolousness with money but rather to the inadequacy of her allowance.[40] Out of sympathy for her genuine need, Uncle Doctor commented to Sir Ralph that Mary never had enough clothing, and she seems to have found it impossible to avoid indebtedness.[41] She was even dependent on Sir Ralph's generosity in the matter of furnishing the bedroom where she was boarding, and had to persuade Sir Ralph to let her borrow the curtains and valance from his son's unused bed at Claydon.[42] In short, the unmarried woman became a perennial supplicant who had little possibility of returning favors; this placed her in an untenable position in a society which placed high priority on reciprocation.

During little more than a three-year period Mary lived with a succession of different relatives. She had left brother Henry's lodge in October of 1646, because the lack of company there proved too 'meloncholy.'[43] For a short time she stayed in London[44] which was preferable to the lodge or any country home in terms of enhancing her chances of finding a husband, but was too expensive for someone in her straightened circumstances. After an attempt to settle her at Claydon,[45] Sir Ralph and his wife subsequently arranged for Cary to take her, since the latter generously agreed not to charge Mary board for the first six months.[46]

Despite Cary's help, Mary was still short of money and argued with Sir Ralph's estate steward because she believed that she was not getting her full share.[47] She also had to borrow from Uncle Doctor to buy some clothes when Sir Ralph did nothing about supplying her with an extra dress which she had twice requested.[48] In fact, Sir Ralph wrote to her as little as possible, probably in order to avoid having to comply with her frequent requests. She complained to her brother because he completely ignored three of her letters.[49]

The disadvantages of the single life were further illustrated by Mary's experience when she visited her sister Susan during the latter's confinement. Susan accused Mary 'of being too familiar' with her husband.[50] Uncle Doctor assured Sir Ralph that Mary was innocent, and fortunately for Mary, Susan was reluctant to spread the story because it might mean a 'breach' with her husband.[51] Mary's difficulties were further compounded by a lengthy illness which left her without money and overdrawn on her allowance.[52] Moreover, this serious illness forced her to move again to some place where she could be cared for until she was 'fit to go to any of [her] sisters,' for while she was still very ill 'it would be too great a trouble for [her] to put them to.'[53]

Mary's difficulties in trying to get a husband illustrate more specifically the reasons why spinsterhood was a condition to be avoided, as well as the kinds of pressures and problems experienced by the unmarried woman and her family. Unlike Elizabeth, who was of a 'cross, proud, lazy disposition,' Mary was 'not at all proud but very thrifty and willing to do anything for anybody' and was considered to have a 'great deal of wit.'[54] It was generally agreed that she was also 'very tractable'[55] and eager to please and would make 'a very good wife' because she was reputed to be 'a very good housewife.'[56]

However, the possibility of marrying her off was considerably reduced by several grave shortcomings. To begin with, she was 'much the plainest' of all the sisters,[57] by which one may fairly conclude that she must have been rather homely, inasmuch as sister Susan, who was considered better looking than Mary, was described as a woman who was not 'for many palates.'[58]

Of course, lack of physical appeal, while a definite disadvantage, was not in itself an insurmountable difficulty. In an arranged marriage society, what nature failed to provide in the way of beauty could be compensated for by instruction in certain socially esteemed activities and graces, such as dancing, needlework, and the cultivation of proper deportment, all of which was described by the contemporary term 'breeding.' In addition, the choice of clothing of a quality in keeping with the lady's station served the marriage market as a ready reference for determining both her social class and her financial condition.

A plain girl like Mary was therefore still marriageable if the head of the family chose to make the effort and investment of providing her with the proper 'breeding.' Unfortunately, Mary became the victim of her own good nature, because she could be more cheaply farmed out to various relatives than sent to school. And since she was 'tractable' and the 'handiest' of the sisters[59] Sir Ralph was permitted an inexpensive alternative. On the other hand the ill-humored Elizabeth was sent to school because there was 'nobody that will take her.'[60]

By the time that various members of the family had succeeded in convincing Sir Ralph that he should do something more for Mary,[61] she was almost 19 and too old for a school.[62] Neither Sir Ralph nor his wife wanted Mary to live with them in France,[63] despite Henry's warning to them that 'breeding she wants much, which at the end will prove her ruin.'[64] Lady Verney, who preferred Mary to any of her sisters-in-law, ended an otherwise flattering description of her with the observation that she was 'wild as a buck,'[65] a simile which confirmed Henry's fears about his sister's lack of breeding and the undesirable effect which that could have on her marriage prospects.

There is every reason to believe, however, that a suitable match could still have been found for Mary if her marriage portion had been available. Of all the variables which affected a woman's preferment, the firm assurance that a generous dowry would be given by an influential family to her prospective groom was more important than any other factor. Since Mary had little else in her favor it was especially vital that she should have a dowry, but wartime financial conditions had made it impossible for Sir Ralph to offer this essential security.[66] The best that he was able to offer was '50 pounds a year for her life' with the understanding that this annuity would cease to be paid as soon as she received her portion.[67]

Sir Ralph was particularly eager to marry 'Mall' off because he realistically feared that she was 'like to stick long.' When he confided to his wife that if a certain match could be concluded for Mary 'Oh how that would joy me!' he was entirely sincere.[68] In addition, since Mary was already 19 at this time and 'a women in years and growth,' if a husband were not found for her it was believed that she would be entitled to something more in the way of support than Sir Ralph was allowing her. The situation was further complicated by the fact that if her brother raised her allowance or offered a larger one as an enticement to a prospective suitor in lieu of her dowry, the other sisters would expect a similar increase.[69]

The only advantage which Sir Ralph enjoyed at this time in attempting to find a husband for Mary was that he had been assured by a Mr Brown that the latter would have Sir Ralph choose him a wife when the time came. When Sir Ralph was informed that the gentleman in question was now a 'stayed man' and ready to entertain the prospect of matrimony, he did what he could to make an attraction offer.[70] But Sir Ralph's assurance that Mary's £1,000 portion, although for the present unattainable, was 'as sure as law can make it'[71] failed to have the desired effect. That meant that Sir Ralph had to place Mary elsewhere, and after an abortive attempt to get sister Margaret's 'crabbed husband' to take her in,[72] Mary was sent to sister Cary.[73]

From Sir Ralph's point of view, the failure of this projected match for Mary was a disappointment on several counts. Her continued spinsterhood not only required him to undertake the costly and bothersome business of finding some other place for her, but he was also put into the position of supplicant to the prospective host, and since this kind of hospitality was viewed as a favor to him it would eventually have to be reciprocated in some way. By contrast, if the match had been successful, the problems involved in maintaining her would have been eliminated, and of equal importance, the act of marriage would have expanded the network of relations upon whom Sir Ralph could have relied for a variety of favors.

It was against this background of financial difficulties and indebtedness, the fear and problems associated with illness, the vulnerability to malicious gossip, the inevitable attrition of hospitality experienced by the unwanted boarder, wearily repeated with a succession of hosts, that one must view Mary's answer to a proposed match which Uncle Doctor found for her in 1648 when she was over 20 years old. The prospective groom was 'reputed' to be worth £700 p.a.,[74] and since the rumored worth of anyone in such discussions was usually found to be something more than his actual income, such a match in normal times would have been considered beneath a Verney daughter. However, Mary was well aware that

> my condition is bad by reason that I cannot enjoy that which my father gave me and I know as my bro[ther] is not in a condition to do much for me . . . I am very sensible of my condition and am willing to settle myself if I can for the better and my friends cannot condemn me for it for a little of my own is better than a great deal of anothers.[75]

She was correct in believing that if this match could be concluded, even if it was not as good a preferment as she might have gotten in normal times, it would be 'for the better.' In this same letter Mary informed her Uncle Doctor that she was moving from brother-in-law Elmes's house because he told her to leave, 'for they will not allow one penny for housekeeping' and she was therefore going once again to sister Susan.[76] In spite of Mary's acceptance of the proposal this match also fell through, but she was spared a lifetime of indignity when she finally did marry Mr Robert Lloyd seven years later.[77]

This brief review of a few years of Mary's rather ordinary and undramatic life is important in understanding the nature of the tragedy of spinsterhood, precisely because her difficulties (with the exception of the unavailability of her dowry) were not of extraordinary proportions. Mary faced the kind of unexceptional problems which must have plagued many husbandless women of her class and accounted for their great desire to be married. Only a husband brought the dual blessings of 'a settled condition' for the woman and relieved her family of the burden 'to think how to dispose of her.'[78]

In addition to these considerations, the disadvantages which derived from the double standard must have weighed more heavily on the spinster than on married women. For one thing, the double standard in its widest sense involved more than an expectation of different sexual behavior for men and women. Women were considered to be intellectually and socially inferior to men, and the nature of social and legal arrangements reflected, reinforced, and in the long run justified that belief. The patriarchal family, the tracing of pedigree in the male line, primogeniture and tail male (descent of property through the male line) as well as the exclusion of women from the universities and professions all testify to the existence of a male-dominated society, in the sense that access to positions of power and authority was reserved to men.

The need and desire to acquire a husband, therefore, was not designed to provide a woman with a lever of power in a male-dominated society. What a woman did derive from her husband was his status. Marriage automatically conferred on the wife the prestige and position which her husband occupied *vis-à-vis* other members of his class. Marriage did not free a woman from the disadvantages of her sex nor did it provide her with any great augmentation of power or control over her own life, but it did give firm definition to her social position, which was extremely important in an authoritarian and status-conscious society.

The spinster, on the other hand, derived her status from her family of origin, and unless she was an only child, her sex alone would guarantee an inferior position within her father's family. The necessarily tentative and ill-defined status of the spinster, whose position within her own class would be precisely defined only at marriage, meant that she, as compared with the married woman of the same class, would occupy an ambiguous and hence inferior position. It was only through the acquisition of a husband that she could attain the preferment to the highest female position within her newly formed conjugal family. In addition, all women, married or not, were considered to be subordinate to men, and therefore the spinster was likely to occupy the lowest ranks within a socially inferior group. This must have served as an added incentive for seeking preferment through marriage.

## THE SISTERS' MARRIAGES: PENELOPE, MARGARET AND SUSAN

Sister Cary was already married[79] in 1643 when Sir Ralph removed to the Continent. Mary, who was 15, was still young enough to wait several years before her age would become a drawback to her marriage prospects. Elizabeth, who was only 10 years old, was still too young to cause the family any immediate anxiety about the problem of finding a husband for her. However, Penelope, Margaret and Susan were in their early twenties, and all of them understandably wished to avoid the disagreeable condition of continued spinsterhood. Since they would soon be past the optimum age for marriage, and they did not know when Sir Ralph would be able to return to England, they could not risk an indefinite delay, despite the fact that their brother's absence and the financial uncertainties of the period would make it more difficult for them to find suitable husbands. Sir Ralph was undoubtedly preaching to the converted when he warned the eldest sister Susan, concerning a proposed match for her, that 'I pray mistake me not, for this is the weightiest business that ever yet befell you, for in this one action consists all your future happiness in this world; therefore, do nothing rashly, good men with good fortunes are very hard to be gotten.'[80] By 1646, all three of them did manage to get husbands. An examination of the financial maneuvers and social departures which were necessary to achieve this *coup*, during that uncertain period, provides illuminating evidence concerning the way in which the family functioned under stress and can also throw considerable light on the nature of the accepted norms.

Although the sisters enjoyed greater freedom in their matrimonial endeavors than they would have had in peacetime, they were still heavily reliant on particular relatives to bring the negotiations to a successful conclusion. The one 'friend' who was to varying degrees influential in effecting their marriages was Henry Verney, the family's youngest son. Ordinarily, in Sir Ralph's absence the next oldest son would have taken his place in the marriage negotiations. However, Thomas who was next in line, was already married, and in addition to his domestic difficulties he had previously shown himself to be entirely untrustworthy in money matters. Edmund, the next brother, was at this time with the Royalist forces in Ireland, and the responsibility therefore descended to Henry. By the mid-1640s he had carved out a sort of temporary career for himself which involved looking after the affairs of his widowed aunt and his recently war-widowed sister Cary as well as assuming increasing responsibilities for the exiled Sir Ralph.[81] The latter included helping with the marriage arrangements for his sisters. Henry's help in these affairs not only served to cement his relationship with Sir Ralph but also provided him with a sense of importance and an exercise of power which in normal times would have been exclusively enjoyed by the oldest brother.

In spite of his mixed motives, Henry did help his sisters to get their preferments. It was he who introduced Penelope to one George Thorne, who was considered a good catch because his elder brother was 'a rich silk man in the City,' who had no issue and who promised to do a great deal for George.[82] In Henry's eagerness to sell Sir Ralph on the proposal, he ticked off the reasons why this prospective brother-in-law should be welcomed into the family. He assured Sir Ralph that

> the man is without exception, and capable of discharging the best office in the kingdom, his own lands and what his brother will settle on him on marriage will amount at least to £200 a year, beside her portion, diet I think they shall have for nothing, the man is to be valued at more than his bare fortune, in respect of his parts.[83]

Moreover, Thorne's older brother wrote to Sir Ralph to assure him that he would put up £1,000 to be invested in 'any convenient purchase' as a jointure.[84] Henry was right in believing that this was a generous offer, considering that Penelope's marriage portion was not then available.[85]

However, after several weeks of negotiating, the match broke off, primarily because Sir Ralph refused to put up security against the future payment of the £1,000 portion.[86] Since he could not be compelled by law to do this,[87] appeals from Penelope, Henry and even brother Thomas were to no avail.[88] If Penelope believed that her description of her unhappy existence at Claydon where the 'outrages of soldiers' and the absence of her two sisters 'will [make for] extreme uncouth housing'[89] would play on Sir Ralph's guilt feelings, she was to be disappointed. Sir Ralph insisted that her portion was 'already secured as sure as law can make it,' though he did admit that 'these unhappy troubles have hitherto delayed the payment of any part of it.'[90] Although Sir Ralph claimed that he was 'desirous to have this match go forward'[91] his best offer was to guarantee to pay her an annuity of £60 a year (about £20 more than he was giving her and £20 less than was asked)[92] until such time as her portion was raised.[93] Sir Ralph's offer of £60 a year in lieu of the portion was much too low. The figure of £80 a year which the groom's side was asking was both realistic and fair because the standard rate of interest was 8 per cent or £80 p.a. on £1,000. Since the prospective groom's friends would not be satisfied with anything less than security for the portion, the negotiations were ended.[94]

There is every reason to believe that Sir Ralph was sincere in his desire to marry off Penelope and her sisters. Marriage would have freed him from the expense of maintaining them, and in the case of a particularly suitable alliance would have added to the list of 'friends' that he could reasonably count on in a pinch. Moreover, Sir Ralph was known to approve especially of Penelope, who was more tractable than the other two sisters and less demanding when it came to money.[95] But, as will become even more evident in the discussion of Susan's marriage, Sir Ralph was determined to marry off his sisters with the least possible financial risk and cost to himself. While it is true that he was having financial difficulties at this time, it is also true that he made no attempt to secure Penelope's portion. By his own admission, the whole sum in normal times could be paid in a year and a half,[96] and the groom's side was asking only that he put up land against default of payment. His refusal was proof that he viewed his obligations to his sister as extending no further than what was legally required of him.

It is possible, of course, to view Sir Ralph's behavior as merely idiosyncratic; a more generous older brother might have stretched himself a bit more to help his sister. But the important point is that Sir Ralph's limited definition of his obligations, if not applauded, was certainly acceptable to his sisters as well as to the rest of the family and kin. If Sir Ralph's attitude had been a gross breach of the norm, he could have suffered badly in reputation and credit. If he fell too far short of what was expected of him, it was possible that some members of the family or kin might retaliate by using their influence with the Royalist side to make trouble for him.[97] Yet he risked refusing to help Penelope on the grounds that he was not legally constrained to do so, because he counted on the fact that she and those acting for her would consider this an acceptable reason for his refusal. They might be disappointed, but they would not be shocked, because they were thoroughly accustomed to the type of relationship in which response was determined by self-interest rather than affection.

When Penelope did marry in the following year, it was without the prior consent of Sir Ralph. Henry again acted for her in the arrangements and pleaded her case to Sir Ralph. He explained that her suitor John Denton (a cousin) had made his proposal without the prior consent of his father, and therefore he saw no reason to delay the proceedings while they waited for Sir Ralph's approval. Henry claimed that this unusual behavior 'staggered us all what to do,' but that he approved of the match.[98] However, he was very careful to assure Sir Ralph that Penelope agreed to accept the proposal without his consent 'not out of disrespect or contempt to you' but because if 'she had stayed for your approbation she must have lost him.' Henry explained that he had decided not to risk such a possibility on that account because Denton was willing to have Penelope without a portion and would settle for 'only a little addition to her yearly maintenance.' Henry was right on the mark when he added that 'on my word I know not one in England would a made her his wife on the like conditions.'[99]

If John Denton's decision to marry Penelope was based on romantic considerations, her reasons for accepting his offer, as Henry outlined them, were nothing of the sort. According to Henry 'she was sensible her portion lay in a desperate condition, besides she grew in years and was not to all men's liking. These reasons made her so ready to yield to his desires having most of her friends consent' that she agreed to it without consulting Sir Ralph.[100]

In addition to this catalogue of reasons, what is known about the dreary existence which Penelope led during the year that elapsed between the first proposal and this one, also helps to explain her desire to marry Denton. When the other match broke off, she was sent from London back into the country to mark time at Claydon, because it was cheaper to maintain her there.[101] In a letter to Will Roads, Sir Ralph's estate agent, written a month before Denton's proposal, one gets a glimpse of the kind of problem she had to face. In this note she asked Roads to advance her £5 against the next payment of her annuity and added that he should take special pains in sending it to her not to let 'my brother Thomas light of [i.e., on] the money for then I shall be disappointed of it.'[102] Under the circumstances it is easy to see why she snapped at the chance to marry, without her brother's prior consent, without the approval of her future in-laws, and without the usual written assurance that she would be provided with a jointure in the event of her husband's death.

Sir Ralph was not at all annoyed that the marriage agreement was concluded without his knowledge. On the contrary, he wrote to Uncle Doctor to ask his help in bringing it to a conclusion. Sir Ralph believed that "twould be a master piece of service, and oblige us all, I thirst after it, therefore I pray try your best skill.'[103] Sir Ralph's optimism concerning the proposal was in part due to his belief that John Denton's land 'is settled,' in which case the groom's father would have little alternative than to accept his son's choice.[104] It was also Sir Ralph's opinion that if Penelope and her husband 'carry themselves wisely, and with respect to him [i.e., the father] a little time and good nature, would procure an act of oblivion.'[105] Sir Ralph also wrote to Henry along this same line to 'advise Pen to be respective [respectful] to her husband and his friends [i.e., her in-laws], for that will induce them to settle somewhat on her and hers.'[106]

Sir Ralph's enthusiasm can in part be accounted for by the fact that he would only have to provide the bride with little more than the £40 p.a. he was already giving her, pay off a £10 debt which she owed, and the £30 which Henry had borrowed to buy her wedding clothes.[107] At least this was what he promised to do for 'Pen' in response to Henry's assurance that 'you are oblige[d] to nothing more than your affection and free will, will allow her.'[108] Sir Ralph readily agreed to the marriage because it cost him so little to bring it off.

Though this is not a charitable interpretation of his actions, it is probably an accurate one. It is known, for example, that when Thomas's wife Joyce asked Sir Ralph for money, he refused on the grounds that he had not been consulted about their marriage.[109] The consistent attitude which marked both these cases was that Sir Ralph was willing to help his relatives only to the extent that he was legally compelled to, or in those instances where he believed that he would benefit from doing so. But it is much too facile an explanation, and does not get one very far in understanding the upper-gentry, to simply conclude that Sir Ralph was tight-fisted about money – though he probably was. The overriding consideration in all his actions and decisions was his desire to preserve the family patrimony against the incursions of all who threatened it, whether family, friends, or parliamentary sequestrators. If this obsession with the patrimony coincided with his self-interest, that should not obscure the fact that he considered his chief responsibility to be the maintenance and, if possible, the expansion of the family estate; the latter provided him with income but it was also the critical variable in determining his social status and influence.

As far as Penelope's marriage was concerned, her brothers' optimism proved unfounded. Her lack of a dowry proved to be an increasingly serious obstacle to the attainment of marital happiness, and her domestic situation deteriorated in direct correspondence to the diminishing possibility of acquiring her marriage portion. By 1649 she had been married for more than two years, and her husband and father-in-law had given up on the possibility of collecting her dowry. Penelope appealed to her brother to save her marriage because 'my father [in-law] tells me ever since my marriage he has been willing to wait with patience but now [that the king had been executed] he is out of all hopes.' Her father-in-law desired 'to provide for his younger children, which he would have done with my portion if my husband had married a wife that had brought him one' but now 'it will be the worst for him, for he [the father-in-law] may give his estate to whom he pleases for he did buy it with his penny and he has not made my husband joint purchaser with him.' Penelope went on to explain that her condition was further compromised in that

> my husband tells me if you will not give me that sum of 500 pounds whereby his father and you may come to some agreement that he may have a settlement of his father['s] estate he will be gone . . . then you may do well to take me home to you again for he knows here will be no stay for me . . . when he is gone.

Penelope therefore told her brother that 'I am at your mercy either to make me forever or to let me sink under your burden.'[110]

When Sir Ralph put her off she tried to get him to agree to less, 'for 200 or 300 pound would do him [her husband] more good than double that sum the time to come.' She further warned Sir Ralph that if he did not cooperate, her husband would give her jointure land to his brother 'and his friends tell him that I have been his undoing by reason that I had not any portion, he is willing to comply with them all in that point.'[111]

Her pleadings were not likely to have the desired effect on Sir Ralph for a number of reasons. In part he was annoyed with her for taking some of his household stuff without his permission, and he was very angry because she had complained to others that Sir Ralph had cheated her.[112] More importantly, as he confided to Lady Verney, he was relatively certain that Penelope could not recover her portion 'out of my estate . . . for I am well assured neither law nor equity will give it her.'[113] Consequently, it was not until Uncle Doctor prevailed on Sir Ralph to help Penelope that he considered the possibility. Sir Ralph was generally more receptive to his uncle than his sister, and in addition he was at that time deeply enmeshed in negotiations with the doctor and was probably reluctant to lose the latter's good opinion of him.[114] At this point Penelope was only asking £10 more than Sir Ralph was already giving her, a sum which she claimed would be enough to get her husband to provide her with a jointure settlement.[115] It is not clear what the final settlement was, but it is obvious that Sir Ralph forced her consistently to reduce her demands.

Penelope's marriage points up the importance of the dowry as a precondition for achieving a workable relationship, even in those rare instances when the groom originally agreed to take his bride without a guaranteed portion. And her situation offers additional evidence of the kind of power and authority that continued to be exercised by the inheriting son over the other siblings after they had reached maturity.

Sir Ralph's sister Margaret was also married off with a minimal drain on the family finances, although she too was unable to obtain her marriage portion at the time. At the age of 21 she had received a gift of money from her Aunt Eure, one of the half dozen aunts on her mother's side. It was probably this money which Sir Ralph had put out at interest to a member of the House of Commons with the expectation that she would receive income from the interest until such time as she married.[116] An MP was an unfortunate choice, because while the Long Parliament was in session no recourse could be taken against a member if he defaulted. As a result, Margaret was so hard pressed for money in the year before her marriage that brother Henry asked Sir Ralph to send her a few pounds to tide her over.[117]

In the spring of 1646, she received a marriage proposal from a Northamptonshire gentleman, Thomas Elmes, who offered her 'five hundred [pounds] a year good security jointure.' This was a generous offer in view of the fact that her portion was unavailable. Elmes did insist that he be paid £100 in cash, however, because 'neither interest nor bonds for the 1,000 [pounds, i.e., her portion] were well paid or secured.' Henry considered the offer a piece of 'good fortune' and to avoid losing Elmes, he and Uncle John borrowed the required £100. Henry expected that Sir Ralph would make good on this loan because the latter was 'in conscience and honor . . . tied in your ability to do something for her.' But to make doubly sure that he would be repaid, Henry assured his brother that after Margaret's marriage took place she would 'engage herself to repay you.'[118]

Sir Ralph was evidently quite pleased and promised to pay back the £100 'as soon as ever I am able . . . and I protest I never parted with an hundred pence with more willingness to any creature when I was in the height of prosperity than I now give this to her,' but he could not forbear adding 'notwithstanding the greatness of my necessity.'[119]

In Henry's glowing reports to Sir Ralph it was chiefly the financial benefits of the marriage that were discussed, and it was not until he had written to Sir Ralph the second time that Henry mentioned that Margaret's new husband 'is so fond of her.'[120] However, in one of sister Susan's letters to Sir Ralph written two months after Margaret's marriage, the latter's relationship with her husband was depicted quite differently. Susan described her new brother-in-law as 'a very humoursome cross boy' who sometimes made his bride 'cry night and day.'[121] These remarks could be brushed aside as the catty observations of an as yet unmarried older sister. But there are reasons for accepting Susan's rather than Henry's version of the relationship.

Margaret's marriage must have been a particularly unhappy one, because despite all the pressures against divorce or separation, Margaret and her husband were formally separated in the 1650s. The exact reasons for the separation are not entirely clear, but it is certain that during one of their arguments her husband struck her,[122] and it must have been shortly after this incident that he abandoned her in England and went to the Continent.[123] Brother Edmund, who was in France at the time, in a kind of comic opera gesture which was typical of him, challenged Elmes to a duel. According to Edmund the duel never took place because while they were still in the coach approaching the place of combat, Elmes saw the error of his ways and agreed to a reconciliation.[124] Despite Edmund's efforts, however, no permanent reunion of Margaret and her estranged husband was possible and surviving documents and letters provide evidence that the original marriage settlements were replaced by new ones which provided her with £160 p.a. 'for [her] own . . . separate use and maintenance as if [she] were sole and unmarried.'[125]

Margaret's case not only suggests the way in which complete breakdown of the marriage was dealt with on the financial level, but also throws some interesting light on the lengths to which the double standard could be carried. Although Sir Ralph knew that it was Margaret's husband who had deserted her and not the other way around, he made a point of asking Edmund to advise Margaret to be especially careful about her public appearances. From Sir Ralph's point of view it was particularly necessary to

> above all charge her not to exceed in clothes (especially in light colours) nor to keep much company for it is not fit for a person in her condition . . . [to] appear often in public as at playhouses and taverns though it be with her own and nearest friends; a refined country life were much better for her.[126]

However, Margaret rebelled against this kind of confinement and Edmund quoted her as having told Uncle Doctor that

> now for my living a retired life, truly I do not know anything I have done as should make me to do so, had I played the whore it had been the fittest course for me, I shall rather give the world leave to talk then to suffer so high a manner of discontent, for I am bad enough in company and should be much worse alone.

After such a bold rejection of brotherly advice, Edmund was obliged to comment to Sir Ralph 'by which passage her indescretion doth so strangely appear that I even blush to repeat it.' Moreover, he assured Sir Ralph 'that unless she will be advised by her friends I shall give her for a lost woman both in her fortune and honour, and shall not intermeddle in her affairs hereafter.'[127]

Sir Ralph's views on the proper behavior to be expected from a woman in Margaret's condition were further clarified in a remarkable letter which he wrote to Elmes some years after the formal separation. In this Sir Ralph complained to 'Brother Elmes' that his sister had no house 'to hide her head in, for you will not suffer her to be there with you' and therefore Sir Ralph wanted Elmes to buy her a house so 'that she may live as becomes your wife.' Then, by way of further persuading him, Sir Ralph added, with absolute seriousness, that he was sure that his sister would be happy to receive Elmes 'whenever you please to come and receive you with all the respect, duty, and affection that becomes a good and loving wife towards her husband.'[128] Whether Margaret was actually capable of performing the emotional gymnastics which this would have required is a moot point. However, her brother believed that this was the way in which a wife should behave in such circumstances, regardless of the fact that her husband had thrown her out, and he apparently counted on Elmes's agreement with this view to persuade him to buy her a house.

Susan, the oldest sister in the family, was married in the same year as the other two (1646), but although the negotiations began much earlier, she was the last of the three to be married. In the course of these unusually lengthy and complicated proceedings, which went on for more than a year and a half, and were the subject of scores of letters, family relationships were severely strained.

Like her sister Penelope, Susan's £1,000 portion was supposed to come from an investment made in an office (the alnage), but the difference in this case was that Sir Ralph had borrowed about £750 of this money from her feoffees and was therefore directly responsible to them for the repayment of that sum plus the interest.[129] He was also indirectly responsible to her for the payment of a £100 bond for a sum which had been lent out and could not be called in because he was unable to find the bond.[130]

Much of the delay in proceeding with the marriage was due to the difficulty of extracting this money, or reasonable security for it, from Sir Ralph. The negotiations were also slowed down by the fact that they were conducted by mail, and that midway in the process Sir Ralph went off on a tour of France.[131] Unlike her sisters, Susan stood to lose about half her portion if she decided to marry without Sir Ralph's consent, but even if she elected to do that she still had to collect the £500 that would then be due to her from Sir Ralph.[132]

To complicate matters further, Susan's future husband, Mr Alport, was a prisoner in the Fleet. Inasmuch as Alport had been imprisoned for debt, his creditors had to be consulted on each new proposal in order to assure themselves that the portion or security for it would be sufficient to cover what was owing to them.[133] For the single man imprisoned for debt, the prospect of marriage had great appeal because he could use the ready cash which the portion provided to free himself, much as Thomas had done in similar circumstances. Neither Susan nor those acting for her had any objection to Alport because he was a prisoner, for it was a common enough experience at the time, and Susan herself had been a prisoner for a brief period shortly before she met Alport.[134] Moreover, Alport was a gentleman whose estate was worth above £600 p.a. and his indebtedness was something less than £1,000.[135]

Susan was certainly eager to marry him, partly because she knew that plain girls who would not appeal to 'many palates' could not expect many offers.[136] Even her Uncle Leeke, who acted for her in arranging the match and who seems to have been genuinely fond of her, did not hesitate to point out to Sir Ralph that Susan 'was not a wife for many men, though it hath pleased God to infuse a great affection into the man [Alport] from the desire to match into your family.'[137]

The practical considerations which originally accounted for Alport's interest in Susan were apparently, in the course of the negotiations, augmented by the blossoming of a romantic relationship between them. At one point in their courtship Susan's friends strongly advised her to break it off when Alport's former girlfriend declared that she had a prior claim to him, and this could have entailed an expensive law suit if Susan persisted in marrying him.[138] However, the feoffees quickly backtracked and allowed the marriage negotiations to proceed because they believed that the relationship between Susan and Alport might have reached, by that time, a level of intimacy which made it impossible for her to break it off. Sir Ralph advised one of the feoffees that if this was the case 'if she have him not she is a lost creature' and therefore 'the trouble, charge, and shame of the suit that is like to follow . . . [if she married him] is rather to be chosen.'[139] Sir Ralph expressed even less doubt about the matter when he confided to a friend of his that 'I think she had best marry him and that quickly too, but in so doing she cannot but expect to reap the reward of her own folly.'[140] It is possible that Susan was pregnant at this time, because she is known to have miscarried during the early months of her marriage.[141] Given the values of the time, however, Sir Ralph and the feoffees would probably have insisted that she go through with the marriage even if she were not pregnant if they had reason to believe that Susan and her fiancé had been intimate. In this connection, there was already a stain on Susan's reputation because the marriage negotiations were so protracted.[142] In cases where it took so long to arrive at a marriage settlement, it was commonly believed that the lady might not be a virgin. The length of time spent in negotiating the marriage treaty, according to conventional opinion, was supposed to be a measure of the lady's chastity as well as of the groom's eagerness to have her.

In addition to her other problems, Susan was also under fire from brother Henry who did not trust Alport and who refused almost from the beginning to be instrumental in promoting a match of which he did not approve.[143] Uncle Leeke, on the other hand, believed Alport was very suitable[144] and in his eagerness to bring the business to a conclusion, risked Sir Ralph's anger by intimating that the latter delayed the proceedings unnecessarily.[145] In order to persuade Sir Ralph that Henry was mistaken, Susan reminded him that her suitor was originally told that the portion was £1,000 and on that basis agreed to £200 a year jointure. After more than a year of haggling, Sir Ralph had succeeded in whittling down his share of the direct payment to Alport from £600 to £400,[146] but Alport still agreed to give Susan £200 a year jointure. Since the amount of the jointure was the groom's greatest lever of power in such treaties, Susan justifiably admired Alport for 'still stand[ing] to his first proposition,' and considered this proof of his good faith.[147] Sir Ralph, for his part, exploited to the full Alport's need for ready cash in order to reduce the size of the payment which he would have to make.[148]

In the course of these lengthy proceedings the discussion gradually degenerated into a series of nasty accusations and counter-accusations. Sir Ralph became increasingly impatient with Uncle Leeke's insistence that he should make a more generous offer so that the treaty could be concluded.[149] Uncle Leeke in his turn was offended because in the last stages Sir Ralph left Leeke's name out of the note of consent nominating those who could treat for Susan in his absence.[150] Susan angrily accused Sir Ralph, among other things, of reneging on his responsibilities to her by offering her worthless land as security.[151] She also fought with Henry because the latter disapproved of her choice.[152] Henry used these disputes as a lever to gain increasing favor with Sir Ralph; he lost no opportunity to commiserate with his brother about the ingratitude of their sister and kin.[153] Sir Ralph defended himself by insisting that he was making the best offers he could in view of his straightened finances, and was greatly incensed by his sister's boldness in accusing him of not doing his best.[154]

While there is little doubt that Sir Ralph was having a difficult time making ends meet during this period, there is also little doubt that his treatment of Susan was quite shabby. Sir Ralph was unwilling to alienate any valuable property from his estate in order to pay what he owed to her. The land that he offered as security was of such poor quality that Uncle Leeke could not raise any money on it although he made repeated attempts all over London.[155] When nothing could be raised on this land, Sir Ralph did offer to pay her cash, but about £700 of this was in money which was owed to him and which Susan would have to collect. Moreover, the money was owed by one Bachus, and Sir Ralph had reason to believe that Bachus was his enemy and something of a conniver who would do his best to avoid payment.[156] It was Bachus's intention to turn the money over to the Parliamentary sequestrators when it came due in order to spite Sir Ralph.[157] Susan only succeeded in getting it because she paid 'the siezers' a larger bribe 'to stay away' than Bachus had offered them to take it.[158] Moreover, when Sir Ralph's figure of what he owed differed from his sister's by £5, he forced her, as much out of cheapness as pique, to have their uncle send him a full list of particulars in order to prove that she was correct.[159]

In spite of all the hard feelings and backbiting which grew out of Susan's attempt to get her portion, when she finally married, tempers cooled and the family relationships were patched up. In each case it was Sir Ralph who was approached by the offending member. Susan tried to make up for some harsh words she had written to Sir Ralph with the observation that 'you are too wise a man, to weigh either the malice or the passion of a foolish woman and your sister.'[160] There was nothing surprising in this because Sir Ralph was still the head of the family and the inheritor of the family patrimony. As such he was the last person that anyone in the family would want to alienate, whatever the provocation. The connection with Sir Ralph was central to all kinds of reciprocal arrangements. For example, after Susan's marriage her husband gave her a flat sum 'to maintain me in clothes, during his life, and to put it out where I have a mind to it [i.e., to lend the money out at interest], servants wages must go out of it too which I had forgot, but I will keep but a few.' She told Sir Ralph that she expected to be able to get together £600 for lending and 'for as far as £600 will go I am a perfect userer.' She furthermore asked him if he would like to borrow it.[161] From Susan's point of view, her offer served the twofold purpose of cementing relations with Sir Ralph by offering him access to credit and also provided her with a safe investment for idle money. Sir Ralph wrote back refusing her offer. However, it is significant of the nature of family interaction that he also took the trouble to make a separate memorandum for his own use, in which he noted the offer and recorded the reason for his refusal which was that 'in these ill times, I should not be able to pay her constantly.'[162] He apparently did not expect his sister to be more charitable in the case of default of payment than someone who was not related to him, and his refusal of her offer also served to reduce her prospects for future claims on him.

However, as long as Sir Ralph controlled the family estate he could offer a favored brother or sister valuable assistance. If he was too tight-fisted to be counted on for much in the way of outright gifts, he still had influence and power which he could exercise on behalf of those whom he believed were worthy to receive it. It was undoubtedly considerations of this sort which made Henry agree to make it up with Susan when Sir Ralph requested him to do so shortly before her marriage.[163] Henry had a great deal more to lose in crossing Sir Ralph than in crossing Susan.

## WIDOWHOOD

Younger brothers of uncertain prospects, living on small annuities, were rarely in a position to flout the demands of the head of the family. The same was true of daughters, especially when they were single, but to some extent even after they married. However, if an upper-class woman outlived her husband, widowhood expanded her options. The widow's jointure served as a dowry, but with no strings attached, for her next preferment.[164] If she chose to remarry the selection of a new husband could be made without reference to parental wishes in the matter or even counter to them.

Sir Ralph's Aunt Poulteney did exactly this when she chose the Catholic Lord Eure for her second husband. Her Anglican family was horrified by the prospect of having a Catholic in-law and strongly objected to her choice. Sir Ralph's father wrote from the field that perhaps Lord Eure would go into battle and 'some lucky bullet may free her of this misfortune.'[165] Her mother had hoped that she would choose Lady Deincourt's son, but Aunt Poulteney was against it despite the fact that

> mother is for it for she hears he [Deincourt] hath a greater estate than this, which I believe is her reason, but for my part I think all the riches in the world without content is nothing, so this liberty I will take to myself that is to make choice of one I can respect.[166]

As to her mother's annoyance with her refusal, Aunt Poulteney agreed

> 'tis true she is my mother and I shall give her what satisfaction as is fit, but I consider my own freedom in my choice or in anything else for what fortune I have, I have had it from my [deceased] hus[band] and a widow is free.[167]

After she had gone through with her marriage to Eure the pressures on her did not immediately subside. She complained to Sir Ralph that

> I understand by your mo[ther] as the town makes havoc of my good name, but let them devise their worst I defy them all, none in the world can call me to an account to my actions for I am not in anyone's tewishion [tuition] as I have sent your mother word.[168]

None the less, her gift to Sir Ralph's sister Margaret of a substantial marriage portion,[169] which was made after her marriage to Eure, provided some assurance that the Verneys would come to look upon her choice with more favor than otherwise.

If few gentlewomen were willing to go quite as far as Aunt Poulteney in exploiting the freedom which widowhood gave them, fewer still seem to have been willing to remain in that condition permanently.[170] As one widow who spoke from experience put it, widowhood was a 'desolate, discontented, estate'[171] from which one was supposed to escape to a new preferment. Similarly, the dowager Elizabeth Lady Russell intended to 'marry and be provided of some one that shall defend me and take care of me living and to bury me, and not thus to live, no man caring for my soul and life.'[172] In a man's world, remarriage was a sensible recourse for a woman alone. With careful management a second marriage could even provide a rise in status. Sir Ralph's patron, Eleanor Countess of Sussex, came from a relatively undistinguished background. She specialized in remarriage to older men and worked her way into the peerage through successive marriages of that kind.[173] After Sussex died she married the second Earl of Warwick. She confided to Sir Ralph that she had decided to marry again because neither Sir Ralph nor his father were available to help her with her many problems,[174] and therefore 'continuall trubles, wantinge a discret and healpful frinde . . . made mee thinke of marrige.'[175] However, previous experience had acquainted her with the need to make an agreement with her newest husband 'which was to keep all my personal estate in my own power.'[176] Sir Ralph's code name for this professional widow was 'Old Man's Wife.'[177]

Whether a widow chose to remarry primarily out of romantic considerations like Aunt Poulteney, or financial and social ambitions like the Countess of Sussex, the choice was usually conceived in terms of which husband one might choose next rather than whether one should remarry. Widowhood does not seem to have been viewed as a permanent alternative to marriage, but rather as a position which provided greater freedom in the choice of marriage partners.

There were too many negative aspects to being husbandless for it to have been otherwise. Widowhood increased a woman's dependence on other male members of the family and kin, and at the same time decreased the pool of kinship connections which she needed in order to reciprocate such favors. At the psychological level, a woman of the type of Lady Verney, whose total definition of herself was in terms of her relationship to a man, would view remarriage as her only practicable alternative. For those women for whom romantic inclinations or sexual needs were unimportant, the financial benefits of remarriage were considerable, especially when the arrangement was carefully managed. A new husband brought at least the prospect of security and, as in the case of the countess, even the possibility of improving one's financial position. In any specific case, of course, the decision to remarry was probably made out of some combination of all three motives, social, psychological and financial.

Moreover, from the new husband's point of view there was little stigma attached to remarriage to a widow. Among the peerage 40 per cent of the widowers married widows,[178] a sufficiently high figure to justify the conclusion that widows were believed to be excellent marriage material. Their jointure settlements made them financially attractive, their previous experience in household management ensured that they would make some positive contribution in that area, and they were also likely to be more compatible sexually and socially since they were more mature.[179] In addition, since they were free to choose the mate to whom they would bring all these advantages, they were more likely to want to make a success of it. Therefore, not only was there great incentive for a widow to remarry, but prevailing modes and values enhanced the possibility that she would seek a new preferment.

# 5

# CHILDREN, SERVANTS AND PARENTS

If family history is a subject which tends to evoke our deepest concerns and passions, perhaps no problem is more controversial and overlaid with special concern, either to justify or condemn the present, than the subject of children. The vagaries and complexities of parent/child relationships seem almost endlessly variable and relentlessly resistant to generalization. Several recent studies have made excellent progress toward providing a better understanding especially of the upper classes, utilizing large samples and a variety of documentation.[1]

Even these extraordinary works, however, raise more questions concerning attitudes and behavior than they were able to answer to complete satisfaction.[2] To take just one example, there seems to be little agreement on the question of whether children were treated with unusual severity in the early modern period. Even if one is persuaded that in the seventeenth century the relatively new concern with the child was apt to express itself in increased discipline, can we view this as an improvement or decline in the condition of children?[3]

Similarly, the practice of sending young children into other people's houses to be reared has been the subject of differing interpretations. Professor Morgan has suggested that this practice was founded primarily on parental concern for their children and their understandable reluctance to administer the kind of discipline on their own progeny which parental goals demanded. At the other end of the spectrum Lloyd de Mause's work and interpretation would view parental reluctance to inflict punishment as the least likely reason for the practice of fostering out.[4]

Given the nature and scope of the debates, a single family study can hardly pretend to offer very much in the way of resolution of the arguments, beyond suggesting the historiographical context in which this study of child rearing practices in the Verney family is set. What it can offer is a kind of precision of detail concerning not only what happened, but why and how the particular action formed part of a network of social interaction. It is at this level of detail that one can best describe actions and attitudes in order to trace their links to the structures and social possibilities which the wider society allows or inhibits. By focusing on interaction within a single family and their social circle this study cannot address the nature of change over time, but neither does it have to rely exclusively on the usually unknowable workings of the interior life of individuals. Instead it relies on the givens of social organization, viz., patriarchy, primogenture, hierarchy and the dependence on rents for family income, all of which are historically verifiable, to help us understand behavior and attitudes.

This kind of approach avoids the difficulties of casting certain problems solely in terms of the psychological needs of children and their parents. It is probably more productive, until we understand personality development much better than at present, to examine the custom of fostering out, for example, as part of the need for social reciprocity and as a familial strategy for avoiding social derogation, rather than attempting to generalize about the psychological consequences of separation trauma. Some parents and children were pained by separation, others were relatively unconcerned or even relieved. What is clear is that fostering out and child swapping served to offer opportunities to children and their families of origin for enlargement of social networks which could be useful in subsequent mate selection, careers and estate management, in a society in which influence mattered and in which psychological trauma was hardly understood to exist.

Their letters do not tell us everything we would like to know. There are the expected omissions of practices so common, like infant swaddling, that little comment is made of them. On the other hand, the correspondence is full of discussions about the ubiquitous presence of servants to the extent that they allow a fairly elaborate profile of attitudes on that subject. In addition, the mnipresence of illness and death among young children is corroborated, but the Verneys' experiences also suggest the ways in which parents coped with what were, to modern sensibilities, incapacitating anguish and grief. Finally, their letters convey a sense of the complexity and range of possibilities in parental attitudes and behavior toward their children as well as the extent to which contextually induced behavior affected parent-child relations.

The Verneys' attitudes toward and treatment of their own and other people's children was of a piece with family strategies and societal expectations. They believed that children were precious, in the sense that they were deemed valuable and necessary to ensure the future of the lineage. In a patriarchal, primogenitural family sons were valued more than daughters and elder sons more than cadets. This did not preclude some favoritism and personal preferences, but it did lay down the probabilities of choice particularly in the extreme circumstances which arose during the Civil War, and especially in the unforeseeable consequences of exile and the threat of expropriation.

But the fact that the family valued its children, as guarantors of futurity, has to be distinguished from parental attitudes toward any individual child. In a specific relationship attitudes were affected by the child's age, birth order and gender. Moreover, the fragility of the individual, the chancy business of survival, made it unlikely that any child should be the exclusive repository of parental hopes and ambitions for the lineage, although death rates and infertility could sometimes combine toward that unwanted prospect.[5] In trying to assess parental attitudes toward children it would be wrongheaded to apply modern notions of individuality in a situation where these concepts were barely palpable, either in mate selection, status and power distribution within the family, styles of salutation, or any of the other signs which underscore the presence of the idea of individual uniqueness.

Heirs, of course, achieved a kind of distinctiveness in parental concerns which other children could not claim. But even they became part of a currency of exchange which circulated in the social reciprocations, favors, and obligations of the kin networks. The realities of high infant mortality combined with poorly articulated notions of individuality to suggest the feasibility of substituting one child for another. Sometimes this attitude, concerning the interchangeability of children, made the permanent loss of a child through death more endurable. A condolence letter to grieving parents could offer that possibility as an acceptable and sympathetic suggestion. Uncle Dr Denton's suggestion to his nephew that 'I should be better pleased to have it [Lady Verney's next baby] a girl for her [Lady Verney's] sake' should not be taken as an expression of his preference for girls. His observation makes better sense in view of the Verneys' loss of their child Margaret the previous year. She had been a favorite, and the doctor expected that the parents would take no offense, in fact be comforted, by the prospect that the new baby might be a replacement for the deceased Margaret.[6] Modern attitudes toward individuality make it unlikely that parents would be comforted by such a suggestion. More likely it would be considered an affront to moderns who are bred on notions of individual uniqueness.

The fragility of infants did little to lessen the effort required if a child were to have a fighting chance for survival. Among this class the parents were supervisors of those who did the actual work. In the middle of the seventeenth century a birth was believed to require not only the attendance of a midwife and perhaps a physician but also the 'nurse and nurse keeper' to whom the godparent was expected to distribute '40 or 50s.'[7] If the baby thrived subsequently there would be governesses and tutors of various kinds depending on the age and sex of the child.

In the lived experience of children and their parents, servants of various kinds were always needed. Not only did they provide for the daily physical needs of the children, but they were expected to help in the care of the frequent illnesses which were so much a part of childhood in that period. In addition, they could be required to provide amusement, to afford protection, supervise and even to instruct them in the rudiments of reading and writing. Although employers agreed that 'a companion [was] not a servant,' notions of specialization had not advanced to the point where the Verneys were precluded from hoping that their French maid, if carefully selected, could teach their 7-year-old to read.[8]

Certainly, children were an important focus of parental concern. But that concern was not apt to be expressed in terms of affection, but rather in offering particular kinds of training, education, skills and discipline. This breeding, in the case of both sexes, was designed to make them personable and malleable in familial relationships and ultimately more attractive in the marriage market.

Almost nothing was understood about psychological needs, but children appear to have been viewed as extremely susceptible not only to disease, but to bad habits and to willfulness. Parental surveillance, or supervision by surrogates for them, was constantly required. There seems to have been little sense of the possibility that children might opt to do the right thing without alert governors to ensure their compliance.

## SERVANTS

The belief that children needed breeding if they were not to revert to wild and uncontrollable creatures was shored up by a set of assumptions concerning character formation which, in part, accounts for the care with which servants were selected. Since the circumstances of the Verneys' lives provided occasions to commit some of these ideas and attitudes to paper, we have a sense of the range of considerations which Sir Ralph and his wife discussed in choosing servants. There was, of course, the perennial cry of the upper classes concerning the outrageous cost of hiring servants and the unwillingness of the latter, in the employer's view, to do as much as they should. The private lives of even the most attentive of servants could also prove to be an inconvenience. Lady Verney's favorite maid, Lucy, had been commanded by her brother to leave the Verneys and to serve in his house. After the brother had made several requests, Lucy confided to her mistress that he was 'so angry with her' that if she did not return he would disown her. This might mean no small inconvenience since he had promised to 'settle seven or eight pounds a year upon her for her life and be good to her' if she agreed to come to him.[9]

The case was further complicated by the fact that he was 'a man of 2 or 3 hundred pound a year and scorns that his sister should serve.' But a woman of this station was precisely the sort of person Lady Verney wanted as a maidservant, one from decent stock who had fallen on hard times. In addition, Lady Verney told her husband that she was very upset 'for I know I cannot expect ever to have so good a sarvant [sic] again and for my greater trouble he will have her away before Christmas which will be so . . . great an inconveniency to me.' Lady Verney had returned temporarily to

England and the uncertainty of her situation there made her grumble that she was unlikely

> to get one that knows how to dress me that will be contend [sic] to do half the work that she doth, for they are all grown so fine that one cannot have any chamber maid that will serve under 4 or 5 pound a year wages at least and beside they will neither wash nor starch.[10]

In their new home in France, the Verneys had an additional problem in keeping desirable upper servants because of the latters' religious scruples. After considerable difficulty Sir Ralph hired a coachman who had been rather dilatory in coming to be interviewed because he had 'a little estate & some business' in the country,[11] but Sir Ralph decided to wait for him. The previous coachman had told the local priest 'he would not live with one of [Sir Ralph's] religion for he was between God & the Devil.' Sir Ralph, on his part, was not afraid of contamination for himself or his children. He wanted 'any honest handsome careful man that is a good coachman and no drunkard.'[12]

The careful calculation that was considered acceptable may be seen in Sir Ralph's offer of 'fifty livres in money, and two suits every year, and a cloak once in 2 years' but he was clear that the servant was not to expect 'shoes nor hats nor washing, nor old coach wheels.' The coachman was expected to take care of the rig 'horses and to keep the coach very clean' as well as 'to serve at table, and bring up wood to my chamber.' This meant that he would be in daily contact with the members of the household, and Sir Ralph characteristically rounded off this list of specific expectations with the cover-all phrase 'in short to do any thing that I appoint him.'[13]

It was this elasticity of demand on servants' time and duties, added to their observability and propinquity within the household, which could make such demands unending, and which could generate the circumstances and angers upon which such relations were apt to break.[14] On the one hand, someone with a little property was apt to be more sober and reliable, acceptable within the household and suitable to be with the children. On the other hand, those like the coachman or Lucy Shephard who had some prospect of other income and possibility could be harder to keep and to control.

Attempts on the servants' part to make distinctions in status in order to elevate their own tended to be resented by employers. When a maid whom the Verneys were trying to hire inquired if there were gentlewomen in the house and if she would have to do laundry, the Verney hiring agent reported himself to be quite restrained because he 'did not tell her I thought it fit for those that took wages to be servants.'[15] The open-ended possibilities of what might be required included having servants play 'the fool' for the children's amusement. Brother Edmund Verney wrote to his nephew and namesake that he would if he could send his servant Dick over for the purpose.[16] Children, like servants, were always alert to any distinctions of rank and power. The Verneys' 12-year-old, 'Mun,' on another occasion wrote to his father and referred to their housekeeper/nanny simply as 'Besse,' but in the same letter made reference to the visiting child of a gentleman as 'Master Busby.'[17] Bess in her turn referred to her charges, the two Verney children, as 'Mr Munn and Mrs Margaret' when she wrote to assure the temporarily absent father that they studied 'their books willingly, as well if not better than when you are present.'[18]

In addition to their other qualifications, it was also important that servants be good-looking. Lady Verney was less than pleased with Lucy's replacement though she admitted the girl was 'a very good wench, but she is not at all handsom [sic] which I know would not please me.'[19] Dr Denton was brought into the search for a maid for Lady Verney. He found a young woman in her mid-twenties who was also eager to go to France. This maid in addition had the much wanted skill of being very good with nursing sick people, a valuable attribute. However, she was very pock-marked and he believed she might not please Lady Verney on that score.[20]

There were other physical requirements besides aesthetic considerations. Wet nurses were not kept if they became pregnant. Lady Verney's infant Ralph had required a change of wet nurses when his was thought to be pregnant. But Lady Verney was hard put to find another because the only replacement that was available was considered not pretty enough and also wanted more money. The superstition that the nurse's traits could be passed through the milk to the suckling child may also have made an unattractive nurse even less appealing.[21] The additional charge of a rise from '3s 6d to 4s' as well as two bundles of wood certainly did nothing to enhance her standing as a prospect.[22]

Since servants of various kinds were deemed necessary to live in anything approaching upper-class style, even the most stringent economies exacted by the early years of the Verneys' exile on the Continent left them with two maids and 'one man and a little boy' in service. This for a family of two children and their parents.[23] It was not unusual for persons of this class to keep one personal servant even in the most reduced circumstances. Brother Thomas had a servant in prison,[24] and his brother Henry and sister Penelope both made inroads on the Verney linens at Claydon Manor in order to supply their respective personal servants with sheets.[25] One had need of servants from one's earliest recollections through one's own reproductive years and into the dependencies attendant on advancing years.

The ever-present servants were inevitably drawn into family squabbles and sometimes became the targets, deserved or not, of their employers' anger. At least one of sister Betty's disputes at the Elmes's household was blamed on her maid Nan. In this case the accusations against Nan as a meddler were made more credible to Sir Ralph by his need to cut expenses in maintaining his sisters in England. He advised Lady Verney to let the maid go and to settle accounts with the long-employed but now 'useless' Nan as inexpensively as possible. The employer's greater power was revealed in the fact that it was always possible to gain great latitude in paying off a departing servant. One might withhold a final gratuity or reduce the sum, and one could manipulate to one's advantage the calculation of 'found' payment, i.e., that part of the servant's pay which was given in the form of room, board, firewood, etc.[26]

Although there was a great deal of indignant sniffing about the effort one had to expend on servants and their propensity to make trouble,[27] it was also necessary to be careful of the feelings of a valued servant. The Verneys' younger son Jack had been left entirely in the care of servants at Claydon. When Lady Verney returned to England, Sir Ralph gave her detailed instructions for the oversight of the child's diet and study habits. But he also warned her to be scrupulous in handling the maid and the housekeeper with tact when relaying all these instructions and to 'do it in as handsome a way as you can.'[28] And when Lady Verney finally had to part with Lucy, she was unwilling to let the maid go to her new employment at the brother's house without giving her a minimum of £5, even though she admitted to her husband that money was 'hard to come by.' Lady Verney believed that the quality of her work deserved this recompense especially since Lucy had been willing to work for wages that even her employer admitted were low.[29]

Aside from the servants' vulnerability in the power relationship and their dependence on the good will of the employer, an additional pressure on these relationships was created by the contemporary practices of household financing. In this period, it was not uncommon for a husband of this class to give his wife a lump payment for clothes and other expenses. This payment enabled the wife to put this money out at interest and in that way enlarge her disposable income. Servants' wages might have to be allowed from this money as well, and this heightened incentive on the wife's part to be as tight-fisted as possible in negotiating servants' wages. After sister Susan was married she decided that 'now all the world grows poor I purpose to turn userer.' She was delighted that her husband allowed her 'to put out [money at interest] where I have a mind to it' but 'servants wages must go out of it too which I had forgot.' She thought she had satisfactorily solved the problem of leaving enough aside to pay the servants by the decision to 'keep but a few.' It is easy to see how in more covetous hands such an arrangement could encourage the wife to extract as much as possible from as few servants as the work and strict management would allow.[30]

This kind of financial arrangement might mean a reduction in the number of servants but even the most impecunious stretched themselves to keep some, because of the variety of services they were expected to provide in households that invariably contained babies and young children. Not the least of their responsibilities was to help in child care and this frequently meant assistance with the sick and dying. Serious illnesses were treated at home, and the correspondence is full of references to children's illnesses and the sometimes revolting cures to which they were subject. Given the ignorance of the medical profession of the period, nursing and ministrations formed an important and laborious part of treatment. A treatment like bleeding was done by a specialist, but many other cures involved brews and recipes of various kinds made in the household. It might be as simple as sending rhubarb to the teething baby's nurse (for her or the child is unclear), or it might involve more exotic concoctions including something called 'Snayle Water.'[31]

When the illnesses were of a severe kind like the then-common small pox and plague, the fears were great, the vigils long, and the work in caring for the patient increased. Of course, the servants were not immune, but their illnesses were usually only recorded in relation to their employers' inconvenience or possible contamination.[32] In discussions about children, one must assume that servants were a continual presence and reality in children's lives, whether the children were well, sick or dying. To the extent that the servants were themselves victimized or abused this may have manifested itself in heightening the animosities of the household or in neglect or abuse of children. The letters indicate little open consciousness of this problem, but the Verneys' general suspiciousness and wariness regarding servants may have been a symptom of their need to depend on those whom they did not entirely trust and whose disaffection could be used against employers or their even more vulnerable children.

## CHILDREN AND ILLNESS

Even if one discounts the preoccupation with illness on the part of those whose ignorance and susceptibility was sufficiently great to lead them to exaggeration, the Verneys' letters indicate a great deal of childhood illness as well as fatalities. Of their six children only two survived to adulthood. Two of them, the infant Ralph and the favored Meg, died within a week of one another.[33] When death did not claim them, the children suffered from a variety of illnesses, everything from the often fatal small pox to the agonies of oozing rashes and the prolonged distress of rotting teeth.

The Verneys had taken two of their children to France, leaving the younger son Jack at the family home in Buckinghamshire. Little Mun and Meg both had small pox when they arrived in France. Although they survived, their parents were very distressed[34] by the threat of losing both of them. It is easy to forget that even toothache, however trivial as a disease, could be excruciating and an added stress on an already weakened child. Contemporaries had very uncertain notions concerning oral hygiene. Toothbrushes were unknown to Sir Ralph and even Dr Denton confessed that he had 'never seen any, nor know of what use they may be.'[35] Sir Ralph's son Mun suffered from toothache and discernible large cavities in his teeth. His father hoped that only the deciduous ones were affected and 'in the meantime we stop them with cotton dipped with Aque Vitae,' a remedy which suggests the inadequacy of the treatment, as well as the largeness and discomfort of the cavities. This child was also suffering from another illness, apparently an oozing rash which the doctors though might be cleared up with some kind of 'issue in the nape of his neck.' It is always risky to attempt diagnoses from this kind of description, but the 'issue' probably referred to the decision to lance a gland in the child's neck. This would jibe with Sir Ralph's concern that the child in that event would have to wear a wig which neither he nor his son wanted.[36]

By modern standards many of the remedies seem like pitiful gestures, but at least they afforded a sense that one could do something useful in response to the seemingly endless afflictions of childhood. Under the circumstances, parents could not have expected all their children to survive to adulthood. In fact, Sir Ralph's generation's hardiness proved to be an embarrassment to the family finances. But the raising of ten or twelve children to adulthood was extremely unusual. Sir Ralph's children were more typical in that babies and children under 5 years of age were most vulnerable to death, but even older children were often claimed before the age of 20, and no age was immune from illness.[37]

Contemporaries lacked the shocking statistics which historians are able to assemble, but many, like the Verneys, endured the most persuasive evidence of the reality and frequency of illness and death. Not only are children's deaths less frequent today, but the death watch is ordinarily experienced only by the parents and hospital professionals. In the seventeenth century, family members died in the household, and the process was viewed by relatives of all ages and degrees of kinship as well as by the inevitable servants. While such familiarity cannot be said to have removed the sense of loss and grief, or fear of death, it may have prepared one better for its inevitability – at least in others.

Because the family was separated in the late 1640s when the pregnant Lady Verney was sent into England to settle the estate, more is known about the loss of two of their children who died during this separation. Certain reservoirs of strength are hinted at in their letters, and the place of religious belief in bolstering the mourners' strength and endurance can also be glimpsed. Other sources of sustenance remain unknowable. What is clear is that a series of losses which today might easily be expected to erode the sanity of a parent to the point of total breakdown, were experienced by the Verneys during a period of great additional personal and political catastrophe, and neither one succumbed.

A more detailed examination of their correspondence does evoke some notion of the price which parents paid for survival. When Sir Ralph sent that nervous inquiry to his Uncle Doctor seeking help with Mun's rash, he was writing only days after the death of 8-year-old Meg. His letter must have crossed in the mail with one from his uncle which could not have brought any relief for Sir Ralph. In the manner of those experienced in being the bearers of bad news, Uncle Doctor chose forthrightness as the kindest way and told his nephew that

> I know that your own discretion and woeful experiences have prepared you for any disasters that any of Job's comforters can present to you, and therefore without any farther preface or apology shall tell you that God hath taken what he gave I mean your youngest son [the infant Ralph] by convulsion fits. My wife met me by the way to let me know so much and that she had broken it to her [Lady Verney].[38]

According to the doctor, who had already been informed of the daughter's passing, at this news the mother became

> very inquisitive of how her other children did. I found her in bed lamenting and as my wife told very inquisitive of me also how her children did expressing that you had sent her noe word of them for a month or longer, so I thought it best to make but one business of both and so I let her know how happy her girl was [i.e., in heaven].

The doctor also expected that Lady Verney's religious beliefs 'with Gods blessing will give her more patience.' His wife and the servant Lucy had seen her and they reported that Lady Verney was looking better. The uncle reassured his nephew that he would 'do what I can to comfort her and to keep her in health' although she was understandably impatient to return to her husband.[39]

Both children were mourned, but the infant's death was not

considered nearly as searing as that of the 8-year-old girl, and it evoked less comment. In that regard, it is probably indicative of the remoteness of nursing infants that the doctor, who provided medical service for the whole family and kin, was informed of the infant's demise by his wife. Little Meg was apt to be mourned more deeply because in addition to her age she was also a parental favorite. When Sir Ralph (who at this point did not know that the infant was dead) wrote to Dr Denton to tell Lady Verney about the death of 'my dear girl' he hoped that his uncle would 'break it to her by degrees' and asked that

> Good Dr. do it the best way you can devise, for I know she loved her tenderly & the child deserved it, for there was never a better natured, more obedient, nor more patient creature born, but she was not too virtuous [for?] heavenly [smudged], though she was too good for me.[40]

Some of his grief was expressed in the conventional phrasing of the bereaved, but there are two reasons to believe that her death caused profound sadness. The first has to do with the circumstances of her death. Sir Ralph had been left in Rouen in a much-shrunken household with few servants and only two of his children (Jack had still not been brought to the Continent) when his pregnant wife departed for England. It was during Lady Verney's confinement with that pregnancy that Meg had become ill. Sir Ralph helped to care for the child himself.[41] He thought she was on the mend, but a few weeks later he wrote in graphic detail to his uncle (Lady Verney was not to be told), that 'in 36 hours (by the clock) [she had] just a hundred stooles, truly hath been in greate extremity and weakness.' Mun apparently had contracted the same complaint despite Sir Ralph's best efforts to keep him out of her room, but the little girl, unlike her brother, was not to recover.[42]

The genuineness of Sir Ralph's protestations of grief can also be corroborated by his subsequent correspondence with his wife. Meg's death was not the first for the Verneys. They had previously lost both an infant and a child of almost 4 years, yet Sir Ralph could write to his wife a couple of months after Meg's death that 'till now I never knew what a grief it was to part with a child.' In this same exchange he also was able to 'confess no creature knew how much you loved that poor child, I ever concealed what passion

I had for her, and rather appeared to neglect her least [sic] our overfondness should spoil her or make the other jealous.' He unburdened his grief further by adding 'but I must needs say I loved her at least equal too [sic] (if not above) any child I had, and truly she deserved it, for there was never a better nor more patient baby born.' Finally, Sir Ralph remembered the recipient and added, 'Enough of this least [sic] in venting my own I increase thy sorrow.'[43]

Infant deaths were so common that it was not to be the custom until later in the century to mourn them formally.[44] This was beginning to change by mid-century and lack of observance could cause some social censure. Sir Ralph's friend, Sir Roger Burgoyne, had been elated at the birth of his first son.[45] The baby was little more than a year old when he died, and his father, who was otherwise quite tireless in his efforts on Sir Ralph's behalf, asked to be excused because he was in mourning.[46] Sir Ralph was rather surprised by this because 'twas not the custom heretofore to mourn for such little children.'[47] Sir Ralph was ordinarily a stickler for propriety and his bemused response to Sir Roger's grief was a measure of the novelty of allowing the death of a baby – even one as in this case past a year old – to interfere greatly with one's daily routine.

Lady Verney certainly took the news of the death of her two children very hard. She was reported to be barely lucid for two days after she was told. Some of that reaction must surely have been for the infant as well as for the daughter, at least those on the scene appear to have thought so.[48] Her grief was harder to bear because this 'affliction, joined with being absent' from her husband was 'without God's great mercy a heavier burden' than she could bear.[49] A few days later she was able to get off a short note, in her own hand, which mentioned not only her grief but also some arrangements about money payments.[50] Within a week of the news, quite lucid, she was able to write a somewhat longer letter which included the sentiment that 'I thank God I can be content to live in any condition so I am with thee, but this [her loss] I confess I have not patience to bear.'[51] But she did bear it. By the following week her letters to her husband took on that mixture of surmise, family gossip, business dealings and information which was their ordinary content.[52]

The following month, just before Christmas, they received hopeful news concerning the lifting of the sequestration and Lady Verney optimistically and accurately predicted that 'I trust in God we shall come off clear' and was looking forward to her return to her husband.[53] Probably buoyed by this change in fortune, and only a little more than a month after the death of her two children, their grief had lessened sufficiently so that, in the custom of the period she was able to suggest to her husband a more formal observation of their loss. She instructed Sir Ralph that if there were sufficient hair of their daughter Meg's to make bracelets for all the sisters, those would be good tokens to offer.[54] The bracelets would serve the dual purposes of gift exchange and memorial.

Sir Ralph, on his part, tried to fill his letters with expressions of endearment and support for his bereaved wife, especially in the weeks immediately following the children's death.[55] These condolence letters were always full of other instructions, however, concerning their business and kindred. This was not unusual practice; announcements of deaths of even close relatives and friends were usually sandwiched in between other business. The uncertainty of the mails and the expense were considerations which probably account for this somewhat crass practice.[56] Only one of Sir Ralph's letters, this to his uncle, written on the day Meg died was marked by the brevity of a grief too acute to allow more. In its entirety it reads

> Oh Dr. Dr.
>
> My poor Meg is happy, but I am
>
> Your most afflicted & most unfortunate
> servant
>
> Tell me how, & when this shall be made known to her mother.[57]

Lady Verney and Sir Ralph also received the expected condolences from other members of the family. These usually emphasized the need to be obedient to God's will and reminded the mourner that a too great or lengthy grief was a sign of resistance to Him. In this, as in other matters, brother Edmund's letter of condolence was a paragon of conventional platitudes and phrasing, and his 'I hope your judgement and discretion will bear that sway with your passion that your grief will be moderated. He that gave him took him and too passionate a sorrow would argue a repining of his decree,' was echoed by others which were sent to the parents.[58]

Sir Ralph may also have derived further satisfaction and relief from the thought that he had been scrupulous and insistent about the need to have the baby christened with some dispatch. And in this Sir Ralph also showed a (for him) relatively rare open-handedness. He had advised his wife not to worry about the cost for getting a good nurse or the expense which the ceremony would entail. He was less concerned and even uncertain about whether godparents were being used in England, a sign that the relationship was becoming minimal, but believed that 'tis no great matter if they are not.' If it were the custom to have them he told his wife rather casually to use 'Harry, Dr. or any other that are next at hand.'[59]

In overcoming one's loss religion offered additional reassurance. If obedience to God's wishes made it possible, in fact imperative to pick up the cares of this world and get on with it, the idea of salvation offered future solace, as well. After the death of the children, Sir Ralph was able to comfort his wife with the consolation that the children were in a better place and that they could look forward to joining them there eventually.[60] Exactly how all of this came together – their religious beliefs, the common bond and needs of the two parents and their remaining children, the support of family and kin, the familiarity with death, and the pervasive knowledge of the fragility of children – to help them through these losses, is finally unknowable.

## ATTITUDES TOWARDS CHILD REARING

What is known about the Verneys' attitudes toward children suggests that their frailty seems to have done little to diminish parental goals and aspirations for them, or to reduce parental desire to have them. The voices in this correspondence are as one in wanting babies even under the uncertain circumstances of political and economic turmoil. At the worst a new pregnancy was accepted with a certain fatalism. Sir Ralph's cousin Nathanial Hobart was one of those obscure country gentlemen connected to the Verneys by marriage to the Leekes. Nathanial and Anne Hobart were for a time displaced persons, driven out of their home by the armies, unable to collect their rents, hence without income, living for a time with a nephew who began hospitably enough and soon chafed at their unwanted presence. In the midst of all this, Hobart's wife became 'great with child.' He saw it as 'an unseasonable blessing' but accepted it because 'God's will must be done.'[61] Other kin were sufficiently disturbed by the sad spectacle of the pregnant and penniless Anne to comment to Lady Verney, whose last child was 5 at the time, that 'God has blest you in keeping you so long without one.'[62]

In that same year, 1645, Sir Roger's wife had another child 'but that it is of another shee,' his second daughter, and on that account understood to be something of a disappointment. But he went on in a more jocular vein to reveal that he 'long[ed] to know how that air [in France] works with my Lady,' because Sir Ralph's wife had till then avoided another pregnancy. Still, he added with a show of piety which allowed him to vent his complaint that 'it is good getting of anything in these hard times, but never had we more reason to trust of God's providence for the keeping of or getting as now.'[63] How easily he was able to conflate the getting and keeping of children with which the observation begins, with the uncertainty of the financial situation, and to count on his friend's shared values to understand his meaning.

Aside from these, under the circumstances of the Civil War, relatively mild comments, there was little to indicate that any of the principals of childbearing age retreated from parenthood. Sir Ralph's female relatives, sisters, cousins and aunts continued to have babies during the worst of the war years, as did the Verneys themselves, even during their most politically and financially precarious year, 1647.[64] When parents of their class had children they seem to have done so through some mixture of motives. The expectation of sex and progeny in marriage combined with inadequate means of birth control, the extremely risky prospect of a baby making it to the age of inheritance, the fear of having no heirs and the gloomy uncertainty of waiting for better times all must have contributed to their acceptance of frequent pregnancies.

In some cases, babies were not viewed as an added strain but as an enhancement of the bond between the spouses. Sister Susan, whose first baby miscarried, seemed delighted by another conception and by the fact that 'now by reason the time is past long since' when she was prone to miscarry again. She was made even happier by the knowledge that 'my hus[band] is extreem [sic] fond of me since I was with child, he was ever a very kind husband to me, but much more since I was with child.' Even vanity about her appearance did not lessen her satisfaction. She seemed to take pride in the cheerful report to her brother than she was 'already as thick as long, within these two months I shal be a monster.'[65]

The desire for children seemed similarly unaffected by the risks and discomforts of childbearing. A pregnant woman who became ill was expected to relinquish recourse to the more heroic cures, which from her point of view was deprivation. But like Lady Verney she 'nevertheless' would have been given 'a world of physic,' the cure-all for all difficulties. Sir Roger's wife was unfortunate to have contracted small pox during her pregnancy and it was considered 'a miracle . . . that notwithstanding her being so full of the small pox her child be very clear from the least spot.'[66] Even without these not unusual complications the childbirth could be dangerous and maternal morbidity was high.[67] That is why it was considered quite remarkable that their recently delivered sister Cary 'in a fortnight time . . . hath been out of her bed a week, because she never was so well of any as of this.'[68]

Not all women were that fortunate. Sister Susan's experience with one of her pregnancies was hardly unusual. Ten weeks after she 'was brought to bed' she wrote to her brother in great detail about her post-partum illness. She began by announcing that 'my child was dead born, it was a boy,' and continued to give details of the 'very sad and weak time' she had 'of it.' She apparently had been far enough gone in the pregnancy that her breasts had swollen with milk for she reported that

> both of them did break, I had 5 holes in one, and one great one in the other, I have endured much pain and misery with them, for a long time not able to turn me in bed, nor to put my hands to my head, I have sat up in a cloak, I am now able to go up and down my house, but not out of doors, I hope I shall gather strength again, but yet I am very weak.[69]

Even when both baby and mother survived the birth many babies, even of this more fortunate class, like the Verneys' infant Ralph, never saw their first birthday. He figures tentatively in the correspondence, and even the report of his death is swallowed up in the overshadowing grief for his elder sibling. In fact those infants who were very short-lived might not in normal times have left many traces. In the scant handful of letters in which baby Ralph is mentioned, references to him are almost parenthetical. The accident of a temporary separation between his parents provides some traces concerning his treatment and accounts for the fact that his father never even saw him. But the surviving evidence indicates that his mother, who was on the scene, hardly saw him either.

He had been sent into the country to be wet nursed as soon after his birth as he seemed strong enough to take the move.[70] Thereafter assurances about his continued well-being were coupled with reports of his elder brother Jack. Lady Verney, for example, assured her husband that 'thy boy Jack [the son they had left in England] appears to me by candlelight to be a brave lusty boy' and she added 'they tell me that the other thrives very well too.' In fact, she apparently had not even seen Jack until then, although at that writing she had been in England more than half a year.[71]

Similarly, it was out of his father's prior concern with reports of the crookedness of 'poor Jack's' legs that he 'much fear[ed] the other child's [i.e., Ralph] nurse being with child, & the change of the milk may bring him to the rickets too.'[72] The next Sir Ralph heard of his namesake was the doctor's communication of the following month that the baby had died of 'convulsion fits.'[73]

By modern standards, the children that did survive must have been rather sad-looking. Sir Ralph was concerned to know if the doctor had a 'remedie for Jack's leggs.'[74] The father believed that the deformity was due to rickets, and that it had been caused by the poor quality of the nurse's milk.[75] Jack also seems to have been a stutterer, and the doctor encouraged the parents with the hope that 'what he will want in retoric I dare say he will have in craft.'[76] Little Peg not only bore the common scars of small pox,[77] but she was also deformed. The relatives viewed it as sufficiently noticeable to offer reassurance that 'she will grow out of her crookedness.'[78] Subsequently, her father was disappointed that she had trouble learning to dance, which he expected would help to correct the difficulty. He hoped that when her mother returned to France 'to order her' she might do better. In the meantime he promised his wife to 'tie up her head, for she holds it worse than ever; not only down, but very much awry.' He justified this resolution by suggesting that 'Madame Testard,' the minister's wife, believed that if their daughter 'be not most carefully looked to, she will never leave it.' Sir Ralph was very loathe to be involved in this rather punitive project for he declared that 'I cannot help it if she be spoiled, for I see her but seldom it must be a mother's work, from whom she must not stir an inch, till she hath left this ill custom.'[79] He apparently had profound faith in the efficacy of discipline over affliction even when, as in this case, he was unwilling to be the dispenser of it.

There was after all very little parents could actually do about their children's illnesses. Disease and contagion were not well understood. Sir Ralph might delay a trip to a city where small pox and plague were rampant, or warn a friend not to handle mail from places having a plague epidemic, but in the end one prayed for protection as the best hope.[80]

This combination of ignorance, the lack of effective remedies or preventative medicine and parental attitudes toward discipline could make childhood a prolonged nightmare. Some of what this was like may be seen in Sir Ralph's relationship with a fellow political exile and lawyer, Mr Robert Busby. Like Sir Ralph, Busby had come to France to escape the war at home and was trying to hold on to his property from the relative safety of the Continent. He had come over accompanied by his young son, and deposited him with the Verneys' tutor M. Testard. Frightened by the specter of sequestration and the possibility that his 'goods will be seized, my rents wholly taken, my trees cut down, my land plowed' which would leave his wife and children unprovided for, Busby decided to return to England, leaving his child in France.[81] Prompted by similar financial pressures, Sir Ralph seized this opportunity to offer to oversee Busby's son, hoping in return to squeeze a series of favors out of the anxious father.

The many tribulations of the child hardly needed to be exaggerated by Sir Ralph who was able to combine steady reports of the son's difficulties with his own requests for a variety of services which he hoped the lawyer father might be in a position to provide.[82] Busby had departed for England late in May 1646 and scarcely a month had passed when Sir Ralph informed him that his son had small pox.[83] When no word was forthcoming from the father, Sir Ralph tried to reopen the connection by volunteering to help in getting payment to the physician who was caring for the child.[84] The letters apparently went astray, but Sir Ralph wrote again this time offering to allow Busby's son to go along with Lady Verney when she returned to England on their business.[85]

Sir Ralph was not easily put off and some time later the now-recovered son's Latin lesson was used as the occasion to pursue the relationship. Sir Ralph's intimacy with the child's condition was implied by his assurances to the father that the Latin was the child's own, not the tutor's, and with the suggestion that Busby should praise the boy to ensure a future performance of the same quality. But Sir Ralph signaled the really important message of the letter with the observation that his own property settlement had been slowed by 'the new disputes between the Parliament and Army.'[86] Shortly thereafter illness again provided an entrée, and Sir Ralph presented himself as the supervisor of both the child's tutor and his physician. Sir Ralph was able to couple the announcement of Busby's son's illness with the news of the death of his own child, a juxtaposition that was hardly calculated to allay fears in Busby. He closed with the request that Busby provide advice to Lady Verney, then in England, on the best way to sue one Lady Denham for arrears owing to the Verneys.[87]

The Busby connection finally paid off when he helped Sir Ralph to settle a debt through his 'very great interest' in one Mr Cleavor.[88] Lady Verney was careful to inform her husband that Mr Busby believed that he had done Sir Ralph a favor, a point which was understood to imply that the Verneys were bound to reciprocate.[89] Not surprisingly, Sir Ralph's next letter to Busby contained reports on the son's health and manners. It was also crowded with the details of Sir Ralph's deeds to land in Berkshire and Oxford, other legal business, and his need for discretion and advice in handling of it because he wished to keep the feoffees and the purchaser ignorant of the deeds.[90] This was rather a tall order and was quickly followed by one in which Sir Ralph shared the news of Busby's son's improving health as well as his concern over all the lessons missed because of illness.[91]

Their growing solidarity can be measured by Sir Ralph's willingness to lay out some money for the child's care at the father's request.[92] The father's letters also treated his concern with his son's ague with some other business matters.[93] Despite all this cultivation of Busby, Lady Verney, who was on the scene, still believed that 'Busby may have to be payed to come and rewarded' to act on their behalf in the sequestration proceedings.[94] Sir Ralph was hoping that his wife might then persuade Busby to come back to France to help him settle some legal matters and was even willing to offer him £20 to sweeten the trip. At least Sir Ralph believed that there would be nothing to be lost 'but lip labor, which few women are nice off [sic].'[95] On the same day, Sir Ralph wrote to Busby and included the by now inevitable description of the son's health as well as a request for some legal work.[96]

In light of Sir Ralph's mixed motives, it is unclear how seriously the father may have taken his next report that the son's fits had resumed. This piece of bad news was offered along with Sir Ralph's forthright confession of his own great need to confer with the lawyer.[97] The picture brightened somewhat with Sir Ralph's subsequent assurance that the boy was recovering but that he and the child were both eager for Busby's return to France.[98] At this point Busby decided to raise the stakes and suggested to Lady Verney in frequent and unmistakable hints that he should like to send his daughter over to France with her when she returned. Lady Verney was not happy about the possibility. She was recovering from her period of mourning and was rather looking forward to meeting her husband alone at Dieppe after their long separation. In a rare fling at coquetry, she vowed to her husband that she was determined to 'break this custom' which she had developed during their separation of going to bed early.[99] The upshot was that Busby did not come over, nor did he send his daughter with Lady Verney. He did decide to leave his son on the Continent until times improved in England.[100]

Months elapsed before the correspondence was resumed. This time it was Busby who rekindled the exchanges. He began with rather vague references to some business for Sir Ralph and gave him assurances that he was concerned to do any favor possible for his friend. Then he moved to what must have been the real purpose of the letter. Busby had recently received disturbing reports from M. Testard that his son was having mental problems and weeping often. The father believed that this strange behavior must have been caused by eating too many grapes or by drinking wine. He wished to remove his son from the Testards' to the Verneys' home, at least during the grape harvest. Busby declared himself quite willing to pay for the service. In addition, he had received news that one of the tutors, one Mauger, and M. Testard were having disputes, and the father was fearful that his son might suffer in the cross-fire between the two.[101]

Sir Ralph's need for Busby had abated considerably since their last correspondence because the sequestration had been lifted. It was more than a month till some business of Sir Ralph's precipitated a reply in which one may get a passing look at the condition of the Busby 'child' whose name was never once used, and who was probably about the age of Sir Ralph's eldest son, 12 years old. The son's unhappiness was in part revealed by the report that he had refused to allow the delivery of a present to 'Madame Bourgignon,' presumably the *pension* keeper, 'she having injured him' – whether in word or deed was not made clear. Mr Busby had also asked Sir Ralph to check on the son's physical condition because he feared that he had been deformed by ill treatment. Sir Ralph's description of him cannot have been reassuring. According to Sir Ralph he was 'but low, [short] & his left shoulder grows out.' There was some disagreement on the last point, the Testards denying any deformity, but Sir Ralph was not in doubt.

On the mental derangement Sir Ralph was more comforting. He had 'questioned him [the boy] in private about crying when he is chid, & he tells me t'was only after his last sickness, & that he hath left it.' The child also confessed that he had fallen out with the tutor Mauger and the latter 'gave him a blow on the side, but Mauger denies it.' Sir Ralph did promise to inquire about the possibility of taking the boy during the *vendage* if both M. Testard and the son were satisfied with the arrangement. In this way, Sir Ralph was able to accommodate Busby and still leave himself a loophole to avoid having to take him.[102]

The father sought solutions in a change of routine or diet rather than in direct parental contact. He wrote to Sir Ralph to tell him that he was sure that the problem had to do with the eating of fruit – the grape rather than the wine – for he requested that the child be given no other kinds of fruit. Furthermore, he was insistent that his son be removed to the Verneys' irrespective of the child's willingness to go because 'As long as I live, but more especially during his minority he ought to subject his will to my desires being his father.' He therefore believed that Sir Ralph need argue nothing else 'to persuade him but only this, that it is my desire that he should be with you for that season [i.e., the *vendage*].'[103] Sir Ralph, who cannot have been eager for the responsibility and whose willingness to oblige was made more flaccid by the fortunate turn in his own affairs, resolved not to take him unless he wished to come. He further reminded the father that 'I know the child desires much to be at Home.'[104]

He was subsequently able to be more reassuring on the matter of the child's tutor. It appears that the father entertained the idea of changing tutors, not because of the tutor's physical abuse of his student but rather because of the Catholic Mauger's unwanted influence in matters religious. He asked Sir Ralph to have the Latin lessons given to their respective sons in the Verney household rather than at the pension.[105] Sir Ralph reassured him that 'I do not find your son in the least way incline to the Romish Religion or to speak in favour of it, however you did well to let him know your dislike of it.' He rounded out this piece of advice with their shared view that 'a father's good example will doubtless prevail much with him, & all other good children.'[106] This was a safe sop to the father as well as a reminder that there were few good examples of the kind except for himself in that part of the world. It might also have been a veiled bid to encourage Mr Busby to take his son home where he might benefit directly from such an example. Either construction served Sir Ralph's purposes.

Even allowing for some exaggeration of the son's difficulties by Sir Ralph in order to gain leverage on the father, the boy's life cannot have been an enviable one. He had been left in a foreign country, in the tutelage of a person who was known to be abusive and in a pension which he disliked. He was a child of 12, small for his age, hunched, frequently ailing, prone to fits, and sometimes weepy to the point of concern. Sir Ralph's ambivalent and intermittent supervision was all that stood between him and the kind of unbridled abuse which went beyond the harsh standards of conventional discipline. The father relied on Sir Ralph's not disinterested judgment in deciding if the limits of acceptable treatment had been breached. The son, for his part, was also forced to make Sir Ralph his main channel of appeal to parental protection.

Both fathers believed themselves self-sacrificing and greatly concerned about the welfare of their respective sons. The evidence of that concern could be seen in their expenditures on tutors, physicians, governors, lessons of various kinds, and tokens of appreciation to those who dispensed physical care of the children. In addition, they were careful to watch for signs of ideological contamination by the available Catholic tutors. To search for tenderness and affection would be to confuse parental devotion with parental love, a quite separable set of feelings which appears not to have been frequently conflated by parents in this period.

## FOSTERING OUT OF CHILDREN

In terms of their investment of time, energy and money, parents displayed great concern and even devotion to their children as well as a suspension of belief in their children's frequently transitory existence. They showed great commitment to the children's future. For example, as the war dragged on, the uncertainty of the situation in England encouraged a number of Verney relatives to view their household on the Continent as preferable to the vagaries of life at home. Child swapping was a long tradition among this class, and the Verneys, after several years, had settled into a sufficiently regular pattern to create the possibility of this kind of exchange. The relatives began to send feelers to see if they were willing to have some children 'over.'

The Verneys were not eager for this kind of reciprocation, even with the Doctor or Aunt Eure, two relations whom they liked. Lady Verney did not want anyone else's children because they 'would make my wound dayly bleed' as reminders of her loss. She also felt that she had little patience left to deal with youngsters.[107] Although she would have liked to oblige her aunt with the favor, the management of two very young 'but weak nice children' the eldest of whom was only 7 at the time, was more than she was willing to assume even in the interests of family solidarity. To complicate matters, 'the Dr. hath a good mind to have his girl there [in France] too,' and the Verneys could hardly oblige the aunt and refuse Dr Denton who was an even greater favorite.[108]

Given family expectations and the nature of social reciprocity, the Verneys were experienced in using circumlocution and graceful refusal, and they had developed it to something of an art. It was difficult but not impossible to ultimately refuse both the aunt and Dr Denton. But the nature of the latter's requests and expectations revealed a good deal about what parents considered important in the way of upbringing, and the circle of kin who might be called on to participate in that process. Their Aunt Eure (now remarried to Captain Sherard) more than a year after her first inquiry was still desirous 'to have them [her two little girls] bred in France for 2 or 3 years' but she was willing to settle for having 'them in the same town' as the Verneys if not the same household. She needed advice on what the cost would be of '2 childrens and one servants diet . . . and their learning to dance and the language will come to.' She believed that they were too young for much more, but 'after one year or two I shall then desire that Peg may learn the guitar.'

The aunt too had been schooled in the nature of familial bargaining and declared herself willing, if Lady Verney thought it best, to keep them at home and bring over a 'French woman' to care for them in England. This latter proposal might have provided an out for the hesitant Lady Verney, except that the aunt concluded her request with the confession that her 'great motive' in sending the girls was that 'my youngest will be apt to a consumption' which residence abroad would presumably preclude.[109] As if this allusion to the more serious motive of the child's health were not enough to persuade, Aunt Sherard concluded with the comment that when the Verneys returned to England they should 'think of no other home but ours for that is both our desires.'[110]

A major and useful strategy in this kind of interchange was to slow the proceedings through delays. Dr Denton had previously sounded Sir Ralph about his orphaned nephew, the son of his eldest brother. Sir Alexander Denton's children had been left to the guardianship of the doctor, and the latter was casting about for ways to place them.[111] The Verneys were not enthusiastic about the possibility of having him come to France, but this boy was 18 and could reside with M. Testard with less supervision than a younger child would have required.[112]

After a number of delays and expressions of confusion concerning which Mun the doctor had reference to in his request, Sir Ralph finally relented to the extent that he addressed the inquiry directly. But his reply was not encouraging. He told his uncle that there were no Protestant teachers where he resided, but that elsewhere 'there are divers universities . . . at more reasonable rates. And not only Protestant schoolmasters but whole colleges of Protestants.' He did not hesitate to review the costs which could be considerable because 'you dare not trust the youth without a governour.' If certain other accomplishments were required, 'Fencing,

Dancing, Riding etc.,' which a young man of his station might be expected to learn, 'the charge . . . [would be] much greater.' Sir Ralph continued in the same vein to string out the requirements. There were 'charges for Schooling, clothes, diet, lodging, washing, etc.' and that in point of cost 'there's little difference between those places & our best schools in England.' This litany provided the myriad of arrangements that needed to be made as well as the sobering note that none of it was cheaper on the Continent than at home.[113]

There were other sticky problems including the fact that 'the charges rise & fall according to the discretion of the youth, or his governour, & the quality of the parents.' Xenophobia was made into an additional stick to beat this dead horse, with the cynical observation that as a stranger 'he will be cheated by his best French Friends.' And as a final warning about the difficulties he cautioned that the trip was expensive and a guide and interpreter would be necessary. Sir Ralph might have considered that this was a bit heavy-handed and tried to mask his evident aversion to the proposal by assuring his uncle that he stood ready to help in any way he could.[114] In the end the boy was sent to Oxford, to the great relief of Lady Verney who told her husband that the nephew was really 'very raw and simple.'[115]

Lady Verney was also on the mark when she intuited that the doctor's next endeavor of this kind would be to send his little daughter 'over.' The negotiations in this case serve to reveal the kind of training that a father might consider appropriate for a favored little girl. The doctor had arranged with M. Testard to swap a son of the minister's for his daughter although he acknowledged to Lady Verney that he would have preferred another girl or a younger boy, presumably because the latter would be more malleable. The doctor's wife was not happy with the arrangement, 'pleading love to the child but the true reason is that she is loath to be at the charges of keeping another that is not her own. And that charge is nothing but the diet for I clothe this and must clothe the other.' He seems to have had some misgivings because he asked his niece to advise him on whether 'this be the exchange that you think fittest for me.'[116]

Despite his wife's objections, he was willing to go ahead with it because he believed that his 7-year-old daughter would get many benefits:

> besides the language which will come of course, I desire especially that she should learn to read & write it, & to draw [?]. As for her needle my highest ambition was never above a plain stitch, but to learn to cut out as much as you will that she may be either seamstress or taylor, anything to get a living by.

This rather ambitious list was not all, for he continued:

> but my highest ambition of all is to have her have so much latin as to understand a latin testament which is enough to understand a Drs. bill & to write one & then I could (if God bless me with life and health) leave her a portion without money, & if this could be done I should stretch my purse strings hard to requite it in his son.[117]

This rather unusual desire to teach a little girl Latin came in part from the fact that she was a special favorite of her father's as well as from the uncertainty of a Royalist's future ability (this was 1648) to provide a dowry.

This kind of arrangement was a slow process because it was complicated, and in the circumstances had to be conducted by mail. Nor was it apt to be moved along by the flabby efforts of the Verneys in an exchange for which they had no enthusiasm. Two years later, he was still in correspondence on the subject. This time the doctor offered as his 'chief aim in sending Babie' his desire

> to wean her from me, to write & speake the language, to dance, & sing if she hath any voice (which I doubt) & to play on the guitar, but especially to write and cast account. I care not for any work [i.e., sewing] but plain work & to cut out, that she may be fit for a [unclear] or a taylor. I would faine have her of as many trades as I could to get her living by, for I am in no great likelihood to provide her a portion.[118]

This list of desired accomplishments comes much closer to conventional expectations. The tag concerning her getting a trade on account of his inability to raise a marriage portion should not be construed as more than a wish on his part to make her handy in the event of spinsterhood. It was also an opportunity for the uncle to complain to his nephew about his dwindling resources, at a period when he was negotiating family financial settlements.

The Verneys' views concerning the training and education of their own children are similarly characterized by prodigious lists of parental expectations. Sir Ralph's correspondence with his wife on the subject was not artificially inflated by other motives or skewed by the necessity to exact one's money's worth in reaching an agreement on fostering out. These were frank exchanges between the parents which expressed their views on child-rearing decisions.

At the time of this particular series of exchanges Sir Ralph had been left with their eldest son Mun and the still living Peg, while the children's mother was in England trying to settle the estate. The family was feeling the pinch of delayed rent payments and uncertain prospects. Still Lady Verney agreed with her husband that the children should be taught dancing, if only for two or three months of the year. But she 'like[d]' her husband's 'motion very well of teaching Mun to sing and play on the guitar, for tis a great deal of pity he should lose his time now he is so young [about 11 years] and capable of breeding.' She was experiencing pressure from the kindred at home who 'much wonder that we make them not learn all exercises, but I have always told them that you have as great a desire they should learn as anybody can have if you had the money.' Then, having justified the quality of their parental care in meeting their responsibilities, she comforted her husband with the invidious comparison to the critics who seemed to be more lax because she went on to note that 'truly, I see nobody here that learnes themselves of anything.' She was also willing to have their 8-year-old daughter 'learn the lute but it may [be] she is of the youngest to do that.' She then turned to the particular needs of her eldest son.

> Now for Mun he hath a good voice which will do well upon the guitar and besides though he have a mind to learn the lute hereafter this for the present will be best to strengthen his fingers. Therefore, I prithee let him begin it and to sing; and I trust God will give wherewithall to give them breeding.[119]

In one of Sir Ralph's letters to her on this subject one notes again the extent of parental agreement on an ambitious program of training. This letter also revealed the way in which distinctions were made between sons and daughters and how the lower intellectual goals which were set for girls provided some convenient financial relief for parents. In this he agreed that two months of dancing was enough because it was 'but for Fashion & Carriage.' In addition, the boy took to it easily but 'pegg learnes it very slowly & scurvily.' She was, of course, younger than the boy, and probably had some degree of scoliosis, but neither her age nor her physical disability were viewed by the father as the cause of her lack of accomplishment as a dancer. Rather the father believed that the reason lay with the instructor who 'hath no heart to teach her.' Sir Ralph proposed that they give dancing lessons only to the son, assuming Lady Verney was able 'to settle things well in England' and 'convert this hour charge . . . to teach him the guitar, & to sing [with] it.' The father did recognize that 'the Lute is so tedious a thing that I doubt (unless he made it his whole business) he would never play well. But this he may do and not neglect his Latin.' He was still in some doubt about the lessons which with singing would raise the fee from £3 a month to £5. He wanted her 'opinion of' this and cautioned her 'to speak not of it to anybody,' trusting her intelligence to 'know why' it needed to be kept quiet.[120]

Having disposed of the needs of his son, he turned to those of his daughter. 'Tis time Peg should learn some work [i.e., needlework], tell me what sort . . . & who can teach her.' He was concerned that 'she grows a great girl and will be spoiled for want of breeding.' Furthermore, he 'never let her go out, because (till you come) there is nobody to look to her.' If her gender required certain constraints, it also had its compensations in that 'being a girl, she shall learn not latin, so she will have the more time to learn breeding hereafter; & work too.' Not only was the training different for a little girl, but the sense of urgency that a boy's needs required was lacking, in part because sons were expected to acquire certain intellectual achievements which were not sought in daughters.[121]

Whatever the gender of the child, a good deal of parental concern and financing was expected to go toward appropriate breeding. There were important social accomplishments which were presumed necessary and useful in career advancement and on the marriage market. These were positive steps which afforded parents a sense of accomplishment in meeting responsibilities, and a modicum of control over what was in reality the risky venture of parenting. Whatever the demographic probabilities, these parents behaved as if they expected their investments to reach future fruition. They seem to have been accepting of the need of high fertility in order to ensure the future of the lineage. The lack of direct and continual interaction with young children, whose care was largely given over to others, probably made it easier to bear their death, although the loss of individual favorites could be very difficult. There does not seem to have been great priority placed on affectionate, personal intimacy of the kind associated with daily contact. Yet parents and guardians took their responsibilities seriously and attempted to provide the care and training necessary for persons of their station.

If the Verneys and their circle were attentive to the training of children they were less concerned with the need for providing affection or even continuity in their children's lives. Parents could not make the kind of emotional investment which would be considered appropriate today. Instead they believed that they should provide appropriate training and 'breeding' to enable the children to take their places in the social hierarchy. The strategies for achieving their goals for their children, as in other matters, included the use of reciprocal favors of all kinds in maintaining and reinforcing the kinship network. Parenting was expected to be undertaken by a spectrum of relations and acquaintances whose capacities for supervision of the children and their servants was judged to be adequate and available.

From the child's point of view, illnesses of various kinds as well as the ever-present possibility of death must have made childhood an unhappy or at least an uncertain period of life. These uncontrollable realities were not often ameliorated by the comforting efforts of warm and affectionate parents or their surrogates. The need for discipline was apt to be seen by the latter as too efficacious to forego in a period that offered few other solutions than prayer and hope for taking positive action on behalf of their children's well-being.

# 6

# CONCLUSION

This attempt to recapture, in some part, the way in which Verney family members and kin treated each other has relied on their formal kin roles and relationships as a point of departure. In addition to emphasizing individual place in the family hierarchy as a key to understanding their values and attitudes, I have also tried to suggest the significance of social context in explaining individual behavior, choices and possibilities. Therefore I have been concerned to suggest the links between the Verney family strategies, including those bearing on family and kin interactions, child-rearing and marriage arrangements and the wider social structure. In all these matters the experiences of the Verneys suggested that their ostensibly private and presumably idiosyncratic personal interactions were very much affected by the structural realities of institutional arrangements, as well as by demographic trends, *rentier* class concerns and ideology.

The picture of family life which emerges here departs considerably from any notion of what Goode has correctly criticized as 'the family of western nostalgia.'[1] The Verneys bear little resemblance to that fictitious family of the rural long ago that lived in harmony under the concerned but firm guidance of a respected father and his adoring wife. But if the family was not notable for its harmonious relations and was marked by continual backbiting and dispute, it was characterized by a high degree of solidarity. One of the puzzles which this study set out to solve was the way in which solidarity endured despite the economic stresses of war and the political schism which ensued among its members, and despite relationships which, even in better times, were seldom dependent on high commitment to feelings of love and affection.

In trying to account for the endurance of family cohesiveness, I have pointed in each set of relations, familial and kin, parents and children, husbands and wives, to the fundamental importance of patriarchal control and primogenitural inheritance patterns as key features of familial interaction. I have also suggested the ramifying significance of the double sexual standard on individual choices and possibilities of men and women. In my assessment of family relationships, I emphasized the way in which these 'givens' of family life, these structural realities, fundamentally tied individual members to the need for Sir Ralph's favor and assistance. I concluded that as much as his younger brothers needed him in a society in which influence and connection mattered more than merit and accomplishment, his sisters, whose gender was a further disadvantage, were even more dependent upon him.

At this level of detail some controls over the family and kin were revealed that are not ordinarily apparent. These included Sir Ralph's capacity to offer or withhold documents in his possession, to help or hinder the business dealings of his relatives as well as his ability to share with them or be silent regarding information he alone might be privy to as head of the family and which affected the disposition of resources belonging to the other members.

In addition, his prestigious position, in itself, could be used to shelter favored relatives against the supplications of debt collectors. His status could also be useful in puffing up one's own possibilities in the outside world with its sensitivity to prestige and with its scarce and elusive professional and marriage preferments. And if 'world opinion' might bridle his personal excesses, it also conferred rather considerable latitude on his personal predispositions in his treatment of the other members. None of this absolutely precluded the possibility of genuine affection, as the relationship of Uncle Doctor Denton and Sir Ralph indicates, but these emotions were hardly central to the endurance of relationships which were based on strategies of survival and the concomitant need for reciprocity in a wide range of exchanges.

The relatively harsh but intense concern demonstrated in parental treatment of children becomes more understandable in light of these social realities. The differential treatment and training of boys and girls, their liability to illness and death, the very tentativeness of children's lives, must have colored parental attitudes and behavior toward them. Among this class, the existence and extensive use of servants in child rearing increased the emotional distance between the generations. The practice of fostering out worked toward the same end. Sending children to live with relatives was a practice which fitted well with the social need to expand networks and to enlarge the numbers of familial allies who might be useful for social reciprocation, but, as the letters indicate, it could sometimes work great hardship on the children. Furthermore, Sir Ralph and Lady Verney's incessant concern with their children's training and socialization reminds us of the need to differentiate between devotion to one's children spurred by notions of duty, and those feelings of parental affection which are the result of perceptions of the child as a unique and irreplaceable being. Not that the Verneys of either generation appear to have been without favorites; little Meg was obviously such a girl, just as Uncle Mun appears to have been a parental favorite in the previous generation. But such children who were loved for their unique personal qualities were the exception rather than the rule, and in any case such love was subversive. In most cases parents could not have allowed themselves, and were not expected to become very attached to young children whose lives were often too short to bring anything but heartbreak to an overly affectionate parent. In this connection, the Verneys' remarkable capacity to accept repeated losses through death, not only of their children but of many of their relatives as well, suggests the support which religious belief afforded in a period of almost unimaginable death rates.

Since marriage practices and attitudes are the acid test of a society's values, and since many family relationships and child rearing practices were connected to marital concerns, they deserve a somewhat lengthier concluding analysis. Their letters have made it possible to examine in detail the motives and values attached to matrimony. The arranged marriage emerges as a procedure which appears to have been used by the propertied classes as a method for establishing new family formations of a kind which would tend to preserve property accumulations. If, for that reason, financial considerations figured prominently in these arrangements, they did not foreclose the possibility of the development of an affectionate and enduring relationship between husband and wife, although this was not ordinarily the primary motive for marriage. Moreover, since individual expectations of marriage were not geared to romantic ideals, workable arrangements between the partners could develop which were based on their mutual need for each other as well as on the variety of other benefits which married life offered.

For the single woman, marriage afforded the only possibility for personal success and preferment. A good match offered financial security and assigned a certain status; it also expanded the woman's capacity to engage in reciprocal social arrangements of the sort which were necessary for success in a patronage society. At the same time, marriage improved her relationship with her family of origin, by relieving them of the responsibility of providing for her as well as by expanding their social resources through increased kinship connections. If her husband were also compatible, that was a gratuitous benefit which she could enjoy; if not, the other advantages of marriage were considered to be adequate compensation. It is also important to point out that modern ideals of romantic marriage educate the prospective bride and groom to expectations of great emotional and physiological satisfactions in marriage, which expectations were not shared by their counterparts in the seventeenth century. The latter, therefore, did not necessarily consider a loveless match a failure, nor were they likely to be disappointed and embittered by that situation.

In addition, the great desire to marry, on the part of both sexes, cannot fully be explained only in terms of the many real advantages which marriage offered as opposed to the dismal prospect of remaining single, even if one adds that it was an important vehicle of upward mobility. In addition to all these justifiably important considerations was the fact that the arranged marriage gave rise to family formations of a particular kind. The families which emerged from this practice fulfilled a variety of vital functions that included and went quite beyond those which they are expected to perform today. The family was a societal institution of vastly greater significance in a wider variety of endeavors than it is today, and at the same time there were fewer specialized institutions which either duplicated its functions or offered alternative possibilities to the individual. The arranged marriage offered *entrée* into new family formations which served not only as nurturing and socializing agencies but also as credit institutions, levers of political power, arbiters of educational and professional advancement and marriage brokers. Marriage heightened one's contact with a whole range of societal modes which were only partially experienced by those adults who were unmarried, and who therefore were limited to operating through their family of origin.

For a variety of reasons the pressure on women to marry was greater, but bachelorhood, at least among the younger sons in the Verney family, seems to have been a status imposed by default rather than choice. It was expected that if they could find a 'good rich wife' they would marry. Marriage placed one in the mainstream of social interaction, and increased one's chances for avoiding social derogation. In fact, in an arranged marriage society, a younger son who managed to accumulate the wherewithal to make a good match could view that accomplishment as a sign of success. Almost without exception, the high-status adults within the Verney family and among the kin were married, and their example as adult models cannot have been ignored by the younger members of the family.

The acceptance and endurance of the arranged marriage procedure cannot be fully understood without recognizing its connection with the double standard. On the one hand the belief in the inferiority of women significantly reduced the demands and expectations which a wife might make on her husband since she was his social subordinate, and at the same time prescribed and justified the necessity for obedience and loyalty to him. In this sense, the subordination of the wife and her dependence on her husband reduced the areas of conflict between two partners who were, in the early stages of the marriage, virtual strangers. This assigned inequality of status of the husband and wife was unlikely to be affected by the subsequent development of genuine affection between them; as in the case of Sir Ralph and his wife, mutual concern and love did not lead to equality of the partners either in terms of their marital obligations and authority or in terms of their personal relationship.

The high priority placed on female virginity increased the value of those who met that requirement *vis-à-vis* other dowered females, and was one of the important variables which determined the choice among them. The insistence on female chastity after marriage reinforced the husband's superior position because it reiterated his control over and property in his wife. The double sexual standard also made the arranged marriage more acceptable from the husband's point of view because it allowed for approved sexual alternatives if the wife was found to be incompatible.

The absence of reciprocal fidelity in marriage does not seem to have diminished its attractiveness. Both sexes were brought up with the idea that the husband would have greater sexual freedom after marriage and a prudent wife was advised to pretend ignorance of her husband's lapses of fidelity. Such behavior on the husband's part, therefore, was not likely to generate criticism or to be viewed as acceptable grounds for dissension between them. Moreover, for a gentlewoman, marriage to a philandering but otherwise suitable husband was certainly preferable to spinsterhood. The latter condition had little to recommend it. The single woman was even more dependent than her married counterpart and less able to reciprocate the multiplicity of demands on her family and kin which her situation forced her to make. And she was denied the chief function of being a woman, the satisfaction and prestige of providing heirs.

The essential characteristics of the arranged marriage which emerge from this study of that practice as it existed shortly before and during the Civil War, remained unchanged after the Restoration. Sir Ralph's godson's marriage in the latter part of the century was quite similar in procedure and reflected the same motives and values as the negotiations of the earlier period. The ideals and practices associated with romantic marriage had little possibility of replacing the arranged marriage as long as the latter served the needs of the propertied classes and until many of the functions of the family were taken over by other institutions.

Widespread preference for romantic marriage, which is based on free choice of partners, with little familial interference, had to wait on the substitution of credentials for familial and kinship influence in educational and career placement, increasing specialization and the widening of career options, the development of impersonal credit agencies as alternative sources of patriarchal and kin generosity, the decline of the family as a prime instrument of social control and its emergence as a humane socializing and nurturing agency devoted to the emotional and psychological welfare of its members. The greater range of personal options in marriage and other life choices which these changes provided, as well as the transformation of values and attitudes which were associated with them, were barely visible even by the end of the seventeenth century. Certainly for the propertied classes of that period neither the aims of marriage nor the varied functions which the family was expected to perform could be contained and executed within the relatively narrow definition of marriage which constitutes the romantic ideal with its almost exclusive concern with the personal desires and physical needs of the partners.[2]

If, however, the upper-gentry did not enjoy the freedom to choose whomever they pleased as marriage partners, they do not seem to have been forced to marry someone whom they actively disliked – a practice which was not unknown in earlier periods. Sir Ralph's sisters appear to have been consulted on the choices that were made for them, and he had even less formal influence on the amorous affairs of his brothers. The fact that the head of the family was in exile probably attenuated his control of them to some extent, but it is not the most important variable in accounting for their ability to have at least a negative vote on the choices which were made for them. Of more importance in explaining the latter was the development of London as a marriage market and the social attraction of the London season. By the seventeenth century the capital had become the chief locus for selection of prospective spouses and marriage negotiations. The legal assistance which was required for the successful negotiation of a marriage settlement was readily available there. Moreover, the season drew families from all over the country to the capital. This practice tended to widen the selection of possible partners and increased the contact among them, providing a basis for comparison and encouraging the development of individual preferences.[3] In addition this expansion of possible choices increased the likelihood that the parents would be willing to respect the child's negative vote on their choice because the difficulty of searching for a different and acceptable partner would be lessened.

The process of selection in the case of widows was similar to modern practice in that she was free to choose a husband without regard to parental wishes. Her situation indicates the extent to which parental authority was based on financial control. The widow's jointure could be used as a marriage portion in her next alliance. Since her parents were not needed to finance the venture she did not need to consult them. However, there were still subtle pressures of various kinds which could be brought to bear and there were probably few widows who were willing to alienate their families completely by making a totally unacceptable choice. This also has certain similarities to modern practice but in the latter case parents are more reluctant to voice their disapproval once the choice has been made, and have fewer avenues for venting their dissatisfaction.

Neither method of selection guarantees personal compatibility but the arranged marriage placed much lower priority on this consideration. However, even if one judges the Verney marriages by the standards of the time, the most successful alliance was that of Sir Ralph and his wife. His sisters' marriages were poor ones by comparison, and his brother Thomas's marriage was a failure. The sisters were all married off to men of lesser social standing than themselves. Only Margaret's husband was armigerous but he was from a cadet branch.[4] Cary was married to her first husband, a Captain Thomas Gardiner, before the family financial difficulties became severe. The other sisters' husbands (and Cary's second husband) all came from undistinguished families. Thomas's wife Joyce came from a sufficiently obscure background to have been left unnamed by one genealogist.

The chief cause of the inferior quality of the Verney daughters' marriages was the unavailability of their marriage portions. In this sense they were the victims of the financial havoc engendered by the Civil War. Despite the fact that none of them (with the possible exception of Cary) seems to have been very pretty, the quality and influence of their family of origin and a £1,000 dowry would have made them attractive to men of greater distinction than they were able to get with the reduced portions, or small annuities in lieu of portions, which they received.

The disastrous nature of Thomas's marriage can be attributed only in part to his personal deficiencies. Thomas's lack of money impelled him to this misalliance and continued to be the main cause of disaffection between himself and his wife. Penelope's dissatisfaction with her marriage proceeded from a similar cause – her lack of dowry. Margaret's marriage failed completely and ended in formal separation. Although the receipt of her dowry might not have been enough to save this marriage the lack of it certainly did nothing to improve it.

Susan seems to have been happy with her choice, but in brother Edmund's opinion she was 'so well tempered that if her husband be not a devil he cannot be unkind to her.'[5] Lady Verney believed that Susan's husband was kind, although she also considered him to be 'very deboche.'[6] However, she and the rest of the family probably would have agreed with cousin Hobart's observation that "'tis true he [Susan's husband] is a good fellow [i.e., he liked to drink] . . . [but] I am persuaded though it may prejudice his health it will never hurt his estate.'[7]

If Sir Ralph's marriage was better than any of the others this was due in large part to his advantageous position as the inheriting son. He was an excellent marriage prospect because he would come to control the family patrimony and exercise the authority and influence that went with it. It is highly unlikely that he could have been matched to an heiress if he had been less favorably endowed. The social and financial compatibility of this couple, as well as their shared values, contributed to the success of their marriage. Since their marriage did not involve social derogation for either partner, they were both spared the frustration and tension which that might generate in their relationship. Their combined inheritance precluded the festering dissatisfactions caused by inadequate income. In normal times a wife of Lady Verney's affluence and social standing enhanced her husband's financial prospects. During the war her wealth and assistance helped to preserve her husband's estate. In either situation her assets were of a kind that would cement their relationship and contribute to the possibility of their achieving a satisfying union. Sir Ralph and his wife were by birth, inheritance and temperament well suited to accommodate the deficiencies as well as to profit by the benefits of the arranged marriage.

# NOTES

## INTRODUCTION: THE VERNEY FAMILY CORRESPONDENCE

1 Oscar Lewis, *La Vida*, New York, 1966, p. xx.

2 See, for example, the provocative anthropological study by Carol B. Stack, *All Our Kin: Strategies for Survival in a Black Community*, New York, 1974. For a discussion of the relationship between historical study of the family and the behavioral sciences see Tamara K. Hareven, 'The history of the family as an interdisciplinary field', in Theodore K. Rabb and Robert I. Rotberg (eds), *The Family in History: Interdisciplinary Essays*, New York, 1973.

3 Mary E. Finch, *The Wealth of Five Northamptonshire Families*, Preface by H. J. Habakkuk, Oxford, 1956, p. xix.

4 If all deeds, trusts, wills, etc. of the entire collection are included the figure is probably over 100,000 items. Note: Unless otherwise stated, references to the Verney correspondence come from microfilmed letters in the Princeton Library, entitled *Claydon House Letters*. The citations include the names of the correspondents, the day, month, and year of the letter, and the microfilm reel number is the Roman numeral following the date. For example, a letter from Sir Ralph Verney to Mary Lady Verney from reel six dated 10 May 1646 will be cited as: Sir Ralph Verney to Mary Verney, 10 May 1646, PUR VI. The dating has been modernized to start the year on 1 January. Letters exchanged between England and the Continent often have two dates, reflecting the ten day differences in dating. In this case I have given both dates. Letters undated by the sender usually have the date of receipt of Sir Ralph Verney's hand; in these cases I have

used that date and noted it as such. Those without any dates are cited as n.d.

## CHAPTER 1 A HISTORY OF THE FAMILY IN THE SEVENTEENTH CENTURY

1 On land ownership as a basis for political and social power as well as style of life see H. J. Habakkuk, 'Economic functions of English landowners in the 17th and 18th centuries,' *Explorations in Entrepreneurial History*, vol. 6, 1953, p. 100.
2 See genealogy of the Verney family, p. 202.
3 George Lipscombe, *The History and Antiquities of the County of Bucks*, London, 1847, The Denton Genealogy, vol. III, p. 17. Margaret's father, Sir Thomas Denton, was eldest son and heir, High Sheriff 1597, knighted July 1603, MP for Bucks, 1603, 1614 and 1620; ibid.; all that remains of Hillesden is the church, containing the family tombs, the manor house having been burnt to the ground by the Parliamentary forces during the Civil War: received 8 May 1644, PUR V; a statement, n.d., next to papers of December 1660, by one John Hersey, a servant of Sir Alexander Denton, referring to the razing of Hillesden, from unmarked box at Claydon.
4 Mary F. Keeler, *The Long Parliament*, Philadelphia, 1945, p. 154. Referring to Sir Alexander Denton, son and heir of Sir Thomas, she says, 'His family were virtually lords of the borough'; his estate was valued at £2,750 which undoubtedly does not include income from office, patents, etc. *Victoria County History of Bucks*, London, 1927, vol. IV, p. 541.
5 *Passim*, letters addressed to the Verneys at Covent Garden, PUR III.
6 Lawrence Stone, *The Crisis of the Aristocracy*, Oxford, 1965, pp. 624–5.
7 H. J. Habakkuk, 'Social attitudes and attributes of the English aristocracy,' in A. Goodwin (ed.), *The European Nobility in the Eighteenth Century*, London, 1953, pp. 1–21; Stone, 1965, op. cit., pp. 57–8; Lawrence Stone, 'The educational revolution in England,' *Past and Present*, no. 28, July 1964, pp. 41–80; G. E. Mingay, *English Landed Society in the 18th Century*, London, 1963, gives estimates of upper-gentry income for this period as £1,500–2,000 p.a., p. 25.
8 Frances P. Verney, *Memoirs of the Verney Family*, London, 1892, vol. I, pedigree of the Verneys, facing p. 360.

9 Indenture of Marriage between Sir Edmund Verney and Margaret Denton. Her marriage portion was £2,300. 27 January 1612, PUR II. Ibid., PUR II, Indenture dated 27 January, 10 James I.
10 Sir Bernard Burke, *Dormant, Abeyant, Forfeited, and Extinct Peerages*, London, 1883, p. 554.
11 *Victoria County History of Bucks*, 1927, op. cit., vol. IV, p. 33.
12 Sir Ralph Verney to Mary Lady Verney, 14 February 1647, PUR VIII; since this information is contained in a letter from Sir Ralph Verney to his wife it is undoubtedly reliable; Sir Ralph Verney to brother Edmund Verney, 24 June 1644, PUR V; the meaning of 'strict settlement' is further discussed in Chapter III, p. 117.
13 Sir Edmund Verney to Sir Ralph Verney, 4 January 1636, PUR III; official agreement on exchange of two parcels of land, 4 January 1636, PUR III; Sir Edmund Verney to Sir Ralph Verney, 5 January 1636, PUR III; Sir Edmund Verney to Sir Ralph Verney, 11 January 1636, PUR III; Sir Edmund Verney to Will Roads, 6 February 1636, PUR III contains detailed instructions for caring for a lame horse as well as Sir Edmund's directions to his estate manager Will Roads on where to sow the hay, posting and raking a close, manuring, etc.; Sir Edmund Verney to Sir Ralph Verney, 6 April 1636, PUR III contains instructions to have certain lands surveyed.
14 Sir Ralph Verney to Mary Lady Verney, 23 January/2 February 1648, PUR VIII.
15 Sir Edward Sidenham to Sir Ralph Verney, 11 November 1642, PUR V.
16 Sir Ralph Verney to Father, 20 April 1639, PUR III; Father to Sir Ralph Verney, 21 July 1639, PUR III.
17 Keeler, 1945, op. cit., p. 373, n. 66.
18 Stone, 1965, op. cit., p. 437.
19 Sir Ralph Verney to Mary Lady Verney, 23 January/2 February 1648, PUR VIII; Stone, 1965, op. cit., p. 422.
20 Thomas Clansey to Will Roads, 18 August 1649, PUR X; according to the indenture dated 1 March 1639, Sir Edmund still retained control of this income, because he could stop payments to any of the children if he desired: Verney, 1892, op. cit., vol. 2, Appendix, p. 435. The alnage income was also supposed to be used to pay off some of Sir Edmund's debts: ibid., p. 436.
21 Mary Lady Verney to [?], 30 July 1634; Mary Lady Verney to [?], 1 August 1634; 8 August 1634, a copy of the agreement, PUR II.
22 There are numerous letters which indicate that Sir Ralph performed the duties of head of the household in his father's absence, catering to the needs of his younger brothers, running the

estate, and maintaining family contacts. On the care of his brothers: brother Thomas Verney to Mary Lady Verney and Sir Ralph Verney, 24 August 1635, PUR III; brother Edmund Verney to Sir Ralph Verney, 2 April 1636, PUR III; brother Henry Verney to Sir Ralph Verney, 19 April 1637, PUR III; Edmund begging Sir Ralph to urge father to remove him from Oxford: brother Edmund Verney to Sir Ralph Verney, 12 July 1637; PUR III; on estate management: Sir Edmund Verney to Sir Ralph Verney, 5 January 1636, PUR III; Sir Edmund Verney to Sir Ralph Verney, 11 January 1636, PUR III; Sir Edmund Verney to Sir Ralph Verney, 6 April 1636, PUR III; on family contacts: Dr William Denton to Sir Ralph Verney, 5 June 1638, PUR III; Sir Ralph Verney to [probably] brother Henry Verney, 3 May 1639, PUR III.

23 Verney, 1892, op. cit., vol. 1, pp. 71–2; ibid., p. 78.

24 Sir Ralph Verney to Dr William Denton, 10 May 1639, PUR III; Sir Ralph also wrote to his uncle Dr Denton to ask the latter to dissuade Sir Edmund: Sir Ralph Verney to Dr William Denton, 10 May 1639, PUR III.

25 Sir Ralph Verney to Madame [undoubtedly the Countess of Sussex], n.d., PUR III; Sir Ralph Verney to 'Sweet Madame,' 24 November 1638, PUR III.

26 Sir Ralph Verney to Dr William Denton, 10 May 1639, PUR III.

27 Sir Edmund Verney to Sir Ralph Verney, 16 May 1639, PUR III.

28 Sir Edward Sidenham to Sir Ralph Verney, 27 October 1642, PUR IV.

29 Brother Edmund Verney to Sir Ralph Verney, 24 November 1638, PUR III.

30 A list in Sir Ralph Verney's hand entitled 'A Schedule of such of my Father's debts as I Yet Stand Engaged for as his Surety,' n.d., from an unmarked box at Claydon. It lists a number of debts due between 1639 and 1642. The bonds come to £4,900 but such bonds were usually made at twice the amount actually borrowed; Sir Ralph Verney to Sir Edmund Verney, 24 June 1644, PUR V, in which Sir Ralph claims that his father 'left 9,000 p. in debt to pay.' Sir Ralph probably was exaggerating to impress his brother with his financial difficulties.

31 During the war taxes rose, rents were slow in coming in and armies living at free quarter and billeted in private homes decreased incomes: Elizabeth Isham to Sir Ralph Verney, received 17 November 1643, PUR V; Elizabeth Isham to Sir Ralph Verney, 4 April 1644, PUR V; Elizabeth Isham to Sir Ralph Verney, 9 December 1644, PUR VI; Sir Ralph Verney to brother Henry

Verney, 28 February 1645, PUR VI; Sir Ralph Verney to Nathanial Hobart, 29 April/9 May 1645, PUR VI. For a detailed examination of Verney family finances see John Broad, 'Gentry finances and the Civil War: the case of the Buckinghamshire Verneys,' in *Economic History Review*, series 2, vol. 32, May 1979, pp. 183–200.

32 Thomas Gardiner to Mary Lady Verney, 5 September 1642, PUR IV; Sir Edmund Verney to Sir Ralph Verney, 14 September 1642, PUR IV; Countess of Sussex to Sir Ralph Verney, received 9 September 1642, PUR IV; Countess of Sussex to Sir Ralph Verney, received 9 September 1642, PUR IV.

33 See genealogy, p. 202; Countess of Barrymore to Sir Ralph Verney, 26 July 1641, PUR IV.

34 Countess of Sussex to Sir Ralph Verney, received 9 September 1642, PUR IV.

35 In this regard, see 21 March 1650, PUR X, in describing how to make a concoction for the ailing Lady Verney, Sir Ralph's uncle Dr Denton alludes to a confection that Ralph and his siblings had had as children, saying it was 'not so long ago since you were a child (if ever you were one) but you may remember it.' For Sir Ralph's character see also: Sir Ralph Verney to Will Roads, 28 March/7 April 1645, PUR VI; Sir Ralph Verney to Mr Trevor, 9 May/19 May 1647, PUR VIII; Sir Ralph Verney to Sir Roger Burgoyne, 14 November/24 November 1647, PUR VIII; Sir Ralph Verney to Dr William Denton, 5 December/15 December 1647, PUR VIII; Sir Ralph Verney to Mary Lady Verney, 27 December/6 January 1647, PUR VIII; Dr William Denton to Sir Ralph Verney, 14 September 1648, PUR IX.

36 Lady Mary Wiseman to Mary Lady Verney, 29 June 1629, PUR II.

37 A deed of 5 May 1631, from an unmarked box at Claydon; Verney, 1892, op. cit., vol. 1, pp. 113–16.

38 Ibid., pp. 115–16.

39 Lady Margaret Verney to Mrs Wiseman [Mary Blacknall's aunt], n.d., PUR II; Mary Blacknall Verney to Mrs Wiseman, n.d., PUR II; Lady Mary Wiseman to Mary Lady Verney, 29 June 1629, PUR II.

40 Stone, 1965, op. cit., pp. 600–5.

41 See for example n.d., [undoubtedly 1629], PUR II; there is no evidence to indicate that Lady Verney had any difficulties with her mother-in-law or father-in-law. References to her in two of Sir Edmund's letters indicate that his relationship with her was satisfactory: Sir Edmund Verney to Sir Ralph Verney, 1 April

1639, PUR III; Sir Edmund Verney to Sir Ralph Verney, 21 June 1639, PUR III.

42 Joseph Foster (ed.), *Alumni Oxonienses*, Oxford, 1891, vol. IV, p. 1541; ibid., vol. I, p. 396; Sir Ralph is not listed among the Oxford alumni but he did attend Magdalen: brother Edmund Verney to Sir Ralph Verney, 15 December 1638, PUR III.

43 See *infra*, Chapter 2, footnotes 36 and 37.

44 The will of Sir Edmund Verney, 26 March, 14 Charles I; Verney, 1892, op. cit., vol. II, Appendix, p. 435.

45 *Victoria County History of Bucks*, 1927, op. cit., vol. III, p. 7; Countess of Sussex to Sir Ralph Verney, received 9 September 1642, PUR IV; brother Henry Verney to Sir Ralph Verney, 30 September 1642, PUR IV; Doll Leeke to Sir Ralph Verney, 10 August 1643, PUR V; brother Edmund Verney to Sir Ralph Verney, 24 October 1643, PUR V.

46 Sir Ralph Verney to Sir Roger Burgoyne, 31 May/10 June 1644, PUR V; Sir Ralph Verney to Sir Roger Burgoyne, 21/31 December 1645, PUR VI.

47 Licence to go Abroad, 4 October, 19 Charles I, PUR V; A Pass for Safe Passage of Ralph Smith alias Verney, 30 November 1643, PUR V; Sir Roger Burgoyne to Sir Ralph Verney, 17 October 1643, PUR V; Sir Ralph Verney to Sir Edward Sidenham, 26 February/7 March 1644, PUR V.

48 Sir Ralph Verney to Dr William Denton, 13/23 September 1646, PUR VII; Sir Ralph Verney to Mary Lady Verney, 17/27 October 1647, PUR VIII.

49 Sir Ralph Verney to Mary Lady Verney, 9/19 January 1648, PUR VIII.

50 See for example Sir Ralph Verney to sister Susan Verney, 20 July 1645, PUR VI; Will Roads to Sir Ralph Verney, 28 October 1648, PUR IX.

51 Thomas Verney to Will Roads, 14 June 1645, PUR VI.

52 Thomas Verney to Will Roads, 20 June 1645, PUR VI.

53 See for example Edmund Verney to Will Roads, 8 July 1645, PUR VI; brother Henry Verney to Sir Ralph Verney, 22 June 1646, PUR VII; Elizabeth Isham to Will Roads, 14 June 1648, PUR IX.

54 Brother Henry Verney to Sir Ralph Verney, 20 July 1645, PUR VI.

55 Sir Ralph Verney to brother Edmund Verney, 24 June 1644, PUR V; 19 October 1646, copies of documents concerning sequestration proceedings of the Committee at Aylesbury, PUR VII; Sir Ralph's 'Dissettlement' from the House dated 22 September 1645.

56 Keeler, 1945, op. cit., p. 122; Sir Roger Burgoyne [his hand] to Sir Ralph Verney, 2 January [no year, probably 1649].
57 Sir Ralph Burgoyne to Sir Ralph Verney, 31 October 1643, PUR V; Sir Roger Burgoyne to Sir Ralph Verney, 17 April 1645, PUR VI; Sir Roger Burgoyne to Sir Ralph Verney, 31 July 1645, PUR VI; Sir Roger Burgoyne to Sir Ralph Verney, 30 September 1647, PUR VIII; on Burgoyne's help with the sequestration, see for example Sir Roger Burgoyne to Sir Ralph Verney, 12 March 1645, PUR VI; Sir Roger Burgoyne to Sir Ralph Verney, 22 January 1646, PUR VII; Mary Lady Verney to Sir Ralph Verney, 16 December 1647, PUR VIII.
58 Sir Ralph Verney to Sir Roger Burgoyne, 14/24 November 1647, PUR VIII.
59 A list of code names in Sir Ralph Verney's hand, n.d., following 1 January 1646, PUR VII.
60 Countess of Sussex to Sir Ralph Verney, n.d. [following 9 January 1639], PUR III; Countess of Sussex to Sir Ralph Verney, received 4 June 1641, PUR IV.
61 G. White (ed.), *The Complete Peerage*, London, 1953, vol. XII, p. 530.
62 Countess of Sussex to Sir Ralph Verney, received 18 January 1639, PUR IV; on Sir Ralph's other services for her, see for example Countess of Sussex to Sir Ralph Verney, 23 July 1639, PUR III; Countess of Sussex to Sir Ralph Verney received 10 May 1641, PUR IV; Countess of Sussex to Sir Ralph Verney, received 20 July 1642, PUR IV; Countess of Sussex to Sir Ralph Verney, received 8 March 1642/3, PUR V.
63 Mary Lady Verney to Sir Ralph Verney, 10 December, 1646, PUR VII.
64 Mary Lady Verney to Sir Ralph Verney, 12 September 1647, PUR VIII.
65 Mary Lady Verney to Sir Ralph Verney, 23 December 1647, PUR VIII; Mary Lady Verney to Sir Ralph Verney, 30 December 1647, PUR VIII; Mary Lady Verney to Sir Ralph Verney, 6 January 1648, for quote, PUR VIII.
66 Dr William Denton to Mary Lady Verney, 11 April 1645, PUR VI; Marie Cottesford to Mr Oakly, n.d., following 21 June 1648, PUR IX; Dr William Denton to Sir Ralph Verney, 27 September 1649, PUR X; Dr William Denton to Sir Ralph Verney, 8 October 1649, PUR X; on his assistance for his nephew Sir Ralph, see for example: Dr William Denton to Sir Ralph Verney, 30 September 1646 (Post Script, 1 October 1646), PUR VII; Dr William Denton to Sir Ralph Verney, 24 December 1646, PUR VII; Dr William

Denton to Mary Lady Verney, 9 September 1647, PUR VIII; Dr William Denton [his hand] to Sir Ralph Verney, 25 November 1647, PUR VIII; Dr William Denton to Sir Ralph Verney, 4 May 1648, PUR IX; Dr William Denton to Sir Ralph Verney, 29 November 1649, PUR X.

67 Sir Ralph Verney to Lord Allington, 14/24 May 1649, PUR X; Sir Ralph Verney to Hatton Rich, 16 February 1649/50, PUR X.

68 Dr William Denton to Mary Lady Verney, 4 January 1643/4, PUR V; brother Thomas Verney to Sir Ralph Verney, 11/21 September 1646, PUR VII; Dr William Denton to Sir Ralph Verney, 4 May 1648, PUR IX; Dr William Denton to Will Roads, 11 September 1648, PUR IX.

69 Dr William Denton [his hand] to Sir Ralph Verney, 6 October 1647, PUR VIII; brother Edmund Verney to Mary Lady Verney, 7 December 1647, PUR VIII; Dr William Denton to Sir Ralph Verney, 15/25 May 1648, PUR IX.

70 Dr William Denton to Sir Ralph Verney, 3 January 1650, PUR X; Verney, 1892, op. cit., vol. II, Appendix, p. 437.

71 For a detailed discussion of the female Verney marriages of this period see *infra*, Chapter 4.

72 Dr William Denton to Sir Ralph Verney, 1 August 1645, PUR VI; Dr William Denton to Sir Ralph Verney, 21 September 1645, PUR VI; Dr William Denton to Sir Ralph Verney, 18 December 1645, PUR VI.

73 Doll Leeke to 'my dear cousin' [Mary Lady Verney], (third undated letter after 28 December/7 January 1646), PUR VI.

74 Sister Cary Gardiner to Mary Lady Verney, 10 March 1646, PUR VII; sister Cary Gardiner to Sir Ralph Verney, 10 March 1646, PUR VII; Mary Lady Verney to Sir Ralph Verney, 22 July 1647, PUR VIII; sister Cary Gardiner to Sir Ralph Verney, 22 April 1649, PUR IX.

75 Elizabeth Isham to Sir Ralph Verney, 13 June 1644, PUR V; Elizabeth Isham to Sir Ralph Verney, 9 December 1644, PUR VI; Elizabeth Isham to Sir Ralph Verney, 31 July 1645, PUR VI; Elizabeth Isham to Sir Ralph Verney, 29 November 1648, PUR IX.

76 Sir Ralph Verney to brother Henry Verney, 30 November/10 December 1645, PUR VI; Mary Lady Verney to Sir Ralph Verney, 4 February 1647, PUR VIII.

77 Brother Henry Verney to Sir Ralph Verney, 26 March 1646, PUR VII; Sir Ralph Verney to Mary Lady Verney, 21/31 March 1647, PUR VIII; Mary Lady Verney to Sir Ralph Verney, 5 September

1647, PUR VIII; sister Mary Verney to Sir Ralph Verney, 15 August 1648, PUR IX.

78 Mary Lady Verney to Sir Ralph Verney, n.d., following 21/31 January 1647, PUR VIII; Sir Ralph Verney to Mary Lady Verney, 19/29 September 1647, PUR VIII; Dr William Denton to Sir Ralph Verney, 4 May 1648, PUR IX.

79 Dr William Denton to Sir Ralph Verney, 29 May 1648, PUR IX.

80 Dr William Denton to Sir Ralph Verney, 30 November 1648, PUR IX.

81 Brother Thomas Verney to Sir Ralph Verney, 13 July 1638, PUR III; Thomas Verney to Sir Edmund Verney, 18 October 1638, PUR III; Thomas Verney to Sir Edmund Verney, 17 April 1642, PUR IV; Thomas Verney to Sir Edmund Verney, 21 May 1642, PUR IV; brother Thomas Verney to Sir Ralph Verney, 8 October 1642, PUR IV; brother Thomas Verney to Sir Ralph Verney, 22 February 1643, PUR V; Thomas Verney to Will Roads, 6 July 1644, PUR V; Sir Ralph Verney to Mr Lavington, 28 March 1645. PUR VI; brother Thomas Verney to Sir Ralph Verney, 29 October 1646, PUR VII; Sir Ralph Verney to sister Susan Alport, 6/16 November 1646, PUR VII; Dr William Denton to Will Roads, 26 February 1648/9, PUR IX.

82 See for example brother Thomas Verney to Sir Ralph Verney, 13 January 1642, PUR V; brother Thomas Verney to Sir Ralph Verney, 12 February 1642/3, PUR V; brother Thomas Verney to Sir Ralph Verney, 5 August, 1646, PUR VII; brother Thomas Verney to Mary Lady Verney, n.d., April 1648, PUR VIII; Thomas Verney to Dr William Denton, 6 September 1648, PUR IX; in this Thomas as the penitent in trouble with the law declares that 'I shall endeavor to spend the remainder of my life in the service of God. . . .' By the following year he was back to his old tricks writing to Uncle Doctor to propose some new deal which Dr Denton described as having too much 'folly' to deserve repetition. Dr William Denton to Sir Ralph Verney, 9 August 1649, PUR X; Thomas Verney to Dr William Denton, 6 March 1650, PUR X.

83 Brother Thomas Verney to Sir Ralph Verney, 16 June 1638, PUR III; brother Thomas Verney to Sir Ralph Verney, 13 July 1638, PUR III; brother Thomas Verney to Sir Ralph Verney, 6 October 1642, PUR IV; Edward Bolle to Sir Ralph Verney, received 20/30 July 1649, PUR VIII.

84 Thomas Verney to Sir Edmund Verney, 17 April 1642, PUR IV; brother Thomas Verney to Sir Ralph Verney, 27 November 1642,

PUR V; brother Thomas Verney to Sir Ralph Verney, 27 February 1642/3, PUR V.

85 Mary Lady Verney to Sir Ralph Verney, 20 September 1647, PUR VIII; Dr William Denton to Sir Ralph Verney, 28 September 1648, PUR IX.

86 Brother Edmund Verney to Sir Ralph Verney, 8/18 May 1648, PUR IX; Dr William Denton to Sir Ralph Verney, 24 August 1648, PUR IX; brother Thomas Verney to Sir Ralph Verney, 19/29 August 1648, PUR IX.

87 Dr William Denton to Sir Ralph Verney, 10 May 1649, PUR X; Dr William Denton to Sir Ralph Verney, 28 June 1649, PUR X, Dr William Denton to Sir Ralph Verney, 6 August 1649, PUR X; Thomas Verney to Will Roads, 24 October 1649, PUR X.

88 Thomas Verney to Dr William Denton, 6 March 1650, PUR X.

89 Brother Edmund Verney to Sir Ralph Verney, 12 July 1637, PUR III; Sir Ralph Verney to brother Edmund Verney, 20 July 1637, PUR III; brother Edmund Verney to Sir Ralph Verney, 9 November 1639, PUR IV; brother Edmund Verney to Sir Ralph Verney, 30 January 1640, PUR IV.

90 Brother Edmund Verney to Sir Ralph Verney, 27 November 1639, PUR IV; brother Edmund Verney to Sir Ralph Verney, 24 September 1641, PUR IV; brother Edmund Verney in Dublin to Sir Ralph Verney, 11 January 1641/2, PUR IV.

91 Brother Edmund Verney to Sir Ralph Verney, 30 May 1642, PUR IV.

92 Brother Edmund Verney to Sir Ralph Verney, 5 December 1643, PUR V; Sir Ralph Verney to brother Edmund Verney, 5/15 September 1647, PUR VIII.

93 Brother Edmund Verney to Sir Ralph Verney, 14 September 1642, PUR IV.

94 Brother Edmund Verney to Sir Ralph Verney, 4 August 1647, PUR VIII; brother Edmund Verney to Sir Ralph Verney, 26 August 1647, PUR VIII; brother Edmund Verney to Sir Ralph Verney, 11/21 May 1648, PUR IX.

95 Brother Edmund Verney to Sir Ralph Verney, 3/13 June 1648, PUR IX.

96 Brother Edmund Verney to Sir Ralph Verney, 14/24 July 1648, PUR IX; brother Edmund Verney to Sir Ralph Verney, 17/27 September 1648, PUR IX; brother Edmund Verney to Sir Ralph Verney, 24 September/4 October 1648, PUR IX.

97 Dr William Denton to Sir Ralph Verney, 26 April 1649, PUR IX.

98 James Buck to Sir Ralph Verney, 8/18 November 1649, PUR X; James Buck to Sir Ralph Verney, 9 December 1649, PUR X.

99 Brother Henry Verney to Sir Ralph Verney, 26 October 1637, PUR III.
100 Sir John Leeke to Sir Ralph Verney, received 20 September 1643, PUR V; Sir Ralph Verney to Colonel Whitehead, 7 October 1643, PUR V.
101 Brother Henry Verney to Sir Ralph Verney , 29 August 1644, PUR VI.
102 Sir Ralph Verney to brother Henry Verney, 6/16 August 1644, PUR VI; Sir Ralph Verney to Doll Leeke, 21/31 August 1644, PUR VI; Elizabeth Isham to Sir Ralph Verney, 31 July 1644, PUR V; brother Henry Verney to Sir Ralph Verney, 29 August 1644, PUR VI.
103 Brother Henry Verney to Sir Ralph Verney, 11 December 1645, PUR VI.
104 For a detailed discussion of Sir Ralph's relationship with Henry see *infra*, Chapter 2; Verney, 1892, op. cit., vol. II, p. 419.
105 A copy of the Committee of Lords and Commons taking off the sequestration and discharged 5 January 1648, PUR VIII.
106 Dr William Denton to Sir Ralph Verney, 20 December 1647, PUR VIII.
107 See for example Sir Ralph Verney to Sir [Francis Drake?], 6 September 1644, PUR VI; Sir Francis Drake to Sir Ralph Verney, 29 January 1645, PUR VII; Dr William Denton [probably] to Sir Ralph Verney, 20 August 1646, PUR VII; Dr William Denton to Sir Ralph Verney, 19 August 1647, PUR VIII; Dr William Denton to Sir Ralph Verney, 4 November 1647, PUR VIII; Mary Lady Verney to Sir Ralph Verney, 20 December 1647, PUR VII; Mary Lady Verney to Sir Ralph Verney, 13 January 1647/8, PUR VIII; FD (undoubtedly Francis Drake) to Sir Ralph Verney, received 25 September/5 October 1648, PUR IX.
108 Sir Ralph Verney to Mary Lady Verney, 16/26 January 1648, PUR VIII; Sir Ralph Verney to Mary Lady Verney 30 January/9 February 1647/8, PUR VIII; Verney, 1892, op. cit., vol. III, p. 54.
109 Dr William Denton to Sir Ralph Verney, 15 March 1649, PUR IX; Dr William Denton to Sir Ralph Verney, 28 February 1650, PUR X; Verney, 1892, op. cit., vol. II, pp. 413–14.
110 *Victoria County History of Bucks*, 1927, op. cit., vol. IV, p. 543.
111 Ibid., p. 545.

## CHAPTER 2 FAMILY RELATIONSHIPS

1 Sir Francis Drake to Sir Ralph Verney, 11 December, 1645, PUR VI. Sir Ralph Verney to Mr Snelling, 8 September 1645, PUR VI. For an insightful discussion of the concept of 'family' and his view that the family should be seen as 'a moving resultant, an uncertain form whose intelligibility can only come from studying the system of relations it maintains with the sociopolitical level,' see Jacques Donzelot, *The Policing of Families*, New York, 1979, p. xxv.

2 Lawrence Stone, *The Crisis of the Aristocracy*, Oxford, 1965, p. 591. Professor Stone refers here to the sixteenth century aristocratic family. His description is equally applicable for the seventeenth century. On the later period see H. J. Habakkuk, 'Social attitudes and attributes,' in A. Goodwin (ed.), *The European Nobility in the 18th Century*, London, 1953, pp. 1–21. Professor Habakkuk includes the upper-gentry in his discussion.

3 Marion J. Levy, Jr, *The Family Revolution in Modern China*, Cambridge, 1949, p. 13, Professor Levy here describes the ideal multilineal conjugal family unit as containing only two generations as compared with the ideal patriarchal family of pre-industrial China which contained at least three generations. I have chosen to describe the upper-gentry family in this way because I believe this comes closer to the mark. The primogenitural patterns argue that this multigenerational ideal was institutionally prescribed at least for the heirs. There is also sufficient evidence to indicate that three-generational household formations did occur, at least in the early years of marriage and childbearing of these heirs. The patrilineal and authoritarian nature of these families, child rearing practices, generational distinctions, and type of residence all testify to a mental set and physical arrangements which belong much more to the multigenerational ideal.

4 Stone, 1965, op. cit., p. 688.

5 Of nineteen Masters of Cambridge who were in office during the period 1600–1605, there were nine who were definitely known to have achieved this distinction through patronage. These figures are based on an unpublished study by the author. To cite just one example, James Montagu became Master of Sidney Sussex College when he was 27 years old. His remarkable precocity can be explained by the fact that he was related to the foundress: John Venn and J. A. Venn, *Alumni Cantabrigienses*, London, 1922, III, p. 201; James Bass Mullinger, *The University of Cambridge*, London, 1873, II, p. 359; Sir Ralph Verney found a preferment for his tutor

in his Aunt Poulteney's household: Mr J. Crowther to Sir Ralph Verney, 14 August 1631, PUR II.

6 Elizabeth Isham to Sir Ralph Verney, 29 November 1648, PUR IX; it was Aunt Isham who stated most clearly the motive for sending a girl to such a school. She admits that it was a 'great charge' but 'I hope this being out abroad [i.e., at school] may do her [Sir Ralph's sister, Elizabeth] more good than if you had given her £500 and no breeding'; for other reasons for the popularity of these schools see Lawrence Stone, 'Literacy and education in England: 1640–1900,' *Past and Present*, no. 42, February 1969, pp. 71–2.

7 Levy, 1949, op. cit., p. 16. In my discussion of the theoretical considerations concerning role differentiation and solidarity I have drawn heavily on Professor Levy's analysis of general concepts in the introduction to this book on Chinese families, especially pp. 15–23. However, I have not attempted to follow in all its detail the theoretical framework which he offers. Of course, the observations and conclusions concerning English propertied families are based on my own research.

8 Levy, 1949, op. cit., p. 18. Although I have obviously departed from a functional analysis, I have found Professor Levy's definition of solidarity useful for examining family dynamics.

9 Ibid., p. 15.

10 Ibid., p. 16.

11 It is becoming increasingly difficult to make any generalizations about contemporary families. In fact, they have only recently begun to receive the complex treatment their study requires. Anthropologists have been among the most interesting and perceptive commentators on modern family life. See for example, Rayna Rapp, 'Family and class in contemporary America: notes toward an understanding of ideology,' *Science and Society*, vol. 42, 1978, pp. 278–300; see also the widely used sociology anthology, Arlene S. Skolnick and Jerome H. Skolnick, *Family in Transition*, Boston, 1977, 2nd edn, especially the Introduction, pp. 1–22.

12 Levy, 1949, op. cit., p. 27–8. Professor Levy believes that control of economic allocations within the family always provides some measure of authority over the other members.

13 The precise role of patriarchal control in cementing family solidarity has been documented in a number of studies. See, for example, an important study which links patriarchalism with control of property by Philip J. Greven, Jr, *Four Generations*, Ithaca and London, 1970, in which Professor Greven concludes his chapter on 'Patriarchalism and the family' with the statement that

'In this seventeenth century American community [Andover], at least, patriarchalism was a reality, based firmly upon the possession and control of land' (p. 99).

14 Christopher Hill, 'The spiritualization of the household,' in *Society and Puritanism in Pre-Revolutionary England*, 2nd edn, New York, 1964, pp. 443–81. Lawrence Stone, *The Family, Sex and Marriage: In England 1500–1800,* London, 1977, pp. 150, 154–5. N. Z. Davis, 'City women and religion,' in *Society and Culture in Early Modern France*, Stanford University Press, 1975, pp. 65–95, suggests the complexities of changes in the status of women which the Reformation effected.

15 N.d. a letter addressed to Sir Edmund Verney or Mr Ralph Verney, Esq. following a copy of a High Constable Warrant dated 10 December 1635, concerning conversion of tillage to pasturage, PUR II. Sir Edmund Verney to Sir Ralph Verney, 4 January 1635/6, PUR III. Sir Edmund Verney to Sir Ralph Verney, 9 March 1635/6, PUR III. Sir Edmund Verney to Sir Ralph Verney, 16 March 1635/6, PUR III. Sir Edmund Verney to Sir Ralph Verney, 6 April 1636, PUR III. A reflection of the high level of trust between father and son can be seen in Sir Edmund Verney to Sir Ralph Verney, 20 April 1639, PUR III. In this Sir Edmund's maneuvers to secure sufficient income brought him into a project concerning a coachman's patent. The father was advised that 'the project is illegal.' Further, Sir Edmund warned his son not to use his own name on the deed, but 'put some other name upon it' so that Sir Ralph would not be liable to action by the Statute of Monopolies.

16 Sir Edmund Verney to Sir Ralph Verney, 26 February, no year, listed as no. 12, PUR III; n.d., listed as no. 47, PUR III; Sir Edmund Verney to Sir Ralph Verney, n.d., 1635/6, PUR III.

17 Sir Edmund Verney to 'My daughter Verney' [Mary Lady Verney], 20 August 1635, PUR III.

18 Sir Edmund Verney to Sir Ralph Verney, 26 February, no year, listed as no. 12, PUR III.

19 Sir Edmund Verney to Sir Ralph Verney, 1 April 1639, PUR III; Sir Edmund Verney to Sir Ralph Verney, 15 June 1639, PUR III; Sir Edmund Verney to Sir Ralph Verney, 17 June 1639, PUR III.

20 Sir Ralph Verney to Lady Susannah Denton, 17 July 1638, PUR III.

21 Lady Mary Wiseman to Mary Lady Verney, 29 June 1629, PUR II.

22 John Crowther to Sir Ralph Verney, 6 November 1632, PUR II.

23 John Crowther to Sir Ralph Verney, 22 September 1631, PUR II;

This was not the advice of a man in his dotage to a youthful pupil. Crowther was only 24 years old when he wrote this letter. Joseph Foster (ed.), *Alumni Oxonienses*, Oxford, 1891, vol. I, p. 358.

24 Sir Edmund Verney to Sir Ralph Verney, 1 April 1639, PUR III.
25 Stone, 1965, op. cit., p. 660.
26 Sir Edmund Verney to Sir Ralph Verney, 1 April 1639, PUR III.
27 Sir Ralph Verney to brother Edmund Verney, 24 June 1644, PUR V; Sir Ralph Verney to Mary Lady Verney, 14/24 February 1647, PUR VIII.
28 Sir Ralph Verney to Dr William Denton, 10 May 1639, PUR III.
29 Sir Ralph Verney to Sir Edmund Verney, 10 May 1639, PUR III.
30 Sir Edmund Verney to Sir Ralph Verney, 16 May 1639, PUR III.
31 Mary Lady Verney to Sir Ralph Verney, 10 December 1646, PUR VII.
32 There are numerous examples of the use of 'friend' as a synonym for kin designations. See, for example, Sir Ralph Verney to brother Henry Verney, 23 November/3 December 1645, PUR VI; Sir Ralph Verney to Sir Francis Drake, 5/15 April 1646, PUR VII. Professor Macfarlane in his study *The Family Life of Ralph Josselin*, Oxford, 1970, notes the use of 'friends' as a synonym for affines, p. 143. According to Professor Macfarlane's interpretation of this usage, 'The fact that Josselin termed his affines "friends" rather than "relations" is . . . significant; they were closer than "neighbors", but more distant than blood relatives.' However, the Verney correspondence offers sufficient evidence to conclude that 'friend' was used to refer to blood relatives as well as affines. In this connection, Professor Macfarlane elsewhere in the Josselin study quotes from the educator John Brinsley. In this passage Brinsley uses 'friends' as a synonym for relatives, but Macfarlane apparently missed this. Ibid., p. 207.
33 Sister Susan Verney to Sir Ralph Verney, 16 January 1645, PUR VI.
34 Mary Lady Verney to Will Roads, 20 March 1647/8, PUR VIII.
35 Thomas Verney to Will Roads, 19 February 1649, PUR IX.
36 Brother Edmund Verney to Sir Ralph Verney, n.d., December 1635, PUR III; brother Henry Verney to Sir Ralph Verney, 19 April 1637, PUR III; brother Edmund Verney to Sir Ralph Verney, 12 July 1637, PUR III; brother Edmund Verney to Sir Ralph Verney, 15 August 1637, PUR III, brother Henry Verney to Sir Ralph Verney, 1 June 1640, PUR IV; brother Thomas Verney to Sir Ralph Verney, 20 September 1639, PUR IV.
37 Brother Henry Verney to Sir Ralph Verney, 22 January 1639, PUR III; brother Henry Verney to Sir Ralph Verney, 9 March

1639, PUR III, brother Edmund Verney to Sir Ralph Verney, 10 September 1639, PUR IV, brother Edmund Verney to Sir Ralph Verney, 30 January 1639/40, PUR IV.

38 Brother Henry Verney to Sir Ralph Verney, 26 October 1637, PUR III.

39 Brother Thomas Verney to Sir Edmund Verney, 11 October 1635, PUR III.

40 Brother Thomas Verney to Sir Edmund Verney, 22 October 1635, PUR III.

41 Brother Thomas Verney to Sir Edmund Verney, 19 July 1638, PUR III.

42 Brother Thomas Verney to Sir Ralph Verney, 11 July 1638, PUR III.

43 Brother Thomas Verney to Sir Ralph Verney, 22 July 1638, PUR III.

44 Ibid.

45 Brother Thomas Verney to Sir Ralph Verney, 27 August 1638, PUR III.

46 Brother Thomas Verney to Sir Edmund Verney, 19 July 1638, PUR III.

47 Brother Thomas Verney to Sir Ralph Verney, 27 August 1638, PUR III.

48 Sir Edmund Verney to Sir Ralph Verney, 5 January 1635/6, PUR III.

49 Brother Edmund Verney to Sir Ralph Verney, 12 July 1637, PUR III; brother Edmund Verney to Sir Ralph Verney, 20 April 1637, PUR III.

50 Sir Ralph Verney to brother Edmund Verney, 20 April 1637, PUR III.

51 Sir Edmund Verney to Mr Crowther, 18 July 1637, PUR III.

52 Sir Ralph Verney to Mr Crowther, 20 July 1637, PUR III.

53 Sir Ralph Verney to Mr Crowther, 18 July 1637, PUR III.

54 Brother Edmund Verney to Sir Ralph Verney, 13 March 1648, PUR IX; for another example among many of this kind written by Edmund see brother Edmund Verney to Sir Ralph Verney, 24 September 1641, PUR IV.

55 Brother Thomas Verney to Sir Ralph Verney, 14 May 1644, PUR V.

56 Brother Henry Verney to Sir Ralph Verney, 20 November 1643, PUR V.

57 The will of Sir Edmund Verney, 26 March, 14th Charles I; for special provisions made for brother Edmund see Uncle John Denton to Sir Ralph Verney, 14 February 1650, PUR X; for Susan

see Uncle John Denton to Sir Ralph Verney, 10 July 1646, PUR VII; Memorandum in Sir Ralph Verney's hand, n.d., following 2 August 1646, PUR VII; for Penelope see sister Penelope Verney to Sir Ralph Verney, 22 May 1645, PUR VI.

58 Thomas Verney to Will Roads, 20 June 1645, PUR VI; Sir Ralph Verney to Mary Lady Verney, 8/18 August 1647, PUR VIII.

59 Brother Henry Verney to Sir Ralph Verney, 15 January 1646, PUR VII.

60 Brother Edmund Verney to Sir Ralph Verney, 29 May/8 June 1648, PUR IX.

61 Sir Ralph Verney to Dr William Denton, 16/26 January 1647/8, PUR VIII.

62 Ibid.; Sir Ralph Verney to Dr William Denton, 5/15 September 1647, PUR VIII; Sir Ralph Verney to sister Susan Verney, 26 September/6 October 1645, PUR VI.

63 Sister Penelope Verney to Sir Ralph Verney, 20 February 1645, PUR VI.

64 Elizabeth Isham to Sir Ralph Verney, 9 December 1644, PUR VI.

65 Sister Susan Verney to Sir Ralph Verney, 19 December 1646, PUR VII.

66 Thomas Verney to Dr William Denton, 6 March 1650, PUR X.

67 Sister Susan Verney to Sir Ralph Verney, 14 August 1640, PUR IV.

68 Copy of letter from Sir Ralph Verney to sister Margaret Verney, 16 August 1639, PUR III; copy of letter from Sir Ralph Verney to sister Margaret Verney, 27 August 1639, PUR III; Sir Ralph Verney to Elizabeth Isham, 27 November 1639, PUR IV; Elizabeth Isham to Sir Ralph Verney, 1 December 1639, PUR IV.

69 Copy of letter from Sir Ralph Verney to sister Margaret Verney, 16 August 1639, PUR III; Sir Ralph Verney to sister Susan Verney, 3 August 1640, PUR IV.

70 Sir Ralph Verney to Aunt Eure, 28 June 1642, PUR IV.

71 Brother Henry Verney to Sir Ralph Verney, 19 April 1637, PUR III; brother Henry Verney to Sir Ralph Verney, 26 October 1637, PUR III; brother Henry Verney to Sir Ralph Verney, 1 June 1640, PUR IV; brother Henry Verney to Sir Ralph Verney, 10 April 1642, PUR IV; brother Henry Verney to Sir Ralph Verney, 25 September 1643, PUR V; Sir Ralph Verney to brother Henry Verney, 7 October 1643, PUR V.

72 Dr William Denton to Mary Lady Verney [probably], 4 January 1643/4, PUR V; brother Henry Verney to Sir Ralph Verney, 29 August 1644, PUR VI.

73 Brother Henry Verney to Sir Ralph Verney, 30 June 1646, PUR

VII; brother Henry Verney to Sir Ralph Verney, 3 September 1646, PUR VII.

74 Brother Thomas Verney to Sir Ralph Verney, 4 October 1643, PUR V; Sir Ralph Verney to brother Henry Verney, 7 October 1643, PUR V.

75 Brother Henry Verney to Mary Lady Verney, 29 May 1644, PUR V; brother Henry Verney to Sir Ralph Verney, 29 May 1644, PUR V.

76 Sir Ralph Verney to brother Henry Verney, 6/16 August 1644, PUR VI; brother Henry Verney to Sir Ralph Verney, 12 September 1644, PUR VI; brother Henry Verney to Sir Ralph Verney, 19 December 1644, PUR VI; brother Henry Verney to Sir Ralph Verney, 4 August 1645, PUR VI.

77 Brother Henry Verney to Sir Ralph Verney, 20 March 1645, PUR VI. See, for example, brother Henry Verney to Sir Ralph Verney, 22 May 1645, PUR VI; brother Henry Verney to Sir Ralph Verney, 29 May 1645, PUR VI; brother Henry Verney to Sir Ralph Verney, 19 June 1645, PUR VI.

78 Brother Henry Verney to Sir Ralph Verney, 19 June 1645, PUR VI; Sir Ralph Verney to brother Henry Verney, 4/14 July 1645, PUR VI.

79 Brother Henry Verney to Sir Ralph Verney, 3 September 1646, PUR VII.

80 Brother Henry Verney to Sir Ralph Verney, 19 December 1644, PUR VI; Sir Ralph Verney to brother Henry Verney, 18/28 April 1645, PUR VI; brother Henry Verney to Sir Ralph Verney, 8 June 1645, PUR VI; brother Henry Verney to Sir Ralph Verney, 4 August 1645, PUR VI.

81 Brother Henry Verney to Sir Ralph Verney, 1 January 1646, PUR VII.

82 Sir Francis Drake to Sir Ralph Verney, 10 November 1645, PUR VI.

83 Brother Henry Verney to Sir Ralph Verney, 11 December 1645, PUR VI; Mary Lady Verney to Sir Ralph Verney, 18 August 1647, PUR VIII.

84 Brother Henry Verney to Sir Ralph Verney, 13 November 1645, PUR VI.

85 Brother Henry Verney to Sir Ralph Verney, 25 December 1645, PUR VI; Henry Verney to Will Roads, 16 February 1646, PUR VII; Sir Ralph Verney to brother Henry Verney, 22 February/4 March 1646, PUR VII; note in brother Henry Verney's hand listing household items which he took from Sir Ralph Verney's

home, n.d., following 29 March/8 April 1646, PUR VII; Sir Ralph Verney to brother Henry Verney, 12/22 April 1646, PUR VII.

86 Brother Henry Verney to Sir Ralph Verney, 25 December 1645, PUR VI.

87 Sister Susan Verney to Sir Ralph Verney, 6 March 1644, PUR VI.

88 Sir Ralph Verney to Will Roads, 14/24 March 1645, PUR VI.

89 Sir Ralph Verney to brother Henry Verney, 19/29 April 1646, PUR VII.

90 Brother Henry Verney to Sir Ralph Verney, 5/15 May 1642, PUR IV; brother Henry Verney to Sir Ralph Verney, 30 September 1642, PUR IV; brother Henry Verney to Sir Ralph Verney, 9 November 1642, PUR IV.

91 Brother Henry Verney to Sir Ralph Verney, 6 March 1645, PUR VI.

92 Brother Henry Verney to Sir Ralph Verney, 14 September 1646, PUR VII.

93 Brother Henry Verney to Sir Ralph Verney, n.d., 1646, PUR VII.

94 Brother Henry Verney to Sir Ralph Verney, 6 April 1646, PUR VII.

95 Sir Ralph Verney to brother Henry Verney, 21 June/1 July 1646, PUR VII.

96 Sir Ralph Verney to brother Henry Verney, 30 October/9 November 1646, PUR VII.

97 Brother Henry Verney to Sir Ralph Verney, 18 February 1647, PUR VIII; brother Henry Verney to Sir Ralph Verney, 25 February 1647, PUR VIII; Sir Ralph Verney to Mary Lady Verney, 14/24 March 1647, PUR VIII.

98 Ibid.

99 Brother Henry Verney to Sir Ralph Verney, 21 January 1647, PUR VIII; brother Henry Verney to Sir Ralph Verney, 25 February 1647, PUR VIII.

100 Sir Ralph Verney to Mary Lady Verney, 14/24 March 1647, PUR VIII.

101 Sir Ralph Verney to Dr William Denton, 20 February/1 March 1648, PUR VIII.

102 Mary Lady Verney to Sir Ralph Verney, 21 January 1647, PUR VIII; Mary Lady Verney to Sir Ralph Verney, 28 January 1647, PUR VIII.

103 Brother Edmund Verney to Mary Lady Verney [unsigned], 5 December 1643, PUR V; brother Edmund Verney to Sir Ralph Verney, 30 November 1644, PUR VI; brother Edmund Verney to Sir Ralph Verney, 17 August 1647, PUR VIII; brother Edmund Verney to Sir Ralph Verney, 26 August 1647, PUR VIII.

104 Sir Ralph Verney to brother Edmund Verney, 17/27 October 1647, PUR VIII.

105 Brother Edmund Verney to Sir Ralph Verney, 26 August 1647, PUR VIII; Mary Lady Verney to Sir Ralph Verney, 5 September 1647, PUR VIII; Mary Lady Verney to Sir Ralph Verney, 12 September 1647, PUR VIII.

106 Mary Lady Verney to Sir Ralph Verney, 5 September 1647, PUR VIII; Sir Ralph Verney to brother Edmund Verney, 17/27 October 1647, PUR VIII; brother Edmund Verney to Sir Ralph Verney, 20 October 1647, PUR VIII; Sir Ralph Verney to brother Edmund Verney, 26 December 1647/5 January 1648, PUR VIII; brother Edmund Verney to 'My dearest Sister' [Mary Lady Verney undoubtedly], 20 January 1647/8, PUR VIII.

107 Brother Edmund Verney to Mary Lady Verney, 17/27 May 1648, PUR IX.

108 Brother Henry Verney to Sir Ralph Verney, 5 February 1646, PUR VII; Henry Verney to Wills Roads, 16 February 1646, PUR VII.

109 Brother Edmund Verney to Sir Ralph Verney, 6/16 June 1648, PUR IX.

110 Sir Ralph's maternal grandfather, Sir Thomas Denton (d. 1633) had been a prominent leader in the county and the Dentons 'were virtually lords of the borough,' Mary F. Keeler, *The Long Parliament*, Philadelphia, 1954, p. 154.

111 George Lipscombe, *The History and Antiquities of the County of Bucks*, London, 1847, vol. III, p. 17. Nine of these are known to have lived to maturity.

112 Sir Ralph Verney to Margaret Eure, 28 June 1642, PUR IV; an indenture dated the 17th year of Charles I, from an unmarked box at Claydon. According to this document Aunt Eure borrowed the money to make this gift, and cousin Nathanial Hobart was one of the parties involved. It is probable that Aunt Eure put up enough money to raise £1,000, rather than the whole sum. See brother Henry Verney to Sir Ralph Verney, 23 April 1646, PUR VII.

113 Sir Ralph Verney to Margaret Eure, 28 June 1642, PUR IV; an indenture dated the 17th year of Charles I, from an unmarked box at Claydon.

114 N.d. following 20 April 1637, PUR II; Aunt Poulteney to Sir Ralph Verney, 1 May 1639, PUR III; Sir Ralph Verney to Aunt Poulteney, 24 May 1638, PUR III.

115 Sir Edmund Verney to Sir Ralph Verney, 9 April 1639, PUR III; Sir Edmund Verney to Sir Ralph Verney, 15 April 1639, PUR III; Sir Ralph Verney to Sir Edmund Verney, 18 April 1639, PUR III;

in a letter to his father, Sir Ralph termed his aunt's marriage to a Catholic 'so foul an act,' Sir Ralph Verney to Father, 18 June 1639, PUR III.

116 Margaret Eure to Mary Lady Verney, 14 April 1642, PUR IV; Margaret Eure to Sir Ralph Verney, 14 April 1642, PUR IV; Margaret Eure to Sir Ralph Verney, 7 May 1642, PUR IV; Margaret Eure to Sir Ralph Verney, 9 July 1642, PUR IV; Margaret Eure to Sir Ralph Verney, 11 September 1642, PUR IV; Margaret Eure to Sir Ralph Verney, 3 April 1643, PUR V; Margaret Eure to Sir Ralph Verney, 15 April 1643, PUR V.

117 Elizabeth Isham to Sir Ralph Verney, 5 [?] 1643, PUR V; Elizabeth Isham to Sir Ralph Verney , 2 October 1645, PUR VI.

118 Countess of Sussex to Sir Ralph Verney, received 13 January 1642/3, PUR V; Countess of Sussex to Sir Ralph Verney, received 5 December 1642, PUR V; Sir Roger Burgoyne to Sir Ralph Verney, 26 December 1644, PUR VI; Lady Peyton to Mary Lady Verney, n.d., following 26 December 1644, PUR VI.

119 On the volume and complexity of estate documents see Stone, 1965, op. cit., pp. 276 ff.

120 Brother Thomas Verney to Sir Ralph Verney, 7 March 1642/3, PUR V; Alexander Denton to Sir Ralph Verney, 28 March/7 April 1644, PUR V; Statement of John Kersey, servant of Sir A. Denton, next to papers of December 1660, from an unmarked box at Claydon.

121 See, for example, Dr William Denton to Sir Ralph Verney, 27 August 1649, PUR X.

122 Elizabeth Isham to Sir Ralph Verney, 2 October 1645, PUR VI.

123 This dispute is the subject of scores of letters. See for example, Elizabeth Isham to Sir Ralph Verney, received 9 May 1643, PUR V; Elizabeth Isham to Sir Ralph Verney, 31 July 1644, PUR V; Elizabeth Isham to Sir Ralph Verney received 1/11 May 1645, [misdated 24 July 1645], PUR VI; Sir Ralph Verney to Elizabeth Isham, 26 September/10 October 1645, PUR VI; Elizabeth Isham to Sir Ralph Verney, 31 December 1646, PUR VII; Elizabeth Isham to Sir Ralph Verney, 19 July 1648, PUR IX.

124 Sir Ralph Verney to Elizabeth Isham, 6/16 August 1648, PUR IX.

125 Ibid.

126 Elizabeth Isham to Sir Ralph Verney, 10 December 1645, PUR VI.

127 Elizabeth Isham to Sir Ralph Verney, 31 July 1644, PUR V; Sir Ralph Verney to Elizabeth Isham, 8/18 November 1644, PUR VI.

128 Sir Ralph Verney to Elizabeth Isham, 26 September/6 October 1645, PUR VI, a memorandum in Sir Ralph Verney's hand which

begins 'Instead of answering my Aunt Isham's letter . . . I writ at large to W[ill] R[oads] . . . .' The memorandum also notes that he 'writ at large to Dr to offer her Brill' with details of the offer; 29 November/6 December 1648, PUR IX.

129 Elizabeth Isham to Sir Ralph Verney, 21 May 1646, PUR VII.

130 Dr William Denton to Sir Ralph Verney, 12 June 1648, PUR IX; Dr William Denton to Sir Ralph Verney, 17 August 1648, PUR IX; Dr William Denton to Sir Ralph Verney, 6 September 1649, PUR X; for a good example of the complexities involved in sorting out family financial arrangements see Dr William Denton to Sir Ralph Verney, 27 August 1649, PUR X.

131 Dr William Denton to Sir Ralph Verney, 5 July 1649, PUR X, the principal and interest owing to Aunt Isham and the doctor's wife came to between £2,800–2,900. The principal alone came to £2,100. Sir Ralph Verney [his hand] to Dr William Denton, n.d., following 5 July 1649, PUR X.

132 Dr William Denton to Sir Ralph Verney, 5 July 1648, PUR X.

133 Dr William Denton to Sir Ralph Verney, 30 July 1649, PUR X.

134 For Dr Denton's character see especially Dr William Denton to Sir Ralph Verney, 1 August 1645, PUR VI; Dr William Denton to Mary Lady Verney, 6 October 1647, PUR VIII; Dr William Denton to Sir Ralph Verney, 13 March 1647/8, PUR VIII; Dr William Denton to Sir Ralph Verney, 4 May 1648, PUR IX; Dr William Denton to Sir Ralph Verney, 25 May 1648, PUR IX; Dr William Denton to Sir Ralph Verney, 17 August 1648. For Sir Ralph's character see Chapter 1, pp. 16–17.

135 Dr William Denton to Sir Ralph Verney, 19 August 1647, PUR VIII; Dr William Denton to Sir Ralph Verney, 9 September 1647, PUR VIII.

136 Mary Lady Verney to Sir Ralph Verney, 6 January 1648, PUR VIII.

137 Joseph Foster (ed.), op. cit., 1891, vol. I, p. 396.

138 Dr William Denton to Sir Ralph Verney, 18 November 1647, PUR VIII.

139 Mary Lady Verney to Sir Ralph Verney, 10 December 1646, PUR VII.

140 For the doctor's help in other business for Sir Ralph see Dr William Denton to Sir Ralph Verney, 26 November 1647, PUR VIII; Sir Ralph Verney to Dr William Denton, 19/29 December 1647, PUR VIII; Dr William Denton, to Sir Ralph Verney, 25 November 1647, PUR VIII; Dr William Denton to Sir Ralph Verney, 10 February 1648, PUR VIII. For Sir Ralph's and Mary Lady Verney's gratitude see Sir Ralph Verney to Dr William

Denton, 10/20 January 1647, PUR VIII; Sir Ralph Verney to Dr William Denton, 27 January 1647, PUR VII; Mary Lady Verney to Sir Ralph Verney, 20 September 1647, PUR VII; Sir Ralph Verney to Mary Lady Verney, 10/20 October 1647, PUR VIII.

141 Sir Ralph Verney to Mary Lady Verney, 10/20 October 1647, PUR VIII; Sir Ralph Verney to Mary Lady Verney, 16/20 January 1648, PUR VIII.

142 Mary Lady Verney to Sir Ralph Verney, 2 March 1648, PUR VIII.

143 Dr William Denton [probably] to Sir Ralph Verney, 20 August 1648, PUR VII.

144 Dr William Denton to Sir Ralph Verney, 4 October 1649, PUR X.

145 Dr William Denton to Sir Ralph Verney, 15 October 1649, PUR X.

146 Henry Harrison to Sir Ralph Verney, 5 January 1649/50, PUR X.

147 Dr William Denton to Sir Ralph Verney, 16 March 1648, PUR VIII; Sir Ralph Verney to Mr Cordell, 24 March/3 April 1648, PUR VIII; Dr William Denton to Sir Ralph Verney, 20 March 1648, PUR VIII.

148 See for example, brother Thomas Verney to Sir Ralph Verney, 11/21 September 1646, PUR VII; Dr William Denton [his hand] to Sir Ralph Verney, 13 October 1647, PUR VIII; Dr William Denton to Sir Ralph Verney, 9 December 1647, PUR VIII; Dr William Denton to Sir Ralph Verney, 28 June 1649, PUR X.

149 Dr William Denton to Mary Lady Verney [probably], 4 January 1643/4, PUR V.

150 Dr William Denton to Will Roads, 7 May 1648, PUR IX.

151 Dr William Denton to Sir Ralph Verney, 28 June 1649, PUR X; Dr William Denton to Sir Ralph Verney, 23 July 1649, PUR X; Dr William Denton to Sir Ralph Verney, 6 August 1649, PUR X; Dr William Denton to Sir Ralph Verney, 29 October 1649, PUR X.

152 Dr William Denton to Sir Ralph Verney, 3 December 1646, PUR VII; sister Susan Alport to Sir Ralph Verney, 3 December 1646, PUR VII.

153 Dr William Denton to Sir Ralph Verney, 18 December 1645, PUR VI.

154 Dr William Denton to Sir Ralph Verney, 1/11 August 1647, PUR VIII.

155 Sister Mary Verney to 'Dear Parent' [Dr Denton undoubtedly], received 19/29 December 1648, PUR IX.

156 Mary Lady Verney to Sir Ralph Verney, 7 December 1647, PUR VIII.

157 Mary Lady Verney to Will Roads, second n.d. letter following 21/31 January 1647, PUR VIII.
158 Lady Ursula Verney to Sir Ralph Verney, 27 June 1647, PUR V; Eleanor Countess of Sussex to Sir Ralph Verney, 29 July 1644, PUR V; Lady Ursula Verney to Sir Ralph Verney, received 8/18 August 1644, PUR VI.
159 Lady Ursula Verney to Sir Ralph Verney, 27 June 1644, PUR V.
160 Eleanor Countess of Sussex to Sir Ralph Verney, 29 July 1644, PUR V; Sir Ralph Verney to Doll Leeke, 21/31 August 1644, PUR VI.
161 Doll Leeke to Sir Ralph Verney, received 15/25 August 1644, PUR VI; brother Henry Verney to Sir Ralph Verney, 12 September 1644, PUR VI.
162 Eleanor Countess of Sussex to Sir Ralph Verney, 29 July 1644, PUR V; Lady Ursula Verney to Sir Ralph Verney, received 8/18 August 1644, PUR VI; brother Henry Verney to Sir Ralph Verney, 12 September 1644, PUR VI.
163 Sister Susan Verney to Sir Ralph Verney, 6 March 1644, PUR VI.
164 Sir John Leeke to Sir Ralph Verney, 5 February 1646, PUR VII.
165 Sir Francis Drake [undoubtedly] to Sir Ralph Verney, 11 December 1645, PUR VI.
166 Sir Francis Drake to Sir Ralph Verney, 30 June 1646, PUR VII; 'A memorandum concerning sequestration,' n.d. following sister Penelope Verney to Sir Ralph Verney, 19 September 1646, PUR VII.
167 Sir Ralph Verney to Sir Francis Drake, 19/29 July 1646, PUR VII.
168 Dr William Denton to Sir Ralph Verney, 24 April 1648, PUR IX.
169 Dr William Denton to Sir Ralph Verney, 12 June 1648, PUR IX.
170 Doll Leeke to Sir Ralph Verney, received 29 August 1646, PUR VII.
171 Eleanor Countess of Sussex to Sir Ralph Verney, 12 August 1639, PUR III; *passim*, letters addressed to the Verneys at the Hobarts' house in London, PUR III.
172 Sir Edmund Verney's will, 14 Charles I.
173 Sir Ralph Verney to Doll Leeke, 21/31 August 1644, PUR VI.
174 Doll Leeke to Sir Ralph Verney, 21 October 1645, PUR VI; Doll Leeke to Sir Ralph Verney, 21 May 1646, PUR VII.
175 Doll Leeke to Sir Ralph Verney, 10 August 1643, PUR V; Doll Leeke to Sir Ralph Verney, 9 July 1645, PUR VI.
176 Doll Leeke to Sir Ralph Verney, 11 December 1644, PUR VI; Doll Leeke to Sir Ralph Verney, 28 March 1648, PUR VIII.
177 Sir Ralph Verney to Sir Edward Sydenham, 14 November 1642,

PUR V; Sir Edward Sydenham to Sir Ralph Verney [undoubtedly], 8 December 1642, PUR V.

178 Sir Ralph Verney to Doll Leeke, 19/29 June 1646, PUR VII.

179 Doll Leeke to Sir Ralph Verney, received 29 August 1646, PUR VII.

180 Mary Lady Verney to Sir Ralph Verney, 12 September 1647, PUR VIII.

181 Mary Lady Verney to Sir Ralph Verney, 2 December 1647, PUR VIII.

182 Sir Ralph Verney to Lady Sydenham, 8/18 October 1648, PUR IX.

183 Doll Leeke to Sir Ralph Verney, 28 March 1648, PUR VIII.

184 Doll Leeke to Sir Ralph Verney, 26 October 1648, PUR IX.

185 Dr William Denton to Mary Lady Verney, 19 October 1648, PUR IX.

186 Mary Lady Verney to Sir Ralph Verney, 11 November 1647, PUR VIII.

187 Doll Leeke to Sir Ralph Verney, 28 March 1648, PUR VIII.

188 Dr William Denton to Mary Lady Verney, 19 October 1648, PUR IX.

189 Sir Ralph Verney to Mary Lady Verney, 14/24 November 1647, PUR VIII.

190 For example, Nathanial Hobart to Sir Ralph Verney, 19 June 1636, PUR III; Mary Lady Verney to Sir Ralph Verney, 10 February 1647/8, PUR VIII.

191 Sir Ralph Verney to brother Henry Verney [undoubtedly], 16/26 May 1645, PUR VI; Sir Ralph Verney to Nathanial Hobart, 12/22 June 1645, PUR VI.

192 Sir Ralph Verney to Anne Hobart, 22 August/1 September 1645, PUR VI; Anne Hobart to Sir Ralph Verney, received 4/14 September 1645, PUR VI; Anne Hobart to Sir Ralph Verney, 18/28 September 1645, PUR VI.

193 Sir Ralph Verney to Anne Hobart, 22 August/1 September 1645, PUR VI.

194 Sister Susan Verney to Sir Ralph Verney, 11 December 1645, PUR VI; John Leeke to Sir Ralph Verney, 24 December 1645, PUR VI; brother Henry Verney to Sir Ralph Verney, 12 February 1646, PUR VII.

195 Sir Ralph Verney to Sir John Leeke, 10/20 May 1646, PUR VII.

196 Anne Hobart to Sir Ralph Verney, received 11/21 February 1646, PUR VII.

197 Sir Ralph Verney to Anne Hobart [undoubtedly], in which Sir

Ralph estimated the cost as £10, 7/17 December 1645, PUR VI; Sir Ralph Verney to Anne Hobart, 1/11 March 1646, PUR VII.

198 Nathanial Hobart to Sir Ralph Verney, 12 March 1646, PUR VII.

199 Sir Ralph Verney to brother Henry Verney [undoubtedly], 16/26 May 1648, PUR VI; Sir Ralph Verney to Sir Roger Burgoyne, 8/18 October 1648, PUR IX.

200 Mary Lady Verney to Sir Ralph Verney, 25 November 1647, PUR VIII.

201 Sir Ralph Verney to Mary Lady Verney, 12/22 December 1647, PUR VIII.

202 For another example of this kind see Dr William Denton to Sir Ralph Verney, 14 September 1648, PUR IX.

203 Anne Hobart to Sir Ralph Verney, received 19/29 January 1647, PUR VIII.

204 G. Lipscombe, *The History and Antiquities of the County of Bucks*, London, vol. III, p. 17; Sir Ralph Verney [his hand] to 'Madam' [Countess of Sussex, probably], 7 June 1641, PUR IV.

205 Sir Ralph Verney to Lady Susannah Denton, 25 June 1639, PUR III; 'Your obedient son,' Sir Ralph Verney to Lady Susannah Denton, 17 June 1638, PUR III.

206 Lady Susannah Denton to Sir Ralph Verney, 4 May 1639, PUR III; Sir Ralph Verney to Lady Susannah Denton, 25 June 1639, PUR III; Lady Susannah Denton to Sir Ralph Verney, 2 July 1639, PUR III; Lady Susannah Denton to Sir Ralph Verney, 3 November 1639, PUR IV.

207 Lady Susannah Denton to Sir Ralph Verney, 5 June 1638, PUR III; Sir Ralph Verney to Lady Susannah Denton, 17 June 1638, PUR III.

208 Brother Edmund Verney to Sir Ralph Verney, 19 January 1638/9, PUR III; brother Edmund Verney to Sir Ralph Verney, 2 February 1638/9, PUR III.

209 Lady Susannah Denton to Sir Ralph Verney, 13 May 1639, PUR III.

210 Lady Susannah Denton to Sir Ralph Verney, received 29 October 1639, PUR IV.

211 Sir Ralph Verney to Sir Edmund Verney, 18 June 1639, PUR III.

212 Ibid.

213 Ibid.; Sir Ralph Verney to Lady Susannah Denton, 25 June 1639, PUR III.

214 Lady Margaret Eure to Sir Ralph Verney, 29 June 1639, PUR III.

215 Lady Susannah Denton to Sir Ralph Verney, received 29 October 1639, PUR IV.

216 Lady Susannah Denton to Sir Ralph Verney, 2 July 1639, PUR

III; Lady Susannah Denton to Sir Ralph Verney, 3 November 1639, PUR IV.

217 For a point of view which emphasizes the importance of individual options and preferences, see Sara Heller Mendelson's critique in *Past and Present*, no. 85, November 1979, pp. 126–35 of my previously published article, 'The weightiest business,' ibid., no. 72, August 1976, pp. 25–54, and my rejoinder, ibid., no. 85, November 1979, pp. 136–40.

218 Bernard Bailyn, *Education in the Forming of American Society*, New York, 1980, p. 25.

219 Recent work has suggested not only that styles of friendship vary over time but that it is necessary to use gender as a category of analysis in recovering the history of friendship. See Carol Smith-Rosenberg, 'The female world of love and ritual,' *Signs*, no. 1, 1975, pp. 1–30.

## CHAPTER 3 MARRIAGE: THE MALE PERSPECTIVE

1 Lawrence Stone, *The Crisis of the Aristocracy*, Oxford, 1965, p. 613. On the subject of arranged marriage see also by the same author, *The Family, Sex and Marriage: In England 1500–1800*, London, 1977, especially Chapter 5, pp. 178–216.

2 Sir John Leeke to Sir Ralph Verney, 5 February 1646, PUR VII.

3 Sir Ralph Verney to Sir Roger Burgoyne, 22 February/4 March 1646, PUR VII; Sir Ralph Verney to Sir Francis Drake, 5/15 April 1646, PUR VII; Alan Macfarlane, *The Family Life of Ralph Josselin*, Oxford, 1970, p. 140. Professor Macfarlane cites the case of Richard Rogers who, 'afraid that his wife might die in childbirth, counted amongst the "uncomfortablenesses which would follow" looseing friendship among her kindred.'

4 Sir Ralph Verney to Sir Roger Burgoyne, 22 February/4 March 1646, PUR VII.

5 Sir Ralph Verney to Sir Roger Burgoyne, 1/11 March 1646, PUR VII; Mary Lady Verney to Sir Ralph Verney, 14 January 1647, PUR VIII.

6 Stone, 1965, op. cit., p. 633.

7 H. J. Habakkuk, 'Social attitudes and attributes,' in A. Goodwin (ed.), *The European Nobility in the 18th Century*, London, 1953, pp. 1–21; Stone, 1965, op. cit., pp. 635–7; G. E. Mingay, *English Landed Society in the 18th Century*, London, 1963, pp. 32–4; J. P. Cooper, 'Patterns of inheritance and settlement by the great landowners from the fifteenth to the eighteenth centuries,' in J. Goody, J.

Thirsk and E. P. Thompson (eds), *Family and Inheritance*, Cambridge, 1976, pp. 192–327.

8 Sir Ralph Verney to Lady Verney, 14/24 February 1647, PUR VIII.

9 Ibid.

10 The will of Sir Edmund Verney, 26 March, 14th Charles I. According to Sir Edmund's will Thomas was to receive £40 p.a. and Henry £30. His son Edmund and all the daughters received only £5 each but were 'otherwise provided for' in separate settlements. Ibid. For special provisions made for brother Edmund see Sir John Denton to Sir Ralph Verney, 14 February 1649/50, PUR X; for Susan see Sir John Denton to Sir Ralph Verney, 10 June 1646, PUR VII, and n.d. a memorandum in Sir Ralph Verney's hand following 2 August 1646, PUR VII; for Penelope see sister Penelope Verney to Sir Ralph Verney, 22 May 1645, PUR VI; Margaret's portion was a gift from Aunt Eure, see Chapter 2, note 112. It is probable that Aunt Eure put up enough money to raise £1,000 rather than the whole sum. Sir John Leeke to Sir Ralph Verney, 23 April 1646, PUR VII; for Mary see Sir Ralph Verney to Mary Lady Verney, 24 January/3 February 1647, PUR VIII. In view of the fact that the other sisters were to receive £1,000 portions it is probable that similar amounts were allotted for Cary and Elizabeth. Sir Ralph seems to have had some latitude in deciding on the amounts to be paid out in annuities. For example, he reduced Penelope's annuity from £50 p.a. to £40 when he was hard pressed for money. Sister Penelope Verney to Sir Ralph Verney, 13 February 1645, PUR VI. For a discussion of inheritance practices see Joan Thirsk, 'The European debate on customs of inheritance,' in J. Goody, *et al.*, 1976, op. cit., pp. 177–91.

11 Deed of 5 May 1631, from an unmarked box at Claydon.

12 See genealogy p. 202; she and Sir Ralph were married in 1629; Lady Mary Wiseman to Lady Margaret Verney, 29 June 1629, PUR II.

13 See genealogy, p. 202.

14 John Crowther to Sir Ralph Verney, 22 September 1631, PUR II; John Crowther to Sir Ralph Verney, 6 November 1632, PUR II.

15 See for example brother Edmund Verney to Mary Lady Verney, 15 February 1644, PUR V. Professor Macfarlane also notes the use of the term 'mother' for mother-in-law, in his study of Ralph Josselin, 1970, op. cit., p. 141. He also indicates use of 'son' for son-in-law, ibid., p. 114.

16 See for example Mary Lady Verney to Doll Leeke, n.d. July 1646,

PUR VII. It is possible that Sir Ralph coached her on that, but see Mary Lady Verney to Sir Ralph Verney, 26 November 1646, PUR VII; Mary Lady Verney to Sir Ralph Verney, 3 December 1646, PUR VII, among others that were written when she was separated from Sir Ralph. For a letter which is more typical of the way other women wrote, see Lady Anne Lee to Mary Lady Verney, 30 September no year, PUR VIII. Lady Verney was also an avid reader: Mr Edmund Brown to Mary Lady Verney, 14 December 1646, PUR VII; Sir Ralph Verney to Mr Bruce, 15/25 December 1646, PUR VIII; Dr William Denton to Sir Ralph Verney, 27 December 1649, PUR X.

17 See for example Sir Ralph Verney to Mary Lady Verney, 18/28 July 1647, PUR VIII; Sir Ralph Verney to Sir Roger Burgoyne, 27 December/6 January 1647, PUR VIII.

18 See genealogy, p. 202.

19 Brother Henry Verney to Sir Ralph Verney, 26 November 1646, PUR VII; she returned to France in the spring of 1648, PUR IX, *passim*.

20 Sir Ralph Verney to Mary Lady Verney, n.d., following 19 December 1646, PUR VII. For a list of the code names used see List in Sir Ralph Verney's hand, n.d., following 1 January 1646, PUR VII.

21 Mary Lady Verney to Sir Ralph Verney, 17 December 1646, PUR VII.

22 Dr William Denton (probably) to Sir Ralph Verney, 20 August 1646, PUR VII.

23 Sir Ralph Verney to Lord Devonshire, 20/30 September 1646, PUR VII.

24 Dr William Denton to Sir Ralph Verney, 17 December 1646, PUR VII.

25 Sir Ralph Verney to Mary Lady Verney, 24 November/4 December 1646, PUR VII.

26 Sir Ralph Verney to Mary Lady Verney, 30 November/10 December 1646, PUR VII.

27 See for example Sir Ralph Verney to Mary Lady Verney, 19/29 December 1646, PUR VII; Sir Ralph Verney to Mary Lady Verney, 7/17 March 1647, PUR VIII.

28 Mary Lady Verney to Sir Ralph Verney, 23 November 1646, PUR VII.

29 Sir Ralph Verney to Mary Lady Verney, 19/29 December 1646, PUR VII; PUR VIII, *passim*.

30 Sir Ralph Verney to Mary Lady Verney, 27 December/6 January 1646/7, PUR VIII.

31 Sir Ralph Verney to Mary Lady Verney, 19/29 December 1646, PUR VII.
32 Sir Ralph Verney to Mary Lady Verney, 29 August/9 September 1647, PUR VIII.
33 Sir Ralph Verney to Mary Lady Verney, 19/29 December 1646, PUR VII; Sir Ralph Verney to Mary Lady Verney, 3/13 January 1647, PUR VIII; Sir Ralph Verney to Mary Lady Verney, 17/27 February 1647, PUR VIII; Sir Ralph Verney to Mary Lady Verney, 19/29 September 1647, PUR VIII; Sir Ralph Verney to Mary Lady Verney, 9/19 January 1648, PUR VIII.
34 Sir Ralph Verney to Mary Lady Verney, 28 February/10 March 1647, PUR VIII.
35 Sir Ralph Verney to Mary Lady Verney, 7/17, February 1647, PUR VIII.
36 Sir Ralph Verney to Mary Lady Verney, 10/20 January 1647, PUR VIII.
37 See for example Mary Lady Verney to Sir Ralph Verney, 7 January 1647, PUR VIII; Mary Lady Verney to Sir Ralph Verney, 3 August 1647, PUR VIII; Mary Lady Verney to Sir Ralph Verney, 5 September 1647, PUR VIII; Mary Lady Verney to Sir Ralph Verney, 12 September 1647, PUR VIII.
38 Mary Lady Verney to Sir Ralph Verney, 10 October 1647, PUR VIII.
39 Mary Lady Verney to Sir Ralph Verney, 25 March 1647, PUR VIII.
40 Mary Lady Verney to Sir Ralph Verney, 7 December 1647, PUR VIII.
41 Mary Lady Verney to Sir Ralph Verney, 15 July 1647, PUR VIII.
42 Sir Ralph Verney to Mary Lady Verney, 28 November/8 December 1647, PUR VIII.
43 Sir Ralph Verney to Dr William Denton, 5/15 December 1647, PUR VIII.
44 Sir Ralph Verney to Dr William Denton, 23 November/3 December 1647, PUR VIII.
45 Mary Lady Verney to Sir Ralph Verney, 16 December 1647, PUR VIII.
46 Ibid.
47 Sir Ralph Verney to Mary Lady Verney, 2/12 January 1648, PUR VIII.
48 Quoted in Keith Thomas, 'The double standard,' *Journal of the History of Ideas*, vol. XX, no. 2, April 1959, p. 209.
49 Mary Lady Verney to Sir Ralph Verney, 2 December 1647, PUR VIII.

50 Sir Ralph Verney to Dr Kirton, 17/27 May 1649, PUR X.
51 Dr William Denton to Sir Ralph Verney, 24 September 1646, PUR VII.
52 Dr William Denton to Sir Ralph Verney, 7 March 1649/50, PUR X.
53 Dr William Denton to Sir Ralph Verney, 6 December 1649, PUR IX; Dr William Denton to Sir Ralph Verney, 28 February 1650; see genealogy, p. 202.
54 Yves-Marie Bercé, 'Aspects de la criminalité au XVLLe siècle,' *Revue historique*, vol. 239, 1968, p. 38.
55 Dr William Denton to Sir Ralph Verney, 5 June 1648, PUR IX.
56 Brother Edmund to Sir Ralph Verney, 6/16 June 1648, PUR IX; brother Edmund Verney's visit to Hillesden to see Sir Ralph's baby who was being boarded there triggered some gossip that Edmund 'came more to see the nurse than the child.' It was Edmund who volunteered this information to Sir Ralph, and the younger brother apparently did not believe that it was necessary to deny this accusation but instead appears to have chosen to repeat it to Sir Ralph as a kind of sly boast; brother Edmund Verney to Sir Ralph Verney, 21 December 1638, PUR III.
57 6 July 1642, PUR IV. Sir Edmund's wife had died in the previous year. It is not known whether the events described in the formal statement by the girl's mother occurred while Sir Edmund's wife was still alive. The date given here is that of the formal statement.
58 Thomas, 1959, op. cit., p. 196.
59 Since Thomas's father was not living, the marriage portion went directly to him. For other evidence that the portion was an inducement for men to marry see Stone, 1965, op. cit., pp. 599, 621.
60 Brother Thomas Verney to Sir Ralph Verney, 10 January 1643, PUR V; Sir Ralph Verney to 'Brother' [Edmund undoubtedly], 21 April 1643, PUR V; brother Thomas Verney to Sir Ralph Verney, 10 June, 1643, PUR V.
61 Sir Ralph Verney to brother Thomas Verney's wife, 1 July 1643, PUR V.
62 Brother Thomas Verney to Sir Ralph Verney, 1 May 1645, PUR VI; brother Thomas Verney to Sir Ralph Verney, 5 August 1646, for quote, PUR VII.
63 Brother Thomas Verney to Will Roads, 4 October 1646, PUR VII.
64 Dr William Denton to Sir Ralph Verney, 30 March 1648, PUR VIII; Dr William Denton to Sir Ralph Verney, 26 April 1649, PUR IX.

65 Sister Susan Verney to Sir Ralph Verney, 3 September 1646, PUR VII.
66 Dr William Denton to Sir Ralph Verney, 28 September 1648, PUR IX.
67 Brother Edmund Verney to Sir Ralph Verney, 26 April/6 May 1648, PUR IX.
68 Brother Edmund Verney to Sir Ralph Verney, 8/18 May 1648, PUR IX.
69 Brother Edmund Verney to Sir Ralph Verney, 21/31 August 1648, PUR IX. Dr William Denton to Sir Ralph Verney, 24 August 1648, PUR IX; brother Thomas Verney to Sir Ralph Verney, 19/29 August 1648, PUR IX.
70 Brother Edmund Verney to Sir Ralph Verney, 23 July/2 August 1648, PUR IX.
71 Brother Edmund Verney to Sir Ralph Verney, 31 August/10 September 1648, PUR IX.
72 Brother Thomas Verney to Sir Ralph Verney, 19/29 August 1648, PUR IX.
73 Brother Thomas Verney to Sir Ralph Verney, 17 July 1648, PUR IX.
74 For Henry's career, *supra*, Chapter 2, pp. 68–73; Edmund was rather more successful than Henry, but even after his promotion to the rank of colonel his prospects were uncertain. He lost favor with his patron and complained of his financial difficulties to Dr Denton: Dr William Denton to Sir Ralph Verney, 26 April 1649, PUR IX. He also attempted to sell his annuity because he needed ready cash: brother Edmund Verney to Sir Ralph Verney, 4 August 1647, PUR VIII.
75 He was murdered at Drogheda: Dr William Denton to Will Roads, 13 August 1649, PUR X; Dr William Denton to Sir Ralph Verney, 16 August 1649, PUR X.
76 Dr William Denton to Sir Ralph Verney, 5 December 1644, PUR VI; Doll Leeke to Sir Ralph Verney, 11 December 1644, PUR VI.
77 Sir Ralph Verney to Sir John Leeke, 6/16 December 1644, PUR VI.
78 See for example brother Edmund Verney to Sir Ralph Verney, 24 February 1643, PUR V; brother Edmund Verney to Sir Ralph Verney, 3/13 June 1648, PUR IX.
79 Brother Edmund Verney to Sir Ralph Verney, 5 December 1643, PUR V.
80 Brother Edmund Verney to Sir Ralph Verney, 23 July/2 August 1648, PUR IX.

81 Dr William Denton to Sir Ralph Verney, 28 October 1648, PUR VII.
82 Dr William Denton to Sir Ralph Verney, 31 May 1649, PUR X; Dr William Denton to Sir Ralph Verney, 28 June 1649, PUR X.
83 Alexander Denton to Sir Ralph Verney, 30 December 1672, from an unmarked box at Claydon.
84 Sir Ralph Verney to Alexander Denton, 6 January 1672/3, from an unmarked box at Claydon.
85 A list in Sir Ralph's hand dated 10 August 1673, from an unmarked box at Claydon.
86 7 November 1673, from an unmarked box at Claydon.

## CHAPTER 4 MARRIAGE: THE FEMALE PERSPECTIVE

1 Sir Ralph Verney to Sir John Denton, 21 June/1 July 1646, PUR VII.
2 Ibid.
3 Sir Ralph Verney to Mary Lady Verney, 1/11 August 1647, PUR VIII.
4 Sister Mary Verney to Mary Lady Verney, 29 September 1647, PUR VIII; Mary Lady Verney to Sir Ralph Verney, 3 October 1647, PUR VIII; Sir Ralph Verney to Mary Lady Verney, 31 October/10 November 1647, PUR VIII.
5 Mary Lady Verney to Sir Ralph Verney, 21 October 1647, PUR VIII.
6 Ibid.
7 Ibid.
8 Elizabeth Isham to Sir Ralph Verney, 29 November 1648, PUR IX.
9 Countess of Sussex to Sir Ralph Verney, received 10 February 1643, PUR V; Countess of Sussex to Sir Ralph Verney, received 17 March 1643, PUR V; sister Susan Verney to Sir Ralph Verney, 5 September 1643; PUR V; Elizabeth Isham to Sir Ralph Verney, 4 April 1644, PUR V; brother Henry Verney to Sir Ralph Verney, 20 July 1645, PUR VI.
10 Countess of Sussex to Sir Ralph Verney, received 13 January 1642, PUR V [probably misdated, should read 13 January 1643]; Countess of Sussex to Sir Ralph Verney, received 5 December 1642, PUR V; Countess of Sussex to Sir Ralph Verney, received 3 April 1643, PUR V; Countess of Sussex to Sir Ralph Verney, received 5 May 1643, PUR V; Will Roads [probably] to Sir Ralph Verney, 30 April 1645, PUR VI.

11 Sister Penelope Verney to Sir Ralph Verney, 13 February 1645, PUR VI.
12 Sister Penelope Verney to Sir Ralph Verney, 4 July 1644, PUR VI.
13 Brother Thomas Verney to Sir Ralph Verney, 20 February 1645, PUR VI.
14 Sister Susan Verney to Sir Ralph Verney [probably], 10 July 1644; PUR V; Elizabeth Isham to Sir Ralph Verney, 9 December 1644, PUR VI; sister Susan Verney to Sir Ralph Verney, 2 October 1645, PUR VI; when Mary moved in with sister Cary, Sir Ralph commented on the latter's kindness in giving Mary a half-year free diet. But Mary was expected to pay for other expenses. Sir Ralph Verney to Mary Lady Verney, 26 September/6 October 1647, PUR VIII.
15 Brother Henry Verney to Sir Ralph Verney, 1 October 1646, PUR VII.
16 Elizabeth Isham to Sir Ralph Verney, 15 August 1644, PUR VI.
17 For a discussion of the sources of patriarchal control see Jean-Louis Flandrin, *Families in Former Times: Kinship, Household and Sexuality*, Cambridge, 1979, especially Chapter 3, pp. 112–73.
18 Richard Vann, 'Toward a new lifestyle: women in preindustrial capitalism,' in R. Bridenthal and C. Koonz, *Becoming Visible: Women in European History*, Boston, 1977, p. 199–214; for his comments on widows' relative freedom see p. 193. See also Lawrence Stone, *The Crisis of the Aristocracy*, Oxford, 1965, pp. 621–2.
19 Keith Thomas, 'The double standard,' *Journal of the History of Ideas*, vol. XX, no. 2, April 1959, pp. 195–216. On this point see especially p. 210.
20 Ibid., pp. 195–7.
21 Brother Edmund Verney to Sir Ralph Verney, 13 October 1641, PUR IV; Sir Ralph Verney to Mary Lady Verney, 26 December 1647/5 January 1648, PUR VIII.
22 Sir Ralph Verney to Sir Roger Burgoyne, 1/11 February 1646, PUR VII.
23 Sir Ralph Verney to Sir John Leeke, 25 January/4 February 1646, PUR VII.
24 Sir Ralph Verney to Countess of Barrymore, 13 November 1641, PUR IV.
25 Sir Ralph Verney to Sir Roger Burgoyne, 20 February/1 March 1648, PUR VIII.
26 Sir Ralph Verney to Sir John Leeke, 25 January/4 February 1646, PUR VII.

27 Dr William Denton to Sir Ralph Verney, 17 May 1649, PUR X.
28 Countess of Sussex to Sir Ralph Verney, received 3 November 1640, PUR IV; Sir Roger Burgoyne to Sir Ralph Verney, 25 June 1645, PUR VI, brother Henry Verney to Sir Ralph Verney, 5 October 1645, PUR VI.
29 Sir Roger Burgoyne to Sir Ralph Verney, 14 October 1645, PUR V.
30 Brother Henry Verney to Sir Ralph Verney, 5 October 1645, PUR VI.
31 Dr William Denton to Sir Ralph Verney, 1 August 1645, PUR VI; Dr William Denton to Sir Ralph Verney, 21 September 1645, PUR VI; brother Henry Verney [his hand] to Sir Ralph Verney, 21 September 1645, PUR VI; brother Henry Verney to Sir Ralph Verney, 3 September 1646, PUR VII; Dr William Denton to Sir Ralph Verney, 25 February 1647, PUR VIII.
32 Magdaline Faulkner to Sir Ralph Verney [probably], 26 September 1641, PUR IV.
33 Ibid.
34 Sir Ralph Verney to Mary Lady Verney, 14/24 March 1647, PUR VIII.
35 Sir Ralph Verney to Mary Lady Verney, 28 February/10 March 1647, PUR VIII.
36 Sir Ralph Verney to brother Henry Verney, 21/31 January 1646, PUR VII.
37 Sister Mary Verney to Will Roads, 17 July 1646, PUR VII.
38 Sister Mary Verney to Mary Lady Verney, 1 May 1648, PUR IX.
39 Sister Mary Verney to Sir Ralph Verney [a copy], 28 August 1648, PUR IX.
40 Sister Mary Verney to Sir Ralph Verney, 15 August 1648, PUR IX.
41 Dr William Denton to Sir Ralph Verney, 25 February 1650, PUR X; Dr William Denton to Will Roads, 5 January 1649, PUR IX; Dr William Denton to Sir Ralph Verney, 4 October 1649, PUR X.
42 Sister Mary Verney to Sir Ralph Verney, 12 June 1648, PUR IX; Sir Ralph Verney to sister Mary Verney, 30 July/9 August 1648, PUR IX; sister Mary Verney to Sir Ralph Verney, 12/22 August 1648, PUR IX.
43 Brother Henry Verney [his hand] to Sir Ralph Verney [undoubtedly], received 19/29 October 1646, PUR VII.
44 Mary Lady Verney to Sir Ralph Verney, 25 February 1647 [probably of that year], PUR VII.
45 Mary Lady Verney to Sir Ralph Verney, 22 July 1647, PUR VIII.

46 Sir Ralph Verney to Mary Lady Verney, 26 September/6 October 1647, PUR VIII.
47 Sister Mary Verney to Sir Ralph Verney, 12/22 August 1648, PUR IX.
48 Sister Mary Verney to Sir Ralph Verney, 15/25 August 1648, PUR IX; sister Mary Verney to Sir Ralph Verney, 15/25 August 1648, PUR IX; Dr William Denton to Will Roads, 5 January 1648/9, PUR IX.
49 Sister Mary Verney to Sir Ralph Verney, 3/13 August 1649, PUR X.
50 Dr William Denton to Sir Ralph Verney, 23 July 1649, PUR X.
51 Dr William Denton to Sir Ralph Verney, 6 August 1649, PUR X.
52 Dr William Denton to Sir Ralph Verney, 4 October 1649, PUR X.
53 Sister Mary Verney to Sir Ralph Verney, 3/13 August 1649, PUR X.
54 Mary Lady Verney to Sir Ralph Verney, 10 August 1647, PUR VIII.
55 Brother Henry Verney to Sir Ralph Verney, 30 October 1645, PUR VI.
56 Mary Lady Verney to Sir Ralph Verney, 4 March 1647, PUR VIII.
57 Ibid. This was Mary Lady Verney's opinion but cousin Doll Leeke made a similar observation. Doll Leeke [her hand] to Mary Lady Verney, n.d., second undated letter after 12/22 December 1647, PUR VIII.
58 Sir John Leeke to Sir Ralph Verney, 11 September 1645, PUR VI.
59 Brother Henry Verney to Sir Ralph Verney, 5 October 1645, PUR VI.
60 Mary Lady Verney to Sir Ralph Verney, 10 August 1647, PUR VIII.
61 Brother Henry Verney to Sir Ralph Verney, 13 November 1645, PUR VI; brother Henry Verney to Sir Ralph Verney, 11 December 1645, PUR VI.
62 When Elizabeth was 14 years old, Mary Lady Verney commented that she was too old for a school. Mary Lady Verney to Sir Ralph Verney, 26 August 1647, PUR VIII.
63 Mary Lady Verney to Sir Ralph Verney, 10 August 1647, PUR VIII.
64 Brother Henry Verney to Sir Ralph Verney, 11 December 1645, PUR VI.
65 Mary Lady Verney to Sir Ralph Verney, 4 March 1647, PUR VIII.
66 Part of Mary's portion had been put out to Sir Martin Lester and

the payment had fallen due in 1642 but had not been collected: Mary Lady Verney to Sir Ralph Verney, 10 February 1648, PUR VIII.

67 Sir Ralph Verney to Mary Lady Verney, 28 February/10 March 1647, PUR VIII.

68 Ibid.

69 Mary Lady Verney to Sir Ralph Verney, 4 February 1647, PUR VIII; Sir Ralph Verney to Mary Lady Verney, 19/29 September 1647, PUR VIII.

70 Sir Ralph Verney to Mr Edmund Brown, 21/31 January 1647, PUR VIII; Sir Ralph Verney to Mary Lady Verney, 24 January/3 February 1647, PUR VIII.

71 Sir Ralph Verney to Mary Lady Verney, 24 January/3 February 1647, PUR VIII.

72 Mary Lady Verney to Sir Ralph Verney, 26 August 1647, PUR VIII.

73 Mary Lady Verney to Sir Ralph Verney, 5 September 1647, PUR VIII.

74 Dr William Denton to Sir Ralph Verney, 22 October 1649, PUR X.

75 Sister Mary Verney to 'Dear Parent' [Dr Denton, undoubtedly], received 19/29 December 1648, PUR IX.

76 Ibid.

77 Frances Parthenope Verney, *Memoirs of the Verney Family*, London, 1892, vol. II, p. 390.

78 Dr William Denton to Sir Ralph Verney, 11 January 1649, PUR IX.

79 Countess of Sussex to Sir Ralph Verney, received 27 May 1642, PUR IV; Lady Cary Gardiner to Sir Ralph Verney, received 28 July 1642, PUR IV. She was the only daughter who was married before Sir Edmund's death.

80 Sir Ralph Verney to sister Susan Verney, 15/25 November 1644, PUR VI.

81 See Chapter 2, pp. 41–4.

82 Brother Henry Verney to Sir Ralph Verney, 6 February 1645, PUR VI.

83 Brother Henry Verney to Sir Ralph Verney, 14 February 1645, PUR VI.

84 Ephraim Thorne to Sir Ralph Verney, 13 February 1645, PUR VI.

85 Sir Ralph Verney to brother Henry Verney, 14/24 February 1645, PUR VI; some of Penelope's money had been invested by Sir Ralph with their uncle, Alexander Denton, but the death of this

uncle and the financial upheavals connected with the war had resulted in her being unable to collect any interest on the bond. Sister Penelope Verney to Sir Ralph Verney, 22 May 1645, PUR VI; her portion had been invested in the alnage, and it is probable that Alexander Denton's involvement was part of the alnage investment: Sir Ralph Verney to brother Henry Verney, 14/24 February 1647, PUR VII.

86 Brother Henry Verney to Sir Ralph Verney, 20 February 1645, PUR VI; Sir Ralph Verney to brother Henry Verney, 28 February 1645, PUR VI; Sir Ralph Verney to brother Henry Verney, 21/31 March 1645, PUR VI.

87 Brother Henry Verney to Sir Ralph Verney, 20 February 1645, PUR VI.

88 Penelope's appeal, sister Penelope Verney to Sir Ralph Verney, 20 February 1645, PUR VI; Henry's appeal, brother Henry Verney to Sir Ralph Verney, 27 February 1645, PUR VI; Thomas's appeal, brother Thomas Verney to Sir Ralph Verney, 20 February 1645, PUR VI.

89 Sister Penelope Verney to Sir Ralph Verney, 20 February 1645, PUR VI.

90 Sir Ralph Verney to brother Henry Verney, 21 February/3 March 1645, PUR VI.

91 Ibid.

92 Sister Penelope Verney to Sir Ralph Verney, 20 February 1645, PUR VI.

93 Sir Ralph Verney to brother Henry Verney, 28 February 1645, PUR VI.

94 George Thorne to Henry Verney, 13 February 1645, PUR VI.

95 Brother Thomas Verney to Sir Ralph Verney, 20 February 1645, PUR VI.

96 Sir Ralph Verney to brother Henry Verney, 21 February/3 March 1645, PUR VI.

97 See Chapter 2, p. 38.

98 Brother Henry Verney [his hand] to Sir Ralph Verney [undoubtedly], 1 October 1646, PUR VII.

99 Ibid.

100 Ibid.

101 Brother Henry Verney to Sir Ralph Verney, 3 April 1645, PUR VI.

102 Penelope Verney to Will Roads, 18 September 1646, PUR VII; on Penelope's life at Claydon see also sister Penelope Verney to Mary Lady Verney, received 20/30 June 1645, PUR VI.

103 Sir Ralph Verney to Dr William Denton, 11/21 October 1646, PUR VII.
104 Ibid.
105 Ibid.
106 Sir Ralph Verney to brother Henry Verney, 30 October/9 November 1646, PUR VII.
107 Ibid.
108 Brother Henry Verney to Sir Ralph Verney, 19 October 1646, PUR VII.
109 Sir Ralph Verney to Joyce Verney, 1 July 1643 [probable year], PUR V.
110 Sister Penelope Verney to Sir Ralph Verney, 3 February 1649, PUR IX
111 Sister Penelope Verney to Sir Ralph Verney, 30 September 1649, PUR X.
112 Sir Ralph Verney to Mary Lady Verney, 5/15 September 1647, PUR VIII.
113 Sir Ralph Verney to Mary Lady Verney, 14/24 February 1647, PUR VIII.
114 Dr William Denton to Sir Ralph Verney, 20 December 1649, PUR X.
115 Sister Penelope Verney to Sir Ralph Verney, 6 November 1649, PUR X.
116 See Chapter 2, note 112.
117 Brother Henry Verney to Sir Ralph Verney, 12 March 1646, PUR VII.
118 Brother Henry Verney to Sir Ralph Verney, 23 April 1646, PUR VII.
119 Sir Ralph Verney to brother Henry Verney, 10/20 May 1646, PUR VII.
120 Brother Henry Verney to Sir Ralph Verney, 14 May 1646, PUR VII.
121 Sister Susan Verney to Sir Ralph Verney, 16 July 1646, PUR VII; on Margaret's husband's personality see also Doll Leeke to Sir Ralph Verney, n.d., second undated letter following 12/22 December 1647, PUR VIII.
122 Brother Edmund Verney to Sir Ralph Verney, 23 July/2 August 1648, PUR IX.
123 Dr William Denton to Sir Ralph Verney, 30 March 1648, PUR VIII.
124 Brother Edmund Verney to Sir Ralph Verney, received 21/31 July 1648, PUR IX.
125 Indenture dated 3 July 1658 from an unmarked box at Claydon;

copy of an agreement in Sir Ralph Verney's hand dated 30 January 1657 from an unmarked box at Claydon.

126 Sir Ralph Verney to brother Edmund Verney, 30 July/9 August 1648, PUR IX.

127 Brother Edmund Verney to Sir Ralph Verney, 16/26 August 1648, PUR IX.

128 5 February 1665 from an unmarked box at Claydon.

129 Sir Ralph Verney to Richard Alport, 16/26 May 1645, PUR VI; Sir Ralph Verney to Sir Roger Burgoyne, 25 January/4 February 1646, PUR VII; Sir John Denton to Sir Ralph Verney, 30 April 1646, PUR VII; for a reliable and detailed account of this complicated business see especially Sir John Denton to Sir Ralph Verney, 10 July 1646, PUR VII.

130 Sister Susan Verney to Sir Ralph Verney, 1 October 1646, PUR VII.

131 Sir Ralph Verney to Mrs Lesly, 4/14 September 1645, PUR VI; Sir John Leeke to Sir Ralph Verney, 28 October 1645, PUR VI; Nathanial Hobart to Sir Ralph Verney, 17/27 June 1646, PUR VII.

132 Sister Susan Verney to Sir Ralph Verney, 7 August 1645, PUR VI; sister Susan Verney to Sir Ralph Verney, 30 April 1646, PUR VII.

133 Brother Henry Verney to Sir Ralph Verney, 13 March 1645, PUR VI; Sir John Leeke to Sir Ralph Verney, received 9/19 May 1645, PUR VI; Sir John Leeke to Sir Ralph Verney, 8 January 1646, PUR VII.

134 Sister Susan Verney to Sir Ralph Verney, received 10/20 October 1644, PUR VI; Doll Leeke to Sir Ralph Verney, 11 December 1644, PUR VI.

135 Sir John Leeke to Sir Ralph Verney, 21 May 1646, PUR VII; in an earlier letter Alport's indebtedness is said to be £800 according to Uncle Leeke; Sir John Leeke to Sir Ralph Verney, 15 May 1645, PUR VI; for a list of Alport's holdings see Sir John Leeke to Sir Ralph Verney, 2 April 1645, PUR VI.

136 Sir John Leeke to Sir Ralph Verney, 11 September 1645, PUR VI.

137 Sir John Leeke to Sir Ralph Verney, 21 August 1645, PUR VI.

138 Sir John Denton to Sir Ralph Verney, 10 June 1646, PUR VII; Sir Ralph Verney to Sir John Leeke, 21 June/1 July 1646, PUR VII.

139 Ibid.

140 Sir Ralph Verney to Sir Roger Burgoyne, 21 June/1 July 1646, PUR VII; cousin Hobart also believed that Susan could not break it off without loss of honor; Nathanial Hobart to Sir Ralph Verney received 17/27 June 1646, PUR VII.

141 Sister Susan Alport to Sir Ralph Verney, 22 July 1647, PUR VIII.

142 Sir Ralph Verney to brother Henry Verney, 6/16 March 1645, PUR VI; brother Henry Verney to Sir Ralph Verney, 5 June 1645, PUR VI; sister Susan Verney to Sir Ralph Verney, 12 June 1645, PUR VI; Sir John Leeke to Sir Ralph Verney, 23 June 1645, PUR VI; sister Susan Verney to Sir Ralph Verney, 31 July 1645, PUR VI; sister Susan Verney to Sir Ralph Verney, 7 August 1645, PUR VI; Sir John Leeke to Sir Ralph Verney, 8 January 1646, PUR VII.

143 Brother Henry Verney to Sir Ralph Verney, 17 April 1645, PUR VI; brother Henry Verney to Sir Ralph Verney, 22 May 1645, PUR VI; brother Henry Verney to Sir Ralph Verney, 1 January 1646, PUR VII.

144 Sir John Leeke to Sir Ralph Verney, received 9/19 May 1645, PUR VI; Sir John Leeke to Sir Ralph Verney, 16 October 1645, PUR VI; Sir John Leeke to Sir Ralph Verney, 21 May 1646, PUR VII.

145 Sir John Leeke to Sir Ralph Verney, 21 August 1645, PUR VI; Sir John Leeke to Sir Ralph Verney, 28 August 1645, PUR VI; Sir John Leeke to Sir Ralph Verney, 11 September 1645, PUR VI; Sir John Leeke to Sir Ralph Verney, 20 November 1645, PUR VI; Sir John Leeke to Sir Ralph Verney, received 24 December 1645, PUR VI; Sir John Leeke to Sir Ralph Verney, 5 February 1646, PUR VII.

146 Sir John Leeke to Sir Ralph Verney, received 9/19 May 1645, PUR VI.

147 Sister Susan Verney to Sir Ralph Verney, 12 February 1646, PUR VI.

148 Sister Susan Verney to Sir Ralph Verney , 20 November 1645; PUR VI; see also Sir Ralph's letter to Sir Roger Burgoyne in which he admits that he is engaged to pay £600 but instructs Burgoyne not to present those documents if his own terms are not accepted by Alport's side: Sir Ralph Verney to Sir Roger Burgoyne, 25 January/4 February 1646, PUR VII.

149 Sir John Leeke to Sir Ralph Verney, 12 June 1645, PUR VI, in which Sir John openly declared his impatience with Sir Ralph's hard bargaining; Sir John Leeke to Sir Ralph Verney, 23 April 1646, PUR VII.

150 Sir Ralph Verney to sister Susan Verney, 23 August/3 September 1646, PUR VII.

151 Sister Susan Verney to Sir Ralph Verney, 23 June 1645, PUR VI.

152 Brother Henry Verney to Sir Ralph Verney, 9 April 1646, PUR VII.

153 Brother Henry Verney to Sir Ralph Verney, 21 September 1645, PUR VI; brother Henry Verney to Sir Ralph Verney, 14 June 1646, PUR VII; brother Henry Verney to Sir Ralph Verney, 3 September 1646, PUR VII.

154 Sir Ralph Verney to brother Henry Verney, 6/16 March 1645, PUR VI; Sir Ralph Verney to Sir John Leeke, 11/21 August 1645, PUR VI; Sir Ralph Verney to Sir John Leeke, 29 August/8 September 1645, PUR VI.

155 Sister Susan Verney to Mary Lady Verney, 3 July 1645, PUR VI; sister Susan Verney to Sir Ralph Verney, 24 July 1645, PUR VI.

156 Sir Ralph Verney to sister Susan Verney, 6/16 November 1646, PUR VII; sister Susan Verney to Sir Ralph Verney, 11 October 1647; Sir Ralph knew that the 'Old Knight', i.e. Bachus, was untrustworthy: Sir Ralph Verney to Sir Roger Burgoyne, 7/17 December 1645, PUR VI.

157 Sir Ralph tried to make it appear that he was surprised by Bachus's behavior: Sir Ralph Verney to Sir Roger Burgoyne, 14/24 December 1645, PUR VI.

158 Sister Susan Verney to Sir Ralph Verney, 19 November 1646, PUR VII; Dr William Denton to Sir Ralph Verney, 19 November 1646, PUR VII; on Bachus see also Burgoyne's letter to Sir Ralph in which he refers to the 'Old Juggler,' undoubtedly referring to Bachus: Sir Roger Burgoyne to Sir Ralph Verney, 19 November 1646, PUR VII; Susan finally succeeded in collecting what was due to her: sister Susan Verney to Sir Ralph Verney, 3 December 1646, PUR VII.

159 Sir Ralph Verney to sister Susan Verney, 23 October/2 November 1646, PUR VII; sister Susan Verney to Sir Ralph Verney, 29 October 1646, PUR VII; Sir Ralph Verney to sister Susan Verney, 6/16 November 1646, PUR VII.

160 Sister Susan Verney to Sir Ralph Verney, 21 August 1645, PUR VI; for other apologies made by Susan to Sir Ralph see sister Susan Verney to Mary Lady Verney, received 10/20 September 1645, PUR VI; sister Susan Verney to Sir Ralph Verney, 11 September 1645, PUR VI; for uncle Leeke's apology to Sir Ralph see Sir John Leeke to Sir Ralph Verney, 21 May 1646, PUR VII.

161 Sister Susan Verney to Sir Ralph Verney, 7 February 1650, PUR X.

162 Memorandum in Sir Ralph Verney's hand, 10/20 March 1650, PUR X.

163 Sir Ralph Verney to brother Henry Verney, 26 April/6 May 1646, PUR VII; brother Henry Verney to Sir Ralph Verney, 7 May 1646, PUR VII.

164 See note 18.
165 Sir Edmund Verney to Sir Ralph Verney, Easter Day 1639, PUR III; Sir Edmund Verney to Sir Ralph Verney, 25 April 1639, PUR III; Sir Ralph's grandmother wrote to Sir Ralph referring to her son-in-law that 'I hear he is without exception, only his religion, but that is such a cut to me that it hath a most killed me': Lady Susannah Denton to Sir Ralph Verney, 21 May 1639, PUR III; Lady Susannah Denton to Sir Ralph Verney, 4 May 1639, PUR III.
166 Lady Margaret Poulteney to Sir Ralph Verney, 28 May 1638, PUR III.
167 Lady Margaret Poulteney to Sir Ralph Verney, 9 May 1639, PUR III.
168 Lady Margaret Poulteney to Sir Ralph Verney, 18 May 1639, PUR III; Stone, 1965, op. cit., p. 622.
169 Sir Ralph Verney to Lady Margaret Eure, 28 June 1642, PUR IV.
170 Stone, 1965, op. cit., p. 621.
171 Joane Lambe to Sir Ralph Verney, 29 November 1649, PUR X.
172 Quoted in Stone, 1965, op. cit., p. 622.
173 C. H. White (ed.), *The Complete Peerage*, London, 1953, vol. XII, p. 530.
174 Countess of Warwick to Sir Ralph Verney, received 19/29 June 1646, PUR VII.
175 Quoted in Stone, 1965, op. cit., p. 622.
176 Countess of Warwick to Sir Ralph Verney, received 19/29 June 1646, PUR VII.
177 A list of code names in Sir Ralph Verney's hand, n.d., following 1 January 1646, PUR VII.
178 Stone, 1965, op. cit., p. 621.
179 Ibid.

## CHAPTER 5 CHILDREN, SERVANTS AND PARENTS

1 J.-L. Flandrin, *Families in Former Times: Kinship, Household and Sexuality*, Cambridge, 1979; Lawrence Stone, *The Family, Sex and Marriage: In England 1500–1800*, London, 1977; see also Professor Stone's earlier book, *The Crisis of the Aristocracy*, Oxford, 1965, especially Chapters XI and XII. Randolph Trumbach, *The Rise of the Egalitarian Family*, New York, 1978, treats the eighteenth century but offers provocative insights into the whole debate about attitudes toward children.
2 Ever since the publication of P. Ariès, *Centuries of Childhood: A*

*Social History of Family Life*, New York, 1962, forced historians to rethink concepts of childhood and parental attitudes, both British and American historians have been debating the nature of attitudes toward children and the causes and nature of changing attitudes and practices regarding them. See for example the relevant articles in M. Gordon (ed.), *The American Family in Social-Historical Perspective*, New York, 1978, now in its second edition, which deals exclusively with American historiography.

3 See for example Flandrin, 1979, op. cit., pp. 130–1; Stone, 1977, op. cit., pp. 174–8. For some sense of the nature of the debate among American historians see Gordon, 1978, op. cit., pp. 153–6.

4 Edmund S. Morgan, *The Puritan Family*, New York, revised edition 1966, especially pp. 75–9; Lloyd de Mause, *The History of Childhood*, New York, 1974, pp. 1–73. Stone believes that one of the reasons infants were sent out to wet nurses was to reduce the personal difficulties evoked by the high infant mortality. Stone, 1977, op. cit., p. 107.

5 For a good brief demographic history of Sir Ralph's generation and children see Stone, 1977, op. cit., p. 74; for the demographic profile of the early seventeenth century see ibid., Chapter 2, pp. 42–82.

6 Dr William Denton to Sir Ralph Verney, 9 November 1648, PUR IX.

7 Sir Ralph Verney to Mary Lady Verney, 8/18 August 1647, PUR VIII; nurse keepers could be hired by the week, Sir Ralph Verney to Mary Lady Verney, 9/19 January 1648, PUR VIII.

8 Richard Trotter to Sir Ralph Verney, 31 October 1648, PUR IX; Sir Ralph Verney to Mary Lady Verney, 5/15 December 1647, PUR VIII.

9 Mary Lady Verney to Sir Ralph Verney, 18 November 1647, PUR VIII.

10 Ibid.

11 Richard Trotter to Sir Ralph Verney, 8 October 1648, PUR IX.

12 Sir Ralph Verney to M. LaBoir, 17/27 August 1648, PUR IX.

13 Ibid.

14 For a sensitive and insightful treatment of the complexities of the master/servant dynamic in a different context, see Eugene D. Genovese, *Roll Jordan Roll: The World the Slaves Made*, New York, 1976, especially pp. 143–9.

15 Richard Trotter to Sir Ralph Verney, 21 October 1648, PUR IX.

16 Brother Edmund Verney to nephew Edmund Verney, 21/31 August 1648, PUR IX.

17 Brother Edmund Verney to 'My Dear Father,' 12 July 1648, PUR IX.
18 Elizabeth Heath to Sir Ralph Verney, 1 November 1646, PUR VII. Edmund was 10 and his sister 7 years old when this was written.
19 Mary Lady Verney to Sir Ralph Verney, 9 March 1647/8, PUR VIII; Richard Trotter to Sir Ralph Verney, 12 November 1648, PUR IX.
20 Dr William Denton to Mary Lady Verney, 5 October 1648, PUR IX.
21 The belief that a mother's milk could transmit character traits was long-standing. See D. Hunt, *Parents and Children in History*, New York, 1972, p. 101; Stone, 1977, op. cit., pp. 426–7.
22 Mary Lady Verney to Sir Ralph Verney, 10 August 1647, PUR VIII.
23 Sir Ralph Verney to Nat Hobart, 3/13 September 1645, PUR VI.
24 Brother Thomas Verney to Sir Ralph Verney, 22 March 1642/3, PUR V.
25 Col. Henry Verney to Will Roads, 16 February 1646, PUR VII.
26 Sir Ralph Verney to Mary Lady Verney, 26 September/6 October 1647, PUR VIII. See also Sir Ralph's accusation against a loose-tongued servant boy: Sir Ralph Verney to Mr Ogleby, 4/14 April 1646, PUR VII; Sir Ralph's displeasure also meant that the boy would have difficulty in finding another place: Mr Ogleby to Mary Lady Verney, 21 May 1646, PUR VII.
27 See for example Mary Lady Verney to Sir Ralph Verney, 3 October 1647, PUR VIII.
28 Sir Ralph Verney to Mary Lady Verney, 17/27 October 1647, PUR VIII.
29 Mary Lady Verney to Sir Ralph Verney, 18 November 1647, PUR VIII.
30 Susan Alport to Sir Ralph Verney, 7 February 1649/50, PUR X. She probably had about £600 to put out at interest.
31 Brother Edmund Verney to Sir Ralph Verney, n.d., following third undated letter May 1681, PUR IX.
32 See for example Aunt Poulteney to Sir Ralph Verney, 31 October 1638, PUR III; Mary Lady Verney to Sir Ralph Verney, 18 August 1647, PUR VIII, in which Lady Verney comments that sister Cary's nurse's house has the pox and the baby was removed.
33 Sir Ralph Verney to Dr William Denton, 24 October/3 November 1647, PUR VIII; Dr William Denton to Sir Ralph Verney, 18 October 1647, PUR VIII: Sir Ralph Verney to Mary Lady Verney, 14/24 November 1647, PUR VIII.

34 Sir Ralph Verney to Doll Leeke, 27 December/6 January 1644, PUR VI.
35 Dr William Denton to Sir Ralph Verney, 22 October 1649, PUR X. The French seem to have already begun using them: William Wakefield to Sir Ralph Verney, 16 August 1649, PUR X.
36 Sir Ralph Verney to Dr William Denton, 24 October/3 November 1647, PUR VIII.
37 Stone, 1977, op. cit., pp. 68–70; P. Laslett, *The World We Have Lost*, London, 1965, pp. 123–6. For a discussion of the high mortality rates and their causes in France, see Flandrin, 1979, op. cit., Chapter IV, especially pp. 198–206. See also Michael W. Flinn, *The European Demographic System*, Baltimore, Maryland, 1981, especially Chapter 4. This also contains an excellent recent bibliography.
38 Dr William Denton to Sir Ralph Verney, 28 October 1647, PUR VIII.
39 Ibid.
40 Sir Ralph Verney to Dr William Denton, 24 October/3 November 1647, PUR VIII.
41 Sir Ralph Verney to Mr Robert Busby, 12/22 September 1647, PUR VIII.
42 Sir Ralph Verney to Dr William Denton, 26 September/6 October 1647, PUR VIII.
43 Sir Ralph Verney to Mary Lady Verney, 5/15 December 1647, PUR VIII.
44 Stone, 1977, op. cit., pp. 105–6; the death of infants who were not heirs sometimes appears to have evoked relief rather than grief among the propertied classes in France: see Flandrin, 1979, op. cit., p. 153.
45 Sir Roger Burgoyne to Sir Ralph Verney, 4 June 1646, PUR VII.
46 Mary Lady Verney to Sir Ralph Verney, 27 July 1647, PUR VIII.
47 Sir Ralph Verney to Mary Lady Verney, 17/27 August 1967, PUR VIII.
48 Dr William Denton to Sir Ralph Verney, 4 November 1647, PUR VIII.
49 Mary Lady Verney to Sir Ralph Verney, n.d. [undoubtedly 28 October 1647], PUR VIII.
50 Mary Lady Verney to Sir Ralph Verney, 1 November 1647, PUR VIII.
51 Mary Lady Verney to Sir Ralph Verney, 4 November 1647, PUR VIII.
52 See for example Mary Lady Verney to Sir Ralph Verney, 11 November 1647, PUR VIII.

53 Mary Lady Verney to Sir Ralph Verney, 23 December 1647, PUR VIII.
54 Mary Lady Verney to Sir Ralph Verney, 30 December 1647, PUR VIII.
55 See, for example, Sir Ralph Verney to Mary Lady Verney, 31 October/10 November 1647, PUR VIII; Sir Ralph Verney to Mary Lady Verney, 14/24 November 1647, PUR VIII; Sir Ralph Verney to Mary Lady Verney, 21 November/1 December 1647, PUR VIII.
56 See for example the announcement of brother Edmund Verney's death: Dr William Denton to Sir Ralph Verney, 11 August 1649, PUR X; James Buck to Sir Ralph Verney, 8/18 November 1649, PUR X; which confirmed the doctor's previous announcement, and in which his comrade-in-arms asks for a settlement of money owed to him 'being confident you will not let so faithfull a friend of your brothers suffer in serving of him the sum being so small and the debt so just.'
57 Sir Ralph Verney to Dr William Denton, 10/20 October 1647, PUR VIII. This is the shortest letter he wrote to any family member during this period.
58 Brother Edmund Verney to Mary Lady Verney [undoubtedly], 28 October 1647, PUR VIII; Margaret Eure Sherard to Sir Ralph Verney, 12/22 December 1647, PUR VIII; Sir Roger Burgoyne to Sir Ralph Verney, 4 November 1647, PUR VIII.
59 Sir Ralph Verney to Mary Lady Verney, 28 February/10 March 1647, PUR VIII.
60 Sir Ralph Verney to Mary Lady Verney, 21 November/1 December 1647, PUR VIII.
61 Nathanial Hobart to Sir Ralph Verney, 26 April/6 May 1645, PUR VI for quote; for the state of their financial affairs see also notes 191 and 192 to Chapter 2.
62 Doll Leeke to Mary Lady Verney, 29 May 1645, PUR VI.
63 Sir Roger Burgoyne to Sir Ralph Verney, 25 June 1645, PUR VI.
64 See for example Aunt Elizabeth Isham to Sir Ralph Verney, 31 December 1646, PUR VII.
65 Susan Alport to Sir Ralph Verney, 22 July 1647, PUR VIII.
66 Mary Lady Verney to Sir Ralph Verney, 31 December 1646, PUR VII.
67 Stone, 1965, op. cit., pp. 619; Flandrin also points to confinements as a cause of deaths of wives, 1979, op. cit., pp. 217–19.
68 Mary Lady Verney to Sir Ralph Verney, 12 June 1648, PUR IX.
69 Sister Susan Verney to Sir Ralph Verney, 11 August 1649 [marked 1647], PUR X.

70 Sir Ralph Verney to Mary Lady Verney, 18/28 July 1647, PUR VIII.
71 Mary Lady Verney to Sir Ralph Verney, 4 August 1647, PUR VIII; having arrived in January she is still the following month relying on the reports of others: Mary Lady Verney to Sir Ralph Verney, 11 February 1647, PUR VIII; in March she is unselfconsciously telling her husband that she had yet to see him herself: Mary Lady Verney to Sir Ralph Verney, 4 March 1647, PUR VIII.
72 Sir Ralph Verney to Mary Lady Verney, 5/15 September 1647, PUR VIII.
73 Dr William Denton to Sir Ralph Verney, 28 October 1647, PUR VIII.
74 Sir Ralph Verney to Mary Lady Verney, 28 February/10 March 1647, PUR VIII.
75 Sir Ralph Verney to Mary Lady Verney, 5/15 September 1647, PUR VIII.
76 Dr William Denton to Sir Ralph Verney, 17 August 1648, PUR IX; Lady Verney also commented that 'he hath an imperfection in his speech'; Mary Lady Verney to Sir Ralph Verney, 10 August 1647, PUR VIII.
77 Sister Susan Verney to Sir Ralph Verney, n.d., following 19 April 1645, PUR VII.
78 Margaret Eure to Sir Ralph Verney, received 20 February 1645, PUR VI.
79 Sir Ralph Verney to Mary Lady Verney, 14/24 March 1647, PUR VIII.
80 Sir Ralph Verney to Mr Lambert, n.d. November 1649, PUR X; Sir Ralph Verney to William Wakefield, 22 August/1 September 1647, PUR VIII contains the warning against poxy letters.
81 Mr Robert Busby to Mary Lady Verney, 26 May 1646, PUR VII.
82 Sir Ralph Verney to Mr Robert Busby, 6/16 September 1646, PUR VII; Sir Ralph Verney to Mr Robert Busby, 30 August/9 September 1646, PUR VII; Mary Lady Verney to Will Roads, 24 July 1647 [probably], PUR VIII which indicates that she borrowed money from Busby; Sir Ralph Verney to Mr Robert Busby, 7/17 November 1647, PUR VIII; Mary Lady Verney to Sir Ralph Verney, 18 November 1647, PUR VIII.
83 Mr Robert Busby to Mary Lady Verney, 26 May 1646, PUR VII; Sir Ralph Verney to Mr Robert Busby, 28 June/8 July 1646, PUR VII.
84 Sir Ralph Verney to Mr Robert Busby, 23 August/2 September 1646, PUR VII.

85 Sir Ralph Verney to Mr Robert Busby, 30 August/9 September 1646, PUR VII.
86 Sir Ralph Verney to Mr Robert Busby, 11/21 July 1647, PUR VIII.
87 Sir Ralph Verney to Mr Robert Busby, 7/17 November 1647, PUR VIII.
88 Mary Lady Verney to Sir Ralph Verney, 18 November 1647, PUR VIII.
89 Ibid.
90 Sir Ralph Verney to Mr Robert Busby, 5/15 December 1647, PUR VIII.
91 Sir Ralph Verney to Mr Robert Busby, 12/22 December 1647, PUR VIII.
92 Mr Robert Busby to Sir Ralph Verney, 23 December 1647, PUR VIII.
93 Mr Robert Busby to Sir Ralph Verney, 2 December 1647, PUR VIII.
94 Mary Lady Verney to Sir Ralph Verney, 23 December 1647, PUR VIII.
95 Sir Ralph Verney to Mary Lady Verney, 26 December/5 January 1647/8, PUR VIII.
96 Ibid.
97 Sir Ralph Verney to Mr Robert Busby, 2/12 January 1647/8, PUR VIII.
98 Sir Ralph Verney to Mr Robert Busby, 9/19 January 1647/8, PUR VIII.
99 Mary Lady Verney to Sir Ralph Verney, 3 January 1647/8, PUR VIII.
100 Mary Lady Verney to Sir Ralph Verney, 10 February 1647/8, PUR VIII.
101 Mr Robert Busby to Sir Ralph Verney, 26 June 1648, PUR IX.
102 Sir Ralph Verney to Mr Robert Busby, 30 July/9 August 1648, PUR IX.
103 Mr Robert Busby to Sir Ralph Verney, 27 July 1648, PUR IX.
104 Sir Ralph Verney to Mr Robert Busby, 1/11 July 1648, PUR IX.
105 Mr Robert Busby to Sir Ralph Verney, 9 December 1648, PUR IX.
106 Sir Ralph Verney to Mr Robert Busby, 7/17 January 1648/9, PUR IX.
107 Mary Lady Verney to Sir Ralph Verney, 18 November 1647, PUR VIII.
108 Ibid.

109 Margaret Sherard to Mary Lady Verney, n.d., following 3/13 March 1649 [probably 1648/49], PUR IX.
110 Ibid.
111 Dr William Denton to Mary Lady Verney, 11 April 1645, PUR VI.
112 Mary Lady Verney to Sir Ralph Verney, 11 February 1647, PUR VIII; Dr William Denton to Sir Ralph Verney, 14 January 1647, PUR VIII.
113 Sir Ralph Verney to Dr William Denton, 23 May/2 June 1645, PUR VI.
114 Ibid.
115 Mary Lady Verney to Sir Ralph Verney, 12 September 1647, PUR VIII.
116 Dr William Denton to Mary Lady Verney, 11 May 1648, PUR IX.
117 Ibid.
118 Dr William Denton to Sir Ralph Verney, 11 April 1650, PUR X.
119 Mary Lady Verney to Sir Ralph Verney, 10 March 1647, PUR VIII.
120 Sir Ralph Verney to Mary Lady Verney, 7/17 March 1647, PUR VIII.
121 Ibid.

## CHAPTER 6 CONCLUSION

1 William Goode, 'World revolutions and family matters,' in Arlene S. Skolnick and Jerome H. Skolnick (eds), *Family in Transition*, Boston and Toronto, 1977, pp. 47–58 (quote p. 48).
2 Clandestine marriages were a reality among the propertied classes. By the end of the seventeenth century pressure on parental control of mate selection and legal confusions allowed circumvention in increasing numbers. This led to the passing of the Marriage Act in the middle of the eighteenth century which made clandestine marriage more difficult. Lawrence Stone, *The Family, Sex and Marriage: In England 1500–1800*, London, 1977, pp. 32–7.
3 Lawrence Stone, *The Crisis of the Aristocracy*, Oxford, 1965, pp. 624–5, p. 671. Flandrin also suggests that the rights of children began to be considered during the seventeenth century. None the less, she points out that 'rather than the rights of the child . . . it was the duties of the parents which underwent development.' J.-L. Flandrin, *Families in Former Times: Kinship, Household and Sexuality*, Cambridge, 1979, p. 136. She concludes that by the eighteenth century the elites

fantasized about the love match but its widespread acceptance had to wait for changes in 'the economic system' which we associate with the current century (p. 173). Flandrin also suggests that they could not institute the love match 'as long as their social power remained based on a material patrimony' (ibid.).

4 Mary Lady Verney to Sir Ralph Verney, 4 February 1647, PUR VIII.

5 Brother Edmund Verney to Sir Ralph Verney, 4/14 September 1648, PUR IX.

6 Mary Lady Verney to Sir Ralph Verney, 4 February 1647, PUR VIII.

7 Nathanial Hobart to Sir Ralph Verney, received 17/27 June 1646, PUR VII.

# BIBLIOGRAPHY


Ariès, P., *Centuries of Childhood: A Social History of Family Life*, New York, Vintage Books, 1962.

Bailyn, B., *Education in the Forming of American Society*, New York, Vintage Books, 1960.

Bercé, Y.-M., 'Aspects de la criminalité au XVLLe siècle,' *Revue historique*, vol. 239, 1968, p. 38.

Broad, J., 'Gentry finances and the civil war: the case of the Buckinghamshire Verneys,' *Economic History Review*, ser. 2, vol. 32, May 1979, pp. 183–200.

Burke, B., *Dormant, Abeyant, Forfeited, and Extinct Peerages*, London, 1883.

Cooper, J. P., 'Patterns of inheritance and settlement by the great landowners from the fifteenth to the eighteenth centuries,' in J. Goody, J. Thirsk and E. P. Thompson (eds), *Family and Inheritance: Rural Society in Western Europe 1200–1800*, Cambridge University Press, Cambridge, 1976.

Davis, N. Z., 'City women and religion,' *Society and Culture in Early Modern France*, Stanford, California, Stanford University Press, 1975.

de Mause, L., *The History of Childhood*, New York, Harper & Row, 1974.

Donzelot, J., *The Policing of Families*, New York, Pantheon, 1979.

Finch, M. E., *The Wealth of Five Northamptonshire Families*, Oxford, Oxford University Press, 1956.

Flandrin, J.-L., *Families in Former Times: Kinship, Household and Sexuality*, Cambridge, Cambridge University Press, 1979.

Flinn, M. W., *The European Demographic System: 1500–1820*, Baltimore, Maryland, Johns Hopkins University Press, 1981.

Foster, J. (ed.), *Alumni Oxonienses*, Oxford, Oxford University Press, vols I and IV, 1891.

Genovese, E. D., *Roll Jordan Roll: The World the Slaves Made*, New York, Vintage Books, 1976.

Goode, W., 'World revolutions and family matters,' in A. S. Skolnick and J. H. Skolnick (eds), *Family in Transition*, Boston, Little Brown, 1977.

Goodwin, A. (ed.), *The European Nobility in the 18th Century*, London, A. and C. Black, 1953.

Goody, J., Thirsk, J. and Thompson, E. P. (eds), *Family and Inheritance: Rural Society in Western Europe 1200–1800,* Cambridge, Cambridge University Press, 1976.

Gordon, M. (ed.), *The American Family in Social-Historical Perspective*, New York, St Martin's Press, 1978.

Greven, P. J., Jr, *Four Generations*, Ithaca, Cornell University Press, 1970.

Habakkuk, H. J., 'Social attitudes and attributes,' in A. Goodwin (ed.), *The European Nobility in the 18th Century*, London, A. and C. Black, 1953.

Habakkuk, H. J., 'Economic functions of English landowners in the 17th and 18th centuries,' *Explorations in Entrepreneurial History*, vol. 6, Madison, University of Wisconsin Press, 1953.

Hareven, T. K., 'The history of the family as an interdisciplinary field,' in T. K. Rabb and R. I. Rotberg (eds), *The Family in History: Interdisciplinary Essays*, New York, Harper & Row, 1973.

Hill, C., 'The spiritualization of the household,' in *Society and Puritanism in Pre-Revolutionary England*, 2nd edn, New York, Schocken Books, 1964.

Hunt, D., *Parents and Children in History*, New York, Harper & Row, 1972.

Keeler, M. F., *The Long Parliament*, Philadelphia, American Philosophical Society, 1954.

Laslett, P., *The World We Have Lost*, London, Methuen, 1965.

Levy, M. J., Jr, *The Family Revolution in Modern China*, Cambridge, Mass., Harvard University Press, 1949.

Lewis, O., *La Vida*, New York, Vintage Books, 1966.

Lipscombe, G., *The History and Antiquities of the County of Bucks*, London, J. and W. Robins, 1847.

Macfarlane, A., *The Family Life of Ralph Josselin*, Cambridge, Cambridge University Press, 1970.

Mendelson, S. H., 'A debate,' *Past and Present*, no. 85, November 1979, pp. 126–35.

Mingay, G. E., *English Landed Society in the 18th Century*, London, Routledge & Kegan Paul, 1963.

Morgan, E. S., *The Puritan Family*, New York, Harper & Row, revised edition 1966.
Mullinger, J. B., *The University of Cambridge*, Cambridge, Cambridge University Press, 1873.
Page, W. (ed.), *Victoria County History of Bucks*, 4 vols, London, St Catherine's Press, 1938.
Rapp, R., 'Family and class in contemporary America: notes toward an understanding of ideology,' *Science and Society*, vol. 42, 1978, pp. 278–300.
Skolnick, A. S. and Skolnick, J. H., *Family in Transition*, Boston, Little Brown, 1977.
Smith-Rosenberg, C., 'The female world of love and ritual,' *Signs*, no. 1, 1975, pp. 1–30.
Stack, C. B., *All Our Kin: Strategies for Survival in a Black Community*, New York, Harper & Row, 1974.
Stone, L., 'The educational revolution in England,' *Past and Present*, no. 28, July 1964, pp. 41–80.
Stone, L., *The Crisis of the Aristocracy, 1558–1641*, Oxford, Clarendon Press, 1965.
Stone, L., 'Literacy and education in England: 1640–1900,' *Past and Present*, no. 42, February 1969, pp. 71–2.
Stone, L., *The Family, Sex and Marriage: In England 1500–1800*, London, Harper & Row, 1977.
Thirsk, J., 'The European debate on customs of inheritance,' in J. Goody, J. Thirsk, and E. P. Thompson (eds), *Family and Inheritance*, Cambridge, Cambridge University Press, 1976.
Thomas, K., 'The double standard,' *Journal of History of Ideas*, vol. XX, no. 2, April 1959, pp. 195–216.
Trumbach, R., *The Rise of the Egalitarian Family*, New York, Academic Press, 1978.
Vann, R., 'Toward a new lifestyle: women in preindustrial capitalism,' in R. Bridenthal and C. Koonz (eds), *Becoming Visible: Women in European History*, Boston, Houghton Mifflin, 1977.
Venn, J. and Venn, J. A., *Alumni Cantabrigienses*, 4 vols, Cambridge, Cambridge University Press, 1922.
Verney, F. P., *Memoirs of the Verney Family*, London, Longmans Green, 1892–4.
White, G. H. (ed.), *The Complete Peerage*, London, 1953.

# THE VERNEY

The Verney family genealogy

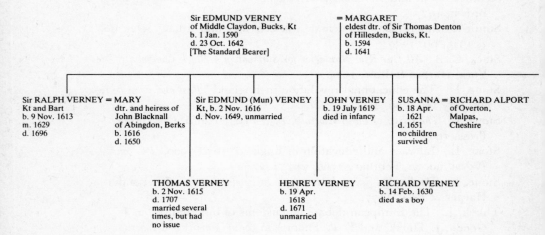

**Sir EDMUND VERNEY** = **MARGARET**

Sir EDMUND VERNEY
of Middle Claydon, Bucks, Kt
b. 1 Jan. 1590
d. 23 Oct. 1642
[The Standard Bearer]

= MARGARET
eldest dtr. of Sir Thomas Denton
of Hillesden, Bucks, Kt.
b. 1594
d. 1641

Children:

Sir RALPH VERNEY = MARY
Kt and Bart
b. 9 Nov. 1613
m. 1629
d. 1696

MARY
dtr. and heiress of
John Blacknall
of Abingdon, Berks
b. 1616
d. 1650

THOMAS VERNEY
b. 2 Nov. 1615
d. 1707
married several
times, but had
no issue

Sir EDMUND (Mun) VERNEY
Kt, b. 2 Nov. 1616
d. Nov. 1649, unmarried

HENREY VERNEY
b. 19 Apr.
1618
d. 1671
unmarried

JOHN VERNEY
b. 19 July 1619
died in infancy

SUSANNA = RICHARD ALPORT
b. 18 Apr.
1621
d. 1651
no children
survived

RICHARD ALPORT
of Overton,
Malpas,
Cheshire

RICHARD VERNEY
b. 14 Feb. 1630
died as a boy

# FAMILY GENEALOGY

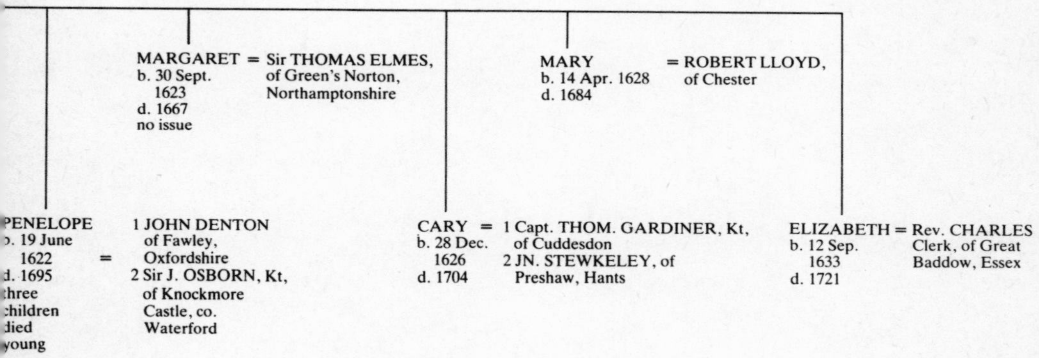

# INDEX

# INDEX

# MATHEMATICS LEARNING in Early Childhood

## Paths Toward Excellence and Equity

Committee on Early Childhood Mathematics

Christopher T. Cross, Taniesha A. Woods, and Heidi Schweingruber, *Editors*

Center for Education
Division of Behavioral and Social Sciences and Education

NATIONAL RESEARCH COUNCIL
*OF THE NATIONAL ACADEMIES*



THE NATIONAL ACADEMIES PRESS
Washington, D.C.
**www.nap.edu**

THE NATIONAL ACADEMIES PRESS   500 Fifth Street, N.W.   Washington, DC 20001

NOTICE: The project that is the subject of this report was approved by the Governing Board of the National Research Council, whose members are drawn from the councils of the National Academy of Sciences, the National Academy of Engineering, and the Institute of Medicine. The members of the committee responsible for the report were chosen for their special competences and with regard for appropriate balance.

This study was supported by Contract No. HHSP23320042509X1,TO#10 between the National Academy of Sciences and the U.S. Department of Health and Human Services; by Contracts No. HHSN267200700434P and HHSN267200800606P with the National Institute of Child Health and Human Development; by Contract No. 20070221 with the Ewing Marion Kauffman Foundation; and by the President's Fund of the National Research Council. Any opinions, findings, conclusions, or recommendations expressed in this publication are those of the author(s) and do not necessarily reflect the views of the organizations or agencies that provided support for the project.

**Library of Congress Cataloging-in-Publication Data**

Mathematics learning in early childhood : paths toward excellence and equity / Christopher T. Cross, Taniesha A. Woods, and Heidi Schweingruber, editors ; Committee on Early Childhood Mathematics, Center for Education, Division of Behavioral and Social Sciences and Education.
p. cm.
Includes bibliographical references and index.
ISBN 978-0-309-12806-3 (hardback) — ISBN 978-0-309-12807-0 (pdf)
1. Mathematics—Study and teaching (Early childhood) 2. Early childhood education. I. Cross, Christopher T. II. Woods, Taniesha A. III. Schweingruber, Heidi A. IV. National Research Council (U.S.). Committee on Early Childhood Mathematics.
QA135.6.M384 2009
372.7—dc22

2009033436

Additional copies of this report are available from National Academies Press, 500 Fifth Street, N.W., Lockbox 285, Washington, DC 20055; (800) 624-6242 or (202) 334-3313 (in the Washington metropolitan area); Internet, http://www.nap.edu.



Printed in the United States of America

Suggested citation: National Research Council. (2009). *Mathematics Learning in Early Childhood: Paths Toward Excellence and Equity.* Committee on Early Childhood Mathematics, Christopher T. Cross, Taniesha A. Woods, and Heidi Schweingruber, Editors. Center for Education, Division of Behavioral and Social Sciences and Education. Washington, DC: The National Academies Press.

# THE NATIONAL ACADEMIES

***Advisers to the Nation on Science, Engineering, and Medicine***

The **National Academy of Sciences** is a private, nonprofit, self-perpetuating society of distinguished scholars engaged in scientific and engineering research, dedicated to the furtherance of science and technology and to their use for the general welfare. Upon the authority of the charter granted to it by the Congress in 1863, the Academy has a mandate that requires it to advise the federal government on scientific and technical matters. Dr. Ralph J. Cicerone is president of the National Academy of Sciences.

The **National Academy of Engineering** was established in 1964, under the charter of the National Academy of Sciences, as a parallel organization of outstanding engineers. It is autonomous in its administration and in the selection of its members, sharing with the National Academy of Sciences the responsibility for advising the federal government. The National Academy of Engineering also sponsors engineering programs aimed at meeting national needs, encourages education and research, and recognizes the superior achievements of engineers. Dr. Charles M. Vest is president of the National Academy of Engineering.

The **Institute of Medicine** was established in 1970 by the National Academy of Sciences to secure the services of eminent members of appropriate professions in the examination of policy matters pertaining to the health of the public. The Institute acts under the responsibility given to the National Academy of Sciences by its congressional charter to be an adviser to the federal government and, upon its own initiative, to identify issues of medical care, research, and education. Dr. Harvey V. Fineberg is president of the Institute of Medicine.

The **National Research Council** was organized by the National Academy of Sciences in 1916 to associate the broad community of science and technology with the Academy's purposes of furthering knowledge and advising the federal government. Functioning in accordance with general policies determined by the Academy, the Council has become the principal operating agency of both the National Academy of Sciences and the National Academy of Engineering in providing services to the government, the public, and the scientific and engineering communities. The Council is administered jointly by both Academies and the Institute of Medicine. Dr. Ralph J. Cicerone and Dr. Charles M. Vest are chair and vice chair, respectively, of the National Research Council.

**www.national-academies.org**

## COMMITTEE ON EARLY CHILDHOOD MATHEMATICS

**CHRISTOPHER T. CROSS** (*Chair*), Cross & Joftus, LLC, Danville, California
**OSCAR BARBARIN,** School of Social Work, University of North Carolina, Chapel Hill
**SYBILLA BECKMANN,** Department of Mathematics, University of Georgia
**SUE BREDEKAMP,** Council for Early Childhood Professional Recognition, Washington, DC
**DOUGLAS H. CLEMENTS,** Department of Learning and Instruction, The State University of New York at Buffalo
**KAREN C. FUSON,** School of Education and Social Policy, Northwestern University
**YOLANDA GARCIA,** E3 Institute for Advancing Excellence in Early Education, WestEd, San Jose, California
**HERBERT GINSBURG,** Department of Human Development, Teachers College, Columbia University
**NANCY C. JORDAN,** School of Education, University of Delaware
**SHARON LYNN KAGAN,** Teachers College, Columbia University
**SUSAN C. LEVINE,** Department of Psychology, Department of Comparative Human Development, and Committee on Education, University of Chicago
**KEVIN MILLER,** Combined Program in Education and Psychology, University of Michigan, Ann Arbor
**ROBERT C. PIANTA,** Curry School of Education, University of Virginia

**TANIESHA A. WOODS,** *Study Director*
**PATRICIA MORISON,** *Interim Director,* Center for Education
**HEIDI SCHWEINGRUBER,** *Deputy Director,* Board on Science Education
**MARY ANN KASPER,** *Senior Program Assistant*

# Preface

Early childhood education has risen to the top of the national policy agenda with recognition that ensuring educational success and attainment must begin in the earliest years of schooling. There is now a substantial body of research to guide efforts to support young children's learning. Over the past 15 years, great strides have been made in supporting young children's literacy. This report summarizes the now substantial literature on learning and teaching mathematics for young children in hopes of catalyzing a similar effort in mathematics.

The need for this study was recognized and championed by the National Research Council's (NRC's) Mathematical Sciences Education Board following the publication in 2001 of *Adding It Up: Helping Children Learn Mathematics*. The tireless efforts of board member Sharon Griffin and then board director David Mandel led the design of this project, which is a comprehensive examination of the evidence base that can guide mathematics education (teaching and learning) for children ages 2 through 6. It represents the further extension of a portfolio of NRC reports focused on mathematics learning and teaching that includes *Adding It Up: Helping Children Learn Mathematics* (2001); *Eager to Learn: Educating Our Preschoolers* (2001); *How Students Learn: Mathematics in the Classroom* (2005); and *On Evaluating Curricular Effectiveness: Judging the Quality of K-12 Mathematics Evaluations* (2004).

The majority of support for this study was provided by the U.S. Department of Health and Human Services, Administration for Children and Families, Office of Head Start. In particular, we thank Frank Fuentes, deputy director of the Office of Head Start, Administration for Children and Families; Amanda Bryans, director of the Educational Development and Partnership Division, Office of Head Start, Administration for Children and Families; and Michele Plutro, education specialist, Office of Head Start, Administration for Children and Families. Additional funding was provided by the Office of Planning, Research, and Evaluation in the Administration for Children and Families, under the leadership of Mary Bruce Webb.

Other sponsors who contributed to the project include the Ewing Marion Kauffman Foundation, under the guidance of Margo Quiriconi and Karen Norwood, and the National Institute of Child Health and Human Development, under the leadership of Daniel Berch and James Griffin. In addition, the National Academies President's Fund provided partial support for the study.

Our work was also advanced by the contributions of able consultants and staff and the input of outside experts. Throughout the study process, the committee benefited from presentations or written input by individuals with a range of perspectives: W. Steven Barnett, National Institute for Early Education Research, Rutgers, The State University of New Jersey; Linda Bevilacqua, Core Knowledge Foundation; Toni Bickart, Creative Curriculum, Teaching Strategies; Bruce D. McCandliss, Sackler Institute for Developmental Psychobiology, Weill Medical College of Cornell University; Holly Rhodes, consultant; Elisa Rosman, consultant for the Georgetown University Center for Child and Human Development; Lawrence Schweinhart, High/Scope Educational Research Foundation; Catherine Snow, Harvard Graduate School of Education; and Prentice Starkey, Graduate School of Education, University of California, Berkeley.

The committee also thanks those who wrote papers that were invaluable to our discussions: Sarah Archibald, Consortium for Policy Research in Education, University of Wisconsin-Madison; Kathryn Bouchard Chval, College of Education, University of Missouri; Jason Downer, Center for the Advanced Study of Teaching and Learning, University of Virginia; Shalom Fisch, MediaKidz Research and Consulting; Michael Goetz, University of Wisconsin, Madison; Bridget K. Hamre, Curry School of Education, University of Virginia; Marilou Hyson, National Association for the Education of Young Children and George Mason University; Carolyn R. Kilday, Graduate Student, Curry School of Education, University of Virginia; Pat McGuire, Graduate Student Curry Leadership Foundations and Policy, School of Education, University of Virginia; Barbara Reys, Department of Learning, Teaching, and Curriculum, University of Missouri; Catherine Scott-Little, Human Development and Family Studies Department, University of North Carolina, Greensboro; and John Switzer, Department of Learning, Teaching, and Curriculum, University of Missouri.

This report has been reviewed in draft form by individuals chosen for their diverse perspectives and technical expertise, in accordance with procedures approved by the Report Review Committee of the NRC. The purpose of this independent review is to provide candid and critical comments that will assist the institution in making its published report as sound as possible and to ensure that the report meets institutional standards for objectivity, evidence, and responsiveness to the study charge. The review comments and draft manuscript remain confidential to protect the integrity of the deliberative process.

We thank the following individuals for their review of this report: Arthur Baroody, Curriculum and Instruction, University of Illinois, Urbana-Champaign; Elena Bodrova, Mid-continent Research for Education and Learning, Lakewood, CO; Karen S. Cook, Department of Sociology, Institute for Research in the Social Sciences, Stanford University; Sharon A. Griffin, Department of Education, Clark University; Jacqueline A. Jones, Division of Early Childhood Education, New Jersey Department of Education; Constance Kamii, Curriculum and Instruction, University of Alabama; Michèle M. M. Mazzocco, Psychiatry and Behavioral Sciences, Johns Hopkins School of Medicine and Math Skills Development Project, Kennedy Krieger West Campus, Baltimore, MD; Sally Moomaw, College of Education, Criminal Justice, and Human Services, University of Cincinnati; Donald G. Saari, Institute for Mathematical Behavioral Sciences, University of California, Irvine; Maria Shea Terrell, Department of Mathematics, Cornell University; and Karen L. Worth, Center for Science Education, Education Development Center, Inc., Newton, MA.

Although the reviewers listed above have provided many constructive comments and suggestions, they were not asked to endorse the conclusions or recommendations nor did they see the final draft of the report before its release. The review of this report was overseen by Jeremy Kilpatrick, Department of Mathematics and Science Education, University of Georgia, Athens, and Charles (Randy) Gallistel, Rutgers University, Rutgers Center for Cognitive Science, The State University of New Jersey. Appointed by the NRC, they were responsible for making certain that an independent examination of this report was carried out in accordance with institutional procedures and that all review comments were carefully considered. Responsibility for the final content of this report rests entirely with the authoring committee and the institution.

We are also grateful to the work of others at the NRC, including Christine McShane, senior editor, Division of Behavioral and Social Sciences and Education (DBASSE), whose work greatly improved the text of the report; Kirsten Sampson Snyder, DBASSE reports officer, who worked with us through several revisions of the report; and Yvonne Wise, DBASSE production editor, who managed the report through final publication. As well, we are thankful to those who assisted committee members with literature searches or background research, including Patricia Harvey, Julie Shuck, and Matthew Von Hendy, at the National Academies.

The committee appreciates the support provided by the Center for

Education, under the leadership of Patricia Morison. Taniesha Woods, the study director, provided invaluable support and guidance to the committee throughout the study. We could not have asked for a better colleague. Senior program assistant Mary Ann Kasper masterfully handled all the logistical aspects of this project, including our four committee meetings. We are also grateful for the leadership and support of Heidi Schweingruber, deputy director of the Board on Science Education, who provided much thoughtful counsel throughout this process and contributed substantially to editing the report in the final stages.

Christopher T. Cross, *Chair*
Committee on Early Childhood Mathematics

# Contents

## APPENDIXES

# Summary

Mathematics education has risen to the top of the national policy agenda as part of the need to improve the technical and scientific literacy of the American public. The new demands of international competition in the 21st century require a workforce that is competent in and comfortable with mathematics. There is particular concern about the chronically low mathematics and science performance of economically disadvantaged students and the lack of diversity in the science and technical workforce. Particularly alarming is that such disparities exist in the earliest years of schooling and even before school entry.

Recognizing the increasing importance of mathematics and encouraged by a decade of success in improving early literacy, the Mathematical Sciences Education Board of the Center for Education at the National Research Council established the Committee on Early Childhood Mathematics. The committee was charged with examining existing research in order to develop appropriate mathematics learning objectives for preschool children; providing evidence-based insights related to curriculum, instruction, and teacher education for achieving these learning objectives; and determining the implications of these findings for policy, practice, and future research.

The committee found that, although virtually all young children have the capability to learn and become competent in mathematics, for most the potential to learn mathematics in the early years of school is not currently realized. This stems from a lack of opportunities to learn mathematics either in early childhood settings or through everyday experiences in homes and in communities. This is particularly the case for economically disadvantaged children, who start out behind in mathematics and will remain so without extensive, high-quality early mathematics instruction.

In fact, well before first grade, children can learn the ideas and skills that support later, more complex mathematics understanding. There is expert consensus that two areas of mathematics are particularly important for young children to learn: (1) number, which includes whole number, operations, and relations; and (2) geometry, spatial thinking, and measurement. A rich body of research provides insight into how children's proficiency develops in both areas and the instruction needed to support it. The committee used this evidence to develop research-based *teaching-learning paths* to guide policy and practice in early childhood education.

Examination of current standards, curricula, and instruction in early childhood education revealed that many early childhood settings do not provide adequate learning experiences in mathematics. The relative lack of high-quality mathematics instruction, especially in comparison to literacy, reflects a lack of attention to mathematics throughout the childhood education system, including standards, curriculum, instruction, and the preparation and training of the teaching workforce.

For example, many widely used early childhood curricula do not provide sufficient guidance on mathematics pedagogy or content. When early childhood classrooms do have mathematics activities, they are often presented as part of an integrated or embedded curriculum, in which the teaching of mathematics is secondary to other learning goals. Emerging research indicates, however, that learning experiences in which mathematics is a supplementary activity rather than the primary focus are less effective in promoting children's mathematics learning than experiences in which mathematics is the primary goal. Finally, education and training for most teachers typically places heavy emphasis on children's social-emotional development and literacy, with much less attention to mathematics. In fact, academic activities such as mathematics can be a context in which social-emotional development and the foundations of language and literacy flourish.

As noted, opportunities to experience high-quality mathematics instruction are especially important for low-income children. These children, on average, demonstrate lower levels of competence with mathematics prior to school entry, and the gaps persist or even widen over the course of schooling. Providing young children with extensive, high-quality early mathematics instruction can serve as a sound foundation for later learning in mathematics and contribute to addressing long-term systematic inequities in educational outcomes.

The committee found that although the research to date about how young children develop and learn key concepts in mathematics has clear implications for practice, the findings are neither widely known nor implemented by early childhood educators or those who teach them. To ensure that all children enter elementary school with the mathematical foundation they need for success requires that individuals throughout the early childhood education system—including the teaching workforce, curriculum developers, program directors, and policy makers—transform their approach to mathematics education in early childhood by supporting, developing, and implementing research-based practices and curricula.

## RECOMMENDATIONS

**Recommendation 1: A coordinated national early childhood mathematics initiative should be put in place to improve mathematics teaching and learning for all children ages 3 to 6.**

A number of specific recommendations for action follow from this overarching recommendation. The specific steps and the individuals or organization that must be involved in enacting them are outlined below. We provide further guidance about how to enact these steps in Chapter 9.

**Recommendation 2: Mathematics experiences in early childhood settings should concentrate on (1) number (which includes whole number, operations, and relations) and (2) geometry, spatial relations, and measurement, with more mathematics learning time devoted to number than to other topics. The mathematical process goals should be integrated in these content areas. Children should understand the concepts and learn the skills exemplified in the teaching-learning paths described in this report.**

**Recommendation 3: All early childhood programs should provide high-quality mathematics curricula and instruction as described in this report.**

**Recommendation 4: States should develop or revise their early childhood learning standards or guidelines to reflect the teaching-learning paths described in this report.**

**Recommendation 5: Curriculum developers and publishers should base their materials on the principles and teaching-learning paths described in this report.**

**Recommendation 6: An essential component of a coordinated national early childhood mathematics initiative is the provision of professional development to early childhood in-service teachers that helps them (a)**

**to understand the necessary mathematics, the crucial teaching-learning paths, and the principles of intentional teaching and curriculum and (b) to learn how to implement a curriculum.**

**Recommendation 7: Coursework and practicum requirements for early childhood educators should be changed to reflect an increased emphasis on children's mathematics as described in the report. These changes should also be made and enforced by early childhood organizations that oversee credentialing, accreditation, and recognition of teacher professional development programs.**

**Recommendation 8: Early childhood education partnerships should be formed between family and community programs so that they are equipped to work together in promoting children's mathematics.**

**Recommendation 9: There is a need for increased informal programming, curricular resources, software, and other media that can be used to support young children's mathematics learning in such settings as homes, community centers, libraries, and museums.**

# Part I

# Introduction and Research on Learning

# 1

# Introduction

> For centuries, many students have learned mathematical knowledge—whether the rudiments of arithmetic computation or the complexities of geometric theorems—without much understanding. . . . Of course, many students tried to make whatever sense they could of procedures such as adding common fractions or multiplying decimals. No doubt many students noticed underlying regularities in the computations they were asked to perform. Teachers who themselves were skilled in mathematics might have tried to explain those regularities. But mathematics learning has often been more a matter of memorizing than of understanding.
>
> Today it is vital that young people understand the mathematics they are learning. Whether using computer graphics on the job or spreadsheets at home, people need to move fluently back and forth between graphs, tables of data, and formulas. To make good choices in the marketplace, they must know how to spot flaws in deductive and probabilistic reasoning as well as how to estimate the results of computations. . . . Public policy issues of critical importance hinge on mathematical analyses. (pp. 15-16)

These words are from an earlier National Research Council (NRC) report called *Adding It Up: Helping Children Learn Mathematics* (National Research Council, 2001a). It focused on examining the evidence about school mathematics and outlining what it means to be mathematically proficient from prekindergarten to eighth grade. The report offers much to guide current policy and practice in elementary and middle schools across the nation. Yet the report also draws attention to the importance of what happens before children enter formal schooling: "Young children show a remarkable ability to formulate, represent, and solve simple mathematical problems and to reason and explain their mathematical activities. They are positively disposed to do and to understand mathematics when they first encounter it" (p. 6).

However, not much attention has been paid historically to teaching mathematics to young children before they enter the period of formal schooling. This stems, at least in part, from generally negative attitudes about mathematics on the part of the American public as well as to beliefs that early childhood education should consist of a nurturing environment that promotes social-emotional development, with academic content primarily focusing on language and literacy development. In fact, a majority of parents report that a positive approach to learning and language development is more important for young children than mathematics (Cannon and Ginsburg, 2008). When asked which subject was more important for her child to learn and why, one mother said (p. 249):

> Language. Definitely. I mean obviously they're both [math and language] very important. But you can find people, even adults, who never learn math. I think that you could survive much better [without mathematics] than if you never learn language. I think communication is so important. If you could learn to be expressive, you could hire someone to do your math for you.

Families are agents of cultural transmission, which includes conveying attitudes about mathematics. Often, mathematics is not viewed as important to young children's cognitive development and later academic success. Evidence shows, however, that learning mathematics is vital for children's early years and for later success in mathematics as well as better overall academic outcomes in such areas as literacy, science, and technology (e.g., Duncan et al., 2007; National Association for the Education of Young Children and National Council of Teachers of Mathematics, 2002).

In addition, early childhood teachers are often uncomfortable teaching mathematics (Clements and Sarama, 2007; Copley, 2004; Ginsburg et al., 2006; Lee and Ginsburg, 2007a). Many teachers avoid teaching mathematics because of their own negative early experiences with mathematics. The quote below, by a pre-service teacher attending a top-ranked university, is illustrative:

> Overall, my personal experiences with math have not been good. . . . Throughout [my] elementary [schooling] it was either you were right or wrong. . . . As a result, I found math very boring and confusing. I am not a natural math learner. . . . I do not like the idea of teaching math to others, because I feel like I am not competent enough to teach math. I remember how hard it was when I was teaching adding and subtracting to first graders, especially when some of them did not understand it. I panicked

> when I made some mistakes myself in adding and subtracting. (Personal communication, comments by student of H. Ginsburg, Teachers College, Columbia University, September 2007.)

In recent years, however, interest in mathematics as a key aspect of early childhood education has increased across both the policy and the practice communities. In 2000, the National Council of Teachers of Mathematics (NCTM), in their revision of the 1989 standards for elementary and secondary school mathematics, included prekindergarten for the first time. Also in 2000, a conference of early childhood and mathematics educators was held to focus more explicitly on standards for preschool and kindergarten children (Clements, Sarama, and DiBiase, 2004). In 2002, Good Start, Grow Smart, an early childhood-focused White House initiative, resulted in the linking of federal funding to the requirement that all states develop voluntary early learning guidelines in language, literacy, and mathematics. The now-suspended National Reporting System for assessing learning outcomes for children participating in Head Start programs, begun in 2002, originally specified four areas of focus for assessment, one of which was early mathematical skills (the other three were language-related: comprehension of spoken English, vocabulary, and letter naming) (National Research Council, 2008). Also in 2002, the National Association for the Education of Young Children and the NCTM approved a joint position statement, "Early Childhood Math: Promoting Good Beginnings," which included recommendations to guide both policy and practice.

In 2006, following on its efforts to improve language and literacy outcomes for the children it serves, the Office of Head Start turned its attention to early mathematics. It convened a mathematics working group composed of parents, local staff, researchers, and other experts in early mathematics learning and has since moved forward on developing strategies for helping Head Start and Early Head Start programs support the early mathematics learning of infants, toddlers, and preschoolers.

## LEARNING FROM THE RESEARCH

Clearly there is growing interest in including mathematics among the learning goals for young children and in improving the teaching of mathematics in developmentally appropriate ways. Over the past several decades, significant investments have been made in research on early development and learning, much of which is ripe for examination and synthesis as it applies to early mathematics.

In the past decade, the NRC has uncovered and synthesized key aspects of the knowledge about learning and development in early childhood. In the reports *From Neurons to Neighborhoods: The Science of Early Child-*

*hood Development* (National Research Council and Institute of Medicine, 2000) and *Eager to Learn: Educating Our Preschoolers* (National Research Council, 2001b) the NRC directed its attention to early childhood institutions, their financing or lack of same, considerations of health and nutrition, and the social, emotional, and cultural components of this territory as they also focused special attention on early literacy. The report *Early Childhood Assessment: Why, What, and How* (National Research Council, 2008) identifies important outcomes for children from birth to age 5 and outlines the quality and purposes of developmental assessments. Although mathematics received attention to some degree in these studies, it was not a central focus of this work.

The NRC study that resulted in the report *How People Learn* (National Research Council, 1999) drew on a large body of research in cognition to offer a set of powerful findings about teaching and learning at all levels and all subjects that, since its publication, have rippled across the research community. The most recent follow-on publication, *How Students Learn: History, Mathematics, and Science in the Classroom* (National Research Council, 2005a), provides several concrete examples of how this research on student learning can translate into improved practice, including one example in early childhood mathematics. Some additional examples of research in this territory also surfaced in *Mathematical and Scientific Development in Early Childhood* (National Research Council, 2005b), which captures the discussion at an NRC workshop. The previously mentioned report, *Adding It Up* (National Research Council, 2001a), synthesized the research on mathematics learning in prekindergarten through eighth grade and provided advice to educators, researchers, publishers, policy makers, and parents. Taken together, these prior initiatives have helped set the stage for an in-depth examination of early learning in mathematics.

## THE COMMITTEE'S CHARGE

In order to synthesize and distill the key lessons from the relevant research, the NRC established the Committee on Early Childhood Mathematics in 2007. The majority of support for the study was provided by the Office of Head Start, under the auspices of the U.S. Department of Health and Human Services; supplementary funding was also provided by the National Institute of Child Health and Human Development, the Ewing Marion Kauffman Foundation, and the NRC. In recognition of the interdisciplinary nature of this work, the committee consists of experts in mathematics, psychology, neuroscience, early childhood education, and teacher education, as well as early childhood practitioners and policy makers. The committee worked on the study over an 18-month period.

The committee charge is as follows:

> To synthesize and analyze the past research on early childhood mathematics from a number of disciplinary fields, draw out the implications for policy and practice affecting young children as they move through the preschool years and begin formal schooling, and provide research-based guidance to increase the number of young children, especially vulnerable children, prepared to get off to a strong start in learning mathematics during their first years of schooling. It is designed to capitalize on the research literature in the field and consider its various implications for policy makers, practitioners and parents.
>
> The committee will assemble the pertinent research literature from the multiple disciplines that have focused attention on the teaching and learning of mathematics by young children. They will analyze this literature in order to develop (1) appropriate mathematics learning objectives for preschool students; and (2) critical evidence-based insights related to curriculum, instruction, and teacher education for achieving these learning objectives. Finally, they will determine the implications of these findings for policy, practice, parent-child relations, future data collection and further research.

See Box 1-1 for questions that the committee might address as part of its charge.

**BOX 1-1**
**Questions the Committee Might Address**

- What does existing research tell us about what preschool children can know about mathematics, and how they develop this knowledge?
- Learning of which mathematical knowledge, skills, and concepts in the preschool years increases the likelihood of successful mathematics learning in school and beyond?
- What do international comparisons with respect to both preschoolers and primary grades students tell us about the nature of early mathematics learning and prospects for its improvement in the United States? What approaches in other countries with respect to interventions and ongoing support could usefully be applied here?
- What policies and practices best lay the foundation for successful mathematics learning?
- What can parents, preschool teachers, and other adults who interact with young children do to promote their mathematical development?
- How can we support the mathematical development of preschool teachers so that they will be able to promote young children's mathematical development?
- How can further research in cognitive development and preschool education be focused to address issues that will lead to improvement in children's mathematical proficiency?

The committee cast its net widely to examine as much of the relevant research as possible. For some issues, the evidence base was limited: Throughout the report, we attempt to recognize and acknowledge the limitations of the evidence base and, at the end of the report, suggest some areas in which the scope and quality of research can be strengthened. The committee was not able to pursue in depth the entire array of possible issues related to mathematics education during early childhood; for example, we lacked the time, resources, and expertise to do a comprehensive international comparative analysis of early childhood education in mathematics. We do discuss the literature on the role of language as a shared cultural experience that shapes children's mathematical learning. In addition, neither program evaluation nor accountability, both of which are important to children's early mathematics education programs, is discussed at length in the report.

In addressing the charge, although the committee did examine research related to the development of number and space concepts for the very early years (i.e., infancy through age 3), our focus was on children ages 3 through 6 and early mathematics education—which includes learning, teaching, teacher education, and curriculum. The committee paid special attention to the learning and teaching practices that underscore mathematical development in children from age 3 through the end of kindergarten. This age range was chosen as the focus because it provides children with key cognitive and social development opportunities associated with successful entry into formal schooling. Evidence demonstrates that preschool-age children are excited about learning and enjoy activities that develop their mathematics competencies (Gelman, 1980; Ginsburg et al., 2006; National Research Council, 2001b; Saxe et al., 1987); this period is thus critical for maintaining and enhancing motivation to learn, especially for children from disadvantaged backgrounds, because enriching early learning experiences can enable them to begin kindergarten on a more level footing with their more advantaged peers.

The committee has put particular emphasis on the need to translate research on early childhood mathematics into practice for *all* children. Still, young children from disadvantaged backgrounds show lower levels of mathematics achievement than children from middle-class and higher status backgrounds (Clements and Sarama, 2007; Ginsburg and Russell, 1981; Hughes, 1986; Jordan, Huttenlocher, and Levine, 1994; Saxe et al., 1987; Starkey and Klein, 2000; Starkey, Klein, and Wakeley, 2004). The committee paid particular attention to issues of equity in early mathematics education throughout the report because of evidence indicating that, whereas all young children can benefit from intentional mathematics instruction, children who are at risk because of particular life circumstances (e.g., low socioeconomic status) will fall further behind their more affluent peers over the course of their schooling if they do not receive more intensive mathematics teaching (Starkey and Klein, 2000).

The committee held four meetings, which provided opportunities for discussions with practitioners, researchers, and other experts in the field of early childhood education. These discussions helped committee members develop a better understanding of the history and positions in the various stakeholder communities as well as the reasoning behind their positions. Our analyses draw on a variety of sources. The committee examined relevant summary data produced by government agencies and professional organizations. We reviewed a wide body of interdisciplinary research and commissioned a number of research synthesis papers by experts. Often, practitioners and policy makers state that the research community is too far removed from what is actually happening in the classroom, causing researchers to make recommendations that cannot be realistically implemented. The committee is keenly aware of this concern, and thus we attempt to put forth here policy recommendations that are grounded in research as well as the action steps necessary to implement them.

## THE EARLY CHILDHOOD EDUCATION AND CARE DELIVERY SYSTEM

One important issue that influenced the committee's thinking about recommendations for policy and practice is the multifaceted and complex nature of the early childhood education "system." Before the beginning of formal schooling, children spend their days in a wide variety of settings. If they are not cared for at home by their parents or relatives, children typically receive care through the country's early education and child care system, which consists of a loosely sewn-together patchwork of different kinds of programs and providers that vary widely in their educational mission and whether they are explicitly designed to provide education services. Data from the nationally representative Early Childhood Longitudinal Study, Birth (ECLS-B) cohort show that about 60 percent of preschool-age children are in center-based care (including Head Start settings), about 21 percent of children are in home-based care arrangements, and about 20 percent have no formal child care arrangements (see Table 1-1) (Jacobson Chernoff, McPhee, and Park, 2007).

In addition, about 43 percent of children younger than age 6 live in low-income families (Chau and Douglas-Hall, 2007). The high cost of high-quality early education and care is unaffordable for many low- and middle-income families (Zigler, Gilliam, and Jones, 2006). For example, the average annual cost for full-day center-based care for preschool-age

**TABLE 1-1** Children Participating in Regular Nonparental Education and Early Care, 2005-2006 (percentage)

| | Home-Based | | Center-Based | | | |
|---|---|---|---|---|---|---|
| Characteristic | Relative Care | Nonrelative Care | Non-Head Start | Head Start | Multiple Arrangements | No Regular Nonparental Arrangement |
| Total | 13 | 8 | 45 | 13 | 2 | 20 |
| **Child Race/Ethnicity** | | | | | | |
| White, non-Hispanic | 11 | 9 | 53 | 7 | 2 | 18 |
| Black, non-Hispanic | 14 | 4 | 37 | 25 | 3 | 16 |
| Hispanic | 16 | 6 | 31 | 19 | 1 | 27 |
| Asian, non-Hispanic | 16 | 3 | 55 | 6 | 2[a] | 18 |
| American Indian and Alaska Native, non-Hispanic | 14 | 5 | 29 | 31 | 1[a] | 20 |
| Other, non-Hispanic | 19 | 9 | 40 | 12 | 2[a] | 18 |
| **Socioeconomic Status[b]** | | | | | | |
| Lowest 20 percent | 15 | 5 | 22 | 25 | 2 | 31 |
| Middle 60 percent | 15 | 7 | 44 | 13 | 2 | 20 |
| Highest 20 percent | 6 | 11 | 71 | 1 | 2 | 10 |

NOTE: Percentages do not sum to 100 because of rounding error.

[a]Standard error is more than one third as large as estimate.

[b]Socioeconomic status (SES) is a measure of social standing. This SES variable reflects the socioeconomic status of the household at the time of the preschool parent interview in 2005. The components used to create the measure of SES were as follows: father/male guardian's education; mother/female guardian's education; father/male guardian's occupation; mother/female guardian's occupation; and household income. SES was collapsed first into quintiles, then into a 20/60/20 percent distribution by collapsing the middle three quintiles.

SOURCE: Jacobson Chernoff, McPhee, and Park (2007).

children ranges from $3,794 in Mississippi to $10,920 in the District of Columbia (National Association of Child Care Resource and Referral Agencies, 2007).

An increase in women's participation in the workforce has also contributed to the demand for high-quality preschool and child care (National Research Council, 2001b). Over the past four and a half decades, women's participation in the workforce has grown from 38 percent in 1960 to 60 percent in 2002 (U.S. Census Bureau, 2003), with 59 percent of mothers of 4-year-olds working outside the home (Jacobson Chernoff, McPhee, and Park, 2007).

Head Start is a large, federally funded early childhood program that promotes school readiness for economically disadvantaged children and families; the program provides comprehensive child development services (education, health, nutritional, social, and other services). In fiscal year 2007, the program served 908,412 children, most of whom were 3- and 4-year-olds (87 percent). The reach of the program is large—in 2007 there were over 49,000 Head Start classrooms located in over 18,000 centers—which makes its policies and practices influential in early childhood education.

Of the 60 percent of children in the United States who attend center-based care, approximately 22 percent are enrolled in state-funded preschool, which is the largest source of public prekindergarten (Barnett et al., 2007). Increasingly, states are moving toward state-funded preschool education to provide early education and care for children, particularly for those whose families would otherwise not be able to afford it. Georgia and Oklahoma, for example, have public preschool programs that enroll (if parents choose) 4-year-olds across the state (Barnett et al., 2007). Voluntary universal preschool is one policy option that has been suggested as a way to provide opportunities for all children, regardless of family income, to receive high-quality early education and care (Zigler et al., 2006).

However, some have argued against voluntary universal preschool in favor of programs that target low-income children (e.g., Ceci and Papierno, 2005; Fuller, 2007). Ceci and Papierno (2005), for example, suggest that targeted programs are more effective in terms of financial and educational benefits because they use (often limited) early education funds to help the most disadvantaged children.

Revisions to legislation and new policy initiatives have also shaped early childhood education policy in recent years. For example, beginning with the National Education Goals of 1990, the No Child Left Behind (NCLB) Act of 2001, and continuing through the 2007 reauthorization of the Head Start Act, interest in young children's preparation for school has increased. Central aims of these pieces of legislation are to support young children's development and learning so that they make a successful transition into kindergarten and to provide equitable educational opportunities for all students.

With the implementation of NCLB, many school districts began to place a major emphasis on the academic success of students in the early elementary grades. NCLB testing requirements do not begin until children reach third grade, but implications from the law exist for lower grades and preschool programs. The emphasis that has been placed on accountability for early childhood learning has caused concern among researchers, parents, and early education stakeholders because of the strong focus on academic development rather than the combination of academic and social-emotional development. This tension is not new; the early childhood education community has grappled with the notion that preschool programs should be more focused on academics, in contrast to the idea that they should focus instead on children's social-emotional development. The consequences of accountability systems have brought an increased emphasis and disagreements about what should be the focus of early education and care.

In addition to NCLB, Good Start, Grow Smart, President Bush's plan to strengthen early learning (White House, n.d.), promoted accountability for preschool children's learning outcomes in literacy and mathematics and also called for program improvements in language and literacy development. A major premise of this initiative was to close the achievement gap between socioeconomic and racial/ethnic groups. Until recently, the focus of these efforts was targeted at improving literacy and language development (e.g., Reading First and Early Reading First). However, with recent research clearly demonstrating the importance of early childhood mathematics to later success in reading and mathematics, policy makers are beginning to see the value of investing in early childhood mathematics. As discussed more fully in Chapter 8, policies aimed at changing or improving the education and learning of 3- to 6-year-olds still need to consider the diverse range of settings and characteristics of those who will do the teaching in these settings.

## ORGANIZATION OF THE REPORT

The report is organized into four parts. Part I focuses on the research on learning and summarizes the nearly 30 years of research demonstrating that young children are able to learn foundational mathematics. As these chapters show, preschool-age children possess a well-developed understanding of informal mathematics (Ginsburg, Klein, and Starkey, 1998), and they are able to learn complex mathematics before school entry (Clements and Sarama, 2007; Ginsburg et al., 2006).

Chapter 2 provides an overview of the important mathematical thinking processes and mathematical ideas for the early childhood period, summarizing the areas in which children need foundational learning opportunities. Chapter 3 reviews the evidence about how young children's everyday mathematics learning begins in infancy with the proximal environments in which they develop. More specifically, it focuses on cognitive development and includes a discussion of the research on infancy. Chapter 4 examines individual variation in children's mathematics learning and performance, with particular attention to mathematics learning disabilities. The chapter also considers sources of individual variation, such as familial practices, and group variation, such as socioeconomic status and race/ethnicity.

Part II focuses on a sequence of milestones for children in the core areas of number (including whole number, relations, and operations) and geometry and measurement. Chapter 5 focuses on number and operations, and Chapter 6 on geometry and measurement.

In Part III the committee turns to topics of implementation of mathematics learning and teaching in the classroom context. Chapter 7 covers the research concerning standards, curriculum, teaching, and formative assessment. Chapter 8 focuses on the early childhood workforce and examines issues of teacher education and professional development.

Part IV contains the committee's synthesis of its major conclusions and outlines the recommendations that flow from these conclusions, focusing particularly on what changes are needed to improve the quality of mathematics learning for young children. The committee also lays out an agenda for future research.

Appendix A is a glossary that defines terminology used throughout the report and Appendix B supplements Chapter 6. Appendix C presents biographical sketches of committee members and staff.

## REFERENCES AND BIBLIOGRAPHY

Barnett, W.S., Hustedt, J.T., Friedman, A.H., Boyd, J.S., and Ainsworth, P. (2007). *The State of Preschool 2007: State Preschool Yearbook*. New Brunswick: Rutgers, The State University of New Jersey, The National Institute for Early Education Research. Available: http://nieer.org/yearbook/pdf/yearbook.pdf#page=6 [accessed August 2008].

Cannon, J., and Ginsburg, H. (2008). "Doing the math": Maternal beliefs about early mathematics versus language learning. *Early Education and Development*, *19*(2), 238-260.

Ceci, S.J., and Papierno, P.B. (2005). The rhetoric and reality of gap closing: When the "have-nots" gain but the "haves" gain even more. *American Psychologist*, *60*(2), 149-160.

Chau, M., and Douglas-Hall, A., (2007, September). *Low-income Children in the United States: National and State Trend Data, 1996-2006*. Mailman School of Public Health at Columbia University, National Center for Children in Poverty. Available: http://www.nccp.org/publications/pdf/text_761.pdf [accessed August 2008].

Clements, D.H., and Sarama, J. (2007). Early childhood mathematics learning. In F.K. Lester, Jr. (Ed.), *Second Handbook of Research on Mathematics Teaching and Learning* (pp. 461-555). New York: Information Age.

Clements, D.H., Sarama, J., and DiBiase, A. (2004). *Engaging Young Children in Mathematics: Findings of the 2000 National Conference on Standards for Preschool and Kindergarten Mathematics Education*. Mahwah, NJ: Erlbaum.

Copley, J.V. (2004). The early childhood collaborative: A professional development model to communicate and implement the standards. In D.H. Clements, J. Sarama, and A-M. DiBiase (Eds.), *Engaging Young Children in Mathematics* (pp. 401-414). Mahwah, NJ: Erlbaum.

Duncan, G.J., Dowsett, C.J., Claessens, A., Magnuson, K., Huston, A.C., Klebanov, P., Pagani, L.S., Feinstein, L., Engel, M., Brooks-Gunn, J., Sexton, H., and Duckworth, K. (2007). School readiness and later achievement. *Developmental Psychology, 43,* 1428-1446.

Fuller, B. (2007). *Standardized Childhood: The Political and Cultural Struggle over Early Education.* Palo Alto, CA: Stanford University Press.

Gelman, R. (1980). What young children know about numbers. *Educational Psychologist, 15,* 54-68.

Ginsburg, H.P., and Russell, R.L. (1981). Social class and racial influences on early mathematical thinking. *Monographs of the Society for Research in Child Development, 46*(6), 1-68.

Ginsburg, H.P., Klein, A., and Starkey, P. (1998). The development of children's mathematical thinking: Connecting research with practice. In I. Sigel and A. Renninger (Eds.), *Handbook of Child Psychology, Volume 4: Child Psychology and Practice* (5th ed., pp. 401-476). New York: Wiley.

Ginsburg, H.P., Goldberg Kaplan, R., Cannon, J., Cordero, M.L., Eisenband, J.G., Galanter, M., and Morgenlander, M. (2006). Helping early childhood educators to teach mathematics. In M. Zaslow and I. Martinez-Beck (Eds.), *Critical Issues in Early Childhood Professional Development* (pp. 171-202). Baltimore: Paul H. Brookes.

Hughes, M. (1986). *Children and Number.* Oxford: Blackwell.

Jacobson Chernoff, J., McPhee, C., and Park, J. (2007). *Preschool: First Findings from the Third Follow-Up of the Early Childhood Longitudinal Study, Birth Cohort (ECLS-B).* Washington, DC: U.S. Department of Education, Institute of Education Sciences, National Center for Education Statistics.

Jordan, N.C., Huttenlocher, J., and Levine, S.C. (1994). Assessing early arithmetic abilities: Effects of verbal and nonverbal response types on the calculation performance of middle- and low-income children. *Learning and Individual Differences, 6,* 413-432.

Kagan, S.L., Kauerz, K., and Tarrant, K. (2008). *The Early Care and Education Teaching Workforce at the Fulcrum: An Agenda for Reform.* New York: Teachers College Press.

Lee, J.S., and Ginsburg, H.P. (2007a). Preschool teachers' beliefs about appropriate early literacy and mathematics education for low- and middle-socioeconomic status children. *Early Education and Development, 18*(1), 111-143.

Lee, J.S., and Ginsburg, H.P. (2007b). What is appropriate mathematics education for four-year-olds?: Pre-kindergarten teachers' beliefs. *Journal of Early Childhood Research, 5*(1), 2-31.

National Association for the Education of Young Children and National Council of Teachers of Mathematics. (2002). *Early Childhood Mathematics: Promoting Good Beginnings.* A joint position statement. Available: http://www.naeyc.org/about/positions/pdf/psmath.pdf [accessed February 2008].

National Association of Child Care Resource and Referral Agencies. (2007). *Parents and the High Price of Child Care.* Arlington, VA: Author.

National Council of Teachers of Mathematics. (2000). *Principles and Standards for School Mathematics.* Reston, VA: Author.

National Research Council. (1999). *How People Learn: Brain, Mind, Experience, and School.* Committee on Developments in the Science of Learning. J.D. Bransford, A.L. Brown, and R.R. Cocking (Eds.). Commission on Behavioral and Social Sciences and Education. Washington, DC: National Academy Press.

National Research Council. (2001a). *Adding It Up: Helping Children Learn Mathematics.* Mathematics Learning Study Committee. J. Kilpatrick, J. Swafford, and B. Findell (Eds.). Center for Education, Division of Behavioral and Social Sciences and Education. Washington, DC: National Academy Press.

National Research Council. (2001b). *Eager to Learn: Educating Our Preschoolers.* Committee on Early Childhood Pedagogy. B.T. Bowman, M.S. Donovan, and M.S. Burns (Eds.). Commission on Behavioral and Social Sciences and Education. Washington, DC: National Academy Press.

National Research Council. (2005a). *How Students Learn: History, Mathematics, and Science in the Classroom.* Committee on How People Learn, A Targeted Report for Teachers. M.S. Donovan and J.D. Bransford (Eds.). Division of Behavioral and Social Sciences and Education. Washington, DC: The National Academies Press.

National Research Council. (2005b). *Mathematical and Scientific Development in Early Childhood.* Mathematical Sciences Education Board and Board on Science Education. A. Beatty (Rapporteur). Center for Education, Division of Behavioral and Social Sciences and Education. Washington, DC: The National Academies Press.

National Research Council. (2007). *Rising Above the Gathering Storm: Energizing and Employing America for a Brighter Economic Future.* Committee on Prospering in the Global Economy of the 21st Century: An Agenda for American Science and Technology. Washington, DC: The National Academies Press.

National Research Council. (2008). *Early Childhood Assessment: Why, What, and How?* Committee on Developmental Outcomes and Assessments for Young Children, C.E. Snow and S.B. Van Hemel (Eds.). Board on Children, Youth and Families, Board on Testing and Assessment, Division of Behavioral and Social Sciences and Education. Washington, DC: The National Academies Press.

National Research Council and Institute of Medicine. (2000). *From Neurons to Neighborhoods: The Science of Early Childhood Development.* Committee on Integrating the Science of Early Childhood Development. J.P. Shonkoff and D.A. Phillips (Eds.). Board on Children, Youth and Families, Commission on Behavioral and Social Sciences and Education. Washington, DC: National Academy Press.

Saxe, G.B., Guberman, S.R., and Gearhart, M. (1987). Social processes in early number development. *Monographs of the Society for Research in Child Development, 52*(2), iii-viii.

Starkey, P., and Klein, A. (2000). Fostering parental support for children's mathematical development: An intervention with Head Start families. *Early Education and Development, 11,* 659-680.

Starkey, P., Klein, A., and Wakeley, A. (2004). Enhancing young children's mathematical knowledge through a prekindergarten mathematics intervention. *Early Childhood Research Quarterly, 19*(1), 99-120.

U.S. Census Bureau. (2003). *No. HS-30 Marital Status of Women in the Civilian Labor Force: 1900 to 2002.* Statistical Abstract of the United States. Bureau of Labor Statistics. Available: http://www.census.gov/statab/hist/HS-30.pdf [accessed August 2008].

White House. (n.d.). *Good Start, Grow Smart: The Bush Administration's Early Childhood Initiative.* Available: http://www.whitehouse.gov/infocus/earlychildhood/earlychildhood.pdf [accessed August 2008].

Zigler, E., Gilliam, W.S., and Jones, S.M. (2006). *A Vision for Universal Preschool Education.* New York: Cambridge University Press.

# 2

# Foundational Mathematics Content

Mathematics provides a powerful means for understanding and analyzing the world. Mathematical ways of describing and representing quantities, shapes, space, and patterns help to organize people's insights and ideas about the world in systematic ways. Some of these mathematical systems have become such a fundamental part of people's everyday lives—for example, counting systems and methods of measurement—that they may not recognize the complexity of the ideas underpinning them. In fact, the mathematical ideas that are suitable for preschool and the early grades reveal a surprising intricacy and complexity when they are examined in depth. At the deepest levels, they form the foundations of mathematics that have been studied extensively by mathematicians over centuries (e.g., see Grattan-Guinness, 2000) and remain a current research topic in mathematics.

In this chapter, we provide an overview of the mathematical ideas that are appropriate for preschool and the early grades and discuss some of the more complex mathematical ideas that build on them. These foundational ideas are taken for granted by many adults and are not typically examined in high school or college mathematics classes. Thus, many people with an interest in early childhood education may not have had adequate opportunities in their preparation to examine these ideas. Chapters 5 and 6 examine these ideas again in some detail, from the perspective of how children come to understand them and the conceptual connections they make in doing so.

This chapter has four sections. The first two describe mathematics for young children in two core areas: (1) number and (2) geometry and measurement. These ideas, which are important preparation for school and for life, are also genuinely mathematical, with importance from a mathematician's perspective. Moreover, they are interesting to children, who enjoy engaging with these ideas and exploring them.

The third section describes mathematical process goals, both general and specific. The general process goals are used throughout mathematics, in all areas and at every level, including in the mathematics for very young children. The specific process goals are common to many topics in mathematics. These process goals must be kept in mind when considering the teaching and learning of mathematics with young children.

The fourth section describes connections across the content described in the first two sections as well as to important mathematics that children study later in elementary school. These connections help to demonstrate the foundational nature of the mathematics described in the first two sections.

## NUMBER CONTENT

Number is a fundamental way of describing the world. Numbers are abstractions that apply to a broad range of real and imagined situations—five children, five on a die, five pieces of candy, five fingers, five years, five inches, five ideas. Because they are abstract, numbers are incredibly versatile ways of explaining the world. "Yet, in order to communicate about numbers, people need representations—something physical, spoken, or written" (National Research Council, 2001, p. 72). Understanding number and related concepts includes understanding concepts of quantity and relative quantity, facility with counting, and the ability to carry out simple operations. We group these major concepts into three core areas: number, relations, and operations. Box 2-1 summarizes the major ideas in each core area. Developing an understanding of number, operations, and how to represent them is one of the major mathematical tasks for children during the early childhood years.

### The Number Core

The number core concerns the list of counting numbers 1, 2, 3, 4, 5, . . . and its use in describing how many things are in collections. There are two distinctly different ways of thinking about the counting numbers: on one hand, they form an ordered list, and, on the other hand, they describe cardinality, that is, how many things are in a set. The notion of 1-to-1 correspondence bridges these two views of the counting numbers and is also central to the notion of cardinality itself. Another subtle and important aspect of numbers is the way one writes (and says) them using the base 10

## BOX 2-1
## Overview of Number, Relations, and Operations Core

**The Number Core: Perceive, Say, Describe/Discuss, and Construct Numbers**

**Cardinality:** giving a number word for the numerosity of a set obtained by perceptual subitizing (immediate recognition of 1 through 3) or conceptual subitizing (using a number composition/decomposition for larger numerosities), counting, or matching.

**Number word list:** knowing how to say the sequence of number words.

**1-to-1 counting correspondences:** counting objects by making the 1-to-1 time and spatial correspondences that connect a number word said in time to an object located in space.

**Written number symbols:** reading, writing, and understanding written number symbols (1, 2, 3, etc.).

**Coordinations across the above,** such as using the number word list in counting and counting to find the cardinality of a set.

**The Relations Core: Perceive, Say, Describe/Discuss, and Construct the Relations More Than, Less Than, and Equal To on Two Sets by**

Using general perceptual, length, density strategies to find which set is more than, less than, or equal to another set, and then later.

Using the unitizing count and match strategies to find which set is more than, less than, or equal to another set, and then later.

Seeing the difference between the two sets, so the relational situation becomes the additive comparison situation listed below.

**The Operations Core: Perceive, Say, Describe/Discuss, and Construct the Different Addition and Subtraction Operations (Compositions/Decompositions of Numbers)**

**Change situations:** addition change plus situations (start + change gives the result) and subtraction change minus situations (start – change gives the result).

**Put together/take apart situations:** put together two sets to make a total; take apart a number to make two addends.

**Compose/decompose numbers:** Move back and forth between the total and its composing addends: "I see 3. I see 2 and 1 make 3."

**Embedded number triads:** Experience a total and addends hiding inside it as a related triad in which the addends are embedded within the total.

**Additive comparison situations:** Comparing two quantities to find out how much more or how much less one is than the other (the Relations Core precedes this situation).

system. The top section of Box 2-1 provides an overview of the number core from the perspective of children's learning; this is discussed in more detail in Chapter 5. Here we discuss the number core from a mathematical perspective, as a foundation for the discussion of children's learning.

### *Numbers Quantify: They Describe Cardinality*

Numbers tell "how many" or "how much." In other words, numbers communicate how many things there are or how much of something there is. One can use numbers to give specific, detailed information about collections of things and about quantities of stuff. Initially, some toy bears in a basket may just look like "some bears," but if one knows there are seven bears in the basket, one has more detailed, precise information about the collection of bears.

Numbers themselves are an abstraction of the notion of quantity because any given number quantifies an endless variety of situations. We use the number 3 to describe the quantity of three ducks, three toy dinosaurs, three people, three beats of a drum, and so on. We can think of the number 3 as an abstract, common aspect that all these limitless examples of sets of three things share.

How can one grasp this common aspect that all sets of three things share? At the heart of this commonality is the notion of 1-to-1 correspondence. Any two collections of three things can be put into 1-to-1 correspondence with each other. This means that the members of the first collection can be paired with the members of the second collection in such a way that each member of the first collection is paired with exactly one member of the second collection, and each member of the second collection is paired with exactly one member of the first collection. For example, each duck in a set of three ducks can be paired with a single egg from a set of three eggs so that no two ducks are paired with the same egg, no two eggs are paired with the same duck, and no ducks or eggs remain unpaired.

### *The Number List*

The counting numbers can be viewed as an infinitely long and ordered list of distinct numbers. The list of counting numbers starts with 1, and every number in the list has a unique successor. This creates a specific order to the counting numbers, namely 1, 2, 3, 4, 5, 6, . . . . It would not be correct to leave a number out of the list, nor would it be correct to switch the order in which the list occurs. Also, every number in the list of counting numbers appears only once, so it would be wrong to repeat any of the numbers in the list.

The number list is useful because it can be used as part of 1-to-1 object counting to tell how many objects are in a collection. Although the number of objects in small collections (up to 3 or 4) can be recognized immediately—this is called *subitizing*—in general, one uses the number list to determine the number of objects in a set by counting. Counting allows one to quantify exactly collections that are larger than can be immediately recognized. To count means to list the counting numbers in order, usually starting at 1, but sometimes starting at another number, as in 5, 6, 7, . . . . (Other forms of counting include "skip counting," in which one counts every second, or third, or fourth, etc., number, such as 2, 4, 6, . . . , and counting backward, as in 10, 9, 8, 7, . . . .)

Although adults take it for granted because it is so familiar, the connection between the list of counting numbers and the number of items in a set is deep and subtle. It is a key connection that children must make. There are also subtleties and deep ideas involved in saying and writing the number list, which adults also take for granted because their use is so common. Because of the depth and subtlety of ideas involved in the number list and its connection to cardinality, and because these ideas are central to all of mathematics, it is essential that children become fluent with the number list (see Box 2-2).

***Connecting the number list with cardinality.*** In essence, counting is a way to make a 1-to-1 correspondence between each object (in which the

**BOX 2-2**
**The Importance of Fluency with the Number List**

All of the work on the relations/operation core in kindergarten serves a double purpose. It helps children solve larger problems and become more fluent in their Level 1 solution methods. It also helps them reach fluency with the number word list in addition and subtraction situations, so that the number word list can become a representational tool for use in the Level 2 counting of solution methods. To get some sense of this process, try to add or subtract using the alphabet list instead of the number word sequence. For counting on, you must start counting with the first addend and then keep track of how many words are counted on. Many adults cannot start counting within the alphabet from D or from J because they are not fluent with this list. Nor do they know their fingers as letters (How many fingers make F?), so they cannot solve D + F by saying D and then raising a finger for each letter said after D until they have raised F fingers. It is these prerequisites for counting on that kindergarten children are learning as they count, add, and subtract many, many times. Of course as they do this, they will also begin to remember certain sums and differences as composed/decomposed triads (as *number facts*).

objects can be any discrete thing, from a doll, to a drumbeat, to the idea of a unicorn) and a prototypical set, namely a set of number words. For example, when a child counts a set of seven bears, the child makes a 1-to-1 correspondence between the list 1, 2, 3, 4, 5, 6, 7 and the collection of bears. To count the bears, the child says the number word list 1, 2, 3, 4, 5, 6, 7 while pointing to one new bear for each number. As a result, each bear is paired with one number, each number is paired with one bear, and there are no unpaired numbers or bears once counting is completed. The pairing could be carried out in many different ways (starting with any one of the bears and proceeding to any other bear next, and so on), but any single way of making such a 1-to-1 correspondence by counting establishes that there are seven bears in the set.

A key characteristic of object counting is that the last number word has a special status, as it specifies the total number of items in a collection. For example, when a child counts a set of seven bears, the child counts 1, 2, 3, 4, 5, 6, 7, pointing to one bear for each number. The last number that is said, 7, is not just the last number in the list, but also indicates that there are seven bears in the set (i.e., cardinality of the set). Thus when counting the 7 bears, the counter shifts from a counting reference (to 7 as the last bear when counting) to a cardinal reference when referring to 7 as the number of bears in all. Counting therefore provides another way to grasp the abstract idea that all sets of a fixed number of things share a common characteristic—that when one counts two sets that have the same number of objects, the last counting word said will be the same for both.

Another key observation about counting is that, for any given number in the list of counting numbers, the next number in the list tells how many objects are in a set that has one more object than do sets of the given number of objects. For example, if there are five stickers in a box and one more sticker is put into the box, then one knows even without counting them all again that there will now be six stickers in the box, because 6 is the next number in the counting list. Generally each successive counting number describes a quantity that is one more than the quantity that the previous number describes.

In a sense, then, counting is adding: Each counting number adds one more to the previous collection (see Figure 2-1). Of course, if one counts backward, then one is subtracting. These observations are essential for children's early methods of solving addition and subtraction problems. Also, each step in the counting process can be thought of as describing the total number of objects that have been counted so far.

***The number word list and written number symbols in the base 10 place-value system.*** Each number in the number list has a unique spoken name and can be represented by a unique written symbol. The names and symbols for the initial numbers in the list have been passed along by tradition, but

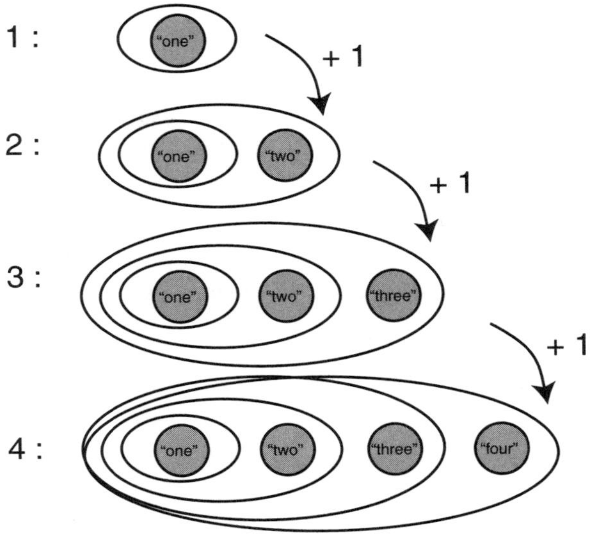


**FIGURE 2-1** Each counting number describes a quantity that is one more than the previous number describes.

the English names of the first 10 (or so) counting numbers and the symbols of the first 9 counting numbers are arbitrary and could have been different. For example, instead of the English word "three," one could be using "bik" or "Russell" or any other word, such as the words for "three" in other languages. Instead of the symbol 3, one could use a symbol that looks completely different.

The list of counting numbers needs to go on and on in order to count ever larger sets. So the problem is how to give a unique name to each number. Different cultures have adopted many different solutions to this problem (e.g., Menninger, 1958/1969; see Chapter 4 of this volume for a discussion of counting words in different languages). The present very efficient solution to this problem was not obvious and was in fact a significant achievement in the history of human thought (Menninger, 1958/1969). Even though the first nine counting numbers, 1, 2, 3, 4, 5, 6, 7, 8, 9, are represented by distinct, unrelated symbols, some mechanism for continuing to list numbers without resorting to creating new symbols indefinitely is desirable.

The decimal system (or base 10 system) is the ingenious system used today to write (and say) counting numbers. The decimal system allows one to use only the 10 digits 0, 1, 2, 3, 4, 5, 6, 7, 8, 9 to write any counting number as a string of digits (such a written representation of a number is often called a *numeral*).

The system is called a base 10 system because it uses 10 distinct digits and is based on repeated groupings by 10. The use of only 10 digits to write any counting number, no matter how large, is achieved by using *place value*. That is, the meaning of a digit in a written number depends (in a very specific way) on its placement. The details about using the decimal system

### BOX 2-3
### Using the Decimal System to Write the List of Counting Numbers

Each of the first nine counting numbers (or number words) "one, two, . . . , nine," requires only one digit to write, 1, 2, . . . , 9. Each digit stands for that many things—in other words, that many "ones," as indicated at the top of Figure 2-2. Each of these digits is viewed as being in the "ones place."

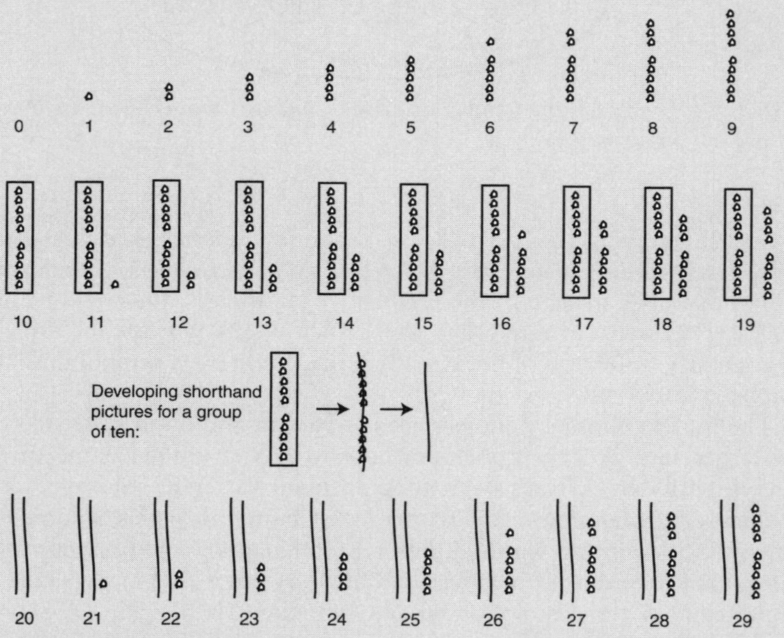


**FIGURE 2-2** Decimal system 1.

The next counting number, ten, requires two digits to write. The 1 stands for 1 ten and the 0 stands for 0 ones, and 10 stands for the combined amount in 1 ten and 0 ones. This way of describing and writing the number ten requires thinking of it as a single group of ten—in other words, as a new entity in its own right, which is created by joining 10 separate things into a new coherent whole, as indicated in the figure by the way 10 dots are shown grouped to form a single unit of 10.

to write the list of counting numbers are given in Box 2-3: A key idea is to create larger and larger units, which are the values of places farther and farther to the left, by taking the value of each place to be 10 times the value of the previous place to its right. One can think of doing this by bundling together 10 of the previous place's value. The greater and greater values

In each of the next two-digit counting numbers, 11, 12, 13, 14, 15, . . . , 20, 21, 22, . . . , 30, 31, . . . , 97, 98, 99, the digit on the right stands for that many ones, so one says this digit is in the "ones place," and the digit on the left stands for that many tens, so one says it is in the "tens place"; the number stands for the combined amount in those tens and ones. For example, in 37, the 3 stands for 3 tens, the 7 stands for 7 ones, and 37 stands for the combined amount in 3 tens and 7 ones. Notice that from 20 on, the way one says number words follows a regular pattern that fits with the way these numbers are written. But the way one says 11 through 19 does not fit this pattern. In fact, 13 through 19 are said backward, because the ones digit is said before the tens digit is indicated.

The number 99 is the last two-digit counting number, and it stands for the combined amount in 9 tens and 9 ones (see Figure 2-3). The next counting number will be the number of dots there are when one more dot is added to the dots on the left of the figure. This additional dot "fills up" a group of ten, as indicated in the middle of the figure. Now there are 10 tens, but there isn't a digit that can show this many tens in the tens place. So the 10 tens are bundled together to make a new coherent whole, as indicated on the right in Figure 2-3, which is called a hundred. From 0 to 9 hundreds can be recorded in the place to the left of the tens place, which is called the hundreds place. So the next counting number after 99 is written as 100, in which the 1 stands for 1 hundred, and the 0s stand for 0 tens and 0 ones.

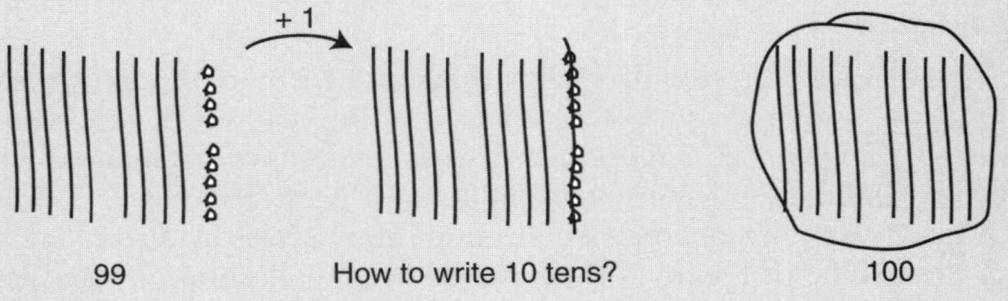


**FIGURE 2-3** Decimal system 2.

The decimal system has a systematic way to make new larger units by bundling 10 previously made units and recording the new unit one place to the left of the given unit's place. Just as 10 ones make a new unit of 10, which is recorded to the left of the ones place, 10 tens make a new unit of a hundred, which is recorded to the left of the tens place, and 10 hundreds make a new unit of a thousand, which is recorded to the left of the hundreds place. This pattern continues on and on to new places on the left.

of the places allow any number, no matter how large, to be expressed as a combination of between 0 and 9 of each place's value. In this way, every counting number can be expressed in a unique way as a numeral made of a string of digits. (See Howe, 2008, for a further discussion of the decimal system and place value.)

Even though most countries around the world now use this system of written numerals, they still use their own list of counting words that relate closely, or not so closely, to the written system of numerals. English and other European lists of counting words have various aspects that do not fit the decimal system so well and that create difficulties in learning the system. These, and ways to compensate for these difficulties, are discussed in Chapter 4.

## The Relations/Operations Core

Numbers do not exist in isolation. They make up a coherent system in which numbers can be compared, added, subtracted, multiplied, and divided. Just as numbers are abstractions of the notion of quantity, the relations "less than," "greater than," and "equal to" and the operations of addition, subtraction, multiplication, and division are abstractions of comparing, combining, and separating quantities. These relations and operations apply to a wide variety of problems. The middle and bottom sections of Box 2-1 are an overview of the relations core and the operations core for young children (which concerns only addition and subtraction, not multiplication or division).

### *Comparing*

In some cases it is visually evident that there are more things in one collection than in another, such as in the case of the two sets of beads shown at the top of Figure 2-4. But in other cases it is not immediately clear which collection (if either) has more items in it.

A basic way to compare two collections of objects is by direct matching (as in the middle of Figure 2-4). If a child has a collection of black beads and another collection of white beads, and if these collections are placed near each other, the child can place each black bead with one and only one white bead. If there is at least one extra white, then there are more whites; if at least one extra black, then more blacks. And if none is left over, then the two groups have the same number (although one may not know and does not need to know exactly what number it is).

When direct matching is not possible, a child can count the number of beads in two collections to determine which collection (if either) has more beads or if they both have the same number of beads. A key observation

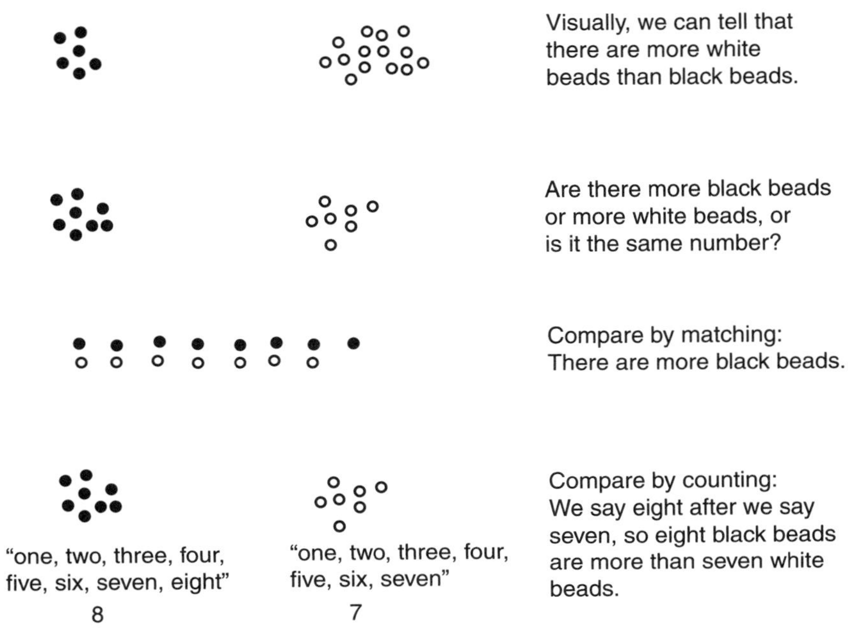


**FIGURE 2-4** Comparing.

about using counting to compare is that a number that is said later in the counting word list corresponds to a collection that has a greater number of objects than does a collection corresponding to a number earlier in the sequence. For example, one knows that there are more beads in a collection of eight black beads than there are in a collection of seven white beads because 8 occurs later in the counting list than 7 (see the bottom of Figure 2-4). Counting thus provides a more advanced way to compare sets of things than direct matching because it relies on knowledge about how numbers compare. Counting is also a more powerful way to compare sets of things than direct matching because it allows sets that are not in close proximity to be compared.

A key point about comparing collections of objects is that counting can be used to do so, and it relies on the link between the number list and cardinality: Numbers later in the list describe greater cardinalities than do numbers earlier in the list. Finding out which collection is more than another collection is easier than determining exactly how many more that collection has than the other, which can be formulated as an addition or subtraction problem. This more specific version of comparison is discussed in the next section.

*Addition and Subtraction Story Problems and Situations*

Addition and subtraction are used to relate amounts before and after combining or taking away, to relate amounts in parts and totals, or to say precisely how two amounts compare. Story problems and situations that can be formulated with addition or subtraction occur in a wider variety than just the simplest and most common "add to" and "take away" story problems. Methods that young children can use to solve addition and subtraction story problems, again, rely on a fluent link between the number list and cardinality. Later methods (in first grade or so) also rely on decomposing numbers and on an initial understanding of the base 10 system, namely that the numbers 11 through 19 can be viewed as a ten and some ones.

Box 2-4 describes the different types of story problems or situations that can be formulated with addition or subtraction. Viewed from a more

**BOX 2-4**
**Types of Addition/Subtraction Situations**

**Change Plus and Change Minus Situations**

Change situations have three quantitative steps over time: start, change, result. Most children before first grade solve only problems in which the result is the unknown quantity. In first grade, any quantity can be the unknown number. Unknown start problems are more difficult than unknown change problems, which are more difficult than unknown result problems.

Change plus: Start quantity + change quantity = result quantity: "Two bunnies sat on the grass. One more bunny hopped there. How many bunnies are on the grass now?"

Change minus: Start quantity – change quantity = result quantity: "Four apples were on the table. I ate two apples. How many apples are on the table now?"

**Put Together/Take Apart Situations**

In these situations, the action is often conceptual instead of physical and may involve a collective term like "animal": "Jimmy has one horse and two dogs. How many animals does he have?"

In put together situations, two quantities are put together to make a third quantity: "Two red apples and one green apple were on the table. How many apples are on the table?"

In take apart situations, a total quantity is taken apart to make two quantities: "Grandma has three flowers. How many can she put in her red vase and how many in her blue vase?"

These situations are decomposing/composing number situations in which children shift from thinking of the total to thinking of the addends. Working with differ-

advanced perspective, most of these situations can be formulated in a natural way with an equation of the form

$$A + B = C \quad \text{or} \quad A - B = C$$

in which two of the three numbers in the equation are known and the problem is to determine the other number that makes the equation true. The types of situations that are naturally formulated with these equations are *change plus* and *change minus* situations, *put together* situations, and *comparison* situations.

In change plus and change minus situations, there is a starting quantity (A), an amount by which this quantity changes (B), and the resulting quantity (C). Problems in which A and B are the known amounts and C is to be determined are the classic, most readily recognized addition and

ent numbers helps them learn number triads related by this total-addend-addend relationship, which they can use when adding and subtracting. Eventually with much experience, children move to thinking of embedded number situations in which one considers the total and the two addends (partners) that are "hiding inside" the total simultaneously instead of needing to shift back and forth.

Equations with the total alone on the left describe take apart situations: $3 = 2 + 1$. Such equations help children understand that the = sign does not always mean *makes* or *results in* but can also mean *is the same number as.* This helps with algebra later.

**Comparison Situations**

Children first learn the comparing relations equal to, more than, and less than for two groups of things or two numbers. They find out which one is bigger and which one is smaller (or if they are equal) by matching and by counting.

Eventually first grade children come to see the third quantity involved in a more than/less than situation: the amount more or less (the difference). Children then can solve additive comparison problems in which a larger quantity is compared to a smaller quantity to find the difference. Children may write different equations to show such comparisons and may also still solve by matching or counting. As with the other addition and subtraction situations, any of the three quantities can be unknown. The language involved in such situations is complex because the comparing sentence gives two kinds of information. "Julie has six more than Lucy" says both that "Julie has more than Lucy" and that the amount more is six. This is a difficult linguistic structure for children to understand and to say.

---

NOTE: Researchers use different names for these types of addition and subtraction situations, and some finer distinctions can be made within the categories. However, there is widespread agreement about the basic types of problem situations despite the use of different terminology.

subtraction problems. Reversing the action in change minus or change plus situations shows the connection between subtraction and addition. For example, if Whitney had 9 dinosaurs and gave away 3 dinosaurs, how many dinosaurs did Whitney have left? This problem can be formulated with the subtraction equation, $9 - 3 = ?$ Starting with the dinosaurs Whitney has left, if she gets the 3 dinosaurs back, she will have her original 9 dinosaurs, which can be expressed with the addition equation $? + 3 = 9$. Subtraction problems can thus be reformulated in terms of addition, which connects subtraction to addition.

In put together situations, there are two parts, A and B, which together make a whole amount, C. These situations are formulated in a natural way with an addition equation, $A + B = C$.

Change plus, change minus, and put together problems in which either A or B (the start quantity, the change quantity, or one of the two parts) is unknown involve an interesting reversal between the operation that formulates the problem and the operation that can be used to solve the problem from a more advanced perspective. For example, consider this "change unknown" problem: "Matt had 5 cards. After he got some more cards, he had 8. How many cards did Matt get?" This problem can be formulated with the addition equation $5 + ? = 8$. Although young children will solve this problem by adding on to 5 until they reach 8 (perhaps with actual cards or other objects), older children and adults may solve the problem by subtracting, $8 - 5 = 3$, which uses the opposite operation than the addition equation that was used to formulate the problem.

Comparison situations concern precise comparisons between two different quantities, A and C. Instead of simply saying that A is greater than, less than, or equal to C, the situation concerns the exact amount by which the two quantities differ. If C is B more than A, then the situation can be formulated with the equation $A + B = C$. If C is B less than A, then the situation can be formulated with the equation $A - B = C$. To consider this precise difference, B, requires one to conceptually create a collection that is not physically present separately in the situation. This difference is either that part of the larger collection that does not match the smaller collection, or it is those objects that must be added to the smaller collection to match the larger collection. Of course, these matches can be done by counting and with specific numbers rather than just by matching. Note that these situations are called additive comparison situations even when formulated with subtraction ($A - B = C$ when C is B less than A) to distinguish them from multiplicative comparison situations, which can be formulated in terms of multiplication or division. Students solve multiplicative comparison problems in the middle and later elementary grades.

In take apart situations, a total amount, C, is known and the problem is to find the ways to break the amount into two parts (which do not have to be equal). Take apart situations are most naturally formulated with an equation of the form

$$C = A + B$$

in which C is known and all the possible combinations of A and B that make the equation true are to be found. There are usually many different As and Bs that make the equation true.

## GEOMETRY/MEASUREMENT CONTENT

Geometry and measurement provide additional, powerful systems for describing, representing, and understanding the world. Both support many human endeavors, including science, engineering, art, and architecture. Geometry is the study of shapes and space, including two-dimensional (2-D) and three-dimensional (3-D) space. Measurement is about determining the size of shapes, objects, regions, quantities of stuff, or quantifying other attributes. Through their study of geometry and measurement, children can begin to develop ways to mentally structure the spaces and objects around them. In addition, these provide a context for children to further develop their ability to reason mathematically.

Every 3-D object or 2-D shape, even very simple ones, has multiple aspects that can be attended to: the overall shape, the particular parts and features of the object or shape, and the relationships among these parts and with the whole object or shape. In determining the size of a shape or object, one must first decide on which particular aspect or measurable attribute to focus.

Space (both 3-D and 2-D) could be viewed initially as an empty, unstructured whole, but objects that are placed or moved within the space begin to structure it. The beginnings of the Cartesian structure of space, a central idea in mathematics, are seen when square tiles are placed in neat arrays to form larger rectangles and when cubical blocks are stacked and layered to make larger box-shaped structures. These are also examples of composing and decomposing shapes and objects more generally. Composing and decomposing shapes and objects are part of a foundation for later reasoning about fractions and about area and volume.

Viewing or imagining an object from different perspectives in space and moving or imagining how to move an object through space to fit in a particular spot links spatial relations with the parts and features of objects and shapes.

Just as numbers are an abstraction of quantity, the ideal, theoretical shapes (2-D and 3-D) of geometry are an abstraction of their approximate physical versions. The angles in a rectangular piece of paper aren't exactly right angles, the edges aren't perfectly straight line segments, and the paper, no matter how thin, has a thickness to it that makes it a solid 3-D shape rather than only 2-D. Measurements of actual physical objects are never exact, either. Even so, valid reasoning about ideal geometric shapes and ideal theoretical measurements can be aided with approximate physical shapes and measurements.

### Measurement

In its most basic form, measurement is the process of determining the size of an object. But the size of an object can be described in different ways, depending on the attribute one chooses. For example, the size of a tower made of cube-shaped blocks might be described by the height of the tower (a length) or in terms of the number of blocks in the tower (a volume). The size of the floor of a room that is covered in square tiles can be described in terms of the number of tiles on the floor (an area). The most important measurable attributes in mathematics are length, area, and volume.

To measure a quantity (with respect to a given measurable attribute, such as length, area, or volume), a unit must be chosen. Once a unit is chosen, the size of an object (with respect to the given measurable attribute) is the number of those units it takes to make (the chosen attribute of) the object.

For length, a stick, for example, 1 foot long, could be chosen to be a unit. With respect to that unit of length, the length of a toy train is the number of those sticks (all identical) needed to lay end to end alongside the train from the front to the end.

For area, a square tile, such as a tile that is 1 inch by 1 inch, could be chosen to be a unit. With respect to that unit of area, the area of a rectangular tray is the number of those tiles (all identical) it takes to cover the tray without gaps or overlaps. Although squares need not be used for units of area, they make especially useful units because they line up in neat rows and columns and fill rectangular regions completely without gaps or overlaps.

For volume, a cube-shaped block, such as a block that is 1 inch by 1 inch by 1 inch, could be chosen to be a unit. With respect to that unit of volume, the volume of a box is the number of those cubes (all identical) it takes to fill the box without any gaps. Although cubes need not be used for units of volume, they make especially useful units because they line up in neat rows and columns and stack in neat layers to fill box shapes completely without gaps.

Once a unit has been chosen, a measurement is a number of those units (e.g., 3 inches, 6 square inches, 12 cubic inches). So measurement is a generalization of cardinality, which describes how many things are in a collection. For young children, measurements will generally be restricted to whole numbers, but measurement is a natural context in which fractions arise. To fill a bucket with sand, a child might pour in 4 full cups of sand and another cup that is only half full of sand, so that the volume of the bucket is approximately 4½ cups.

An important but subtle idea about units, which children learn gradually, is that when measuring a given object, the larger the unit used to measure, the smaller the total number of units. For example, suppose there are two sizes of sticks to use as units of length: short sticks and longer sticks. More short sticks than long ones are needed to measure the same length. In other words, there is an inverse relation between the size of a measuring unit and the number of units needed to measure some characteristic.

Young children may also not grasp the importance of using standard units, which allow one to compare objects that are widely separated in space or time (see Chapter 3 for further discussion).

## 2-D Shapes

Shapes found in nature, such as flowers, leaves, tree trunks, and rocks, are complex, intricate, and 3-D rather than 2-D. In contrast, the familiar 2-D shapes studied in geometry, such as triangles, rectangles, and circles, are relatively simple. Compared with most shapes in the natural world, these shapes are relatively easy to draw or create and also to describe and analyze. Many manufactured objects, such as tabletops and appliances, have parts that are approximate triangles, rectangles, or circles. Many shapes in the natural world are approximate combinations of parts of these simpler geometric shapes. For example, a birch leaf might look like a triangle joined to a half-circle.

Although geometric shapes can be described and discussed informally and children can simply be told the names of some prototypical examples of these shapes (for ease of reference and discussion), these shapes also have mathematical definitions, which teachers should know.

### *Parts and Features of 2-D Shapes*

Geometric shapes have parts and features that can be observed and analyzed. The shapes all have an "inside region" and an "outer boundary." Distinguishing the inside region of a 2-D shape from its outer boundary is an especially important foundation for understanding the distinction between the perimeter and area of a shape in later grades. Except for circles, the outer boundary of the common 2-D geometric shapes consists of straight sides, and the nature of these sides and their relationships to each other are important characteristics of a shape. One can attend to the number of sides and the relative length of the sides: Are all the sides of the same length, or are some longer than others? Where two sides meet, there is a corner point or vertex (plural: vertices). One interesting observation is that the number of vertices is the same as the number of sides. One can attend to how "pointy" a shape is at its vertex. In this case, one is attending to the angle formed by the sides that meet at the vertex. In some shapes, all the angles are the same, such as rectangles. In some shapes, some angles are the same and others are different, such as a rhombus that is not a square. The study of geometry is not only about seeing shapes as wholes; it's about finding and analyzing their properties and features.

#### *Additional Characteristics of 2-D Shapes Beyond Their Defining Characteristics*

In studying shapes, young children's attention will be drawn to the many different characteristics and features of a given shape. But from a more advanced standpoint, mathematicians have made definitions of shapes precise and spare by selecting only some of the characteristics of a shape as defining characteristics. For example, the definition of a triangle is a 2-D shape with three straight sides. A triangle also has three vertices and three angles, but these are not mentioned in the definition of triangle. Similarly, the opposite sides in a rectangle are the same length, but this is not mentioned in the definition of rectangle. Young children, however, can observe and describe these additional properties of shapes. For example, when one folds a rectangle out of paper by folding right angles, one can see that the opposite sides of the rectangle are the same length. The rectangle wasn't constructed with the explicit intent of making opposite sides the same length, yet it turns out that way. Similarly, if one joins four sticks end to end to make a quadrilateral and if the sticks were chosen so that the opposite sides are the same length, one can see that the opposite angles are also the same. Although the shape wasn't constructed with the explicit intent of making opposite angles the same, it nevertheless turns out that way.

### 3-D Shapes

The common simple geometric 3-D shapes are cubes, prisms, cylinders, pyramids, cones, and spheres. Many common objects are approximate versions of these ideal, theoretical shapes. For example, a building block is a rectangular prism, and a party hat can be in the shape of a cone. As with 2-D shapes, the study of 3-D shapes is not only about seeing these shapes as wholes and learning their names, but also about finding and analyzing their properties and features.

The 3-D geometric shapes have parts and features that can be observed. The shapes all have an "inside" and an "outer surface." The outer surface may consist of several parts. For example, the outer surface of a prism can consist of rectangles. If the outer surface of a 3-D shape consists of flat surfaces, these are often called faces. For example, a long wooden building block has two faces at each end that are small rectangles and four faces around the middle that are long rectangles. Faces are joined along straight edges, and edges meet at points called vertices. Children might observe that some shapes (like that building block) have pairs of faces on opposite sides that are the same (congruent). Children might also observe that some shapes, like cylinders (like a pole or a can), cones (like a party hat), and spheres (like a ball), have outer surfaces that are not flat.

Although the outer surface of a 3-D shape is usually visible, unless one cuts the shape open, or the shape is made of clear plastic, or the shape is hollow and a face can be removed to look inside, one must usually imagine and visualize the inside. One exception is rooms, which are often (roughly) in the shape of a rectangular prism, and which one experiences from the inside. Distinguishing the inside of a 3-D shape from its outer surface is an especially important foundation for understanding the distinction between the surface area and volume of a shape in later grades.

### Composing and Decomposing Shapes

Just as 10 ones can be composed to make a single unit of 10, shapes can also be composed to make new, larger shapes. And just as a 10 can be decomposed into 10 ones, so too shapes can be decomposed to make new, smaller shapes. Figure 2-5 presents a few examples of relationships among shapes obtained by composing and decomposing shapes based on equilateral triangles. Figure 2-6 shows relationships among shapes obtained by composing and decomposing rectangles.

Composing and decomposing 2-D shapes is an important foundation for understanding area in later grades. In particular, viewing rectangles as

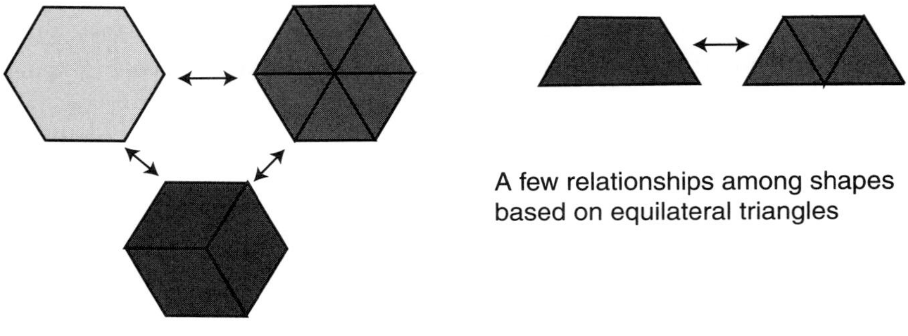
A few relationships among shapes based on equilateral triangles

**FIGURE 2-5** Relationships among shapes based on equilateral triangles.

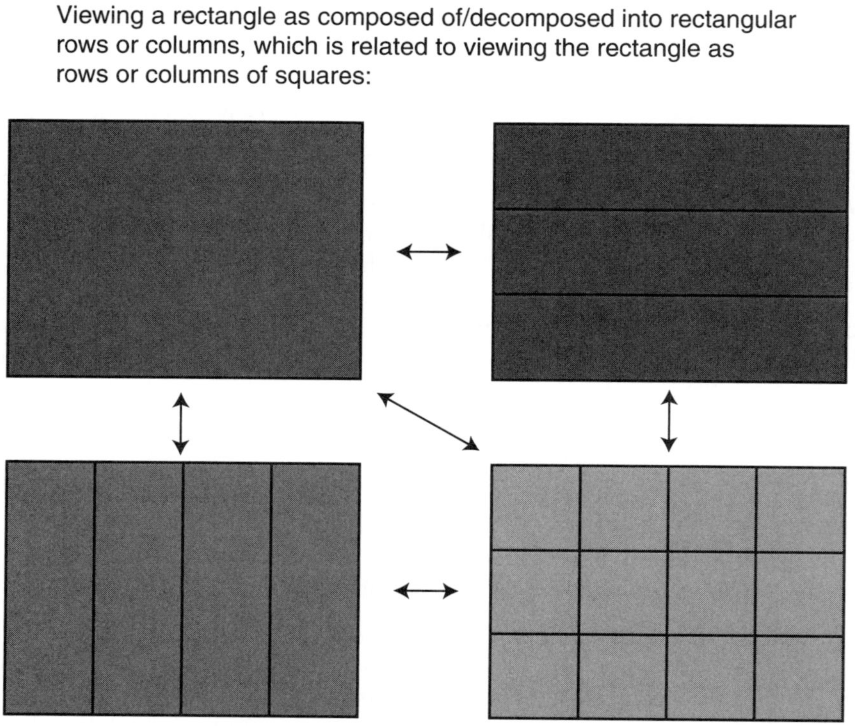

Viewing a rectangle as composed of/decomposed into rectangular rows or columns, which is related to viewing the rectangle as rows or columns of squares:


**FIGURE 2-6** Relationships among rectangles.

composed of rows and columns of squares, as illustrated in Figure 2-6, is key to understanding areas of rectangles.

Likewise, composing and decomposing 3-D shapes is an important foundation for understanding volume in later grades. In particular, viewing rectangular prisms as composed of layers of rows and columns of cubes is key to understanding volumes of rectangular prisms (see Figure 2-7). Also, reasoning about fractions often takes place in a context of reasoning about decomposing shapes into pieces.

Composition and decomposition is discussed in greater detail in the section on mathematical connections across content areas and to later mathematics.

### Motion, Relative Location, and Spatial Structuring

Part of the study of geometry is the analysis of both 2-D and 3-D space. A flat tabletop or piece of paper (imagined to extend infinitely in all

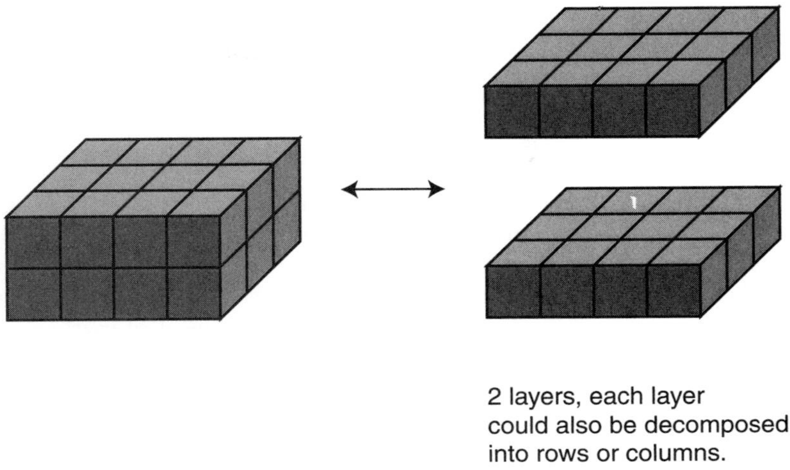

2 layers, each layer
could also be decomposed
into rows or columns.


**FIGURE 2-7** Viewing a rectangular box as composed of layers of rows and columns.

directions) is a model for 2-D space. The space around one is a model for 3-D space. For young children, the study of space begins with movement through space and with describing relative location in space.

Space is oriented by relative location. Think of one object as at a fixed location in 3-D space. Another object may be above or below the fixed object, which indicates relative location along a vertical axis (line). Another object may be in front of or behind a fixed object, or it may be to the left or right of a fixed object. These two descriptions indicate relative location along two distinct (and perpendicular) horizontal axes (lines). A related way to begin to structure space is to join squares into neat arrays of rows and columns for 2-D space and to stack cubes in layers of rows and columns for 3-D space.

Although objects can be moved through space in many different ways, in 2-D space (think of a 2-D shape on a tabletop) there are some special motions that are of particular interest in advanced geometry that are also accessible to young children. Using elementary school terminology, these motions are called slides, flips, and turns (and in more advanced settings they are called translations, reflections, and rotations).

A slide moves a shape in a single direction for a specified distance without turning the shape. A flip reflects the shape across a line (so that the top and bottom of the shape become reversed). A turn rotates the shape around a fixed point with a specified amount of turning (e.g., a half turn or a quarter turn). (Technically, the center point of rotation need not be the center of the shape or even within the shape, although for young children it will be chosen that way.)

## MATHEMATICAL PROCESS GOALS

In addition to coming to understand the specific mathematical concepts discussed so far, children need to develop proficiency in the reasoning processes used in mathematics. In this section we describe two categories of mathematical processes: (1) general mathematical reasoning processes, which are central in every content area and at every level of mathematics, and (2) specific mathematical reasoning processes, which weave through many different content areas. Note that many of the specific reasoning processes were already touched on in the discussions of number, geometry, and measurement. In fact, these specific processes represent powerful, cross-cutting ideas that connect multiple concepts, procedures, or problems and can help children begin to see coherence across topics in mathematics. One major goal of early education should be to stimulate and foster mathematical reasoning.

### General Mathematical Reasoning Processes

The National Council of Teachers of Mathematics (NCTM) identified five process standards essential for meaningful and substantive mathematics learning and teaching (National Council of Teachers of Mathematics, 2000): (1) representing (including analyzing representations mathematically and visualizing internally), (2) problem solving, (3) reasoning, (4) connecting, and (5) communicating. These processes are vehicles for children to deepen, extend, elaborate, and refine their thinking and to explore ideas and lines of reasoning. According to NCTM, these processes are to be continually interwoven throughout the teaching and learning of mathematics content—even at the preschool level (see Chapters 5 and 6 for further discussion).

Representing is central in mathematics. Mathematics at every level uses simplified pictures or diagrams to represent a situation and subject it to mathematical analysis. For example, a child hears the story of The Three Bears. She forms a mental image of the three, with the papa bear largest in size, the mama bear next, and then the baby bear. She draws a crude picture of the three, or perhaps uses stick figures, or even lines. All of these are representations—the mental image, the picture, the stick figures, and the lines. The child can use the representations to reason about the objects and to explore ideas about size. Is the mama bear smaller than the papa bear? Is she also bigger than the baby bear? How can she be both bigger and smaller at the same time? Much later, the student can represent this situation as

A > B and B > C and reason that, if this is the case, then A > C. Here the representations are mathematical in the conventional sense. But when used to understand a situation quantitatively or geometrically, images and simple drawings are no less mathematical than are such representations as written numbers or equations, which are universally recognized as mathematical.

According to mathematical educators, "problem solving and reasoning are the heart of mathematics" (National Association for the Education of Young Children and National Council of Teachers of Mathematics, 2002, p. 6). In fact, solving problems is both a goal of mathematics learning and a mechanism for doing so. Young children will need support to formulate, struggle with, and solve problems and to reflect on the reasoning they use in doing so. By developing their ability to reason mathematically, children will begin to note patterns or regularities in the world and across the mathematical ideas they are introduced to. They will become increasingly sophisticated in their ability to recognize and analyze the mathematics inherent in the world around them.

Connecting and communicating are particularly important in the preschool years. Children must learn to describe their thinking (reasoning) and the patterns they see, and they must learn to use the language of mathematical objects, situations, and notation. Children's informal mathematical experiences, problem solving, explorations, and language provide bases for understanding and using this formal mathematical language and notation. The informal and formal representations and experiences need to be continually connected in a nurturing "math talk" learning community, which provides opportunities for all children to talk about their mathematical thinking and produce and improve their use of mathematical and ordinary language. Children also need to connect ideas across different domains of mathematics (e.g., geometry and number) and across mathematics and other subjects (e.g., literacy) and aspects of everyday life.

### *Applying the Process Standards: Mathematizing*

Together, the general mathematical processes of reasoning, representing, problem solving, connecting, and communicating are mechanisms by which children can go back and forth between abstract mathematics and real situations in the world around them. In other words, they are a means both for making sense of abstract mathematics and for formulating real situations in mathematical terms—that is, for *mathematizing* the situations they encounter.

The power of mathematics lies in its ability to unify a wide variety of situations and thereby to apply a common problem-solving strategy in seemingly disparate examples. For example, the number 3 applies not only to concrete situations, such as three pencils or three apples, but also to any collection of three things, real or imagined. Thus, the addition problem $3 + 2 = ?$ provides an abstract formulation for a vast number of actual situations in the world around one. The abstract nature of mathematics is part of its power: Because it is abstract, it can apply to a virtually limitless number of situations. But for children to use this mathematical power requires that they take situations and problems from the world around them and formulate them in mathematical terms. In other words, it requires children to *mathematize* situations.

Mathematizing happens when children can create a model of the situation by using mathematical objects (such as numbers or shapes), mathematical actions (such as counting or transforming shapes), and their structural relationships to solve problems about the situation. For example, children can use blocks to build a model of a castle tower, positioning the blocks to fit with a description of relationships among features of the tower, such as a front door on the first floor, a large room on the second floor, and a lookout tower on top of the roof. Mathematizing often involves representing relationships in a situation so that the relationships can be quantified.

For example, if there are three green toy dinosaurs in one box and five yellow toy dinosaurs in another box, children might pair up green and yellow dinosaurs and then determine that there are two more yellow dinosaurs than green ones because there are two yellow dinosaurs that do not have a green partner. With experience and guidance, children create increasingly abstract representations of the mathematical aspects of the situation. For example, drawing five circles instead of five yellow ducks or drawing a rectangle to represent the side of a box of tissues and, later, writing an equation to model a situation. Children become able to visualize these mathematical attributes mentally, which helps in various kinds of problem solving. Children also need eventually to learn to read and to write formal mathematical notation, such as numerals (1, 2, 6, 10) and other symbols (=, +, −) and to use these symbols in mathematizing situations. Thus, mathematizing involves reinventing, redescribing, reorganizing, quantifying, structuring, abstracting, and generalizing what is first understood on an intuitive and informal level in the context of everyday activity (Clements and Sarama, 2007).

### Specific Mathematical Reasoning Processes

Mathematics learning in early childhood requires children to use several specific mathematical reasoning processes, also known as "big ideas," across domains. These big ideas are overarching concepts that connect multiple concepts, procedures, or problems within or across domains or topics and are a particularly important aspect of the process of forming connections. Big ideas "invite students to look beyond surface features of procedures and concepts and see diverse aspects of knowledge as having the same underlying structure" (Baroody, Feil, and Johnson, 2007, p. 26).

### *Unitizing*

Unitizing—finding or creating a mathematical unit—occurs in numerical, geometric, and spatial contexts. When children count, they must create mental units of what they are going to count: single cats, the paws on several cats, or groups of two cats. To measure length, children must select a unit of length measure (for example, they will lay along a length and then count new crayons, feet stepped heel-to-toe along some distance, or inch lengths). To create repeating patterns, children must select and repeat a unit. For example, they might make a bead necklace by repeatedly stringing two cubes then a sphere (their unit). In designing a block building, they might repeatedly place a square, then a triangular block, repeating that unit around the top of their building. When making designs or pictures with pattern blocks, children might join several shapes to make a unit that they repeat throughout the design. To begin to understand the base 10 place-value system, children must be able to view ten ones as forming a single unit of ten. Research suggests a link between being able to view a collection of shapes as a higher order unit and being able to view two-digit numbers as groups of tens and some ones (Clements et al., 1997; Reynolds and Wheatley, 1996). Because the concept of unit underlies core ideas in number and in geometry and measurement, it has been recommended as a central focus for early childhood mathematics education (Sophian, 2007).

### *Decomposing and Composing*

Decomposing and composing are used throughout mathematics at every level and in all topics. In the realm of numbers and operations (addition, subtraction, multiplication, and division), composing and decomposing are used in recognizing the number of objects in a collection, in the meaning of the operations themselves, and in the place-value system. Children can sometimes quickly determine the number of objects in a small collection by viewing the collection as composed of two immediately recognizable collections, such as seeing four counters as composed of a set of three counters and another counter. Composing and decomposing are the basis for the operations of addition and subtraction and later for the operations of multiplication and division. Some key steps toward developing proficiency with arithmetic involve decomposing and composing. Children must be able to decompose numbers from 1 to 10 into all possible pairs and to recognize numbers from 11 to 19 as composed of a ten and some ones. The base 10 place-value system relies on repeated bundling in groups of ten. Proficiency with multidigit addition and subtraction requires being able to compose ten ones as one ten and to decompose one ten as ten ones.

In geometry, shapes can be viewed as composed of other shapes, such as viewing a trapezoid as made from three triangles, or viewing a house shape as made from a triangle placed above a square. Children can compose rows of squares to make rectangles (see Figure 2-6). Many 3-D shapes seen in everyday life can be viewed as composed of shapes that are found in sets of building blocks (or at least approximately so). A juice box might look like a rectangular prism with a (sideways) triangular prism on top. Children can compose layers of cubes to make larger cubes and rectangular prisms.

In measurement, units are composed to make larger units and decomposed to make smaller units. Measurement itself requires viewing the attribute to be measured as composed of units. In effect, using a unit of measure to partition a continuous quantity, such as a length or area, into discrete and equal size pieces transforms it into a countable quantity.

### *Relating and Ordering*

Relating and ordering allow one to decide which is more and which is less in various domains: number, length, area. Having children see and discuss relating and ordering across domains can deepen mathematical understanding. By broadening the ways in which things can be compared, children are led to the idea of different measurable attributes. For example, two stacks of blocks might be made from the same number of blocks, but one stack might be taller than the other. Relating is a first step toward measurement, because measurement is a quantified form of relating. A measurement specifies how many of one thing (the unit) it takes to make the other thing (the attribute that is measured). When relating and number are joined via measurement, both realms are extended. On one hand, relating becomes more precise when it becomes measurement, and, on the other hand, numbers extend into fractions and decimals in the context of measurement. For example, a bucket of sand might be filled with 2½ smaller pails of sand.

### *Looking for Patterns and Structures and Organizing Information*

Looking for patterns and structures and organizing information (including classifying) are crucial mathematical processes used frequently in mathematical thinking and problem solving. They also have been viewed as distinct content areas in early childhood mathematics learning. Such pattern "content" usually focuses on repeated patterns, such as *abab* or *abcabc*, that are done with colors, sounds, body movements, and so forth (such as the bead and block patterning examples discussed in the section on unitizing). Such activities are appropriate in early childhood and can help to introduce children to seeing and describing patterns more broadly in mathematics. The patterns *abab*, *abcabc*, and *aabbaabb* can be learned by many young children, and many children in kindergarten can do more complex patterns (Clements and Sarama, 2007). Learning to see the unit in one direction (from left to right or from top to bottom or bottom to top) (*ab* in *abab*, *abc* in *abcabc*) and then repeating it consistently is the core of such repeated pattern learning. Learning to extend a given pattern to other modalities (for example, from color to shape, sounds, and body movements) is an index of abstracting and generalizing the pattern.

Counting involves some especially important patterns that go beyond simple repeating patterns. For example, the pattern of counting is a critical idea in number. The list of counting numbers has an especially important and intricate pattern, which involves a coordinated cycling of the digits 0 through 9 in the ones, tens, hundreds, etc., places (see Box 2-2). Although this intricate pattern will not be fully understood by children until later in elementary school, the foundation for this understanding is laid in early childhood as they identify and use the repeating patterns in the number words to 100.

Organizing information, including classifying, has also been seen as early childhood mathematics content, as children use attribute blocks and other collections of entities in which attributes are systematically varied so that they can sort them in multiple ways. Attribute blocks usually vary in color, shape, size, and sometimes thickness, so that children can sort on any of these dimensions and also describe a given block using multiple terms. For example, in small groups, a teacher may first ask children to sort the blocks on one or two dimensions: "Find all the big blue blocks." As children become more proficient, the teacher adds challenge, such as "Find the small blue thin rectangle." Later on, in preschool and in kindergarten, the teacher may ask children to generate their own descriptions of how groups of blocks are similar and different.

Recognizing patterns and organizing information are part of recognizing structure. At all levels in mathematics, one looks for structure. Some experiences in recognizing structure can be part of a foundation for later algebraic thinking. For example, recognizing that if there were 3 birds and then 2 more birds flew in versus if there were 2 birds at first and then 3 more birds flew in results in the same total number of birds either way is a step toward recognizing the commutative property of addition, that $a + b = b + a$ for all numbers a and b.

Although these content examples of looking for patterns and structures and organizing information are appropriate activities, they form a small part of the mathematics content for early childhood. Similarly, the specific skills in these examples are but a small part of the role that these processes play in mathematics.

## MATHEMATICAL CONNECTIONS

In this section we discuss some of the main connections across content areas of early childhood mathematics and into later mathematics. Mathematics as a whole is a web of interconnected ideas, and the mathematics of early childhood is no exception. Mathematics is also deep, in that every mathematical idea, including those of early childhood, is embedded in long chains of related ideas. As this section shows, the foundational and achievable mathematical ideas discussed in the previous sections are tightly interwoven with each other and with other important ideas that are studied later in mathematics.

### Connections in Structuring Numbers, Shapes, and Space

Throughout mathematics, structure is found and analyzed by composing and decomposing. A group of objects can be joined to form a new composite object. An object can be decomposed to reveal its finer structure. Some of the most important connections in elementary mathematics concern structuring of numbers and space via composition and decomposition. We now discuss several of these connections.

#### *Making Units by Grouping*

Numbers are structured by composition because the decimal place-value system relies on grouping by tens. In the realm of number, 10 individual counters are viewed as forming a single composite unit of 10. A geometric version of this grouping idea occurs when several shapes are put together to form another larger shape, which is then viewed as a unified shape in its own right, such as if the unified shape is seen as a possible substitute for another shape or as able to fill a space in a puzzle.

When children (or adults) make a repeating pattern, they might focus mainly on maintaining a certain order. But repeating patterns can also be viewed as made from a single composite unit that is copied over and over. This is not unlike viewing the counting numbers as a sequence that is structured in groups of 10 (see Figure 2-8).

Repeating patterns and, more generally, making groups of equal size are the basis for multiplication and division. Later in elementary school, when children skip count by fives, by counting 5, 10, 15, 20, . . . to list the multiples of 5, this pattern can be viewed as a growing pattern, but it can also be viewed as counting every fifth entry in a repeating pattern of 5. When children study division with remainders (in around fourth or fifth grade), they may observe a repeating pattern in the remainders. For example, when dividing successive counting numbers by 5, say, the remainders cycle through 0, 1, 2, 3, and 4.

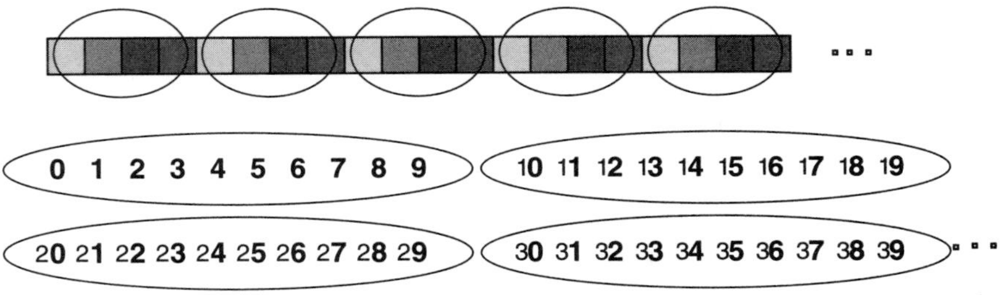


**FIGURE 2-8** A repeating pattern is formed by repeating a unit. In counting, the ones digits form a repeating pattern.

### *Groups of Groups: Numbers, Shapes, and 2-D Space*

The compositional structure of the decimal system is more complex than just making groups of 10 from 10 ones, since every 10 groups of 10 are composed into a unit of 100. A geometric version of this group's idea occurs when shapes are put together to form a new, composite shape, and composite shapes are then put together to make another composite shape—a composite of the composite shapes.

An especially important case of geometric structuring as composites of composites occurs when analyzing rectangles and their areas. When considering the area of a rectangle, one views the rectangle as composed of identical square tiles that cover the rectangle without gaps or overlaps. Each square tile has area one square unit. The area of the rectangle (in square units) is the number of squares that cover the rectangle. Although these squares can be counted one by one, to develop and understand the *length* × *width* formula for the area of a rectangle, the squares must be seen as grouped, either into rows or into columns (see Figure 2-6). Each row has the same number of squares in it, and the number of rows in the rectangle is equal to the number of squares in a column (likewise, each column has the same number of squares in it, and the number of columns is the number of squares in a row). Because of this grouping structure, the area of the rectangle is # *rows* × # *in each row* or *length* × *width* (square units). Similarly, the decimal system has a multiplicative structure because 100 is formed (by definition) by making 10 groups of 10, and so 100 = 10 × 10.

The idea of structuring rectangles as arrays of squares can be extended to structuring an entire infinite plane (in the imagination) as an infinite array of squares. This idea of a plane structured by an infinite array is essentially the idea of the Cartesian coordinate plane, in which each point in the plane is described by a pair of numbers that indicate its location relative to two coordinate lines (axes) (see Figure 2-9).

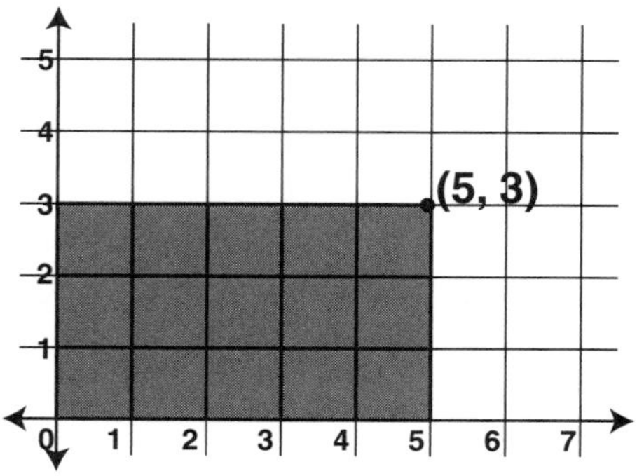


**FIGURE 2-9** The coordinate plane.

*Groups of Groups of Groups: Numbers, Shapes, and 3-D Space*

The compositional structure of the decimal system consists not only of making groups of 10 from 10 ones and groups of 100 from 10 groups of 10, but also groups of 1,000 from 10 groups of 100, so that $1,000 = 10 \times 10 \times 10$. The grouping structure of the decimal system continues in such a way that all successive groupings are obtained by repeatedly grouping by 10. The geometric counterpart of this grouping structure of the decimal system takes one into 3-D space and then higher dimensional space. Just as 2-D rectangles can be structured as 2-D arrays of squares, so, too, 3-D rectangular prisms (box shapes) can be structured as 3-D arrays of cubes. As in the case of rectangles, the multiplicative structure of a 3-D array of cubes explains why one multiplies the three dimensions of length, width, and height of a box to find its volume. Box shapes can be built as layers of identical cubes, as in Figure 2-12, and each layer can be viewed as groups of rows, so a box built from cubes can be viewed as a group of a group of cubes in the same way that 1,000 is 10 groups of 10 groups of 10.

When one extends the array structure of rectangular prisms to all of 3-D space, one gets essentially the idea of coordinate space, in which the location of each point in space is described by a triple of numbers that indicate its location relative to three coordinate lines.

*Motion, Decomposing and Composing, Symmetry, and Properties of Arithmetic*

The properties (or laws) of arithmetic are the fundamental structural properties of addition and multiplication from which all of arithmetic is derived. These properties include the commutative properties of addition and of multiplication, the associative properties of addition and multiplication, and the distributive property of multiplication over addition. The commutative properties of addition and multiplication state that

$$A + B = B + A \text{ for all numbers A, B}$$

$$A \times B = B \times A \text{ for all numbers A, B.}$$

The associative properties of addition and multiplication state that

$$A + (B + C) = (A + B) + C \text{ for all numbers A, B, C}$$

$$A \times (B \times C) = (A \times B) \times C \text{ for all numbers A, B, C.}$$

The distributive property states that

$$A \times (B + C) = A \times B + A \times C \text{ for all numbers A, B, C.}$$

Each property can be illustrated by moving and reorganizing objects, sometimes also by decomposing and recomposing a grouping, and sometimes even in terms of symmetry.

The report *Adding It Up: Helping Children Learn Mathematics* has a good discussion and an illustration of the commutative and associative properties of addition, the commutative and associative properties of multiplication, and the distributive property (National Research Council, 2001, Chapter 3 and Box 3-1). The commutative property of addition is illustrated by switching the order in which two sets are shown. The commutative property is especially useful in conjunction with counting on strategies for solving addition problems (see Chapter 5 for further discussion of children's problem-solving strategies for addition and subtraction). For example, instead of counting on 6 from 2 to calculate 2 + 6, a child can switch the problem to 6 + 2 and count on 2 from 6. The associative property involves starting with three separate sets, two of which are close together, separating the two that are close together, and moving one of those sets to reassociate with the other set. The associative property of addition is used in make-a-ten methods, when one number is decomposed so that one of the pieces can be recomposed with another number to make a group of 10.

Early experiences with properties of addition then extend to multiplication in third and fourth grade. The commutative and associative properties of multiplication and the distributive property are essential to understanding relationships among basic multiplication facts and to understanding multidigit multiplication and division. For example, knowing that $3 \times 5 = 5 \times 3$ and that $7 \times 8$ can be obtained by adding $5 \times 8$ and $2 \times 8$ lightens the load in learning the multiplication tables. The commutative property of multiplication is illustrated by decomposing a rectangular array in two different ways: by the rows or by the columns (as shown in Figure 2-6) or in terms of a rotation (see National Research Council, 2001, Box 3-1). The associative property of multiplication can be illustrated by decomposing a 3-D array (or box shape built of blocks) in different ways (one way is shown in Figure 2-7). The distributive property is illustrated by viewing objects as grouped in two different ways (see National Research Council, 2001, Box 3-1).

The properties of multiplication can be illustrated with arrays and rectangles, and they are also visible in the multiplication tables, which contain many relationships and have important structure. One structural aspect of the multiplication tables is their diagonal symmetry. This diagonal symmetry corresponds with the commutative property of multiplication, namely that $a \times b = b \times a$ for all numbers a and b. Recognizing this symmetry allows children to learn multiplication facts more efficiently. In other words, once they know the upper right-hand triangular portion of the multiplication tables in around third grade, they can fill in the rest of the table by reflecting across the diagonal (see Figure 2-10).

Patterns associated with horizontal or vertical shifts (slides) can also be seen in the multiplication tables. For example, the entries in two columns are related by the column that is associated with the amount of shift between the columns (see Figure 2-10). This structural relationship corresponds with the distributive property.

## Connections in Measurement and Number: Fractions

Once children encounter measurement situations, the possibility of fractions arises naturally. Fractions can be shown well in the context of

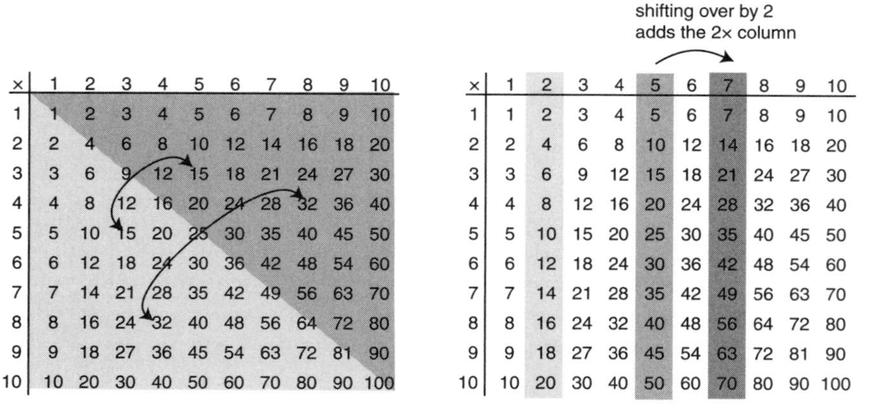


The diagonal symmetry in the multiplication table is due to the commutative property.

The relationship among the columns is due to the distributive property, e.g., $6 \times 7 = 6 \times 5 + 6 \times 2$.

**FIGURE 2-10** Symmetry and relationships in the multiplication table.

length and on number lines (in around second or third grade). A number line is much like an infinitely long ruler, so number lines can be viewed as unifying measurement and number in a one-dimensional space. A number on a number line can be thought of as representing the length from 0 to the number (see Figure 2-11).

Because of the close connection between number lines and length, number lines are difficult for children below about second grade. In contrast, the number paths on most number board games used for preschoolers are a count model, not a number line. There is a path of squares, circles, or rocks, each has a number on it, and players move along this path by counting the squares or other objects or saying the number on them as they move. These are appropriate for younger children because they can support their knowledge of counting, cardinality, comparing, and number symbols.

In measurement, there is an important relationship between the size of a unit and the number of units it takes to make a given, fixed quantity. For example, if the triangle in Figure 2-5 is designated to have 1 unit of area, then the hexagon has an area of 6 units. But if one picks a new unit of area, such as designating the area of the rhombus in Figure 2-5 to be 1 unit, which is twice the size of the triangle, then the hexagon has an area of only 3 units.

Later in elementary school (in around second grade), children see this inverse relationship between the size of a unit of measurement and the number of units it takes to make a given quantity reflected in the inverse relationship between the ordering of the counting numbers and the ordering of the unit fractions (see Figure 2-12).

### Connections in Data Analysis, Number, and Measurement

To use data to answer (or address) a question, one must analyze the data, which often involves classifying the data into different categories,

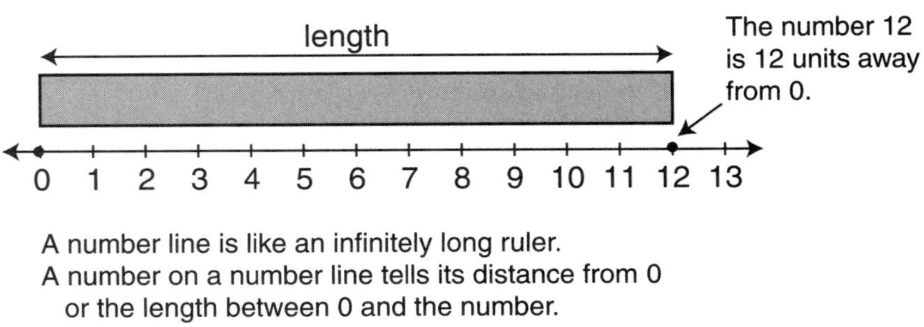
length
The number 12
is 12 units away
from 0.
0 1 2 3 4 5 6 7 8 9 10 11 12 13
A number line is like an infinitely long ruler.
A number on a number line tells its distance from 0
or the length between 0 and the number.

**FIGURE 2-11** Number lines relate numbers to lengths.

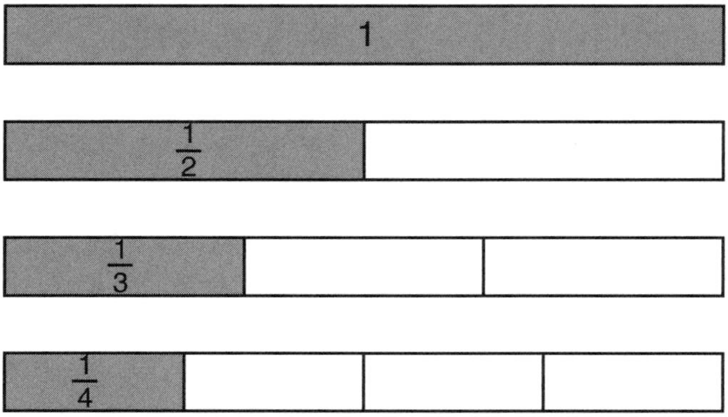


**FIGURE 2-12** 1 > ½ > ⅓ > ¼.

displaying the categorized data graphically, and describing or comparing the categories. Because the process of describing or comparing categories usually involves number or measurement, number and measurement are central to data analysis, and data analysis provides a context to which number and measurement can be applied.

The collection of data should ideally start with a question of interest to children. For example, children in a class might be interested in how everyone got to school in the morning and might wonder what way was most popular. To answer this question, children might divide themselves into different groups according to how they got to school in the morning (by bus, by car, by walking, or by bike). The children could then make "real graphs" (graphs made of real objects) either by lining up in their categories or by each placing a small toy or token to represent a bus, a car, a pair of shoes, or a bike into predrawn squares, as shown on the left in Figure 2-13 (the predrawn squares ensure that each object occupies the same amount of space in the graph). Instead of a real graph, children could display the data somewhat more abstractly in a pictograph by lining up sticky notes in categories, as on the right in the figure. Each child places a sticky note in the category for how the child got to school.

In general, pictographs use small, identical pictures to represent data. In this case, each sticky note stands for a single piece of data and functions as a small picture in a pictograph. Children can then use these real graphs or pictographs to answer such questions as "How many children rode a bus to get to school today?" or "Did more children ride in a car or walk to school today?" or even "If it were raining today, how do you think the graph might be different?" Data displays that are used in posing and answering such quantitative questions serve a purpose and help children mathematize their daily experiences. In contrast, data displays that are only

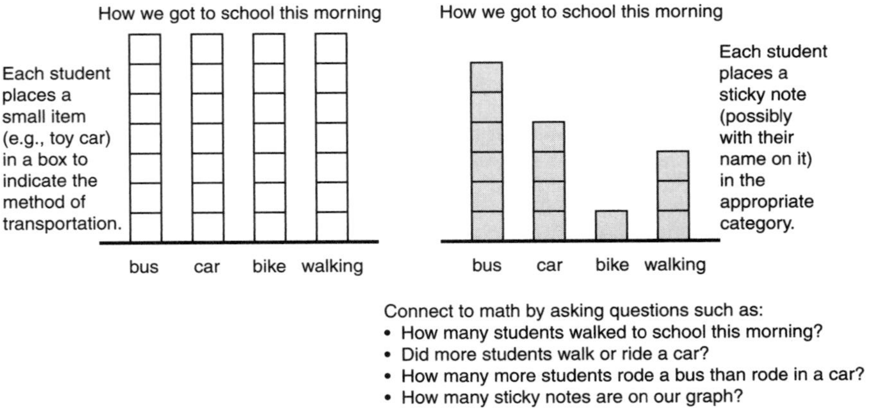

How we got to school this morning
Each student places a small item (e.g., toy car) in a box to indicate the method of transportation.
bus car bike walking
How we got to school this morning
Each student places a sticky note (possibly with their name on it) in the appropriate category.
bus car bike walking
Connect to math by asking questions such as:
• How many students walked to school this morning?
• Did more students walk or ride a car?
• How many more students rode a bus than rode in a car?
• How many sticky notes are on our graph?


**FIGURE 2-13** A template for a "real graph" and a pictograph made with sticky notes.

made but not discussed are not likely to help children develop or extend their mathematical thinking.

In around second or third grade, once children have worked with linear measurement, they can begin to work with bar graphs. One can think of bar graphs as arising from pictographs by fusing the separated entries in a pictograph to make the bars in a bar graph. In this way, the discrete counting of separate entries in a pictograph gives way to the length measurement of a bar in a bar graph.

In third grade or so, once children have begun to skip count and to multiply, the entries in a pictograph can be used to represent more than one single piece of data. For example, each picture might represent 2 pieces of data or 10 pieces of data.

## SUMMARY

This chapter describes the foundational and achievable mathematics content for young children. The focus of this chapter is on the mathematical ideas themselves rather than on the teaching or learning of these ideas. These mathematical ideas are often taken for granted by adults, but they are surprisingly deep and complex. There are two fundamental areas of mathematics for young children: (1) number and (2) geometry and measurement as identified in NCTM's Curriculum Focal Points and outlined by this committee. There are also important mathematical reasoning processes that children must engage in. This chapter also describes some of the most important connections of the mathematics for young children to later mathematics.

In the area of number, a fundamental idea is the connection between the counting numbers as a list and for describing how many objects are in a set. We can represent arbitrarily large counting numbers in an efficient, systematic way by means of the remarkable decimal system (base 10). We can use numbers to compare quantities without matching the quantities directly. The operations of addition and subtraction allow us to describe how amounts are related before and after combining or taking away, how parts and totals are related, and to say precisely how two amounts compare.

In the area of geometry and measurement, a fundamental idea is that geometric shapes have different parts and aspects that can be described, and they can be composed and decomposed. To measure the size of something, one first selects a specific measurable attribute of the thing, and then views the thing as composed of some number of units. The shapes of geometry can be viewed as idealized and simplified approximations of objects in the world. Space has structure that derives from movement through space and from relative location within space. An important way to think about the structure of 2-D and 3-D space comes from viewing rectangles as composed of rows and columns of squares and viewing box shapes as composed of layers of rows and columns of cubes.

## REFERENCES AND BIBLIOGRAPHY

Clements, D.H., and Sarama, J. (2007). Early childhood mathematics learning. In F.K. Lester, Jr. (Ed.), *Second Handbook of Research on Mathematics Teaching and Learning* (pp. 461-555). New York: Information Age.

Clements, D.H., Battista, M.T., Sarama, J., Swaminathan, S., and McMillen, S. (1997). Students' development of length measurement concepts in a logo-based unit on geometric paths. *Journal for Research in Mathematics Education*, *28*(1), 70-95.

Grattan-Guinness, I. (2000). *The Search for Mathematical Roots 1870-1940: Logics, Set Theories, and the Foundations of Mathematics from Cantor Through Russell to Gödel.* Princeton, NJ: Princeton University Press.

Howe, R. (2008). *Taking Place Value Seriously: Arithmetic, Estimation and Algebra.* Available: http://www.maa.org/pmet/resources/PlaceValue_RV1.pdf [accessed September 2008].

Menninger, K. (1958/1969). *Number Words and Number Symbols: A Cultural History of Numbers.* (P. Broneer, Trans.). Cambridge, MA: MIT Press. (Original work published 1958.)

National Association for the Education of Young Children and National Council of Teachers of Mathematics. (2002). *Early Childhood Mathematics: Promoting Good Beginnings.* A joint position statement of the National Association for the Education of Young Children and National Council of Teachers of Mathematics. Available: http://www.naeyc.org/about/positions/pdf/psmath.pdf [accessed August 2008].

National Council of Teachers of Mathematics. (2000). *Principles and Standards for School Mathematics.* Reston, VA: Author.

National Research Council. (2001). *Adding It Up: Helping Children Learn Mathematics.* Mathematics Learning Study Committee. J. Kilpatrick, J. Swafford, and B. Findell (Eds.). Center for Education, Division of Behavioral and Social Sciences and Education. Washington, DC: National Academy Press.

Reynolds, A., and Wheatley, G.H. (1996). Elementary students' construction and coordination of units in an area setting. *Journal for Research in Mathematics Education, 27*(5), 564-581.

Sophian, C. (2007). Rethinking the starting point for mathematics learning. In O.N. Saracho and B. Spodek (Eds.), *Contemporary Perspectives in Early Childhood Education: Mathematics, Science, and Technology in Early Childhood Education* (pp. 21-44). New York: Information Age.

Wheatley, G.H. (1990). Spatial sense and mathematics learning. *Arithmetic Teacher*, *37*(6), 10-11.

# 3

# Cognitive Foundations for Early Mathematics Learning

Over the past two decades, a quiet revolution in developmental psychology and related fields has demonstrated that children have skills and concepts relevant to mathematics learning that are present early in life, and that most children enter school with a wealth of knowledge and cognitive skills that can provide a foundation for mathematics learning. At the same time, these foundational skills are not enough—children need rich mathematical interactions, both at home and at school in order to be well prepared for the challenges they will meet in elementary school and beyond. (Chapter 4 discusses supporting children's mathematics at home, and Chapters 5 and 6 discuss children's mathematical development and related instructional practices.) The knowledge and interest that children show about number and shape and other mathematics topics provide an important opportunity for parents and preschool teachers to help them develop their understanding of mathematics (e.g., Gelman, 1980; Saxe, Guberman, and Gearhart, 1987; Seo and Ginsburg, 2004).

In this chapter we review research on the mathematical development of infants and young children to characterize both the resources that most children bring to school and the limitations of preschoolers' understanding of mathematics. Because this literature is vast, it is not possible to do it justice in a single chapter. However, we attempt to provide an overview of key issues and research findings relevant to early childhood education settings. These include

- What is the nature of early universal starting points? These are generally thought to provide an important foundation for subsequent mathematical development (e.g., Barth et al., 2005; Butterworth, 2005; Dehaene, 1997; but see Holloway and Ansari, 2008, and Rips, Bloomfield, and Asmuth, 2008, for contrasting views). We examine two domains that are foundational to mathematics in early childhood: (1) number, including operations, and (2) spatial thinking, geometry, and measurement.

- What are some of the important developmental changes in mathematical understandings in these domains that occur during the preschool years?
- What is the relation of mathematical development to more general aspects of development needed for learning mathematics, such as the ability to regulate one's behavior and attention?

## EVIDENCE FOR EARLY UNDERSTANDING OF NUMBER

### Preverbal Number Knowledge

Delineating the starting points of knowledge in important domains is a major goal in developmental psychology. These starting points are of theoretical importance, as they constrain models of development. They are also of practical importance, as a basic tenet of instruction is that teaching that makes contact with the knowledge children have already acquired is likely to be most effective (e.g., Clements et al., 1999). Thus, it is not surprising that infant researchers have been actively mapping out the beginnings of preverbal number knowledge—knowledge that appears to be shared by humans from differing cultural backgrounds as well as with other species, and thus part of their evolutionary endowment (e.g., Boysen and Berntson, 1989; Brannon and Terrace, 1998, 2000; Brannon et al., 2001; Cantlon and Brannon, 2006; Dehaene, 1997; Dehaene, Dehaene-Lambertz, and Cohen, 1998, Meck and Church, 1983). A large body of research has examined a set of numerical skills, including infants' ability to discriminate between different set sizes, their ability to recognize numerical relationships, and their ability to understand addition and subtraction transformations. The study of numerical knowledge in infants represents a major departure from previously held views, which were heavily influenced by Piaget's (1941/1965) number conservation findings and stage theory. These older findings showed that children do not conserve number in the face of spatial transformations until school age, and they led many to believe that before this age children lack the ability to form concepts of number (see Mix, Huttenlocher, and Levine, 2002, for a review). Although Piaget recognized that children acquire some mathematically relevant skills at earlier ages, success on the conservation task was widely regarded as the sine qua non of numerical understanding.

Beginning in the 1960s and 1970s, researchers began to actively examine early numerical competencies, which led to a revised understanding of children's numerical competence. This research identified a great deal of competence in preschool children, including counting and matching strategies that children use on Piaget's conservation of number task (see the discussion in Chapter 5).

As we detail, infant and toddler studies have largely focused on the natural numbers (also called counting numbers). However, they have also examined representations of fractional amounts and proportional relations as well as geometric relationships, shape categories, and measurement. Moreover, although there is some disagreement in the field about the interpretation of the findings of infant and toddler studies as a whole, these findings are generally viewed as showing strong starting points for the learning of verbal and symbolic mathematical skills.

### *Infants' Sensitivity to Small Set Size*

Infant studies typically use habituation paradigms to examine whether infants can discriminate between small sets of objects, either static or moving (Antell and Keating, 1983; Starkey and Cooper, 1980; Strauss and Curtis, 1981; Van Loosbroek and Smitsman, 1990; Wynn, Bloom, and Chiang, 2002). In a typical habituation study, infants are repeatedly shown sets containing the same number of objects (e.g., 2) until they become bored and their looking time decreases to a specified criterion. The infant is then shown a different set size of objects or the same set size, and looking times are recorded. Longer looking times indicate that the infant recognizes that the new display is different from an earlier display. Results show that infants (ranging in age from 1 day old to several months old) can discriminate a set of two objects from a set of three objects, yet they are unable to discriminate four objects from six objects, even though the same 3:2 ratio is involved. These findings indicate that infants' ability to discriminate small set sizes is limited by number rather than by ratio. Huttenlocher, Jordan, and Levine (1994) suggest that infants' ability to discriminate small sets (2 versus 3) could be based on an approximate rather than on an exact sense of number.

Several studies suggest that the early quantitative sensitivity displayed by infants for small set sizes is actually based on their sensitivity to amount (surface area or contour length) which covaries with numerosity, rather than on number per se (Clearfield and Mix, 1999, 2001). That is, unless these variables are carefully controlled, the more items there are, the greater the amount of stuff there is. In studies that independently vary number and amount, Clearfield and Mix (1999, 2001) found that infants ages 6 to 8 months detected a change in amount (contour length or area) but not a change in number. Thus, if they were habituated to a set of two items, they did not dishabituate to a set of three items if that set was equivalent to the original set in area or contour length.

However, recent findings indicate that infants are sensitive to both continuous quantity and to number (Cordes and Brannon, 2008, in press; Kwon et al., 2009). Furthermore, Cordes and Brannon (2008) report that, although 6-month-old infants are sensitive to a two-fold change in number, they are sensitive to a three-fold change only in cumulative area across elements, suggesting that early sensitivity to set size may be more finely tuned than early sensitivity to continuous quantity. Other studies that provide support for early number sensitivity include a study showing that 6-month-old infants can discriminate between small sets of visually presented events (puppet jumps) (e.g., Wynn, 1996). This result is not subject to the alternative explanation of discrimination based on amount rather than number, like the findings involving sets of objects. However, it is possible that even though the rate and duration of the events have been controlled in these studies, infants' discrimination is based on nonnumerical cues, such as rhythm (e.g., Demany, McKenzie, and Vurpillot, 1977; Mix et al., 2002). Indeed, in one study in which the rate of motion was not a reliable cue to numerosity, 6-month-olds did not discriminate old and new numerosities (Clearfield, 2004).

A set size limitation also is seen in the behavior of 10- to 14-month-olds on search tasks (Feigenson and Carey, 2003, 2005; Feigenson, Carey, and Hauser, 2002). For example, in one study 12-month-olds saw crackers placed inside two containers. The toddlers chose the larger hidden quantity for 1 versus 2 and 2 versus 3 crackers, but they failed to do so on 3 versus 4, 2 versus 4, and 3 versus 6 crackers (Feigenson, Carey, and Hauser, 2002). The authors suggest that this failure is due to the set size limitation of the object file system.[1] When cracker size was varied, the toddlers based their search on the total cracker amount rather than on number. Similarly, 12- to 14-month-olds searched longer in a box in which two balls had been hidden after they saw the experimenter remove one ball, than they did in a box in which one ball had been hidden and the experimenter removed one ball (in actuality there were no more balls in either box, as the experimenter surreptitiously removed the remaining ball). They also succeeded on 3 versus 2 balls but failed on 4 versus 2 balls. That is, they did not search longer in a box in which four balls were hidden and they saw two removed than in a box in which they had seen two hidden and two were removed. The failure

[1]The object file system refers to the representation of an object in a set that consists of small numbers, the objects are in a 1-to-1 correspondence with each mental symbol, and there is no summary representation of set size (e.g., three items are represented as "this," "this," "this" rather than "a set of three things") (Carey, 2004).

on 2 versus 4, which has the same ratio as the 2 versus 1 problem, suggests that they were using the object file system rather than the analog magnitude system, which is second system that represents large set sizes (4 or more) approximately. Furthermore, in this study, the toddlers based their search on the number of objects they saw hidden rather than on the total object volume. Thus, at least by 12 months of age, it appears that children can represent the number of objects in sets up to three (Feigenson and Carey, 2003). A subsequent study shows that this set size limit can be extended to four if spatiotemporal cues allow the toddlers to represent the sets as two sets of two (Feigenson and Halberda, 2004).

### *Infants' Sensitivity to Large Set Size*

Recent studies have shown that infants can approximate the number of items in large sets of visual objects (e.g., Brannon, 2002; Brannon, Abbott, and Lutz, 2004; Xu, 2003; Xu and Spelke, 2000; Xu, Spelke, and Goddard, 2005), events (puppet jumps) (Wood and Spelke, 2005), and auditory sets (Lipton and Spelke, 2003) that are well beyond the range of immediate apprehension of numerosity (*subitizing* range). Consistent with the accumulator model, which refers to a nonverbal counting mechanism that provides approximate numerical representations in the form of analog magnitudes, infants' discrimination of large sets is limited by the ratio of the two sets being compared rather than by set size. Thus, at 6 months of age, when infants are habituated to an array of dots, they dishabituate to a new set as long as the ratio between two sets is at least 2:1. By 10 months of age, infants are able to discriminate visual and auditory sets that differ by a 2:3 ratio but not by a 4:5 ratio (Lipton and Spelke, 2003, 2004; Xu and Arriaga, 2007). Importantly, these studies controlled for many continuous variables, suggesting that the discriminations were based on number rather than amount (e.g., Brannon, Abbott, and Lutz, 2004; Cordes and Brannon, 2008; Xu, 2003; Xu and Spelke, 2000).

### *Do Infants Have a Concept of Number?*

Infants may be able to discriminate between sets of different sizes but have no notion that all sets that have the same numerosity form a category or equivalence class (the mathematical term for such a category). This notion is referred to as the cardinality concept (e.g., the knowledge that three flowers, three jumps, three sounds, and three thoughts are equivalent in number). Number covers such matters as the list of counting numbers (e.g., 1, 2, 3, . . .) and its use in describing how many things are in collections. It also covers the ordinal position (e.g., first, second, third, . . .), the idea of cardinal value (e.g., how many are there?), and the various operations on number (e.g., addition and subtraction). The notion of 1-to-1 correspondences connects the counting numbers to the cardinal value of sets. Another important aspect of number is the way one writes and says them using the base 10 system (see Chapters 2 and 5 for further discussion). Knowledge of number is foundational to children's mathematical development and gradually develops over time, so not all aspects of the number are present during the earliest years.

Several studies (e.g., Starkey, Spelke, and Gelman, 1990; Strauss and Curtis, 1984) examined whether infants understand that small sets that share their numerosity but contain different kinds of entities form a category (e.g., two dogs, two chicks, two jumps, two drumbeats). Starkey and colleagues (1990) examined this question by habituating infants to sets of two or three aerial photographs of different household objects. At test, infants were shown novel photographs that alternated between sets of two and sets of three. Infants dishabituated to the novel set size, suggesting that they considered different sets of two (or three) as similar. Whereas these studies might be regarded as suggesting that infants form numerical equivalence classes over visual sets containing disparate objects, these studies may have tapped infants' sensitivity to continuous amount rather than number, as described above (Clearfield and Mix, 1999, 2001). That is, unless careful controls are put in place, sets with two elements will on average be smaller in amount than sets of three elements (e.g., Clearfield and Mix, 1999, 2001; Mix et al., 2002).

Findings showing that infants consider two objects and two sounds to form a category would not be subject to this criticism and thus could be considered as strong evidence for abstract number categories. In an important study, Starkey, Spelke, and Gelman (1983) tested whether infants have such categories. While the results seemed to indicate that 7-month-olds regarded sets of two (or three) objects and drumbeats as similar, several attempts to replicate these important findings have called them into question (Mix, Levine, and Huttenlocher, 1997; Moore et al., 1987). Thus, whether infants have an abstract concept of number that allows them to group diverse sets that share set size remains an open question. The findings, reviewed below, showing that 3-year-olds have difficulty matching visual and auditory sets on the basis of number, and that this skill is related to knowledge of conventional number words, suggest that the ability to form equivalence classes over sets that contain different kinds of elements may depend on the acquisition of conventional number skills. Kobayashi, Hiraki, Mugitani, and Hasegawa (2004) suggest that the methods used may be too abstract to tap this intermodal knowledge and that when the sounds made are connected to objects, for example, the sound of an object landing on a surface, evidence of abstract number categories may be revealed at younger ages, perhaps even in infants.

### *Infant Sensitivity to Changes in Set Size*

Several studies report that infants track the results of numerically relevant transformations—adding or taking away objects from a set. That is, when an object is added to a set, they expect to see more objects than were previously in the set and when an object is taken away, they expect to see fewer objects than were previously in the set. Wynn (1992a) found that after a set was transformed by the addition or subtraction of an object, 5-month-old infants looked longer at the "impossible" result (e.g., 1 + 1 = 1) than at the "correct" result. However, as for numerical discrimination, subsequent studies suggest that their performance may reflect sensitivity to continuous (cumulative size of objects) amount rather than to numerosity (Feigenson, Carey, and Spelke, 2002). For the problem 1 + 1, infants looked longer at 2, the expected number of objects, when the cumulative size of the two objects was changed than at three, the impossible number of objects, when the cumulative size of the objects was correct—that is, when the cumulative area of the three objects was equivalent to the area that would have resulted from the 1 + 1 addition.

Cohen and Marks (2002) suggested an alternative explanation for Wynn's results. In particular, they suggest that the findings could be attributable to a familiarity preference rather than to an ability to carry out numerical transformations. For the problem 1 + 1 = 2, they point out that infants more often see one object, as there was a single object in the first display of every trial and thus, based on familiarity, look more at 1 (the incorrect answer). A similar argument was made for looking more at 2 for the problem 2 − 1.

Although their findings support this hypothesis, a more recent study by Kobayashi et al. (2004) provides evidence that infants look longer at 1 + 1 = 3 and 1 + 2 = 3 than at 1 + 1 + 2 and 1 + 2 = 3 when the first addend is a visual object and the second addend consists of a tone(s). This paradigm cannot be explained by the familiarity preference because, for each problem, infants see only one element on the stage.

### *Order Relations*

A few studies have examined infants' sensitivity to numerical order relations (more than, less than). One habituation study showed that 10- and 12-month-olds discriminated equivalent sets (e.g., a set of two followed by another set of two) from nonequivalent sets (e.g., a set of two followed by a set of three) (Cooper, 1984). In another study, Cooper (1984) habituated 10-, 12-, 14-, and 16-month-old infants to sequences that were nonequivalent. In the "less than" condition, the first display in the pair was always less than the second (e.g., infants were shown two objects followed by three objects). The reverse order was shown for the "greater than" condition. At test, the 14- and 16-month-olds showed more interest in the opposite relation than the one that was shown, suggesting that they represented the less than and greater than relations, whereas 10- and 12-month-olds did not. However, Brannon (2002) presents evidence that infants are sensitive to numerical order relations by 11 months of age.

*Summary*

The results of infant studies using small set sizes show that, very early in life, infants have a limited ability to discriminate sets of different sizes from each other (e.g., 2 versus 3 but not 4 versus 6). The set size limitation has been interpreted as reflecting one of two core systems for number—the object file system. They also expect the appropriate result from small number addition and subtraction transformations (e.g., $1 + 1 = 2$ and $2 - 1 = 1$), at least when amount covaries with number. Somewhat later, by 10 months of age, infants discriminate equivalent from nonequivalent sets, and by 14 months of age they discriminate greater than from less than relationships. Because many of these studies did not control for continuous variables that covary with number (i.e., contour length and surface area), the basis of infant discriminations is debated. However, recent studies indicate that infants are sensitive to both number of objects in small sets and to continuous variables, and they may be more sensitive to number than to cumulative surface area. Infant studies also have examined sensitivity to approximate number by using larger sets of items (e.g., 8 versus 16). These studies have found that infants can discriminate between sets with a 2:1 ratio by age 6 months and between those with 2:3 ratios by age 9 months as long as all set sizes involved are greater than or equal to 4, that is, 6-month-olds fail to discriminate 2 versus 4.

We also note that infants' early knowledge of number is largely implicit and has important limitations that are discussed below. There were no number words involved in any of the studies described above. This means that learning the number words and relating them to sets of objects is a major new kind of learning done by toddlers and preschoolers at home and in care and education centers. This learning powerfully extends numerical knowledge, and children who acquire this knowledge at earlier ages are provided with a distinct advantage.

## Mental Number Representations in Preschool Children

Just as much of the infant research has a focus on theorizing about and researching the nature of infant representations of number, so, too, does some research on toddlers and preschool children. The goal is to understand how and when young children represent small and larger numbers. To do this, special tasks are used that involve hidden objects, so that children must use mental representations to solve the task. Sometimes objects are shown initially and are then hidden, and sometimes objects are never shown and numbers are given in words. These tasks are quite different from situations in which young children ordinarily learn about numbers in the home or in care and educational centers, and they can do tasks in home and naturalistic settings considerably earlier than they can solve these laboratory tasks (e.g., Mix, 2002). In home and in care and educational settings, numbers are presented with objects (things, fingers), and children and adults may see, or count, or match, or move the objects. The objects do not disappear, and they are not hidden. Children's learning under these ordinary conditions is described in Chapter 5. Here we continue to focus on theoretical issues of representations of numbers.

*Small Set Sizes*

Like infants, 2- to 3-year-olds show more advanced knowledge of number than would be predicted by previous views. As noted previously, conservation of number was considered to be a hallmark of number development (Piaget, 1941/1965). However, Gelman's (1972) "magic experiment" showed that much younger children could conserve number if the spatial transformation was less salient and much smaller set sizes were used. In this study, 3- to 6-year-olds were told that either a set of two mice or a set of three mice was the "winner." The two sets were then covered and moved around. After children learned to choose the winner, the experimenter altered the winner set, either by changing the spatial arrangement of the mice or by adding or subtracting a mouse. Even the 3-year-olds were correct in recognizing that the rearrangement maintained the status of the winner, whereas the addition and subtraction transformations did not.

Huttenlocher, Jordan, and Levine (1994) examined the emergence of exact number representation in toddlers. They posited that mental models representing critical mathematical features—the number of items in the set and the nature of the transformation—were needed to exactly represent the results of a calculation. Similarly, Klein and Bisanz (2000) suggest that young children's success in solving nonverbal calculations depends on their ability to hold and manipulate quantitative representations in working memory as well as on their understanding of number transformations.

Huttenlocher, Jordan, and Levine (1994) gave children ages 2 to 4 a numerosity matching task and a calculation task with objects (called nonverbal; see Box 3-1). On the matching task, children were shown a set of disks that was subsequently hidden under a box. They were then asked to lay out the same number of disks. On the calculation task, children were

**BOX 3-1**
**Clarifying Experimental Misnomers**

Researchers have used tasks in which two conditions vary in two important ways, such as in Huttenlocher, Newcombe, and Sandberg (1994). In one condition, children are first shown objects, and then the objects are hidden. Number words are not used in this condition. In the other condition, children never see objects but must imagine or generate them (e.g., by raising a certain number of fingers). Here the numbers involved are conveyed by using number words, either as a story problem or just as words (e.g., "2 and 1 make what?"). In their reports, researchers call the first condition *nonverbal* and the second condition *verbal.* But these labels are a bit misleading, because they sound as if nonverbal and verbal are describing the children's solution methods. In this report we use language that mentions both aspects that were varied: with objects (called nonverbal) and without objects (called verbal).

shown a set of disks that was subsequently covered. Following this, items were either added or taken away from the original set. The child's task was to indicate the total number of disks that were hidden by laying out the same number of disks ("Make yours like mine").

On both the matching and transformation tasks, performance increased gradually with age. Children were first successful with problems involving low numerosities, such as 1 and 2, gradually extending their success to problems involving higher numerosities. Importantly, when children responded incorrectly, their responses were not random, but rather were approximately correct. Approximately correct responses were seen in children as young as age 2, the youngest age group included in the study. On the basis of these findings, Huttenlocher, Jordan, and Levine (1994) argue that representations of small set sizes begin as approximate representations and become more exact as children develop the ability to create a mental model. Exactness develops further and extends to larger set sizes when children map their nonverbal number representations onto number words.

Toddlers' performance on numerosity matching tasks indicates that, as they get older, they get better at representing quantity abstractly. This achievement appears to be related to the acquisition of number words (Mix, 2008). Mix showed that preschoolers' ability to discriminate numerosities is highly dependent on the similarity of the objects in the sets. Thus, 3-year-olds could match the numerosities of sets consisting of pictures of black dots to highly similar black disks. Between ages 3 and 5, children were able to match the numerosities of increasingly dissimilar sets (e.g., black dots to pasta shells and black dots to sequential black disks at age 3½; black dots to heterogeneous sets of objects at age 4).

The abstractness of preschoolers' numerical representations was also assessed in a study (Mix, Huttenlocher, and Levine, 1996) examining their ability to make numerical matches between auditory and visual sets, an ability that Starkey, Spelke, and Gelman (1990) had attributed to infants. The researchers presented 3- and 4-year-olds with a set of two or three claps and were asked to point to the visual array that corresponded to the number of claps. The 3-year-olds performed at chance on this task, but by age 4, the children performed significantly above chance. In contrast, both age groups performed above chance on a control task that involved matching sets of disks to pictures of dots. Another study assessed the effect of the heterogeneity of sets on the ability of 3- to 5-year-olds to make numerical matches and order judgments. The results replicate Mix's (1999b) finding that the heterogeneity of sets decreases children's ability to make equivalence matches. However, heterogeneity versus homogeneity of sets did not affect their ability to make order judgments (i.e., to judge which of two sets is smaller) (Cantlon et al., 2007).

Mix (2002) has also examined the emergence of numerical knowledge through a diary study of her son, Spencer. In this study, she found indications of earlier knowledge than the experiments described above might indicate. Spencer was able to go into another room and get exactly two dog biscuits for his two dogs at 21 months of age, long before children succeed on the homogeneous or heterogeneous set matching tasks described above. Indeed, Spencer himself had failed to perform above chance on these laboratory tasks. Thus, it appears that early knowledge of numerical equivalence may arise piecemeal, and first in highly contextualized situations. For Spencer, his earliest numerical equivalence matches occurred in social situations (e.g., biscuits for dogs, sticks for guests). Whether this is a general pattern or whether there are wide individual differences in such behaviors is an open question (also see Mix, Sandhofer, and Baroody, 2005, for a review).

Levine, Jordan, and Huttenlocher (1992) compared the ability of preschool children to carry out calculations involving numerosities of up to six with objects (called nonverbal) and without objects (called verbal) (the former calculations were similar to those described above in the Huttenlocher, Jordan, and Levine, 1994 study). The calculations without objects (called verbal) were given in the form of story problems ("Ellen has 2 marbles and her father gives her 1 more. How many marbles does she have altogether?") and in the form of number combinations (e.g., "How much is 2 and 1?"). Children ages 4 to 5½ performed significantly higher on the calculation task when they could see objects and transformations than on the calculation tasks when they could not see objects or transformations. This was true for both addition and subtraction calculations. This difference in performance between nonverbal and verbal calculations was particularly marked for children from low socioeconomic backgrounds. Children from low socioeconomic backgrounds appear to have more difficulty accessing the numerical meaning of the number words (Jordan et al., 2006), which may be related to their exposure to cultural learning tools (e.g., number symbols, number words) (see Chapter 4 for further discussion).

*Large Set Sizes*

To investigate how preschoolers carry out approximate calculations with large numbers, 5-year-olds were presented with comparison and addition problems shown on a computer screen (Barth et al., 2005, 2006). On comparison problems, they were shown a set of blue dots (set sizes ranged from 10 to 58) that were then covered up. Next, they were shown a set of red dots and were asked whether there are more blue dots or red dots. On addition problems, they were shown a set of blue dots that were then covered up. They were then shown another set of blue dots that moved behind the same occluder. Finally, they were shown a set of red dots and were asked whether there were more blue dots or red dots. Subsequent experiments showed that children performed as well when the red dots were presented as a sequence of auditory tones as when they were presented visually. In each condition, performance was above chance and equivalent on comparison and addition problems, decreasing as the ratio of the red to blue dots approached 1. The ratio dependence of performance indicates that children are using the analogue magnitude system. This system differs from the exact representations of larger numbers that are built up by working with objects arranged in groups of tens and ones (see Chapter 5).

*Summary*

Toddlers and preschoolers continue to build on the two representational systems identified for infants: the object file system, which is limited to sets of three or less and provides a representation for each element in a set but no summary representation of set size, and the analogue magnitude system, which provides an approximate summary representation of set size but no representation of the individual elements in a set and no way to differentiate between adjacent set sizes, such as 10 and 11 (Carey, 2004; Feigenson, Dehaene, and Spelke, 2004; Spelke and Kinzler, 2007). Existing research also shows that children's early numerical knowledge is highly context-dependent, often depending on the presence of objects or fingers to represent sets. Although their numerical abilities are limited, young children have considerably more numerical competence than was inferred from Piaget's research. They are even building early informal knowledge in many other mathematics areas besides representation of the counting numbers (see sections below). However, the path from informal to formal knowledge is not necessarily a smooth one.

Impressive growth of numerical competence from age 2 to age 6 is stimulated by children's learning of important cultural numerical tools: spoken number words, written number symbols, and cultural solution methods, like counting and matching. As shown by Wynn's (1990, 1992b) research, the acquisition of the understanding of the cardinal meanings of number words is a protracted process. In a longitudinal study, Wynn found that it takes about a year for a child to move from succeeding in giving a set of "one" when requested to do so to being able to give the appropriate number for all numbers in his or her count list. The acquisition of such symbolic knowledge is important in promoting the abstractness of number concepts, that is, the concept of cardinality (that all sets of a given numerosity form an equivalence class). It is also important in promoting the exactness of number representations and the understanding of numerical relations, as only children who have acquired this knowledge understand that adding one item to a set means moving to the very next number in the count list (Sarnecka and Carey, 2008). The research concerning these cultural learning achievements is summarized in Chapter 5 in identifying foundational and achievable goals for teaching and learning. It is discussed in Chapter 4 as a major source of socioeconomic differences, connected to differential exposure to talk about number at home and at preschool.

## DEVELOPMENT OF SPATIAL THINKING AND GEOMETRY

Spatial thinking, like numerical thinking, is a fundamental component of mathematics that has its roots in foundational skills that emerge early in life. Spatial thinking is critical to a variety of mathematical topics, including geometry, measurement, and part-whole relations (e.g., Ansari et al., 2003; Fennema and Sherman, 1977, 1978; Guay and McDaniel, 1977; Lean and Clements, 1981; Skolnick, Langbort, and Day, 1982; see Chapter 6, this volume). Spatial thinking has been found to be a significant predictor of achievement in mathematics and science, even controlling for overall verbal and mathematical skill (e.g., Clements and Sarama, 2007; Hedges and Chung, in preparation; Lean and Clements, 1981; Shea, Lubinski, and Benbow, 2001; Stewart, Leeson, and Wright, 1997; Wheatley, 1990). One reason that spatial thinking is predictive of mathematics and science achievement is because it provides a way to conceptualize relationships in a problem prior to solving it (Clements and Sarama, 2007).

The mental functions encompassed by spatial thinking include categorizing shapes and objects and encoding the categorical and metric relations among shapes and objects. Spatial thinking is also crucial in representing object transformations and the outcomes of these transformations (e.g., rotation, translation, magnification, and folding) as well as perspective changes that occur as one moves to new locations. Spatial thinking is involved in navigating in the environment to reach goal locations and to find one's way back to one's starting point. Use of spatial symbolic systems, including language, maps, graphs, and diagrams, and spatial tools, such as measuring devices, extend and refine the ability to think spatially.

As is the case for the development of number knowledge, recent research has shown strong starting points for spatial thinking. In contrast to Piaget's view, which is in opposition to the gradual unfolding of spatial skills over the course of development, recent evidence shows that infants are able to code spatial information about objects, shapes, distances, locations, and spatial relations. This early emergence of spatial skills is consistent with an evolutionary perspective that emphasizes the adaptive importance of navigation for all mobile species (e.g., Newcombe and Huttenlocher, 2000, 2006; Wang and Spelke, 2002). That said, humans are unique in that their spatial skills are extended through symbolic systems, such as spatial language, measurement units, maps, graphs, and diagrams. Thus, it is not surprising that the trajectory of children's spatial development depends heavily on their spatially relevant experiences, including those involving spatial language and spatial activities, such as block building, puzzle play, and experience with certain video games.

### Starting Points in Infancy

Even young infants are able to segment their complex visual environments into objects that have stable shapes, using such principles as cohesion, boundedness, and rigidity (e.g., see Spelke, 1990). Infants also perceive the similarities between three-dimensional objects and photographs of these objects (DeLoache, Strauss, and Maynard, 1979). In habituation studies, infants show sensitivity to shape similarities across exemplars (e.g., Bomba and Siqueland, 1983). In addition, they are able to recognize invariant aspects of a shape shown from different angles of view (e.g., Slater and Morison, 1985).

Infants are also capable of forming categories of spatial relations—a claim that is widely supported; however, different views exist regarding the developmental sequence for children's understanding of space categories (Quinn, 1994, 2004; van Hiele, 1986). As stated by Bruner, Goodnow, and Austin (1956), categorization entails treating instances that are discriminable as the same. Using this criterion, Quinn showed that 3-month-old infants are sensitive to the categories above versus below (e.g., Quinn, 1994) and left versus right (e.g., Quinn, 2004). Both of these categories involve the relationship of an object and a single referent object (e.g., a horizontal or vertical bar). However, infants are not able to code the relationship between an object and a diagonal bar, showing that certain kinds of spatial relationship are privileged over others. Somewhat later, at 6 to 7 months, they are sensitive to the category of *between* relationships (Quinn et al., 1999). This spatial category is more complex than above/below or left/right, as it involves the relation of an object to two referent objects (e.g., two bars). At around this same age, infants form other, rather subtle spatial concepts. For example, they are sensitive to the functional difference between a container and a cylindrical object that does not have a bottom, even though these objects are highly similar visually (Aguiar and Baillargeon, 1998; Baillargeon, 1995).

Infants and toddlers also have impressive abilities to locate objects in space using both landmarks and geometric cues. Infants as young as 5 months are also able to use enclosed spaces that define a shape (e.g., walls of a sandbox) to code the location of objects (Newcombe, Huttenlocher, and Learmonth, 1999). By 12 months, children code distance and direction and use this information to search for objects hidden in displays (Bushnell et al., 1995). By 16 to 17 months, they are able to use the rectangular shape of an enclosure as well as landmark cues (both adjacent to the hiding location and at a distance from it) to search for objects (Hermer and Spelke, 1994, 1996; Huttenlocher, Newcombe, and Sandberg, 1994; Learmonth, Newcombe, and Huttenlocher, 2001).

### Mental Transformation of Shapes

Mental rotation (the ability to visualize and manipulate the movement of two-dimensional and three-dimensional objects) and spatial visualization (holding a shape in mind and finding the shape in more complex figures, combining shapes, or matching orientations) are fundamental spatial skills essential for mathematics learning (Linn and Peterson, 1985). Several recent studies have shown that preschool children are able to mentally rotate shapes in the picture plane. In one study, Marmor (1975) showed that children as young as age 5 years are able to mentally rotate visual images in the picture plane to determine whether one image is the same as another. Similarly, Levine et al. (1999) showed that children as young as age 4½ are able to perform above chance on mental transformations involving rotation and translation.

In tasks requiring spatial visualization (e.g., holding an image, such as a block letter, in mind for later comparison to a standard block letter), children between ages 4 and 5 perform poorly unless the visualized image is in the same orientation as the comparison object, whereas children between ages 6 and 10 were not adversely affected by differences in orientation (Smothergill et al., 1975). Furthermore, spatial ability in manipulating orientation at age 7, but not at ages 3 to 5 (Rod-and-Frame Test, Preschool

Embedded Figures Test), predicted spatial visualization abilities much later, at age 18 (Ozer, 1987). This developmental shift in spatial visualization ability is most likely to reflect differences in mental rotation ability and perspective-taking. Thus, when children are better able to mentally manipulate images held in mind (e.g., imagining the letter "F" and mentally rotating it clockwise or counterclockwise), they will be more accurate at determining how these images will appear from various viewpoints.

Similarly, when a child is asked to imagine what an object would look like from another person's perspective, this task is more easily accomplished when the child can mentally imagine the scene and move either themselves or the objects in order to match another person's perspective of the scene. For example, a child is sitting at a desk that has a toy car to the left of a pencil on top of the desk. A teacher is sitting on the other side of the desk, opposite the child, and asks the child to arrange the toy car and the pencil so that they would match what the teacher sees. The task becomes easier if the child can imagine the desk with the two objects and mentally "walk" to the other side of the desk to figure out the answer (pencil on the left, toy car on the right) or can imagine the objects and mentally rotate them so that they are in the 180 degree position.

As mental rotation and perspective-taking ability increase over time, such factors as changes in orientation become less problematic in tasks in which one must match something displayed in a different orientation than the visualized object. The fact that early spatial visualization measures during preschool were not correlated with later spatial visualization may suggest that the foundations for spatial abilities, such as mental rotation and perspective-taking, are molded in these formative years and are highly susceptible to change, more so than during later elementary education. This has important implications for findings that display gender differences in spatial performance on such tasks as mental rotation by age 4½ (Levine et al., 1999) and socioeconomic differences by second grade (Levine et al., 2005). That is, these differences in spatial ability may largely be the result of experiential differences during early childhood, and the preschool period may be an especially important time to begin addressing these issues through educational programs that foster spatial learning.[2]

The early emergence of mental rotation ability may be related to preschoolers' success with map use. Given simple maps, 4-year-olds and a majority of 3-year-olds can locate a hidden object in a sandbox (Huttenlocher, Newcombe, and Vasilyeva, 1999), children ages 3 to 5½

[2]Recent evidence shows a sex difference in mental rotation for 4- and 5-month-old infants that is not attributable to experimental factors (see Moore and Johnson, 2008; Quinn and Liben, 2008). Implications from these studies suggest there may be an advantage in early spatial learning for boys.

can find a hidden toy in an open field (Stea et al., 2004) and children ages 5 and 6 can navigate the hallways of an unfamiliar school (Sandberg and Huttenlocher, 2001). In order to succeed on these tasks, children must recognize the correspondence between the map and the actual space of a similar shape, scale distance (which we discuss further in the section on measurement), and perform mental rotation of the map with respect to actual space. Successful use of maps among preschoolers has occurred when the maps were oriented with respect to the space and mental rotation was limited to the vertical plane (in order to match ground-based perception of the space). Increasing the complexity of mental rotations required to realign spaces causes maps to become increasingly difficult for preschool children and is most likely to explain some of the difficulty children show in interpreting maps even into the elementary school years (Liben and Downs, 1989; Liben and Yekel, 1996; Piaget and Inhelder, 1967; Uttal, 1996; Wallace and Veek, 1995). Although the level of sophistication in mental transformation matures dramatically throughout childhood, the initial ability to mentally transform objects in space at the preschool age allows for productive interactions with spatial representations, such as maps.

### Learning Spatial Terms: Relation to Spatial Mathematical Skills

As summarized above, infants form spatial categories from an early age (e.g., Quinn, 1994, 2004). These visual categories may lay the foundation for the later learning of the spatial terms that label these categories (e.g., Mandler, 1992). However, it is also possible that linguistic input guides the learning of spatial concepts, highlighting certain preverbal spatial concepts and not others, perhaps leading to the formation of new spatial concepts. An example of how language can shape a preexisting nonverbal concept is provided by recent evidence showing that English-speaking infants form categories for tight/loose fit, a relation that is labeled in Korean but not in English (e.g., Casasola and Cohen, 2002; Hespos and Spelke, 2004; McDonough, Choi, and Mandler, 2003). By 29 months of age, English-speaking infants still categorized tight-fit containment relations when these were contrasted with loose-fit containment, but they no longer categorized loose-fit containment. By adulthood, English speakers do not pay attention to fit, categorizing tight and loose fit as "in" (McDonough, Choi, and Mandler, 2003). Thus, in this case exposure to English seems to play a selective function, highlighting some preexisting categories (in versus on) while downplaying others (tight fit/loose fit).

Exposure to spatial language during spatial experiences also appears to be particularly useful in "the learning and retention [of spatial concepts by] . . . inviting children to store the information and its label" (Gentner, 2003, pp. 207-208). Gentner found that children who heard specific spatial labels during a laboratory experiment that involved hiding objects ("I'm putting this on/in/under the box") were better able to find the objects than children who heard a general reference to location ("I'm putting this here"). Moreover, this was true even two days later, without further exposure to the spatial language (Loewenstein and Gentner, 2005). Similarly, Szechter and Liben (2004) observed parents and children in the lab as they read a children's book with spatial-graphic content. These researchers found a relation between the frequency with which parents drew children's attention to spatial-graphic content during book reading (e.g., "the rooster is really tiny now") and children's performance on spatial-graphic comprehension tasks.

Cannon, Levine, and Huttenlocher (2007) have also examined the parents' use of spatial language during puzzle play in a longitudinal study in which parent-child dyads were observed during naturalistic interactions every four months from age 26 to 46 months. Their findings show that puzzle play is correlated with children's mental rotation skill at 54 months for boys and girls. However, for girls but not boys, amount of parent spatial language during puzzle play (controlling for overall language input) is also a significant predictor of mental rotation skill at 54 months. This finding may be related to gender differences in the way in which spatial information is coded (e.g., Kail, Carter, and Pellegrino, 1979; Lourenco, Huttenlocher, and Fabian, under review).

### Understanding of Geometric Shape and Shape Composition

Various proposals have influenced views on children's shape categories. Piaget and Inhelder (1967) proposed a developmental sequence in which children first discriminate objects on the basis of topological features (e.g., a closed shape, which has an internal space defined by the closed boundary, versus an open shape, which has no defined internal or external boundaries) and only later on the basis of Euclidean features, such as rectilinear versus curvilinear. Still later, according to this theory, children are able to discriminate among rectilinear shapes (e.g., squares and diamonds). However, this sequence has been called into question on the basis of evidence that young children are able to represent the projective (e.g., curvilinear or rectilinear) as well as the Euclidean aspects of shape (e.g., Clements and Battista, 1992; Ginsburg et al., 2006; Kato, 1986; Lovell, 1959).

A different stage framework, proposed by van Hiele (1986), posits that children first identify shapes at the visual level on the basis of their appearance, then represent shapes at the "descriptive" level on the basis of their properties, and finally progress to more formal kinds of geometric thinking that are based on logical reasoning abilities. Consistent with van Hiele's first stage, preschoolers' early shape categories are centered on prototypes and the similarity of perceptual surface qualities of a shape are used to determine category inclusion. For example, preschoolers do not accept an inverted triangle as a triangle or nonisosceles triangles as triangles (e.g., Clements et al., 1999). Moreover, they tend to regard squares as a distinct category and not as a special kind of rectangle with four sides that are equal in length (Clements et al., 1999). Preschoolers sometimes overextend shape labels to nonexemplars. For example, they sometimes extend the label "rectangle" to right trapezoids as well as to nonrectangular parallelograms that have two sides that are much longer than the other two (Hannibal and Clements, 2008).

By the elementary school years, children's shape categories incorporate deeper knowledge of rules and theories that are definitional (Burger and Shaughnessy, 1986; Satlow and Newcombe, 1998). The timing of the shift from relying on characteristic perceptual features to relying on defining features varies depending on the shape. For example, Satlow and Newcombe (1998) report that this shift occurs between ages 3 and 5 for circles and rectangles, prior to second grade for triangles, and during second grade for pentagons. During the preschool years, the main change in shape categories is an increasing tendency to accept atypical exemplars of shapes as members of the category—that is, to extend shape categories beyond prototypical examples (e.g., Burger and Shaughnessy, 1986; Usiskin, 1987). The ability to broaden shape categories to include nonprotoypical examples depends on exposure to a variety of exemplars rather than to just prototypical examples such as equilateral and isosceles triangles (e.g., Clements et al., 1999). Neither Piaget's nor van Heile's stage theories recognize preschoolers' ability to represent and categorize shapes.

Children's learning of specific spatial terms also helps highlight spatial categories. These spatial terms include shape words (e.g., circle, square, triangle, rectangle), as well as words describing spatial features (e.g., curved, straight, line, side, corner, angle), spatial dimensions (e.g., big, little, tall, short, wide, narrow), and spatial relationships (e.g., in front of, behind, next to, between, over, under). Between ages 2 and 4, children learn terms for novel shapes more readily than other features, such as novel color or texture words (Heibeck and Markman, 1987; O'Hanlon and Roberson, 2006). Fuson and Murray (1978) found that over 60 percent of 3-year-old children could name a circle, a square, and a triangle. By age 5, 85 percent of children could name a circle, 78 percent a square, and 80 percent a triangle. In addition, 44 percent could correctly name a rectangle (Klein, Starkey, and Wakesley, 1999). In a shape word comprehension study, results were similar.

Clements et al. (1999) report that over 90 percent of children, ranging in age from 3 years 5 months to 4 years 4 months, could correctly point out a circle, and by age 6 years, 99 percent of children could do so. Only a few children in the younger group incorrectly chose an ellipse or another curved shape. For a square these numbers were also high yet somewhat lower: 82 percent of children in the younger group responded correctly, and 91 percent of 6-year-olds did so. Some children in the younger group incorrectly identified nonsquare rhombi as squares. Accuracy for triangles and rectangles was significantly lower (60 and 50 percent, respectively, for children ranging in age from 4 to 6).

Children also learn spatial words for shape dimensions (e.g., big, small, tall, short, wide, narrow) and words for the relationships of shapes (e.g., in, on, under, in front of, behind, between). For example, Clark (1972) reports that for each pair of dimensional adjectives, children learned the unmarked term before the marked term, that is, they learned big before little. Note that asking how big something is does not presuppose its being big or little, whereas asking how little something is carries the presupposition that one is asking about little things. The same is true for other pairs such as tall/short. The learning of these terms, like other words, is highly related to their frequency of occurrence in child-directed speech (e.g., Levine et al., 2008).

Children who hear greater amounts of spatial language have been found to perform at higher levels on a variety of nonverbal spatial tasks, including the WPPSI-3 Block Design subtest and a mental rotation task (Levine et al., 2008). This correlation may rest on the association of spatial language and spatial activities. Furthermore, spatial language may serve to focus children's attention on spatial relationships and lead to deeper processing of this information (e.g., forming categories of shapes and spatial relations). However, parents' spatial language to 3- to 5-year-old children has been found to occur more frequently during such activities as block and puzzle play than during other activities, such as book reading (Levine et al., 2008; Shallcross et al., 2008). Furthermore, higher amounts of parent spatial language occur during guided block play in which there is a goal than during free play with blocks (Shallcross et al., 2008). Thus, it is possible that spatial activities, spatial language, or both promote the development of spatial skills, such as block building and mental rotation.

## Summary

As for number, there are strong starting points during infancy for learning about space, including shapes, locations, distances, and spatial relations. These early starting points, however, like those for number, undergo major developments during the preschool years and beyond. Moreover, developmental rates and the competencies achieved are highly dependent on access to spatial activities, spatial language, and learning opportunities at home and at school.

Children are equipped to comprehend and reason about shape at an earlier age and in more complex detail than originally thought. By preschool, they benefit from learning about a variety of shapes, both typical and atypical, and this knowledge is impacted by their acquisition of spatial language. Language input and spatial activities appear to be highly influential in the development of spatial categories and spatial skills during the preschool years.

## DEVELOPMENT OF MEASUREMENT

Measurement is a fundamental aspect of mathematics, which "bridges two main areas of school mathematics—geometry and number" through the attachment of number to spatial dimensions (National Council of Teachers of Mathematics, 2000). The development of measurement skills usually starts with directly comparing objects along one dimension. Thus, children generally succeed in measuring length prior to area and volume (Hart, 1984; but see Curry and Outhred, 2005, for early success in measuring volume when the task involves successive filling of a container).

Certain skills, such as sensitivity to variations in amount, can be thought of as precursors to mature measurement skills and have been observed in infants. The ability to directly compare the lengths of objects is an early emerging skill and initially appears to be perceptually based (Boulton-Lewis, 1987). Infants demonstrate awareness of variations in amount in one dimension (e.g., noticing height) as early as 4 months (Baillargeon, 1991) and can discriminate between two objects based on height at 6 months (Gao, Levine, and Huttenlocher, 2000). For example, 6-month-old infants and 2-year-old toddlers are able to discriminate the length of dowels when they appear in the presence of a constant, aligned standard but not when there is no standard available with which to compare them (Huttenlocher, Duffy, and Levine, 2002).

Subsequent studies show that infants and toddlers are responding to the relative size of the standard and the test objects (Duffy, Huttenlocher, and Levine, 2005a, 2005b). This result is in line with the theory (Bryant, 1974) that relative coding precedes absolute coding. The ability to discriminate lengths in a more precise manner (distinguishing two heights that are fairly close without a present, aligned standard) develops some time between ages 2 and 4. However, even by age 4, children's sensitivity to variations in size is often influenced by the relation between two objects.

This early reliance on a standard to assess size may seem to contrast with findings by Piaget and his colleagues showing that young children do not spontaneously use a standard to measure objects (Piaget, Inhelder, and Szeminska, 1960). Piaget and colleagues argue that before school age, children's ability to encode metric information is limited because they lack the ability to make transitive inferences that are involved in measurement—that is, if A = B (the measure) and B = C, then A and B are equivalent. However, unlike Piaget and colleagues' task, in which the child was required to spontaneously use a stick to compare the heights of two towers that were not aligned, the experiments showing much earlier skill involve a visually aligned standard.

So far we have been discussing the development of the ability to discriminate linear extents and not the understanding of equivalence/nonequivalence of these extents, or sensitivity to amount transformations (adding or subtracting amounts). Although, as reviewed above, researchers have examined these topics with respect to discrete sets, there is little work on these topics with respect to continuous amounts. However, some evidence indicates that the ability to order continuous amounts is present at least by the preschool years. For example, Brainerd (1973) found that kindergartners could arrange three balls of clay according to weight and could arrange three sticks according to length.

### Understanding Units and Conventional Measurement

Early sensitivity to linear extent in relation to a standard is far from the mature ability to measure length. It is not until age 8 that children typically succeed in discriminating between objects of different lengths when there is not a constant aligned standard present. This ability is much closer to conventional measurement than the skill displayed by children up to age 4 (Duffy et al., 2005a). These changes in sensitivity to variation in amount from age 4 to age 8 may be related to exposure to conventional measurement at school and the ability to form and maintain images with certain attributes. However, developing a sophisticated conceptual understanding of linear measurement has a surprisingly long developmental time course (e.g., Copeland, 1979; Hiebert, 1981, 1984; Miller, 1984, 1989).

Conventional measurement involves several basic operations. First, it is important to realize that the units must be equal in size and must be specified. Second, the chosen unit must be repeated if it is smaller than the object being measured. Finally, the chosen unit must be subdivided when a whole unit does not fully cover the object or the remaining part of an object (Nunes, Light, and Mason, 1993).

Young children have difficulty understanding the importance of using an equal size unit. Miller (1984) showed that preschoolers between ages 4 and 5 have difficulty appreciating that the size of pieces (or units) must remain constant in measurement situations. In a well-known example, Miller found that preschool children who are asked to divide candy evenly among children consider it fair to break the last piece in half if they run out of pieces. In other words, as long as everyone gets a piece, they are not concerned that the pieces are unequal in size. In a study in which 5- and 6-year-olds were asked to make rulers by writing in the numbers, Nunes and Bryant (1996) found that they failed to space the numbers even approximately equally. In another study reported by Nunes and Bryant, children ages 5 to 7 had no trouble answering whether a 7 cm or 6 cm ribbon is longer. However, when asked whether a 2 inch or 2 cm ribbon is longer, 5-year-olds performed at chance. Although 7-year-olds performed above chance, they still performed significantly worse when the units were unequal than when they were equal, even though all the children knew that an inch is longer than a centimeter. Even first through third graders have difficulty understanding the importance of equal size units on rulers. Pettito (1990) gave children in elementary school a choice of rulers with which they could measure a line. She found that the majority of first and second graders were content to use a ruler with units that varied in size—in fact, only about half the third graders chose the standard unit.

Preschool children also have difficulty understanding that changes in the units of measure change the numerical answer (1 foot = 12 inches), but they do not change the length of the object being measured. Preschool children commonly fail to grasp the fundamental property of a unit, that a whole object can be segmented into parts of various sizes without changing the overall amount of what is being measured. They often count discrete parts of objects as being examples of a whole rather than grouping objects and counting amounts based on meaningful units (e.g., the two halves of a plastic egg each count as eggs versus the combination of the two pieces is one egg) (Shipley and Shepperson, 1990; Sophian and Kailihiwa, 1998). Similarly, Galperin and Georgiev (1969) gave kindergarten children two equal cups of rice and had them empty the cups by putting spoonfuls of rice into piles on a table using either a tablespoon or a teaspoon. When asked which group of piles contained more rice (correct answer is neither), a majority of the children chose the one made with the teaspoon because it contained more piles rather than choosing the group made with the tablespoon, which had fewer but larger piles. Thus, they were influenced by their propensity to count the overall number of piles. In this sense, children's skill at counting can interfere with their understanding of measurement. These findings highlight that part-whole relationships are fundamental to understanding the relationship between units and wholes (see Sophian, 2002, for a review).

A mature understanding of units of measure also entails the realization that the smaller the size of the unit, the larger the number of units the object will encompass. Research by Sophian, Garyantes, and Chang (1997) showed that preschool children have difficulty understanding this inverse relation, but that with instruction they can learn it. Young children do demonstrate some understanding of measurement principles, such as the inverse relation between unit size and the number of units after training or when measurement activities are set in a familiar context (e.g., part of a normal everyday routine or using familiar objects). Sophian (2002) taught preschool children ages 3 and 4 to correctly judge whether more small objects or more large ones would fit in a designated space. In pretest trials, the children incorrectly chose the larger object, but after six demonstration trials of watching the experimenter place objects of the two sizes, one by one, into two identical containers, they performed significantly better on posttest trials. These results identify the difficulties very young children have with understanding units and suggest that preschoolers (ages 2 years, 9 months to 4 years, 7 months) benefit from instructional intervention highlighting the relation between unit size and number. Thus, young children show some understanding of fundamental mathematical concepts that are relevant to measurement if given the opportunity to explore these concepts in interactive, supportive contexts.

### Scaling and Proportion

Children demonstrate early use of fundamental skills related to measurement and proportional reasoning in their use of maps. A critical factor for success in map use is scaling, which is related to measurement and proportional thinking. Scaling refers to the ability to code distance and understand how distance on a map corresponds to distance in the real world (Huttenlocher et al., 1999). Newcombe and Huttenlocher (2000, 2005) review the hierarchical nature of spatial coding, suggesting that various systems of coding spatial location are available, and their use depends on a mix of factors (e.g., cue salience in the external environment, complexity of movements required for action by the viewer). Furthermore, the availability of these systems appears as early as 6 months for both externally referenced and viewer-centered systems, which is much earlier than is predominantly reported in the literature. In relation to map use, children not only need to code locations in space but also to accommodate changes in scale, which requires a form of measurement (e.g., comparing the distance between two locations on a map and the corresponding distance between two locations in the real world). Scaling has been assumed to involve proportional reasoning and therefore to occur much later in development, between ages 10 and 12 (Piaget and Inhelder, 1967). However, evidence of early success using maps by children ages 3 to 6 indicates that scaling, at least in these cases, may represent a precursor to more precise measurement and is accomplished using spatial coding (Huttenlocher et al., 1999; Sandberg and Huttenlocher, 2001; Stea et al., 2004).

## REGULATING BEHAVIOR AND ATTENTION

Infants' and young children's mathematical development also takes place in the context of cognitive and behavior regulation, which when stimulated and supported can promote mathematical learning. Research suggests that executive function is more strongly associated with successful transition to formal schooling than IQ or entry-level reading or mathematics skills (Diamond, 2008). Executive function is defined as having three core components (Diamond, 2008). The first is inhibitory control, which is the ability to stay on task and do what is most necessary, even in the face of an inclination or impulse to do something else. The second is working memory, which is the ability to keep information in mind while still manipulating it or changing it mentally; "working memory may be thought of as a short-term 'working space' that can temporarily hold information while a participant is involved in other tasks" (Passolunghi, Vercelloni, and Schadee, 2007, p. 166). In mathematics specifically, this allows for performing mental arithmetic, such as addition or subtraction. The third component is cognitive flexibility, which allows for shifting between different tasks, demands, priorities, or perspectives. As Diamond explains, executive function, particularly the inhibitory control component, is very similar to self-regulation but tends to focus more on cognitive tasks and less on social situations. Multiple executive function skills may be valuable in early math learning. These include the ability to stay on task and ignore distractions, the ability to follow the teacher's directions, the ability to keep two strategies in mind at the same time, the motivation to succeed, the ability to plan and reflect on one's actions, and the ability to cooperate (Leong, n.d.; McClelland et al., 2007).

The link between mathematics success and executive function may have different underlying causes. Blair and colleagues (2007) review neuroscience research indicating that, in adults, there may be a relationship between mathematical skills and executive functioning at the neural level. Reviewing changes in mathematics curriculum for children, they also found that, increasingly, automatized knowledge is emphasized less and tasks that require executive function skills (pattern-solving, relational reasoning, and geometry concepts) are emphasized more. This is an area that will continue to shed light on the relationship between executive function and mathematical development as more research is conducted.

Some studies have explicitly found a link between executive function and early math skills.[3] In a study of 170 Head Start children, Blair and Razza (2007) found that multiple aspects of self-regulation (including inhibitory control, effortful control, and false belief understanding, along with fluid intelligence) all made independent contributions to children's early math knowledge. Similarly, McClelland and colleagues (2007) administered the Heads-to-Toes task to more than 300 preschool-age children. The

[3]Different studies use different terms for concepts encompassed by executive function, such as self-regulation and behavioral regulation.

Heads-to-Toes task asks children to do the opposite of what the instructor tells them. So, for example, if the instructor asks the children to touch their head, they are to touch their toes. This task measures behavioral regulation (a component of self-regulation), in that it requires children to employ inhibitory control, attention, and working memory. The researchers found that behavioral regulation scores significantly predicted emergent math scores. The researchers conclude that "strengthening attention, working memory, and inhibitory control skills prior to kindergarten may be an effective way to ensure that children also have a foundation of early academic skills" (p. 956). Espy and colleagues (2004) specifically studied the roles of working memory and inhibitory control with almost 100 preschoolers. They found that both components of executive function contributed to the children's mathematical proficiency, with inhibitory control being the most prominent. Passolunghi and colleagues (2007) studied 170 6-year-olds in Italy. They examined the roles of working memory, phonological ability, numerical competence, and IQ in predicting math achievement. They found that working memory skills significantly predicted math learning at the beginning of elementary school (primary school in Italy).

## SUMMARY

This chapter underscores that young children have more mathematics knowledge, in terms of number and spatial thinking, than was previously believed. Very early in life, infants can distinguish between larger set sizes, for example 8 versus 16 items, but their ability to do so is only approximate and is limited by the ratio of the number of items in the sets. The set size limitation is thought to reflect one of the two core systems for number (Feigenson, Dehaene, and Spelke, 2004; Spelke and Kinzler, 2007). Furthermore, young infants' early knowledge of quantity is implicit, in that they do not use number words, which means that learning number words and relating them to objects is one of the major developmental tasks to occur during early childhood.

Toddlers and preschool children move from the implicit understanding of number seen during infancy to formal number knowledge. Spoken number words, written number symbols, and cultural solution methods are important tools that support this developmental progression.

Young children also learn about space, including shapes, locations, distances, and spatial relations, which also go through major development during the early childhood years. Children's acquisition of spatial language plays an important role in the development of spatial categories and skills. In addition to learning about number and shape, early childhood also includes development of measurement, which is a fundamental aspect of mathematics that connects geometry and number. Young children's understanding of measurement begins with length, which is perceptually based, and an important feature of their learning during this period is that they have difficulty understanding units of measure. Young children can become successful at this when given appropriate instruction.

It is also important to note that across early childhood, mathematical development that is situated in an environment that promotes regulation of cognitive activities and behavior can improve mathematical development. More specifically, when young children have an opportunity to practice staying on task, to keep information in mind while manipulating or changing it mentally, and to practice shifting between differing tasks, mathematics learning is improved and in turn improves these regulatory processes.

Although we discuss universal starting points for mathematics development in this chapter, there are, of course, differences in children's mathematical development. The next chapter explores variation in children's mathematical development and learning outcomes and the sources of this variation. We also discuss the role of the family and informal mathematics learning experiences in supporting children's mathematical development.

## REFERENCES AND BIBLIOGRAPHY

Aguiar, A., and Baillargeon, R. (1998). Eight-and-a-half-month-old infants' reasoning about containment events. *Child Development*, *69*, 636-653.

Ansari, D., Donlan, C., Thomas, M.S.C., Ewing, S.A., Peen, T., and Karmiloff-Smith, A. (2003). What makes counting count: Verbal and visuo-spatial contributions to typical and atypical number development. *Journal of Experimental Child Psychology*, *85*, 50-62.

Antell, S.E., and Keating, L.E. (1983). Perception of numerical invariance by neonates. *Child Development*, *54*, 695-701.

Baillargeon, R. (1991). Reasoning about the height and location of a hidden object in 4.5 and 6.5 month-old children. *Cognition*, *38*, 13-42.

Baillargeon, R. (1995). Physical reasoning in infancy. In M.S. Gazzaniga (Ed.), *The Cognitive Neurosciences* (pp. 181-204). Cambridge, MA: Bradford Press.

Barth, H., LaMont, K., Lipton, J. and Spelke, E.S. (2005). Abstract number and arithmetic in preschool children. *Proceedings of the National Academy of Sciences*, *102*, 14116-14121.

Barth, H., LaMont, K., Lipton, J., Dehaene, S., Kanwisher, N., and Spelke, E. (2006). Non-symbolic arithmetic in adults and young children. *Cognition*, *98*, 199-222.

Blair, C., and Razza, R.P. (2007). Relating effortful control, executive function, and false belief understanding to emerging math and literacy ability in kindergarten. *Child Development*, *78*, 647-663.

Blair, C., Knipe, H., Cummings, E., Baker, D.P., Gamson, D., Eslinger, P., and Thorne, S.L. (2007). A developmental neuroscience approach to the study of school readiness. In R.C. Pianta, M.J. Cox, and K.L. Snow (Eds.), *School Readiness and the Transition to Kindergarten in the Era of Accountability* (pp. 149-174). Baltimore, MD: Paul H. Brookes.

Bomba, P.C., and Siqueland, E.R. (1983). The nature and structure of infant form categories. *Journal of Experimental Child Psychology*, *35*, 294-328.

Boulton-Lewis, G.M. (1987). Recent cognitive theories applied to sequential length measuring knowledge in young children. *British Journal of Educational Psychology*, *57*, 330-342.

Boysen, S.T. and Berntson, G.G. (1989). Numerical competence in a chimpanzee (*Pan troglodytes*). *Journal of Comparative Psychology*, *103*, 23-31.

Brainerd, C.J. (1973). Mathematical and behavioral foundations of number. *Journal of General Psychology, 11*, 369-381.

Brannon, E.M. (2002). The development of ordinal numerical knowledge in infancy. *Cognition, 83*, 223-240.

Brannon, E.M., and Terrace, H.S. (1998). Ordering of the numerosities 1 to 9 by monkeys. *Science, 282*, 746-749.

Brannon, E.M., and Terrace, H.S. (2000). Representation of the numerosities 1-9 by rhesus macaques (*Macaca mulatta*). *Journal of Experimental Psychology: Animal Behavior Processes, 26*, 31-49.

Brannon, E.M., Wushoff, C.J., Gallistel, C.R., and Gibbon, J. (2001). Numerical subtraction in the pigeon: Evidence for a linear subjective number scale. *Psychological Science, 12*, 238-243.

Brannon, E.M., Abbott, S., and Lutz, D. (2004). Number bias for the discrimination of large visual sets in infancy. *Cognition, 93*, B59-B68.

Bruner, J., Goodnow, J., and Austin, A. (1956). *A Study of Thinking*. New York: Wiley.

Bryant, P.E. (1974). *Perception and Understanding in Young Children*. London: Methuen.

Burger, W.F., and Shaughnessy, J.M. (1986). Characterizing the van Hiele levels of development in geometry. *Journal for Research in Mathematics Education, 17*, 31-48.

Bushnell, E.W., McKenzie, B.E., Lawrence, D., and Connell, S. (1995). The spatial coding strategies of 1-year-old infants in a locomotor search task. *Child Development, 66*, 937-958.

Butterworth, B. (2005). The development of arithmetical abilities. *Journal of Child Psychology and Psychiatry, 46*(1), 3-18.

Cannon, J., Levine, S.C., and Huttenlocher, J. (2007, March). *Sex Differences in the Relation of Early Puzzle Play and Mental Rotation Skill.* Paper presented at the biennial meeting of the Society for Research on Child Development, Boston, MA.

Cantlon, J.F., and Brannon, E.M. (2006). Shared system for ordering small and large numbers in monkeys and humans. *Psychological Science, 17*, 401-406.

Cantlon, J., Fink, R., Safford, K., and Brannon, E. (2007). Heterogeneity impairs numerical matching but not numerical ordering in preschool children. *Developmental Science, 10*, 431-441.

Carey, S. (2004). Bootstrapping and the origins of concepts. *Daedalus*, 59-68.

Casasola, M., and Cohen, L.B. (2002). Infant categorization of containment, support and tight-fit spatial relationships. *Developmental Science, 5*, 247-264.

Clark, E. (1972). On the child's acquisition of antonyms in two semantic fields. *Journal of Verbal Learning and Verbal Behavior, 11*, 750-758.

Clearfield, M.W. (2004). Infants' enumeration of dynamic displays. *Cognitive Development, 19*(3), 309-324

Clearfield, M.W., and Mix, K.S. (1999). Number versus contour length in infants' discrimination of small visual sets. *Psychological Science, 10*, 408-411.

Clearfield, M.W., and Mix, K.S. (2001). Infants' use of area and contour length to discriminate small sets. *Journal of Cognition and Development, 2*, 243-260.

Clements, D.H., and Battista, M.T. (1992). Geometry and spatial reasoning. In D.A. Grouws (Ed.), *Handbook of Research on Mathematics Teaching and Learning* (pp. 420-464). New York: Macmillan.

Clements, D.H., and Sarama, J. (2007). Early childhood mathematics learning. In F.K. Lester (Ed.), *Second Handbook of Research on Mathematics Teaching and Learning* (pp. 461-555). New York: Information Age.

Clements, D.H., Swaminathan, S., Hannibal, M.A.Z., and Sarama, J. (1999). Young children's concept of shape. *Journal for Research in Mathematics Education, 30*, 192-212.

Cohen, L.B., and Marks, K.S. (2002). How infants process addition and subtraction events. *Developmental Science, 5*, 186-201.

Cooper, R.G., Jr. (1984). Early number development: Discovering number space with addition and subtraction. In C. Sophian (Ed.), *Origins of Cognitive Skills* (pp. 157-192). Hillsdale, NJ: Erlbaum.

Copeland, R.W. (1979). *How Children Learn Mathematics: Teaching Implications of Piaget's Research* (3rd ed.). New York: Macmillan.

Cordes, S., and Brannon, E.M. (2008). The difficulties of representing continuous extent in infancy: Using numbers is just easier. *Child Development*, *79*, 476-489.

Cordes, S., and Brannon, E.M. (in press). The relative salience of discrete and continuous quantity in infants. *Developmental Science*.

Curry, M., and Outhred, L. (2005). Conceptual understanding of spatial measurement. In P. Clarkson, A. Downton, D. Gronn, M. Horne, A. McDonough, R. Pierce, and A. Roche (Eds.), *Building Connections: Theory, Research and Practice* (Proceedings of the 27th Annual Conference of the Mathematics Education Research Group of Australasia, Melbourne, pp. 265-272). Sydney: MERGA.

Dehaene, S. (1997). *The Number Sense: How the Mind Creates Mathematics*. New York: Oxford University Press.

Dehaene, S., Dehaene-Lambertz, G., and Cohen, L. (1998). Abstract representations of numbers in the animal and human brain. *Trends in Neurosciences*, *21*, 355-361.

DeLoache, J.S., Strauss, M., and Maynard, J. (1979). Picture perception in infancy. *Infant Behavior and Development*, *2*, 77-89.

Demany, L., McKenzie, B., and Vurpillot, E. (1977). Rhythm perception in early infancy. *Nature*, *266*, 218-219.

Diamond, A. (2008, June). Cognitive control (executive functions) in young children: Relevance of what we know to what can be done to help children. In *Emotion Regulation, Children's Brains and Learning*, plenary session presented at Head Start's Ninth National Research Conference, Washington, DC.

Diamond, A., Barnett, W.S., Thomas, J., and Munro, S. (2007). Preschool program improves cognitive control. *Science*, *318*, 1387-1388.

Duffy, S., Huttenlocher, J., and Levine, S.C. (2005a). It's all relative: How young children encode extent. *Journal of Cognition and Development*, *6*, 51-63.

Duffy, S., Huttenlocher, J., and Levine, S.C. (2005b). How infants encode spatial extent. *Infancy*, *8*, 81-90.

Espy, K.A., McDiarmid, M.M., Cwik, M.F., Stalets, M.M., Hamby, A., and Senn, T.E. (2004). The contribution of executive functions to mathematic skills in preschool children. *Developmental Neuropsychology*, *26*, 465-486.

Feigenson, L., and Carey, S. (2003). Tracking individuals via object-files: Evidence from infants' manual search. *Developmental Science*, *6*, 568-584.

Feigenson, L., and Carey, S. (2005). On the limits of infants' quantification of small object arrays. *Cognition*, *97*, 295-313.

Feigenson, L., and Halberda, J. (2004). Infants chunk object arrays into sets of individuals. *Cognition*, *91*, 173-190.

Feigenson, L., Carey, S., and Hauser, M. (2002). The representations underlying infants' choice of more: Object files vs. analog magnitudes. *Psychological Science*, *13*, 150-156.

Feigenson, L., Carey, S., and Spelke, L. (2002). Infants' discrimination of number vs. continuous extent. *Cognitive Psychology*, *44*, 33-66.

Feigenson, L., Dehaene, S., and Spelke, E. (2004). Core systems of number. *Trends in Cognitive Sciences*, *8*, 307-314.

Fennema, E.H., and Sherman, J.A. (1977). Sex-related differences in mathematics achievement, spatial visualization, and affective factors. *American Education Research Journal*, *14*, 51-71.

Fennema, E.H., and Sherman, J.A. (1978). Sex-related differences in mathematics achievement and related factors. *Journal for Research in Mathematics Education*, *9*, 189-203.

Fuson, K.C., and Murray, C. (1978). The haptic-visual perception, construction, and drawing of geometric shapes by children aged two to five: A Piagetian extension. In R. Lesh and D. Mierkiewicz (Eds.), *Concerning the Development of Spatial and Geometric Concepts* (pp. 49-83). Columbus, OH: ERIC Clearinghouse for Science, Mathematics, and Environmental Education.

Galperin, P., and Georgiev, L. (1969). The formation of elementary mathematical notions. In J. Kilpatrick and I. Wirzup (Eds.), *The Learning of Mathematical Concepts. Soviet Studies in the Psychology of Learning and Teaching Mathematics (Vol. 1)*. Palo Alto, CA: SMSG.

Gao, F., Levine, S.C., and Huttenlocher, J. (2000). What do infants know about continuous quantity? *Journal of Experimental Child Psychology*, *77*, 20-29.

Gelman, R. (1972). Logical capacity of very young children: Number invariance rules. *Child Development*, *43*, 75-90.

Gelman, R. (1980). What young children know about numbers. *Educational Psychologist, 15,* 54-68.

Gentner, D. (2003). Why we're so smart. In D. Gentner and S. Goldin-Madow (Eds.), *Language in Mind: Advances in the Study of Language and Thought* (pp. 195-235). Cambridge: MA: MIT Press.

Ginsburg, H.P., Cannon, J. Eisenband, and Pappas, S. (2006). Mathematical thinking and learning. In K. McCartney and D. Phillips (Eds.), *Handbook of Early Child Development* (pp. 208-229). Oxford, England: Blackwell.

Guay, R.B., and McDaniel, E. (1977). The relationship between mathematics achievement and spatial abilities among elementary school children. *Journal for Research in Mathematics Education*, *8*, 211-215.

Hannibal, M.A.Z., and Clements, D.H. (2008). Young children's understanding of basic geometric shapes. Manuscript submitted for publication, Indiana University of Pennsylvania, Indiana, PA.

Hart, K. (1984). Which comes first—length, area, or volume? *Arithmetic Teacher*, *31*, 16-18, 26-27.

Hedges, L.V., and Chung, V. (in preparation). Does spatial ability predict STEM college major and employment?: An examination of two longitudinal studies. University of Chicago.

Heibeck, T.H., and Markman, E.M. (1987). Word learning in children: An examination of fast mapping. *Child Development*, *67*, 850-866.

Hermer, L., and Spelke, E.S. (1994). A geometric process for spatial reorientation in young children. *Nature*, *370*, 57-59.

Hermer, L., and Spelke, E.S. (1996). Modularity and development: The case of spatial reorientation. *Cognition*, *61*, 195-232.

Hespos, S.J., and Spelke, E.S. (2004). Conceptual precursors to language. *Nature*, *430*, 453-456.

Hiebert, J. (1981). Cognitive development and learning linear measurement. *Journal for Research in Mathematics Education*, *12*, 197-210.

Hiebert, J. (1984). Why do some children have trouble learning measurement concepts? *Arithmetic Teacher*, *31*, 19-24.

Holloway, I., and Ansari, D. (2008). Domain-specific and domain-general changes in children's development of number comparison. *Developmental Science*, *11*, 644-649.

Huttenlocher, J., Jordan, N.C., and Levine, S.C. (1994). A mental model for early arithmetic *Journal of Experimental Psychology: General*, *123*, 284-296.

Huttenlocher, J., Newcombe, N., and Sandberg, E.H. (1994). The coding of spatial location in young children. *Cognitive Psychology*, *27*, 115-148.

Huttenlocher, J., Newcombe, N. and Vasilyeva, M. (1999). Spatial scaling in young children. *Psychological Science*, *10*, 393-398.

Huttenlocher, J., Duffy, S., and Levine, S.C. (2002). Infants and toddler discriminate amount: Are they measuring? *Psychological Science, 13*, 244-249.

Jordan, N.C., Kaplan, D., Nabors Oláh, L. and Locuniak, M.N. (2006). Number sense growth in kindergarten: A longitudinal investigation of children at risk for mathematics difficulties. *Child Development, 77,* 153-175.

Kail, R., Carter, P. and Pellegrino, J. (1979). The locus of sex differences in spatial skill. *Perception and Psychophysics, 26*, 182-186.

Kato, Y. (1986). Development of spatial recognition in preschool children: On Piaget and Inhelder's hypothesis of topological space. *Perceptual and Motor Skills, 63*, 443-450.

Klein, A., Starkey, P., and Wakesley, A. (1999). *Enhancing Pre-kindergarten Children's Readiness for School Mathematics.* Paper presented at the American Educational Research Association, Montreal, Canada.

Klein, J.S., and Bisanz, J. (2000). Preschoolers doing arithmetic: The concepts are willing but the working memory is weak. *Canadian Journal of Experimental Psychology, 54*, 105-114.

Kobayashi, T., Hiraki, K., Mugitani, R., and Hasegawa, T. (2004). Baby arithmetic: One object plus one tone. *Cognition, 91*, B23-B34.

Kwon, M.-K., Levine, S.C., Suriyakham, L.W., and Ehrlich, S.B. (2009). *Infants' Quantitative Sensitivity: Number, Continuous Extent or Both.* Presented at the Society for Research on Child Development Biennial Meeting, Denver, CO.

Lean, G., and Clements, M.A. (1981). Spatial ability, visual imagery, and mathematical performance. *Educational Studies in Mathematics, 12*, 267-299.

Learmonth, A., Newcombe, N., and Huttenlocher, J. (2001). Toddlers' use of metric information and landmarks to reorient. *Journal of Experimental Child Psychology, 80*(3), 225-244.

Leong, D.J. (n.d.). *Tools of the Mind: Pre-K, Preschool.* Available: http://www.mscd.edu/extendedcampus/toolsofthemind/assets/pdf/Preschool%20Brochure%20(acrobat).pdf [accessed June 2008].

Levine, S.C., Jordan, N.C., and Huttenlocher, J. (1992). Development of calculation abilities in young children. *Journal of Experimental Child Psychology, 53*, 72-103.

Levine, S.C., Huttenlocher, J., Taylor, A., and Langrock, A. (1999). Early sex differences in spatial ability. *Developmental Psychology, 35*, 940-949.

Levine, S.C., Vasilyeva, M., Lourenco, S., Newcombe, N., and Huttenlocher, J. (2005). Socioeconomic status modifies the sex difference in spatial skill. *Psychological Science, 16*, 841-845.

Levine, S.C., Huttenlocher, J., Pruden, S., Ratliff, K, and Saunders, J. (2008, June). *Learning to Think Spatially: Role of Early Spatial Language and Activities.* Paper presented at The Ins and Outs of Spatial Language: From Theory to Practice, Chicago, IL.

Liben, L.S., and Downs, R.M. (1989). Understanding maps as symbols: The development of map concepts in children. *Advances in Child Development and Behavior, 22*, 145-201.

Liben, L.S., and Yekel, C.A. (1996). Preschoolers' understanding of plan and oblique maps: The role of geometric and representational correspondence. *Child Development, 67*, 2780-2796.

Linn, M.C., and Peterson, A.C. (1985). Emergence and characterization of sex difference in spatial ability: A meta-analysis. *Child Development, 56*, 1479-1498.

Lipton, J., and Spelke, E.S. (2003). Origins of number sense: Large number discrimination in human infants. *Psychological Science, 14*, 396-401.

Lipton, J., and Spelke, E.S. (2004). Discrimination of large and small numerosities by human infants. *Infancy, 5*, 271-290.

Loewenstein, J., and Genter, D. (2005). Relational language and the development of relational mapping. *Cognitive Psychology, 50*, 315-353.

Lourenco, S.F., Huttenlocher, J., and Fabian, L. (under review). Early sex difference in weighting geometric cues.

Lovell, K. (1959). A follow-up study of some aspects of the work of Piaget and Inhelder on the child's conceptions of space. *British Journal of Educational Psychology, 29*, 104-117.

Mandler, J.M. (1992). How to build a baby II: Conceptual primitives. *Psychological Review, 99*, 587-604.

Marmor, G.S. (1975). Development of kinetic images: When does the child first represent movement in mental images? *Cognitive Psychology, 7*, 548-559.

McClelland, M.M., Cameron, C.E., Connor, C.M., Farris, C.L., Jewkes, A.M., and Morrison, F.J. (2007). Links between behavioral regulation and preschoolers' literacy, vocabulary, and math skills. *Developmental Psychology, 43*, 947-959.

McDonough, L., Choi, S., and Mandler, J.M. (2003). Understanding spatial relations: Flexible infants, lexical adults. *Cognitive Psychology, 46*, 229-259.

Meck, W.H., and Church, R.M. (1983). A mode control model of counting and timing processes. *Journal of Experimental Psychology: Animal Behavior Processes, 9*, 320-334.

Miller, K.F. (1984). Child as the measurer of all things: Measurement procedures and the development of quantitative concepts. In C. Sophian (Ed.), *Origins of Cognitive Skills* (pp. 193-228). Hillsdale, NJ: Erlbaum.

Miller, K.F. (1989). Measurement as a tool for thought: The role of measurement procedures in children's understanding of quantitative invariance. *Developmental Psychology, 25*, 589-600.

Mix, K.S. (1999a). Preschoolers' recognition of numerical equivalence: Sequential sets. *Journal of Experimental Child Psychology, 74*, 309-322.

Mix, K.S. (1999b). Similarity and numerical equivalence: Appearances count. *Cognitive Development, 14*, 269-297.

Mix, K.S. (2002). The construction of number concepts. *Cognitive Development, 17*, 1345-1363.

Mix, K.S. (2008). Surface similarity and label knowledge impact early numerical comparisons. *British Journal of Developmental Psychology, 26*, 13-32.

Mix, K.S., Huttenlocher, J., and Levine, S.C. (1996). Do preschool children recognize auditory-visual numerical correspondences? *Child Development, 67*, 1592-1608.

Mix, K.S., Levine, S.C., and Huttenlocher, J. (1997). Numerical abstraction in infants: Another look. *Developmental Psychology, 33*, 423-428.

Mix, K.S., Huttenlocher, J, and Levine, S.C. (2002). *Quantitative Development in Infancy and Early Childhood.* New York: Oxford University Press.

Mix, K.S., Sandhofer, C.M., and Baroody, A. (2005). Number words and number concepts: The interplay of verbal and nonverbal processes in early quantitative development. In R.V. Kail (Ed.), *Advances in Child Development and Behavior* (vol. 3, pp. 305-346). New York: Elsevier.

Moore, D.S., and Johnson, S.P. (2008). Mental rotation in human infants: A sex difference. *Psychological Science, 19*(11), 1063-1066.

Moore, D., Benenson, J., Reznick, J.S., Peterson, M., and Kagan, J. (1987). Effect of auditory numerical information on infants' looking behavior: Contradictory evidence. *Developmental Psychology, 23*, 665-670.

National Council of Teachers of Mathematics. (2000). *Principles and Standards for School Mathematics: An Overview.* Reston, VA: Author.

Newcombe, N., and Huttenlocher, J. (2000). *Making Space: The Development of Spatial Representation and Reasoning.* Cambridge, MA: MIT Press.

Newcombe, N., and Huttenlocher, J. (2006). Development of spatial cognition. In D. Kuhn and R.S. Siegler (Eds.), *Handbook of Child Psychology* (6th ed., pp. 734-776). New York: Wiley.

Newcombe, N., Huttenlocher, J., and Learmonth, A. (1999). Infants' coding of location in continuous space. *Infant Behavior and Development*, *22*, 483-510.

Nunes, T., and Bryant, P. (1996). *Children Doing Mathematics*. Cambridge, MA: Blackwell.

Nunes, T., Light, P., and Mason, J. (1993). Tools for thought: The measurement of length and area. *Learning and Instruction*, *3*, 39-54.

O'Hanlon, C.G., and Roberson, D. (2006). Learning in context: Linguistic and attentional constraints on children's color term learning. *Journal of Experimental Child Psychology*, *94*, 25-300.

Ozer, D. (1987). Personality, intelligence, and spatial visualization: Correlates of mental rotation test performance. *Journal of Personality and Social Psychology*, *53*, 129-134.

Passolunghi, M.C., Vercelloni, B., and Schadee, H. (2007). The precursors of mathematics learning: Working memory, phonological ability, and numerical competence. *Cognitive Development*, *22*, 165-184.

Pettito, A.L. (1990). Development of numberline and measurement concepts. *Cognition and Instruction*, *7*, 55-78.

Piaget, J. (1941/1965). *The Child's Conception of Number.* New York: Norton.

Piaget, J., and Inhelder, B. (1967). *The Child's Conception of Space.* (F.J. Langdon and J.L. Lunzer, Trans.). New York: Norton. (Original work published in 1948).

Piaget, J., Inhelder, B., and Szeminska, A. (1960). *The Child's Conception of Geometry.* London: Routledge and Kegan Paul.

Quinn, P.C. (1994). The categorization of above and below spatial relations by young infants. *Child Development*, *65*, 58-69.

Quinn, P.C. (2004). Spatial representation by young infants: Categorization of spatial relations or sensitivity to a crossing primitive? *Memory and Cognition*, *32*, 852-861.

Quinn, P.C., and Liben, L.S. (2008). A sex difference in mental rotation in young infants. *Psychological, Science*, *19*(11), 1067-1070.

Quinn, P.C., Norris, C.M., Pasko, R.N., Schmader, T.M. and Mash, C. (1999). Formation of a categorical representation for the spatial relation between by 6- to 7 month old infants. *Visual Cognition*, *6*, 569-585.

Rips, L.J., Bloomfield, A., and Asmuth, J. (2008). From numerical concepts to concepts of number. *Behavioral and Brain Sciences*, *6*, 623-642.

Sandberg, E.H., and Huttenlocher, J. (2001). Advanced spatial skills and advance planning: Components of 6-year-olds navigational map use. *Journal of Cognition and Development*, *2*, 51-70.

Sarnecka, B.W., and Carey, S. (2008). How counting represents numbers: What children must learn and when they learn it. *Cognition*, *108*, 662-674.

Satlow, E., and Newcombe, N. (1998). When is a triangle not a triangle? Young children's developing concepts of geometric shape. *Cognitive Development*, *13*, 547-559.

Saxe, G.B., Guberman, S.R., and Gearhart, M. (1987). Social processes in early number development. *Monographs of the Society for Research in Child Development*, *52*(2), iii-viii.

Seo, K.-H., and Ginsburg, H.P. (2004). What is developmentally appropriate in early childhood mathematics education? In D.H. Clements, J. Sarama and A.-M. DiBiase (Eds.), *Engaging Young Children in Mathematics: Standards for Early Childhood Mathematics Education* (pp. 91-104). Mahwah, NJ: Erlbaum.

Shallcross, W.L., Göksun, T., Golinkoff, R. M., Hirsh-Pasek, K., Lloyd, M., Newcombe, N., and Roseberry, S. (2008, March). *Building Talk: Parental Utterances During Construction Play.* Poster presented at the 16th International Conference on Infant Studies, Vancouver, Canada.

Shea, D.L., Lubinski, D., and Benbow, C.P. (2001). Importance of assessing spatial ability in intellectually talented young adolescents. *Journal of Educational Psychology*, *93*, 604-614.

Shipley, E.F., and Shepperson, B. (1990). Countable entities: developmental changes. *Cognition, 32*, 109-136.

Skolnick, J., Langbort, C., and Day, L. (1982). *How to Encourage Girls in Mathematics and Science: Strategies for Parents and Educators.* Englewood Cliffs, NJ: Prentice-Hall.

Slater, A., and Morison, V. (1985). Shape constancy and slant perception at birth. *Perception, 14*, 337-344.

Smothergill, D.W., Hughes, F.P., Timmons, S.A., and Hutko, P. (1975). Spatial visualizing in children. *Developmental Psychology, 11*, 4-13.

Sophian, C. (2002). Learning about what fits: Preschool children's reasoning about effects of object size. *Journal of Research in Mathematics Education, 33*, 290-302.

Sophian, C., and Kailihiwa, C. (1998). Units of counting: Developmental changes. *Cognitive Development, 13*, 561-585.

Sophian, C., Garyantes, D., and Chang, C. (1997). When three is less than two: Early development in children's understanding of fractional quantities. *Developmental Psychology, 33*, 731-744.

Spelke, E.S. (1990). Principles of object perception. *Cognitive Science, 14*, 29-56.

Spelke, E.S., and Kinzler, K.D. (2007). Core knowledge. *Developmental Science, 10*, 89-96.

Starkey, P., and Cooper, R. (1980). Perception of numbers by human infants. *Science, 210*, 1033-1034.

Starkey, P., Spelke, E.S., and Gelman, R. (1983). Detection of intermodal numerical correspondences by human infants. *Science, 222*, 179-181.

Starkey, P., Spelke, E.S., and Gelman, R. (1990). Numerical abstraction by human infants. *Cognition, 36*, 97-128.

Stea, D., Kerkman, D.D., Phinon, M.F., Middlebrook, N.N., and Rice, J.L. (2004). Preschoolers use maps to find a hidden object outdoors. *Journal of Environmental Psychology, 24*, 341-345.

Stewart, R., Leeson, N., and Wright, R.J. (1997). Links between early arithmetical knowledge and early space and measurement knowledge: An exploratory study. In F. Biddulph and K. Carr (Eds.), *Proceedings of the Twentieth Annual Conference of the Mathematics Education Research Group of Australasia* (vol. 2, pp. 477-484). Hamilton, New Zealand: MERGA.

Strauss, M.S., and Curtis, L.E. (1981). Infant perception of numerosity. *Child Development, 52*, 1146-1152.

Strauss, M.S., and Curtis, L.E. (1984). Development of numerical concepts in infancy. In C. Sophian (Ed.), *Origins of Cognitive Skills* (pp. 131-155). Hillsdale, NJ: Erlbaum.

Szechter, L.E., and Liben, L. (2004). Parental guidance in preschoolers' understanding of spatial-graphic representation. *Child Development, 75*, 869-885.

Usiskin, Z. (1987). Resolving the continuing dilemmas in school geometry. In M.M. Lindquist and A.P. Shulte (Eds.), *Learning and Teaching Geometry, K-12* (pp. 1-31), Reston, VA: National Council of Teachers of Mathematics.

Uttal, D.H. (1996). Angles and distances. Children's and adults' reconstruction and scaling of spatial configurations. *Child Development, 67*, 2763-2779.

van Hiele, P.M. (1986). *Structure and Insight: A Theory of Mathematics Education.* Orlando, FL: Academic Press.

Van Loosbroek, E., and Smitsman, A.W. (1990). Visual perception of numerosity in infancy. *Developmental Psychology, 26*, 916-922.

Wallace, J.R., and Veek, A.L. (1995). *Children's Use of Maps for Direction and Distance Estimation.* Paper presented at the Biennial Meeting of the Society for Research on Child Development, Indianapolis, IN.

Wang, R.F., and Spelke, E.S. (2002). Human spatial representation: Insights from animals. *Trends in Cognitive Sciences, 6*, 376-382.

Wheatley, G.H. (1990). Spatial sense and mathematics learning. *Arithmetic Teacher*, *37*, 10-11.

Wood, J.N., and Spelke, E.S. (2005). Infants' enumeration of actions: Numerical discrimination and its signature limits. Developmental *Science*, *8*, 173-181.

Wynn, K. (1990). Children's understanding of counting. *Cognition, 36*, 155-193.

Wynn, K. (1992a). Addition and subtraction by human infants. *Nature*, *358*, 749-750.

Wynn, K. (1992b). Children's acquisition of the number words and the counting system. *Cognitive Psychology*, *24*, 220-251.

Wynn, K. (1996). Infants' individuation and enumeration of actions. *Psychological Science*, *7*, 164-169.

Wynn, K., Bloom, P., and Chiang, W-C. (2002). Enumeration of collective entities by 5-month-old infants. *Cognition*, *83*, B55-B62.

Xu, F. (2003). Numerosity discrimination in infants: Evidence for two systems of representations. *Cognition*, *89*, B15-B25.

Xu, F., and Arriaga, R.I. (2007). Number discrimination in 10-month-old infants. *British Journal of Developmental Psychology*, *25*, 103-108.

Xu, F., and Spelke, E.S. (2000). Large number discrimination in 6-month-old infants. *Cognition*, *74*, B1-B11.

Xu, F., Spelke, E., and Goddard, S. (2005). Number sense in human infants. *Developmental Science*, *8*, 88-101.

# 4

# Developmental Variation, Sociocultural Influences, and Difficulties in Mathematics

There is evidence that most children bring foundational resources and knowledge about mathematics to school. However, this is not the whole story. Research findings reveal enormous discrepancies in young children's levels of mathematics competence, and these discrepancies appear to be larger in the United States than they are in some other countries (e.g., China) (Starkey and Klein, 2008). This chapter describes the kinds of differences that exist and reviews what is known about the nature and sources of developmental variations among children.

Most children bring core number sense or number competencies to school (National Research Council, 2001). Number sense refers to interconnected knowledge of numbers and operations. Although preverbal number sense begins in infancy and appears to be universal, preschool and kindergarten number sense involves understanding of number words and symbols, which is heavily influenced by experience and instruction. The number sense children bring to kindergarten is highly predictive of their later mathematics achievement. The term "number sense" means different things in different fields of research, and almost no two researchers define it in exactly the same way (Gersten, Jordan, and Flojo, 2005; Jordan et al., 2006). The term "number sense" is used in this chapter because much of the research summarized here uses it. When the discussion is more general, the term "number competencies" is used along with number sense to remind the reader that we are talking about knowledge and skills that can be taught and learned. The word "competencies" is used as a balanced term meaning both knowledge and skills. The competencies encompassed by the term "number sense" as used here are described more fully in Chapter 5.

Despite strong universal starting points, striking individual differences in number sense emerge early in life and are present by the time children enter preschool (e.g., Klibanoff et al., 2006). These differences are apparent both on standardized tests (e.g., Arnold et al., 2002; Starkey, Klein, and Wakeley, 2004) and on specific measures tapping early number competencies, such as determining set size, comparing sets, and carrying out calculations (e.g., Entwisle and Alexander, 1990; Ginsburg and Russell, 1981; Griffin, Case, and Siegler, 1994; Jordan, Huttenlocher, and Levine, 1992; Levine et al., in preparation; Saxe, Guberman and Gearheart, 1987). The level of number sense in kindergarten is highly of predictive future mathematics success in first through third grades (Fuchs et al., 2007; Jordan, Glutting, and Ramineni, in press; Locuniak and Jordan, in press; Mazzocco and Thompson, 2005) as well as into the later school years (Duncan et al., 2007).

In this chapter, we explore individual differences in children's mathematics competence. We begin by describing the differences associated with key social groups specifically defined by socioeconomic status, gender, race/ethnicity, and English language ability. We then discuss the contextual factors and early experiences that appear to be linked to these differences, giving particular attention to the role of the family and language. We then discuss learning disabilities. We end with a brief discussion of potential intervention.

## GROUP DIFFERENCES IN MATHEMATICS PERFORMANCE

Researchers have explored several key social factors that are linked to systematic, average differences in children's mathematical performance. Socioeconomic status (SES), which includes income level as well as level of parental education, is strongly linked to differences in mathematics competence. Evidence related to gender differences in mathematics competence is less clear, although some differences have been found.

### Socioeconomic Status

Mathematical skills of young children from low-income families lag behind those of their middle-income peers. Preschoolers who attend Head Start Programs perform significantly below children who attend preschools serving middle-income children on standardized tests of mathematical readiness (Ehrlich and Levine, 2007). The gulf between low- and middle-income children is wide and includes spatial/geometric and measurement as well as number competencies (Clements, Sarama, and Gerber, 2005; Klein and Starkey, 2004; Saxe et al., 1987).

Jordan and colleagues (Jordan et al., 2006, 2007) found that low-income children enter kindergarten far behind their middle-income peers on tasks assessing counting skills, knowledge of number relations (e.g., recognizing which number is smaller), and number operations. Moreover, longitudinal assessment over six data points revealed that low-income children were four times more likely than their middle-income peers to show flat growth in these areas throughout kindergarten and early first grade. Underlining the importance of early number sense to school success, the researchers found that level of performance on a battery assessing number sense in kindergarten as well as rate of growth between kindergarten and first grade accounted for 66 percent of the variance in mathematics learning at the end of first grade (Jordan et al., 2007). In other words, number sense in kindergarten in strongly related to competence in mathematics at the end of first grade and the rate of growth over the first grade year. Income status, gender, age, and reading ability did not account for additional variance in first grade mathematics outcomes over and above initial performance and growth in number sense. This suggests that SES differences found at the end of first grade are due to initial differences in number sense in kindergarten.

Several studies indicate that SES differences in preschoolers' number skills are more marked on tasks tapping number skills without objects (called verbal tasks) than on tasks tapping number skills with objects (called nonverbal tasks). When kindergarten and first grade children are presented with verbal calculation problems with no objects, either as number combination problems ("How much is 3 and 2?") or story problems ("Mike had 3 pennies. Jen gave him 2 more pennies. How many pennies does Mike have now?"), middle-income children perform much better than do low-income children (Jordan et al., 2006; Jordan, Huttenlocher, and Levine, 1992; Jordan, Levine, and Huttenlocher, 1994). Middle-income children also achieve at a faster rate on calculation problems without objects in kindergarten (Jordan et al., 2006, 2007). In contrast, SES differences are smaller if the same calculations are presented in a nonverbal format with objects (e.g., the child is shown 3 disks that are then hidden with a cover. The tester then slides 2 disks under the cover and the child indicates how many are now hidden).

Jeong and Levine (2005) have shown that knowing number words is associated with very early performance on numerosity matching tasks that do not require verbal responses (e.g., matching arrays of visual dots). Specifically, performance on these tasks is more exact for children who have acquired the meaning of a few number words. For instance, 2- to 3-year-olds were more exact in their ability to match small set sizes when they have better knowledge of the cardinal meanings of number words. Although low-income children performed worse than middle-income children on such numerosity matching tasks, this difference was eliminated if answers that were plus or minus 1 from the correct answer were counted as correct

(Ehrlich, Levine, and Goldin-Meadow, 2006). Thus, low-SES preschoolers appear to have approximate representations of set sizes and number words at a time when their higher SES peers have gained exact representations. Therefore, low-SES preschoolers need experiences to learn number words and to use them to help on these matching tasks.

The sources of these differences are difficult to pinpoint. Research on children's early experiences point to the amount of support for mathematics at home as well as other language and contextual factors. Some findings show that young children from low-income families receive less support for mathematics in their home environment than do their middle-income peers (Blevins-Knabe and Musun-Miller, 1996; Holloway et al., 1995; Saxe et al., 1987; Starkey et al., 1999). Compounding the situation, public preschool programs serving low-income families tend to provide fewer learning opportunities and supports for mathematical development than ones serving middle-income families (Clements and Sarama, 2008). These factors are discussed in greater detail in the section on the influence of context and experience.

### Gender

Results and opinions vary regarding gender differences in early mathematics. Some studies have no revealed gender differences in mathematics performance (e.g., Clements and Sarama, 2008; Lachance and Mazzocco, 2006; Levine, Jordan, and Huttenlocher, 1992; Sarama et al., 2008). Some have found differences favoring boys: Jordan et al. (2006) found small but statistically significant gender effects on calculation with objects and on numerical estimation. In particular, boys had an edge over girls even when income level, age, and reading ability were controlled for in the analyses, and there were more boys than girls in the highest performing group. However, Coley's (2002) analysis of the Early Childhood Longitudinal Study database indicated small advantages in kindergarten in different areas for each gender: Girls were somewhat better in recognizing numbers and shapes, and boys were somewhat better in numerical operations.

Some research with older children indicates that girls in the primary grades may tend to use less advanced strategies than do boys (Fennema et al., 1998), and other work suggests no gender differences in the mathematics performance of older students (Hyde et al., 2008). Recent research (e.g., Carr et al., 2007) suggests spatial skills may promote the use of more advanced computational strategies, and boys seem to have an advantage in the more general area of spatial cognition, even in preschool. There are differences in the mean level of performance of boys and of girls on mental rotation tasks by 4½ years of age, ranging from small but significant differences (Levine et al., 1999) to large differences with girls performing at chance levels (Rosser et al., 1984). Preschool boys also perform better than preschool girls on solving problems involving mazes (e.g., Fairweather and Butterworth, 1977; Wechsler, 1967; Wilson, 1975) and are faster at copying a three-dimensional Lego (plastic blocks) model (Guiness and Morley, 1991). However, it appears that at least some of these differences are created by lack of particular types of experiences (Ebbeck, 1984).

Spatial skill may reflect or at least interact with greater engagement of boys than girls in spatial activities, such as building with Legos (Baenninger and Newcombe, 1989). Young boys typically spend more time playing with Legos and putting puzzles together than do girls, suggesting that engagement in spatial activities promotes skill development (Levine et al., 2005). The amount of puzzle play for both boys and girls was related to the mental transformation performance (McGuinness and Morley, 1991). Parents' spatial language may be more important for girls than for boys; use of such language by parents related to mental transformation performance of girls but not of boys (Cannon, Levine, and Huttenlocher, 2007). Boys tend to be more interested in movement and action from the first year of life and girls more focused on social interactions (e.g., Lutchmaya and Baron-Cohen, 2002). Boys also may gesture more on spatial tasks (e.g., Ehrlich, Levine, and Goldin-Meadow, 2006), indicating that encouraging gesture, especially for girls, may be helpful in spatial learning.

Given the finding that boys seem to have an advantage in spatial cognition and that this seems to result partly from the number of experiences they have that support such learning, it seems particularly important for both numerical and spatial learning that girls be given opportunities for spatial learning. Importantly, intervention studies with preschoolers using a research-based mathematics curriculum did not find an interaction with gender, indicating that girls can learn as much as boys in both numerical and spatial tasks (Clements and Sarama, 2008; Sarama et al., 2008). Simple modifications to everyday preschool activities, such as block building (Kersh, Casey, and Young, in press) and the use of stories about spatial topics (Casey et al., 2008), have been shown to be effective in developing girls' spatial cognition. Teachers should ensure that girls play with blocks and provide them with challenges that ensure that they extend their block-building skills, such as building windows, bridges, and arches.

## Race and Ethnicity

Over the past several decades, research has found differences in children's mathematics learning outcomes as a function of their race/ethnicity (e.g., Ginsburg and Russell, 1981). This section discusses differences in mathematics learning outcomes, but readers should keep in mind that using a fixed trait based on a single dimension can lead to a cultural deficit model

(Lubienski, 2007). Racial/ethnic groups are heterogeneous, and children in particular racial/ethnic groups have mathematical knowledge and skills that range from low to high mastery levels.

Generally, African American, Hispanic, and American Indian/Alaska Native children achieve at lower levels than their white peers in mathematics (National Center for Education Statistics, 2007). Few data exist on early childhood mathematics teaching and learning in relation to race/ethnicity, but one can extrapolate from K-12 studies. Findings suggest that this achievement disparity is related to differences in mathematics learning before school entry and fewer meaningful pedagogical experiences once children of color enter school (Magnuson and Waldfogel, 2008). For example, the National Assessment of Educational Progress (NAEP) survey data show that fourth grade black and Hispanic students and those with low SES report that mathematics mainly consists of memorizing facts, a belief that is negatively correlated with achievement even after controlling for race/ethnicity and SES (Lubienski, 2006, 2007). Furthermore, teachers' reports indicate that black and Hispanic children were more likely to be routinely assessed with multiple-choice tests than white students (Lubienski, 2006). These practices do not represent the best pedagogy for high-quality mathematics education (National Council of Teachers of Mathematics, 2000).

Teachers who build on children's everyday mathematical experiences promote genuine mathematics learning (Civil, 1998; Ladson-Billings, 1995). For example, Ladson-Billings (1995) found that urban and suburban students' community experiences shaped the way they approached a mathematics problem-solving task and that students' differing approaches to learning could be used by teachers to inform their instruction. Instructional practices that extend children's out-of-school experiences are more likely to produce meaningful mathematics learning.

## English Language Learners

Surprisingly little research has examined the mathematics performance of English language learners. Findings for other subject areas show that children who have limited proficiency in English perform more poorly than their native English-speaking peers in other academic subjects (McKeon, 2005). A major issue for educating English language learners (ELL) is the language of instruction (Barnett et al., 2007; Genesee et al., 2006). In research conducted by Barnett and colleagues (2007) with 3- and 4-year-olds, they tested whether children in a two-way immersion (English and Spanish) or those in English-only programs made gains in English language measures of mathematics, vocabulary development, and literacy. They found that children in both types of programs made gains on all academic measures and the two-way immersion classrooms saw improvements in Spanish language development for both ELL and English-speaking children without losses to English language learning (Barnett et al., 2007). It is important to note that classrooms in both types of program employed a licensed teacher and an assistant with a child development associate credential. A review of the K-12 literature on the language of instruction provides evidence that conflicts with the findings of Barnett and colleagues; specifically, Lindholm-Leary and Borasato (2006) suggest that bilingual education may be related to more positive educational outcomes for older ELL students. Given these disparate findings, additional research in high-quality early childhood settings on this topic is warranted.

One of the few studies focused specifically on mathematics competence with this population of students suggests there may not be performance differences in mathematics. Secada (1991) found that first grade Hispanic students were not at a disadvantage to their native English-speaking peers in solving addition and subtraction word problems. However, with the growing number of ELL in the student population, it vital that more attention be paid to the relationship between language status and early mathematics learning so that early childhood education can effectively accommodate and support these children.

## INFLUENCE OF CONTEXT AND EXPERIENCE

As noted in the previous section, research has identified consistent, average differences in mathematics competence and performance depending on membership in a particular social group. Why group membership is linked to such differences is a complicated question. Research suggests that early experiences play an important role in shaping the observed differences. In this section we explore the contributions of context and early experience. We begin with a general discussion of the role of families in shaping early experience, including parents' knowledge and beliefs about mathematics, and the support they provide for mathematics through engagement in mathematics activities. We then look more specifically at how differences in experiences at home are linked to the observed SES differences in performance. Finally, we consider the role of language in mathematics learning.

### Role of Families

Families are one of the critical social settings in which children develop and learn (Bronfenbrenner, 2000; Iruka and Barbarin, 2008). Families influence children's development in many ways, including parenting practices, provision of resources, interactions with school, and involvement in the community (Weiss, Caspe, and Lopez, 2006; Woods and Kurtz-Costes, 2007). Parents have different attitudes, values, and beliefs in raising young children, which result in difference emphasis on educational activities in the home. Families support mathematics learning through their activities at home, conversations, attitudes, materials they provide to their children, expectations they have about their performance, the behaviors they model, and the games they play. Parents also build connections with their children's educational settings—all of which can shape children's early mathematics development.

### *Parents' Knowledge and Beliefs About Early Childhood Mathematics*

Although there are only a few empirical studies about parental beliefs and behaviors related to early mathematics, those that exist suggest that parents place more importance on literacy development (Barbarin et al., 2008). Barbarin and colleagues examined the beliefs of parents whose children were enrolled in public prekindergarten regarding the skills children need to be prepared for school. Mathematical skills and such tasks as counting were rated less important than other social and cognitive tasks. Specifically, language/early literacy was mentioned 50 percent of the time, whereas numeracy was mentioned only 3.5 percent of the time (Barbarin et al., 2008). Similarly, Cannon and Ginsburg (2008) found that mothers thought it was more important that their children learn daily living skills and develop language skills in preschool than that their children learn mathematical skills. Most mothers in the study reported they themselves spent more time teaching their children language skills than mathematics skills at home.

### *Engagement in Mathematics Activities*

Children's mathematical competence is supported and shaped by the math-related activities they engage in as part of their daily lives (Benigno and Ellis, 2008). Parenting practices in which parents engage children in conversations about number concepts, play with puzzles and shapes, encourage counting, and use number symbols to represent quantity in their interactions in the physical world can facilitate mathematics learning (see Box 4-1 for examples of how parents can engage children in mathematics activities). Acquiring mathematics knowledge involves more than learning numbers. It also includes learning shapes and patterns. It is facilitated by conversations about what children are doing when they compute, solve puzzles, and develop patterns and discussions of why they took a particular approach to a problem.

In fact, one study demonstrates how parents and their children can engage in mathematics-related activities. In a groundbreaking study of

**BOX 4-1**
**Supporting Children's Mathematics at Home**

Parents play an important role in supporting mathematics learning through the mathematics-related activities in which they engage their children. Incorporating mathematics-focused activities during play is one strategy for enhancing mathematics. Another is to capitalize on situations in which mathematics is a natural part of everyday tasks, such as grocery shopping or cooking. During daily activities, parents can:

- Observe their children carefully, seeing what they do and encouraging and extending their fledgling use of number symbols and processing.
- Say the number word list. For example, they can count small food items or the number of cups at the table.
- Ask children to tell them about their problem solving. For example, they can ask "What did you mean by that?" or "Why did you do it that way?"
- Engage in activities that involve playing with blocks, building things, and board games.

Given the prevalence of the Internet, television, and videogames in the lives of children, even young children (for a review, see Fisch, 2008), these means of communication provide interesting opportunities for impacting early mathematics skills. Fisch (2008) provides a review of existing media that include a mathematical component. These include television shows, such as *Sesame Street*; mathematics-based software games, such as *Building Blocks* and *Millie's Math House*; websites that include mathematics content, such as that of Sesame Street and Disney; and electronic, interactive toys.

The Internet can be a tool to help families devise mathematics-related activities for their young children. Such websites as *FAMILY MATH*, from the Lawrence Hall of Science at the University of California, Berkeley, can provide this kind of help. Although there are no effectiveness data available for this website, *FAMILY MATH* offers fun activities that maintain mathematical integrity and uses inexpensive materials that families may already have at home (see http://sv.berkeley.edu/showcase/pages/fm_act.html).

early childhood mathematics in family contexts, Saxe and colleagues (1987) found that many of the children in the 78 families they studied, both low and middle income, were spontaneously engaging in number-related activities (counting toys, using numbers in play, etc.), but the nature of their numerical knowledge and environment differed. Mothers in the study reported that both they and their children had a high level of interest in number play, but middle-income children performed better than low-income children on both the cardinality and arithmetic tasks.

There are numerous opportunities on a daily basis for children and families to explore mathematical terms and concepts. These include mealtimes, shopping, playtime, sports, television, and reading (Benigno and Ellis, 2008). In fact, Blevins-Knabe and Musun-Miller (1996) provide evidence to support the effects of parental modeling, reporting a relation between parental participation in number activities and children's involvement in similar activities. Moreover, they found that parental reports of children's number activities at home predicted their scores on a standardized test of early mathematical ability.

Several studies suggest that exposure to the language and symbol system of mathematics powerfully extends the universal starting points of children's quantitative knowledge and contributes to observed differences in mathematics competence. This is true in terms of exposure to the language of mathematics in preschool (Klibanoff et al., 2006) as well as at home between ages 14 and 30 months (Levine et al., in preparation). These studies show that the range of number words used in these settings is enormous. For example, in the home study, a longitudinal project in which families were visited every 4 months for five 90-minute sessions during which they were asked to go about their normal activities, the use of number words ranged from a low of 3 to a high of 175 instances. Similarly, in the classroom studies, the amount of number input provided by teachers during a 1-hour period that included circle time ranged from 1 to 104 coded instances.

While research suggests that families do incorporate mathematics into their everyday lives, they may also need reminders of the importance of mathematics. An observational study of 39 preschoolers and their families (Tudge and Doucet, 2004) found that the children engaged in a very low rate of explicit mathematics lessons over the course of a day and also demonstrated low levels of mathematics-related play. Of the mathematics lessons that were observed, the most common were lessons involving numbering, and the most common types of mathematical play involved toys that featured numbers (puzzles, computer programs, etc.). Furthermore, parents may overestimate their children's mathematical skills. Fluck and colleagues (2005) found that parents believed their children had a much better grasp of the concept of cardinality (beyond mere counting) than the children actually displayed.

### *Differences in Children's Experiences and Learning Opportunities as a Function of Socioeconomic Status*

Evidence suggests that SES differences in children's mathematics competence are linked to parallel differences in experiences provided in the home. For parents in some low-SES families, involvement in fostering the acquisition of mathematics skills in their children may be hampered by multiple factors. Poverty and uncertainty related to inadequate resources and residential instability can easily become all-consuming, leaving room for little else. Parents in low-SES families, though concerned about their children's education, may feel less ready to assist them due to limitations in their own education, the strains of inadequate financial resources, unmet mental health needs, and specific discomfort with their own mathematical skills and a lack of awareness of the importance of early mathematics development (for research on the effects of poverty on parenting see, e.g., Knitzer and Lefkowitz, 2006; McLoyd, 1990; see Clements and Sarama, 2007, for a specific discussion of low-income families and mathematics).

Research shows that low-income parents provide fewer mathematics activities than middle-class parents (Starkey et al., 1999). This includes free activities, such as those that are integrated into everyday experiences and made-up games, suggesting that, to some extent, lack of financial resources does not explain the difference. Starkey and Klein (2008) suggest that the difference may instead stem from educational background and exposure to mathematics courses. The difference may be resource-based as well. Ramani and Siegler (2008), in a study of board game activities, found that, although 80 percent of middle-class preschool-age children reported playing one or more board games outside preschool, only 47 percent of Head Start children did so. However, such board games could easily be made and used at home.

It is also vital to remember that, in many cases, children and families from low-SES backgrounds are involved with many more agencies and programs than their more well-off peers. "Exploring the contribution of these additional settings is important because interpreting SES effects as emanating exclusively from the family or the child means that policy and program interventions may focus too narrowly as they attempt to improve the educational outcomes of low-SES children" (Aikens and Barbarin, 2008, p. 236). Policy makers, researchers, and practitioners should not neglect the importance of the interactions and experiences of the multiple contexts and the nature of development in everyday life. Thus, at the level of a mother and child interacting in a larger social context unique to cultural environments, the entire dynamic may influence a child's learning and specifically reinforce or hinder the development of mathematical thinking and understanding.

The SES gap prior to preschool entry suggests that the home environment plays a major role, yet it is important to note that formal preschool programs do not appear to be ameliorating it. In fact, the gap widens during the preschool years. "In the United States, neither the home nor preschool learning environments of low-SES children provide sufficient enrichment to close or even maintain early SES-related differences in mathematical knowledge" (Starkey and Klein, 2008, p. 266). The issue of how to better support low-income children in mathematics and address the gap is taken up in detail in Chapter 7.

## Role of Language

Languages vary in the ways they represent mathematical concepts. This variation appears to be linked to variation in children's mathematics learning. For example, several recent studies have shown that characteristics of speakers' language influence the quantitative skills of children and adults. One set of studies provides evidence that variations in the structure of a morphological marker, which refers to a language element that identifies quantity in different languages, is associated with the age at which children learn the meaning of specific cardinal numbers. That is, children who speak a language that marks the singular-plural distinction through a morphological marker (e.g., the *s* on the end of dog*s*, which indicates that the word is plural, is the morphological marker) acquire the meanings of small cardinal numbers sooner than children whose language does not make such a distinction (e.g., LeCorre, Li, and Lee, 2004; Li et al., 2003; Sarnecka et al., 2007). Even more strikingly, recent evidence has shown that adults in cultural groups with few number words perform worse than adults from cultural groups with more elaborated number systems in matching set sizes, performing arithmetic operations, and other cognitive tasks requiring knowledge of exact numbers (Gordon, 2004; Pica et al., 2004). There is also a large body of evidence regarding the implications of number naming systems for mathematics learning.

### *Language Differences in Number Names*

Language differences in number names have received in-depth attention in the literature. Such differences appear to be linked to the ease with which children learn to count, an essential task during early childhood. Names and symbols for numbers can be (and have been) generated according to a bewildering variety of systems (see Ifrah, 1985; Menninger, 1958/1969). Because the base-ten system is so familiar and widespread and because humans have 10 fingers, it may appear that the development of a base-ten system is somehow natural and inevitable. Historically, base 4 and base 8 systems were also common (Menninger, 1958/1969). However, most modern languages now use systems that are organized around a base of 10, although languages vary in the consistency and transparency of that structure. For example, number words in English, Spanish, and Chinese differ in important ways. In all three languages, number names can be described to a first approximation as a base-ten system, but the languages differ in the clarity and consistency with which the base-ten structure is reflected in actual number names.

Representations for numbers from 1 to 9 consist of an unsystematically organized list. There is no way to predict that "5" or "five" or "wu" comes after "4," "four," and "si," in the Arabic numeral, English, or

Chinese systems, respectively. Names for numbers above 10 also diverge in interesting ways among the three languages. The Chinese number-naming system maps directly onto the Hindu-Arabic number system used to write numerals. For example, a word-for-word translation of "shi qi" (17) into English produces "ten-seven." English has unpredictable names for "11" and "12" that bear only a historical relation to "one" and "two" from the Old Saxon *ellevan* (one left over) and *twelif* (two left over) (Menninger, 1958/1969). Whether the boundary between 10 and 11 is marked in some way is very significant, because this is the first potential clue to the fact that number names are organized according to a base-ten system.

English names for teen numbers beyond twelve do have an internal structure, but this relation is obscured by phonetic modifications of many of the elements from those used for 1 through 10 (e.g., "ten" becomes "teen," "three" becomes "thir," and "five" becomes "fif"). Furthermore, the order of formation reverses place value compared with the Hindu-Arabic and Chinese systems (and with English names above 20), naming the smaller value before the larger value (e.g., say "fourteen" but write 14 with the 4 second). Spanish follows the same basic pattern for English to begin the teens, although there may be a clearer parallel between "uno, dos, tres" and "once, doce, trece" than between "one, two, three" and "eleven, twelve, thirteen." The biggest difference between Spanish and English is that, after 15, number names in Spanish abruptly take on a different structure. Thus, the name for 16 in Spanish "diez y seis" (literally "ten and six"), follows the same basic structure as do Arabic numerals and Chinese number names (starting with the tens value and then naming the ones place), rather than the structure used by teens names in English from 13 to 19 and by teens names in Spanish from 11 to 15 (starting with the ones place and then naming the tens value).

Above 20, all these number-naming systems converge on the Chinese structure of naming the larger value before the smaller one, consistent with the order of writing the values in numerals. Despite this convergence, the systems continue to differ in the clarity of the connection between decade names and the corresponding unit values. Chinese numbers are consistent in forming decade names by combining a unit value and the base (10). Decade names in English and Spanish generally can be derived from the name for the corresponding unit value, with varying degrees of phonetic modification (e.g., "five" becomes "fif" in English as in fifty rather that fivety, "cinco" becomes "cincuenta" in Spanish) and some notable exceptions, primarily the special name for twenty ("veinte") used in Spanish.

### *Consequences for Learning to Count*

Although languages differ in the length and complexity of the irregular portion of the system of names that must be learned, in general children must learn quite a few number names prior to coming across data supporting the induction that they are dealing with an ordered base-ten system of names. Looking at the extent to which differences in learning reflect differences in counting terms can assess effects of number-naming systems on children's early mathematics.

Research on children's acquisition of number names (Fuson, Richards, and Briars, 1982; Miller and Stigler, 1987; Siegler and Robinson, 1982) suggests that children in America learn to recite the list of number names through at least the teens in essentially a rote learning task. When first counting above twenty, U.S. preschoolers often produce idiosyncratic number names, indicating that they fail to understand the base-ten structure underlying larger number names, often counting "twenty-eight, twenty-nine, twenty-ten, twenty-eleven, twenty-twelve." This kind of mistake is extremely rare for Chinese children, indicating that the base-ten structure of number names is more accessible for learners of Chinese than it is for children learning to count in English.

The cognitive consequences of the relative complexity of English number names are not limited to obstacles placed in the way of early counting. Speakers of English and other European languages (Fuson, Fraivillig, and Burghardt, 1992; Séron et al., 1992) face a complex task in learning to write Arabic numerals, one more difficult than that faced by speakers of Chinese (compare the mapping between name and numeral for "twenty-four" with that for "fourteen" in the two languages). Work by Miura and her colleagues (Miura, 1987; Miura and Okamoto, 1989; Miura et al., 1988, 1993) suggests that the lack of transparency of base-ten markings in English has conceptual consequences as well. They have found that speakers of languages whose number names are patterned after Chinese (including Korean and Japanese) are better able than speakers of English and other European languages to represent numbers using base-ten blocks and to perform other place-value tasks. Because school arithmetic algorithms are largely structured around place value, this indication that the complexity of number names affects the ease with which children acquire this basic concept is a finding with real educational significance.

When learning to count, children must acquire a combination of conventional knowledge about number names (they must learn their own cultural number word list in order), a conceptual understanding of the mathematics principles that underlie counting, and an ability to apply this knowledge to mathematical problem solving. Language differences during preschool appear to be limited to the first aspect of learning to count. For example, Miller and colleagues (1995) found no differences between Chinese and U.S. preschoolers in the extent to which they violated counting principles when counting objects, or in their ability to use counting to produce sets of a given size in the course of a game. The effects of differences in number-name structure on early mathematical development appear to be very specific to those aspects of mathematics that require one to learn and use these symbol systems. These effects have implications for learning Arabic numerals and thus for acquiring the primary symbol system used in school-based mathematics.

The nature and timing of differences in early counting between Chinese-speaking and English-speaking preschoolers correspond to predictions based on the morphology of number names. Evidence from object counting indicates that these differences are also limited to aspects of counting that involve number naming. Miller and colleagues (1995) looked at children's object counting for sets that were small (3-6 items), medium (7-10 items), and large (14-17 items). They found that Chinese-speaking children were significantly more likely to report the correct number word for a set than English-speaking children, but this was entirely due to the greater likelihood of Chinese children to correctly recite the sequence of names. The task of completely coordinating saying number words and designating objects in counting is quite difficult for many young preschoolers, and equally so for U.S. and Chinese children: 37 percent of U.S. and 38 percent of Chinese preschoolers either pointed to an object and did not produce the number name or the reverse. Double counting or skipping objects was even more common, but again did not differ between the Chinese and U.S. preschoolers.

### *Consequences for Using the Base-ten Structure in Problem Solving*

The structure of number names is associated with a specific, limited difference in the course of counting acquisition between English-speaking and Chinese-speaking children. One area in which there may be conceptual consequences of these linguistic differences is in children's understanding of the base-ten principle that underlies the structure of Arabic numerals. This structure is a feature of a particular representational system rather than a fundamental mathematical fact, but it is a feature that is incorporated into many of the algorithms children learn for performing arithmetic and thus is a powerful concept in early mathematical development. Because English number names do not show a base-ten structure as consistently or as early in the count sequence as do Chinese number names, English-speaking children's conceptual understanding of this base-ten structure may be delayed compared with their Chinese-speaking peers.

Miura and her colleagues (Miura, 1987; Miura and Okamoto, 2003; Miura et al., 1993) have looked at the base-ten understanding of two groups of first grade children: speakers of East Asian languages, whose number-naming systems incorporate a clear base-ten structure, usually based on Chinese, and speakers of European languages, which generally do not show a clear base-ten structure in their number names. The primary task used is asking children to represent the cardinal value associated with a given number name using sets of blocks representing units and tens. Children whose native language is Chinese, Korean, or Japanese are consistently more likely to represent numbers as sets of tens and ones as either a first or second choice than are children whose native language is English, French, or Swedish.

Ho and Fuson (1998) compared the performance of Chinese-speaking preschool children in Hong Kong with English-speaking children in Britain and the United States. They found that half of the Chinese-speaking 5-year-olds (but none of the English-speaking children) who could count to at least 50 were able to take advantage of the base-ten structure of number names to quickly determine the answer to addition problems of the form "10 + n = ?," compared with other problems. Fuson and Kwon (1992) argued that the Chinese number-naming structure facilitates the use of a tens-complement strategy for early addition. In this approach, when adding numbers whose sum is greater than 10 (e.g., 8 + 7), the smaller addend is partitioned into the tens-complement of the first addend (2) and the remainder (5); the answer is 10 plus that remainder (10 + 5). In Chinese-structured number-naming systems, the answer corresponds to the result of the calculation ("shi wu" – "10 5"); in English, there is an additional step as the answer is converted into a different number name ("fifteen"). Fuson and Kwon reported that most Korean first graders they tested used this method before it was explicitly taught in school. Explicit instruction may be required for English-speaking children, but there is evidence that it can be quite successful, even with children from at-risk populations. Fuson and her colleagues (Fuson, Smith, and Lo Cicero, 1997) report success with explicitly teaching low-SES urban first graders about the base-ten structure of numbers, with the result that their end-of-year arithmetic performance approximated that reported for East Asian children.

## LEARNING DISABILITIES IN MATHEMATICS

Mathematics learning disabilities appear in 6 to 10 percent of the elementary school population (Barberisi et al., 2005). Many more children struggle in one or more mathematics content area at some point during their school careers (Geary, 2004). Although less research has been devoted to mathematical than to reading disabilities (Geary and Hoard, 2001; Ginsburg, 1997), considerable progress has been made over the past two decades with respect to understanding the nature of the mathematics difficulties and disabilities that children experience in school (Gersten, Jordan, and Flojo, 2005).

### Characteristics of Learning Difficulties

Poor computational fluency is a signature characteristic of mathematics learning disabilities in elementary school (e.g., Geary, 2004; Hasselbring, Goin, and Bransford, 1988; Jordan and Montani, 1997; Jordan, Hanich, and Kaplan, 2003a, 2003b; Ostad, 1998; Russell and Ginsburg, 1984). Computational fluency refers to accurate, efficient, and flexible computation with basic operations. Weak knowledge of facts reduces cognitive and attentional resources that are necessary for learning advanced mathematics (Goldman and Pellegrino, 1987). Computational fluency deficits can be reliably identified in the first few years of school and, if not addressed, are very persistent throughout elementary and middle school (Jordan, Hanich, and Kaplan, 2003b).

Children around the world move through a learning path of levels of solution methods for addition and subtraction problems. These levels become progressively more abstract, abbreviated, embedded, and complex. As they move through the levels, many children use a mix of strategies that vary according to number size and aspects of the problem situation (Geary and Burlinghman-Dubree, 1989; Siegler and Jenkins, 1989; Siegler and Robinson, 1982; Siegler and Shipley, 1995).

In contrast, young children with a mathematics learning disability rely on the most primitive Level 1 methods for extended periods in elementary school, do not use efficient counting procedures (e.g., counting on from the larger addend), and make frequent counting errors while learning to add and subtract (Geary, 1990). They also lag behind other children in the accuracy and linearity of their number line estimates (Geary et al., 2007). Researchers have differentiated children with a specific mathematics learning disability from those with a comorbid learning disability in both mathematics and reading. Jordan and colleagues (Hanich et al., 2001; Jordan, Hanich, and Kaplan, 2003a; Jordan, Kaplan, and Hanich, 2002) as well as other researchers (e.g., Geary, Hamson, and Hoard, 2000; Landerl, Bevan, and Butterworth, 2004) suggest that the nature of the mathematical deficits is similar for both groups, although children with the comorbid condition show lower performance overall. What differentiates children with a mathematics-only disability from those with combined mathematics and reading learning disabilities is that the former group performs better on word problems in mathematics, which depend on language comprehension as well as calculation facility. The potential for catching up in mathematics is much better for children with a mathematics-only disability, who can exploit their relative strength in general language to compensate for their deficiencies with numbers.

Some research shows that mathematics learning disabilities can be traced to early weaknesses in number, number relationships, and number operations as opposed to more general cognitive deficits (e.g., Gersten et al., 2005; Malofeeva et al., 2004). Weak number competency is reflected in poorly developed counting procedures, slow fact retrieval, and inaccurate computation, all characteristics of the disability (Geary et al., 2000; Jordan, Hanich, and Kaplan, 2003a). Skill with number combinations is tied to fundamental number knowledge (Baroody and Rosu, 2006; Locuniak and Jordan, in press). Accurate and efficient counting procedures can lead to strong connections between a problem and its solution (Siegler and Shrager, 1984). Developmental dyscalculia, a severe form of mathematics disability that has a known neurological basis, is explained more by domain-specific impairments in number knowledge than by domain-general deficits related to memory, spatial processing, or language (Butterworth and Reigosa, 2007). Although debate continues about the underpinnings of mathematics learning disabilities and diagnostic criteria (e.g., Geary et al., 2007), weakness in number sense appears to be a common theme in the literature. This finding has instructional implications for young children's mathematics education. Specifically, early interventions that focus on number sense have the potential to improve children's mathematics learning outcomes.

### Helping High-Risk Children

Early number competencies serve as a foundation for learning formal mathematics (Griffin et al., 1994; Miller, 1992). Deficits in these can prevent children from benefiting from formal mathematics instruction when they enter school, regardless of whether they are associated with environmental disadvantages or with genuine learning differences or disabilities (Baroody and Rosu, 2006; Griffin, 2007). In a recent study, Jordan and colleagues (in press) found that poor mathematics achievement is mediated by low number sense regardless of children's social class. That is, deficits in number sense are a better predictor of poor mathematics achievement than SES when all else is equal. Implications of this work suggest that children from low-income backgrounds and those with mathematics difficulties would benefit from a mathematics intervention during the early years (Jordan et al., in press).

Number competencies appear to have neurological origins, with their core components (e.g., subitization and approximate number representations) developing without much formal instruction (Berch, 2005; Dehaene, 1997; Feigenson, Dehaene, and Spelke, 2004). These early foundations provide support for learning more complex number skills involving number words, number comparisons, and counting. Children with mathematics difficulties seem to have problems with the symbolic system of number, rather than the universal analog magnitude system. Knowledge of the symbolic number system is heavily influenced by experience and instruction (Geary,

1995; Levine et al., 1992). Engaging young children in number activities (e.g., a mother or preschool teacher asking a child to give her 4 cookies) and simple games (e.g., board games that emphasize 1-to-1 correspondences, counting, and moving along number paths) are important for strengthening foundations and building conventional number knowledge (Gersten et al., 2005, Klibanoff et al., 2006; Levine et al., in preparation). Case and Griffin (1990) report that number sense learning is closely associated with children's home experiences with number concepts (e.g., reading number books with children). Moreover, efforts to teach number-related skills to high-risk kindergartners show promise for improving mathematics achievement (Griffin et al., 1994). In a recent study, Ramani and Siegler (2008) showed that playing a number board game that involved counting on squares on a number path improved the performance of 5-year-olds from low-income backgrounds on counting, numeral identification, numerical magnitude estimation, and number line estimation, and that the gains held after a follow-up several weeks later. Importantly, children playing this game said the number words written on the squares as they counted on one or two more, rather than saying "one" or "two" as they counted on. Playing games to help children master basic number, counting, and arithmetic concepts and skills has long been advocated by mathematics educators (e.g., Baroody, 1987; Ernest, 1986; Wynroth, 1986)—a proposition that is supported by research (for reviews, see, e.g., Baroody, 1999; Bright, Harvey, and Wheeler, 1985).

The effects of weaknesses in early mathematics, if not addressed, are likely to be felt throughout the school years and beyond. There is good reason to believe that early intensive instruction, both at home and at school, will give children the background they need to achieve at grade level in elementary school mathematics and help "shape the course of their mathematical journey" (Griffin, 2007, p. 392).

## REFERENCES AND BIBLIOGRAPHY

Aikens, N.L., and Barbarin, O. (2008). Socioeconomic differences in reading trajectories: The contribution of family, neighborhood, and school contexts. *Journal of Educational Psychology, 100*(2), 235-251.

Arnold, D.H., Fisher, P.H., Doctoroff, G.L., and Dobbs, J. (2002). Accelerating math development in Head Start classrooms. *Journal of Educational Psychology*, *94*(4), 762-770.

Baenninger, M., and Newcombe, N. (1989). The role of experience in spatial test performance: A meta-analysis. *Sex Roles*, *20*, 327-344.

Barbaresi, M.J., Katusic, S.K., Colligan, R.C., Weaver, A.L., and Jacobsen, S.J. (2005). Math learning disorder: Incidence in a population-based birth cohort, 1976-1982, Rochester, Minn. *Ambulatory Pediatrics*, *5*(5), 281-289.

Barbarin, O.A., Early, D., Clifford, R., Bryant, D., Frome, P., Burchinal, M., Howes, C., and Pianta, R. (2008). Parental conceptions of school readiness: Relation to ethnicity, socioeconomic status, and children's skills. *Early Education & Development*, *19*(5), 671-701.

Barnett, W.S., Yarosz, D.J., Thomas, J., Jung, K., and Blanco, D. (2007). Two-way monolingual English immersion in preschool education: An experimental comparison. *Early Childhood Research Quarterly*, *22*, 277-293.

Baroody, A.J. (1987). *Children's Mathematical Thinking: A Developmental Framework for Preschool, Primary, and Special Education Teachers.* New York: Teachers College Press.

Baroody, A.J. (1999). The development of basic counting, number, and arithmetic knowledge among children classified as mentally handicapped. In L.M. Glidden (Ed.), *International Review of Research in Mental Retardation* (vol. 22, pp. 51-103). San Diego, CA: Academic Press.

Baroody, A.J., and Rosu, L. (2006). *Adaptive Expertise with Basic Addition and Subtraction Combinations: The Number Sense View.* Paper presented at the American Educational Research Association, San Francisco, CA.

Benigno, J.P., and Ellis, S. (2008). Do parents count? The socialization of children's numeracy. In O.N. Saracho and B. Spodek (Eds.), *Contemporary Perspectives on Mathematics in Early Childhood Education* (pp. 291-308). Charlotte, NC: Information Age.

Berch, D.B. (2005). Making sense of number sense: Implications for children with mathematical disabilties. *Journal of Learning Disabilities, 38*(4), 333-339.

Blevins-Knabe, B., and Musun-Miller, L. (1996). Number use at home by children and their parents and its relationship to early mathematical room. *Early Development and Parenting*, *5*(1), 35-45.

Bright, G.W., Harvey, J.G., and Wheeler, M.M. (1985). Learning and mathematics games. *Journal for Research in Mathematics Education Monograph* (whole volume). Reston, VA.

Bronfenbrenner, U. (2000). Ecological system theory. In A.E. Kazdin (Ed.) *Encyclopedia of Psychology* (vol. 3, pp. 129-133). Washington, DC: American Psychological Association.

Butterworth, B., and Reigosa, V. (2007). Information processing deficits in dyscalculia. In D. Berch and M. Mazzocco (Eds.), *Why Is Math So Hard for Some Children?* (pp. 65-81). Baltimore, MD: Paul H. Brookes.

Cannon, J., and Ginsburg, H.P. (2008). "Doing the math": Maternal beliefs about early mathematics versus language learning. *Early Education and Development*, *19*, 238-260.

Cannon, J., Levine, S.C., and Huttenlocher, J. (2007, March). *Sex Differences in the Relation of Early Puzzle Play and Mental Transformation Skill.* Paper presented at the biennial meeting of the Society for Research on Child Development, Boston, MA.

Carr, M., Shing, Y.L, Janes, P., and Steiner, H. (2007). *Early Gender Differences in Strategy Use and Fluency: Implications for the Emergence of Gender Differences in Mathematics.* Paper presented at the biennial meeting of the Society for Research in Child Development, March, Boston, MA.

Case, R., and Griffin, S. (1990). Child cognitive development: The role of central conceptual structures in the development of scientific and social thought. In E.A. Hauert (Ed.), *Developmental Psychology: Cognitive, Perceptuo-Motor, and Neurological Perspectives* (pp. 193-230). North-Holland, Amsterdam: Elsevier Science.

Casey, M.B., Erkut, S., Ceder, I., and Young, J.M. (2008). Use of a storytelling context to improve girls' and boys' geometry skills in kindergarten. *Journal of Applied Developmental Psychology*, *29*, 29-48.

Civil, M. (1998). *Bridging In-School Mathematics and Out-of-School Mathematics: A Reflection.* Paper presented at the annual meeting of the American Education Research Association, April, San Diego, CA.

Clements, D.H., and Sarama, J. (2007). Early childhood mathematics learning. In J.F.K. Lester (Ed.), *Second Handbook of Research on Mathematics Teaching and Learning* (pp. 461-555). New York: Information Age.

Clements, D.H., and Sarama, J. (2008). Experimental evaluation of the effects of a research-based preschool mathematics curriculum. *American Educational Research Journal*, *45*, 443-494.

Clements, D.H., Sarama, J., and Gerber, S. (2005). *Mathematics Knowledge of Low-Income Entering Preschoolers.* Paper presented at the annual meeting of the American Educational Research Association, Montreal, Quebec, Canada.

Coley, R.J. (2002). *An Uneven Start: Indicators of Inequality in School Readiness.* Princeton, NJ: Educational Testing Service.

Dehaene, S. (1997). *The Number Sense: How the Mind Creates Mathematics.* New York: Oxford University Press.

Duncan, G.J., Dowsett, C.J., Classens, A., Magnuson, K., Huston, A.C., Klebanov, P., Pagani, L.S., Feinstein, L., Engel, M., Brooks-Gunn, J., Sexton, H., Duckworth, K., and Japel, C. (2007). School readiness and later achievement. *Developmental Psychology, 43*(6), 1428-1446.

Ebbeck, M. (1984). Equity for boys and girls: Some important issues. *Early Child Development and Care, 18*, 119-131.

Ehrlich, S.B., and Levine, S.C. (2007, March). *What Low-SES Children Do Know About Number: A Comparison of Head Start and Tuition-Based Preschool Children's Number Knowledge.* Paper presented at the biennial meeting of the Society for Research on Child Development, Boston, MA.

Ehrlich, S.B., Levine, S.C., and Goldin-Meadow, S. (2006). The importance of gesture in children's spatial reasoning. *Developmental Psychology, 42*, 1259-1268. Available: http://babylab.uchicago.edu/research_files/Ehrlich_2006.pdf [accessed October 2008].

Entwisle, D.R., and Alexander, K.L. (1990). Beginning school math competence: Minority and majority comparisons. *Child Development, 61*, 454-471.

Ernest, P. (1986). Games: A rationale for their use in the teaching of mathematics in school. *Mathematics in School, 15*(1), 2-5.

Fairweather, H., and Butterworth, G. (1977). The WPPSI at four years: A sex difference in verbal-performance discrepancies. *British Journal of Educational Psychology, 47*, 85-90.

Feigenson, L., Dehaene, S., and Spelke, E. (2004). Core systems of number. *Trends in Cognitive Sciences, 8*(7), 307-314.

Fennema, E., Carpenter, T.P., Jacobs, V.R., Franke, M.L., and Levi, L.W. (1998). A longitudinal study of gender differences in young children's mathematical thinking. *Educational Researcher, 27*, 6-11.

Fisch, S.M. (2008). *The Role of Educational Media in Preschool Mathematics Education.* Teaneck, NJ: Mediakidz Research and Consulting.

Fluck, M., Linnell, M., and Holgate, M. (2005). Does counting count for 3- to 4-year-olds? Parental assumptions about preschool children's understanding of counting and cardinality. *Social Development, 14*, 496-513.

Fuchs, L.S., Fuchs, D., Compton, D.L., Bryant, J.D., Hamlett, C.L., and Seethaler, P.M. (2007). Mathematics screening and progress monitoring at first grade: Implications for responsiveness to intervention. *Exceptional Children, 73*(3), 311-330.

Fuson, K.C., and Kwon, Y. (1992). Korean children's single-digit addition and subtraction: Numbers structured by ten. *Journal for Research in Mathematics Education, 23*(2), 148-165.

Fuson, K.C., Richards, J., and Briars, D.J. (1982). The acquisition and elaboration of the number word sequences. In C. Brainerd (Ed.), *Progress in Cognitive Development: Volume 1. Children's Logical and Mathematical Cognition* (pp. 33-92). New York: Springer-Verlag.

Fuson, K.C., Fraivillig, J.L., and Burghardt, B.H. (1992). Relationships children construct among English number words, multiunit base-ten blocks, and written multi-digit addition. In J.I.D. Campbell (Ed.), *The Nature and Origins of Mathematical Skills* (pp. 39-112). New York: North-Holland.

Fuson, K.C., Smith, S.T., and Lo Cicero, A.M. (1997). Supporting Latino first graders' ten-structured thinking in urban classrooms. *Journal for Research in Mathematics Education, 28*, 738-766.

Geary, D.C. (1990). A componential analysis of an early learning deficit in mathematics. *Journal of Experimental Child Psychology, 49*, 363-383.

Geary, D.C. (1995). Reflections of evolution and culture in children's cognition: Implications for mathematical development and instruction. *American Psychologist, 50*(1), 24-37.

Geary, D.C. (2004). Mathematics and learning disabilities. *Journal of Learning Disabilities, 37*(1), 4-15.

Geary, D.C., and Burlingham-Dubree, M. (1989). External validation of the strategy choice model for addition. *Journal of Experimental Child Psychology, 47*, 175-192.

Geary, D.C., and Hoard, M.K. (2001). Numerical and arithmetical deficits in learning-disabled children: Relation to dyscalculia and dyslexia. *Aphasiology, 15*(7), 635-647.

Geary, D.C., Hamson, C.O., and Hoard, M.K. (2000). Numerical and arithmetical cognition: A longitudinal study of process and concept deficits in children with learning disability. *Journal of Experimental Child Psychology, 77*, 236-263.

Geary, D.C., Hoard, M.K., Byrd-Craven, J., Nugent, L., and Numtee, C. (2007). Cognitive mechanisms underlying achievement deficits in children with mathematical learning disability. *Child Development, 78*(4), 1343-1359.

Genesee, F., Lindholm-Leary, K., Saunders, W., and Christian, D. (2006). *Educating English Language Learners*. New York: Cambridge University Press.

Gersten, R., Jordan, N.C., and Flojo, J.R. (2005). Early identification and interventions for students with mathematics difficulties. *Journal of Learning Disabilities, 38*(4), 293-304.

Ginsburg, H.P. (1997). Mathematics learning disabilities: A view from developmental psychology. *Journal of Learning Disabilities, 30*(1), 20-33.

Ginsburg, H.P., and Russell, R.L. (1981). Social class and racial influences on early mathematical thinking. *Monographs of the Society for Research in Child Development, 46*(6, Serial No. 193), 1-69.

Goldman, S.R., and Pellegrino, J.W. (1987). Information processing and educational microcomputer technology: Where do we go from here? *Journal of Learning Disabilities, 20*, 144-154.

Gordon, P. (2004). Numerical cognition without words: Evidence from Amazonia. *Science, 306*, 496-499.

Griffin, S. (2007). Early intervention for children at risk of developing mathematical learning difficulties. In D.B. Berch and M.M. Mazzocco (Eds.), *Why Is Math So Hard for Some Children? The Nature and Origins of Mathematical Learning Difficulties and Disabilities* (pp. 373-396). Baltimore, MD: Paul H. Brookes.

Griffin, S., Case, R., and Siegler, R.S. (1994). Classroom lessons: Integrating cognitive theory and classroom practice. In K. McGilly (Ed.), *Rightstart: Providing the Central Conceptual Prerequisites for First Formal Learning of Arithmetic to Students at Risk for School Failure* (pp. 25-50). Cambridge, MA: MIT Press.

Guiness, D., and Morley, C. (1991). Sex differences in the development of visuo-spatial ability in pre-school children. *Journal of Mental Imagery, 15*, 143-150.

Hanich, L., Jordan, N.C., Kaplan, D., and Dick, J. (2001). Performance across different areas of mathematical cognition in children with learning difficulties. *Journal of Educational Psychology, 93*(3), 615-626.

Hasselbring, T.S., Goin, L.I., and Bransford, J.D. (1988). Developing math automaticity in learning handicapped children: The role of computerized drill and practice. *Focus on Exceptional Children, 20*(6), 1-7.

Ho, C.S., and Fuson, K.C. (1998). Children's knowledge of teen quantities as tens and ones: Comparisons of Chinese, British, and American kindergartners. *Journal of Educational Psychology, 90*(3), 536-544.

Holloway, S.D., Rambaud, M.F., Fuller, B., and Eggers-Pierola, C. (1995). What is "appropriate practice" at home and in child care? Low-income mothers' views on preparing their children for school. *Early Childhood Research Quarterly*, *10*(4), 451-473.

Hyde, J.S., Lindberg, S.M., Linn, M.C., Ellis, A.B., and Williams, C.C. (2008). Gender similarities characterize math performance. *Science*, *321*, 494-495.

Ifrah, G. (1985). *From One to Zero: Universal History of Numbers.* (Lowell Blair, Trans.) New York: Viking Penguin.

Iruka, I., and Barbarin, O. (2008). African American children's early learning and development: examining parenting, schools, and neighborhoods. In H. Neville, B. Tynes, and S. Utsey (Eds.), *Handbook of African American Psychology* (Ch. 13, pp. 175-186). Thousand Oaks, CA: Sage.

Jeong, Y., and Levine, S.C. (2005, April). *How Do Young Children Represent Numerosity?* Paper presented at the biennial meeting of Society for Research on Child Development, Atlanta, GA.

Jordan, N.C., and Montani, T.O. (1997). Cognitive arithmetic and problem solving: A comparison of children with specific and general mathematics difficulties. *Journal of Learning Disabilities*, *30*(6), 624-634.

Jordan, N.C., Huttenlocher, J., and Levine, S.C. (1992). Differential calculation abilities in young children from middle- and low-income families. *Developmental Psychology*, *28*(4), 644-653.

Jordan, N.C., Levine, S.C., and Huttenlocher, J. (1994). Development of calculation abilities in middle- and low-income children after formal instruction in school. *Journal of Applied Developmental Psychology*, *15*, 223-240.

Jordan, N.C., Kaplan, D., and Hanich, L.B. (2002). Achievement growth in children with learning difficulties in mathematics: Findings of a two-year longitudinal study. *Journal of Educational Psychology*, *94*(3), 586-597.

Jordan, N.C., Hanich, L.B., and Kaplan, D. (2003a). A longitudinal study of mathematical competencies in children with specific mathematics difficulties versus children with comorbid mathematics and reading difficulties. *Child Development*, *74*(3), 834-850.

Jordan, N.C., Hanich, L.B., and Kaplan, D. (2003b). Arithmetic fact mastery in young children: A longitudinal investigation. *Journal of Experimental Child Psychology*, *85*, 103-119.

Jordan, N.C., Kaplan, D., Nabors Oláh, L., and Locuniak, M.N. (2006). Number sense growth in kindergarten: A longitudinal investigation of children at risk for mathematics difficulties. *Child Development*, *77*, 153-175.

Jordan, N.C., Kaplan, D., Locuniak, M.N., and Ramineni, C. (2007). Predicting first-grade math achievement from developmental number sense trajectories. *Learning Disabilities Research and Practice*, *22*(1), 36-46.

Jordan, N.C., Glutting, J., and Ramineni, C. (in press). A number sense screening tool for young children at risk for mathematical difficulties. In A. Dowker (Ed.), *Mathematical Difficulties: Psychology, Neuroscience and Intervention.* New York: Elsevier.

Jordan, N.C., Kaplan, D., Ramineni, C., and Locuniak, M.N. (in press). Early math matters: Kindergarten number competence and later mathematics outcomes. *Developmental Psychology.*

Kersh, J., Casey, B., and Young, J.M. (in press). Research on spatial skills and block building in girls and boys: The relationship to later mathematics learning. In B. Spodek and O.N. Saracho (Eds.), *Mathematics, Science, and Technology in Early Childhood Education.* Charlotte, NC: Information Age.

Klein, A., and Starkey, P. (2004). Fostering preschool children's mathematical knowledge: Findings from the Berkeley Math Readiness Project. In. D.H. Clements, J. Sarama, and A-M. DiBiase (Eds.), *Engaging Young Children in Mathematics: Findings of the 2000 National Conference on Standards for Preschool and Kindergarten Mathematics Education.* Mahwah, NJ: Erlbaum.

Klibanoff, R.S., Levine, S.C., Huttenlocher, J., Vasilyeva, M., and Hedges, L.V. (2006). Preschool children's mathematical knowledge: The effect of teacher "Math Talk". *Developmental Psychology*, *42*(1), 59-69.

Knitzer, K., and Lefkowitz, J. (2006). *Helping the Most Vulnerable Infants, Toddlers, and Their Families*. New York: National Center for Children in Poverty. Available: http://www.nccp.org/publications/pdf/text_669.pdf [accessed April 2008].

Lachance, J.A., and Mazzocco, M.M.M. (2006). A longitudinal analysis of sex differences in math and spatial skills in primary school age children. *Learning and Individual Differences*, *16*, 195-216.

Ladson-Billings, G. (1995). Making mathematics meaningful in a multicultural context. In W.G. Secada, E. Fennema, and L.B. Adajian (Eds.), *New Direction for Equity in Mathematics Education* (pp. 126-145). Cambridge, England: Cambridge University Press.

Landerl, K., Bevan, A., and Butterworth, B. (2004). Developmental dyscalculia and basic numerical capacities: A study of 8-9-year-old students. *Cognition*, *93*, 99-125.

LeCorre, M., Li, P., and Lee, Y. (2004). Numerical bilingualism: Count list acquisition in Korean. (Unpublished raw data.)

Levine, S.C., Jordan, N.C., and Huttenlocher, J. (1992). Development of calculation abilities in young children. *Journal of Experimental Child Psychology*, *53*, 72-103.

Levine, S.C., Huttenlocher, J., Taylor, A., and Langrock, A. (1999). Early sex differences in spatial ability. *Developmental Psychology*, *35*, 940-949.

Levine, S.C., Vasilyeva, M., Lourenco, S.F., Newcombe, N.S., and Huttenlocher, J. (2005). Socioeconomic status modifies the sex difference in spatial skill. *Psychological Science*, *16*(11), 841-845.

Levine, S.C., Suriyakham, L., Rowe, M. and Huttenlocher, J. (in preparation). What counts in preschoolers' development of cardinology knowledge? A longitudinal investigation.

Li, P., LeCorre, M., Shui, R., Jia, G., and Carey, S. (2003, October). *Effects of Plural Syntax on Number Word Learning: A Cross-Linguistic Study.* Paper presented at the 28th Boston University Conference on Language Development, Boston, MA.

Lindholm-Leary, K. and Borasato, G. (2006). Academic achievement. In F. Genesee, K. Lindholm-Leary, W.M. Saunders, and D. Christian (Eds.), *Educating English Language Learners: A Synthesis of Research Evidence*. New York: Cambridge University Press.

Locuniak, M.N., and Jordan, N.C. (in press). Using kindergarten number sense to predict calculation fluency in second grade. *Journal of Learning Disabilities*.

Lubienski, S.T. (2006). Examining instruction, achievement, and equity with NAEP mathematics data. *Education Policy Analysis Archives*, *14*(14). Available: http://epaa.asu.edu/epaa/v14n14/ [accessed January 2009].

Lubienski, S.T. (2007). What we can do about achievement disparities. *Educational Leadership*, *65*(3), 54-59.

Lutchmaya, S., and Baron-Cohen, S. (2002). Human sex differences in social and nonsocial looking preferences at 12 months of age. *Infant Behaviour and Development*, *25*, 319-325.

Magnuson, K., and Waldfogel, J. (2008). *Steady Gains and Stalled Progress: Inequality and the Black-White Test Score Gap*. New York: Russell Sage Foundation.

Malofeeva, E., Day, J., Saco, X., Young, L., and Ciancio, D. (2004). Construction and evaluation of a number sense test with Head Start children. *Journal of Educational Psychology*, *96*(4), 648-659.

Mazzocco, M.M.M., and Thompson, R.E. (2005). Kindergarten predictors of math learning disability. *Learning Disabilities Research and Practice*, *20*(3), 142-155.

McGuinness, D., and Morley, C. (1991). Sex differences in the development of visuo-spatial ability in preschool children. *Journal of Mental Imagery*, *15*, 143-150.

McKeon, D. (2005). *Research Talking Points: English Language Learners*. Available: http://www.nea.org/achievement/talkingells.html [accessed September 2008].

McLoyd, V.C. (1990). The impact of economic hardship on Black families and children: Psychological distress, parenting, and socioemotional development. *Child Development*, *61*, 311-346.

Menninger, K. (1958/1969). *Number Words and Number Symbols: A Cultural History of Numbers.* (P. Broneer, Trans.). Cambridge, MA: MIT Press. (Original work published 1958.)

Miller, K.F. (1992). What a number is: Mathematical foundations and developing number concepts. In J.I.D. Campbell (Ed.), *The Nature and Origin of Mathematical Skills* (pp. 3-38). New York: Elsevier Science.

Miller, K.F., and Stigler, J.W. (1987). Counting in Chinese: Cultural variation in a basic cognitive skill. *Cognitive Development*, *2*, 279-305.

Miller, K.F., Smith, C.M., Zhu, J., and Zhang, H. (1995). Preschool origins of cross-national differences in mathematical competence: The role of number-naming systems. *Psychological Science*, *6*(1), 56-60.

Miura, I.T. (1987). Mathematics achievement as a function of language. *Journal of Educational Psychology*, *79*(1), 79-82.

Miura, I.T., and Okamoto, Y. (1989). Comparisons of U.S. and Japanese first graders' cognitive representation of number and understanding of place value. *Journal of Educational Psychology*, *81*(1), 109-114.

Miura, I.T., and Okamoto, Y. (2003). Language supports for mathematics understanding and performance. In A.J. Baroody and A. Dowker (Eds.), *The Development of Arithmetic Concepts and Skills—Constructing Adaptive Expertise: Studies in Mathematical Thinking and Learning* (pp. 229-242). Hillsdale, NJ: Erlbaum.

Miura, I.T., Kim, C.C., Chang, C., and Okamoto, Y. (1988). Effects of language characteristics on children's cognitive representation of number: Cross-national comparisons. *Child Development*, *59*, 1445-1450.

Miura, I.T., Okamoto, Y., Kim, C.C., Steere, M., and Fayol, M. (1993). First graders' cognitive representation of number and understanding of place value: Cross-national comparisons—France, Japan, Korea, Sweden, and the United States. *Journal of Educational Psychology*, *85*(1), 24-30.

National Center for Education Statistics. (2007). *The Nation's Report Card, Mathematics 2007: National Assessment of Educational Progress at Grades 4 and 8.* Washington, DC: Institute of Education Sciences, U.S. Department of Education.

National Council of Teachers of Mathematics. (2000). *Principles and Standards for School Mathematics.* Reston, VA: Author.

Ostad, S.A. (1998). Developmental differences in solving simple arithmetic word problems and simple number-fact problems: A comparison of mathematically normal and mathematically disabled children. *Mathematical Cognition*, *4*(1), 1-19.

Pica, P., Lemer, C., Izard, V., and Dehaene, S. (2004). Exact and approximate arithmetic in an Amazonian Indigene group. *Science*, 499-503.

Ramani, G.B., and Siegler, R.S. (2008). Promoting broad and stable improvements in low-income children's numerical knowledge through playing number board games. *Child Development*, *79*, 375-394. Available: http://www.psy.cmu.edu/~siegler/Ram-Sieg2008.pdf [accessed October 2008].

Rosser, R.A., Ensing, S.S., Glider, P.J., and Lane, S. (1984). An information processing analysis of children's accuracy in predicting the appearance of rotated stimuli. *Child Development*, *55*, 2204-2211.

Russell, R.L., and Ginsburg, H.P. (1984). Cognitive analysis of children's mathematic difficulties. *Cognition and Instruction*, *1*(2), 217-244.

Sarama, J., Clements, D.H., Starkey, P., Klein, A., and Wakeley, A. (2008). Scaling up the implementation of a pre-kindergarten mathematics curriculum: Teaching for understanding with trajectories and technologies. *Journal of Research on Educational Effectiveness*, *1*, 89-119.

Sarnecka, B.W., Kamenskaya, V.G., Yamana, Y., Ogura, T., and Yudovina, Y.B. (2007). From grammatical number to exact numbers: early meanings of "one", "two", and "three" in English, Russian, and Japanese. *Cognitive Psychology*, *55*, 136-168.

Saxe, G.B., Guberman, S.R., and Gearhart, M. (1987). Social processes in early number development. *Monographs of the Society for Research in Child Development*, *52*(2).

Secada, W.G. (1991). Degree of bilingualism and arithmetic problem solving in Hispanic first graders. *Elementary School Journal*, *92*, 213-231.

Séron, X., Pesenti, M., Noël, M.-P., Deloche, G., and Cornet, J.-A. (1992). Images of numbers, or "when 98 is upper left and 6 sky blue." *Cognition*, *44*(1-2), 159-196.

Siegler, R.S., and Jenkins, E. (1989). *How Children Discover New Strategies*. Hillsdale, NJ: Erlbaum.

Siegler, R.S., and Robinson, M. (1982). The development of numerical understandings. In H.W. Reese and L.P. Lipsitt (Eds.), *Advances in Child Development and Behavior, Volume 16* (pp. 242-312). New York: Academic Press.

Siegler, R.S., and Shipley, C. (1995). Variation, selection, and cognitive change. In T. Simon and G. Halford (Eds.), *Developing Cognitive Competence: New Approaches to Process Modeling* (pp. 31-76). Hillsdale, NJ: Erlbaum.

Siegler, R.S., and Shrager, J. (1984). Strategy choices in addition and subtraction: How do children know what to do? In C. Sophian (Ed.), *Origins of Cognitive Skills* (pp. 229-293). Hillsdale, NJ: Erlbaum.

Starkey, P., and Klein, A. (2008). *Sociocultural Influences on Young Children's Mathematical Knowledge: Contemporary Perspectives on Mathematics in Early Childhood Education*. Charlotte, NC: Information Age.

Starkey, P., Klein, A., Chang, I., Qi, D. Lijuan, P., and Yang, Z. (1999). *Environmental Supports for Young Children's Mathematical Development in China and the United States*. Paper presented at the biennial meeting of the Society for Research in Child Development, Albuquerque, NM.

Starkey, P., Klein, A., and Wakeley, P. (2004). Enhancing young children's mathematical knowledge through a pre-kindergarten mathematics intervention. *Early Childhood Research Quarterly*, *19*, 99-120.

Stipek, D.J., and Byler, P. (1997). Early childhood teachers: Do they practice what they preach? *Early Childhood Research Quarterly*, *12*, 305-325.

Tudge, J.R.H., and Doucet, F. (2004). Early mathematical experiences: Observing young black and white children's everyday activities. *Early Childhood Research Quarterly*, *19*, 21-39.

Wechsler, D. (1967). *Manual for the Wechsler Preschool and Primary Scale of Intelligence*. New York: Psychological Corporation.

Weiss, H., Caspe, M., and Lopez, M.E. (2006). *Family Involvement Makes a Difference: Family Involvement in Early Childhood Education (No. 1)*. Available: http://www.gse.harvard.edu/hfrp/projects/fine/resources/research/earlychildhood.html [accessed April 2008].

Wilson, R.S. (1975). Twins: Patterns of cognitive development as measured on the Wechsler preschool and primary scale of intelligence. *Developmental Psychology*, *11*, 126-134.

Woods, T.A., and Kurtz-Costes, B. (2007). Race identity and race socialization in African American families: Implications for social workers. *Journal of Human Behavior and the Social Environment*, *15*, 99-116.

Wynroth, L. (1986). *Wynroth Math Program—The Natural Numbers Sequence*. Ithaca, NY: Wynroth Math Program.

# Part II

# Teaching-Learning Paths

In Part II, we lay out a sequence of milestones for children ages 2-7 in the core areas of number (which includes whole number, relations, and operations) and geometry and measurement. We call this sequence a *teaching-learning path*. A teaching-learning path consists of the significant steps in learning in a particular topic; each new step in the learning path builds on the earlier steps. These paths are based on research that shows that young children generally follow particular paths when learning number-relations-operations and geometry-measurement (Clements and Sarama, 2007, 2008; Fuson, 1992a, 1992b; Ginsburg, 1983). Of course, learning is a continuous process, but to overview the process, we have identified four related steps organized by age/grade. The four steps move from children 2 and 3 years old, to children age 4 or in prekindergarten, to children in kindergarten, to children in Grade 1. Grade 1 is included to indicate how the knowledge from the earlier step is used—and vital for doing well—in Grade 1.

For our purposes, we define the core mathematical ideas as those that are mathematically central and coherent, consistent with the thinking of children who have had adequate mathematical experiences, and generative of future learning. Thus, they are foundational mathematically and developmentally. They are achievable for children of these ages. That is, they are consistent with children's ways of thinking, developing, and learning when they have experience with mathematics ideas. In addition, they are interesting to children. The committee recommends that all children learn this mathematics by the end of kindergarten.

In Chapter 2, we discussed why these core ideas are important mathematically. Here we focus on how they develop in children who have opportunity to learn them as the ideas become increasingly sophisticated and interconnected over these years. Relationships among the ideas as well as some of children's common errors are also discussed. Vital ideas for Grade 1 are briefly overviewed to indicate how younger children's knowledge is developed and extended into Grade 1.

As noted in Chapter 2, we are building on earlier efforts to articulate appropriate mathematics content for young children. In 1989, the National Council of Teachers of Mathematics (NCTM) issued *Curriculum and Evaluation Standards for School Mathematics*. This document described 13 curriculum standards for the grade band K-4 (as well as for the grade bands 5-8 and 9-12). Although these standards have been influential, they do not describe the mathematics to be learned in detail and did not give guidance by grade level, nor for children younger than kindergarten.

In 2000, NCTM released *Principles and Standards for School Mathematics* (PSSM) after an extensive process of revision of the 1989 standards. Prekindergarten (pre-K) was included this time, in the grade band pre-K–2. PSSM described five content standards—number and operations, algebra, geometry, measurement, and data analysis and probability—and five process standards—problem solving, reasoning and proof, communication, connections, and representations—for each of four grade bands (pre-K–2, 3-5, 6-8, 9-12), covering all of school mathematics from pre-K through the end of high school. Although PSSM discussed the mathematics to be learned at the grade bands in greater detail than the 1989 standards did, it still did not specify what was to be learned at individual grade levels.

Recognizing the need for more in-depth attention to prekindergarten, early childhood educators and mathematics educators convened in 2000 and publish a conference report on the development of mathematics standards for young children. The resulting book, *Engaging Young Children in Mathematics: Findings of the 2000 National Conference on Standards for Preschool and Kindergarten Mathematics Education* (Clements, Sarama, and DiBiase, 2004), contains 17 recommendations for early childhood mathematics education. They concern equity, programs, teaching, teachers and their development, assessment, appropriate mathematics for young children, and broader efforts to inform stakeholders and encourage collaboration in early childhood education and addressing the need for age/grade level standards. That report grouped the mathematics content for early childhood into four topic areas: number and operations, geometry, measurement, and algebra, patterns, and data analysis.

In 2002, the National Association for the Education of Young Children (NAEYC) and NCTM approved a joint position statement, "Early Childhood Mathematics: Promoting Good Beginnings." The statement includes 10 research-based recommendations to guide practice and 4 policy recommendations. The statement includes sample charts of learning paths related to a number goal and a geometry goal with activity examples.

In 2006, NCTM released *Curriculum Focal Points for Prekindergarten through Grade 8 Mathematics: A Quest for Coherence* (hereafter *Curriculum Focal Points*). These were developed in response to inconsistency in placement of topics by grade level in the United States and the lack of focus ("a mile wide and an inch deep") typical of U.S. mathematics curricula. Although much shorter than PSSM (and developed over a much shorter time), this report gives grade-level recommendations for each individual grade from pre-K to grade 8. These grade-level recommendations do not specify a full curriculum but rather describe the most significant mathematical concepts and skills at each grade level. There are three focal points at each grade level, each of which is a coherent cluster of skills and ideas, sometimes cutting across NCTM's five content strands. *Curriculum Focal Points* recommends that instruction at a grade level should devote the vast majority of attention to the content identified in the three focal points (p. 6). At pre-K and kindergarten, the three focal points concern number and operations, geometry, and measurement.

In addition to the three focal points at each grade level, *Curriculum Focal Points* describes connections, which consist of related content, including contexts and material to receive continuing development from previous grade levels. At pre-K, the connections concern data analysis, number and operations, and algebra. At kindergarten, the connections concern data analysis, geometry, and algebra. Collectively, these previous reports form the basis for the descriptions of foundational and achievable mathematics content in this report. The current report provides guidance on the two most critical mathematical areas during early childhood: number and operation and geometry and measurement, and as will be discussed later, number and operations is the area where young children need to spend the most time. Meaningful learning experiences in these content areas provide young children with the foundation that is necessary for them to be successful in later mathematics.

## SUPPORTING LEARNING IN MATHEMATICS

Our view of children is one of powerful and intrinsically motivated mathematics learners who, in a supportive physical and social environment, spontaneously learn some aspects of mathematics and make connections and extensions. However, children need adult guidance to help them learn the many culturally important aspects of mathematics, such as language and counting. In preschools and care centers, all children will bring to each mathematical topic area some initial competencies and knowledge on which to build. The major teaching challenge is to build a mathematical learning and teaching environment in which children will learn at least the basics of each topic area. This will enable them to practice and build on their own knowledge, with guidance from adults, peers, and family members, and be supported to move through learning paths to learn the foundational and achievable content identified in this report. These teaching and learning environments need to be consistent with the process goals outlined in Chapter 2, and they need to support children to be active in thinking about and discussing mathematical ideas.

Children require significant amounts of time to develop the foundational mathematical skills and understandings they have the desire and potential to learn and that they will need for success at school. Although some children have a sufficiently enriched home environment and enough mathematically focused interactions with family members so that they develop many of the necessary foundational mathematical understandings and skills at home, others do not. For the sake of equity, preschool programs should help children develop foundational mathematical understandings and skills; high-quality preschool programs that devote sufficient time to mathematics are able to do so (see Chapter 7). Even children who learn mathematical ideas at home will benefit from a consistent high-quality program experience in the preschool and kindergarten years. It is therefore critical that sufficient time is devoted to mathematics instruction in preschool programs so that children develop the foundational mathematical skills and understandings described here. Time must be allocated not only for the more formal parts of mathematics instruction and discussions that occur in the whole group or in small groups, but also for children to elaborate and extend their mathematical thinking by exploring, creating, and playing.

The time that is allotted for mathematics in early childhood programs must be allocated across various topics. The typical description of mathematics content is divided into the five strands of number and operations, algebra, geometry, measurement, and data analysis and probability. These are used to describe and categorize all of school mathematics, from pre-K through high school, and these strands are intended to receive different amounts of emphasis at different grade levels.

The committee is concerned that inclusion of all five strands for young children has led some programs and teachers to spread their mathematics time equally across these different content areas, thus spreading mathematical experiences too thinly and not going deeply enough into the core foundations that children need to establish firmly. It is important to concentrate on number and operations and on geometry and measurement in the early childhood period, with a greater portion of time spent on number and operations. Number is critically important to all of later mathematics. Geometry and measurement play an important supporting role in the development of number concepts and are themselves important to later mathematics. In addition, research on programs that result in positive learning gains for children indicate that children need sufficient time working with these ideas in order to achieve a level of proficiency that prepares them for continuing success in mathematics. Of course, many activities overlap these topic areas and could be counted in either if there is a balanced focus on both. The time spent on number and operations and on geometry and measurement can also include connections to data analysis and patterns, as listed in *Curriculum Focal Points* and discussed in the chapters of Part II.

The kind of learning involved in various number and operation components and in various aspects of geometry and measurement is different, as we describe. Major themes of these variations in the kinds of learning are the need for achieving fluency, the use of patterns, generalizing, and extending. All of these require many repeated experiences with the same numbers and related similar tasks. This is part of what makes learning mathematics require so much time focused on mathematical content.

Mathematics is a participant sport. Children must play it frequently to become good at it. They do need frequent modeling of correct performance, discussion about the concepts involved, and frequent feedback about their performance. Both modeling and feedback can come from other students as well as from adults, and feedback also sometimes comes from the situation. All children must have sustained and frequent times in which they themselves enact the core mathematical content and talk about what they are doing and why they are doing it. In mathematics learning, effort creates ability.

## REFERENCES AND BIBLIOGRAPHY

Clements, D.H., and Sarama, J. (2007). Early childhood mathematics learning. In F.K. Lester, Jr. (Ed.), *Second Handbook of Research on Mathematics Teaching and Learning* (pp. 461-555). New York: Information Age.

Clements, D.H., and Sarama, J. (2008). Experimental evaluation of a research-based preschool mathematics curriculum. *American Educational Research Journal*, *45*, 443-494.

Clements, D.H., Sarama, J., and DiBiase, A. (2004). *Engaging Young Children in Mathematics: Findings of the 2000 National Conference on Standards for Preschool and Kindergarten Mathematics Education.* Mahwah, NJ: Erlbaum.

Fuson, K.C. (1992a). Research on learning and teaching addition and subtraction of whole numbers. In G. Leinhardt, R.T. Putnam, and R.A. Hattrup (Eds.), *The Analysis of Arithmetic for Mathematics Teaching* (pp. 53-187). Hillsdale, NJ: Erlbaum.

Fuson, K.C. (1992b). Research on whole number addition and subtraction. In D. Grouws (Ed.), *Handbook of Research on Mathematics Teaching and Learning* (pp. 243-275). New York: Macmillan.

Ginsburg, H.P. (1983). *The Development of Mathematical Thinking.* New York: Academic Press.

National Association for the Education of Young Children and National Council of Teachers of Mathematics. (2002). *Early Childhood Mathematics: Promoting Good Beginnings.* A joint position statement of the National Association for the Education of Young Children and National Council of Teachers of Mathematics. Available: http://www.naeyc.org/about/positions/pdf/psmath.pdf [accessed August 2008].

National Council of Teachers of Mathematics. (1989). *Curriculum and Evaluation Standards for School Mathematics.* Reston, VA: Author.

National Council of Teachers of Mathematics. (2000). *Principles and Standards for School Mathematics*. Reston, VA: Author.

National Council of Teachers of Mathematics. (2006). *Curriculum Focal Points for Prekindergarten through Grade 8 Mathematics: A Quest for Coherence*. Reston, VA: Author.

# 5

# The Teaching-Learning Paths for Number, Relations, and Operations

In this chapter we describe the teaching-learning paths for number, relations, and operations at each of the four age/grade steps (2- and 3-year-olds, 4-year-olds [prekindergarten], kindergarten, and Grade 1). As noted, the four steps are convenient age groupings, although, in fact, children's development is continuous. There is considerable variability in the age at which children do particular numerical tasks (see the reviews of the literature in Clements and Sarama, 2007, 2008; Fuson, 1992a, 1992b; also see Chapter 4). However, a considerable amount of this variability comes from differences in the opportunities to learn these tasks and the opportunity to practice them with occasional feedback to correct errors and extend the learning. Once started along these numerical learning paths, children become interested in consolidating and extending their knowledge, practicing by themselves and seeking out additional information by asking questions and giving themselves new tasks. Home, child care, and preschool and school environments need to support children in this process of becoming a self-initiating and self-guiding learner and facilitate the carrying out of such learning. Targeted learning path time is also needed—time at home or in an early childhood learning center—that will support children in consolidating thinking at one step and moving along the learning path to the next step.

Although we consider the mathematics goals described in this and the next chapter foundational and achievable for all children in the designated age range for that step, we recognize that some children's learning will be advanced while others' functioning will be significantly behind. Children at particular ages/grades may be able to work correctly with larger numbers or more complex geometric ideas than those we specify in the various tables and text. Each subsequent step assumes that children have had sufficient experiences with the topics in the previous step to learn the earlier content well. (See Box 5-1 for a discussion of what it means to learn something well.) However, many children can still learn the content at a given step without having fully mastered the previous content if they have sufficient time to learn and practice the more challenging content. Of course, some children have difficulty in learning certain kinds of mathematical concepts, and a few have really significant difficulties. But most children are capable of learning the foundational and achievable mathematics content specified in the learning steps outlined here.

In both the number and operations and the geometry and measurement core areas, children learn about the basic numerical or geometric concepts and objects (numbers, shapes), and they also relate those objects and compose/decompose (operate on) them. Therefore, each core area begins by discussing the basic objects and then moves to the relations and operations on them. In all of these, it is important to consider how children perceive, say, describe/discuss, and construct these objects, relations, and operations.

The development of the elements of the number core across ages is described first, and then the development of the relations and operations core

**BOX 5-1**
**Learning Something Well**

In most aspects of the number and the relations/operation core, children need a great deal of practice doing a task, even after they can do it correctly. The reasons for this vary a bit across different aspects, and no single word adequately captures this need, because the possible words often have somewhat different meanings for different people.

*Overlearning* can capture this meaning, but it is not a common word and might be taken to mean something learned beyond what is necessary rather than something learned beyond the initial level of correctness. *Automaticity* is a word with technical meaning in some psychological literature as meaning a level of performance at which one can also do something else. But to some people it carries only a sense of rote performance. *Fluency* is the term used by several previous committees, and we have therefore chosen to continue this usage. *Fluency* also carries for some a connotation of flexibility because a person knows something well enough to use it adaptively. We find this meaning useful as well as the usual meaning of doing something rapidly and relatively effortlessly. Research on reading in early childhood has recently used *fluency* only in the latter sense as measured by performance on standardized tests of reading, such as the Dynamic Indicators of Basic Early Literacy Skills (DIBELS). We do not mean *fluency* to be restricted to this rote sense. By *fluent* we mean accurate and (fairly) rapid and (relatively) effortlessly with a basis of understanding that can support flexible performance when needed.

is summarized. These cores are quite related, and their relationships are discussed. Box 5-2 summarizes the steps along the teaching-learning paths in the core areas. As children move from age 2 through kindergarten, they learn to work with larger and more complicated numbers, make connections across the mathematical contents of the core areas, learn more complex strategies, and move from working only with objects to using mental representations. This journey is full of interesting discoveries and patterns that can be supported at home and at care and education centers.

## THE NUMBER CORE

The four mathematical aspects of the number core identified in Chapter 2 involve culturally specific ways that children learn to perceive, say, describe/discuss, and construct numbers. These involve

1. Cardinality: Children's knowledge of cardinality (how many are in a set) increases as they learn specific number words for sets of objects they see (*I want two crackers*).
2. Number word list: Children begin to learn the ordered list of number words as a sort of chant separate from any use of that list in counting objects.
3. 1-to-1 counting correspondences: When children do begin counting, they must use one-to-one counting correspondences so that each object is paired with exactly one number word.
4. Written number symbols: Children learn written number symbols through having such symbols around them named by their number word (*That is a two*).

Initially these four aspects are separate, and then children make vital connections. They first connect saying the number word list with 1-to-1 correspondences to begin counting objects. Initially this counting is just an activity without an understanding of the total amount (cardinality). If asked the question *How many are there?* after counting, children may count again (repeatedly) or give a number word different from the last counted word. Connecting counting and cardinality is a milestone in children's numerical learning path that coordinates the first three aspects of the number core.

As noted, we divide the teaching-learning path into four broad steps. In Step 1, for 2- and 3-year-olds, children learn about the separate aspects of number and then begin to coordinate them. In Step 2, for approximately 4-year-olds/prekindergartners, children extend their understanding to larger numbers. In Step 3, for approximately 5-year-olds/kindergartners, children integrate the aspects of number and begin to use a ten and some ones in teen numbers. In Step 4, approximately Grade 1, children see, count, write, and work with tens-units and ones-units from 1 to at least 100.

## BOX 5-2
## Overview of Steps in the Number, Relations, and Operations Core

### Steps in the Number Core

**Step 1 (ages 2 and 3):** Beginning 2- and 3-year-olds learn the number core components for very small numbers: cardinality, number word list, 1-1 counting correspondences, and written number symbols; later 2- and 3-year-olds coordinate these number core components to count **n** things and, later, say the number counted.

**Step 2 (age 4/prekindergarten):** Extend all four core components to larger numbers and also use conceptual subitizing if given learning opportunities to do so.

**Step 3 (age 5/kindergarten):** Integrate all core components, see a ten and some ones in teen numbers, and relate ten ones to one ten and extend the core components to larger numbers.

**Step 4 (Grade 1):** See, say, count, and write tens-units and ones-units from 1 to 100.

### Steps in the Relations (More Than/Less Than) Core

**Step 1 (ages 2 and 3):** Use perceptual, length, and density strategies to find which is more for two numbers $\leq 5$.

**Step 2 (age 4/prekindergarten):** Use counting and matching strategies to find which is more (less) for two numbers $\leq 5$.

**Step 3 (age 5/kindergarten):** Kindergartners show comparing situation with objects or in a drawing and match or count to find out which is more and which is less for two numbers $\leq 10$.

**Step 4 (Grade 1):** Solve comparison word problems that ask, "How many more (less) is one group than another?" for two numbers $\leq 18$.

### Steps in the Addition/Subtraction Operations Core

**Step 1 (ages 2 and 3):** Use subitized and counted cardinality to solve situation and oral number word problems with totals $\leq 5$; these are much easier to solve if objects present the situation rather than the child needing to present the situation and the solution.

**Step 2 (age 4/prekindergarten):** Use conceptual subitizing and cardinal counting of objects or fingers to solve situation, word, and oral number word problems with totals $\leq 8$.

**Step 3 (age 5/kindergarten):** Use cardinal counting to solve situation, word, oral number word, and written numeral problems with totals $\leq 10$.

**Step 4 (Grade 1):** Use counting on solution procedures to solve all types of addition and subtraction word problems: Count on for problems with totals $\leq 18$ and find subtraction as an unknown addend.

## Step 1 (Ages 2-3)

At this step, children first begin to learn the core components of number: cardinality, the number word list, 1-to-1 correspondences, and written number symbols (see Box 5-3).

### BOX 5-3
### Step 1 in the Number Core

Children at particular ages/grades may exceed the specified numbers and be able to work correctly with larger numbers. The numbers for each age/grade are the foundational and achievable content for children at this age/grade. The major types of new learning for each age/grade are given in italics. Each level assumes that children have had sufficient learning experiences at the lower level to learn that content; many children can still learn the content at a level without having fully mastered the content at the lower level if they have sufficient time to learn and practice.

**Beginning 2- and 3-Year-Olds Learn the Number Core Components**

**Cardinality:** *How many animals (crackers, fingers, circles, . . . )?* uses perceptual subitizing to give the number for 1, 2, or 3 things.
**Number word list:** *Count as high as you can (no objects to count)* says 1 to 6.
**1-to-1 counting correspondences:** *Count these animals (crackers, fingers, circles, . . . )* or *How many animals (crackers, fingers, circles, . . . )?* counts accurately 1 to 3 things with 1-1 correspondence in time and in space.
**Written number symbols:** *This (2, 4, 1, etc.) is a______?* knows some symbols; will vary.

**Later 2- and 3-Year-Olds Coordinate the Number Core Components**

**Cardinality:** *Continues to generalize perceptual subitizing to new configurations and extends to some instances of conceptual subitizing for 4 and 5:* can give number for 1 to 5 things.
**Number word list:** *Continues to extend and may be working on the irregular teen patterns and the early decade twenty to twenty-nine, etc., pattern:* says 1 to 10.
**1-to-1 counting correspondences:** *Continues to generalize to counting new things, including pictures, and to extend accurate correspondences to larger sets (accuracy will vary with effort):* counts accurately 1 to 6 things.
**Written number symbols:** *Continues to learn new symbols if given such learning opportunities.*
**Coordinates counting and cardinality into cardinal counting** in which the last counted word tells how many and (also or later) tells the cardinality (the number in the set).

*Cardinality*

The process of identifying the number of items in a small set (cardinality) has been called *subitizing*. We will call it *perceptual subitizing* to differentiate it from the more advanced form we discuss later for larger numbers called *conceptual subitizing* (see Clements, 1999). For humans, the process of such verbal labeling can begin even before age 2 (see Chapter 3). It first involves objects that are physically present and then extends to nonpresent objects visualized mentally (for finer distinctions in this process, see Benson and Baroody, 2002). This is an extremely important conceptual step for attaching a number word to the perceived cardinality of the set. In fact, there is growing evidence that the number words are critical to toddlers' construction of cardinal concepts of even small sets, like three and four and possibly one and two (Benson and Baroody, 2002; Spelke, 2003; also see Baroody, Lai, and Mix, 2006; and Mix, Sanhofer, and Baroody, 2005).

Children generally learn the first 10 number words by rote first and do not recognize their relation to quantity (Fuson, 1988; Ginsburg, 1977; Lipton and Spelke, 2006; Wynn, 1990). They do, however, begin to learn sets of fingers that show small amounts (cardinalities). This is an important process, because these finger numbers will become tools for adding and subtracting (see research literature summarized in Clements and Sarama, 2007; Fuson, 1992a, 1992b). Interestingly, the conventions for counting on fingers vary across cultures (see Box 5-4).

In order to fully understand cardinality, children need to be able to both generalize and extend the idea. That is, they need to generalize from a specific example of two things (two crackers), to grasp the "two-ness" in any set of two things. They also need to *extend* their knowledge to larger and larger groups—from one and two to three, four, and five, although these are more difficult to see and label (Baroody, Lai, and Mix, 2006; Ginsburg, 1989). Children's early notions of cardinality and how and when they learn to label small sets with number words are an active area of research at present. The timing of these insights seems to be related to the grammatical structure of the child's native language (e.g., see the research summarized in Sarnecka et al., 2007).

Later on, children can learn to quickly see the quantity in larger sets if these can be decomposed into smaller subitized numbers (e.g., *I see two and three, and I know that makes five*). Following Clements (1999), we call such a process *conceptual subitizing* because it is based on visually apprehending the pair of small numbers rather than on counting them. Conceptual subitizing requires relating the two smaller numbers as addends within the conceptually subitized total. With experience, the move from seeing the smaller sets to seeing and knowing their total becomes so rapid that one can experience this as seeing 5 (rather than as seeing 2 and 3). Children may also learn particular patterns, such as the 5 pattern on a die. Because these

**BOX 5-4**
**Using Fingers to Count: Cultural Differences**

Around the world, most children learn from their family one of the three major ways of raising (or in some cultures, lowering) fingers to show numbers. All of these methods can be seen in centers or schools with children coming from different parts of the world, as well as some less frequent methods (the Indian counting on cracks of fingers with the thumb, Japanese lowering and raising fingers). The most common way is to raise the thumb first and then the fingers in order across to the small finger. Another way is to raise the index finger, then the next fingers in order to the smallest finger, and then the thumb. The third way is to begin with the little finger and move across in order to the thumb. The first way is very frequent throughout Latin America, and the third way also is used by some children coming from Latin America. The second way is the most usual in the United States. It is the common way to show ages (for example, *I am two years old* by holding up the index and largest finger). This method allows children to hold down unused fingers with their thumb. But the other two methods show numbers in a regular pattern going across the fingers. Children in a center or school where children show numbers on fingers in different ways may come to use multiple methods. Because fingers are such an important tool for numerical problem solving, it is probably best not to force a child to change his or her method of showing numbers on fingers if it is well established. It is important for teachers to be aware and accepting of these differences.

kinds of patterns can also be considered in terms of addends that compose them, they are included in conceptual subitizing. Such patterns can help older children learn mathematically important groups, such as five and ten; these are discussed in the later levels and in the relations and operation core discussion of addition and subtraction composing/decomposing.

Children also learn to assign a number to sets of entities they hear but do not see, such as drum beats or ringing bells. There is relatively little research on auditory quantities, and they play a much smaller role in everyday life or in mathematics than do visual quantities. For these reasons, and because auditory quantities relate to music and rhythm and body movements, it seems sensible to have some activities in the classroom in which children repeat simple or complex sets they hear (clap clap or, later, clap clap clap pause clap clap), tell the number they hear (of bells, drumbeats, feet stamping, etc.), and produce sounds with body movements for particular quantities (*Let me hear three claps*).

In home and care/educational settings, it is important that early experiences with subitizing be provided with simple objects or pictures. Textbooks or worksheets often present sets that discourage subitizing and depict collections of objects that are difficult to count. Such complicating factors include embedded or overlapping pictures, complex noncompact things or pictures (e.g., detailed animals of different sizes rather than circles or squares), lack of symmetry, and irregular arrangements (Clements and Sarama, 2007).

The importance of facilitating subitizing is underscored by a series of studies, which first found that children's spontaneous tendency to focus on numerosity was related to counting and arithmetic skills, then showed that it is possible to enhance such spontaneous focusing, and then found that doing so led to better competence in cardinality tasks (Hannula, 2005). Increasing spontaneous focusing on numerosity is an example of helping children mathematize their environment (seek out and use the mathematical information in it). Such tendencies can stimulate children's self-initiated practice in numerical skills because they notice those features and are interested in them.

### *Number Word List*

A common activity in many families and early childhood settings is helping a child learn the list of number words. Children initially may say numbers in the number word list in any order, but rapidly the errors take on a typical form. Children typically say the first part of the list correctly, and then may omit some numbers in the next portion of the list, or they say a lot of numbers out of order, often repeating them (e.g., one, two, three, four, five, eight, nine, four, five, two, six) (Fuson, 1988; Fuson, Richards, and Briars, 1982; Miller and Stigler, 1987; Siegler and Robinson, 1982). Children need to continue to hear a correct number list to begin to include the missing numbers and to extend the list.

Children can learn and practice the number word list by hearing and saying it without doing anything else, or it can be heard or said in coordination with another activity. Saying it alone allows the child to concentrate on the words, and later on the patterns in the words. However, it is also helpful to practice in other ways to link the number words to other aspects of the number core. Saying the words with actions (e.g., jumping, pointing, shaking a finger) can add interest and facilitate the 1-to-1 correspondences in counting objects. Raising a finger with each new word can help in learning how many fingers make certain numbers, and flashing ten fingers at each decade word can help to emphasize these words as made from tens.

### *Counting: 1-to-1 Correspondences*

In order to count a group of objects the person counting must use some kind of action that matches each word to an object. This often involves moving, touching or pointing to each object as each word is said. This counting action requires two kinds of correct matches (1-to-1 correspondences): (1) the matching in a moment of *time* when the action occurs and a word is said, and (2) the matching in *space* where the counting action points to an object once and only once. Children initially make errors in both of these kinds of correspondences (e.g., Fuson, 1988; Miller et al., 1995). They may violate the matching in time by pointing and not saying a word or by pointing and saying two or more words. They may also violate the matching in space by pointing at the same object more than once or skipping an object; these errors are often more frequent than the errors in time.

Four factors strongly affect counting correspondence accuracy: (1) amount of counting experience (more experience leads to fewer errors), (2) size of set (children become accurate on small sets first), (3) arrangement of objects (objects in a line make it easier to keep track of what has been counted and what has not), and (4) effort (see research reviewed in Clements and Sarama, 2007, and in Fuson, 1988). Small sets (initially up to three and later also four and five) can be counted in any arrangement, but larger sets are easier to count when they are arranged in a line. Children ages 2 and 3 who have been given opportunities to learn to count objects accurately can count objects in any arrangement up to 5 and count objects in linear arrangements up to 10 or more (Clements and Sarama, 2007; Fuson, 1988).

In groundbreaking research, Gelman and Gallistel (1978) identified five counting principles that stimulated a great deal of research about aspects of counting. Her three how-to-count principles are the three mathematical aspects we have just discussed: (1) the *stable order principle* says that the number word list must be used in its usual order, (2) the *one-one principle* says that each item in a set must be tagged by a unique count word, and (3) the *cardinality principle* says that the last number word in the count list represents the number of objects in the set. Her two what-to-count principles are mathematical aspects we have also discussed: (1) the *abstraction principle* states that any combination of discrete entities can be counted (e.g., heterogeneous versus homogeneous sets, abstract entities, such as the number of days in a week) and (2) the *order irrelevance principle* states that a set can be counted in any order and yield the same cardinal number (e.g., counting from right to left versus left to right).

Gelman took a strong position that children understand these counting principles very early in counting and use them in guiding their counting activity. Others have argued that at least some of these principles are understood only after accurate counting is in place (e.g., Briars and Siegler, 1984). Still others, taking a middle ground between the "principles before" view and the "principles after" view, suggest that there is a mutual (e.g., iterative) relation between understanding the count principles and counting skill (e.g., Baroody, 1992; Baroody and Ginsburg, 1986; Fuson, 1988; Miller, 1992; Rittle-Johnson and Siegler, 1998).

Each of these aspects of counting is complex and does not necessarily exist as a single principle that is understood at all levels of complexity at once. Children may initially produce the first several number words and not even separate them into distinct words (Fuson, Richards, and Briars, 1982). They may think that they need to say the number word list in order as they count, but early on they cannot realize the implication that they need a unique last counted word, or they would not repeat words so frequently as they say the number word list.

The what-to-count principles also cover a range of different understandings. It takes some time for children to learn to count parts of a thing (Shipley and Shepperson, 1990; Sophian and Kailihiwa, 1998), a later use of the abstraction principle. And the order irrelevance principle (counting in any order will give the same result) seems to be subject to expectations about what is conventional "acceptable" counting (e.g., starting at one end of a row rather than in the middle) as well as involving, later on, a deeper understanding of what is really involved in 1-to-1 correspondence: Count-

**BOX 5-5**
**Common Counting Errors**

There are some common counting errors made by young children as they learn the various principles that underpin successful counting. Counting requires effort and continued attention, and it is normal for 4-year-olds to make some errors and for 5-year-olds to make occasional errors, especially on larger sets (of 15 or more for 4-year-olds and of 25 or more for 5-year-olds). Younger children may initially make quite a few errors. It is much more important for children to be enthusiastic counters who enjoy counting than for them to worry so much about errors that they are reluctant to count. If one looks at the proportion of objects that receive one word and one point, children's counting often is pretty accurate. Letting errors go sometimes or even somewhat frequently if children are trying hard and just making the top four kinds of errors is fine as long as children *understand* that correct counting requires one point and one word for each object and are trying to do that. As with many physical activities, counting will improve with practice and does not need to be perfect each time. Teachers do not have to monitor children's counting all of the time. It is much more important for all children to get frequent counting practice and watch and help each other, with occasional help and corrections from the teacher.

Very young children counting small rows with high effort make more errors in which their say-point actions do not correspond than errors in the matching of the points and objects. Thus, they may need more practice coordinating their actions of saying one word and pointing at an object. Energetic collective practice in which children rhythmically say the number word list and move down their hand with a finger pointed as each word is said can be helpful. To vary the practice, the words can sometimes be said loudly and sometimes softly, but always with emphasis (a regular beat). The points can involve a large motion of the whole arm or a smaller motion, but, again, in a regular beat with each word. Coordinating these actions

ing is correct if and only if each object receives one number word (LeFevre et al., 2006). An aspect of the 1-to-1 principle that is difficult even for high school students or adults to execute is remembering exactly which objects they have already counted with a large fixed set of objects scattered irregularly around (such as in a picture) (Fuson, 1988).

The principles are useful in understanding children's learning to count, but they should not be taken as simplistic statements that describe knowledge that is all-or-nothing or that has a simple relationship to counting skill. It can be helpful for teachers or parents to make statements of various aspects of counting (e.g., *Remember that each object needs one point and one number word, You can't skip any, Remember where you started in the circle so you stop just before that.*). But children will continue to make counting errors even when they understand the task, because counting is a complex activity (see Box 5-5).

of saying and pointing is the goal for overcoming this type of error. For variety, these activities can involve other movements, such as marching around the room with rhythmic arm motions or stamping a foot saying a count word each time.

Counting an object twice or skipping over an object are errors made occasionally by 4-year-olds and even by 5-year-olds on larger sets. These seem to stem from momentary lack of attention rather than lack of coordination. Trying hard or counting slowly can reduce these errors. However, when two counts of the same set disagree, many children of this age think that their second count is correct, and they do not count again. Learning the strategy of counting a third time can increase the accuracy of their counts. If children are skipping over many objects, they need to be asked to *count carefully and don't skip any.*

Young children sometimes make multiple count errors on the last object. They either find it difficult to stop or think they need to say a certain number of words when counting and just keep on counting so they say that many. When they say the number word list, more words are better, so they need to learn that saying the number word list when counting objects is controlled by the number of objects. Reminding them that even the last object only gets one word and one point can help. They also may need the physical support of holding their hand as they reach to point to the last object so that the hand can be stopped from extra points and the last word is said loudly and stretched out (e.g., *fii-i-i-ve*) to inhibit saying the next word.

Regularity and rhythmicity are important aspects of counting. Activities that increase these aspects can be helpful to children making lots of correspondence errors. Children who are not discouraged about their counting competence generally enjoy counting all sorts of things and will do so if there are objects they can count at home or in a care or education center. Counting in pairs to check each other find and correct errors is often fun for the pairs. Counting in other activities, such as building towers with blocks, should also be encouraged.

### *Written Number Symbols*

Learning to read written number symbols is quite variable and depends considerably on the written symbols in children's environment and how often these are pointed out and read with a number word so that they can learn the symbol-word pair (Clements and Sarama, 2007; Mix, Huttenlocher, and Levine, 2002). Unlike much of the number core discussed so far, learning these pairs is rote learning with hardly any possibility of finding and using sequential information. Component parts of particular numbers, or an overall impression (e.g., an 8 looks like a snowman) can be identified and discussed using perceptual learning principles (Baroody, 1987; Baroody and Coslick, 1998; Gibson, 1969; Gibson and Levin, 1975). Learning to recognize the numerals is not a hugely difficult task, and 2- and 3-year-olds can often read some numerals; 4-year-olds can learn to read many of the numerals to 10. Kindergarten children with such experiences can then concentrate on reading and understanding the numerals for the teens, and first graders can master the cardinal tens and ones connections in the numerals from 20 to 100 (see discussions at those levels).

Learning to write number symbols (numerals) is a much more difficult task than is reading them and often is not begun until kindergarten. Writing numerals requires children to have an accurate mental image of the symbol, which entails left-right orientation, and a motor plan to translate the mental image into the correct sequence of motor actions to form a numeral (e.g., see details in Baroody, 1987; Baroody and Coslick, 1998; Baroody and Kaufman, 1993). Some numerals are much easier than others. The loops in 6 and 9, the curve and straight line in the 2, and the crossovers in the 8 are difficult but can be mastered by kindergarten children with effort. The easier numerals 1, 3, 4, 5, and 7 can often be mastered earlier. Whenever children do learn to write numerals, learning to write correct and readable numerals is not enough. They must become fluent at writing numerals (i.e., writing numerals must become overlearned) so that writing them as part of a more complex task is not so slow or effortful as to be discouraging when solving several problems. It is common for children at this step and even later to reverse some numerals (such as 3) because the left-right orientation is difficult for them. This will become easier with age and experience.

### *Coordinating the Components of the Number Core*

We discussed above how children coordinate their knowledge of the number word list and 1-to-1 correspondences in time and in space to count groups of objects in space. They also gradually generalize what they can count and extend their accurate counting to larger sets and to sets in various arrangements not in a row (circular, disorganized). However, accuracy for the latter comes quite late, except for small sets (Fuson, 1988). Generalization of counting involves taking as a unit each object they are counting so that each object can receive one count word. For example, when they are counting toy animals, each animal is a unit regardless of how big it is, what color it is, or what kind of animal it is. Later, 2- and 3-year-olds continue to generalize the range of objects they can count. Children with little experience with print may have more difficulty counting pictures of objects rather than objects themselves, and so they may especially need practice counting pictures of objects (Murphy and Wood, 1981).

The next crucial coordination of components is connecting counting and cardinality (Fuson, 1988; Gelman and Gallistel, 1978). When counting things (objects or pictures), the counting action matches each count word to one thing (see discussion above and in Chapter 2). But a cardinal number word refers to how many things there are in the whole set of things. So when anyone counts, they must at the end of the counting action make a mental shift from thinking of the last counted word as referring to *the last counted thing* to thinking of that word as referring to *all of the things* (the number of things in the whole set, i.e., the cardinality of the set). For example, when counting 7 toy animals 1, 2, 3, 4, 5, 6, 7, the 7 refers to the one last animal you count when you say 7. But then you must shift to thinking of all of the animals and think of the 7 as meaning all of them: There are 7 animals. This is a major conceptual milestone for young children.

When children discover this relationship, they tend to apply it to all counts no matter the size of the set of objects (Fuson, 1988). Therefore, this is a type of rule/principle of learning that children immediately generalize and apply fairly consistently. It is relatively easy to teach children that the last word said in counting tells how many there are (see Fuson, 1988). For example, a statement of this principle followed by three demonstrations followed by another statement of the principle was sufficient to move 20 of 22 children ages 2 years 8 months to 3 years 11 months who did not use the principle to using it (Fuson, 1988).

However, not all children really understand cardinality, even when they understand the importance of the last counted word (Fuson, 1988). Some children initially understand only that the last word answers the "How many?" question. They do not fully grasp the more abstract idea of cardinality. Thus, they give their last counted word when asked how many there are, but they do not point to all of the objects when asked the cardinality question *"Show me the seven animals."* Instead, they point at the last animal again. It is important to note that responding with the last word is progress. Earlier when asked *"How many are there?"* children may have recounted or given a number other than the last counted word. Children who recount are understanding the question *"How many are there?"* as a request to count, not as a cardinal request. Such children may recount several if the question is repeated and may protest *But I already did it* or *I already said it* because they don't understand the reason for the repeated requests (to them, each count is a correct response to the *How many are there?* question). Children making the other error (giving a number that differs from the last word) are understanding that the question *How many are there?* is a request for cardinal information about the whole set, but they do not yet understand that the cardinal information is given by counting, and, in particular, by the last word said in counting.

Verbal knowledge is also required for full competence in discriminating the use of individual number words for each thing counted versus the use of the final number word to refer to the whole set. Even children who gesture correctly to show their count meaning (gesture to one thing) or their cardinal meaning (gesture to the whole set) may struggle with correct verbal expressions (see Box 5-6). Mastering these is a later achievement that will be learned with modeling and practice.

**BOX 5-6**
**Learning the Correct Counting Language**

Learning the singular and plural forms that go with counting (single) and with cardinal (plural) references to objects takes some time. Here are typical examples of errors that children initially make while they are sorting out all of these conceptual and linguistic issues. After children counted a row of objects, they were asked a count-reference question and a cardinality-reference question (the order varied across children). The count-reference question was *Is this the soldier (chip) where you said **n**?* where **n** was the last word said by the child. The experimenter asked the question three times and pointed to the last item, the next-to-last item, and all the items in the row. The cardinal-reference question was *Are these the **n** soldiers (chips)?* The correct answer was always in the middle, because research indicated that young children have a strong bias toward choosing the last alternative. In the examples below, children spontaneously verbalized cardinality or counting references that disagreed with their gesture.

| | |
|---|---|
| Response to cardinality question: | *Those are five soldiers*, said as child points to the last soldier. |
| Response to cardinality question: | *This one's the five chips*, said as child points to the last chip. |
| Response to cardinality question: | *This is the six soldiers*, said as child points to each soldier (said six times). |
| Response to cardinality question: | *This is the four chips*, said as child points to the last chip. |
| Response to cardinality question: | *This is where I said chip four*, said as child's hands gesture to all of the chips. |
| Response to count question: | *All of these animals I said five.* |

SOURCE: Fuson (1988, p. 232).

### Step 2 (Age 4 or Prekindergarten)

As children become acquainted with the components of number, they extend cardinal counting and conceptual subitizing to larger numbers. The major advances for children at this step who have had opportunities at home or in a care center to learn the previous foundational and achievable number core content involve extending their competency to larger numbers. This means that teachers or caregivers who must support children at different levels, or support a mixture of children who have learned and those who have not had sufficient opportunity to learn the previous number core content, can frequently combine these groups by allowing children to choose set sizes with which they feel comfortable and can succeed (see Box 5-7).

**BOX 5-7**
**Step 2 in the Number Core**
**Age 4 or Prekindergarten**

**Extend Cardinal Counting and Conceptual Subitizing to Larger Numbers**

Children at particular ages/grades may exceed the specified numbers and be able to work correctly with larger numbers. The numbers for each age/grade are the foundational and achievable content for children at this age/grade. The major types of new learning for each age/grade are given in italics. Each level assumes that children have had sufficient learning experiences at the lower level to learn that content; many children can still learn the content at a level without having fully mastered the content at the lower level if they have sufficient time to learn and practice.

**Cardinality:** *Extends conceptual subitizing to 5-groups with 1, 2, 3, 4, 5 to see 6 through 10:* can see the numbers 6, 7, 8, 9, 10 as 5 + 1, 5 + 2, 5 + 3, 5 + 4, 5 + 5 and can relate these to the fingers (5 on one hand). May do other such numerical compose/decompose patterns also.

**Number word list:** *Continues to extend and learns the irregular teen patterns and extends the early decade twenty to twenty-nine, etc., pattern to higher decades:* says 1 to 39.

**1-to-1 counting correspondences:** *Continues to generalize to counting new things and to extend accurate correspondences to larger sets (accuracy will vary with effort):* counts accurately 1 to 15 things in a row.

**Written number symbols:** *Continues to learn new symbols if given such learning opportunities:* reads 1 to 10; writes some numerals.

**Reverses the cardinal counting principle (the count-to-cardinal shift) to count out n things (makes the cardinal-to-count shift):** *Must have fluent counting to have the attentional space to remember the number to which you're counting so you can stop there.*

*Cardinality*

Children at this level continue to extend to larger numbers their conceptual subitizing of small groups to make a larger number, for example, *I see one thumb and four fingers make my five fingers* (this is part of the relation and operation core and is discussed more there). The 5-groups are particularly important and useful. These 5-groups provide a good way to understand the numbers 6, 7, 8, 9, 10 as 5 + 1, 5 + 2, 5 + 3, 5 + 4, 5 + 5 (see Figure 5-1). The convenient relationship to fingers (5 on one hand) provides a kinesthetic component as well as a visual aspect to this knowledge. Without focused experience with 5-groups, children's notions of the numbers 6 through 10 tend to be hazy beyond a general sense that the numbers are getting larger. Knowing the 5-groups is helpful at the next level, as children add and subtract numbers 6 through 10; the patterns are problem-solving tools that can be drawn or used mentally. Children in East Asia learn and use these 5-group patterns throughout their early numerical learning (Duncan, Lee, and Fuson, 2000). Children can continue to experience and begin remembering other addends that make totals (e.g., 3 and 3 make 6, 8 is 4 and 4).

*Number Word List*

As noted, beyond the first ten words, which are arbitrary in most languages (e.g., see the extensive review in Menninger, 1958/1969), most languages begin to have patterns that make them easier to learn. English, however, has irregularities that are challenging for children. A major difficulty in understanding the meaning of the teens words is that English words do not explicitly say the *ten* that is in the teen number (*teen* does not mean *ten* even to many adults), so English-speaking children can benefit

5-groups that show 6 as 5 + 1, 7 as 5 + 2, 8 as 5 + 3, 9 as 5 + 4, and 10 as 5 + 5

| 6 | 7 | 8 | 9 | 10 |
|---|---|---|---|---|
| ooooo | ooooo | ooooo | ooooo | ooooo |
| o | oo | ooo | oooo | ooooo |

**FIGURE 5-1** Five groups to understand the numbers 6, 7, 8, 9, and 10.

from visual representations that show the ten inside teen numbers in order to understand what quantities these words represent (see the discussion in the kindergarten level).

There are two patterns in the English number words from 20 to 100 that children need to understand if each word is to have its value as some number of tens and some number of ones, as in Chinese words (52 is said as *five ten two*). One is the irregular pattern in the decade words that name the tens multiples: *twenty (twin-tens), thirty (three-tens), forty, fifty (five tens), sixty, seventy, eighty, ninety*. As with the teens, the relationships of the decade words to the numbers below ten become really clear only for the last four words because only then are the *six*, *seven*, *eight*, *nine* said. The irregularities in *twenty* through *fifty* interfere with seeing the meaning of these words as two tens, three tens, four tens, five tens, etc., and thus with learning these in order by using the list below ten, as Chinese-speaking children can do (see Chapter 4). Also, as with the teen words, the *ten* is not said explicitly but is said as a different suffix, *–ty*. Therefore, as discussed later for Grade 1, children need to work explicitly with groups of tens and ones to understand these meanings for the number words from 20 to 100.

The second pattern is the pattern of a decade word followed by the decade word with the numbers one through nine: *twenty, twenty-one, twenty-two, twenty-three, . . . , twenty-nine*. Children can begin to learn this second pattern quite early. Because the transition to ten and the teens words is not clear in English, children often initially do not stop at *twenty-nine* but continue to count *twenty-nine, twenty-ten, twenty-eleven, twenty-twelve, twenty-thirteen* (Fuson, 1988). This error can be a mixture of not yet understanding that the pattern ends at nine and difficulty stopping the usual counting at nine in order to shift to another decade.

Children in the United States tend to learn the pattern of the decade word followed by a number (1-9) before learning the order of the decade words (e.g., Fuson, 1988; Fuson, Richards, and Briars, 1982; Miller and Stigler, 1987; Siegler and Robinson, 1982). Although some 2- and 3-year-olds begin learning and practicing the patterns for the teens and decade words, the teen pattern can be mastered by almost all 4-year-olds with support and practice, as can the early decades (two cycles of the pattern from twenty through thirty-nine). Many 4-year-olds learn more than this, but mastering the correct order of the decades and using this with the ***n-ty* *through n-ty-nine*** pattern is for many children a kindergarten achievement (e.g., Fuson, 1988; Fuson, Richards, and Briars, 1982; Miller et al., 1995). Structured learning experiences can decrease the time it takes to learn this pattern of decades to 100, but without such experiences this learning effort can continue even to age 6. Counting by tens to 100 to learn this decade sequence is a goal for kindergarten and is discussed in that section.

*Counting Correspondences*

At this step, children extend considerably the set size they are able to count accurately. They move from considerable inaccuracy with counting larger sets to only occasional errors, even with large sets of 15 and above, unless the sets are arranged in a disorganized way and children are not able to move objects to keep track of which have been counted (i.e., make a counted and an uncounted pile) (Fuson, 1988). As before, effort continues to be important. Children who are tired or discouraged may make many more errors than they make after a simple prompt to try hard or count slowly. Children at this step also continue to generalize what they can count.

Children at this step are working on counting linear arrangements correctly in the teens or above, and many make few errors, showing considerably more accuracy than children a year younger (Clements and Sarama, 2007; Fuson, 1988). Of course, accurate counting also depends on knowing an accurate number word list, so accuracy with these larger sets depends on three things:

1. Knowing the patterns discussed above in the number word list so that a correct number word list can be said.
2. Correctly assigning one number word to one object (1-to-1 correspondence).
3. Keeping track of which objects have already been counted so that they are not counted more than once.

Differentiating counted from uncounted entities is most easily done by moving objects into a counted set, but this is not possible with things that cannot be moved, such as pictures in a book. For pictures or objects that cannot be moved, counting objects arranged in a row is easiest because one can start at the end of a row and continue to the other end. However, if objects are arranged in a circle, children may initially count on and on around the circle. Strategies for keeping track of messy, large sets continue to develop for many years (Fuson, 1988), with even adults not being entirely accurate.

Children in kindergarten who have had adequate counting experiences earlier continue to extend their counting of objects as high as 100, often with correct correspondences (and perhaps occasional errors). There may or may not still be errors in the number word list.

*Written Number Symbols*

Children at this step continue to extend the number of written number symbols they can read, now often reading many of the numerals 1, 2, 3,

4, 5, 6, 7, 8, 9, and 10. However, the 10 at this level means ten ones, the counted number *ten* that comes after *nine*. Not until the next level does it come to mean what the 10 symbols actually say: 1 ten and 0 ones. Children at this level can begin to write some numerals, often beginning with the easier numerals 1, 3, 4, and 7.

### *Counting Out "n" Things*

Children at this level make one major conceptual advance. They move from knowing that the last number stated represents the amount in the group to knowing how to count out a given number of objects (Clements and Sarama, 2007; Fuson, 1988). Lots of counting of objects and saying the number word list enables their counting to become fluent enough that they can count out a specified number of things, for example, count out 6 things. Counting out **n** things requires a child to remember the number **n** while counting. This is more difficult for larger numbers because the child has to remember the number longer. So children may initially count past **n** because their counting is not fluent (overlearned) enough to count a long sequence of words, remember a number, and monitor with each count whether they have reached the number yet. Counting out a specified number is needed for solving addition and subtraction problems and for doing various real-life tasks, so this is an important milestone. Children can practice this conceptual task by counting out **n** things for various family and school purposes; such practice can also occur in game-like activities.

Counting out **n** things also requires a conceptual advance that is the reverse of learning that the last count word tells how many there are. To count out 6 things, a child is being told how many there are (a cardinal meaning) and must then shift to a count meaning of that 6 in order to monitor the count words as they are said (*Have I said 6 yet?*) so that they can stop when they say 6 as a counting word that corresponds to one object. They then have the set of 6 things they need.

## Step 3 (Kindergarten)

At this step children work to integrate all of the core components of number. They are able to see that teen numbers are made up of tens and some ones. They also can come to understand that ten ones make one group of ten (see Box 5-8).

Kindergarten children can begin the process with seeing and making tens in teen numbers, and first graders can continue the process for tens and ones in numbers 20 to 100. At both grades this process helps children integrate the number components into a related web of cardinal, counting, and written number symbol knowledge. The first conceptual step is for chil-

**BOX 5-8**
**Step 3 in the Number Core**
**Age 5 or Kindergarten**

**Integrate All Core Components, See a Ten and Some Ones in Teen Numbers, Relate Ten Ones to One Ten, and Extend the Core Components to Larger Numbers**

Children at particular ages/grades may exceed the specified numbers and be able to work correctly with larger numbers. The numbers for each age/grade are the foundational and achievable content for children at this age/grade. The major types of new learning for each age/grade are given in italics. Each level assumes that children have had sufficient learning experiences at the lower level to learn that content; many children can still learn the content at a level without having fully mastered the content at the lower level if they have sufficient time to learn and practice.

**Cardinality:** *Extends conceptual subitizing to a new visual group, a group of tens:* can see a ten in each teen number (18 = 10 + 8).

**Number word list:** *Extends to learn all of the decades in order as a new number word list counting by tens; uses this decade order with the decade pattern to count to 100 by ones:* says the tens list 10, 20, 30, . . . , 90, 100; says 1 to 100 by ones.

**1-to-1 counting correspondences:** *Continues to extend accurate correspondences to larger sets; accuracy will still vary with effort:* counts 25 things in a row with effort.

**Written number symbols:** *Coordinates knowledge of symbols 1 to 9 to write teen numbers:* reads and writes 1 to 19; reads 1 to 100 arranged in groups of ten when counting 1 to 100.

**Integrates all of the above for teen numbers** so that ten ones = 1 ten, relating the unitary cardinality relationship *ten ones + eight ones make eighteen ones* to the written symbols 18 as 10 with an 8 on top of the 0 ones in ten.

dren to understand each cardinal teen number as consisting of two groups: 1 group of ten things and a group of the ones (the extra over ten). So, for example, 11 is 1 group of ten and 1 one (11 = 10 + 1), 14 is 1 group of ten and 4 ones (14 = 10 + 4), and 18 is 1 group of ten and 8 ones (18 = 10 + 8). The second crucial understanding that builds on the above is that ten ones equal one ten. That is, the written teen number symbols such as 18 mean 1 group of ten (1 ten rather than ten ones) and 8 ones. Being able to see ten ones as one ten is a crucial step on the learning path.

It can be helpful for English-speaking children to have experiences seeing 18 things separated into ten and eight and relating these quantities to both the number words *"eighteen is ten and eight"* and to the written number symbols (18). It may also be helpful to use the written symbol version of this as 18 = 10 + 8. Repeated experiences with all of these relationships can help children overcome the second kind of typical error in writing teen numbers, in which children write first what they say first. They hear *eighteen* and know that teens have a 1 in them (they may not yet think of this as one ten) and so they write 81.

Kindergarten children can also experience and learn all of the decade words in order from 20 to 100. Doing so while looking at a list of these number symbols grouped in tens can help to reinforce the pattern of the groups of ten.

Many states require that kindergarten children understand some aspects of money, but sometimes they have goals that are not sensible for this age group, even children who have had strong earlier mathematical experiences. The mathematical aspects of money that are most appropriate are the groups of ten pennies in dimes and the groups of five pennies in nickels. Children have been working with these cardinal groups of tens in this level and with 5-groups in the 4-year-old/prekindergarten level, so it is easy to build this understanding by extending this knowledge to coins by using any visual support that relates a 5-group of pennies to one nickel and one 10-group of pennies to one dime. Such supports were used successfully for first graders to construct the relationships for understanding two-digit numbers described next for first graders (Fuson, Smith, and Lo Cicero, 1997; Hiebert et al., 1997).

Learning the values of a dime and a nickel are of course particularly complicated because their values are not in the order of the sizes of the coins. In size, a dime < a penny < a nickel, but in value a penny < a nickel < a dime. For this reason, it is too difficult to work with these coins alone rather than with visual supports that show the values of these coins in pennies, as discussed above. Counting mixed collections of dimes, nickels, and pennies requires shifting counts from counting by tens when counting dimes to counting by fives when counting nickels to counting by ones when counting pennies. Such shifts are too complex for many children at this level, especially if they are looking at the coins rather than looking at their values as pennies. Practice just on the names of the coins and on their visual features, rather than on their value as ones, fives, or tens, is also not appropriate. It is the quantitative values that are mathematically important.

### Step 4 (Grade 1)

At this step children see, say, count, and write tens and ones from 1 to 100 (see Box 5-9). To do this, they build on the integrations among cardinality, counting, and written number symbols that they have made in kindergarten. The major advance has two parts. First, children learn to count by two different units, units of ten and units of one. Second, they learn to shift from counting by units of ten to counting by units of one so that they can count cardinal sets up to 100. Children who have mastered

**BOX 5-9**
**Step 4 in the Number Core**
**Grade 1**

**See, Say, Count, and Write Tens-Units and Ones-Units from 1 to 100**

Children at particular ages/grades may exceed the specified numbers and be able to work correctly with larger numbers. The numbers for each age/grade are the foundational and achievable content for children at this age/grade. The major types of new learning for each age/grade are given in italics. Each level assumes that children have had sufficient learning experiences at the lower level to learn that content; many children can still learn the content at a level without having fully mastered the content at the lower level if they have sufficient time to learn and practice.

**Cardinality:** *Relates patterns in number word list to 100 to quantities of tens and of ones:* can see the tens and ones quantities in numbers from 10 to 99 (e.g., 68 = 60 + 8); sees the 60 both as 60 ones (*sixty*) and as *6 tens*; can make drawn quantities to show tens and ones.

**Number word list:** *May count groups of ten using a tens list (1 ten, 2 tens, etc.) as well as the decade list 10, 20, 30, . . . .*

**1-to-1 counting correspondences:** *Extends counting single units to counting a group of ten as a 10-unit and shifts from counting these units of ten to counting by ones when counting left-over ones units:* arranges things in groups of ten (or uses prearranged groups or drawings) and counts the groups by tens and then shifts to a count by ones for the leftover single things: 10, 20, 30, 40, 50, 60, 61, 62, 63, 64, 65, 66, 67, 68, or 1 ten, 2 tens, 3 tens, 4 tens, 5 tens, 6 tens, 6 tens and 1 one, 6 tens and 2 ones, 6 tens and 3 ones, 6 tens and 4 ones, 6 tens and 5 ones, 6 tens and 6 ones, 6 tens and 7 ones, 6 tens and 8 ones.

**Written number symbols:** *Extends reading and writing to all two-digit numbers 1 to 99 and understands that the tens digit refers to groups of tens and the ones digit refers to groups of ones;* also sees that the 0 from the tens number is hiding behind the ones number so can see 68 as 60 + 8.

**Integrates all of the above for numbers 1 to 100** so that ***n–ty*** = ***n tens*** (e.g., 60 is 6 tens); the counting by tens and by ones represents sets of tens and of ones; a 2-digit numeral like 68 = 60 + 8 and 68 also means 6 tens and 8 ones.

the kindergarten concept that *ten ones equal one ten* can learn to use visual representations of tens that show each ten as *one ten.*

Children at this step need to be able to make drawings of tens and of ones so that they can represent numbers to use when adding and subtracting. Making such drawings can also help with the consolidation of the two-digit numerals, for example, 68 = 60 + 8 as *sixty plus eight* and as *six tens plus eight.* Place value cards in which the ones card covers the 0 in the tens card can also help eliminate the typical errors of children hearing 68 as *sixty eight* and therefore writing what they hear: 608 instead of 68.

## THE RELATIONS AND OPERATIONS CORE

The main mathematical categories in the relations and operations core were discussed in Chapter 2, and the steps through which our four age groups move were summarized in Box 5-2. These steps are elaborated in Box 5-10.

In the relations core, children learn to perceive, say, discuss, and create the relations *more than*, *less than*, and *equal to* on two sets. Initially they use general perceptual, or length, or density strategies to decide whether one set is *more than*, *less than*, or *equal to* another set. Gradually these are replaced by more accurate strategies: They match the entities in the sets to find out which has leftover entities, or they count both sets and use understandings of *more than/less than* order relations on numbers (see research reviewed in Clements and Sarama, 2007; Fuson, 1988). Eventually, in Grade 1, children begin to see the third set potentially present in relational situations, the *difference* between the smaller and the larger set (see research reviewed in Fuson, 1992a, 1992b). In this way, relational situations become the third kind of addition/subtraction situations: comparison situations.

In the operations core, children learn to see addition and subtraction situations in the real world by focusing on the mathematical aspects of those situations and making a model of the situation (called *mathematizing* these situations, as explained in Chapter 2). Initially such mathematizing may involve only focusing on the number of objects involved rather than on their color or their use (*I see **two** red spoons and **one** blue spoon*) and using those same objects to find the answer by refocusing on the total or counting it (*I see **three** spoons in all*). The three types of addition/subtraction situations that children must learn to solve were discussed in Chapter 2 and summarized in Box 2-4. These types are change plus/change minus, put together/take apart (sometimes called combine), and comparisons.

Addition and subtraction situations, and the word problems that describe such situations, provide many wonderful opportunities for learning language. Word problems are short and fairly predictable texts, so children can vary words in them while keeping much of the text. This enables them to say word problems in their own words and help everyone's understanding. English language learners can repeat such texts and vary particular words as they wish, all with the support of visual objects or acted-out situations. Although children need to learn the special mathematics vocabulary involved in addition and subtraction, these problems also give them wonderful opportunities to integrate art (drawing pictures) and language practice and pretend play while also generalizing their growing mathematical knowledge.

**BOX 5-10**
**Steps in Addition/Subtraction Operations and Relations**

**Step 1 (ages 2 and 3)**

- Use subitized and counted cardinality to solve situation and oral number word problems with totals $\leq 5$.
- Act out numerical situations with objects and say them in words; see answer at the end.
- Determine that something is bigger or has more using perceptual, length, and density strategies.

Examples of problems they can solve:
- Change plus: Two blocks and two blocks make four blocks.
- Change minus: Four apples take away one apple is three apples.
- Put together/take apart: I see three apples. I see two and one make three.

**Step 2 (age 4/prekindergarten)**

- Use conceptual subitizing and cardinal counting to solve situation, word, and oral number word problems with totals $\leq 8$.
- Solve numerical situations and word problems by modeling actions with objects, fingers, or mentally (or just know the answer); or see or count the answer.
- Solve number word problems by modeling actions with objects, fingers, or mentally (or just know the answer); or see or count the answer.
- Learn the partners for 3, 4, 5 (e.g., $5 = 4 + 1$, $5 = 3 + 2$).
- For relations, understand and say *this is/has less/fewer than that.*
- For more than/less than relations with totals $\leq 5$, act out or show situation, and count or match to solve.

Examples of problems they can solve:
- Change plus: Two and two make ?

## Levels in Children's Numerical Solution Methods

There is a large research base from around the world describing three levels through which children's numerical solution methods for addition and subtraction situations move (e.g., see the research summarized in Baroody, 1987, 2004; Baroody, Lai, and Mix, 2006; Clements and Sarama, 2007, 2008; Fuson, 1988, 1992a, 1992b; Ginsburg, 1983; Saxe, 1982; Sophian, 1984). These levels are summarized in Box 5-11. At all levels, the solution methods require mathematizing the real-world situation (or later the word problem or the problem represented with numbers) to focus on only the

- Change minus: Four take away one is ?
- Put together/take apart: Three has ? and ?

**Step 3 (Kindergarten)**

- Use conceptual subitizing and cardinal counting to solve situation, word, oral number word, and written numeral problems with totals $\leq 10$.
- For word problems, model action with objects or fingers or a math drawing and count or see to solve; write an expression or equation.
- For oral or written numeral problems, use fingers, objects, or a math drawing to solve.
- Engage in learning the partners for 6, 7, 8, 9, 10.
- For relations, act out or show with objects or a drawing, then count or match to solve.
- Use $=$, $\neq$ symbols.

**Step 4 (Grade 1)**

- Use Level 2 or Level 3 solution procedures: count on or use a derived fact method for problems with totals $\leq 18$ and find subtraction as an unknown addend.
- Solve change plus problems by counting on to find the total $6 + 3 = ?$
- Solve change minus problems by counting on to find the unknown addend $9 - 6 = ?$ is $6 + ? = 9$.
- Solve put together/take apart problems by counting on to find the unknown addend $6 + ? = 9$.
- Advanced first graders use Level 3 solution procedures: (a) doubles and doubles $\pm$ 1. (b) they experience make-a-ten methods: $8 + 6 = 8 + 2 + 4 = 10 + 4 = 14$; $14 - 8$ is $8 + ? = 14$, so $8 + 2 + 4 = 14$, so $? = 6$ (not all children master these in Grade 1).
- Solve comparison situations or determine how much/many more/less by counting or matching for totals $\leq 10$, then for totals $\leq 18$.

mathematical aspects—the numbers of things and the additive or subtractive operation in the situation. As we discuss each level, we also describe ways in which children can be helped to learn methods appropriate for that level and the prerequisite knowledge. Children need opportunities to relate strategies to actual objects or pictures of objects and to discuss and explain their thinking.

The solution methods at Level 1 use direct modeling of every object. In direct modeling children must carry out the actions in the situation using actual objects or fingers. Until around age 6, children primarily use such direct modeling to solve situations presented in objects, word problems

**BOX 5-11**
**Levels in Children's Numerical Solution Methods**

**Level 1: Direct modeling** of all quantities in a situation; used at the first three number/operation levels:

**Counting all:** Count out things or fingers for one addend, count out things or fingers for the other addend, and then count all of the things or fingers.
**Take away:** Count out things or fingers for the total, take away the known addend number of things or fingers, and then count the things or fingers that are left.

**Level 2: Count on** can be done in first grade (some children can do so earlier): They use embedded number understanding to see the first addend within the total and so see that they do not need to count all of the total, but instead could make a cardinal-to-count shift and count on from the first addend.

**Count on to find the total:** On fingers or with objects or with conceptual subitizing, children keep track of how many words to count on so that they stop when they have counted on the second addend number of words and the last word they say is the total:
6 + 3 = ? would be "six, seven, eight, nine, so the total is nine. I counted on 3 more from 6 to make 9."
After learning counting on from the first addend, children learn to count on from the larger addend.
**Count on to find the unknown addend:** Children stop counting when they say the total, and the fingers (or other keeping track method) tell the answer (the unknown addend number of words they counted on past the first addend).
6 + ? = 9 would be "six, seven, eight, nine, so I added on 3 to 6 to make 9. I counted on 3 more from 6 to make 9. Three is my unknown addend."

(situations expressed in words, perhaps with an accompanying picture), oral numerical problems such as *three plus two*, and written numerical problems such as 3 + 2. Chapter 4 summarized research reporting that more children from low-income families had trouble with the last three kinds of problems than with the first kind and than did their middle-income peers. Therefore, such children especially need help and practice in generating models using objects or fingers for such situations.

At Grade 1, children who have not yet moved to the Level 2 general counting on methods (see Box 5-8 and Box 5-11 for more details) can do so with help. In these methods, children shift from the cardinal meaning of the first addend to the counting meaning as they count on from it: For 5 + 2, they think *five*, shift to the counting word *five* in the number word list, and count on two more words—*five, six, seven*. This ability to count on can be

**Level 3: Derived fact methods** in which known facts are used to find related facts (mastery by some/many at first grade).

Doubles are totals of two of the same addend: 1 + 1, 2 + 2, 3 + 3, etc., up to 9 + 9. These are learned by many children in the United States because of the easy pattern in their totals (2, 4, 6, 8, etc.). **Doubles ± 1** is a Level 3 more advanced strategy that uses a related double to find the total of two addends in which one addend is one more or less than the other addend (6 + 7 = 6 + 6 + 1 = 12 + 1 = 13).

**Make-a-ten methods** are general methods for adding or subtracting to find a teen total by changing a problem into an easier problem involving 10. Children first make a 10 from the first addend and then learn to make a 10 from the larger addend.

**Make a ten to find a total:** 8 + 6 becomes 10 + 4 by separating the 6 into the amount that makes 10 with the 8. Then solving 6 = 2 + ? gives the leftover 4 within the 6 to become the ones number in the teen total: 8 + 6 = 8 + 2 + 4 = 10 + 4 = 14.

**Make a ten to find an unknown addend:** 14 – 8 = ? is 8 + ? = 14, so 8 + 2 is 10 plus the 4 in 14 makes 14. So 8 + 6 = 14. In this method subtraction requires adding, which is easier than making a ten to find a total. The first step can also be thought of as subtracting the 8 from 10.

**Three prerequisites** for fluency with make-a-ten methods can be built up before first grade:

1. knowing the number that makes 10 (the partner to 10) for each number 3 to 9;
2. knowing each teen number as a 10 and some ones (e.g., knowing that 14 = 10 + 4 and that 10 + 4 = 14 without counting); and
3. knowing all the partners of numbers 3 to 9 so that the second number can be broken into a partner to make 10 and the leftover partner that will make the teen number.

facilitated by children's earlier work with embedded number experiences of finding partners of a total (e.g., *Inside seven, I see five and two*) and by fluency with the count word sequence, so they can begin counting from any number (most 2-, 3-, and 4-year-olds need to start at 1 when counting and cannot start from just any number). With larger second addends, children also need a method of keeping track of how many they have counted on. These counting on methods are sufficient for all further quantitative work, especially if children are helped to see subtraction as finding an unknown addend, so that they can use counting on to find that addend. Counting down to subtract is difficult, and children make many errors at it (Baroody, 1984; Fuson, 1984). Just counting backward is difficult, and children make various count-cardinal errors in counting down. Counting forward to find an unknown addend for subtraction (e.g., solving 9 – 5 = ? as 5 + ? = 9) is much easier and can make subtraction as easy as addition (e.g., Fuson, 1986b; Fuson and Willis, 1988). It also emphasizes addition and subtraction as inverse operations.

The derived fact methods (Level 3) are mastered by some children at Grade 1, depending on how many of the prerequisites shown in Box 5-8 have been made accessible for 4- and 5-year-olds and then have been practiced so that they become fluent. These methods require recomposing the given numbers into a new, easier problem (e.g., 9 + 4 becomes 10 + 3). The make-a-ten methods are taught in East Asian countries and are very useful in multidigit computation (see the discussion in Chapter 2). The prerequisites are discussed later in the summaries of the 4- and 5-year-olds because children can begin building these prerequisites then. Enabling 4- and 5-year-olds to learn the prerequisites for the counting on and derived facts methods can help low-income children to learn more advanced strategies, which fewer of them do now. This can also help children with learning difficulties in mathematics because they often continue to use the Level 1 modeling methods for too many years unless they are helped to learn more advanced strategies. The general counting on methods for addition and subtraction can be learned meaningfully and done accurately and rapidly by most children in Grade 1 (Fuson, 2004).

Throughout the process of learning and using more advanced approaches to solving addition and subtraction problems, children also become fluent with individual sums and differences. Small numbers, such as plus 1 and minus one, and doubles (2 + 2, 3 + 3) become fluent early. Others become fluent over time.

## Step 1 (Ages 2 and 3)

Children at this step use subitized and counted cardinality to solve situation and oral number word problems. They also use perceptual, length, and density strategies to find which is more with totals ≤ 5 (see Box 5-10).

### *Relations: More Than, Equal To, Less Than*

Children ages 2 and 3 begin to learn the language involved in relations (Clements and Sarama, 2007, 2008; Fuson, 1992a, 1992b; Ginsburg, 1977). *More* is a word learned by many children before they are 2. Initially it is an action directive that means: *Give me more of this.* But gradually children become able to use perceptual subitizing and length or density strategies to judge which of two sets has more things: *She has more than I have.* Such comparisons may not be correct at this age level if the sets are larger than three because children focus on length or on density and cannot yet coordinate these dimensions or use the strategies of matching or counting effectively (see research reviewed in Fuson, 1988, 1992a, 1992b, and in Clements and Sarama, 2007, 2008).

*Operations: Addition and Subtraction*

The 2- and 3-year-old children can solve change plus/change minus situations and put together/take apart situations with small numbers (totals ≤ 5) if the situation is presented with objects or if they are helped to use objects to model these situations (Clements and Sarama, 2007; Fuson, 1988). Children can have experience in learning how to do such adding and subtracting from family members, in child care centers, and from media such as television and CDs. Children may subitize groups of one and two or count these or somewhat larger numbers. To find the total, they may count or put together the subitized quantity into a pattern that is also just seen and not really counted (e.g., *two and two make four*).

**Step 2 (Age 4 or Prekindergarten)**

At this step, children learn to use conceptual subitizing and cardinal counting to solve situation, word, and oral number word problems with totals ≤ 8 and begin to count and to match to find out which set has more or less (see Box 5-10).

Cardinal counters at this age level can extend their understanding of relations and of all of the addition/subtraction situations and generalize them to a wider range of settings because their real-world knowledge is more extensive than it was at the previous level. Children can now also count out a specified number of objects, so they can carry out the count all and take away solution methods (Level 1 in Box 5-11) for numbers in their counting accuracy range. They also begin to use counting and matching as well as the earlier perceptual strategies to find which of two sets is more and begin to learn the meaning of the word *less*.

*Relations*

Children at this level continue to use the perceptual strategies they used earlier (general perceptual, length, density) but they can also begin to use matching and counting to find *which is less* and *which is more* (see research summarized in Clements and Sarama, 2007, 2008; Fuson, 1988, 1992a, 1992b; Sophian, 1988). However, they can also be easily misled by perceptual cues. For example, the classic tasks used by Piaget (1941/1965) involved two rows of objects in which the objects in one row were moved apart so one row was longer (or occasionally, moved together so one row was shorter). Many children ages 4 and 5 would say that the longer row has more. These children focused either on length or on density, but they could not notice and coordinate both. However, when asked to count in such situations, many 4-year-olds can count both rows accurately, remember both count words, and change them to cardinal numbers and find the order relation on the cardinal numbers (Fuson, 1988). Thus, many 4-year-olds need encouragement to count in *more than/less than/equal to* situations, especially when the perceptual information is misleading.

To use matching successfully to find more than/less than, children may need to learn how to match by drawing lines visually to connect pairs or draw such matching lines if the compared sets are drawn on paper. Then they need to know that the number with any extra objects is more than the other set. It is also helpful to match using actual objects.

To use counting successfully, children need to be able to count both sets accurately and remember the first count result while counting the second set. Here is another example of the need for fluency in counting (see Box 5-1). Without such fluency, some children forget their first count result by the time they have counted the second set. They need more counting practice in such situations. Children also need to know order relations on cardinal numbers. They need to learn the general pattern that most children do derive from the order of the counting words: *The number that tells more is farther along (said later) in the number word list than the smaller number* (e.g., Fuson, Richards, and Briars, 1982). Activities in which children make sets for both numbers, match them in rows and count them, and discuss the results can help them establish this general pattern.

There was an early period in which the counting and matching research had not been done and many researchers and educators suggested that teachers had to wait until children conserved number (said that rows in the classic Piagetian task were equal even in the face of misleading perceptual transformations) to do any real number activities, such as adding and subtracting. However, newer research shows that there is a crucial stage for 4- and 5-year-olds in which using counting and matching are important to learn and can lead to correct relational judgments (see the research summarized in Clements and Sarama, 2007, 2008; Fuson, 1992a, 1992b). It is true that children typically do not understand that the rows are equal out of a logical necessity until age 6 or 7 (sometimes not until age 8). These older children (ages 6-7) judge the rows to be equal based on mental transformations that they apply to the situation. They do not see the need to count or match after one row is made shorter or longer by moving objects in it together or apart to see that they are equal. They are certain that simply moving the objects in the set does not change the numerosity. This is what Piaget meant by conservation of number. But children can work effectively with situations involving more and less long before they demonstrate this meaning of conservation of number.

For progress in relations, it is important that children hear, and try to use, the less common comparative terms such as *less, shorter, smaller* instead of only hearing or using *more, taller, bigger*. Initially some children think that *less* means *more* because almost all of their experience has been focused on selecting the set with *more* (e.g., Fuson, Carroll, and Landis, 1996). So children need to hear many examples of *fewer* and *less*, although it is not vital that they differentiate these from each other because that is difficult (*fewer* is used with things you can count, *less* is used with measured quantities and with numbers). Teachers can also use the comparative terms (for example, *bigger* and *smaller* rather than just *big* and *small*) so that children gain experience with them, although all children may not become fluent in their use at this level.

### *Operations*

Problems expressed in words (word problems) can now be solved, although many children may need to act out some word problems in order to understand the meanings of the situation or of some of the words (see research summarized in Fuson 1992a, 1992b). Through such experiences relating actions and words, children gradually extend their vocabulary of words that mean to add—*in all, put together, altogether, total*—and of words that mean to subtract—*are left, take away, eat, break*. Discussing and sharing solutions to word problems and acting out addition/subtraction situations can provide extended experiences for language learning. Children can begin posing such word problems as well as solving them, although many will need help with asking the questions, the most difficult aspect of posing word problems. As with all language learning, it is very important for children to talk and to use the language themselves, so having them retell a word problem in their own words is a powerful general teaching strategy to extend their knowledge and give them practice speaking in English.

Drawing the solution actions using circles or other simple shapes instead of pictures of real objects can be helpful. The two addends can be separated just by space or encircled separately or separated by a vertical line segment. Some children can also begin to make mathematical drawings to show their solutions. Teacher and child drawings leave a visual record of the full solution that facilitates children's reflecting on the solution, as well as discussing and explaining it. For children, making math drawings is also a creative activity in which they are somehow showing in space actions that occur over time. Children do this in various interesting ways that can lead to productive discussions.

Children also become able to use their fingers to add or to subtract using the direct modeling solution methods counting all or taking away (see Box 5-11, Level 1). When counting all, they will count out and raise fingers for the first addend, then for the second addend, and then count all of the raised fingers. (See Box 5-4 for a discussion of different conventions for counting on fingers.)

Some children learn at home or in a care center to put the addends on separate hands, while others continue on to the next fingers for the second addend. The former method makes it easier to see the addends, and the latter method makes it easier to see the total. Both methods can be modeled by the teacher. As children become more and more familiar with which group of fingers makes 4 or 5 or 7 fingers, they may not even have to count out the total because they can feel or see the total fingers. Similarly, children using the method of putting fingers on separate hands eventually can just raise the fingers for the addends without counting out the fingers. But they do need initially to count the total. Children who put addends on separate hands may have difficulty with problems with addends over 5 (e.g., 6 + 3) because one cannot put both such numbers on a separate hand. They can, however, continue raising fingers from 6 fingers. Because these problems involve adding 1 or 2, such continuations of 1 and 2 are relatively easy.

By now children who have had experience with adding and subtracting situations when they were younger can generalize to solve decontextualized problems that are posed numerically, as in *Two and two make how many?* (Clements and Sarama, 2007; Fuson, 1988). For some small numbers, children may have solved such a problem so many times that they know the answer as a verbal statement: *Two and two make four.* If such knowledge is fluent, children may be able to use it to solve a more complex unknown addend problem. For example, *Two and how many make four? Two.*

For larger numbers, children will need to use objects or fingers to carry out a counting all or taking away solution procedure (Box 5-11) (see research summarized in Fuson 1992a, 1992b). Children will learn new composed/decomposed numerical triads as they have such experiences. The doubles that involve the same addends (2 is 1 and 1, 4 is 2 and 2, 6 is 3 and 3, 8 is 4 and 4) are particularly easy for children to learn because the perceptual and verbal task is simplified by have the same addends (e.g., see research summarized in Fuson, 1992a, 1992b). The visual 5-groups (e.g., 8 is made from 5 and 3) discussed for the number core are also useful. Research about powerful patterns for conceptual subitizing for very small numbers would be helpful, including the extent to which flexibility is important beyond a single powerful visual core that will work for all numbers.

The put together/take apart situations, and especially the take apart situation, can be used to provide varied numerical experiences with given numbers that help children see all of the addends (*partners*) hiding inside a given number. For example, children can take apart five to see that it can be made from a three and two and also from four and one. Later on these decomposed/composed triads can be symbolized by equations, such as 5 =

3 + 2 and 5 = 4 + 1, giving children experiences with the meaning of the = symbol as *is the same number as* and with algebraic equations with one number on the left. Initially children shift from seeing the total and then seeing the partners (addends), but with experience and fluency, they can simultaneously see the addend within the total. This is called *embedded numbers*: The two addends are embedded within the total. Such embedded numbers, along with the number word sequence skill of starting counting at any number, allow children to move to the second level of addition/subtraction solution procedures, *counting on*. Initially composed/decomposed number triads and even embedded number triads are constructed with small numbers using conceptual subitizing, but eventually counting is used with larger numbers to construct larger triads.

Many children from low-income backgrounds cannot initially solve such oral numerical problems, even with very small numbers (see Chapter 4). They need opportunities to learn and practice the Level 1 solution methods with objects and with fingers and experience composing/decomposing numbers to be able to see the addends (partners) hiding inside the small numbers 3, 4, 5. Such alternating focusing on the total and then on the partners (addends) will enable them to answer such oral numerical problems and also begin the learning path toward embedded numbers that is vital for the Level 2 addition/subtraction solution methods.

### Step 3 (Kindergarten)

At this step, children extend cardinal counting and use math drawings as well as objects to solve situation, word, oral number word, written numeral, and which-is-more/less problems with totals ≤ 10 (see Box 5-10). Written work, including worksheets, is appropriate in kindergarten if it follows up on activities with objects or presents supportive visualizations. Children at these ages need practice that builds fluency after related experiences with objects to build mathematical understanding, and they need experience relating symbols for quantities to actual or drawn quantities.

Kindergarten children can extend their addition and subtraction problem solving to all problems with totals ≤ 10. Close to half of these problems have one addend of six or more. For these problems, knowing the 5-patterns using fingers for 6 through 10 can be helpful (5 + 1 = 6, 5 + 2 = 7, etc., to 5 + 5 = 10). All children can begin to make math drawings themselves, even for these larger numbers. This allows them to reflect on and discuss their solution methods. Math drawings involving circles or other simple shapes also enable more advanced children to explore problems with totals greater than ten. It is difficult to solve such problems with fingers until one advances to the general counting on solution methods (see Box 5-11, Level 2), which typically does not occur until Grade 1. Children can discuss general patterns they see in addition and subtraction, such as +1 is just the next counting number or –1 is the number just before. Children can discuss adding and subtracting 0 and the pattern it gives: adding or subtracting 0 does not change the original number, so the result (the answer) is the same as the original number. Many children can now informally use the commutative property (A + B = B + A) especially when one number is small (e.g., Baroody and Gannon, 1985; Carpenter et al., 1993; DeCorte and Verschaffel, 1985; for a review of the literature, see Baroody, Wilkins, and Tiilikainen, 2003). Experience with put together addition situations in which the addends do not have different roles provides better support for learning the commutative property than does experience with the change situation (see research described in Clements and Sarama, 2007, 2008; Fuson, 1992a, 1992b) because these addends have such different roles in the action. To the child, it actually feels different to have 1 and then get 8 more than to have 8 and get 1 more. It feels better to gain 8 instead of gaining 1, even though you end up with the same amount. In contrast, the numerical work on put together/take apart partners facilitates understanding that the order in which one adds does not matter. Looking at composed/decomposed triads with the same addends also enables children to see and understand commutativity in these examples (for example, see that 9 = 1 + 8 and 9 = 8 + 1 and that the addends are just switched in order but still total the same).

All of the work on the relations/operation core in kindergarten serves a double purpose. It helps children solve larger problems and become more fluent in their Level 1 direct modeling solution methods. It also helps them reach fluency with the number word list in addition and subtraction situations, so that the number word list can become a representational tool for use in the counting on solution methods.

Different children learn and remember some sums and differences at each level, and it is very useful to know these for small numbers, for example for totals ≤ 8. But the more important step at the kindergarten level is that children are learning general numerical solution methods that they can extend to larger numbers. Simultaneously they are becoming fluent with these processes and with the number word list, so that they can advance to the Level 2 counting on methods that are needed to solve single-digit sums and differences with totals over ten. Children later in the year can begin to practice the number word list prerequisite for counting on by starting to count at a given number instead of always at one.

Kindergarten children are also working on all of the prerequisites for the Level 3 derived fact methods, such as make-a-ten (see Box 5-11). One prerequisite, seeing the tens in teen numbers, was discussed in the number core. The other two prerequisites involve knowing partners of numbers (decomposed/composed numerical triads) to permit flexible breaking apart and combining of numbers to turn them into teen addition or subtraction problems. For example, all of the following addition problems—9 + 2, 9 + 3, 9 + 4, . . . , 9 + 9—require the same first step: 9 needs 1 more to make ten, so separate the second number into 1 + ?. This triad then becomes 9 + 1 + ? = 10 + ?, which is an easier problem to solve if you know the tens in teen numbers. However, each problem requires a different second step: decomposing the second number to identify the rest of the second addend that will be added to ten (prerequisite 3 for derived facts methods in Box 5-11). For example, 9 + 4 = 9 + 1 + 3 = 10 + 3 = 13, but 9 + 6 = 9 + 1 + 5 = 10 + 5 = 15. So kindergarten children need experiences with finding and learning the partners of various numbers under 10.

Children's counting and matching knowledge is now sufficient to extend to relations on sets up through 10 and to more abstract ways of presenting such relational situations as two rows of drawings that can be matched by drawing lines connecting them. As discussed above for Step 2, children will be more accurate when these objects are already matched instead of being visually misleading (for example, the longer row has less). They therefore can start with the simpler nonmisleading situations and extend to the visually misleading situations when they have mastered such matched situations. Again, differentiating length and number meanings of *more* will be helpful (which *looks like more* and which *really is more*). Children who have not had sufficient experiences matching objects at Step 2 will need such experiences to support the more advanced activities in which matching is done by drawing lines.

Working with the terms *more* and *less* can also be an opportunity to discuss and emphasize that length units used in measuring a length must touch each other and cover the whole length from beginning to end to get an accurate length measurement. But things children are counting can be spread apart or moved around and they will still have the same number of things. Comparing objects spaced evenly in two rows can also be related to picture graphs, which record numbers of different kinds of data as a row of the same pictures (see the Chapter 2 discussion in the Mathematical Connections section). Activities in which children compare two rows of drawings by counting or matching them can be considered as using picture graphs if each drawing in one row is the same. What is important about such activities is that children talk about them using comparison language (*There are more suns than clouds* or *There are fewer clouds than suns*) and describe how they found their answer.

Children at this level can also prepare for the comparison problems at Grade 1 by beginning to equalize two related sets. For example, for a row of 5 above a row of 7, they can be asked to add more to the row of 5 to make it equal to the row of 7 and write their addition 5 + 2. This 2 is the difference between 5 and 7, it is the amount extra 7 has, so such exercises help children begin to see this third quantity in the comparison situation.

*Writing Equations*

There is not sufficient evidence to indicate the best time for teachers to start writing addition and subtraction problems in equations or for students to do so. The equation form can be confusing to some students even in Grade 1, and students may confuse the symbols + = and –. This confusion and limited meanings for the = sign often continue for many years and are of concern for the later learning of algebra. Because the fundamental aspect of an equation is that the sides are equal to each other, it is important for children to learn to conceptually chunk each side. Thus, some children may need extensive experience just with expressions, such as 3 + 2 or 7 – 5, before these are used in equations. These forms might be introduced before the full equation is introduced, perhaps even with 4-year-olds. It may also help for the teacher to circle or underline these expressions to indicate that this group of symbols is a chunk that represents a single number. Future research directed at such issues of when and how to write such pre-equation forms would be helpful.

The other issue with equations is the form of the equation to write. As mentioned earlier, it is important for later algebraic understanding of acceptable forms of equations for children to see equations with only one number on the left, such as 6 = 4 + 2 to show that 6 breaks apart to make 4 and 2. This equation form can be written for take apart situations in which the total is being separated into two parts, for example, *Grammy has 6 flowers. She put four flowers in one vase and two flowers in the other vase.* Children can show this situation with objects or fingers (*Count out 6 objects and then separate them into 4 and 2*) or make a math drawing of it while the teacher records the situation in an equation. This form can also be used in practice activities with objects in which children find all of the partners (addends) of a given number. For example, children can make 5 using two different colors of objects, and each color can show the partners. The teacher can record all of the partners that children find: 5 = 1 + 4, 5 = 2 + 3, 5 = 3 + 2, 5 = 4 + 1. This can be in a situation (*Let's find all of the ways that Grammy can put her 5 flowers in her 2 vases*) or just an activity with numbers (*Let's find all of the partners of 5*).

Change plus and change minus situations can be recorded by equations with only one number on the right because that is the action in these situations (see Box 2-4), for example, 3 + 1 = 4 or 5 – 2 = 3. In these equations the = sign is really more like an arrow, meaning *gives* or *results in*. As discussed, this is often the only meaning of = that students in the United States know, and this interferes with their use of algebra. So it is really important that they also see and use forms like 5 = 3 + 2 to show the numbers hiding inside a number, the partners (addends) that make that number.

### Step 4 (Grade 1)

At this step, children build on their earlier number and relations/operation knowledge and skills to advance to Level 2 counting on solution methods. They also come to understand that addition is related to subtraction and can think of subtraction as finding an unknown addend (see Box 5-10).

Grade 1 addition and subtraction is the culmination of all of the number core and relations/operation core experiences and expertise that have been building since birth, for those who have been given sufficient opportunities to build such competence. Foundational and achievable relations and operations content for Grade 1 children is summarized in Box 5-9.

For all of the earlier experiences to come together into the Level 2 counting on solution methods, some children may still need some targeted practice in beginning counting at any number instead of always starting at one (one of the prerequisites for counting on). It is also helpful to begin counting on in some kind of structured visual setting, so that children can conceptualize the relationships between the counting and cardinal meanings of number words.

Counting on is not a rote method. It requires a shift in word meaning for the first addend from its cardinal meaning of the number in that first addend to a counting meaning, as children count on from that first addend to the total. Children then must shift from that last counted word to its cardinal meaning of how many objects there are in total. For example, seeing circles for both addends in a row with the problem printed above enables children to count both addends and then count all to find the total (their usual Level 1 direct modeling solution method). But after several times of counting all, they can be asked what number they say when they count the last circle in the group of 6 and whether they need to count all of the objects or could they just start at 6. Going back and forth between this counting on and the usual counting all enables children to see that counting on is just an abbreviation of counting all, in which the initial counts are omitted (e.g., Fuson, 1982; Fuson and Secada, 1986; Secada, Fuson, and Hall, 1983).

| | | |
|---|---|---|
| | 6 + 3 | *Six* is a cardinal number. |
| o o o o o o | o o o | |
| 1 2 3 4 5 6 | 7 8 9 | *Six* here is a count number when counting all. |

siiiixxx 7 8 9 To count on like this, a child must shift from the cardinal meaning above to the count meaning of *six* and then keep counting 7, 8, 9.

Trying this with different problems enables many children to see this general pattern and begin counting on. Transition strategies, such as counting 1, 2, 3, 4, 5, 6 very quickly or very softly or holding the 6 (*siiiiiiixxxxxx*), have been observed in students who are learning counting on by themselves; these can be very useful in facilitating this transition to counting on (e.g., Fuson, 1982; Fuson and Secada, 1986; Secada, Fuson, and Hall, 1983). Some weaker students may need explicit encouragement to *trust the six* and to let go of the initial counting of the first addend, and they may need to use these transitional methods for a while.

Counting on has two parts, one for each addend. The truncation of the final counting all by starting with the cardinal number of the first addend was discussed above. Counting on also requires keeping track of the second addend—of how many you count on so that you count on from the first addend exactly the number of the second addend. When the number is small, such as for 6 + 3, most children use perceptual subitizing to keep track of the 3 counted on. This keeping track might be visual and involve actual objects, fingers, or drawn circles. But it can also use a mental visual image (some children say they see 3 things in their head and count them). Some children use auditory subitizing (they say they hear 7, 8, 9 as three words). For larger second addends, children use objects, fingers, or conceptual subitizing to keep track as they count on. For 8 + 6, they might think of 6 as 3 and 3 and count with groups of three: 8 9 10 11 12 13 14 with a pause after the 9 10 11 to mark the first three words counted on. Other children might use a visual (*I saw 3 circles and another 3 circles*) or an auditory rhythm to keep track of how many words they counted on. So here we see how the *perceptual subitizing* and the *conceptual subitizing*, which begin very early, come to be used in a more complex and advanced mathematical process. This is how numerical ideas build, integrating the levels of thinking visually/holistically and thinking about parts into a complex new conceptual structure that relates the parts and the whole. Children can discuss the various methods of keeping track, and they can be helped to use one that will work for them. Almost all children can learn to use fingers successfully to keep track of the second addend.

Many experiences with composing/decomposing (finding partners hiding inside a number) can give children the understanding that a total is any number that has partners (addends) that compose it. When subtracting, they have been seeing that they take away one of those addends, leaving the other one. These combine into the understanding that subtracting means finding the unknown addend. Therefore, children can always solve subtraction problems by a forward method that finds the unknown addend, thus avoiding the difficult and error-prone counting down methods (e.g., Baroody, 1984; Fuson, 1984, 1986b). So 14 – 8 = ? can be solved as 8 + ? = 14, and students can just count on from 8 up to 14 to find that 8 plus 6 more is 14.

Some first graders will also move on to Level 3 derived fact solution methods (see Box 5-11) such as doubles plus or minus one and the general method that works for all teen totals: the make-a-ten methods taught in East Asia (see Chapter 4 and, e.g., Geary et al., 1993; Murata, 2004). These make-a-ten methods are particularly useful in multidigit addition and subtraction, in which one decomposes a teen number into a ten to give to the next column while the leftover ones remain in their column. More children will be able to learn make-a-ten methods if they have learned the prerequisites for them in kindergarten or even in Grade 1.

The comparison situations compare a large quantity to a smaller quantity to find the difference. These are complex situations that are usually not solvable until Grade 1. The third quantity, the difference, is not physically present in the situation, and children must come to see the differences as the extra leftovers in the bigger quantity or the amount the smaller quantity needs to gain in order to be the same as the bigger quantity. The language involved in comparison situations is challenging, because English gives two kinds of information in the same sentence. Consider, for example, the sentence *Emily has five more than Tommy*. This says both that Emily has more than Tommy and that she has five more. Many children do not initially hear the five. They will need help and practice identifying and using the two kinds of information in this kind of sentence (see the research reviewed in Clements and Sarama, 2007, 2008; Fuson, 1992a, 1992b; Fuson, Carroll, and Landis, 1996).

Learning to mathematize and model addition and subtraction situations with objects, fingers, and drawings is the foundation for algebraic problem solving. More difficult versions of the problem situations can be given from Grade 1 on. For example, the start or change number can be the unknown in change plus problems: *Joey drew 5 houses and then he drew some more. Now he has 9 houses. How many more houses did he draw?* Children naturally model the situation and then reflect on their model (with objects, fingers, or a drawing) to solve it (see research summarized in Clements and Sarama, 2007; Fuson, 1992a, 1992b). From Grade 2 on they can also learn to represent the situation with a situation equation (e.g., 5 + ? = 9 as in the example above, or ? + 4 for an unknown start number) and then reflect on that to solve it. This process of mathematizing (including representing the situation) and then solving the situation representation is algebraic problem solving.

## Issues in Learning Relations and Operations

### *The Extensive Learning Path for Addition and Subtraction*

The teaching-learning path we describe shows that even the most advanced solution strategies for adding and subtracting single-digit numbers have their roots before age 2 and may not culminate until Grade 1 or even Grade 2. The paths also illustrate how children coordinate several different complex kinds of understandings and skills beginning with *perceptual subitizing* through *conceptual subitizing* and then counting and matching to employ more sophisticated problem-solving strategies. This makes it clear that one cannot characterize the learning of single-digit addition and subtraction as simply "memorizing the facts" or "recalling the facts," as if children had been looking at an addition table of numbers and memorizing these. Children do remember particular additions and subtractions as early as age 2, but each of these has some history as perceptually or conceptually subitized situations, counted situations over many examples, or additions/subtractions derived from other known additions/subtractions. It is therefore much more appropriate to set learning goals that use the terminology *fluency with single-digit additions and their related subtractions* rather than the terms *recalled* or *memorized facts*. The latter terms imply simplistic rote teaching/learning methods that are far from what is needed for deep and flexible learning.

### *The Mental Number Word List as a Representational Tool*

We have demonstrated how children come to use the number word list (the number word sequence) as a mental tool for solving addition and subtraction problems. They are able to use increasingly abbreviated and abstract solution methods, such as counting on and the make-a-ten methods. The number words themselves have become unitized mental objects to be added, subtracted, and ordered as their originally separate sequence, counting, and cardinal meanings become related and finally integrated over several years into a truly numerical mental number word sequence. Each number can be seen as embedded within each successive number and as seriated: related to the numbers before and after it by a linear ordering created by the order relation *less than* applied to each pair of numbers (see Box 5-12). This is what Piaget (1941/1965) called *truly operational cardinal number*: Any number in the sequence displays both class inclusion (the embeddedness) and seriation (see also Kamii, 1985). But this fully Piagetian integrated sequence will not be finished for most children until Grade 1 or Grade 2, when they can do at least some of the Step 3 derived fact solution methods, which depend on the whole teaching-learning path we have discussed.

**BOX 5-12**
**Ordering and Ordinal Numbers**

There is frequent confusion in the research literature in the use of the terms *ordered* or *ordering*, *ordinal number*, and *order relation*. Some of this confusion stems from the fact that adults can flexibly and fluently use the counting, cardinal, and ordinal meaning of number words without needing to consciously think about the different meanings. As a result, they may not be able to differentiate the meanings very clearly. But young children learn the meanings separately and need to connect them.

When counting to find the total number in a set, the order for connecting each number word to objects is arbitrary and could be done in any order. As noted previously, the last number takes on a cardinal meaning and refers to the total numbers of items counted. Thus, the cardinal meaning of a number refers to a set with that many objects. Cardinal numbers can be used to create an order relation. That is the idea that one set has more members than another set. An order relation (one number or set is less than or more than another number or set) tells how two quantities are related. This order relation produces a linear ordering on these numbers or sets. An ordinal number tells where in the ordering a particular number or set falls. A child can subitize for the small ordinal numbers (see whether an object in an ordered set is first, second, or third), but needs to count for larger ordinal numbers and shift from a count meaning to an ordinal meaning (e.g., count *one, two, three, four, five, six, seven* [count meaning]. *That person is seventh* [ordinal meaning and ordinal work] *in the line to buy tickets.*).

We have not emphasized ordinal words in this chapter because they are so much more difficult than are cardinal words, and children learn them much later (e.g., Fuson, 1988). Although 4- and 5-year-olds could learn to use the ordinal words *first, second,* and *last,* it is not crucial that they do so. The ordinal words *first* through *tenth* could wait until Grade 1.

Many researchers have noted how the number word list turns into a mental representational tool for adding and subtracting. A few researchers have called this a *mental number line*. However, for young children this is a misnomer, because children in kindergarten and Grade 1 are using the number word list (sequence) as a count model: Each number word is taken as a unit to be counted, matched, added, or subtracted. In contrast, a number line is a length model, like a ruler or a bar graph, in which numbers are represented by the length from zero along a line segmented into equal lengths. Young children have difficulties with the number line representation because they have difficulty seeing the units—they need to see things, so they focus on the numbers instead of on the lengths. So they may count the starting point 0 and then be off by one, or they focus on the spaces and are confused by the location of the numbers at the end of the spaces. The report *Adding It Up: Helping Children Learn Mathematics* (National

Research Council, 2001a) recognized the difficulties of the number line representation for young children and recommended that its use begin at Grade 2 and not earlier.

The number line is particularly important when one wants to show parts of one whole, such as one-half. In early childhood materials, the term *number line* or *mental number line* often really means a number path, such as in the common early childhood games in which numbers are put on squares and children move along a numbered path. Such number paths are count models—each square is an object that can be counted—so these are appropriate for children from age 2 through Grade 1. Some research summarized in Chapter 3 did focus on children's and adult's use of the analog magnitude system to estimate large quantities or to say where specified larger numbers fell along a number line. Again, it is not clear, especially for children, whether they are using a mental number list or a number line; the crucial research issue is the change in the spacing of the numbers with age, and this could come either from children's use of a mental number list or a number line. The use of number lines, such as in a ruler or a bar graph scale, is an important part of measurement and is discussed in Chapter 6. But for numbers, relations, and operations, physical and mental number word lists are the appropriate model.

### *Variability in Children's Solution Methods*

The focus of this chapter is on how children follow a learning path from age 2 to Grade 1 in learning important aspects of numbers, relations, and operations. We continually emphasize that there is variability within each age group in the numbers and concepts with which a given child can work. As summarized in Chapter 3, much of this variability stems from differences in opportunities to learn and to practice these competencies, and we stress how important it is to provide such opportunities to learn for all children. We close with a reminder that there is also variability within a given individual at a given time in the strategies the child will use for a given kind of task. Researchers through the years have shown that children's strategy use is marked by variability both within and across children (e.g., Siegler, 1988; Siegler and Jenkins, 1989; Siegler and Shrager, 1984). Even on the same problem, a child might use one strategy at one point in the session, and another strategy at another point. As children gain proficiency, they gradually move to more mature and efficient strategies, rather than doing so all at once. The variability itself is thought to be an important engine of cognitive change. Similarly, as discussed above, accuracy can vary with effort, particularly with counting. The variability in the use of strategies within or across children can provide important opportunities to discuss different methods and extend understandings of all participants. The variability in results with different levels of effort can lead to discussions about how learning mathematics depends on effort and practice and that everyone can get better at it if they practice and try hard. Effort creates competencies that are the building blocks for the next steps in the learning path for numbers, relations, and operations.

## SUMMARY

The teaching-learning path described in this chapter shows how young children learn, integrate, and extend their knowledge about cardinality, the number word list, 1-to-1 counting correspondences, and written number symbols in successive steps from age 2 to 7. Much of this knowledge requires specific cultural knowledge—for example, the number word list in English, counting, matching, vocabulary about relations and operations. Children require extensive, repeated experiences with small numbers and then similar experiences with larger and larger numbers. Counting must become very fluent, so that it can become a mental representational tool for problem solving. As we have shown, even young children can have experiences in the teaching-learning path that support later algebraic learning. To move through the steps in the teaching-learning path, children require teaching and interaction in the context of explicit, real-world problems with feedback and opportunities for reflection provided. They also require accessible situations in which they can practice (consolidate), deepen, and extend their learning and their own.

## REFERENCES AND BIBLIOGRAPHY

Baroody, A.J. (1984). Children's difficulties in subtraction: Some causes and questions. *Journal for Research in Mathematics Education, 15*(3), 203-213.

Baroody, A.J. (1987). *Children's Mathematical Thinking: A Developmental Framework for Preschool, Primary, and Special Education Teachers.* New York: Teachers College Press.

Baroody, A.J. (1992). The development of preschoolers' counting skills and principles. In J. Bideaud, C. Meljac, and J.P. Fischer (Eds.), *Pathways to Number* (pp. 99-126). Hillsdale, NJ: Erlbaum.

Baroody, A.J., and Coslick, R.T. (1998). *Fostering Children's Mathematical Power: An Investigative Approach to K-8 Mathematics Instruction.* Mahwah, NJ: Erlbaum.

Baroody, A.J., and Gannon, K.E. (1984). The development of the commutativity principle and economical addition strategies. *Cognition and Instruction, 1*, 321-329.

Baroody, A.J., and Ginsburg, H.P. (1986). The relationship between initial meaning and mechanical knowledge of arithmetic. In J. Hiebert (Ed.), *Conceptual and Procedural Knowledge: The Case of Mathematics.* Hillsdale, NJ: Erlbaum.

Baroody, A.J., and Kaufman, L.C. (1993). The case of Lee: Assessing and remedying a numerical-writing difficulty. *Teaching Exceptional Children, 25*(3), 14-16.

Baroody, A.J., Wilkins, J.L.M., and Tiilikainen, S.H. (2003). The development of children's understanding of additive commutativity: From protoquantitative concept to general concept? In A.J. Baroody and A. Dowker (Eds.), *The Development of Arithmetic Concepts and Skills: Constructing Adaptive Expertise* (pp. 127-160). Mahwah, NJ: Erlbaum.

Baroody, A., Lai, M-L., and Mix, K.S. (2006). The development of young children's early number and operation sense and its implications for early childhood education. In B. Spodek and O. Saracho (Eds.), *Handbook of Research on the Education of Young Children* (pp. 187-221). Mahwah, NJ: Erlbaum.

Benson, A.P., and Baroody, A.J. (2002). *The Case of Blake: Number-Word and Number Development.* Paper presented at the annual meeting of the American Educational Research Association, April, New Orleans, LA.

Briars, D., and Siegler, R.S. (1984). A featural analysis of preschoolers' counting knowledge. *Developmental Psychology, 20*(4), 607-618.

Carpenter, T.P., Ansell, E., Franke, M.L., Fennema, E.H., and Weisbeck, L. (1993). Models of problem solving: A study of kindergarten children's problem-solving processes. *Journal for Research in Mathematics Education, 24*, 428-441.

Case, R. (1991). *The Mind's Staircase: Exploring the Conceptual Underpinnings of Children's Thought and Knowledge.* Hillsdale, NJ: Erlbaum.

Clements, D.H. (1999). Subitizing: What is it? Why teach it? *Teaching Children Mathematics, 5*, 400-405.

Clements, D.H., and Sarama, J. (2007). Early childhood mathematics learning. In F.K. Lester, Jr. (Ed.), *Second Handbook of Research on Mathematics Teaching and Learning* (pp. 461-555). New York: Information Age.

Clements, D.H., and Sarama, J. (2008). Experimental evaluation of a research-based preschool mathematics curriculum. *American Educational Research Journal, 45*, 443-494.

Clements, D.H., Sarama, J., and DiBiase, A. (2004). *Engaging Young Children in Mathematics: Findings of the 2000 National Conference on Standards for Preschool and Kindergarten Mathematics Education.* Mahwah, NJ: Erlbaum.

DeCorte, E., and Verschaffel, L. (1985). Beginning first graders' initial representation of arithmetic word problems. *Journal of Mathematical Behavior, 1*, 3-21.

Duncan, A., Lee, H., and Fuson, K.C. (2000). Pathways to early number concepts: Use of 5- and 10-structured representations in Japan, Taiwan, and the United States. In M.L. Fernandez (Ed.), *Proceedings of the Twenty-Second Annual Meeting of the North American Chapter of the International Group for the Psychology of Mathematics Education, Vol. 2* (p. 452). Columbus, OH: ERIC Clearinghouse for Science, Mathematics, and Environmental Education.

Fuson, K.C. (1982). An analysis of the counting-on solution procedure in addition. In T. Romberg, T. Carpenter, and J. Moser (Eds.), *Addition and Subtraction: A Developmental Perspective* (pp. 67-81). Hillsdale, NJ: Erlbaum.

Fuson, K.C. (1984). More complexities in subtraction. *Journal for Research in Mathematics Education, 15*, 214-225.

Fuson, K.C. (1986a). Roles of representation and verbalization in the teaching of multi-digit addition and subtraction. *European Journal of Psychology of Education, 1*, 35-56.

Fuson, K.C. (1986b). Teaching children to subtract by counting up. *Journal for Research in Mathematics Education, 17*, 172-189.

Fuson, K.C. (1988). *Children's Counting and Concept of Number.* New York: Springer-Verlag.

Fuson, K.C. (1992a). Research on learning and teaching addition and subtraction of whole numbers. In G. Leinhardt, R.T. Putnam, and R.A. Hattrup (Eds.) *The Analysis of Arithmetic for Mathematics Teaching* (pp. 53-187). Hillsdale, NJ: Erlbaum.

Fuson, K.C. (1992b). Research on whole number addition and subtraction. In D. Grouws (Ed.), *Handbook of Research on Mathematics Teaching and Learning* (pp. 243-275). New York: Macmillan.

Fuson, K.C. (2004). Pre-K to grade 2 goals and standards: Achieving 21st-century mastery for all. In D.H. Clements, J. Sarama, and A. DiBiase (Eds.), *Engaging Young Children in Mathematics* (pp. 105-148). Mahwah, NJ: Erlbaum.

Fuson, K.C., and Kwon, Y. (1991). Chinese-based regular and European irregular systems of number words: The disadvantages for English-speaking children. In K. Durkin and B. Shire (Eds.), *Language and Mathematical Education* (pp. 211-226). Milton Keynes, England: Open University Press.

Fuson, K.C., and Kwon, Y. (1992a). Korean children's understanding of multidigit addition and subtraction. *Child Development, 63*, 491-506.

Fuson, K.C., and Kwon, Y. (1992b). Korean children's single-digit addition and subtraction: Numbers structured by ten. *Journal for Research in Mathematics Education, 23*, 148-165.

Fuson, K.C., and Secada, W.G. (1986). Teaching children to add by counting with finger patterns. *Cognition and Instruction, 3*, 229-260.

Fuson, K.C., and Willis, G.B. (1988). Subtracting by counting up: More evidence. *Journal for Research in Mathematics Education, 19*, 402-420.

Fuson, K.C., Richards, J., and Briars, D. (1982). The acquisition and elaboration of the number word sequence. In C.J. Brainerd (Ed.), *Children's Logical and Mathematical Cognition: Progress in Cognitive Development Research* (pp. 33-92). New York: Springer-Verlag.

Fuson, K.C., Carroll, W.M., and Landis, J. (1996). Levels in conceptualizing and solving addition/subtraction compare word problems. *Cognition and Instruction, 14*(3), 345-371.

Fuson, K.C., Smith, S.T., and Lo Cicero, A. (1997). Supporting Latino first graders' ten-structured thinking in urban classrooms. *Journal for Research in Mathematics Education, 28*, 738-766.

Geary, D.C., Fan, L., Bow-Thomas, C.C., and Siegler, R.S. (1993). Even before formal instruction, Chinese children outperform American children in mental addition. *Cognitive Development, 8*, 517-529.

Gelman, R., and Gallistel, C.R. (1978). *The Child's Understanding of Number.* Cambridge, MA: Harvard University Press.

Gibson, E.J. (1969). *Principles and Perceptions of Learning Development.* New York: Appleton-Century Crofts.

Gibson, E.J., and Levin, H. (1975). *The Psychology of Reading,* Cambridge, MA: MIT Press.

Ginsburg, H.P. (1983). *The Development of Mathematical Thinking.* New York: Academic Press.

Ginsburg, H.S. (1977). *Children's Arithmetic.* New York: Van Nostrand.

Hannula, M.M. (2005). *Spontaneous Focusing on Numerosity in the Development of Early Mathematical Skills.* Turku, Finland: University of Turku.

Hiebert, J., Carpenter, T., Fennema, E., Fuson, K.C., Wearne, D., Murray, H., Olivier, A., and Human, P. (1997). *Making Sense: Teaching and Learning Mathematics with Understanding.* Portsmouth, NH: Heinemann.

Kamii, C. (1985). *Young Children Reinvent Arithmetic: Implication of Piaget's Theory.* New York: Teachers College Press.

LaFevre, J., Smith-Chant, B.L., Fast, L., Skwarchuk, S., Sargla, E., Arnup, J.S., Penner-Wilger, M., Bisanz, J., and Kamawar, D. (2006). What counts as knowing? The development of conceptual and procedural knowledge of counting from kindergarten through grade 2. *Journal of Experimental Child Psychology, 93*(4), 285-303.

Lipton, J.S., and Spelke, E.S. (2006). Preschool children master the logic of number word meanings. *Cognition, 98*(3), 57-66.

Menninger, K. (1958/1969). *Number Words and Number Symbols: A Cultural History of Numbers.* (P. Broneer, Trans.). Cambridge, MA: MIT Press. (Original work published 1958).

Miller, K.F. (1992). What a number is: Mathematical foundations and developing number concepts. In J.I.D. Campbell (Ed.), *The Nature and Origins of Mathematical Skills* (pp. 3-38). New York: Elsevier.

Miller, K.F., and Stigler, J.W. (1987). Counting in Chinese: Cultural variation in a basic cognitive skill. *Cognitive Development*, 2, 279-305.

Miller, K.F., Smith, C.M., Zhu, J., and Zhang, H. (1995). Preschool origins of cross-national differences in mathematical competence: The role of number naming systems. *Psychological Science*, 6, 56-60.

Mix, K.S., Huttenlocher, J., and Levine, S.C. (2002). *Quantitative Development in Infancy and Early Childhood.* New York: Oxford University Press.

Mix, K.S., Sandhofer, C.M., and Baroody, A.J. (2005). Number words and number concepts: The interplay of verbal and nonverbal processes in early quantitative development. In R. Kail (Ed.), *Advances in Child Development and Behavior* (vol. 33, pp. 305-346). New York: Academic Press.

Murata, A. (2004). Paths to learning ten-structured understandings of teen sums: Addition solution methods of Japanese grade 1 students. *Cognition and Instruction*, *22*(2), 185-218.

Murphy, C.M., and Wood, D.J. (1981). Learning from pictures: The use of pictorial information by young children. *Journal of Experimental Child Psychology*, *32*, 279-297.

National Association for the Education of Young Children and National Council of Teachers of Mathematics. (2002). *Early Childhood Mathematics: Promoting Good Beginnings.* A joint position statement of the National Association for the Education of Young Children and National Council of Teachers of Mathematics. Available: http://www.naeyc.org/about/positions/pdf/psmath.pdf [accessed August 2008].

National Council of Teachers of Mathematics. (2006). *Curriculum Focal Points.* Reston, VA: Author.

National Research Council. (1999). *How People Learn: Brain, Mind, Experience, and School.* Committee on Developments in the Science of Learning. J.D. Bransford, A.L. Brown, and R.R. Cocking (Eds.). Commission on Behavioral and Social Sciences and Education. Washington, DC: National Academy Press.

National Research Council. (2001a). *Adding It Up: Helping Children Learn Mathematics.* Mathematics Learning Study Committee. J. Kilpatrick, J. Swafford, and B. Findell (Eds.). Center for Education, Division of Behavioral and Social Sciences and Education. Washington, DC: National Academy Press.

National Research Council. (2001b). *Eager to Learn: Educating Our Preschoolers.* Committee on Early Childhood Pedagogy. B.T. Bowman, M.S. Donovan, and M.S. Burns (Eds.). Commission on Behavioral and Social Sciences and Education. Washington, DC: National Academy Press.

National Research Council and Institute of Medicine. (2000). *From Neurons to Neighborhoods: The Science of Early Childhood Development.* Committee on Integrating the Science of Early Childhood Development. J.P. Shonkoff and D.A. Phillips (Eds.). Board on Children, Youth and Families, Commission on Behavioral and Social Sciences and Education. Washington, DC: National Academy Press.

Pepperberg, I.M. (1987). Evidence for conceptual quantitative abilities in the African grey parrot: Labeling of cardinal sets. *Ethology*, *75*, 37-61.

Piaget, J. (1941/1965). *The Child's Conception of Number.* New York: Norton. (Original work published 1941).

Rittle-Johnson, B., and Siegler, R.S. (1998). The relation between conceptual and procedural knowledge in learning mathematics: A review. In C. Donlan (Ed.), *The Development of Mathematical Skills* (pp. 75-110). East Sussex, England: Psychology Press.

Sarnecka, B., Kamenskaya, G., Yamana, Y., Ogura, T., and Yudovina, Y.B. (2007). From grammatical number to exact numbers: Early meaning of 'one', 'two', and 'three', in English, Russian, and Japanese. *Cognitive Psychology, 55*, 136-168.

Saxe, G.B. (1982). Culture and the development of numerical cognition: Studies among the Oksapmin of Papua New Guinea. In C.J. Brainerd ((Ed.), *Progress in Cognitive Development Research, Vol. 1. Children's Logical and Mathematical Cognition* (pp. 157-176). New York: Springer-Verlag.

Secada, W.G., Fuson, K.C., and Hall, J.W. (1983). The transition from counting-all to counting-on in addition. *Journal for Research in Mathematics Education, 14*, 47-57.

Shipley, E.F., and Shepperson, B. (1990). Countable entities: Developmental changes. *Cognition, 34*, 109-136.

Siegler, R.S. (1988). Individual differences in strategy choices: Good students, not-so-good students, and perfectionists. *Child Development, 59*, 833-851.

Siegler, R.S., and Jenkins, E. (1989). *How Children Discover New Strategies*. Hillsdale, NJ: Erlbaum.

Siegler, R.S., and Robinson, M. (1982). The development of numerical understandings. In H.W. Reese and L.P. Lipsitt (Eds.), *Advances in Child Development and Behavior* (vol. 16, pp. 242-312). New York: Academic Press.

Siegler, R.S., and Shrager, J. (1984). Strategy choices in addition and subtraction: How do children know what to do? In C. Sophian (Ed.), *The Origins of Cognitive Skills* (pp. 229-293). Hillsdale, NJ: Erlbaum.

Sophian, C. (Ed.) (1984). *The Origins of Cognitive Skills*. Hillsdale, NJ: Erlbaum.

Sophian, C. (1988). Early developments in children's understanding of number: Inferences about numerosity and one-to-one correspondence. *Child Development, 59*, 1397-1414.

Sophian, C., and Kailihiwa, C. (1998). Units of counting: Developmental changes. *Cognitive Development, 13*, 561-585.

Spelke, E. (2003). What make us smart? Core knowledge and natural language. In D. Genter and S. Goldin-Meadow (Eds.), *Language in Mind* (pp. 277-311). Cambridge, MA: MIT Press.

Wynn, K. (1990). Children's understanding of counting. *Cognition, 36*, 155-193.

# 6

# The Teaching-Learning Paths for Geometry, Spatial Thinking, and Measurement

Geometry, spatial thinking, and measurement make up the second area of mathematics we emphasize for young children. In this chapter we provide an overview of children's development in these domains, lay out the teaching-learning paths for children ages 2 through kindergarten in each broad area, and discuss instruction to support their progress through these teaching-learning paths. As in Chapter 5, the discussion of instruction is closely tied to the specific mathematical concepts covered in the chapter. Chapter 7 provides a more general overview of effective instruction.

## GEOMETRY AND SPATIAL THINKING

The Dutch mathematician Hans Freudenthal stated that geometry and spatial thinking are important because "Geometry is grasping space. And since it is about the education of children, it is grasping that space in which the child lives, breathes, and moves. The space that the child must learn to know, explore, and conquer, in order to live, breath and move better in it. Are we so accustomed to this space that we cannot imagine how important it is for us and for those we are educating?" (Freudenthal, 1973, p. 403). This section describes the two major ways children understand that space, starting with smaller scale perspectives on geometric shape, including composition and transformation of shapes, and then turning to larger spaces in which they live. Although the research on these topics is far less developed than in number, it does provide guidelines for developing young children's learning of both geometric and spatial abilities.

## Shape

Shape is a fundamental idea in mathematics and in development. Beyond mathematics, shape is the basic way children learn names of objects, and attending to the objects' shapes facilitates that learning (Jones and Smith, 2002).

### *Steps in Thinking About Shape*

Children tend to move through different levels in thinking as they learn about geometric shapes (Clements and Battista, 1992; van Hiele, 1986). They have an innate, implicit ability to recognize and match shapes. But at the earliest, prerecognition level, they are not explicitly able to reliably distinguish circles, triangles, and squares from other shapes. Children at this level are just starting to form unconscious visual schemes for the shapes, drawing on some basic competencies. An example is pattern matching through some type of feature analysis (Anderson, 2000; Gibson et al., 1962) that is conducted after the visual image of the shape is analyzed by the visual system (Palmer, 1989).

At the next level, children think visually or holistically about shapes (i.e., syncretic thought, a fusion of differing systems; see Clements, Battista, and Sarama, 2001; Clements and Sarama, 2007b) and have formed schemes, or mental patterns, for shape categories. When first built, such schemes are holistic, unanalyzed, and visual. At this visual/holistic step, children can recognize shapes as wholes but may have difficulty forming separate mental images that are not supported by perceptual input. A given figure is a rectangle, for example, because "it looks like a door." They do not think about shapes in terms of their attributes, or properties. Children at this level of geometric thinking can construct shapes from parts, but they have difficulty integrating those parts into a coherent whole.

Next, children learn to describe, then analyze, geometric figures. The culmination of learning at this descriptive/analytic level is the ability to recognize and characterize shapes by their properties. Initially, they learn about the parts of shapes—for example, the boundaries of two-dimensional (2-D) and three-dimensional (3-D) shapes—and how to combine them to create geometric shapes (initially imprecisely). For example, they may explicitly understand that a closed shape with three straight sides is a triangle. In the teaching-learning path articulated in Table 6-1, this is called the "thinking about parts" level.

Children then increasingly see relationships between parts of shapes, which are properties of the shapes. For instance, a student might think of a parallelogram as a figure that has two pairs of parallel sides and two pairs of equal angles (angle measure is itself a relation between two sides, and

**TABLE 6-1** Space and Shapes in Two Dimensions

| | Goals | | |
|---|---|---|---|
| Steps/Ages (Level of Thinking) | A. Perceive, Say, Describe/Discuss, and Construct Objects in 2-D Space | B. Perceive, Say, Describe/ Discuss, and Construct Spatial Relations in 2-D Space | C. Perceive, Say, Describe/Discuss, and Construct Compositions and Decompositions in 2-D Space |
| **Step 1 (Ages 2 and 3)** | | | |
| Thinking visually/ holistically | Recognition and informal description (including at least circles, squares, then triangles, rectangles). | Recognize shapes in many different orientations and sizes. Trial-and-error geometric movements (informal, not quantified).<br>• Use relational language, including vertical directionality terms as "up" and "down," referring to a 2-D environment.<br>• Informally recognizes area as filling 2-D space (e.g., "I need more papers to cover this table"). | Solve simple puzzles involving things in the world.<br>Create pictures by representing single objects, each with a different shape. |
| Thinking about parts | Shapes by number of sides (starting with restricted cases, e.g., prototypical equilateral triangle, square). | | |
| **Step 2 (Age 4)** | | | |
| Thinking visually/ holistically | Recognition and informal description at multiple orientations, sizes, and shapes (includes circles and half/quarter circles, squares and rectangles, triangles, and others [the pattern block rhombus, trapezoids, hexagons regular]). | Recognize shapes (to the left) in many different orientations, sizes, and shapes (e.g., "long" and "skinny" rectangles and triangles).<br>• Match shapes by using geometric motions to superimpose them.<br>• Use relational words of proximity, such as "beside," "next to," and "between," referring to a 2-D environment. | |

*continued*

**TABLE 6-1** Continued

| Steps/Ages (Level of Thinking) | Goals: A. Perceive, Say, Describe/Discuss, and Construct Objects in 2-D Space | B. Perceive, Say, Describe/ Discuss, and Construct Spatial Relations in 2-D Space | C. Perceive, Say, Describe/Discuss, and Construct Compositions and Decompositions in 2-D Space |
|---|---|---|---|
| Thinking about parts | Describe and name shapes by number of sides (up to the number they can count).<br>Describe and name shapes by number of corners (vertices). | Move shapes using slides, flips, and turns.<br>• Use relational language involving frames of reference, such as "to this side of," "above."<br>• Compare areas by superimposition.<br>For rectangular spaces<br>• Tile a rectangular space with physical tiles (squares, right triangles, and rectangles with unit lengths) and guidance. | Move shapes using slides, flips, and turns to combine shapes to build pictures.<br>For rectangular spaces<br>• Copy a design shown on a grid, placing squares onto squared-grid paper. |
| Relating parts and wholes | Sides of same/ different length.<br>• Right vs. nonright angles. | Predict effects of rigid geometric motions. | Combine shapes with intentionality, recognizing them as new shapes.<br>• In an "equilateral triangle world," create pattern block blue rhombus, trapezoid, and hexagons from triangles. |
| **Step 3 (Age 5)** | | | |
| Thinking visually/ holistically | Recognition and informal description, varying orientation, sizes, shapes (includes all above, as well as octagons, parallelograms, convex/concave figures). | | |

**TABLE 6-1** Continued

| Steps/Ages (Level of Thinking) | Goals<br>A. Perceive, Say, Describe/Discuss, and Construct Objects in 2-D Space | B. Perceive, Say, Describe/ Discuss, and Construct Spatial Relations in 2-D Space | C. Perceive, Say, Describe/Discuss, and Construct Compositions and Decompositions in 2-D Space |
|---|---|---|---|
| Thinking about parts | Shape by number of sides and corners (including new shapes). | Create and record original compositions made using squares, right triangles, and rectangles on grid paper. Extend to equilateral grids and pattern blocks (those with multiples of 60° and 120° angles).<br>• Begin to use relational language of "right" and "left."<br>• Draw a complete covering of a rectangle area. Count squares in rectangular arrays correctly and (increasingly) systematically. | |
| Relating parts and wholes | Measure of sides (simple units), gross comparison of angle sizes. | Compare area using superimposition.<br>• For rectangular regions, draw and count by rows (initially may only count some rows as rows).<br>• Identify and create symmetric figures using motions (e.g., paper folding; also mirrors as reflections). | Composition on grids and in puzzles with systematicity and anticipation, using a variety of shape sets (e.g., pattern blocks; rectangular grids with squares, right triangles, and rectangles; tangrams). |

NOTE: Most of the time should be spent on 2-D, about 85 percent (there are many beneficial overlapping activities).

equality of angles another relation). Owing usually to a lack of good experiences, many students do not reach this level until late in their schooling. However, with appropriate learning experiences, even preschoolers can begin to develop this level of thinking. In Table 6-1 this is called the "relating parts and wholes" level.

### *Development of Shape Concepts*

What ideas do preschool children form about common shapes? Decades ago, Fuson and Murray (1978) reported that, by 3 years of age, over

60 percent of children could name a circle, a square, and a triangle. More recently, Klein, Starkey, and Wakeley (1999) reported the shape-naming accuracy of 5-year-olds as circle, 85 percent; square, 78 percent; triangle, 80 percent; rectangle, 44 percent. In one study (Clements et al., 1999), children identified circles quite accurately (92, 96, and 99 percent for 4-year-olds, 5-year-olds, and 6-year-olds, respectively), and squares fairly well (82, 86, and 91 percent). Young children were less accurate at recognizing triangles and rectangles, although their averages (e.g., 60 percent for triangles for all ages 4-6) were not remarkably smaller than those of elementary students (64-81 percent). Their visual prototype for a triangle seems to be of an isosceles triangle. Their average for rectangles was a bit lower (just above 50 percent for all ages). Children's prototypical image of a rectangle seems to be a four-sided figure with two long parallel sides and "close to" square corners. Thus, young children tended to accept long parallelograms or right trapezoids as rectangles.

In a second study (Hannibal and Clements, 2008), children ages 3 to 6 sorted a variety of manipulable forms. Certain mathematically irrelevant characteristics affected children's categorizations: skewness, aspect ratio, and, for certain situations, orientation. With these manipulatives, orientation had the least effect. Most children accepted triangles even if their base was not horizontal, although a few protested. Skewness, or lack of symmetry, was more important. Many rejected triangles because "the point on top is not in the middle." For rectangles, many children accepted nonright parallelograms and right trapezoids. Also important was aspect ratio, the ratio of height to base. Children preferred an aspect ratio near one for triangles; that is, about the same height as width. Children rejected both triangles and rectangles that were "too skinny" or "not wide enough."

## Spatial Structure and Spatial Thinking

Spatial thinking includes two main abilities: spatial orientation and spatial visualization and imagery. Other important competencies include knowing how to represent spatial ideas and how and when to apply such abilities in solving problems.

### *Spatial Orientation*

Spatial orientation involves knowing where one is and how to get around in the world. As shown in Chapter 3, spatial orientation is, like number, a core cognitive domain, for which competencies, including the ability to actively and selectively seek out information, are present from birth (Gelman and Williams, 1997). Children have cognitive systems that are based on their own position and their movements through space, and external references. They can learn to represent spatial relations and movement through space using both of these systems, eventually mathematizing their knowledge.

Children as young as age 2 can implicitly use knowledge of multiple landmarks and distances between them to determine or remember locations. By about age 5, they can explicitly represent that information, even interpreting or creating simple models of spaces, such as their classroom. Similarly, they can implicitly use distance and direction when they move at age 1-2. They do so more reliably when they move themselves, another justification for providing children of all ages with opportunities to explore large spaces in which they can navigate safely. By age 4, children explicitly use distance and direction and reason about their locations. For example, they can point to one location from another, even though they never walked a path that connected the two (Uttal and Wellman, 1989).

Language for spatial relationships is acquired in a consistent order, even across different languages (Bowerman, 1996). The first terms acquired are *in*, *on*, and *under*, along with such vertical directionality terms as *up* and *down*. These initially refer to transformations (e.g., "on" not as a smaller object on top of another, but only as making an object become physically attached to another; Gopnik and Meltzoff, 1986). Children then learn words of proximity, such as "beside" and "between." Later, they learn words referring to frames of reference, such as "in front of," "behind." The words "left" and "right" are learned much later, and are the source of confusion for several years.

In these early years, children also can learn to analyze what others need to hear in order to follow a route through a space. Such learning is dependent on relevant experiences, including language. Learning and using spatial terminology can affect spatial competence (Wang and Spelke, 2002). For example, teaching preschoolers the spatial terms "left" and "right" helped them reorient themselves more successfully (Shusterman and Spelke, 2004). However, language provides better support for simpler representations, and more complex spatial relationships are difficult to capture verbally. In such cases, children benefit from learning to interpret and use external representations, such as models or drawings.

Young children can begin to build mental representations of their spatial environments and can model spatial relationships of these environments. When very young children tutor others in guided environments, they build geometrical concepts (Filippaki and Papamichael, 1997). Such environments might include interesting layouts inside and outside classrooms, incidental and planned experiences with landmarks and routes, and frequent discussion about spatial relations on all scales, including distinguishing parts of their bodies (Leushina, 1974/1991), describing spatial movements (forward, back), finding a missing object ("under the table that's next to the door"), putting objects away, and finding the way back home from an excursion. As for many areas of mathematics, verbal interaction is important. For example, parental scaffolding of spatial communication helped both 3- and 4-year-olds perform direction-giving tasks, in which they had to clarify the directions (disambiguate) by using a second landmark ("it's in the bag on the table"), which children are more likely to do the older they are. Both age groups benefited from directive prompts, but 4-year-olds benefited more quickly than younger children from nondirective prompts (Plumert and Nichols-Whitehead, 1996). Children who received no prompts never disambiguated, showing that interaction and feedback from others is critical to certain spatial communication tasks.

Children as young as 3½ to 5 years of age can build simple but meaningful models of spatial relationships with toys, such as houses, cars, and trees (Blaut and Stea, 1974), although this ability is limited until about age 6 (Blades et al., 2004). Thus, younger children create relational, geometric correspondences between elements, which may still vary in scale and perspective (Newcombe and Huttenlocher, 2000).

As an example, children might use cutout shapes of a tree, a swing set, and a sandbox in the playground and lay them out on a felt board as a simple map. These are good beginnings, but models and maps should eventually move beyond overly simple iconic picture maps and challenge children to use geometric correspondences. Four questions arise: direction (which way?), distance (how far?), location (where?), and identification (what objects?). To answer these questions, children need to develop a variety of skills. They must learn to deal with mapping processes of abstraction, generalization, and symbolization. Some map symbols are icons, such as an airplane for an airport, but others are more abstract, such as circles for cities. Children might first build with objects, such as model buildings, then draw pictures of the objects' arrangements, then use maps that are miniaturizations and those that use abstract symbols. Teachers need to consistently help children connect the real-world objects to the representational meanings of map symbols.

As noted in Chapter 4, equity in the education of spatial thinking is an important issue. Preschool teachers spend more time with boys than girls and usually interact with boys in the block, construction, sand play, and climbing areas and with girls in the dramatic play area (Ebbeck, 1984). Boys engage in spatial activities more than girls at home, both alone and with caretakers (Newcombe and Sanderson, 1993). Such differences may interact with biology to account for early spatial skill advantages for boys (note that some studies find no gender differences (e.g., Brosnan, 1998, Chapter 15; Ehrlich, Levine, and Goldin-Meadow, 2006; Jordan et al., 2006; Levine et al., 1999; Rosser et al., 1984).

### *Spatial Visualization and Imagery*

Spatial images are internally experienced, holistic representations of objects that are to a degree isomorphic to their referents (Kosslyn, 1983). Spatial visualization is understanding and performing imagined movements of 2-D and 3-D objects. To do this, you need to be able to create a mental image and manipulate it, showing the close relationship between these two cognitive abilities.

An image is not a "picture in the head." It is more abstract, more malleable, and less crisp than a picture. It is often segmented into parts. Some images can cause difficulties, especially if they are too inflexible, vague, or filled with irrelevant details. People's first images are static. They can be mentally recreated, and even examined, but not transformed. For example, one might attempt to think of a group of people around a table. In contrast, dynamic images can be transformed. For example, you might mentally "move" the image of one shape (such as a book) to another place (such as a bookcase, to see if it will fit). In mathematics, you might mentally move (slide) and rotate an image of one shape to compare that shape to another one. Piaget argued that most children cannot perform full dynamic motions of images until the primary grades (Piaget and Inhelder, 1967, 1971). However, preschool children show initial transformational abilities (Clements et al., 1997a; Del Grande, 1986; Ehrlich et al., 2005; Levine et al., 1999). With guidance, 4-year-olds and some younger children can generate strategies for verifying congruence for some tasks, moving from more primitive strategies, such as edge matching (Beilin, 1984; Beilin, Klein, and Whitehurst, 1982) to the use of geometric transformations and superposition. Interventions can improve the spatial skills of young children, especially when embedded in a story context (Casey, 2005). Computers are especially helpful, as the screen tools make motions more accessible to reflection and thus bring them to an explicit level of awareness for children (Clements and Sarama, 2003; Sarama et al., 1996).

Similarly, other types of imagery can be developed. Manipulative work with shapes, such as tangrams (a puzzle consisting of seven flat shapes, called tans, which are put together in different ways to form distinct geometric shapes), pattern blocks, and other shape sets, provides a valuable foundation (Bishop, 1980). After such explorations, it is useful to engage children in puzzles in which they see only the outline of several pieces and have them find ways to fill in that outline with their own set of tangrams. Similarly, children can begin to develop a foundation for spatial structuring by forming arrays with square tiles and cubes (this is discussed in more detail in the section on measurement).

Also challenging to spatial visualization and imagery are "snapshot" activities (Clements, 1999b; Yackel and Wheatley, 1990). Children briefly see a simple arrangement of pattern blocks, then try to reproduce it. The configuration is shown again for a couple of seconds as many times as necessary. Older children can be shown a line drawing and try to draw it themselves (Yackel and Wheatley, 1990). This often creates interesting discussions revolving around "what I saw."

Spatial visualization and imagery have been positively affected by interventions that emphasize building and composing with 3-D shapes (Casey et al., in press). Another series of activities described above that develops imagery is the sequence of tactile-kinesthetic exploration of shapes.

## Achievable and Foundational Geometry and Spatial Thinking

Although longitudinal research is needed, extant research provides guidance about which geometric and spatial experiences are appropriate for and achievable by young children and will contribute to their mathematical development. First, of the mathematics children engage in spontaneously in child-centered school activities, the most frequent deals with shape and pattern. Second, each of the recently developed, research-based preschool mathematics curricula includes geometric and spatial activities (Casey, Paugh, and Ballard, 2002; Clements and Sarama, 2004; Ginsburg, Greenes, and Balfanz, 2003; Klein, Starkey, and Ramirez, 2002), with some of these featuring such a focus in 40 percent or more of the activities. Third, pilot-testing has shown that these activities were achievable and motivating to young children (Casey, Kersh, and Young, 2004; Clements and Sarama, 2004; Greenes, Ginsburg, and Balfanz, 2004; Starkey, Klein, and Wakeley, 2004), and formal evaluations have revealed that they contributed to children's development of both numerical and spatial/geometric concepts (Casey and Erkut, 2005, in press; Casey et al., in press; Clements and Sarama, 2007c, in press; Starkey et al., 2004, 2006).

Fourth, previous work has shown that well-designed activities can effectively build geometric and spatial skills and general reasoning abilities (e.g., Kamii, Miyakawa, and Kato, 2004). Fifth, results with curricula in Israel that involved only spatial and geometric activities (Eylon and Rosenfeld, 1990) are remarkably positive. Children gained in geometric and spatial skills and showed pronounced benefits in the areas of arithmetic and writing readiness (Razel and Eylon, 1990). Similar results have been found in the United States (Swaminathan, Clements, and Schrier, 1995). Children are better prepared for all school tasks when they gain the thinking tools and representational competence of geometric and spatial sense.

In this section, we describe teaching-learning paths for spatial and geometric thinking in 2-D and 3-D contexts. For each area outlined below, children should be engaged in activities that cover a range of difficulty, including perceive, say, describe/discuss, and construct (measurement in one, two, and three dimensions is described in the following section). Tables 6-1 and 6-2 summarize development of spatial and geometric thinking, as well as measurement, in two and three dimensions. Ages are grouped in the same was as in the previous chapter in order to illustrate how children's engagement with mathematics should build and develop over the prekindergarten years.

In the tables, children's competence within each band is described on the basis of the level of sophistication in their thinking. These levels are called *thinking visually/holistically*, *thinking about parts*, and *relating parts and wholes*.

## Step 1 (Ages 2 and 3)

### *2-D and 3-D Objects*

Very young children match shapes implicitly in their play. Working at the visual/holistic level (see Table 6-1), they can describe pictures of objects of all sorts, using the shape implicitly in their recognition. By age 2 to 3, they also learn to name shapes, with 2-D shapes being more familiar in most cultures, beginning with the familiar and symmetric circle and square and extending to at least prototypical triangles. Although they may name 3-D shapes by the name of one of its faces (calling a cube a square), their ability to match 2-D to corresponding 2-D (and similar for 3-D) indicates their intuitive differentiation of 2-D and 3-D shapes.

Children also learn to recognize and name additional shapes, such as triangles and rectangles—at least in their prototypical forms—and can begin to describe them in their own words. With appropriate knowledge of number, they can begin to describe these shapes by the number of sides they have, just starting to learn the concepts and terminology of the thinking about parts level of geometric thinking.

### *Spatial Relations*

From the first year of life, children develop an implicit ability to move objects. They also learn relationship language, such as "up" and "down" and similar vocabulary. They learn to apply that vocabulary in both 3-D contexts and in 2-D situations, such as the "bottom" of a picture that they are drawing on a horizontal surface.

### *Compositions and Decompositions*

At the visual/holistic level, children can solve simple puzzles involving things in the world (e.g., wooden puzzles with insets for each separate ob-

**TABLE 6-2** Space and Shapes in Three Dimensions

| Steps/Ages (Levels of Thinking) | Goals: A. Perceive, Say, Describe/Discuss, and Construct Objects in 3-D Space | B. Perceive, Say, Describe/Discuss, and Construct Spatial Relations in 3-D Space | C. Perceive, Say, Describe/ Discuss, and Construct Compositions and Decompositions in 3-D Space |
|---|---|---|---|
| **Step 1 (Ages 2 and 3)** | | | |
| Thinking visually/ holistically | See and describe pictures of objects of all sorts (3-D to 2-D).* | Understand and use relational language, including "in," "out," "on," "off," and "under," along with such vertical directionality terms as "up" and "down. | Represent real-world objects with blocks that have a similar shape.<br>• Combine unit blocks by stacking. |
| Thinking about parts | Discriminate between 2-D and 3-D shapes intuitively, marked by accurate matching or naming. | | |
| **Step 2 (Age 4)** | | | |
| Thinking visually/ holistically | Describe the difference between 2-D and 3-D shapes, and names common 3-D shapes informally and with mathematical names ("ball"/sphere; "box" or rectangular prism, "rectangular block," or "triangular block"; "can"/cylinder). | Match 3-D shapes.<br>• Uses relational words of proximity, such as "beside," "next to" and "between," "above," "below," "over," and "under." | |
| Thinking about parts | Identify faces of 3-D objects as 2-D shapes and name those shapes.<br>• Use relational language involving frames of reference such as "in front of," "in back of," "behind," "before." | Identify (matches) the faces of 3-D shapes to (congruent) 2-D shapes, and match faces of congruent 2-D shapes, naming the 2-D shapes.<br>• Represent 2-D and 3-D relationships with objects. | Combine building blocks, using multiple spatial relations. |

**TABLE 6-2** Continued

| Steps/Ages (Levels of Thinking) | Goals: A. Perceive, Say, Describe/Discuss, and Construct Objects in 3-D Space | B. Perceive, Say, Describe/Discuss, and Construct Spatial Relations in 3-D Space | C. Perceive, Say, Describe/Discuss, and Construct Compositions and Decompositions in 3-D Space |
|---|---|---|---|
| Relating parts and wholes | Informally describe why some blocks "stack well" and others do not. | | Compose building blocks to produce composite shapes. Produce arches, enclosures, corners, and crosses systematically. |
| **Step 3 (Age 5)** | | | |
| Thinking visually/ holistically | Name common 3-D shapes with mathematical terms (spheres, cylinder, rectangle, prism, pyramid). | | |
| Thinking about parts | Begin to use relational language of "right" and "left." | Fill rectangular containers with cubes, filling one layer at a time. | |
| Relating parts and wholes | Describe congruent faces and, in context (e.g., block building), parallel faces of blocks. | Understand and can replicate the perspective of a different viewer. | Substitution of shapes. Build complex structures.<br>• Build structures from pictured models. |

NOTE: Less time on 3-D than on 2-D, about 10 percent of the time on 3-D.
*Research indicates that very young children mainly use shape for object identification. Research says children with lower socioeconomic status have difficulty with describing objects and need to learn the vocabulary to do so.

ject pictured). They create pictures with geometric shapes (circles, circle sections, polygons), often representing single objects with different shapes, but eventually combining shapes to make, for example, the body of a vehicle or an animal. That is, initially children manipulate shapes individually, but they are unable to combine them to compose a larger shape. For example, they might use a single shape for a sun, a separate shape for a tree, and another separate shape for a person. Initially, they cannot accurately match shapes to even simple frames.

Later, children learn to place 2-D shapes contiguously to form pictures. In free-form "make a picture" tasks, for example, each shape used represents a unique role or function in the picture (e.g., one shape for one leg). Children can fill simple frame-based shapes puzzles using trial and error, but they may have limited ability to use turns or flips to do so; they cannot use motions to see shapes from different perspectives. Thus, children view shapes only as wholes and see few geometric relationships between shapes or between parts of shapes (i.e., a property of the shape).

Composition with 3-D shapes usually begins with stacking blocks. Children then learn to stack congruent blocks and make horizontal "lines." Next they build a vertical and horizontal structure, such as a floor or a simple wall. Later, some 3-year-olds begin to extend their buildings in multiple directions, possibly creating arches, enclosures, corners, and crosses, but often using unsystematic trial and error and simple addition of pieces.

## Step 2 (Age 4)

### *2-D and 3-D Objects*

Beginning at the visual/holistic level, preschoolers learn to recognize a wide variety of shapes, including shapes that are different sizes and are presented at different orientations. They also begin to recognize that geometric figures can belong to the same shape class, but have different measures and proportions. Similarly, preschoolers learn to describe the differences between 2-D and 3-D shapes informally. They also learn to name common 3-D shapes informally and with mathematical names (ball/sphere, box/rectangular prism, rectangular block, triangular block, can/cylinder). They name and describe these shapes, first using their own descriptions and increasingly adopting mathematical language. For example, "diamond" gives way to "rhombus" and "corners" become "angles" (or vertices). Eventually, they adopt the terminology of the thinking about parts level, such as identifying shapes as triangles because they have three sides. Faces of 3-D shapes are identified as specific 2-D shapes.

Such descriptions build geometric concepts, as well as reasoning skills and language. They encourage children to view shapes analytically. Children begin to describe some shapes in terms of their properties, such as saying that squares have four sides of equal length, and thus make initial forays into thinking at the relating parts and wholes step. They informally describe the properties of blocks in functional contexts, such as that some blocks roll and others do not.

### *Spatial Relations*

Also beginning at the visual/holistic level, preschool children learn to extend their vocabulary of spatial relations with such terms as "beside," "next to," and "between," which they can apply in 3-D and 2-D spaces. Later, they extend this to terms that involve frames of reference, such as "to the side of," "above," and "below."

Later, at the thinking about parts level, preschoolers recognize "matching" shapes at different orientations. They can learn to check if pairs of 2-D shapes are congruent by using geometry motions intuitively, moving from less accurate strategies, such as side-matching, or using lengths, to the use of superimposition (placing one shape on top of the other). They begin to use the geometric motions of slides, flips, and turns explicitly and intentionally, in discussing their solutions to puzzles or in applying such motions in computer environments to manipulate shapes. They learn to predict the effects of geometric motions, thus laying the foundation for thinking at the relating parts and wholes level.

Children also begin to be able to cover a rectangular space with physical tiles and represent their tilings with simple drawings, although they may initially leave gaps in each and may not align all the squares. This is mainly a competence of spatial structuring but it has close connections to the ability to construct compositions in 2-D space.

Preschoolers also learn about the parts of 3-D shapes, using motions to match the faces of 3-D shapes to 2-D shapes and representing 2-D and 3-D relationships with objects. For example, they may make a simple model of the classroom, using a rectangular block for the teacher's desk, small cubes for chairs, and so forth.

### *Compositions and Decompositions*

At the thinking about parts level, preschoolers can place shapes contiguously to form pictures in which several shapes play a single role (e.g., a leg might be created from three contiguous squares), but they use trial and error and do not anticipate creation of new geometric shapes. When filling in a frame or picture outline, children use gestalt configuration or one component, such as side length (Sarama et al., 1996). For example, if several sides of the existing arrangement form a partial boundary of a shape (instantiating a schema for it), children can find and place that shape. If such cues are not present, they match by a side length. Children may attempt to match corners but do not understand angle as a quantitative entity, so they try to match shapes into corners of existing arrangements in which their angles do not fit. Rotating and flipping are used, usually by trial and error, to try different arrangements (a "picking and discarding" strategy). Thus, they can complete a frame that suggests placement of the individual shapes but in which several shapes together may play a single semantic role in the picture.

Later, preschoolers begin to develop relating parts and wholes thinking.

For example, they might combine pattern block shapes (angles that are multiples of 30°) to make composites that they recognize as new shapes and to fill puzzles with growing intentionality and anticipation ("I know what will fit"). Shapes are chosen using angles as well as side lengths. The equilateral triangle world of pattern blocks provides a microworld, in which matching by sides (all of which are equal in length or double the unit length), fitting angles (multiples of 30°), and composing (two equilateral triangles can "make" the blue rhombus, a rhombus and a triangle make a trapezoid, etc.) are facilitating at this beginning step. Eventually, children consider several alternative shapes with angles equal to the existing arrangement. Rotation and flipping are used intentionally (and mentally, i.e., with anticipation) to select and place shapes (Sarama et al., 1996). Children can fill complex frames (Sales, 1994) or cover regions (Mansfield and Scott, 1990).

Related to their ability to tile the rectangular section of a plane, children can copy designs made from squares (and, for some, also isosceles right triangles) and place these shapes onto squared-grid paper. This square-based microworld is simple and not only facilitates composition, but also develops the foundations of much of mathematics (spatial structuring, multiplication, area, volume, coordinates, etc.).

Using 3-D shapes, preschoolers combine building blocks using multiple spatial relations, extending in multiple directions and with multiple points of contact among components, showing flexibility in integrating parts of the structure. Thus, they can reliably produce arches, enclosures, corners, and crosses, including enclosures that are several blocks in height. Later, they can learn to compose building blocks with anticipation, understanding what 3-D shape will be produced with a composition of 2 or more other (simple, familiar) 3-D shapes.

## Step 3 (Age 5)

### *2-D and 3-D Objects*

Kindergartners learn to recognize additional shapes, such as parallelograms, and, more importantly, learn to describe why a certain figure is classified into a given class of shapes (at the relating parts and wholes level). They may therefore discuss that parallelograms have two pairs of sides that are equal in length and two pairs of angles of equal size. This remains just the beginning of this type of thinking, as concepts of parallelism, perpendicularity, and angle measure develop over many years thereafter.

Kindergartners also learn the names of more 3-D shapes, such as spheres, cylinders, prisms, and pyramids. They describe congruent faces of such shapes and begin to understand and discuss such properties as parallel faces in some contexts (e.g., building with blocks).

### *Spatial Relations*

Kindergartners begin to use relational terms "right" and "left" in both 3-D and 2-D contexts, using scaffolds and other guidance as needed. They can also continue to develop the ability to tile a plane with square tiles without gaps and begin to represent such a tiling by drawing. They can learn to count the squares in their tiling, using more systematic strategies for keeping track, such as counting one row at a time. Finally, kindergartners can understand and can replicate the perspectives of different viewers. These competencies reflect an initial development of thinking at the relating parts and wholes level.

### *Compositions and Decompositions*

Kindergartners continue to develop the ability to intentionally and systematically combine shapes to make new shapes and complete puzzles. They do so with increasing anticipation, based on the shapes' attributes, indicating development of mental images of the component shapes. A significant advance is that they can combine shapes with different properties, extending the pattern block (30°) shapes common at early steps to such shapes as tangrams (angles multiples of 45°), and with sets of various shapes that include angles that are multiples of 15° as well as sections of circles.

Using 3-D shapes, kindergartners can substitute a composite shape for a congruent whole shape. They learn to build complex structures, such as bridges with multiple arches, with ramps and stairs at the ends. They can build structures with cubes or building blocks from 2-D pictures of these structures. Children of this age also can learn to move squares and right triangles on grids to create original designs. They can also record these designs on squared-grid paper.

## Instruction to Support the Teaching-Learning Paths

### *Learning and Teaching About Shape*

Without good experiences—"educative" rather than "mis-educative" (Dewey, 1933)—students often rely on impoverished visual prototypes that they develop based on limited examples and limited experiences with language. In contrast, good experiences include providing a variety of examples—for example, with triangles, not all equilateral or isosceles, and not all with a horizontal base, as well as discussions about triangles and their attributes that go beyond simple memorized definitions. Most children in the United States do not have these good experiences. Teachers and curriculum writers assume that children in early childhood classrooms have little or no knowledge of geometric figures. And teachers have had few experiences with geometry in their own education or in their professional development. Thus, it is unsurprising that most classrooms exhibit limited geometry instruction. One early study found that kindergarten children had a great deal of knowledge about shapes and matching shapes before instruction began. Their teacher tended to elicit and verify this prior knowledge but did not add content or develop new knowledge. That is, about two-thirds of the interactions had children repeat what they already knew (Thomas, 1982). Furthermore, many of their attempts to add content were mathematically inaccurate ("every time you cut a square, you get two triangles").

Such neglect is reflected in student achievement. U.S. students are not prepared for learning more sophisticated geometry, especially when compared with students of other nations (Carpenter et al., 1980; Fey et al., 1984; Kouba et al., 1988; Starkey et al., 1999; Stevenson, Lee, and Stigler, 1986; Stigler, Lee, and Stevenson, 1990). In some international studies, they score at or near the bottom in every geometry task (Beaton et al., 1997; Lappan, 1999).

The research reviewed to this point suggests that development of geometric knowledge is fueled by experience and education, not just maturation. If the shape categories children experience are limited, so will be their concepts of shapes. If the examples and nonexamples children experience are rigid, so will be their mental prototypes. Many children learn to accept only isosceles triangles, for example. Others learn richer concepts, even at a young age. Such children are likely to have had good experiences with shapes, including rich, varied examples and nonexamples and discussions about shapes and their characteristics.

Good experiences should begin early. Children need to experience varied examples and nonexamples and understand the attributes of shapes that are mathematically relevant as well as those (orientation, size) that are not. So, examples of triangles and rectangles should include a wide variety of shapes, including "long," "skinny," and "fat" examples. Direct empirical support for this finding is strongest for 4-year-olds, who are motivated to explore shape (Seo and Ginsburg, 2004) and have achieved substantial gains in geometric knowledge through curricular interventions, often surpassing the concepts of much older students in business-as-usual curricula (Casey and Erkut, in press; Casey et al., in press; Clements and Sarama, 2007c, in press; Starkey et al., 2006; Starkey, Klein, and Wakeley, 2004).

Beyond perceiving and naming shapes, children can and should discuss the parts and attributes of shapes. Again, there are several reasons for this recommendation. First, such descriptive activity encourages children to move beyond visual prototypes to the use of mathematical criteria. Second, discussions redirect attention and build strong concepts, mutually affecting and benefiting mental images (Clements and Sarama, 2007b). Third, these types of discussions are interesting to, and beneficial for, children as young as ages 3 and 4 (as the evaluations of the research-based curricula show; see also Spitler, Sarama, and Clements, 2003). Instructional activities that promote such reflection and discussion include building shapes from components. For example, children might build squares and other polygons with toothpicks and marshmallows. They might also form shapes with their bodies, either singly or with their friends.

Another sequence of activities involves tactile-kinesthetic exploration of shapes (feeling shapes hidden in a box). Such nonvisual exploration of shapes does not allow simple matching to prototypes. Instead, they force children to carefully put the parts of the shape into relationship with each other. First, teachers place a small number of shapes on the table and hide a shape congruent to one of these in the box (Clements and Sarama, 2007a). Children feel the shape and point to the matching shape, then pull out the hidden shape to check. Later, children do not have the shapes on the table. Instead, they have to name the shape they are feeling. Even later, they have to describe the shape without using its name, so that their friends could name the shape. In this way, children learn the properties of the shape, moving from intuitive to explicit knowledge.

The sequence in Table 6-1 indicates that 3-year-olds may begin to associate certain shapes with a known small number, even if only at an intuitive level. In comparison, 4-year-olds can explicitly adopt terminology of the thinking about parts step, illustrated by a preschooler stating that an obtuse triangle "must be a triangle, because it has three sides." As 4-year-olds start to see that some shapes have four sides that are the same length, they begin a long journey into the relating parts and wholes level of geometric thinking. Kindergartners can explicitly discuss why they call a certain shape a rectangle. Teachers might start by having children gather rectangles and have them describe why their shapes are rectangles in their own words. They could also show children a variety of shapes and have them decide whether they were or were not rectangles and why. Another useful instructional task is to challenge children to use sticks or straws of varying lengths to make triangles. Older children could draw a series of rectangles, increasing in size. Some children increase the lengths in both dimensions (e.g., length and width), some in only one dimension, leading to rich discussions.

Early childhood curricula traditionally introduce shapes in four basic categories: circle, square, triangle, and rectangle. The separation of the square and the rectangle sets up a misconception that violates the mathematical relationship between these shapes: A square is a rectangle; it is a special kind of rectangle in which all sides are the same length. The idea that a square is not a rectangle, however, is rooted by age 5 (Clements et al., 1999; Hannibal and Clements, 2008). It is time to change the presentation of squares as an isolated set. Instead, recent approaches present many examples of squares and rectangles, varying orientation, size, and so forth, including squares as examples of rectangles. If children say "that's a square," teachers respond that it is a square that is a special type of rectangle, using double-naming ("it's a square-rectangle"). This approach has been shown to be successful with preschoolers and kindergartners (Clements and Sarama, 2007c, in press; Clements, Sarama, and Wilson, 2001; Sarama and Clements, 2002). Kindergarten and first graders can discuss general categories, such as quadrilaterals and triangles, counting the sides of various figures to choose their category. They can then build hierarchical relationships of subsets of these general categories (Kay, 1987).

Children should also learn about composing and decomposing shapes from other shapes. This competence is significant in that the concepts and actions of creating and then iterating units and higher order units in the context of constructing patterns, measuring, and computing are established bases for mathematical understanding and analysis (Clements et al., 1997b; Reynolds and Wheatley, 1996; Steffe and Cobb, 1988). In addition, there is empirical support that this type of composition corresponds with, and supports, children's ability to compose and decompose numbers (Clements et al., 1996).

The sequence in Table 6-1 is based on a series of developmental studies describing children's capabilities (Clements, Sarama, and Wilson, 2001; Mansfield and Scott, 1990; Sales, 1994; Sarama, Clements, and Vukelic, 1996). These studies were synthesized into an empirically verified developmental progression that identified skills that are achievable for children at different ages, especially if provided opportunities to learn (Clements, Wilson, and Sarama, 2004). Starting with a lack of competence in composing geometric shapes, they gain abilities to combine shapes into pictures, and finally synthesize combinations of shapes into new shapes (composite shapes). As further evidence, interventions at the preschool level have shown notable gains in this ability for 2-D shapes (Casey and Erkut, in press). Intentional interventions with 3-D shape construction (i.e., building with unit blocks) have also resulted in statistically significant gains (Casey et al., in press).

Many activities develop these abilities. With a variety of groups of shapes, such as pattern blocks, tangrams, or groups with a greater variety of shapes, children can be encouraged to combine shapes creatively to create pictures and designs. Noting children's developmental level, teachers can make suggestions and pose challenges that will facilitate their learning of more sophisticated thinking.

Outline puzzles that can be filled with those same groups of shapes are also motivating and particularly useful because they can be designed to promote a particular level of thinking. Teachers can then view children's active problem solving and provide them with puzzles that will be attainable but challenging—that is, that will promote their development to the next level of thinking for 2-D geometric composition.

Similar teaching strategies can develop composition of 3-D shapes. Discussions about children's own creative constructions may make explicit ideas about length and symmetry, among others. Also, problems can be designed to encourage spatial and mathematical thinking and sequenced to match developmental progressions (Casey et al., in press; Kersh, Casey, and Young, 2008) early problem for children might be to build an enclosure with walls that are at least two blocks high and include an arch. This introduces the problem of bridging, which involves balance, measurement, and estimation. A second problem might be to build more complex bridges, such as ones with multiple arches and ramps or stairs at the end. This introduces planning and seriation. The third problem might be to build a complex tower with at least two floors, or stories. Children could be provided with cardboard ceilings, so they to make the walls fit the constraints of the cardboard's dimensions.

The recommended approaches and activities in this section have been performed successfully with 3- and 4-year-olds in classrooms serving low- and middle-income children, with strong positive results on child outcomes (Clements and Sarama, 2007c, in press; Starkey et al., 2006; Starkey, Klein, and Wakeley, 2004).

### *Use of Manipulatives, Pictures, and Computers*

Research suggests that the use of manipulatives can help young children develop geometric and spatial thinking (Clements and McMillen, 1996). Using a greater variety of manipulatives is beneficial (Greabell, 1978). Such tactile-kinesthetic experiences as body movement and manipulating geometric solids help young children learn geometric concepts (Gerhardt, 1973; Prigge, 1978). Children also fare better with solid cutouts than with printed forms, the former encouraging the use of more senses (Stevenson and McBee, 1958). However, such benefits are not straightforward or certain (Clements, 1999a; National Mathematics Advisory Panel, 2008). These materials must be used in the context of a complete mathematics program to intentionally develop specific skills and concepts. Also, from the beginning, manipulatives should be used to help children—even young children—develop mental representations that are increasingly abstract.

Pictures can also support learning. Children as young as 5 or 6 (but not most younger children) can use information in pictures to build a pyramid, for example (Murphy and Wood, 1981). Thus, pictures can give students an immediate, intuitive grasp of certain geometric ideas. Instructionally, pictures need to be sufficiently varied so the ideas that students form are not too limited. With experience, children can become sophisticated in interpreting geometric relationships in pictures. Diagrams are also useful tools for visualizing numerical and arithmetic problems, and the more experience children have with the geometric and measurement attributes of pictures and shapes, the more competence they will have in constructing and interpreting such diagrams. However, research indicates that it is rare for pictures to be superior to manipulatives. In fact, in some cases, pictures may not differ in effectiveness from instruction with symbols (Sowell, 1989). The reason may lie not so much in the nonconcrete nature of the pictures as in their nonmanipulability—that is, that children cannot act on them as flexibly and extensively. This is one reason that manipulatives on computers—even though 2-D—can benefit learning and teaching.

In fact, computers may have some specific advantages (Clements and McMillen, 1996). For example, some computer manipulatives offer more flexibility than their noncomputer counterparts. Computer-based pattern blocks, for example, can be composed and decomposed in more ways than physical pattern blocks. As another example, children and teachers can save and later retrieve any arrangement of computer manipulatives. Similarly, computers allow storage and replay of sequences of actions on manipulatives. Computers can also be used to carry out mathematical processes that are difficult or impossible to perform with physical manipulatives. For example, a computer environment might automatically draw shapes symmetrical to anything the child constructs or draws.

As a final illustration, computers can help children become aware of, and mathematize, their actions. For example, very young children can move puzzle pieces into place, but they do not think about their actions. Using the computer, however, helps children become aware of and describe these motions (Clements and Battista, 1991; Johnson-Gentile, Clements, and Battista, 1994).

Manipulatives—physical or computer—are one tool that can assist children in constructing mathematical meaning. They do not always do that, however, and the point of using them lies not in their use in promoting manipulations or random play, but to develop abstract ideas. In this view, manipulatives are successful to the extent that they become unnecessary because children have built mental images and concepts that they use for mathematical thinking (Clements, 1999a).

## MEASUREMENT

Geometric measurement connects and enriches the two critical domains of geometry and number. Children's understanding of measurement has its roots in infancy and the preschool years, and it grows over many years, as the research described in Chapter 3 shows. Even preschoolers can be guided to learn important concepts if provided appropriate measurement experiences. They naturally encounter and discuss quantities (Seo and Ginsburg, 2004). They initially learn to use words that represent quantity or magnitude of a certain attribute. Then they compare two objects directly and recognize equality or inequality (Boulton-Lewis, Wilss, and Mutch, 1996). At age 4-5, most children can learn to overcome perceptual cues and make progress in reasoning about and measuring quantities. They are ready to learn to measure, connecting number to the quantity, yet the average child in the United States, with limited measurement experience, exhibits limited understanding of measurement until the end of the primary grades. We examine this development in more detail for the attribute of length.

## Length Measurement

Length is a characteristic of an object found by quantifying how far it is between the end points of the object. Distance is often used similarly to quantify how far it is between any two points in space. Measuring length or distance consists of two aspects: (1) identifying a unit of measure and *subdividing* (mentally and physically) the object by that unit; (2) placing that unit end to end (*iterating*) alongside the object. Subdividing and unit iteration are complex mental accomplishments that are too often ignored in traditional measurement curriculum materials and instruction. Many researchers therefore go beyond the physical act of measuring to investigate children's understandings of measuring as covering space and quantifying that covering. Appendix B describes concepts that are basic to understanding length measurement.

Before kindergarten, many children lack understanding of measurement ideas and procedures, such as lining up end points when comparing the lengths of two objects. Even 5- to 6-year-olds, given a demarcated ruler, write in numerals haphazardly, with little regard to the size of the spaces. Few use zero as a starting point, showing a lack of understanding of the origin concept. At age 4-5, however, many children can, with opportunities to learn, become less dependent on perceptual cues and thus make progress in reasoning about or measuring quantities. From kindergarten to Grade 2, children can significantly improve in measurement knowledge (Ellis, 1995). They learn to represent length with a third object, using transitivity to compare the length of two objects that are not compared directly in a wider variety of contexts (Hiebert, 1981). They can also use given units to find the length of objects and associate higher counts with longer objects (Hiebert, 1981, 1984). Some 5-year-olds and most 7-year-olds can use the concept of unit to make inferences about the relative size of objects; for example, if the numbers of units are the same, but the units are different, the total size is different (Nunes and Bryant, 1996).

Children as young as kindergartners may be proficient with a conventional ruler and understand quantification in limited measurement contexts. However, their skill decreases when features of the ruler deviate from the convention. Thus, measurement is supported by characteristics of measurement tools, but children still need to develop understanding of key measurement concepts. For example, they may initially iterate a unit leaving gaps between subsequent units or overlapping adjacent units (Horvath and Lehrer, 2000; Lehrer, 2003). These children may think of measuring as the physical activity of placing units along a path in some manner, rather than the activity of covering the space/length of the object with no gaps. Furthermore, children often begin counting at the numeral 1 on a ruler (Lehrer, 2003) or, when counting paces heel-to-toe, start their count with the movement of the first foot, missing the first foot and counting the second foot as one (Lehrer, 2003; Stephan et al., 2003). Again, children may not be thinking about measuring as covering space. Rather, the numerals on a ruler (or the placement of a foot) signify when to start counting, not an amount of space that has already been covered (i.e., 1 is the space from the beginning of the ruler to the hash mark, not the hash mark itself). Many children initially find it necessary to iterate the unit until it "fills up" the length of the object and will not extend the unit past the end point of the object they are measuring (Stephan et al., 2003). Finally, many children do not understand that units must be of equal size. They will even measure with tools subdivided into different size units and conclude that quantities with more units are larger (Ellis et al., 2000). This may be a deleterious side effect of counting, in which children learn that the size of objects does not affect the result of counting (Mix, Huttenlocher, and Levine, 2002). However, the researchers base this interpretation on the assumption that units are always "given" in counting contexts. In fact, there are counting contexts in which this is not the case, such as counting whole toy people constructed in two parts, top and bottom, when some are fastened and some are separated (Sophian and Kailihiwa, 1998).

Thus, significant development occurs in the early childhood years. However, the foundational ideas about length are usually not integrated, even by the primary grades. For example, children may still not understand the importance of, or be able to create, equal size units (Clements et al., 1997a; Lehrer, Jenkins, and Osana, 1998; Miller, 1984). This indicates that children have not necessarily differentiated fully between counting discrete objects and measuring. Even if they show competence with rulers and are given identical units, children may not spontaneously iterate those they have if they do not have a sufficient number to measure an object (Lehrer, Jenkins, and Osana, 1998)—even when the units are rulers themselves (Clements, 1999c). Some children can or do not mentally partition the object to be measured.

Many recent curricula or other instructional guides advise a sequence of instruction in which children compare lengths, measure with nonstandard units, incorporate the use of manipulative standard units, and measure with a ruler (Clements, 1999c; Kamii and Clark, 1997). The basis for this sequence is, explicitly or implicitly, the theory of measurement of Piaget et al. (1960). The argument is that this approach motivates children to see the need for a standard measuring unit.

Although such an approach has been shown to be effective, it may not be necessary to follow a nonstandard-to-standard units approach. For example, Boulton-Lewis et al. (1996) found that children used nonstandard units unsuccessfully but were successful at an earlier age with standard units and measuring instruments. The researchers concluded that nonstandard units are not a good way to initially help children understand the need for standardized conventional units in the length measuring process. Just as interesting were children's strategy preferences. Children of every age preferred to use standard rulers, even though their teachers were encouraging them to use nonstandard units.

Furthermore, children measured correctly with a ruler before they could devise a measurement strategy using nonstandard units. To realize that arbitrary units are not reliable, a child must reconcile the varying lengths and numbers of arbitrary units. Emphasizing nonstandard units too early may defeat the purpose it is intended to achieve. That is, early emphasis on various nonstandard units may interfere with children's development of the basic measurement concepts required to understand the need for standard units. In contrast, using manipulative standard units, or even standard rulers, is less demanding and appears to be a more interesting and meaningful real-world activity for young children (Boulton-Lewis et al., 1996). These findings have been supported by additional research (Boulton-Lewis, 1987; Clements and Battista, 2001; Clements et al., 1997b; Héraud, 1989).

Thus, early experience measuring with different units may be exactly the wrong thing to do. Another study (Nunes, Light, and Mason, 1993) suggests that children can meaningfully use rulers before they reinvent such ideas as units and iteration. In it, children ages 6 to 8 communicated about lengths using string, centimeter rulers, or one ruler and one broken ruler starting at 4 cm. The traditional ruler supported the children's reasoning more effectively than the string; their accurate performance almost doubled. Their strategies and language (it is as long as the "little line just after three") indicated that children gave "correct responses based on rigorous procedures, clearly profiting from the numerical representation available through the ruler" (p. 46). They did even better with the *broken* ruler than the string, showing that they were not just reading numbers off the ruler. The unusual context confused children only 20 percent of the time. The researchers concluded that conventional units already chosen and built into the ruler do not make measurement more difficult. Indeed, children benefited from the numerical representation provided by even the broken ruler.

Such research has led several authors to argue that early rule use should be encouraged, not avoided or delayed (Clements, 1999c; Nührenbörger, 2001; Nunes et al., 1993). Rulers allow children to connect instruction to their previous measurement experiences with conventional tools. In contrast, dealing with informal, 3-D units deemphasizes the one-dimensional (1-D) nature of length and focuses on the counting of discrete objects. In this way, it deemphasizes both the zero point and the iteration of line segment lengths as units (Bragg and Outhred, 2001).

The Piagetian-based argument, that children must conserve length before they can make sense of ready-made systems, such as rulers (or computer tools, such as those discussed in the following section), may be an overstatement. Findings of these studies support a Vygotskian perspective (Ellis et al., 2000; Miller, 1989), in which rulers are viewed as cultural instruments children can appropriate. That is, children can use rulers, appropriate them, and so build new mental tools. Not only do children prefer using rulers, but also they can use them meaningfully and in combination with manipulable units to develop understanding of length measurement. In general, measurement procedures can serve as cognitive tools (Miller, 1989) developed to solve certain practical problems and organize the way children think about amount. Measurement concepts may originally be organized in terms of the contexts and procedures used to judge, compare, or measure specific attributes (Miller, 1989). If so, transformations that do not change length but do change number, such as cutting, may be particularly difficult for children, more so than traditional conservation questions. Children need to learn to distinguish the different attributes (e.g. length, number) and learn which transformations affect which attributes.

Another Piagetian idea, from the field of social cognition, is that conflict is the genesis of cognitive growth. One series of studies, however, indicates that this is not always so. If two strategies, measurement and direct comparison, were in conflict, children learned little and benefited little from verbal instruction. However, if children saw that the results of measurement and direct comparison agreed, then they were more likely to use measurement later than were children who observed both procedures but did not have the opportunity to compare their results (Bryant, 1982). This is a case in which presenting children with conflicting information (between strategies or between results of measuring with different units) too soon is unhelpful or deleterious.

Whatever the specific instructional approach taken, research demonstrates several implications. Measurement should not be taught as a simple skill. It is a complex combination of concepts and skills that develops over years. Teachers who understand the foundational concepts of measurement will be better able to interpret children's understanding and ask questions that will lead them to construct these ideas. Both research with children and interviews with teachers support the claims that (a) the principles of measurement are difficult for children, (b) they require more attention in school than is usually given, (c) time needs to first be spent in informal measurement, in which the use of measurement principles is evident, and (d) transition from informal to formal measurement needs much more time and care, with instruction in formal measure always returning to basic principles (see Irwin, Vistro-Yu, and Ell, 2004).

The sequence in Table 6-3 summarizes achievable goals in linear measurement that have been employed in pilot-testing of research-based curricula (Casey et al., 2004; Clements and Sarama, 2004; Greenes et al., 2004; Starkey et al., 2004). Again, evaluations confirm the appropriateness of the sequencing (Clements and Sarama, 2007c, in press; Starkey et al., 2004, 2006).

## Area Measurement and Spatial Structuring

Area is an amount of 2-D surface that is contained within a boundary. Area measurement assumes that a suitable 2-D region is chosen as a unit, congruent regions have equal areas, regions do not overlap, and the area of the union of two regions that do not overlap (disjoint union) is the sum of their areas (Reynolds and Wheatley, 1996). Thus, finding the area of a region can be thought of as tiling (or equal partitioning) a region with a 2-D unit of measure. Such understandings are complex, and children develop them over time. These area understandings do not develop well in traditional U.S. instruction (Carpenter et al., 1975), not only for young children, but also for preservice teachers (Enochs and Gabel, 1984). A study of children from Grades 1, 2, and 3 revealed little understanding of area measurement (Lehrer, Jenkins, and Osana, 1998). Asked how much space a square (and a triangle) cover, 41 percent of children used a ruler to measure length. Although area measurement is typically emphasized in the intermediate grades, the literature suggests that some less formal aspects of area measurement can be introduced in earlier years. Concepts that are essential to understanding and learning area measurement are described in Appendix B. One especially important one, spatial structuring, is discussed next.

Nascent awareness of area is often noticed in informal observations, such as when a child asks for pieces of colored paper to cover their table. A way to more formally assess children's understanding of area is through comparison tasks. Some researchers report that preschoolers use only one dimension or one salient aspect of the stimulus to compare the area of two surfaces (Bausano and Jeffrey, 1975; Maratsos, 1973; Mullet and Paques, 1991; Piaget et al., 1960; Raven and Gelman, 1984; Russell, 1975; Sena

**TABLE 6-3** Linear Measurement (Space in One Dimension)

| Steps/ Ages (Levels of Thinking) | Goals: A. Perceive, Say, Describe/Discuss, and Construct Objects in 1-D Space | B. Perceive, Say, Describe/Discuss, and Construct Spatial Relations in 1-D Space | C. Perceive, Say, Describe/Discuss, and Construct Compositions and Decompositions in 1-D Space |
|---|---|---|---|
| **Step 1 (Ages 2 and 3)** | | | |
| Thinking visually/ holistically | Informally recognize length as extent of 1-D space. Compare 2 objects directly, noting equality or inequality. | | Informally combine objects in linear extent. |
| **Step 2 (Age 4)** | | | |
| Thinking about parts | Compare the length of two objects by representing them with a third object.<br>• Initial measurement by laying units end to end, often with units that are notably square or cubical (to facilitate physical concatenation). | | Understand that lengths can be concatenated. |
| Relating parts and wholes | Seriate up to six objects by length (e.g., connecting cube towers). | | |
| **Step 3 (Age 5)** | | | |
| Thinking about parts | Measure by repeated use of a unit, moving from units that are notably square or cubical to those that more closely embody one dimension (e.g., sticks or stirrers). | | |
| Relating parts and wholes | Seriate any number of objects by length, even if differences between consecutive lengths are not palpable perceptually.<br>• Initial measurement with simple unit rulers, including sticks with unit lengths marked off and other unit rulers.<br>• Explore the relationship between the size and number of units.<br>Interpret bar graphs to answer questions such as "more," "less," as well as simple trends, using length of the bars. | | Add two lengths to obtain the length of a whole. |

NOTE: Less time on 1-D than on 2-D; about 5 percent of the time on 1-D.

and Smith, 1990). For example, 4- and 5-year-olds may match only one side of figures when attempting to compare their areas (Silverman, York, and Zuidema, 1984). Others claim that children can integrate more than one feature of a region but judge areas with additive combination, for example, making implicit area judgments based on the longest single dimension (Mullet and Paques, 1991) or height + width rules (Cuneo, 1980; Rulence-Paques and Mullet, 1998). Children ages 6 to 8 use a linear extent rule, such as the diagonal of a rectangle. Only after this age do most children move to explicit use of spatial structuring of multiplicative rules to solve those studies' tasks. Note that this does not imply formal use of multiplication, but only that their estimates are best approximated by the area formula.

In most of these studies, children did not interact with the materials. Doing so often changes their strategies and improves their estimates. Children as young as age 3 are more likely to make estimates consistent with multiplicative rules when using manipulatives than when just asked to make a perceptual estimation. For example, they are more accurate when they are asked to count out the right number of square tiles to cover a floor and put them in a cup (Miller, 1984). Similarly, children ages 5 to 6 were more likely to use strategies consistent with multiplicative rules after playing with the stimulus materials (Wolf, 1995).

A more accurate strategy for comparing areas than visual estimation is superimposition. Children as young as age 3 have a rudimentary concept of area based on placing regions on top of one another, but it is not until age 5 or 6 that their strategy is accurate and efficient. As an illustration, when asked to manipulate regions, preschoolers in one study used superimposition instead of the less precise strategies of laying objects side-by-side or comparing single sides, both of which use one dimension at best in estimating the area (Yuzawa, Bart, and Yuzawa, 2000). Again, the facilitative effect of manipulation is shown. Children were given target squares or rectangles and asked to choose one that was equal to two standard rectangles in area. They performed better when they placed the standard figures on the targets than when they made perceptual judgments. They also performed better when one target could be overlapped completely with the standard figures (even in the perceptual condition, which suggests that they performed a mental superposition).

Higher steps in thinking about area may have their roots in the internalization of such procedures as placing figures on one another, which may be aided by cultural tools (manipulatives) or scaffolding by adults (see Vygotsky, 1934/1986). For example, kindergartners who were given practice with origami (paper folding) increased the spontaneous use of the procedure of placing one figure on another for comparing sizes (Yuzawa et al., 1999). Because origami practice includes the repeated procedure of folding one sheet into two halves, origami practice might facilitate the development of an area concept, which is related to the spontaneous use of the procedure.

To measure, a unit must be established. Teachers often assume that the product of two lengths structures a region into an area of 2-D units for students. However, the construction of a 2-D array from linear units is nontrivial. Young children often cannot partition and conserve area and instead use counting as a basis for comparing. For example, when it was determined that one share of pieces of paper cookie was too little, preschoolers cut one of that share's pieces into two and handed them both back, apparently believing that the share was now "more" (Miller, 1984).

As with length measurement, children often cover space, but they do not initially do so without gaps or overlapping (i.e., they do not tile the region with units). They also initially do not extend units over the boundaries when a subdivision of that unit is needed to fill the surface (Stephan et al., 2003). Even more limiting, children often choose units that physically resemble the region they are covering; for example, choosing bricks to cover a rectangular region and beans to cover an outline of their hands (Lehrer, 2003; Lehrer, Jenkins, and Osana, 1998; Nunes et al., 1993). They also mix different shapes (and areas), such as rectangular and triangular, to cover the same region and accept a measure of "7" even if the seven covering shapes are of different sizes (84 percent of primary grade children; Lehrer, Jenkins, and Osana, 1998). These concepts have to be developed before children can use iteration of equal units to measure area with understanding. Once these problems have been solved, children need to structure 2-D space into an organized array of units to achieve multiplicative thinking in determining volume, a concept to which we now turn.

### Volume Measurement

Volume introduces even more complexity, not only in adding a third dimension and thus presenting a significant challenge to students' spatial structuring, but also in the very nature of the materials that are measured using volume. This leads to two ways to measure volume, illustrated by "packing" a space, such as a 3-D array with cubic units, and "filling" with iterations of a fluid unit that takes the shape of the container. For the latter, the unit structure may be psychologically 1-D for some children (i.e., simple iterative counting that is not processed as geometric 3-D), especially, for example, in filling a cylindrical jar in which the (linear) height corresponds to the volume (Curry and Outhred, 2005). Given the possible complexities, is either of these more or less appropriate for young children, beyond, say, informal experiences?

For children in Grades 1-4, competence in filling volume (e.g., estimating and measuring the number of cups of rice that filled a container) was about equivalent to their competence in corresponding length tasks (Curry and Outhred, 2005). The relationship is consistent with the notion that the structure of the task is 1-D, exemplified by some students' treating the height of the rice in the container as if it were a unit length and iterating it, either mentally or using their fingers, up the side of the container. Some students performed better on length, others on filling volume, giving no evidence of a relationship between the two. The task contained some extra demands, such as creating equal measurements; even many first graders made sure that the cup was not over- or underfilled for each iteration. In another study, 3- and 4-year-olds understood that unit size affects the measurement of the object's volume (Sophian, 2002). Thus, simple experience with filling volume may be appropriate for young children.

On the other hand, packing volume is more difficult than length and area (Curry and Outhred, 2005). Most children had little idea of how to estimate or measure on packing tasks. There were substantial increases from Grades 2 to 4, but even the older students' scores were below the corresponding scores for the area task. Furthermore, there was a suggestion that understanding of area is a prerequisite to understanding packing volume. Therefore, children should have many experiences building with blocks and filling boxes with cubes. A developmental progression is provided in Table 6-2. A full conceptual understanding of 3-D space will develop only over several years for most children.

## Achievable and Foundational Measurement in One, Two, and Three Dimensions

In this section, we describe children's development of measurement in one, two, and three dimensions. We do not consider measurement of nongeometric attributes, such as weight/mass, capacity, time, and color, because these are more appropriately considered in science and social studies curricula. Again, for each area outlined below, children should be engaged in activities that cover a range of difficulty, including perceive, say, describe/discuss, and construct. Table 6-3 outlines the path for measurement of length.

### Step 1 (Ages 2 and 3)

#### *Objects and Spatial Relations*

Young children naturally encounter and discuss quantities in their play (Ginsburg, Inoue, and Seo, 1999). They first learn to use words that represent quantity or magnitude of a certain attribute. Facilitating this language is important not only to develop communication abilities, but for the development of mathematical concepts. Simply using labels such as

"Daddy/Mommy/Baby" and "big/little/tiny" helped children as young as 3 years to represent and apply higher order seriation abilities, even in the face of distracting visual factors, an improvement equivalent to a 2-year gain.

At the visual/holistic level (see Table 6-3), children begin by informally recognizing length as extent of 1-D space. For example, they may remark of a road made with building blocks, "This is long." They can then compare two objects directly and recognize and describe their equality (e.g., "You are just as tall as I am!") or inequality (e.g., "My pencil is longer than yours") in length.

*Compositions and Decompositions*

At the visual/holistic level, children compose lengths intuitively. For example, they may lay building blocks along a path to "make a long road."

**Step 2 (Age 4)**

*Objects and Spatial Relations*

At the thinking about parts level, preschool children learn to compare the length of two objects by representing them with a third object and using transitive reasoning (i.e., indirect comparison) (Boulton-Lewis et al., 1996). Again, language, such as the differences between counting-based terms (e.g., a toy, two trucks) and mass terms (e.g., some sand), can help children form relationships between counting and continuous measurement (Huntley-Fenner, 2001).

Preschoolers also begin actual measurement by laying physical units end to end and counting them to measure a length. However, they may not recognize the need for equal-length units and initially may make errors, such as leaving gaps between units. One way to engage in discussions of such concepts is to apply the resulting measures to comparison situations. These concepts and skills develop in parallel with competencies in seriating lengths, which emerge last and mark the first level of thinking about relating parts and wholes.

Preschoolers also begin to be able to cover a rectangular space with physical tiles and represent their tilings with simple drawings, although they may leave gaps in each and may not align all the squares.

*Compositions and Decompositions*

At the thinking about parts level, preschoolers understand that lengths can be concatenated in this way. This understanding, initially implicit, is revealed as children operate on objects.

### Step 3 (Age 5)

*Objects and Spatial Relations*

Kindergartners move to more sophisticated understanding at the thinking about parts level by measuring via the repeated use of a unit. However, they initially may not be precise in such iterations. Beginning to develop aspects of thinking at the level of relating parts and wholes, they can explore the concept of the inverse relationship between the size of the unit of length and the number of units required to cover a specific length or distance, recognizing it at least at an intuitive level. However, they may not appreciate the need for identical units. Work with manipulative units of standard measure (e.g., 1 inch or 1 cm), along with related use of rulers and consistent discussion, will help children learn both the concepts and procedures of linear measurement.

Kindergartners also can learn to fill containers with cubes, filling one layer at a time, intentionally, all of which involves relationships at the thinking about parts level of thinking. In a similar vein, they can learn to accurately count the number of squares in a rectangular array, using increasingly systematic strategies, including counting in rows or columns. They represent a complete covering of a rectangle's area (although initially there may be some inaccuracies, such as in the alignment of drawn shapes).

*Compositions and Decompositions*

Kindergartners understand length composition explicitly. For example, they can add to lengths to obtain the length of the whole. They can use a simple ruler (or put a length of connecting cubes together) to measure one plastic snake and measure the length of another snake to find the total of their lengths. Or, more practically, they can measure all sides of a table with unmarked (foot) rulers to measure how much ribbon they would need to decorate the perimeter of the table. Their use of rows or columns in covering a rectangular area also implies at least an implicit composition of units into a composite unit.

### Instruction to Support the Teaching-Learning Path

*Length*

To move children through the teaching-learning path, teachers of the youngest children should observe children in their play, because they encounter and discuss measurable quantities frequently (Ginsburg, Inoue, and Seo, 1999). Using such words as "bigger/larger/smaller," and, as soon as possible, "longer/shorter" and "taller/shorter" directs children's attention to these attributes and also helps them apply seriation abilities. Teachers should listen carefully to see how they are interpreting and using language (e.g., length as the distance between end points or as "one end sticking out").

Children should be given a variety of experiences comparing the size of objects. Once they can do so by direct comparison, they should compare several items to a single item, such as finding all the objects in the classroom longer than their forearm. Ideas of transitivity can then be explicitly discussed. Next, children should engage in experiences that allow them to connect number to length. Teachers should provide children with both conventional rulers and manipulative units using standard units of length, such as centimeter cubes (specifically labeled "length-units"; from Dougherty and Slovin, 2004). As they explore with these tools, the ideas of length-unit iteration (e.g., not leaving space between successive length-units), correct alignment (with a ruler), and the zero-point concept can be developed. Having older (or more advanced) children draw, cut out, and use their own rulers can be used to discuss these aspects explicitly.

In all activities, teachers should focus on the meaning that the numerals on the ruler have for children, such as enumerating lengths rather than discrete numbers. In other words, classroom discussions should focus on "What are you counting?" with the answer in length-units. Given that counting discrete items often correctly teaches children that the length-unit size does not matter, teachers should plan experiences and reflections on the nature of properties of the length-unit in various discrete counting and measurement contexts. Comparing results of measuring the same object with manipulatives and with rulers and using manipulative length-units to make their own rulers help children connect their experiences and ideas.

In second or third grade, teachers might introduce the need for standard length-units and the relation between the size and number of length-units. The relationship between the size and number of length-units, the need for standardization of length-units, and additional measuring devices can be explored at this time. The early use of multiple nonstandard length-units would not be used until this point (see Carpenter and Lewis, 1976). Instruction focusing on children's interpretations of their measuring activity can enable them to use flexible starting points on a ruler to indicate measures successfully (Lubinski and Thiessen, 1996). Without such attention, children are just reading off whatever ruler number aligns with the end of the object into the intermediate grades (Lehrer, Jenkins, and Osana, 1998).

By kindergarten, length is used in other areas, such as understanding addition and graphing. For example, bar graphs use length to represent counts or measures. Kindergartners can answer such questions as "more" and "less," as well as simple trends, using length of the bars.

Emphasis on children's solving real measurement problems and, in so doing, building and iterating units, as well as units of units, helps them develop strong concepts and skills. Teachers should help children closely connect the use of manipulative units and rulers. When conducted in this way, measurement tools and procedures become tools for mathematics and tools for thinking about mathematics (Clements, 1999c; Miller, 1984, 1989). Well before first grade, children have begun the journey toward that end.

### *Area*

Children need to structure an array to understand area as truly 2-D (see Appendix B). Play with structured materials, such as unit blocks, pattern blocks, and tiles, can lay the groundwork for children's spatial structuring, although achieving the conceptual benchmark will not be achieved until after the primary grades for most children, even with high-quality instruction. In brief, the too-frequent practice of simple counting of units to find area (achievable by preschoolers) leading directly to teaching formulas may not build the requisite foundational concepts (Lehrer, 2003). Instead, educators should build on young children's initial spatial intuitions and appreciate their need to construct the idea of measurement units—including development of a measurement sense for standard units, for example, finding common objects in the environment that have a unit measure. Children need to have many experiences covering quantities with appropriate measurement units, counting those units, and spatially structuring the object they are to measure, in order to build a firm foundation for eventual use for formulas. For example, children might build rectangular arrays with square tiles and learn to count the number of manipulatives used in each. Eventually, they need to link counting by groups to reflect the structure of rectangular arrays, for example, counting the squares in an array by skip-counting the number in each row.

This long developmental process usually only begins in the years before first grade. However, we should also appreciate the importance of these early conceptualizations. For example, 3- and 4-year-olds' use of a linear rating scale to judge area, even if using an additive rule, indicates an impressive level of quantitative ability and, according to some, nascent mental structures for algebra at an early age (Cuneo, 1980).

Competencies in the major realms of geometry/spatial thinking and number are connected throughout development. The earliest competencies may share common perceptual and representational origins (Mix, Huttenlocher, and Levine, 2002). Infants are sensitive to both the amount of liquid in a container (Gao, Levine, and Huttenlocher, 2000) and the distance away a toy is hidden in a long sandbox (Newcombe, Huttenlocher, and Learmonth, 1999). Visual-spatial deficits in early childhood are detrimental to children's development of numerical competencies (Semrud-Clikeman and Hynd, 1990; Spiers, 1987). Other evidence shows specific spatially related learning disabilities in arithmetic, possibly more so for boys than girls (Share, Moffitt, and Silva, 1988). Primary school children's thinking about units and units of units was found to be consistent in both spatial and numerical problems (Clements et al., 1997a). In this and other ways, specific spatial abilities appear to be related to other mathematical competencies (Brown and Wheatley, 1989; Clements and Battista, 1992; Fennema and Carpenter, 1981; Wheatley, Brown, and Solano, 1994). Geometric measurement connects the spatial and numeric realms explicitly.

## SUMMARY

This chapter describes geometry and spatial thinking and measurement, which comprise the second essential domain for young children's mathematical development. The research in this domain is less developed than for number, but it does provide guidance for educators regarding what young children can and should do to develop competence in these areas. The teaching-learning path for geometry and spatial relations demonstrates how young children move through levels of thinking as they learn about 2-D and 3-D objects. The use of manipulatives, pictures, and computers play an important role in facilitating children's progress along this path. Early childhood teachers should help children extend their thinking by building on simple conventional models (e.g., child represents classroom with cut out pictures) and challenge them by asking them to use geometric correspondences (e.g., direction—which way?, identification—which object?) to solve problems.

Measurement, the second major area covered in this chapter, connects and enriches the two crucial domains of geometry and number. The teaching-learning path for measurement describes children's developing competence in linear measurement and initial steps toward understanding areas and volume. The teaching-learning path outlined for length emphasizes the need to provide experiences that allow children to compare the size of objects and to connect number to length. Children also need opportunities to solve real measurement problems which can help build their understanding of units, length-unit iteration, correct alignment and the zero-point concept. Children's early competency in measurement is facilitated by play with structured materials, such as unit blocks, pattern blocks, and tiles and strengthened through opportunities to reflect on and discuss their experiences.

It is important to note that the potential of young children's learning in geometry and measurement if a conscientious, sequenced development of spatial thinking and geometry were provided to them throughout their earliest years is not yet known. Research on the learning of shapes and certain aspects of visual literacy suggests the inclusion of these topics in the early years can be powerful. Specific spatial abilities appear to be related to other mathematical competencies and geometric measurement connects the spatial and numeric realms explicitly (Brown and Wheatley, 1989; Clements and Battista, 1992; Fennema and Carpenter, 1981; Wheatley et al., 1994). However, there is insufficient evidence on the effects (efficacy and efficiency) of including such topics as congruence, similarity, transformations, and angles in curricula and teaching at specific age levels (Clements and Sarama, 2007b; National Mathematics Advisory Panel, 2008). Such research, as well as longitudinal research on many such topics, is needed.

## REFERENCES AND BIBLIOGRAPHY


Anderson, J.R. (2000). *Cognitive Psychology and Its Implications* (5th ed.). New York: W.H. Freeman.

Ansari, D., Donlan, C., Thomas, M.S.C., Ewing, S.A., Peen, T., and Karmiloff-Smith, A. (2003). What makes counting count? Verbal and visuo-spatial contributions to typical and atypical number development. *Journal of Experimental Child Psychology, 85*, 50-62.

Battista, M.T., and Clements, D.H. (1996). Students' understanding of three-dimensional rectangular arrays of cubes. *Journal for Research in Mathematics Education, 27*, 258-292.

Battista, M.T., Clements, D.H., Arnoff, J., Battista, K., and Borrow, C.V.A. (1998). Students' spatial structuring of 2D arrays of squares. *Journal for Research in Mathematics Education, 29*, 503-532.

Bausano, M.K., and Jeffrey, W.E. (1975). Dimensional salience and judgments of bigness by three-year-old children. *Child Development, 46*, 988-991.

Beaton, A.E., Mullis, I.V.S., Martin, M.O., Gonzalez, E J., Kelly, D.L., and Smith, T.A. (1997, November). *Mathematics Achievement in the Middle School Years: IEA's Third International Mathematics and Science Study (TIMSS)*. Available: http://timss.bc.edu/timss1995i/MathB.html [accessed October 2008].

Beilin, H. (1984). Cognitive theory and mathematical cognition: Geometry and space. In B. Gholson and T.L. Rosenthal (Eds.), *Applications of Cognitive-Developmental Theory* (pp. 49-93). New York: Academic Press.

Beilin, H., Klein, A., and Whitehurst, B. (1982). *Strategies and Structures in Understanding Geometry.* New York: City University of New York.

Bellugi, U., Lichtenberger, L., Jones, W., Lai, Z., and St. George, M. (2000). The neurocognitive profile and Williams syndrome: A complex pattern of strengths and weaknesses. *Journal of Cognitive Neuroscience, 12*(Suppl.), 7-29.

Bishop, A.J. (1980). Spatial abilities and mathematics achievement—A review. *Educational Studies in Mathematics, 11*, 257-269.

Blades, M., Spencer, C., Plester, B., and Desmond, K. (2004). Young children's recognition and representation of urban landscapes: From aerial photographs and in toy play. In G.L. Allen (Ed.), *Human Spatial Memory: Remembering Where* (pp. 287-308). Mahwah, NJ: Erlbaum.

Blaut, J.M., and Stea, D. (1974). Mapping at the age of three. *Journal of Geography, 73*(7), 5-9.

Bornstein, M.H., Ferdinandsen, K., and Gross, C.G. (1981). Perception of symmetry in infancy. *Developmental Psychology, 17*, 82-86.

Boulton-Lewis, G.M. (1987). Recent cognitive theories applied to sequential length measuring knowledge in young children. *British Journal of Educational Psychology, 57*, 330-342.

Boulton-Lewis, G.M., Wilss, L.A., and Mutch, S.L. (1996). An analysis of young children's strategies and use of devices of length measurement. *Journal of Mathematical Behavior, 15*, 329-347.

Bowerman, M. (1996). Learning how to structure space for language: A cross-linguistic perspective. In P. Bloom, M.A. Peterson, L. Nadel, and M.F. Garrett (Eds.), *Language and Space* (pp. 385-436). Cambridge, MA: MIT Press.

Bragg, P., and Outhred, L. (2001). So that's what a centimetre looks like: Students' understandings of linear units. In M.V.D. Heuvel-Panhuizen (Ed.), *Proceedings of the 25th Conference of the International Group for the Psychology in Mathematics Education* (vol. 2, pp. 209-216). Utrecht, The Netherlands: Freudenthal Institute.

Bronowski, J. (1947). Mathematics. In D. Thompson and J. Reeves (Eds.), *The Quality of Education*. London, England: Muller.

Brosnan, M.J. (1998). Spatial ability in children's play with Lego blocks. *Perceptual and Motor Skills, 87*, 19-28.

Brown, D.L., and Wheatley, G.H. (1989). Relationship between spatial knowledge and mathematics knowledge. In C.A. Maher, G.A. Goldin, and R.B. Davis (Eds.), *Proceedings of the Eleventh Annual Meeting, North American Chapter of the International Group for the Psychology of Mathematics Education* (pp. 143-148). New Brunswick, NJ: Rutgers University.

Bryant, P.E. (1982). The role of conflict and of agreement between intellectual strategies in children's ideas about measurement. *British Journal of Psychology, 73*, 242-251.

Burger, W.F., and Shaughnessy, J.M. (1986). Characterizing the van Hiele levels of development in geometry. *Journal for Research in Mathematics Education, 17*, 31-48.

Carpenter, T.P., and Lewis, R. (1976). The development of the concept of a standard unit of measure in young children. *Journal for Research in Mathematics Education, 7*, 53-58.

Carpenter, T.P., Coburn, T., Reys, R., and Wilson, J. (1975). Notes from national assessment: Basic concepts of area and volume. *Arithmetic Teacher, 22*, 501-507.

Carpenter, T.P., Corbitt, M.K., Kepner, H.S., Lindquist, M.M., and Reys, R.E. (1980). National assessment. In E. Fennema (Ed.), *Mathematics Education Research: Implications for the 1980s* (pp. 22-38). Alexandria, VA: Association for Supervision and Curriculum Development.

Casey, B., Paugh, P., and Ballard, N. (2002). *Sneeze Builds a Castle*. Bothell, WA: The Wright Group/McGraw-Hill.

Casey, B., Kersh, J.E., and Young, J.M. (2004). Storytelling sagas: An effective medium for teaching early childhood mathematics. *Early Childhood Research Quarterly, 19*, 167-172.

Casey, M.B. (2005, April). *Evaluation of NSF-Funded Mathematics Materials: Use of Storytelling Contexts to Improve Kindergartners' Geometry and Block-Building Skills*. Paper presented at the National Council of Supervisors of Mathematics, Anaheim, CA.

Casey, M.B., and Erkut, S. (2005, April). *Early Spatial Interventions Benefit Girls and Boys*. Paper presented at the Biennial Meeting of the Society for Research in Child Development, Atlanta, GA.

Casey, M.B., and Erkut, S. (in press). Use of a storytelling context to improve girls' and boys' geometry skills in kindergarten. *Journal of Applied Developmental Psychology.*

Casey, M.B., Nuttall, R.L., and Pezaris, E. (2001). Spatial-mechanical reasoning skills versus mathematics self-confidence as mediators of gender differences on mathematics subtests using cross-national gender-based items. *Journal for Research in Mathematics Education, 32*, 28-57.

Casey, M.B., Andrews, N., Schindler, H., Kersh, J.E., and Samper, A. (in press). The development of spatial skills through interventions involving block building activities. *Cognition and Instruction.*

Clements, D.H. (1999a). Concrete manipulatives, concrete ideas. *Contemporary Issues in Early Childhood, 1*(1), 45-60.

Clements, D.H. (1999b). Subitizing: What is it? Why teach it? *Teaching Children Mathematics, 5*, 400-405.

Clements, D.H. (1999c). Teaching length measurement: Research challenges. *School Science and Mathematics, 99*(1), 5-11.

Clements, D.H. (2003). Teaching and learning geometry. In J. Kilpatrick, W.G. Martin, and D. Schifter (Eds.), *A Research Companion to Principles and Standards for School Mathematics* (pp. 151-178). Reston, VA: National Council of Teachers of Mathematics.

Clements, D.H., and Barrett, J. (1996). Representing, connecting and restructuring knowledge: A micro-genetic analysis of a child's learning in an open-ended task involving perimeter, paths and polygons. In E. Jakubowski, D. Watkins, and H. Biske (Eds.), *Proceedings of the 18th Annual Meeting of the North America Chapter of the International Group for the Psychology of Mathematics Education* (vol. 1, pp. 211-216). Columbus, OH: ERIC Clearinghouse for Science, Mathematics, and Environmental Education.

Clements, D.H., and Battista, M.T. (1991). *The Development of a Logo-Based Elementary School Geometry Curriculum.* Final Report, NSF Grant No. MDR 8651668. Buffalo, NY/Kent State, OH: State University of New York and Kent State University Presses.

Clements, D.H., and Battista, M.T. (1992). Geometry and spatial reasoning. In D.A. Grouws (Ed.), *Handbook of Research on Mathematics Teaching and Learning* (pp. 420-464). New York: Macmillan.

Clements, D.H., and Battista, M.T. (2001). Length, perimeter, area, and volume. In L.S. Grinstein and S.I. Lipsey (Eds.), *Encyclopedia of Mathematics Education* (pp. 406-410). New York: RoutledgeFalmer.

Clements, D.H., and McMillen, S. (1996). Rethinking "concrete" manipulatives. *Teaching Children Mathematics, 2*(5), 270-279.

Clements, D.H., and Sarama, J. (1998). *Building Blocks—Foundations for Mathematical Thinking, Pre-Kindergarten to Grade 2: Research-based Materials Development.* NSF Grant No. ESI-9730804. Buffalo: State University of New York. Available: http://www.gse.buffalo.edu/org/buildingblocks/ [accessed July 2009].

Clements, D.H., and Sarama, J. (2003). Young children and technology: What does the research say? *Young Children, 58*(6), 34-40.

Clements, D.H., and Sarama, J. (2004). Building blocks for early childhood mathematics. *Early Childhood Research Quarterly, 19*, 181-189.

Clements, D.H., and Sarama, J. (2007a). *Building Blocks—SRA Real Math Teacher's Edition, Grade PreK.* Columbus, OH: SRA/McGraw-Hill.

Clements, D.H., and Sarama, J. (2007b). Early childhood mathematics learning. In F.K. Lester, Jr. (Ed.), *Second Handbook of Research on Mathematics Teaching and Learning* (pp. 461-555). New York: Information Age.

Clements, D.H., and Sarama, J. (2007c). Effects of a preschool mathematics curriculum: Summative research on the building blocks project. *Journal for Research in Mathematics Education, 38*, 136-163.

Clements, D.H., and Sarama, J. (in press). Experimental evaluation of the effects of a research-based preschool mathematics curriculum. *American Educational Research Journal.*

Clements, D.H., and Stephan, M. (2004). Measurement in preK-2 mathematics. In D.H. Clements, J. Sarama and A.-M. DiBiase (Eds.), *Engaging Young Children in Mathematics: Standards for Early Childhood Mathematics Education* (pp. 299-317). Mahwah, NJ: Erlbaum.

Clements, D.H., Sarama, J., Battista, M.T., and Swaminathan, S. (1996). Development of students' spatial thinking in a curriculum unit on geometric motions and area. In E. Jakubowski, D. Watkins, and H. Biske (Eds.), *Proceedings of the 18th Annual Meeting of the North America Chapter of the International Group for the Psychology of Mathematics Education* (vol. 1, pp. 217-222). Columbus, OH: ERIC Clearinghouse for Science, Mathematics, and Environmental Education.

Clements, D H., Battista, M.T., Sarama, J., and Swaminathan, S. (1997a). Development of students' spatial thinking in a unit on geometric motions and area. *The Elementary School Journal, 98*, 171-186.

Clements, D.H., Battista, M.T., Sarama, J., Swaminathan, S., and McMillen, S. (1997b). Students' development of length measurement concepts in a logo-based unit on geometric paths. *Journal for Research in Mathematics Education, 28*(1), 70-95.

Clements, D.H., Swaminathan, S., Hannibal, M.A.Z., and Sarama, J. (1999). Young children's concepts of shape. *Journal for Research in Mathematics Education, 30*, 192-212.

Clements, D.H., Battista, M.T., and Sarama, J. (2001). Logo and geometry. *Journal for Research in Mathematics Education Monograph Series, 10*.

Clements, D.H., Sarama, J., and Wilson, D.C. (2001). Composition of geometric figures. In M.v.d. Heuvel-Panhuizen (Ed.), *Proceedings of the 25th Conference of the International Group for the Psychology of Mathematics Education* (vol. 2, pp. 273-280). Utrecht, The Netherlands: Freudenthal Institute.

Clements, D.H., Wilson, D.C., and Sarama, J. (2004). Young children's composition of geometric figures: A learning trajectory. *Mathematical Thinking and Learning, 6*, 163-184.

Cooper, T.J., and Warren, E. (2007, April). *Developing Equivalence of Expressions in the Early to Middle Elementary Years.* Paper presented at the Research Pre-session of the 85th Annual Meeting of the National Council of Teachers of Mathematics, Atlanta, GA.

Cuneo, D. (1980). A general strategy for quantity judgments: The height + width rule. *Child Development, 51*, 299-301.

Curry, M., and Outhred, L. (2005). Conceptual understanding of spatial measurement. In P. Clarkson, A. Downtown, D. Gronn, M. Horne, A. McDonough, R. Pierce and A. Roche (Eds.), *Building Connections: Research, Theory, and Practice: Proceedings of the 28th Annual Conference of the Mathematics Education Research Group of Australasia* (pp. 265-272). Melbourne, Australia: MERGA.

Dehaene, S., Izard, V., Pica, P., and Spelke, E.S. (2006). Core knowledge of geometry in an Amazonian indigene group. *Science, 311*, 381-384.

Del Grande, J.J. (1986). Can grade two children' spatial perception be improved by inserting a transformation geometry component into their mathematics program? *Dissertation Abstracts International, 47*, 3689A.

Dewey, J. (1933). *How We Think: A Restatement of the Relation of Reflective Thinking to the Educative Process.* Boston, MA: D.C. Heath.

Dougherty, B.J., and Slovin, H. (2004). Generalized diagrams as a tool for young children's problem solving. In M.J. Høines and A.B. Fuglestad (Eds.), *Proceedings of the 28th Conference of the International Group for the Psychology in Mathematics Education* (vol. 2, pp. 295-302). Bergen, Norway: Bergen University College.

Ebbeck, M. (1984). Equity for boys and girls: Some important issues. *Early Child Development and Care, 18*, 119-131.

Ehrlich, S.B., Levine, S.C., and Goldin-Meadow, S. (2005, April). *Early Sex Differences in Spatial Skill: The Implications of Spoken and Gestured Strategies.* Paper presented at the Biennial Meeting of the Society for Research in Child Development, Atlanta, GA.

Ellis, S. (1995). *Developmental Changes in Children's Understanding of measurement Procedures and Principles.* Paper presented at the biennial meetings of the Society for Research in Child Development, Indianapolis, IN.

Enochs, L.G., and Gabel, D.L. (1984). Preservice elementary teaching conceptions of volume. *School Science and Mathematics, 84*, 670-680.

Eylon, B.-S., and Rosenfeld, S. (1990). *The Agam Project: Cultivating Visual Cognition in Young Children.* Rehovot, Israel: Department of Science Teaching, Weizmann Institute of Science.

Fennema, E.H., and Carpenter, T.P. (1981). Sex-related differences in mathematics: Results from national assessment. *Mathematics Teacher, 74*, 554-559.

Fennema, E.H., and Sherman, J. (1977). Sex-related differences in mathematics achievement, spatial visualization, and affective factors. *American Educational Research Journal, 14*, 51-71.

Fennema, E.H., and Sherman, J.A. (1978). Sex-related differences in mathematics achievement and related factors. *Journal for Research in Mathematics Education, 9*, 189-203.

Fey, J., Atchison, W.F., Good, R.A., Heid, M.K., Johnson, J., Kantowski, M.G., et al. (1984). *Computing and Mathematics: The Impact on Secondary School Curricula.* College Park: University of Maryland.

Filippaki, N., and Papamichael, Y. (1997). Tutoring conjunctions and construction of geometry concepts in the early childhood education: The case of the angle. *European Journal of Psychology of Education, 12*(3), 235-247.

Fisher, N.D. (1978). Visual influences of figure orientation on concept formation in geometry. *Dissertation Abstracts International, 38*, 4639A.

Freudenthal, H. (1973). *Mathematics as an Educational Task.* Dordrecht, The Netherlands: Reidel.

Fuson, K.C., and Hall, J.W. (1982). The acquisition of early number word meanings: A conceptual analysis and review. In H.P. Ginsburg (Ed.), *Children's Mathematical Thinking* (pp. 49-107). New York: Academic Press.

Fuson, K.C., and Murray, C. (1978). The haptic-visual perception, construction, and drawing of geometric shapes by children ages two to five: A Piagetian extension. In R. Lesh and D. Mierkiewicz (Eds.), *Concerning the Development of Spatial and Geometric Concepts* (pp. 49-83). Columbus, OH: ERIC Clearinghouse for Science, Mathematics, and Environmental Education.

Fuys, D., Geddes, D., and Tischler, R. (1988). *The van Hiele Model of Thinking in Geometry Among Adolescents.* Reston, VA: National Council of Teachers of Mathematics.

Gagatsis, A., and Patronis, T. (1990). Using geometrical models in a process of reflective thinking in learning and teaching mathematics. *Educational Studies in Mathematics, 21*, 29-54.

Gao, F., Levine, S.C., and Huttenlocher, J. (2000). What do infants know about continuous quantity? *Journal of Experimental Child Psychology, 77*, 20-29.

Gelman, R., and Williams, E.M. (1997). Enabling constraints for cognitive development and learning: Domain specificity and epigenesis. In D. Kuhn and R. Siegler (Eds.), *Cognition, Perception, and Language, Volume 2: Handbook of Child Psychology* (5th ed., pp. 575-630). New York: Wiley.

Gerhardt, L.A. (1973). *Moving and Knowing: The Young Child Orients Himself in Space.* Englewood Cliffs, NJ: Prentice-Hall.

Gibson, E.J., Gibson, J.J., Pick, A.D., and Osser, H. (1962). A developmental study of the discrimination of letter-like forms. *Journal of Comparative and Physiological Psychology, 55*, 897-906.

Ginsburg, A., Cooke, G., Leinwand, S., Noell, J., and Pollock, E. (2005). *Reassessing U.S. International Mathematics Performance: New Findings from the 2003 TIMSS and PISA.* Washington, DC: American Institutes for Research.

Ginsburg, H.P., Inoue, N., and Seo, K.-H. (1999). Young children doing mathematics: Observations of everyday activities. In J.V. Copley (Ed.), *Mathematics in the Early Years* (pp. 88-99). Reston, VA: National Council of Teachers of Mathematics.

Ginsburg, H.P., Greenes, C., and Balfanz, R. (2003). *Big Math for Little Kids.* Parsippany, NJ: Dale Seymour.

Gopnik, A., and Meltzoff, A.N. (1986). Words, plans, things, and locations: Interactions between semantic and cognitive development in the one-word stage. In S.A. Kuczaj, II, and M.D. Barrett (Eds.), *The Development of Word Meaning* (pp. 199-223). Berlin, Germany: Springer-Verlag.

Greabell, L.C. (1978). The effect of stimuli input on the acquisition of introductory geometric concepts by elementary school children. *School Science and Mathematics, 78*(4), 320-326.

Greenes, C., Ginsburg, H.P., and Balfanz, R. (2004). Big math for little kids. *Early Childhood Research Quarterly, 19*, 159-166.

Guay, R.B., and McDaniel, E. (1977). The relationship between mathematics achievement and spatial abilities among elementary school children. *Journal for Research in Mathematics Education, 8*, 211-215.

Hannibal, M.A.Z., and Clements, D.H. (2008). *Young Children's Understanding of Basic Geometric Shapes.* Manuscript submitted.

Héraud, B. (1989). A conceptual analysis of the notion of length and its measure. In G. Vergnaud, J. Rogalski, and M. Artique (Eds.), *Proceedings of the 13th Conference of the International Group for the Psychology of Mathematics Education* (pp. 83-90). Paris, France: City University.

Hiebert, J.C. (1981). Cognitive development and learning linear measurement. *Journal for Research in Mathematics Education, 12*, 197-211.

Hiebert, J.C. (1984). Why do some children have trouble learning measurement concepts? *Arithmetic Teacher, 31*(7), 19-24.

Hofmeister, A.M. (1993). Elitism and reform in school mathematics. *Remedial and Special Education, 14*(6), 8-13.

Horvath, J., and Lehrer, R. (2000). The design of a case-based hypermedia teaching tool. *International Journal of Computers for Mathematical Learning, 5*, 115-141.

Howlin, P., Davies, M., and Udwin, U. (1998). Syndrome specific characteristics in Williams syndrome: To what extent do early behavioral patterns persist into adult life? *Journal of Applied Research in Intellectual Disabilities, 11*, 207-226.

Huntley-Fenner, G. (2001). Why count stuff?: Young preschoolers do not use number for measurement in continuous dimensions. *Developmental Science, 4*, 456-462.

Inhelder, B., Sinclair, H., and Bovet, M. (1974). *Learning and the Development of Cognition.* Cambridge, MA: Harvard University Press.

Irwin, K.C., Vistro-Yu, C.P., and Ell, F.R. (2004). Understanding linear measurement: A comparison of Filipino and New Zealand children. *Mathematics Education Research Journal, 16*(2), 3-24.

Johnson-Gentile, K., Clements, D.H., and Battista, M.T. (1994). The effects of computer and noncomputer environments on students' conceptualizations of geometric motions. *Journal of Educational Computing Research, 11*(2), 121-140.

Jones, S.S., and Smith, L.B. (2002). How children know the relevant properties for generalizing object names. *Developmental Science, 2*, 219-232.

Jordan, N.C., Kaplan, D., Oláh, L.N., and Locuniak, M.N. (2006). Number sense growth in kindergarten: A longitudinal investigation of children at risk for mathematics difficulties. *Child Development, 77*, 153-175.

K-13 Geometry Committee. (1967). *Geometry: Kindergarten to Grade Thirteen.* Toronto, Canada: Ontario Institute for Studies in Education.

Kabanova-Meller, E.N. (1970). The role of the diagram in the application of geometric theorems. In J. Kilpatrick and I. Wirszup (Eds.), *Soviet Studies in the Psychology of Learning and Teaching Mathematics* (vol. 4, pp. 7-49). Chicago: University of Chicago Press.

Kamii, C., and Clark, F.B. (1997). Measurement of length: The need for a better approach to teaching. *School Science and Mathematics*, *97*, 116-121.

Kamii, C., Miyakawa, Y., and Kato, Y. (2004). The development of logico-mathematical knowledge in a block-building activity at ages 1-4. *Journal of Research in Childhood Education*, *19*, 13-26.

Kay, C.S. (1987). *Is a Square a Rectangle?* The Development of First-Grade Students' Understanding of Quadrilaterals with Implications for the van Hiele Theory of the Development of Geometric Thought. Doctoral dissertation, University of Georgia, 1986. *Dissertation Abstracts International*, *47*(08), 2934A.

Kersh, J., Casey, B., and Young, J.M. (2008). Research on spatial skills and block building in girls and boys: The relationship to later mathematics learning. In B. Spodek and O.N. Saracho (Eds.), *Contemporary Perspectives on Mathematics, Science, and Technology in Early Childhood Education*. Charlotte, NC: Information Age.

Klein, A., Starkey, P., and Wakeley, A. (1999). *Enhancing Pre-kindergarten Children's Readiness for School Mathematics*. Paper presented at the American Educational Research Association.

Klein, A., Starkey, P., and Ramirez, A.B. (2002). *Pre-K Mathematics Curriculum*. Glenview, IL: Scott Foresman.

Kosslyn, S.M. (1983). *Ghosts in the Mind's Machine*. New York: W.W. Norton.

Kouba, V.L., Brown, C.A., Carpenter, T.P., Lindquist, M.M., Silver, E.A., and Swafford, J.O. (1988). Results of the fourth NAEP assessment of mathematics: Measurement, geometry, data interpretation, attitudes, and other topics. *Arithmetic Teacher*, *35*(9), 10-16.

Lappan, G. (1999). Geometry: The forgotten strand. *NCTM News Bulletin*, *36*(5), 3.

Lean, G., and Clements, M.A. (1981). Spatial ability, visual imagery, and mathematical performance. *Educational Studies in Mathematics*, *12*, 267-299.

Lehrer, R. (2003). Developing understanding of measurement. In J. Kilpatrick, W.G. Martin, and D. Schifter (Eds.), *A Research Companion to Principles and Standards for School Mathematics* (pp. 179-192). Reston, VA: National Council of Teachers of Mathematics.

Lehrer, R., Jenkins, M., and Osana, H. (1998). Longitudinal study of children's reasoning about space and geometry. In R. Lehrer and D. Chazan (Eds.), *Designing Learning Environments for Developing Understanding of Geometry and Space* (pp. 137-167). Mahwah, NJ: Erlbaum.

Lehrer, R., Jacobson, C., Thoyre, G., Kemeny, V., Strom, D., Horvarth, J., et al. (1998). Developing understanding of geometry and space in the primary grades. In R. Lehrer and D. Chazan (Eds.), *Designing Learning Environments for Developing Understanding of Geometry and Space* (pp. 169-200). Mahwah, NJ: Erlbaum.

Leushina, A.M. (1974/1991). *The Development of Elementary Mathematical Concepts in Preschool Children* (vol. 4). Reston, VA: National Council of Teachers of Mathematics.

Levine, S.C., Huttenlocher, J., Taylor, A., and Langrock, A. (1999). Early sex differences in spatial skill. *Developmental Psychology*, *35*(4), 940-949.

Lubinski, C.A., and Thiessen, D. (1996). Exploring measurement through literature. *Teaching Children Mathematics*, *2*, 260-263.

Mansfield, H.M., and Scott, J. (1990). Young children solving spatial problems. In G. Booker, P. Cobb and T.N. deMendicuti (Eds.), *Proceedings of the 14th Annual Conference of the International Group for the Psychology of Mathematics Education* (vol. 2, pp. 275-282). Oaxlepec, Mexico: International Group for the Psychology of Mathematics Education.

Maratsos, M.P. (1973). Decrease in the understanding of the word "big" in preschool children. *Child Development*, *44*, 747-752.

Miller, K.F. (1984). Child as the measurer of all things: Measurement procedures and the development of quantitative concepts. In C. Sophian (Ed.), *Origins of Cognitive Skills: The Eighteenth Annual Carnegie Symposium on Cognition* (pp. 193-228). Hillsdale, NJ: Erlbaum.

Miller, K.F. (1989). Measurement as a tool of thought: The role of measuring procedures in children's understanding of quantitative invariance. *Developmental Psychology, 25*, 589-600.

Mix, K.S., Huttenlocher, J., and Levine, S.C. (2002). *Quantitative Development in Infancy and Early Childhood.* New York: Oxford University Press.

Mullet, E., and Paques, P. (1991). The height + width = area of a rectangle rule in five-year-olds: Effects of stimulus distribution and graduation of the response scale. *Journal of Experimental Child Psychology, 52*(3), 336-343.

Mulligan, J., Prescott, A., and Mitchelmore, M.C. (2004). Children's development of structure in early mathematics. In M.J. Høines and A.B. Fuglestad (Eds.), *Proceedings of the 28th Conference of the International Group for the Psychology in Mathematics Education* (vol. 3, pp. 393-401). Bergen, Norway: Bergen University College.

Mullis, I.V.S., Martin, M.O., Beaton, A.E., Gonzalez, E.J., Kelly, D.L., and Smith, T.A. (1997). *Mathematics Achievement in the Primary School Years: IEA's Third International Mathematics and Science Study (TIMSS).* Chestnut Hill, MA: Center for the Study of Testing, Evaluation, and Educational Policy, Boston College.

Murphy, C.M., and Wood, D.J. (1981). Learning from pictures: The use of pictorial information by young children. *Journal of Experimental Child Psychology, 32*, 279-297.

National Council of Teachers of Mathematics. (1989). *Curriculum and Evaluation Standards for School Mathematics.* Reston, VA: Author.

National Mathematics Advisory Panel. (2008). *Foundations for Success: The Final Report of the National Mathematics Advisory Panel.* Washington, DC: U.S. Department of Education. Available: http://www.ed.gov/about/bdscomm/list/mathpanel/report/final-report.pdf [accessed August 2008].

Newcombe, N.S., and Huttenlocher, J. (2000). *Making Space: The Development of Spatial Representation and Reasoning.* Cambridge, MA: MIT Press.

Newcombe, N., and Sanderson, H.L. (1993). *The Relation Between Preschoolers' Everyday Activities and Spatial Ability.* New Orleans, LA: Society for Research in Child Development.

Newcombe, N.S., Huttenlocher, J., and Learmonth, A. (1999). Infants' coding of location in continuous space. *Infant Behavior and Development, 22*, 483-510.

Nührenbörger, M. (2001). Insights into children's ruler concepts—Grade-2 students' conceptions and knowledge of length measurement and paths of development. In M.V.D. Heuvel-Panhuizen (Ed.), *Proceedings of the 25th Conference of the International Group for the Psychology in Mathematics Education* (vol. 3, pp. 447-454). Utrecht, The Netherlands: Freudenthal Institute.

Nunes, T., and Bryant, P. (1996). *Children Doing Mathematics.* Cambridge, MA: Blackwell.

Nunes, T., Light, P., and Mason, J.H. (1993). Tools for thought: The measurement of length and area. *Learning and Instruction, 3*, 39-54.

Outhred, L.N., and Mitchelmore, M.C. (1992). Representation of area: A pictorial perspective. In W. Geeslin and K. Graham (Eds.), *Proceedings of the Sixteenth Psychology in Mathematics Education Conference* (vol. II, pp. 194-201). Durham, NH: Program Committee of the Sixteenth Psychology in Mathematics Education Conference.

Palmer, S.E. (1989). Reference frames in the perception of shape and orientation. In B.E. Shepp and S. Ballesteros (Eds.), *Object Perception: Structure and Process* (pp. 121-163). Hillsdale, NJ: Erlbaum.

Petitto, A.L. (1990). Development of number line and measurement concepts. *Cognition and Instruction, 7*, 55-78.

Piaget, J., and Inhelder, B. (1967). *The Child's Conception of Space.* (F.J. Langdon and J.L. Lunzer, Trans.). New York: W.W. Norton.

Piaget, J., and Inhelder, B. (1971). *Mental Imagery in the Child.* London, England: Routledge and Kegan Paul.

Piaget, J., Inhelder, B., and Szeminska, A. (1960). *The Child's Conception of Geometry.* London, England: Routledge and Kegan Paul.

Plumert, J.M., and Nichols-Whitehead, P. (1996). Parental scaffolding of young children's spatial communication. *Developmental Psychology, 32*(3), 523-532.

Prigge, G.R. (1978). The differential effects of the use of manipulative aids on the learning of geometric concepts by elementary school children. *Journal for Research in Mathematics Education, 9*, 361-367.

Raven, K.E., and Gelman, S.A. (1984). Rule usage in children's understanding of "big" and "little." *Child Development, 55*, 2141-2150.

Razel, M., and Eylon, B.-S. (1990). Development of visual cognition: Transfer effects of the Agam program. *Journal of Applied Developmental Psychology, 11*, 459-485.

Reynolds, A., and Wheatley, G.H. (1996). Elementary students' construction and coordination of units in an area setting. *Journal for Research in Mathematics Education, 27*(5), 564-581.

Rosch, E. (1975). Cognitive representations of semantic categories. *Journal of Experimental Psychology: General, 104*, 192-233.

Rosser, R.A., Horan, P.F., Mattson, S.L., and Mazzeo, J. (1984). Comprehension of Euclidean space in young children: The early emergence of understanding and its limits. *Genetic Psychology Monographs, 110*, 21-41.

Rulence-Paques, P., and Mullet, E. (1998). Area judgment from width and height information: The case of the rectangle. *Journal of Experimental Child Psychology, 69*(1), 22-48.

Russell, J. (1975). The interpretation of conservation instructions by five-year-old children. *Journal of Child Psychology and Psychiatry, 16*, 233-244.

Sales, C. (1994). *A Constructivist Instructional Project on Developing Geometric Problem Solving Abilities Using Pattern Blocks and Tangrams with Young Children.* Unpublished Masters, University of Northern Iowa, Cedar Falls.

Sarama, J., and Clements, D.H. (2002). Building blocks for young children's mathematical development. *Journal of Educational Computing Research, 27*(1 and 2), 93-110.

Sarama, J., Clements, D.H., and Vukelic, E.B. (1996). The role of a computer manipulative in fostering specific psychological/mathematical processes. In E. Jakubowski, D. Watkins, and H. Biske (Eds.), *Proceedings of the 18th Annual Meeting of the North America Chapter of the International Group for the Psychology of Mathematics Education* (vol. 2, pp. 567-572). Columbus, OH: ERIC Clearinghouse for Science, Mathematics, and Environmental Education.

Semrud-Clikeman, M., and Hynd, G.W. (1990). Right hemispheric dysfunction in nonverbal learning disabilities: Social, academic, and adaptive functioning in adults and children. *Psychological Bulletin, 107*, 196-209.

Sena, R., and Smith, L.B. (1990). New evidence on the development of the word big. *Child Development, 61*, 1034-1052.

Seo, K.-H., and Ginsburg, H.P. (2004). What is developmentally appropriate in early childhood mathematics education? In D.H. Clements, J. Sarama, and A.-M. DiBiase (Eds.), *Engaging Young Children in Mathematics: Standards for Early Childhood Mathematics Education* (pp. 91-104). Mahwah, NJ: Erlbaum.

Share, D.L., Moffitt, T.E., and Silva, P.A. (1988). Factors associated with arithmetic and reading disabilities and specific arithmetic disability. *Journal of Learning Disabilities, 21*, 313-320.

Shepard, R.N. (1978). Externalization of mental images and the act of creation. In B.S. Randhawa and W.E. Coffman (Eds.), *Visual Learning, Thinking and Communication*. New York: Academic Press.

Shepard, R.N., and Cooper, L.A. (1982). *Mental Images and Their Transformations*. Cambridge, MA: MIT Press.

Shusterman, A., and Spelke, E. (2004). Investigations in the development of spatial reasoning: Core knowledge and adult competence. In P. Carruthers, S. Laurence, and S. Stich (Eds.), *The Innate Mind: Structure and Contents*. New York: Oxford University Press.

Silverman, I.W., York, K., and Zuidema, N. (1984). Area-matching strategies used by young children. *Journal of Experimental Child Psychology, 38*, 464-474.

Smith, I. (1964). *Spatial Ability*. San Diego, CA: Knapp.

Sophian, C. (2002). Learning about what fits: Preschool children's reasoning about effects of object size. *Journal for Research in Mathematics Education, 33*, 290-302.

Sophian, C., and Kailihiwa, C. (1998). Units of counting: Developmental changes. *Cognitive Development, 13*, 561-585.

Sowell, E.J. (1989). Effects of manipulative materials in mathematics instruction. *Journal for Research in Mathematics Education, 20*, 498-505.

Spiers, P.A. (1987). Alcalculia revisited: Current issues. In G. Deloche and X. Seron (Eds.), *Mathematical Disabilities: A Cognitive Neuropyschological Perspective*. Hillsdale, NJ: Erlbaum.

Spitler, M.E., Sarama, J., and Clements, D.H. (2003). *A Preschooler's Understanding of a Triangle: A Case Study*. Paper presented at the 81st Annual Meeting of the National Council of Teachers of Mathematics.

Starkey, P., Klein, A., Chang, I., Qi, D., Lijuan, P., and Yang, Z. (1999, April). *Environmental Supports for Young Children's Mathematical Development in China and the United States*. Paper presented at the Society for Research in Child Development, Albuquerque, NM.

Starkey, P., Klein, A., and Wakeley, A. (2004). Enhancing young children's mathematical knowledge through a pre-kindergarten mathematics intervention. *Early Childhood Research Quarterly, 19*, 99-120.

Starkey, P., Klein, A., Sarama, J., and Clements, D.H. (2006). *Preschool Curriculum Evaluation Research*. Paper presented at the American Educational Research Association.

Steffe, L.P. (1991). Operations that generate quantity. *Learning and Individual Differences, 3*, 61-82.

Steffe, L.P., and Cobb, P. (1988). *Construction of Arithmetical Meanings and Strategies*. New York: Springer-Verlag.

Stephan, M., Bowers, J., Cobb, P., and Gravemeijer, K.P.E. (2003). *Supporting Students' Development of Measuring Conceptions: Analyzing Students' Learning in Social Context* (vol. 12). Reston, VA: National Council of Teachers of Mathematics.

Stevenson, H.W., and McBee, G. (1958). The learning of object and pattern discrimination by children. *Journal of Comparative and Psychological Psychology, 51*, 752-754.

Stevenson, H.W., Lee, S.-Y., and Stigler, J.W. (1986). Mathematics achievement of Chinese, Japanese, and American children. *Science, 231*, 693-699.

Stewart, R., Leeson, N., and Wright, R.J. (1997). Links between early arithmetical knowledge and early space and measurement knowledge: An exploratory study. In F. Biddulph and K. Carr (Eds.), *Proceedings of the Twentieth Annual Conference of the Mathematics Education Research Group of Australasia* (vol. 2, pp. 477-484). Hamilton, New Zealand: MERGA.

Stigler, J.W., Lee, S.-Y., and Stevenson, H.W. (1990). *Mathematical Knowledge of Japanese, Chinese, and American Elementary School Children*. Reston, VA: National Council of Teachers of Mathematics.

Swaminathan, S., Clements, D.H., and Schrier, D. (1995). *The Agam Curriculum in Kindergarten Classes: Effects and Processes.* Buffalo: University of Buffalo, State University of New York.

Tasuoka, K., Corter, J.E., and Tatsuoka, C. (2004). Patterns of diagnosed mathematical content and process skills in TIMSS-R across a sample of 20 countries. *American Educational Research Journal, 41*, 901-926.

Thomas, B. (1982). *An Abstract of Kindergarten Teachers' Elicitation and Utilization of Children's Prior Knowledge in the Teaching of Shape Concepts:* Unpublished manuscript, School of Education, Health, Nursing, and Arts Professions, New York University.

Usiskin, Z. (1997, October). The implications of geometry for all. *Journal of Mathematics Education Leadership, 1*(3), 5-14. Available: http://ncsmonline.org/NCSMPublications/1997journals.html#oct97mel [accessed October 2008].

Uttal, D.H., and Wellman, H.M. (1989). Young children's representation of spatial information acquired from maps. *Developmental Psychology, 25*, 128-138.

van Hiele, P.M. (1986). *Structure and Insight: A Theory of Mathematics Education.* Orlando, FL: Academic Press.

Vinner, S., and Hershkowitz, R. (1980). Concept images and common cognitive paths in the development of some simple geometrical concepts. In R. Karplus (Ed.), *Proceedings of the Fourth International Conference for the Psychology of Mathematics Education* (pp. 177-184). Berkeley: Lawrence Hall of Science, University of California.

Vygotsky, L.S. (1934/1986). *Thought and Language.* Cambridge, MA: MIT Press.

Wang, R.F., and Spelke, E.S. (2002). Human spatial representation: Insights from animals. *Trends in Cognitive Sciences, 6*, 376-382.

Wheatley, G.H. (1990). Spatial sense and mathematics learning. *Arithmetic Teacher, 37*(6), 10-11.

Wheatley, G.H., Brown, D.L., and Solano, A. (1994). Long-term relationship between spatial ability and mathematical knowledge. In D. Kirshner (Ed.), *Proceedings of the Sixteenth Annual Meeting of the North American Chapter of the International Group for the Psychology of Mathematics Education* (vol. 1, pp. 225-231). Baton Rouge: Louisiana State University.

Wolf, Y. (1995). Estimation of Euclidian quantity by 5- and 6-year-old children: Facilitating a multiplication rule. *Journal of Experimental Child Psychology, 59*, 49-75.

Yackel, E., and Wheatley, G.H. (1990). Promoting visual imagery in young pupils. *Arithmetic Teacher, 37*(6), 52-58.

Yuzawa, M., Bart, W.M., Kinne, L.J., Sukemune, S., and Kataoka, M. (1999). The effects of "origami" practice on size comparison strategy among young Japanese and American children. *Journal of Research in Childhood Education, 13*(2), 133-143.

Yuzawa, M., Bart, W.M., and Yuzawa, M. (2000). Development of the ability to judge relative areas: Role of the procedure of placing one object on another. *Cognitive Development, 15*, 135-152.

Zykova, V.I. (1969). Operating with concepts when solving geometry problems. In J. Kilpatrick and I. Wirszup (Eds.), *Soviet Studies in the Psychology of Learning and Teaching Mathematics* (vol. 1, pp. 93-148). Chicago: University of Chicago.

# Part III

# Contexts for Teaching and Learning

# 7

# Standards, Curriculum, Instruction, and Assessment

In this chapter, we address the topic of effective mathematics curriculum and teaching—what is known about how teachers can effectively support children's learning of important foundational mathematics content. We begin the chapter with a description and analysis of current state standards for early learning. Standards are intended to influence the development of curriculum and assessment tools, and therefore they have the potential to serve as a bridge between what research says about children's learning and the kinds of teaching and learning that actually occur.

Next, the chapter provides an overview about the state of mathematics teaching and learning experiences in early childhood settings and reviews the literature on effective practices for teaching young children mathematics. Following this is a discussion of formative assessment, an essential and often overlooked element of effective instruction. The chapter concludes with a discussion of research on effective curricula.

## DEFINITIONS

To enhance understanding of the content of this chapter, we first define some of the most frequently used early childhood education terminology.

### Teacher-Initiated and Child-Initiated Experiences

Early childhood practices are often described as either teacher-initiated or child-initiated. *Teacher-initiated* or *teacher-guided* means that teachers plan and implement experiences in which they provide explicit information, model or demonstrate skills, and use other teaching strategies in which they take the lead. Teacher-initiated learning experiences are determined by the teacher's goals and direction, but they should also reflect children's active engagement (Epstein, 2007). Ideally, teacher-initiated instruction actively involves children. Indeed, when appropriately supportive and focused, teacher-initiated instruction can lead to significant learning gains (French and Song, 1998; Howes et al., 2008). In practice, however, most teacher-initiated instruction is associated with the passive engagement of children (Pianta et al., 2005).

By contrast, *child-initiated* or *child-guided* means that children acquire knowledge and skills through their own exploration and through interactions with objects and with peers (Epstein, 2007, p. 2). Child-initiated experience emanates primarily from children's interests and actions with support from teachers. For child-initiated learning to occur, teachers organize the environment and materials and provide the learning opportunities from which children make choices (Epstein, 2007). Teachers thoughtfully observe children during child-initiated activity, gauging their interactions and the provision of new materials, as well as reorganization of the environment, to support their continued learning and development.

During optimal child-initiated experience, teachers are not passive, nor are children entirely in control—although this ideal is not always realized in practice. For example, classroom observational research reveals that teachers tend to spend little time with children during free play (Seo and Ginsburg, 2004), or they focus their interactions on behavior management rather than on helping children learn (Dickinson and Tabors, 2001; Kontos, 1999).

## Instruction and Intentional Teaching

In early childhood education, the term *instruction* is most often used to mean "direct instruction," implying that teachers are entirely in control and children are passive recipients of information. The term is also used pejoratively to refer to drill and practice on isolated skills. *Direct instruction* is more accurately defined as situations in which teachers give information or present mathematics content directly to children. The National Mathematics Advisory Panel (2008) uses the term *explicit instruction* to refer to the many ways that teachers can intentionally structure children's experiences so that they support learning in mathematics.

Throughout the day and across various contexts—whole group, small group, centers, play, and routines—teachers need to be active and draw on a repertoire of effective teaching strategies. This skill in adapting teaching to the content, type of learning experience, and individual child with a clear learning target as a goal is called *intentional teaching* (Epstein, 2007;

National Association for the Education of Young Children, 1997). To be effective, intentional teaching requires that teachers use formative assessment to determine where children are in relation to the learning goal and to provide the right kind and amount of support for them to continue to make progress. Intentional teaching is useful to get beyond the dichotomies that arise when teaching is characterized as either teacher-directed or child-initiated.

### Integrated and Focused Curriculum

Early childhood curriculum is often integrated across content domains or subject matter disciplines. *Integration* is the blending together of two or more content areas in one activity or learning experience (Schickedanz, 2008). The purpose of an integrated curriculum is to make content meaningful and accessible to young children. Integration also enables more content to be covered during the limited school day.

Integration typically occurs in two ways. One approach is to add a mathematics content goal to a storybook reading. In this situation, language and literacy goals related to storybook reading are primary, and mathematics learning is secondary. Another way of integrating curriculum is to use a broad topic of study, a theme (such as animals or plants), or a project of interest to children through which mathematics content goals are addressed. Projects are extended investigations into a topic that intellectually engages and interests children, such as how to create a garden or build a house (Katz and Chard, 1989). In both of these approaches to integration, mathematics learning is a secondary objective, rather than the primary focus of attention. In this report, we use both *integrated learning experience* and *secondary focus* on mathematics (which some studies have referred to as *embedded mathematics*) to reflect the teaching/exposure to mathematics content as an ancillary activity.

By contrast, *focused* curriculum or primary focus on mathematics refers to experiences in which mathematics is the major learning goal. A focused mathematics curriculum should also be meaningful and connect to children's interests and prior knowledge. In this report, we use the terms, "primary focus on mathematics" and "focused mathematics time" to refer to dedicated time for a learning experience with mathematics as the primary goal.

## STANDARDS FOR CHILDREN'S MATHEMATICS LEARNING

State standards for students' learning have had an increasingly important role in education over at least the past decade, particularly in K-12 education. More recently, standards have begun to play a role in early childhood education as well. Standards have great potential for shaping instruction, curricula, and assessment; however, the impact of standards on learning depends heavily on the content and specific learning goals laid out in them.

The number of states with published early learning standards has grown over the past eight years from 27 in 2002 to 49 as of 2008. To inform their early learning standards in mathematics, states have used a variety of National Council of Teachers of Mathematics (NCTM) resources, including *Principles and Standards for School Mathematics* (2000) (14 states) and *Early Childhood Mathematics: Promoting Good Beginnings*, issued by NCTM and National Association for the Education of Young Children (NAEYC). *Engaging Young Children in Mathematics* (2004) is also a widely recognized guide for state early learning standards.

*Curriculum Focal Points* (National Council of Teachers of Mathematics, 2006), the most recent set of guidelines provided by NCTM, was developed after most states had already established their standards. The *Curriculum Focal Points* provides guidance about the most significant mathematical concepts and skills (i.e., number and operations, geometry and measurement) that should be addressed during children's early education. *Curriculum Focal Points* also has a clear emphasis on the PSSM process standards, which are essential for meaningful and substantive mathematics learning. The process strands of communication, reasoning, representation, connections, and particularly problem solving allow children to understand their mathematics learning as a coherent and connected body of knowledge (National Council of Teachers of Mathematics, 2006). *Curriculum Focal Points* does not, however, provide the kind of in-depth coverage of what children should know and can do that this report does.

In order to gain a more systematic understanding of the content of states' mathematics standards, the committee commissioned two content analyses of current standards for young children: one at the prekindergarten level (here termed "early learning standards") and one at the kindergarten level (Reys, Chval, and Switzer, 2008; Scott-Little, 2008).

## Early Learning Standards

Many states developed early learning standards to improve classroom instruction and professional development; they also serve as a component of accountability systems. The age levels addressed in the standards documents vary across states. In 17 states the standards targeted children ages 3 to 5, 12 states targeted 3- and 4-year-olds, and 11 states targeted children finishing prekindergarten or starting kindergarten.

State-funded prekindergarten programs are the most common target audience for the early learning standards (42 states), which are usually required to implement the standards (39 states) (Scott-Little et al., 2007).

Currently, 17 states have developed monitoring systems to ensure that standards are being implemented, and 4 others are in the process of developing such a system. States also report that they intend for the early learning standards to be used in child care (39 states), Head Start (38 states), the Individuals with Disabilities Education Act (26 states), and Even Start (27 states) programs, although the use of the standards in these programs is typically voluntary.

For the early learning standards it was possible to evaluate how much emphasis each state has given to mathematics across all of the standards as a whole. On average, states devoted 15 percent of the total number of early learning standards to mathematics, although there was wide variation across states (from a low in New Mexico of only 4 percent to a high in Colorado of 54 percent).

In the content analysis of the mathematics early learning standards (Scott-Little, 2008), each standard was first coded into 1 of the 10 mathematics content and process areas in the PSSM. These categories include the three content areas emphasized in this report and in the *Curriculum Focal Points*—number and operations and geometry and measurement. After the mathematics standards items from a state's document were coded, the total number of items in each area was summed. Because the total number of items varied from state to state, the total for each area was divided by the total number of mathematics items to produce a percentage that was comparable across documents. In effect, the percentage represents the relative emphasis given to each area of mathematics. Table 7-1 presents these results.

**TABLE 7-1** Percentages of States Early Learning Mathematics Standards That Fall in Each of the PSSM Areas

| PSSM Area | Mean | SD | Min. | Max. |
|---|---|---|---|---|
| Content | | | | |
| Numbers and operations | 32.3 | 9.8 | 9 | 50 |
| Algebra | 19.0 | 8.8 | 0 | 50 |
| Geometry | 17.8 | 7.9 | 0 | 44 |
| Measurement | 15.8 | 8.7 | 0 | 50 |
| Data analysis | 5.3 | 5.8 | 0 | 17 |
| Process | | | | |
| Problem solving | 3.7 | 6.2 | 0 | 25 |
| Communication | 1.4 | 3.6 | 0 | 4 |
| Reasoning | 1.3 | 3.1 | 0 | 13 |
| Representation | 0.6 | 1.8 | 0 | 11 |
| Connections | 0.4 | 1.3 | 0 | 7 |
| Other | 2.5 | 3.4 | 0 | 15 |

NOTE: PSSM = *Principles and Standards for School Mathematics*, n = 49 states.
SOURCE: Scott-Little (2008).

These data show a focus on the area of number and operations; on average, states devoted 32 percent of their mathematics standards to this area, and all states had at least some standards in this area. Geometry received less emphasis than number in the early learning standards (18 percent), and measurement accounted for 16 percent of standards in mathematics. In addition, there was much greater overall emphasis on the content standards areas than on the process standards areas (see Table 7-1).

A more detailed analysis was conducted of all standards in each of the three content areas that are the focus of this report (as well as the NCTM *Curriculum Focal Points*): (1) number and operations, (2) geometry, and (3) measurement. Table 7-2 provides the details of the results for each area.

In the area of number and operations, states have most often addressed number sense (an average of 24 percent of the number/operations standards); however, there is considerable variation among states—from 11 states with no standards in this area, to 4 states for which number sense accounted for 100 percent of their number and operations standards. Three other core areas of number were relatively frequent—the number word list, 1-to-1 counting correspondences, and written number symbols—and each is addressed by 11 to 14 percent of the standards. Cardinality and the three basic kinds of addition/subtraction situations received minimal attention.

In the geometry early learning standards, there was an emphasis on children's knowledge of properties of shapes (40 percent) and spatial reasoning (25 percent) (e.g., knowledge related to spatial location and direction), although, again, there was considerable variability among states. Some important aspects of geometry for young children receive little attention, including transformation and visualization of shapes.

In the measurement standards, areas most often emphasized are measurement of objects (34 percent of the standards), comparing objects (27 percent), and understanding of concepts related to time (27 percent). Again there was variability—for example, 2 states had no measurement standards at all, and 15 states had no standard related to comparisons of objects and the concept of time (see Table 7-2).

## Kindergarten Standards

The committee also commissioned an analysis of the 10 states with the largest student populations that publish kindergarten-specific mathematics standards: California, Florida, Georgia, Michigan, New Jersey, New York, North Carolina, Ohio, Texas, and Virginia (Reys, Chval, and Switzer, 2008). These states were selected for analysis because they represent approximately 50 percent of the U.S. school population and therefore influence the intended curriculum for a substantial population of students. Given their size, these 10 states are also likely to influence textbook development and materials that are produced by commercial curriculum publishers.

**TABLE 7-2** Classification of State Mathematics Early Learning Standards by Content Area and Focal Area

| Content/Focal Area | Mean% | SD | Minimum% | Maximum% |
|---|---|---|---|---|
| *Number and Operations* | | | | |
| Number sense | 24.1 | 26.6 | 0 | 100 |
| 1-to-1 correspondence | 13.8 | 10.3 | 0 | 43 |
| Number word list | 13.1 | 10.2 | 0 | 50 |
| Written number symbols | 11.4 | 11.6 | 0 | 40 |
| Perceptional comparisons | 9.6 | 10.3 | 0 | 50 |
| Combining/taking apart | 7.3 | 9.6 | 0 | 33 |
| Cardinality | 5.4 | 7.2 | 0 | 25 |
| Estimation | 4.7 | 8.4 | 0 | 33 |
| Change | 3.9 | 7.9 | 0 | 33 |
| Ordinal numbers | 3.8 | 6.6 | 0 | 25 |
| Counting comparisons | 2.2 | 9.0 | 0 | 60 |
| Additive comparisons | 0.6 | 2.1 | 0 | 11 |
| Place value | 0.2 | 1.6 | 0 | 11 |
| *Geometry* | | | | |
| Properties of shapes | 39.6 | 17.9 | 0 | 100 |
| Spatial reasoning | 25.3 | 23.2 | 0 | 100 |
| Analyzing and comparing shapes | 13.3 | 15.8 | 0 | 67 |
| Location and directionality | 12.2 | 15.5 | 0 | 50 |
| Composing/decomposing shapes | 6.6 | 10.7 | 0 | 40 |
| Symmetry | 1.6 | 5.3 | 0 | 25 |
| Transformation of shapes | 1.5 | 6.0 | 0 | 33 |
| Visualization of shapes | 0.0 | 0.0 | 0 | 0 |
| *Measurement* | | | | |
| Measurement of objects | 33.9 | 25.3 | 0 | 100 |
| Comparing objects | 27.1 | 26.0 | 0 | 100 |
| Time | 26.9 | 23.3 | 0 | 100 |
| Measurable attributes | 12.7 | 16.0 | 0 | 50 |
| Composing objects | 0.0 | 0.0 | 0 | 0 |

NOTE: For number and operations n = 49 states; for geometry n = 48 as one state had no geometry standards; for measurement n = 47 as two states had no measurement standards. Percentages represent the number of a state's standards in a focal area divided by the total number of standards in the content area (content areas are number and operation, geometry, and measurement).
SOURCE: Scott-Little (2008).

The kindergarten learning standards for each state were coded into the five PSSM mathematical content areas or strands: (1) number and operation, (2) geometry, (3) measurement, (4) algebra, and (5) data analysis/probability (Clements, 2004; National Council of Teachers of Mathematics, 2000). Results allow an examination of which of these mathematical strands are emphasized across and within states. Relative emphasis devoted to each strand was calculated as a percentage of standards in that strand within the total number of mathematics standards.

There was considerable variability across the 10 states studied. The total number of mathematics standards varied widely, from 11 in Florida to 74 in Virginia (average number of standards was 29). Of the "total set" of 103 specific standards identified in the analysis, only 1 standard was common to all 10 states (extending a pattern) and another 3 standards were common to 9 states. Only 20 percent of the 103 standards were common to 6 or more states.

In kindergarten (as with the early learning standards), the greatest emphasis across all the mathematics standards is placed on number and operations—40 percent of a state's mathematics standards on average (with a range from a low of 27 percent to a high of 56 percent among states). Geometry and measurement each receive less emphasis than number (19 and 21 percent, respectively), although, again, variability is high (from 9 to 45 percent across states for geometry and from 11 to 28 percent for measurement).

In the number strand, the heaviest emphasis is placed on counting. Areas of emphasis (meaning at least 6 of the 10 states had standards in this focal area) include counting objects, reading and writing numerals, identifying ordinal numbers, comparing the relative size of groups of objects, and modeling and solving problems using addition and subtraction. Consistent with the theme of state variability, however, no single number/operations standard appeared in all 10 state documents.

In both geometry and measurement, few learning standards were common across the states; only 6 topics (of 43 total across geometry and measurement) appeared in the documents of 6 or more states. In geometry, these topics were identifying and naming two-dimensional (2-D) shapes and knowing the relative position of objects. In measurement, the most common topics were comparing the weight of objects; sort, compare, and/or order objects; compare length of objects; and know days of the week.

Taken together, the three focal areas emphasized by the committee (number, geometry, and measurement) account for 80 percent of the content of the kindergarten standards across the 10 states. However, many states also include some specific standards that would not be considered core or primary mathematics by the committee—such as knowing the names of the months, parts of the day, seasons, ordering events by time, comparing time, understanding the concept of time, identifying the time of everyday events to the nearest hour, and measurement of weight, capacity, and temperature.

Process strands were addressed quite differently by different states, so no systematic analyses could be done. Specifically, three states make no mention of process standards at the kindergarten level (Florida, North Carolina, and Virginia), and three other states include identification of specific standards by process strand (Georgia, New York, and Texas). Notably, although these strands are specified for kindergarten, these process standards are very similar, if not identical, at each grade, K-8. Two states (Arizona and Massachusetts) provide a general description of process standards in the introductory material of their K-6 or K-8 document. These descriptions emphasize the importance of the process strands outlined in the PSSM (National Council of Teachers of Mathematics, 2000). The California and Ohio documents include process standards organized within one strand ("Mathematical Reasoning" in the California document and "Mathematical Process Standard" in the Ohio document) for each grade. The California document lists process standards that are common across kindergarten and Grade 1. Likewise, the Ohio document includes a list of process standards that are common to Grades K-2.

### Summary

A total of 49 states have early learning standards in mathematics; on average, states devote the greatest emphasis to the area of number (32 percent of the standards on average). Specific emphasis within the areas of number, geometry, and measurement showed considerable state-to-state variation. According to our analysis for the 10 largest states, the greatest emphasis in kindergarten is also placed on number (40 percent of the standards on average). However, there is also considerable variation in content of the specific standards across all of the areas. In fact, of the 103 total standards across the 10 states, 47 are unique to just 1 or 2 state documents.

A pattern of wide variation across states in emphasis given to mathematics as a whole and relative emphasis given to various topics in mathematics emerges from these analyses of standards. Thus, while some common topics could be identified, when taken as a whole, the state standards do not communicate a clear consensus about the most important mathematical ideas for young children to learn.

## THE CLASSROOM CONTEXT

We begin with a description of the classroom context in which mathematics instruction takes place. We then focus specifically on what is known about mathematics teaching and learning practices in preschool and kindergarten classrooms—when it occurs, how often, and in what contexts.

Results from several large studies of prekindergarten (pre-K) and kindergarten classrooms paint a detailed picture of how young children spend their time in these settings and the quality of their learning experiences. We draw particularly on two studies conducted by the National Center for

Early Development and Learning (NCEDL) and on the Early Childhood Longitudinal Study-Kindergarten[1] (ECLS-K).

The NCEDL conducted two major studies of state-funded pre-K and kindergarten classrooms: the six-state Multi-State Study of Preschool (MS) and the five-state State-wide Early Education Programs (SWEEP) Study (Early et al., 2005). While neither of these studies included a nationally representative sample, as of 2001-2002, almost 80 percent of all children in the United States who were participating in state-funded prekindergarten were in one of these 11 states (Early et al., 2005). When combined, these two studies provide observational data on over 700 preschool and 800 kindergarten classrooms across the United States and offer a unique window on children's classroom experiences.

It is important to note that classrooms were included in these studies only if they received state pre-K funding, so the results are not representative of the larger segment of schooling opportunities for 4-year-olds. State-funded pre-K classrooms are a small subset of early childhood classrooms, generally with greater funding and tighter regulation and monitoring, than the larger set of early childhood classrooms. The studies must be interpreted in this context.

In both studies, classrooms were observed using a variety of measures to capture the content and quality of learning opportunities and materials afforded to children, including the Early Childhood Environment Rating Scale (ECERS-R; Harms, Clifford, and Cryer, 1998), Classroom Assessment Scoring System (CLASS; Pianta, La Paro, and Hamre, 2008), and Emerging Academics' Snapshot (Ritchie et al., 2001).[2]

### How Children Spend Their Time in Prekindergarten and Kindergarten

Results from both of the NCEDL studies (the MS and the SWEEP) indicate that children in state pre-K programs spend a great deal of time *not* engaged in any type of instructional activity. Using the Emerging Academics Snapshot, both NCEDL studies recorded the proportion of time spent in all major areas of curriculum, assessing the amount of time students spent in

---

[1]Material in this section is based on a paper prepared for the committee by Hamre et al. (2008), which included a review of the published literature related to these studies as well as some reanalysis of the data conducted for this report.

[2]During pre-K, observation days lasted from the beginning of class until the end of class in part-day rooms and until nap in full-day rooms. In pre-K, observers stayed with the children all day, including lunch, outside time, and special activities. In kindergarten, the observations were slightly different because the days were generally longer. Snapshot and CLASS observations lasted the entire day, but no observations were made during lunch, recess, or nap. For this reason, pre-K and kindergarten Snapshot percentages of time spent are discussed separately. More information about these studies can be found on the NCEDL website (http://www.fpg.unc.edu/~ncedl/) and in several published articles (Clifford et al., 2005; Howes et al., 2008; Pianta et al., 2005).

reading, oral language and phonemic awareness activities, writing, mathematics, science, social studies, aesthetics, and fine and gross motor activities. Each area was broadly defined so that time spent in dramatic play, block areas, coloring with markers, talking with teachers about things outside school, and singing songs were included in one of these areas. During the preschool day, the average student spent 44 percent of the time engaged in none of these curriculum activities. Data from kindergarten classrooms revealed that the average student was not engaged in any instructional activity in 39 percent of the observed intervals.

What were children doing during this noninstructional time? In preschool classrooms, much of the time (22 percent) was spent engaged in routine activities, such as transitioning, waiting in line, or washing hands. Some time (11 percent) was also spent in meals and snacks (Early et al., 2005). Importantly, routine, meal, and snack times could be included as instructional time if, for example, teachers and children engaged in a conversation, sang a song, or played a number game during a transition. But few preschool or kindergarten teachers appeared to take advantage of the learning opportunities that arose during transitional periods or employed strategies for getting the most out of this time in the classroom.

Which types of instructional opportunities are young children exposed to most often? Of all content areas, young children spent more time in language and literacy activities than any other—14 percent of the observed day in preschool and 28 percent of the observed day in kindergarten (La Paro et al., 2008). None of the other major areas occurred much more than 10 percent, on average, in any given day. Pre-K children in the NCEDL studies were exposed to mathematics content in only 6 percent of the observations, and kindergarten children were exposed to mathematics an average of 11 percent of the day.

Another relevant question concerns the use of various instructional contexts, such as free choice/center time or whole-group instruction. Data from the NCEDL studies suggest there is a major shift in the preferred instructional context from preschool to kindergarten. Children in preschool classrooms spent an average of 33 percent of the school day in free choice or center time, compared with only 6 percent of the day in kindergarten classrooms. Once in kindergarten, both whole-group instruction and individual time, in which children work independently at desks, becomes much more frequent. Across kindergarten and preschool, teachers rarely made use of small-group instruction.

### Quality of Teacher-Child Interactions in Preschool and Kindergarten

The NCEDL data also provide a window into the quality of teacher-child interactions and instruction to which young children are exposed, using the *CLASS Framework for Children's Learning Opportunities in*

*Early Childhood and Elementary Classrooms* (CLASS framework; Pianta, La Paro, and Hamre, 2007). The CLASS framework captures three broad domains of classroom interactions—emotional supports, classroom organization, and instructional supports—as well as more specific dimensions in each domain. The CLASS framework was derived from basic, theory-driven research on classroom environments and research on effective teaching practices, and it aligns well with a variety of conceptualizations of effective teaching and empirical evidence on effective practices (see Hamre and Pianta, 2007, for a more detailed discussion).

### *Emotional Supports in Preschool and Kindergarten*

NCEDL results indicate that across preschool and kindergarten, children, on average, experienced moderately positive interactions with teachers in moderately well-managed classrooms (La Paro et al., 2008). Approximately one-third of children in this study were in classrooms characterized by high-quality emotional supports in both pre-K and kindergarten.

Teachers' emotional support may have direct links to students' learning (e.g., Connor, Son, and Hindman, 2005), as well as indirect links in which emotional support fosters engagement, which in turn leads to greater achievement (Rimm-Kaufman, Early, and Cox, 2002). Children's social and emotional functioning in the classroom is increasingly recognized as an indicator of school readiness (Blair, 2002; Denham and Weissberg, 2004; Raver, 2004) and a potential target for intervention (Greenberg, Weissberg, and O'Brien, 2003; Zins et al., 2004). Children who are more motivated and connected to others in the early years of schooling are much more likely to establish positive trajectories of development in both social and academic domains (Hamre and Pianta, 2001; Pianta, Steinberg, and Rollins, 1995; Silver et al., 2005). Furthermore, there is some evidence that emotional supports may be particularly important for supporting the academic development of students with social and emotional difficulties (Hamre and Pianta, 2005). Recent nonexperimental research in elementary classrooms suggests that there may be direct links between emotional supports and students' mathematics knowledge (Pianta et al., 2008).

### *Classroom Organization and Management*

Classrooms function best and provide the most opportunities to learn when students are well behaved, consistently have things to do, and are interested and engaged in learning tasks (Pianta et al., 2005). In short, children are better regulated in well-regulated classroom environments. In the NCEDL studies, this dimension of classrooms was measured using the CLASS.

In general, the quality of classroom organization and management in the early childhood classrooms observed in the NCEDL studies was moderately positive. The typical classroom was characterized by a mix of productive periods, with children engaged in learning, and other periods, in which significant behavior problems disrupted learning or teachers failed to actively engage children in learning opportunities.

### *Instructional Supports*

Of greatest concern are results suggesting very low levels of instructional supports across pre-K and kindergarten, as measured by both the CLASS and ECERS-R. In the CLASS, instructional supports include the three dimensions of support for concept development, quality of feedback, and language modeling. Interactions between adults and children are the key mechanism through which these instructional supports are provided to children in the early years of schooling. A child gets more out of an activity if the teacher is either directly interacting with the child in an intentional way or if the child's participation in the activity has been sufficiently supported by the teacher prior to the start of the activity, so that the child, in playing, is more intentional in the purpose of the activity (the section below called "Research on Effective Mathematics Pedagogy" is a more detailed discussion of instructional supports).

## Mathematics Practices in U.S. Preschools and Kindergartens

Little is known about the math-specific learning opportunities that are provided to children in early childhood settings. This may reflect, in part, the focus on early literacy and language development that has consumed much of early childhood policy and research attention for the past decade. Although more recent attention has focused on early childhood mathematics (Clements and Sarama, 2007a), there is not yet detailed, national-level information on the typical mathematical practices to which children are exposed. In this section, we again draw on the NCEDL MS Study and on data from the nationally representative ECLS-K cohort. We begin with a more detailed analysis of observational data from pre-K classrooms in the NCEDL MS Study and end with a description of kindergarten teachers' self-reported mathematics practices from the ECLS-K. Although the ECLS-K is nationally representative, the information about mathematics instruction is limited.

### *Mathematics Instruction in Prekindergarten*

The most relevant NCEDL MS data come from observations conducted during visits to pre-K classrooms in the fall and the spring. The average amount of time focused on mathematics content in the pre-K classrooms was minimal (6.5 percent in the fall, and 6.7 percent in the spring).[3]

More detailed analysis of the actual activities that took place during this mathematics time suggests that, for about half of the time, mathematics content occurred during whole-group activities (49 percent in the fall and 48 percent in the spring). Free choice/center time was the second most common mathematics setting (31 and 29 percent in the fall and spring respectively), with small group instruction third (11 and 12 percent).

Another important question is whether mathematics is taught alone or in conjunction with other content. Data indicate that mathematics content co-occurred with other academic content during the majority of the time (61 percent in the fall and 55 percent in the spring). About 20 percent of the time, when mathematics co-occurred with something else, it was with an art or music activity (aesthetics), and between 15 and 18 percent of the time it was with a fine motor activity. Other academic content occurred simultaneously with mathematics about 11 percent of the time for reading (a combination of being read to, prereading, and letter-sound), 13 percent for social studies, and 11 percent for science. These findings indicate that, when they do teach mathematics, early childhood education programs rely on integrated or embedded mathematics experiences a majority of the time, rather than including activities with a primary focus on mathematics. The selection of materials and activities such as puzzles, blocks, games, songs, and fingerplays seem to constitute mathematics for many teachers (Clements and Sarama, 2007a).

Using the Emerging Academics Snapshot, researchers found that teachers' interactions with children during mathematics content were likely to be either encouraging or didactic in nature. *Encouraging* was coded when teachers provided feedback about effort and persistence, including praise, personal comments, and general statements that helped children stay engaged in their work. *Didactic* was coded when teachers focused on giving instructions, asking questions with one correct answer, and engaging children in instruction focused on mastering a discrete set of materials. Less often, teachers spent time scaffolding while delivering mathematics content. *Scaffolding* was coded when teachers showed an awareness of an individual child's needs and responded in a manner that supported and expanded the child's learning.

---

[3]Note that *math* was coded when a child was verbally counting, counting with 1-to-1 correspondence, skip counting, identifying written numerals, matching numbers to pictures, making graphs, playing counting games (e.g., dice, dominoes, Candyland, Chutes and Ladders), keeping track of how many days until a special event, counting marbles in a jar, playing Concentration or Memory with numbers, working on mathematics worksheets, identifying shapes, talking about the properties of shapes (e.g., how many sides), finding shapes in the room, identifying same and different (e.g., big/little, biggest), sorting (by color, size, shape), discerning patterns (red, blue, red, blue), or measuring for cooking or size.

To summarize, in the state-funded pre-K classrooms observed in the NCEDL MS Study, mathematics was often taught in conjunction with art, music, and fine motor activities, suggesting that perhaps teachers were integrating mathematics with activities that they assumed would heighten children's engagement and were making use of manipulatives. However, the committee thinks that the integration of mathematics with other activities may or may not be effective in supporting children's development of mathematics knowledge, depending on the integrity of, and emphasis on, the mathematical ideas. It is also evident that mathematics, like literacy, was often taught in a manner in which teachers focused on student performance of a discrete skill or display of factual knowledge. Children were less often exposed to instruction that was conversational, interactive, and focused on understanding and problem solving.

### *Mathematics Instruction in Kindergarten*

The ECLS-K cohort is a nationally representative sample of 22,000 students in approximately 1,000 classrooms across the United States. This cohort of students entered the study in 1998-1999 as they began kindergarten and will be followed through eighth grade. The most relevant ECLS-K data for our purposes are items from a survey of kindergarten teachers who reported how often their students were exposed to classroom instruction in mathematics, including (1) broad exposure to mathematics, (2) instructional emphasis on specific mathematics concepts and skills, and (3) exposure to specific mathematics instructional strategies and activities.

The committee commissioned a reanalysis of these teacher survey items because existing published analyses did not provide sufficient detail on mathematics (Hamre et al., 2008a). For the purposes of our analysis, the items were organized conceptually according to the *NCTM Content Standards* (National Council of Teachers of Mathematics, 2000) into the areas of number and operations, geometry, measurement, algebra, and data analysis and probability.

The vast majority of teachers (81 percent) indicated that mathematics instruction is a part of their daily classroom routine, with over half of the teachers (65 percent) reporting that they provide more than 30 minutes of mathematics instruction each day. Teachers also indicated the frequency with which they taught a list of 27 specific mathematics concepts and skills. By far, teachers reported concepts and skills associated with number and operations to be the most common emphasis of mathematics instruction. However, in contrast to the recommendations in this report for focusing on learning paths in a few key areas, concepts and skills associated with all of the NCTM standards were the emphasis of mathematics instruction to some extent in a given academic week.

Specific to number and operations, the most common concepts and skills teachers reported teaching were correspondence between number and quantity, writing all numbers between 1 and 10, and reading two-digit numbers—all of these were frequently (77, 55, and 52 percent, respectively) reported to be the emphasis of instruction three or more times per week.

Counting by 2s, 5s, and 10s was fairly common, with 44 percent of teachers reporting this to occur at least three times per week. Instruction was slightly less often focused on ordinal numbers (35 percent reported at least three times per week), adding single-digit numbers (40 percent), and subtracting single-digit numbers (28 percent). Research on children's number and operations learning discussed in previous chapters suggests that such emphases are out of balance. For example, time dedicated to skip counting—especially if involving only verbal counting—might be better used to address concepts, strategies, and skills related to addition and subtraction.

As for measurement concepts and skills, the most commonly endorsed items were identification of relative quantity (e.g., most, least, more, less), ordering objects by size or other properties, and sorting objects into subgroups according to a rule, all of which were reported to be the emphasis of instruction once a week or more for 56-76 percent of teachers. Measurement concepts and skills received less frequent emphasis but still were reportedly the focus of instruction at least once a month for most classrooms, as were using measurement instruments accurately, telling time, estimating quantities, and recognizing the value of coins and currency.

Geometry, algebra, and data analysis/probability consisted of the fewest survey items. The lone geometry skill in the survey, recognizing and naming geometric shapes, was reported to be the emphasis of instruction once per week or more by more than 66 percent of teachers. Similarly, related to algebra, over two-thirds of teachers (72 percent) reported teaching copying, making, and extending a pattern at least once a week. Under data analysis and probability, over half of the teachers emphasized reading simple graphs once per week or more, while simple data collection and graphing was less often emphasized (54 percent reported doing this two to three times per month or less). The majority of teachers (59 percent) noted that estimating probability was a skill to be taught at a higher grade level.

Another set of survey items asked teachers about the extent to which they used various instructional activities or strategies. In numbers and operations, the most common math-related activity reported by teachers was verbal counting, which happened on a daily basis in more than 79 percent of the kindergarten classrooms. Another relatively common activity involved use of counting manipulatives to learn basic operations, with 66 percent of teachers reporting this to occur three or more times per week. The use of geometric manipulatives was also fairly common, with 45 percent of teachers reporting their use three or more times a week. In contrast, work with rulers, measuring cups, spoons, and other measuring instruments was fairly infrequent, with two-thirds of teachers (66 percent) reporting use of them three times per month or less.

Generalized teaching strategies and activities are defined as those that can apply to a variety of the NCTM mathematics standards. The most prominent generalized strategy was calendar-related activities, which occurred on a daily basis in over 90 percent of the classrooms surveyed, this despite the fact that mathematics educators do not consider most calendar activities to be useful early childhood mathematics instruction and have serious questions about the efficacy of "doing the calendar" every day (see Box 7-1).

More than half of the teachers reported using the following strategies and activities twice a week or more: playing mathematics-related games, explaining how a mathematical problem is solved, doing mathematical

**BOX 7-1**
**How Using the Calendar Does Not Emphasize Foundational Mathematics**

Many preschool and kindergarten teachers spend time each day on the calendar, in part because they think it is an efficient way to teach mathematics. Although the calendar may be useful in helping children begin to understand general concepts of time, such as "yesterday" and "today," or plan for important events, such as field trips or visitors, these are not core mathematical concepts. The main problem with the calendar is that the groups of seven days in the rows of a calendar have no useful mathematical relationship to the number 10, the building block of the number system. Therefore, the calendar is not useful for helping students learn the base 10 patterns; other visual and conceptual approaches using groups of 10 are needed because these patterns of groups of 10 are foundational.

Time spent on the calendar would be better used on more effective mathematics teaching and learning experiences. "Doing the calendar" is not a substitute for teaching foundational mathematics.

| | | | | | | | | | | | |
|---|---|---|---|---|---|---|---|---|---|---|---|
| 1 | 11 | 21 | 31 | 41 | 51 | 61 | 71 | 81 | 91 | 101 | 111 |
| 2 | 12 | 22 | 32 | 42 | 52 | 62 | 72 | 82 | 92 | 102 | 112 |
| 3 | 13 | 23 | 33 | 43 | 53 | 63 | 73 | 83 | 93 | 103 | 113 |
| 4 | 14 | 24 | 34 | 44 | 54 | 64 | 74 | 84 | 94 | 104 | 114 |
| 5 | 15 | 25 | 35 | 45 | 55 | 65 | 75 | 85 | 95 | 105 | 115 |
| 6 | 16 | 26 | 36 | 46 | 56 | 66 | 76 | 86 | 96 | 106 | 116 |
| 7 | 17 | 27 | 37 | 47 | 57 | 67 | 77 | 87 | 97 | 107 | 117 |
| 8 | 18 | 28 | 38 | 48 | 58 | 68 | 78 | 88 | 98 | 108 | 118 |
| 9 | 19 | 29 | 39 | 49 | 59 | 69 | 79 | 89 | 99 | 109 | 119 |
| 10 | 20 | 30 | 40 | 50 | 60 | 70 | 80 | 90 | 100 | 110 | 120 |

worksheets, solving mathematical problems in small groups or with a partner, working on mathematical problems that reflect real-life situations, working in mixed achievement groups on mathematics activities, and using computers to learn mathematics. A somewhat different pattern was evident for using music to understand mathematics, using creative movement or creative drama to understand mathematical concepts, completion of mathematical problems on the chalkboard, and engaging in peer tutoring. A quarter or more of the teachers indicated that they never asked students to do these activities, whereas another quarter or more used these activities at least one to two times per week.

### *Mathematics Practices Across Diverse Preschool Settings*

Findings from the few smaller scale studies that examined mathematics in early childhood settings show a similar pattern. In one study, teachers in two states from a range of preschool settings, including family and group child care providers, were surveyed about their mathematics instruction (Sarama, 2002; Sarama and DiBiase, 2004). Most teachers reported using manipulatives (95 percent), number songs (74 percent), and games (71 percent). Only 33 percent used software, and 16 percent reported using mathematical worksheets. Teachers reported a preference for children to explore mathematics activities and engage in free play rather than participate in large group lessons or do mathematical worksheets. The mathematics topics teachers reported were counting (67 percent), sorting (60 percent), numeral recognition (51 percent), patterning (46 percent), number concepts (34 percent), spatial relations (32 percent), making shapes (16 percent), and measuring (14 percent). The least popular topics were geometry and measurement.

In an observational study of New Jersey preschools, teachers were found to provide little support for children's mathematical skill development and seldom used mathematics terminology (Frede et al., 2007). Of particular interest is that over 40 percent of the classrooms in this study were rated as good to excellent quality on the ECERS-R measure of the environmental quality of early childhood programs. Apparently, mathematics teaching and learning is relatively rare even in classrooms that are otherwise judged to be of high quality.

## RESEARCH ON EFFECTIVE MATHEMATICS INSTRUCTION

The majority of research that is focused specifically on mathematics taught in early childhood examines the effectiveness of a particular mathematics curriculum (e.g., Clements and Sarama, 2008a; Sophian, 2004; Starkey, Klein, and Wakeley, 2004). Although much of this work meets very high empirical standards, it is often difficult to derive information about specific types of effective instructional practices from general information on whether or not a curriculum is successful. Nevertheless, this research base does provide some guidance on effective mathematics instruction. (Curriculum research is discussed later in the chapter.)

There is also a large body of research on effective instruction in early childhood that is not specific to mathematics. The general principles of effective instruction that emerge from this research can and should be taken into consideration when designing mathematics instruction for young children. Both of these bodies of research are briefly reviewed below. Taken together, they provide guidance on effective instruction, although further research on strategies specific to mathematics is needed.

The large body of research on effective instruction informed the development of the CLASS system for observation described briefly in the previous section. Since the domain of the CLASS most closely associated with the development of mathematics knowledge and skill is instructional supports, we begin with a discussion of various kinds of instructional supports as defined in the CLASS. We then move to discussion of other aspects of instruction that are important for supporting learning in mathematics.

### Instructional Supports

The theoretical foundation for the CLASS conceptualization of instructional supports comes primarily from research on children's cognitive and language development (e.g., Catts et al., 2002; Fujiki, Brinton, and Clarke, 2002; Romberg, Carpenter, and Dremlock, 2005; Taylor et al., 2003; Vygotsky, 1991; Wharton-McDonald and Pressley, 1998). This literature highlights the distinction between simply learning facts and gaining usable knowledge, which is built on learning how facts are interconnected, organized, and conditioned on one another (Mayer, 2002; National Research Council, 1999). A child's cognitive and language development is contingent on the opportunities adults provide to express existing skills and scaffold more complex ones (Davis and Miyake, 2004; Skibbe, Behnke, and Justice, 2004; Vygotsky, 1991). The development of metacognitive skills, including children's awareness and understanding of their own thinking processes as well as their executive function skills, are also critical to their academic development (Blair, 2002; Veenman, Kok, and Blote, 2005; Williams, Blythe, and White, 2002).

The CLASS assessment system has been validated, both in terms of its factor structure (Hamre et al., 2008b) and in relation to preschool children's language, literacy, and mathematics knowledge and social and emotional development (Burchinal et al., 2008; Howes et al., 2008; Mashburn et al., 2008). Children in classrooms that score higher on the instructional dimensions of concept development and quality of feedback, as measured by the CLASS, display greater gains in mathematics knowledge over the course of the year, although the effect sizes are small (between .10 and .20; Mashburn et al., 2008). These two dimensions of instructional support are discussed in greater detail below.

### *Promoting Conceptual Development*

Concept development describes the instructional behaviors, conversations, and activities that teachers use to help stimulate students' higher order thinking skills (Pianta et al., 2007), which refers not only to the acquisition of knowledge, but also to the ability to access and apply this knowledge in new situations (Mayer, 2002). The four key elements of high-quality concept development are (1) analysis and reasoning, (2) creating, (3) integration, and (4) connections to the real world.

In classrooms that fall at the high end of concept development, teachers not only plan activities in ways that will stimulate higher order thinking, but also they take advantage of the moment-to-moment opportunities in their daily interactions to push children toward deeper thinking. In contrast, classrooms that are low on conceptual development lack instructional opportunities or focus instruction solely on remembering facts or on simple tasks that require only recognition or recall.

### *Providing Scaffolding and Feedback*

In order for students to get the most benefit from instructional opportunities, they need feedback about their learning. Feedback refers to a broad range of interactions through which the teacher provides some information back to the students about their performance or effort. There are five major types of feedback interactions described in the CLASS: (1) scaffolding, (2) feedback loops, (3) prompting of thought processes, (4) provision of information, and (5) encouragement or affirmation. Feedback is a key element of formative assessment, which is discussed in greater detail later in this chapter.

***Scaffolding.*** Teachers scaffold children's learning by providing hints and assistance that enable them to perform at a higher level than they might be able to do on their own. This may occur during a whole-group or small-group discussion or individually during center time or children's play (scaffolding is also discussed in the section on formative assessment in this chapter).

***Feedback loops.*** Effective feedback is also characterized by sustained exchanges with a child (or group of children), leading them to a better or deeper understanding of a particular idea. This is in contrast to a teacher who might give a single hint to a child but then move on, even if the child does not seem to understand.

*Prompting thought processes.* This feedback strategy asks students to explain their thinking or actions. Prompting thought processes helps to identify children who may have completed an activity or answered a question correctly, but who cannot yet clearly articulate their reasoning. By having a child articulate his or her thought process, the teacher discovers erroneous thinking and can intervene. This learning opportunity is in contrast to one in which the teacher just tells the child that he or she was correct or incorrect.

*Providing information.* In the context of instructional interactions, children often give the wrong answer or action. Each instance provides an opportunity for effective feedback by expanding on children's answers and actions, clarifying incorrect answers, or providing very specific information about the correct answer. These are all in contrast to a teacher who simply tells students they are wrong.

*Encouragement and affirmation.* Another form of feedback consists of strategies that can motivate children to sustain their efforts and engagement. Simple recognition statements, such as "You are working really hard on that puzzle" reinforce students' effort and encourage persistence. This may be especially important in the area of mathematics, in which older children in the United States have been found to assume that mathematics achievement is a product of ability rather than effort (National Mathematics Advisory Panel, 2008). Young children may need help to learn that effort leads to improved results in learning mathematics.

### The Importance of Math Talk

In a mathematics context, teachers' use of language can facilitate connections between numbers, words, and ideas. In an elegant demonstration of the importance of mathematical language for young children, Klibanoff and colleagues (2006) showed that children exposed to more math talk in their preschool classrooms displayed greater gains in mathematical knowledge from October to April. The authors transcribed an hour of teachers' utterances, including circle time, and coded the transcripts for the number of mathematical inputs in the following categories: counting, cardinality, equivalence, nonequivalence, number symbols, conventional nominative (as in naming an address or phone number), ordering, calculation, and placeholding. There was a wide range of mathematical inputs among the 26 classrooms (a range from 1 to 104, with an average of 28). References to cardinality were the most common, accounting for 48 percent of all inputs. Many of the inputs, such as equivalence, nonequivalence, ordering, calculation, and placeholding, were rare, each accounting for less than 5 percent of all inputs.

After controlling for children's prior performance, those in classrooms with a higher number of mathematics inputs displayed better performance in April on a short (15-item), multiple-choice test of general mathematical knowledge. Klibanoff et al. (2006) found only a small correlation between teachers' syntactic complexity and frequency of math talk ($r = .18$). And only math talk, not syntactic complexity, was associated with gains in mathematical skills. As the authors point out, this is the first study to examine the specific effects of math talk on children's knowledge, and research is needed to understand more about the direct role of math talk in early childhood classrooms.

In general, the amount and kind of language that occurs in the classroom among teachers and children is frequently related to outcomes for children. Correlational research with preschoolers demonstrates that, during large-group times, teachers' explanatory talk and use of cognitively challenging vocabulary are related to better learning outcomes for children (Dickinson and Tabors, 2001).

The use of open-ended questions also has the potential to increase the math talk in a classroom or in a home. Effective teachers make greater use of open-ended questions than less effective teachers. They ask children "Why?" and "How do you know?" They expect children, as young as preschool, to share strategies, explain their thinking, work together to solve problems, and listen to each other (Askew et al., 1997; Carpenter et al., 1998, 1999; Clarke et al., 2001; Clements and Sarama, 2007a, 2008a; Cobb et al., 1991; Thomson et al., 2005). As the questions become internal, children can increasingly become self-sustaining mathematical learners who carry and use a mathematical lens for seeing and understanding their world. Examples of such open-ended mathematical questions are

- Where do you see this (mathematical idea) in our classroom?
- Tell me how you figured out (this mathematical idea).
- What is (insert mathematical idea, such as adding or subtracting)?
- What happens when I break this apart/put these together?
- How does this compare with something else? (Which one is smaller/larger? Longer/shorter?)
- Where are the units? What are the units (that children are familiar with)?
- Do you see a pattern? What is the pattern?
- How can I describe this idea for myself or for someone else (such as, can you draw a picture, describe it in words, or use your body)?

## Grouping as an Instructional Strategy

As described previously, data from the NCEDL studies and the ECLS-K indicate that mathematics is taught in a whole group most of the time, especially in kindergartens, where little time is allocated for centers or small groups. The almost nonexistent use of small groups in early childhood programs, documented in these studies, is of concern given that small-group instruction has been found to be an effective context for enhancing young children's learning (Dickinson and Smith, 1993; Karweit and Wasik, 1996; Morrow, 1988).

Various mathematics curricula that use small groups as one of several or as the main instructional strategy have shown substantial positive effects (e.g., Clements, 2007; Clements and Sarama, 2008a; Preschool Curriculum Evaluation Research Consortium, 2008; Sarama et al., 2008; Starkey et al., 2006). The results suggest that small-group work can significantly increase children's scores on tests aligned with that work (Klein and Starkey, 2004; Klein, Starkey, and Wakeley, 1999), and can transfer to knowledge and abilities that have not been taught (Clements and Sarama, 2007a). Guidelines in these curricula generally suggest four children with a teacher as the small-group size, although teachers have been observed using group sizes of two (for low achievers, for children with special needs, or to introduce an idea or activity for the first time) to six (usually for efficiency's sake; often used for easily managed activities).

Whole groups can also be effective for supporting mathematics learning. In one program, children as young as kindergarten engaged in teacher- and peer-scaffolded mathematics learning, problem solving, and discussion during whole-class instruction (Fuson and Murata, 2007). Based on teaching-learning paths, the program successfully enabled teachers to individualize mathematics in large-group activities—a promising strategy to give mathematics needed attention in the already packed schedule of half-day kindergarten. French and Song (1998) document extensive use of whole-group instruction to good effect in Korean preschools. Effective whole-group interactions include brief demonstrations and discussions, problem solving in which children talk to and work with the person next to them (other children and possibly adults), and physically active activities, such as marching around the room while counting (Clements, 2007; Clements and Sarama, 2007a, 2008a). Box 7-2 provides an example.

## Play as a Teaching and Learning Context

A highly motivating learning context for young children is child-initiated play (Wiltz and Klein, 2001). Preschool children engage in different types of play that have potentially different benefits for learning and develop-

**BOX 7-2**
**Mathematics Activities with Different Size Groups**

The Building Blocks Program dedicates several weeks to shape composition. One theme is puzzles. In a whole-group setting, the teacher asks the children what puzzles they like to solve at home and at school. She discusses various types of puzzles and what puzzles are, showing some examples, telling the children she will put them all out in the mathematics centers. She then introduces a new kind of puzzle: outline puzzles that can be completed with geometric shapes (e.g., pattern blocks or tangram pieces). She solves a simple puzzle with the children, using their ideas as to solutions.

Later, with small groups of four children, the teacher introduces several of the outline puzzles. She carefully observes children's solutions to these, evaluating where each child is in the learning trajectory for shape composition. Based on these observations, she provides individuals with puzzles at different levels of the learning trajectory (or mathematics teaching-learning paths), individualizing the challenge for each child.

Meanwhile, the teacher's assistant observes and discusses children's work with the puzzles in the mathematics center, as well as supervising those in other centers, allowing the teacher to concentrate on the small-group work. One special center involves a series of computer activities, the Piece Puzzler series, in which children also solve puzzles by manipulating pattern blocks or tangram pieces to complete similar outline puzzles. They use icons of the geometric motions to slide, turn, and flip the shapes into place. Individualized help and feedback are offered to them immediately. For example, if they put on too large a shape, covering the puzzle and also other areas, the computer activity makes the shape transparent and shows them that it covers too much (something difficult to show with physical manipulatives). Also, the computer activity automatically adjusts the levels of the puzzle to match the children's development along the learning trajectory.

ment. Among the typically observed play experiences in an early childhood classroom are constructive play, such as block building; play with table toys (manipulatives, puzzles, Lego blocks); pretend play; mathematical play; and games, including ones in which mathematics is a secondary focus, as well as ones in which mathematics is the primary focus. (Of course children also engage in outdoor play, rough-and-tumble play, and other forms of play that have benefits as well.)

### *Block Building*

Play, especially block play, provides valuable opportunities for children to explore and engage in mathematical activity on their own (Ginsburg, 2006; Hirsch, 1996). Young children enjoy playing with blocks, and there is evidence that they naturally engage in mathematical play with them (Seo and Ginsburg, 2004). However, mathematics learning is enhanced if teachers engage children in a discussion of mathematical principles during block play (Clements and Sarama, 2007a), such as introducing new terminology (e.g., edges, faces) and commenting on children's rotation of objects during construction. The provision of these supports by teachers during play enhances children's learning during the specific interaction as well as in future play sessions, when the child may incorporate these new ideas.

Research also indicates that teachers should incorporate planned, systematic block building into their curriculum, which they rarely do (Kersh, Casey, and Young, 2008). Preschoolers who are provided such scaffolding display significant increases in the complexity of their block building (Gregory, Kim, and Whiren, 2003). Important to our teaching-learning paths approach (also called learning trajectories), the teachers' scaffolding was based on professional development aimed at helping them recognize developmental progressions in the levels of complexity of block building. Teachers learned to provide verbal scaffolding based on those levels but not to directly assist children or engage in any block building themselves. Interventions that incorporate full teaching-learning paths—that is, a goal, a developmental progression, and matched activities—appear to be effective in developing children's skills. Groups of kindergartners who experienced such a learning trajectory improved in block-building skill more than control groups who received an equivalent amount of block-building experience during unstructured free play sessions (Kersh et al., 2008).

One longitudinal study indicated that block building may help lay a foundation for mathematics achievement in later years (Wolfgang, Stannard, and Jones, 2001). More specifically, block building has been linked to improved spatial skills, although most of these studies are correlational (Brosnan, 1998; Serbin and Connor, 1979). Similarly, in a preschool population, two types of block-building skills were associated with two measures of spatial visualization: block design and analyzing and reproducing abstract patterns (Caldera et al., 1999). In an experimental study, children who received instruction on spatial-manipulation improved in spatial visualization skills, whereas the control group did not (Sprafkin et al., 1983).

### *Sociodramatic Play*

One particularly valuable form of play is mature sociodramatic play—pretend play that lasts 10 minutes or more and involves a theme, props, roles, rules for roles, and language interaction. An example would be four children playing grocery store with play food, a cash register, and shopping carts, and different children playing the roles of store manager, cashier, and customers. Rules restrict the behavior of each player—for example, only the cashier can use the register. A Vygotskian-based curriculum, Tools of the Mind, uses this type of mature sociodramatic play as a primary format for children's learning and development (Bodrova and Leong, 2007). In this approach, teachers scaffold children's play skills by engaging them in preparing written play plans and reflecting after play is finished. Teachers work with children to make play more complex over time and to encourage the use of sophisticated vocabulary.

Studies of Tools of the Mind show positive impacts on language and early literacy (Barnett et al., 2006, 2008) and on self-regulation and executive functioning (Diamond et al., 2007). The latter is relevant for mathematics learning, as executive function and self-regulation are important for academic success. Executive function has been found to predict academic outcomes in school independent of intelligence or family background (Blair and Razza, 2007). Importantly, the approaches used in Tools of the Mind have been shown to be effective with children from low-income families.

### *Practice During Play*

Learning many early mathematics skills, such as counting, requires large amounts of practice to become fluent. Play can be an excellent context for children to practice developing abilities. For example, 3- and 4-year-old children will repeatedly attempt to build a block tower or string a set of beads in a pattern until they have mastered the skill to their personal satisfaction. Many mathematics competencies, such as counting, require repeated, often massive amounts of experience, as well as demonstrations, modeling, or scaffolding from adults (Fuson, 1988). Practice is important for consolidating skills, but such practice can be done in the meaningful and motivating context of children's play and with teachers' assistance as needed. For example, after a walk in the park, children can return to the classroom and examine their collections of leaves, trying to find out who has the most. The teacher can help the children to count their leaf collections, which they choose to do again and again. After repeatedly counting the separate collections, they can work as a group to count the total.

Children's play and self-selected activities can provide valuable contexts for mathematics teaching and learning experiences. Capitalizing on their everyday experience is likely to motivate and help them see the relevance in mathematics, as well as lead to complex child-centered projects that include mathematics. Early childhood education has a strong tradition of teachers' observation of children's play for the purpose of determining how best to respond to support their learning. Teachers can and should be intentional in supporting and mathematizing children's play experiences. However, using only "teachable moments" during child-initiated play is unlikely to lead to an effective, comprehensive mathematics program (Ginsburg, Lee, and Boyd, 2008).

### *Mathematical Play*

These examples bring us to another type of play, *mathematical play*, or *play with mathematics itself* (Sarama and Clements, 2009; see Steffe and Wiegel, 1994). The following features of mathematical play may be important for supporting learning: (a) it is a solver-centered activity with the solver in charge of the process; (b) it uses the solver's current knowledge; (c) it develops links between the solver's current schemes while the play is occurring; (d) it will, via "c," reinforce current knowledge; (e) it will assist future problem solving/mathematical activity as it enhances future access to knowledge; and (f) these behaviors and advantages apply irrespective of the solver's age (Holton et al., 2001).

### *Games*

One recent study provides evidence that board games in which young children count on (1 or 2) along a number list (squares with numbers on them) can be an effective instructional tool for developing their numerical knowledge (Siegler and Ramani, in press). In an experiment conducted in a Head Start program, children played a board game, similar to Chutes and Ladders, four times (for 15 to 20 minutes) over a two-week period. The game used numbered squares for the experimental group and colored squares for the control group. Children using the numbered squares said the numbers on the squares as they moved their token one or two spaces. At the end of the intervention, children who played the number game demonstrated increased knowledge of four different number skills: numerical magnitude comparison, number line estimation, numeral identification, and counting. The gains were still apparent nine weeks later (Siegler and Ramani, in press). To achieve such gains through play, however, requires that important mathematical structures are used by children within the game.

## Using Concrete Materials and Manipulatives

Using concrete materials, such as puzzles and matching games, with task selection and scaffolding adjusted to children's strategies, is effective in moving them through mathematics teaching-learning paths (Clements and Sarama, 2007a). Manipulatives, such as small blocks, cubes, beads, and pegs, are ubiquitous in high-quality early childhood classroom environments. There is evidence suggesting that the use of manipulatives enhances mathematical knowledge for young children (Clements and Sarama, 2007a). This is an area in which there has been a fair amount of mathematics-specific research (Clements and McMillen, 1996), although most work in this area has focused on elementary school children (e.g., Greabell, 1978;

Prigge, 1978). Concrete objects are needed for preschoolers to learn nonverbal and counting strategies for addition and subtraction. In fact, children need objects to solve larger number problems until about age 5½ (Jordan, Huttenlocher, and Levine, 1992). The manipulatives give meaning to the task, count words, and order (Clements and Sarama, 2007a). That is, at a certain level, number is an adjective rather than a noun for children—"5 kittens" is meaningful, but "5" as an abstract quantity is not.

Pictures can be useful in several ways, such as to illustrate concepts, and young children can learn to interpret pictures (Scott and Neufeld, 1976). However, manipulatives can be more effective than pictures for teaching certain mathematical concepts, because pictures are not manipulable, that is, they cannot be acted on extensively and flexibly (Clements and McMillen, 1996; Gerhardt, 1973; Prigge, 1978; Sowell, 1989; Stevenson and McBee, 1958). For example, in one study children benefited more from using pipe cleaners than pictures to make nontriangles into triangles (Martin, Lukong, and Reaves, 2007). They merely drew on top of the pictures, but they transformed the pipe cleaners.

The suggestion that manipulatives and other materials are effective should not be interpreted to mean that young children should always be provided with manipulatives or that simply providing these manipulatives is sufficient. Rather, teachers should be thoughtful about the most appropriate manipulative for a specific lesson. Once children have mastered a task using manipulatives, they can often solve simple arithmetic tasks without them (Grupe and Bray, 1999).

### Using Computers

As all-purpose tools, computers can also constitute quite different environments that support mathematics teaching and learning. They can provide effective experiences, ranging from complex problem solving to practice with concepts and skills, managed at the children's level of thinking and at the level of individual tasks.

The computer aids the metacognitive aspect of spatial activity, enabling the child to go beyond the physical world limitations (Clements and Battista, 1991; Johnson-Gentile, Clements, and Battista, 1994). For example, children can cut shapes and put them together in new ways. They become aware of and describe the geometric motions they use to solve geometric puzzles (Sarama and Clements, 2009; Sarama, Clements, and Vukelic, 1996)—that is, doing physical puzzles, they move shapes intuitively. However, on the computer, they choose the geometric motion—slide, flip, or turn—that they need. This helps them become explicitly aware of those motions and intentional in their use.

Children as young as age 3 have been shown to benefit from focused computer activities (Clements, 2003). Connected representations in practice or tutorial computer environments help them form concepts that are interrelated and thus mutually reinforcing. Computer environments can also foster deeper conceptual thinking, including a valuable type of "cognitive play" (Steffe and Wiegel, 1994). That is, children will pose problems for themselves and explore the computer objects or shapes with the same playful attitude—and the same beneficial learning—found in other types of play.

Several characteristics of effective computer software can guide its creation and selection (Clements and Sarama, 2005, 2008b; Sarama and Clements, 2002a, 2006):

- Actions and graphics should provide a meaningful context for children.
- Reading level, assumed attention span, and way of responding should be appropriate for the age level. Instructions should be clear, such as simple choices in the form of a picture menu.
- After initial adult support, children should be able to use the software independently. There should be multiple opportunities for success.
- Feedback should be informative.
- Children should be in control. Software should provide as much manipulative power as possible.
- Software should allow children to create, program, or invent new activities. It should have the potential for independent use but should also challenge. It should be flexible and allow more than one correct response.

As with using manipulatives, initial adult support and active mentoring has significant positive effects on children's learning with computers (Sarama and Clements, 2002b). Effective teachers closely guide children's learning of basic tasks; then they encourage experimentation with open-ended problems. These teachers are frequently encouraging, questioning, prompting, and demonstrating, without offering unnecessary help or limiting children's opportunity to explore. The teachers redirect inappropriate behaviors, model strategies, and give children choices. Whole-group discussions that help children communicate about their solution strategies and reflect on what they've learned are also essential components of good teaching with computers.

### Using Movement

Another context for learning mathematics is teachers' use of movement to engage children. There is evidence suggesting that young children benefit from engaging in self-directed movement during instruction, particularly in learning spatial concepts (Poag, Cohen, and Weatherford, 1983; Rieser, Garing, and Young, 1994). During a mapping activity, for example, children are more likely to benefit from actually taking a tour around the classroom than simply thinking about the classroom and being asked to represent it abstractly (Ginsburg and Amit, 2008).

### Book Reading

Book reading is used frequently in early childhood settings. Earlier studies have produced equivocal results with relation to the effect of book reading on mathematics achievement (Hong, 1996). However, several recent studies provide evidence that this can be an effective learning context for mathematics instruction (Casey, Kersh, and Young, 2004; Casey et al., 2008; Young-Loveridge, 2004). Young-Loveridge (2004) provides evidence that children exposed to a seven-week pull-out[4] mathematics program, using storybooks, rhymes, and games, made greater gains pre- to posttest on mathematical knowledge than did children not receiving this program. Casey and colleagues (2008) provide evidence that mathematics content (spatial and number skills) delivered in a storytelling context produced greater mathematics learning than delivering the content alone. Notably, the approach, Storytelling Sagas, is based on a series of specially written mathematics storybooks for preschool through Grade 2 that are primarily mathematical and secondarily for literacy. However, the approach demonstrates the important role of language in children's mathematics learning. In this study, researchers compared an intervention that taught a specific set of geometry skills in a storytelling context and alone. Kindergarten children who learned the geometry content in a storytelling context appeared to gain more knowledge, as assessed on both near- and far-transfer tasks. The authors suggest that the storytelling context engages children in the content in ways that more decontextualized instruction does not.

## FORMATIVE ASSESSMENT

A core instructional principle of early childhood education is that teaching must be child-centered and "developmentally appropriate" (Copple and Bredekamp, 2009). To promote genuine and enthusiastic learning, the teacher must be sensitive to the individual child's emotions and must establish a trusting and supportive relationship with him or her. But child-centered and developmentally appropriate teaching requires cognitive as well as emotional sensitivity: to support mathematics learning, the teacher

[4]Pull-out programs remove children from the regular classroom for some portion of the day to give specialized instruction.

must acquire an understanding of the child's current mathematical performance and knowledge.

Formative assessment is the process of gaining insight into children's learning and thinking in the classroom and using that information to guide instruction (Black and Wiliam, 1998b) and improve it (Black and Wiliam, 2004). According to the National Mathematics Advisory Panel (2008), "Teachers' regular use of formative assessments improves their students' learning, especially if teachers have additional guidance on using the assessment results to design and individualize instruction" (p. 47).

Formative assessment does not involve formal testing conducted outside the classroom (with results usually left there); however, it can provide teachers a way in which to track children's progress toward high-quality early learning standards. Formative assessment entails the use of several methods—observation, task, and flexible interview—to collect information about children's thinking and learning and then adapt teaching methods to help them learn. It is often inseparable from teaching and usually not distinctly identified as assessment. Teachers assess children all the time, often unaware that they do so. But formative assessment can also be more deliberate and organized than is usually the case. This section provides guidance about how teachers can use formative assessment to improve classroom teaching practices so that students' learning needs are best met.

### Rationale for Formative Assessment

The need for sound formative assessment is evident from a variety of theoretical perspectives. Approaches that stress the need to capitalize on the teachable moment (Dodge, Colker, and Heroman, 2002) require teachers to understand when that moment occurs—that is, when the child is ready to learn—and then to exploit it so as to help the child undertake further learning. Using observation to identify the teachable moment is one use of formative assessment (Seo, 2003).

Early childhood educators often draw on Vygotsky's theory to advocate effective scaffolding. Scaffolding in turn involves first determining the child's "actual developmental level" so that one can help the child reach his or her potential "through problem solving under adult guidance or in collaboration with more capable peers" (Vygotsky, 1978, p. 86). Determining both actual and potential developmental level, as well as the scaffolding useful to help the child traverse this "zone of proximal development," requires formative assessment.

Piaget's theory stresses the distinction between overt performance and underlying thought (Piaget and Inhelder, 1969). To illustrate: A child says that the sum of 3 apples and 2 apples is 6 apples. The incorrect response is clearly important and needs to be corrected, but even more important is the method used to obtain the response. The child may have got it by faulty memory ("I just knew it"), faulty calculation (the child miscounts the objects in front of him or her), or faulty reasoning ("I know that 3 and 2 is more than 4 and 6 is 2 more than 4"). Identifying and promoting underlying thought requires formative assessment.

Contemporary cognitive theories often stress establishing a link between the child's informal knowledge and what is to be taught (Baroody, 1987; National Research Council, 1999; Resnick, 1989, 1992). The child brings to the task of learning a body of prior knowledge—an "everyday mathematics" that is often relatively powerful and sometimes a source of misconceptions. In either case, the teacher needs to understand the child's current cognitive state (the everyday mathematics) in order to adjust instruction to it. Sometimes the everyday mathematics can serve as a fruitful basis for further development; the child's learning may in part involve mathematizing what she or he already knows. Sometimes the teacher needs to employ methods to help the child abandon everyday concepts in favor of more accurate notions, as when the child believes that the symbol = means "get an answer" instead of an equivalence relation (Seo and Ginsburg, 2003), or that a long, skinny scalene triangle is not an acceptable triangle (Clements, 2004).

Those who practice behavior modification also need to employ formative assessment to acquire an accurate account of the child's current behavior so they know what to shape. Careful observation of behavior and decisions about appropriate reinforcement can also be conceptualized under the rubric of formative assessment.

In brief, many theoretical approaches advocate getting information about the child's current behavior, thinking, and learning so that effective teaching can be implemented. It is hard to imagine a theory of teaching that would advocate ignorance of the child's mind or behavior.

## Three Kinds of Formative Assessment

Formative assessment is a very natural and commonplace activity for teachers, who do it all the time without necessarily knowing that what they do is assessment. Here we discuss three major kinds of formative assessment: everyday observations, tasks, and interviews (see Box 7-3). These everyday practices of observation, presenting tasks, and interviewing involve an informal, often unplanned, implementation of formative assessment, which is so bound up with everyday teaching that it often goes unrecognized. Yet the three types of formative assessment can be rigorous, focused, and deliberate. The early childhood assessment systems discussed here include widely used integrated programs as well as mathematics-specific programs: Big Math for Little Kids, Building Blocks, Core Knowledge, Creative Curriculum, High/Scope, and Number Worlds.

**BOX 7-3**
**Formative Assessment**

Teachers often use *everyday observations* to make inferences about children's abilities. The teacher sees that Juanita often spontaneously names shapes as she places them on the table. She can identify large and small objects and red and green objects as rectangles, and she even knows the name for a trapezoid. The teacher concludes that she can see the differences among various shapes, understands that color and size are irrelevant, and even knows some shape names. She is now ready to learn to mathematize her knowledge—that is, to analyze the properties of shapes so that she will understand explicitly what defines a rectangle and other shapes.

Teachers also give children specific *tasks* to elicit their understanding. The teacher has seen that Juanita spontaneously names rectangles and trapezoids but has never seen her name a square. So the teacher shows her a large red square and a small green one and asks what they are. Juanita says that the red one is a square but that the green one is not. Having given this specific task, the teacher now concludes that Juanita knows the name for square but applies it in a rather unusual way. The teacher is puzzled because Juanita was able to identify small green rectangles as rectangles, but she cannot ignore size or color in the case of squares.

Why does she do this? To find out, the teacher goes a step further. She wants to know how Juanita thinks about squares. What makes something a square? What's the role of color and size? Can she talk about it? So she *interviews* Juanita. She asks her why she said this large red object was a square, whereas this small green one was not. Juanita says that color does not matter, but that squares have to have 4 sides the same length and have to be big. Why do they have to be big? She does not know.

The teacher concludes that her lessons on shape should include specific attention to issues of size and when it is relevant or not relevant. And the teacher has a clue about how to proceed. She will put Juanita in a situation of cognitive conflict, which, according to Piaget (1985), is a major impetus to cognitive growth (Limon, 2001). She points out to Juanita that color and size do not matter for rectangles. Why should they matter for squares? Juanita looks puzzled. But then she quickly agrees that of course squares can be small, too. Her expression says: How silly to think otherwise! Assessments like these take place in many classrooms. Teachers observe their children, set them brief everyday tasks, and question them about their thinking. They do these classroom assessments on the fly, spontaneously, and without special preparation. Sometimes children learn a good deal, and sometimes they don't.

### *Observation*

Observation involves several components. One is obtaining useful information. The teacher needs to observe relevant aspects of an individual child's mathematical behavior. For example, she needs to observe that, in free play, the child is not only comparing the lengths of two blocks but also makes the mistake of failing to use a common baseline. This is not easy to do when the teacher must observe and supervise a room full of young children who have many needs and who exhibit complex patterns of behavior. There is an enormous amount of behavior taking place at any one moment in the classroom day. Nevertheless, it is possible for teachers to focus observations on at least a few children in order to provide activities that promote further mathematics learning.

A second important component of observation is interpretation of the evidence. The observer needs to understand what the behavior means. In the example above, the child's failure to use a common baseline in comparing the length of blocks indicates a common misconception of a fundamental idea underlying measurement (Clements, 2004; Piaget and Inhelder, 1967). Teachers need to be aware of and understand this misconception in order to interpret behavior accurately. Observation is very theoretical. To interpret everyday behavior, the teacher needs to be familiar with the development of mathematical thinking, as well as with the mathematics about which the child is thinking. Teachers need to receive professional development about learning in early childhood to be able to effectively interpret their observations of children's mathematical thinking.

A third component of observation is careful evaluation of evidence. Suppose the teacher sees a child spontaneously place a red and a blue isosceles triangle into one collection. But the child does not place a red skinny irregular (scalene) triangle into that same collection. Does this evidence suggest that the child has an understanding of triangles? On one hand, maybe the child did not see the small triangle and, had she seen it, perhaps would have placed it with the others, thus demonstrating at least some understanding of what defines a triangle. On the other hand, maybe she did see it and decided not to include it with the others because it was so strange looking, not an isosceles triangle, thus revealing that she had a narrow concept of a triangle. The evidence is inconclusive, and one cannot make a firm conclusion; both interpretations are possible. Evaluation of evidence requires skills of critical thinking that do not come easily and often need to be taught (Kuhn, 2005).

How well do teachers observe mathematical behavior? Research on this issue appears to be lacking. But there are reasons to be pessimistic about the likelihood that they make useful and insightful observations. Teachers seldom have time to observe behavior during free play; they tend to have their hands full with management and discipline (Kontos, 1999). Also, teachers may not know what to look for. As Piaget said, observation requires knowledge of what is to be observed—in this case, mathematical thinking: "if they are not on the lookout for anything . . . they will never find anything" (Piaget, 1976a, p. 9). In addition, as Chapter 8 discusses, early childhood teachers have little training in either early mathematics education or mathematics, especially in the analysis of mathematical behavior.

***Organized systems of observation.*** Teachers need guidance in the observation of mathematical behavior. Their college or university education may have provided some useful experience in observation. And although popular textbooks on the subject (e.g., Boehm and Weinberg, 1997; Cohen, Stern, and Balaban, 1997) discuss general issues of observation, they do not discuss in any depth the observation of mathematical behavior in particular.

Several widely used curricula offer guidance in observation of mathematical behavior. They may provide checklists for observation of various topics with directions about which behaviors should be recorded. For example, one form instructs teachers to record their observations of a child's knowledge of number and operations. The checklist specifically focuses on counting aloud in the correct order and grouping objects. A checklist like this is broad and provides teachers with little guidance for assessing children's mathematical knowledge. Rather, teachers should use the checklist as a start to assessing where children are on the mathematics teaching-learning path. Ideally, teachers would use follow-up questions and various tasks in conjunction with observation to ascertain the child's level of mathematical knowledge. At best, the observations give only an extremely crude idea of the child's interests and provide very little information about his or her knowledge.

Other widely used early childhood mathematics assessment systems offer the opportunity for the teacher to collect interesting anecdotes about individual children. For example, teachers create a personal log of each child's actions and abilities with spaces for writing numerous anecdotes—brief reports on individual children's classroom behavior and work samples that highlight their developing abilities. Again, we note that observation of mathematical behavior requires training and theoretical background. These assessment systems do not seem to provide evidence concerning the quality of observations or their usefulness.

Other curricula and their related assessment systems stress the analysis of various products of learning activities. The Reggio Emilia group in Italy uses "pedagogical documentation to capture learning moments through observation, transcriptions and visual representations that provoke reflection and inspire teachers, children, and parents to consider the significance of the interactions taking place, and the next steps to be taken in teaching and learning" (MacDonald, 2007, p. 232).

***Strengths and weaknesses of observation.*** Observation can be an extremely powerful method. It may provide insight into the child's spontaneous interests and everyday competence in the absence of adult pressure or constraint. Observation deals with behavior in "authentic" situations, like block play or snack time. The teacher may learn from careful observation that the child possesses a competence that is not expressed when he or she is tested or given instruction.

At the same time, no single method of assessment is perfect, always accurate, or completely informative, and observation has some limitations. Sometimes, the teacher can wait indefinitely before observing truly important behavior. Sometimes, the child's behavior does not express the true extent of her or his competence. As Piaget said: "How many inexpressible thoughts must remain unknown so long as we restrict ourselves to observing the child without talking to him?" (Piaget, 1976a, pp. 6-7). Thus, observation may show that the child does not seem to sort objects by common shapes, putting triangles into one group and rectangles into another. Instead, he or she places them all into one messy collection and tells stories about them. Does this mean that the child does not understand the difference between triangles and rectangles? The observer will never know without explicitly asking the child to sort them. This is a *task*, the next type of assessment.

### *Task*

Sometimes to find out about a child's learning, thinking, or performance, one presents him or her with some kind of task, a simple problem to solve. The teacher may ask, "What do you see in this picture book? What is the clown doing?" Or the teacher may say, "What do you call this thing [a triangle]?" The child's response may give an indication of his or her competence. If the child says, "The clown is juggling three balls," then the teacher may learn something about the accuracy of his or her counting skills. If in response to the question about the triangle the child says, "I don't know," then the teacher has learned that the child may not be able to produce the correct word or apply it to at least a certain kind of triangle. Yet from Vygotsky's perspective, the child's response to this task may be an indication only of current developmental level. The teacher therefore goes on to provide a little scaffolding, asking, "What shape is it?" The child then answers, "a triangle," and this indicates his level of potential development.

In brief, tasks are initiated by the teacher to learn about the child's performance with respect to a particular topic of interest to the teacher. Basically, the teacher wants to know whether the child can do something—count, recognize a triangle, or make a pattern—perhaps with a little help.

Evidence about how well teachers employ tasks in the classroom appears to be lacking. Yet it may be relatively easy for the teacher to ask the child to respond to simple tasks with which the child is engaged during free play ("What is that block called?") or to ask questions about the topic of the teacher's instruction ("Which animal is first in line?"). Of course the teacher must interpret the child's response with accuracy and is therefore faced with some of the same difficulties as discussed in the case of observation. The teacher must understand the development of mathematical thinking to appreciate the meaning of the child's response.

*Organized systems of tasks.* Some early childhood curricula present a series of tasks as the basis of their assessment system. For example, an item might instruct the teacher to use manipulative counters (e.g., blocks) to create different groups of objects containing between one and four items and to arrange the groups in different configurations (e.g., straight line, random grouping). The teacher would need to be sure that the child had several opportunities to correctly count, and she would record whether the child counted correctly and, for incorrect counts, the kinds of mistakes the child made.

The task employed, namely to count a given number of objects, is common both in the research literature and in some tests at this age level (e.g., Ginsburg and Baroody, 2003). What appears to be lacking, however, is any indication of how to interpret the results. What does it mean, for example, if the child can count a randomly arranged set of 3 but not 4, which he or she can count if it is placed in a line? Several primary mathematics curricula have a large collection of tasks with a clear theoretical basis (Case and Okamoto, 1996; Griffin, 2004).

*Strengths and weaknesses of tasks.* The strength of this method is that it provides information about the child's performance on a task in which the teacher has an interest. The teacher is attempting to teach something about pattern and needs to know whether the child is "getting it" so that she can take the next appropriate instructional step. There is some evidence that, at least at the elementary school level, frequent monitoring of student behavior can improve performance (Fuchs et al., 1999).

But there are at least two basic weaknesses in using tasks. The first is also its strength, namely that the teacher's interests determine the choice of task. The teacher is trying to teach pattern, but the child may in fact be more interested in or dealing with another topic, like the shapes of the objects intended to comprise the pattern. Because children do not always learn what teachers teach, teachers' questions about what they are trying to teach do not necessarily reveal what the child is learning. Second, the child's behavior may indicate success or failure on the task but does not necessarily reveal how the child construes or solves the task. As Piaget pointed out, it is not enough to ascertain the child's answer; one must in addition learn how the child got it. It is possible for the correct answer to be the result of a mechanical process devoid of understanding and for an incorrect answer to be the result of insightful thinking.

### *Flexible Interview*

A constructivist and child-centered perspective demands that the teacher go beyond observation and tasks to probe the child's thinking. Observation and tasks can provide useful information about performance, but the flexible interview is needed to dig below the surface to learn what the child is thinking. A truly child-centered, cognitively sensitive approach requires asking how the child solved the problem, how she got the answer, and why she said what she did. This kind of questioning originated in Piaget's "clinical interview method" (Piaget, 1976a), which we term "flexible interviewing," so as to avoid any connotation of the "clinical interview" devoted to the investigation and cure of pathological phenomena.

Flexible interviewing involves several steps (Ginsburg, 1997). First, the interviewer notices what seems to be an important child behavior worthy of further investigation. Sometimes this occurs in the course of naturalistic observation of everyday classroom activities. More frequently it occurs when the child gives an interesting response to a task. In either event, the interviewer follows up in various ways. He may rephrase the initial question, ask the child to talk about how she or he solved the problem, or request that the child expand on an answer or justify it. Occasionally the interviewer may challenge a child's response and ask her to prove why it is not correct. The essential questions include: "How did you figure it out? How did you know? How did you get the answer? Tell me more about it. How do you know you are right?"

In general, the rationale is that, if the goal is to learn what the child is thinking, the teacher must engage in flexible interviewing, asking the child to elaborate on his or her ways of interpreting and approaching a problem. Note that the flexible interview involves elements of both the task and observation. The interviewer frequently begins with a simple task for the child to solve ("What do you call this figure?") and then follows up on the child's response ("Why do you think it is a triangle?"). And as the child seems to be thinking about the problem or provides an answer, the interviewer carefully observes the child's behavior to determine, for example, whether he points to a certain object or looks confused or seems to whisper his thought aloud. Indeed, Piaget maintained that the interview method combines the best of observation and task.

Flexible interviewing involves a good deal of skill and mental agility. It requires the same kind of observational sensitivity, critical thinking, and interpretive skills discussed in connection with observation and task. It also requires the interviewer to think on her feet, to improvise, and to come up with the right follow-up question on the spot.

How frequently and well do teachers employ the flexible interview in the classroom? Research on the issue seems to be lacking. At the same time, flexible interviewing, although difficult, is a natural form of human interaction in which the participants attempt to make sense of problems and how they can be solved—"clinical interviewing is a species of naturally occurring mutual inquiry" (diSessa, 2007, p. 534). Asking a person why he or she said or did something is an entirely familiar form of discourse and not necessarily artificial or lacking in ecological validity.

***Organized systems.*** Few curricula provide extensive guidance in flexible interviewing. D.M. Clarke and colleagues (Clarke et al., 2001) have used a developmental trajectory theory as the basis for development of an extensive collection of "task-based interviews" for children beginning at age 5.

The collection of interview items is intended to form the basis for a comprehensive program of professional development, as well as to serve as a formative assessment tool for the teacher. "The [theoretical] framework of growth points provides a means for *understanding* young children's mathematical thinking in general, the interview provides a tool for *assessing* this thinking for particular individuals and groups, and the professional development program is geared towards *developing* further such thinking" (p. 2). In many respects, the work is a model for what should be done in this area. To date, few early childhood curricula provide guidance on flexible interview. Big Math for Little Kids (Ginsburg, Greenes, and Balfanz, 2003), however, includes extensive guidance on flexible interviewing for each major topic. The Number Worlds curriculum (Griffin, 2007) offers an assessment system that largely involves a series of tasks (boldly called "tests"), some of which include flexible interview follow-ups. For example, "How many *more* smiley faces does the hexagon have than the triangle has? How did you figure that out?" (p. 72). After these instructions, an example of a possible child response is presented: "2 more; I counted to 3 and there were 2 left that I didn't count" (p. 72). In general, the focus on flexible interviewing, even though it is at the very heart of a child-centered approach, is limited in current curricula.

***Strengths and weaknesses.*** The flexible interview can provide basic and often surprising information about children's knowledge. It sometimes shows that the child who seems to know something really doesn't, and the child who doesn't seem to know something really does. This kind of information can help teachers overcome preconceptions they might have about children's abilities. For example, teachers may expect low-income children to be more capable of procedural than conceptual knowledge.

The results of a flexible interview may help to disabuse the teachers of this preconception.

The flexible interview allows the interviewer to make sense of puzzling observations of everyday behavior or responses to tasks. The benefits accruing from this knowledge may be considerable: Understanding the child's perspective can provide a sensitive guide to instruction. If the child's wrong response was the result of a misinterpretation of the question, the teaching solution is different from what is needed if the response resulted from a basic misunderstanding.

Also, use of the method entails secondary benefits. Flexible interviewing requires that teachers talk a great deal with children. Furthermore, flexible interviewing not only promotes the teacher's language but also requires it from the child. Flexible interviewing stresses to the child the importance of talking about one's thinking, justifying one's conclusions, and in general engaging in mathematical communication, which as we have seen is one of the main goals of mathematics education at all levels (National Council of Teachers of Mathematics, 2000; National Research Council, 2001a). Indeed, the very process of being interviewed may have a salutary effect on the child. There is some evidence with older children that self-explanation (providing an explanation of material recently studied) promotes increased understanding (Chi et al., 1994). Similarly, the requirement to explain one's thinking might help one to examine, organize, and in the process even improve it.

Interviewing can be hard to do well, especially when very young children are involved. As noted, it demands interpretative skill, creativity, and flexibility in questioning. It is easy to ask misleading or uninformative questions and distort results; it requires considerable skill and sophistication to do really well. It is hard for young children to be aware of their mental processes or to describe them in words (Flavell, Green, and Flavell, 1995; Kuhn, 2000; Piaget, 1976). The strength of the method—its flexibility and sensitivity to the individual—is at the same time its weakness.

## Some General Remarks

In general, children's developmental characteristics make it difficult, although not impossible, to assess their learning, thinking, or performance. They can be shy, uncooperative, nonverbal, impatient, noncommunicative, and so on. Their self-regulation skills are imperfectly developed (Bronson, 2000), and they are egocentric (Piaget, 1955). The result is that assessment of the child at any one point in time may be inaccurate. But that does not mean teachers should not attempt to assess. It means that assessment needs to be done as sensitively as possible. Similarly, it is hard to diagnose a 2-year-old child's hearing, but there is a moral obligation to do it as well as possible.

Similarly, because of the natural fluctuation and rapid development of children's behavior, a single assessment—whether done by observation, task, or interview—may not provide accurate information. It is necessary to assess young children frequently and to base educational decisions on multiple sources of information (National Research Council, 2001b, 2008). Formative assessment should be complementary to program evaluation, which is conducted outside the classroom (see Box 7-4). Also, it is possible and sometimes desirable to blend the three methods. Thus, the teacher can observe in the natural setting and at the same time give the children simple tasks and even interview them.

The importance of teachers' understanding of their students cannot be overemphasized. According to the National Research Council report *Adding It Up: Helping Children Learn Mathematics*, "information about students is crucial to a teacher's ability to calibrate tasks and lessons to students' current understanding. . . . In addition to tasks that reveal what students know and can do, the quality of instruction depends on how teachers interpret and use that information. Teachers' understanding of their students' work and the progress they are making relies on . . . their ability to use that understanding to make sense of what the students are doing" (National Research Council, 2001a, pp. 349-350). Teachers' understanding of their students is the key, or at least one key to successful teaching.

Finally, although formative assessment shows great promise, the methods of assessment have not been clearly linked to instructional interventions. In fact, there seem to be few if any research studies that investigate the power of formative assessment to improve student achievement (exceptions include Black and Wiliam, 1998a, 1998b; Heritage, Kim, and Vendlinkskil, 2008). One of these studies suggests that, although elementary school teachers are reasonably skilled in interpreting student behavior, they have difficulty linking the assessment to subsequent teaching (Heritage, Kim, and Vendlinski, 2008). Clearly, further research and development are required. Development is needed to create links between assessment and instruction, and research is needed to investigate the effectiveness of those links. All of this should be easier to do in the teaching-learning paths described in this report because they keep the teacher situated in an organized set of goals with directionality both for individual children and for the class.

## RESEARCH ON THE EFFECTIVENESS OF MATHEMATICS CURRICULUM

Although this chapter addresses the topics of pedagogy and curriculum separately, in practice there is often no clear distinction between the two. This is especially true in early childhood education. Early childhood curriculum has traditionally emphasized the process of teaching and learning rather than the content of what children are learning (National Association

**BOX 7-4**
**Comments on Program Evaluation**

Programs for young children, like those for older ones, need to be held accountable. People want their children to receive the best early childhood mathematics education possible. There is no dispute as to the necessity for evaluation of programs, but the evaluation has to be as fair, sound, and based on scientific evidence and theory as much as possible.

Current evaluations are informative but limited. Several obstacles need to be overcome to improve the quality of evaluation efforts. First, it is hard to assess young children. Just as in the case of formative assessment, observation alone is insufficient, and the adult must employ some form of task or interview. But as pointed out earlier, even when a friendly adult does the assessment on a 1-to-1 basis, young children can be shy, uninterested, uncooperative, or inconsistent. Conditions like these require highly trained adult assessors who can engage children and approach the assessment with sensitivity and intelligence. This in turn "creates significant feasibility issues for large-scale accountability initiatives. Relatively large numbers of assessors must be trained and supervised. Quality assurance is another major challenge: the consistency, credibility and integrity of child assessment reports must be established and monitored" (National Early Childhood Accountability Task Force, 2007, p. 23).

Second, and even more important, there are few psychometrically valid assessment instruments to use in the evaluation of early mathematics education programs. Current instruments either focus on a narrow aspect of early mathematics, like number (e.g., Ginsburg and Baroody, 2003), or lack extensive psychometric support. A useful assessment should cover a broad array of mathematical knowledge, from number to pattern to space. Also, it should examine the "productive disposition," that is, the "habitual inclination to see mathematics as sensible, useful, and worthwhile, coupled with a belief in diligence and one's own efficacy" (National Research Council, 2001a, p. 5). And the evaluation it should be easy to administer and enjoyable to take. Such an instrument with sound psychometric qualities is not yet available. Because evaluations are only as valuable as the measures they employ, current evaluations must be considered of limited value.

Finally, it is as important to assess program quality, including teaching, to assess the children's performance. At present there are few psychometrically sound measures of early mathematics teaching or program quality (for an in-depth discussion on this topic, see National Research Council, 2008).

Just as early mathematics education has been neglected for many years, so have the methods needed to evaluate it. In view of the former, the latter should come as no surprise. As a result, considerable research and development need to be conducted to create evaluation methods appropriate for examining the quality of programs and their success in educating children.

for the Education of Young Children, 1997). Given this view of curriculum, research and debate have focused on which curriculum model is most effective in supporting children's short-term and long-term development (Epstein, Schweinhart, and McAdoo, 1996).

Many early childhood educators are not comfortable with defining curriculum as a written plan or specifying scope and sequence in advance. This concern grows out of the strong tradition of emergent curriculum in early childhood education (Jones and Nimmo, 1994). According to this perspective, the focus should be on children, not on curriculum. Advocates of emergent curriculum believe that children's interests and needs should determine what goes on in a classroom rather than a predetermined plan. They also assume that a planned scope and sequence cannot be responsive to children's individual and cultural variations.

Emergent curriculum is often implemented using the project approach (Katz and Chard, 1989), in which children and teachers engage in an intensive investigation of a topic of interest. Sometimes people refer to the project approach as a curriculum model, but it is more akin to a teaching strategy or context. In recent years, advocates of the project approach have been more specific about how state standards can be incorporated and met during the planning and implementation of a project (Helm and Katz, 2000). To help children achieve learning goals, educators have begun to emphasize intentional teaching in an emergent curriculum or project approach (Epstein, 2007).

During the past 15 years, early childhood practice in the United States (and throughout the world) has been influenced by the Reggio Emilia approach (Edwards, Gandini, and Forman, 1998). The approach is not a curriculum, nor is it a model. It is a coherent set of principles and practices that reflect a sociocultural perspective on learning and development. A key element of the approach is serious project work involving small groups of children collaborating with teachers to undertake investigations, theorizing, representing, revisiting experiences, and revising conceptualizations. Project work often arises from real rather than contrived situations. For example, one school needed a new table and the carpenter asked for measurements, a project documented in a book called *Shoe and Meter* (Reggio Children, 1997). The children worked together to figure out how to measure the table. They tried measuring using their various body parts but were dismayed to discover that each person's foot was a different length. Finally, they chose one child's foot to be their standard length. Then, they held his foot up to the ruler and determined how it compared, and so on.

In the past decade in the United States, there has been an explosion in commercially published early childhood curriculum resources. In 2007, the PreK Now website listed 27 research-based curricula for preschool children (see http://www.preknow.org). Some of these curricula are comprehensive—designed to address all domains of children's learning and development. These comprehensive programs tend to be organized into units, often called themes, based on children's predictable interests, but they are also broad enough to connect many different experiences and achieve multiple goals. Such themes usually include such topics as weather, animals, or construction. Comprehensive curricula are sometimes integrated curricula, in which one topic or experience is designed to meet goals across subject matter areas, such as reading a book that includes scientific information. Some comprehensive curricula have a limited number of themes, six to nine, allowing for more in-depth attention to the topic. Others change the topic weekly. In the past (and today as well), teacher-developed preschool "curriculum" was often theme-based, consisting of a series of activities related to the changing seasons, holidays, and events in children's lives, such as visits to the firehouse.

Often newly available curriculum resources are designed to provide instruction focusing on language, literacy, and/or mathematics. In some of these resources, learning and instruction are devoted to a single content domain, such as mathematics or literacy skills. Sometimes, a curriculum resource focuses on only one aspect of one domain rather than on an entire domain, such as phonological awareness or social-emotional development. These resources require teachers to figure out how to offer a coherent curriculum that covers all important learning goals.

Little research is available on the extent to which preschool programs use specific curriculum. The six-state study of prekindergarten conducted by the National Center for Early Development and Learning provides some evidence about curriculum use in state-funded preschool programs (Early et al., 2005). Only 4 percent of teachers reported having no curriculum, 14 percent used a locally developed curriculum, and 9 percent used a state curriculum. The most widely used curricula are High/Scope, with 38 percent of classrooms, and Creative Curriculum, accounting for 19 percent (National Center for Early Development and Learning Prekindergarten Study, 2005). These two curricula are also the most widely used in Head Start programs (U.S. Department of Health and Human Services, 2006).

There is increasing agreement over many early childhood teaching practices, often called developmentally appropriate practice (see previous section on effective instruction; see also Copple and Bredekamp, 2006, 2009). Developmentally appropriate practice as defined by the National Association for the Education of Young Children (Copple and Bredekamp, 2009) calls for teachers to make decisions that are informed by knowledge of child development and learning, knowledge about individual children, and knowledge about the social and cultural context in which they live. The concept is that teachers adapt the curriculum and teaching strategies for the age, experience, and abilities of individual children to help them make learning progress.

Despite the support for developmentally appropriate practice in the field, there is less acceptance of the need for a written curriculum, especially if that curriculum provides a planned sequence of teaching and learning opportunities (Lee and Ginsburg, 2007). Yet such a curriculum organized by research-based teaching-learning paths, such as those described in Chapters 5 and 6, or at least some learning path organization of the mathematics activities over the year, is needed to ensure that all children have a chance to learn the topics in the learning path. Such systematic opportunities are needed to help improve mathematical outcomes for all young children.

## Mathematics Curriculum

A limited amount of research is available on the effectiveness of specific mathematics curricula or curricular approaches. As described earlier, most early childhood programs do not include primary mathematics experiences or focused mathematics time but rather rely on integrated mathematics experiences in which mathematics is a secondary goal and often incidental (Preschool Curriculum Evaluation Research Consortium, 2008). However, incidental mathematics instruction appears to be less effective than activities with a primary focus on mathematics, although this evidence is only correlational (Starkey et al., 2006).

In addition, reliance on incidental or integrated mathematics may contribute to the fact that little time is spent on math. For example, in the Preschool Curriculum Evaluation Research (PCER) Study, conducted by the U.S. Department of Education, a literacy-oriented curriculum (Bright Beginnings, available at http://www.brightbeginningsinc.org/) and a developmentally focused one (Creative Curriculum, available at http://www.teachingstrategies.com/) engendered no more mathematics instruction than a control group (Aydogan et al., 2005). Other research (Farran et al., 2007) found a negligible time devoted to mathematics in a literacy-oriented comprehensive curriculum.

It is important to note, however, that in response to changing standards and current research, the developers of Creative Curriculum have recently added a mathematics component to their approach (Copley, Jones, and Dighe, 2007). In addition, the High/Scope curriculum (Hohmann and Weikart, 2002) is developing a more challenging focused mathematics component (Schweinhart, 2007).

Large effect sizes support the strategy of designing a mathematics curriculum built on comprehensive research-based principles, including an emphasis on hypothesized teaching-learning paths (Clarke, Clarke, and Horne, 2006; Clements and Sarama, 2007b, 2008a; Thomas and Ward, 2001; Wright et al., 2002). Most of these studies also emphasized key developmental milestones in the main teaching-learning paths, promoting deep, lasting learning of critical mathematical concepts and skills.

Teaching-learning paths or learning trajectories are useful instructional, as well as theoretical, constructs (Bredekamp, 2004; Clements and Sarama, 2004; Simon, 1995; Smith et al., 2006). The developmental progressions—levels of understanding and skill, each more sophisticated than the last—are essential for high-quality teaching based on understanding both mathematics and learning. Early childhood teachers' knowledge of young children's mathematical development is related to their students' achievement (Carpenter et al., 1988; Peterson, Carpenter, and Fennema, 1989). In one study, the few teachers that actually led in-depth discussions in reform mathematics classrooms saw themselves not as moving through a curriculum, but as helping students move through levels of understanding (Fuson, Carroll, and Drueck, 2000). Furthermore, research suggests that professional development focused on developmental progressions increases not only teachers' professional knowledge but also their students' motivation and achievement (Clarke, 2004; Clarke et al., 2001, 2002; Fennema et al., 1996; Kühne, van den Heuvel-Panhulzen, and Ensor, 2005; Thomas and Ward, 2001; Wright et al., 2002). Thus, teaching-learning paths can facilitate developmentally appropriate teaching and learning for all children (see Brown et al., 1995).

A few words of caution are in order in interpreting findings about mathematics curriculum research. In the early childhood context, randomized control trials in mathematics may tend to overstate effect sizes because teaching some mathematics will always be more effective than teaching no or almost no mathematics (which is usually what the control classrooms are doing). Comparing the large effect sizes of the mathematics PCER study (Starkey et al., 2006) with the results of no significant differences for most of the literacy PCER studies does not mean that mathematics curricula are effective while literacy curricula are not. Preschools have had a decade of focus on literacy, so the control groups in those studies were doing a lot of literacy as well as the experimental groups. Curricular research does have great potential to advance understanding of effective instructional strategies, but only if this research is conducted with this explicit goal in mind. The inclusion of observational measures, both of fidelity to the curriculum and generalized instructional processes, greatly enhances the ability of the research to speak to specific teaching strategies that may be most important for student learning.

For example, Clements and Sarama (2008a) included extensive observation using the Classroom Observation of Early Mathematics Environment and Teaching (COEMET) and Fidelity of Implementation during a randomized control trial of two mathematics curricula—Building Blocks and Preschool Mathematics Curriculum (PMC; Klein, Starkey, and Ramirez, 2002)—and a control condition. The results indicate that research-based mathematics preschool curricula can be implemented with good fidelity, if teachers are provided ongoing training and support.

Using data from the COEMET the researchers identified instructional strategies that significantly predicted gains in children's mathematical knowledge over the course of the year: (1) the percentage of time the teacher was actively engaged in activities, (2) the degree to which the teacher built on and elaborated children's mathematical ideas and strategies, and (3) the degree to which the teacher facilitated children's responding. Examples are provided in Box 7-5. In addition, the researchers' inclusion of multiple curricula also facilitates generalization beyond the effects of a specific curriculum to the broader approaches that may be embedded in it.

The ability of curricular research to inform effective practice would also be enhanced if individual curricula more clearly defined the instructional approaches embedded in them. Often curricula distinguish themselves in terms of content (e.g., covering geometry or not) and generalized approach (e.g., whole-group versus small-group instruction) more than in the instructional strategies that are endorsed and supported in the activities. Thus, any findings that one curriculum is more effective than another provides little knowledge about specific teaching strategies that may be useful.

### Improving Mathematics Outcomes for Children in Poverty

The limited amount of time devoted to the subject of mathematics may account for why Head Start children make little or no gain in mathematics. For example, using randomized assignment, the Head Start Impact Study found no significant impacts for the early mathematics skills of 3- or 4-year-olds (U.S. Department of Health and Human Services, 2005). Other examples include control groups from experiments (Clements and Sarama, 2007b; Clements and Lewis, 2009; Starkey et al., 2006). The control group in one study, for example, made small gains in number, but little or no gain in geometry (Clements and Sarama, 2007b) and Head Start children made no significant gain in any area of mathematics during the school year (control classrooms continued using their school's mathematics activities, which were informed by a mixture of influences ranging from commercially published curricula to homegrown materials based on state standards).

Research demonstrates that interventions with a primary focus on mathematics have the potential to increase the mathematics achievement of children living in poverty and those with special needs (Campbell and Silver, 1999; Clements and Lewis, 2009; Fuson, Smith, and Lo Cicero, 1997; Griffin, 2004; Griffin, Case, and Capodilupo, 1995; Ramey and Ramey, 1998), which can be sustained into first (Magnuson et al., 2004) to third grade (Gamel-McCormick and Amsden, 2002). For example, both the Building Blocks and Big Math for Little Kids curricula significantly and substantially increase the mathematical knowledge of children from low-income families (e.g., Clements and Lewis, 2009; Clements and Sarama, 2007b, 2008a). The success, even in comparison to other curricula, is probably due to the shared core of learning trajectories (teaching-learning paths) emphasized in the curriculum and the professional development that ensures that teachers spend time teaching appropriate mathematics topics during the year.

Another example, the Rightstart program[5] (Griffin, Case, and Siegler,

[5]Now published as Number Worlds (Griffin, 2004, 2007).

**BOX 7-5**
**Examples of Low-Quality and High-Quality Mathematics Teaching**

1. The teacher was actively engaged.

*Consider a situation in which the teacher has put out a mathematics center with play dough.*

A nonengaged teacher talks for several minutes exclusively to another adult in the room.

An engaged teacher works with several children at the center until she observes they "have the idea" of the activity. She keeps her eye on the center and encourages children to keep building.

Another works with children in another area of the room, but neither she nor the aide visits the math center.

In another room, the teacher works with children in another area of the room, while the aide visits the center and helps or acknowledges the children's mathematics work.

2. The teacher built on and elaborated children's mathematical ideas and strategies.

*Consider a situation in which children are to put some dinosaurs on a play scene and describe what they did. One child put out dinosaurs, but then just pointed.*

A teacher who did not build on or elaborate children's ideas, merely says, "OK."

A teacher who does build on or elaborate children's ideas says, "What do you have there?" The child does not respond.

Another teacher asks, "What are the dinosaurs doing?" "Fighting!" says the child, as he picks up the dinosaurs and loudly demonstrates the fighting. The teacher says, "That's enough of that!" excuses this child and calls another child to the activity.

"What are these two dinosaurs doing?" "Fighting." "How many are in your pond?" "Two." "What are they going to see? On the hill here? "A T-rex. One T-rex." "Wow! Four dinosaurs, two here and two on the pond, are seeing that Tyrannosaurus Rex. I'll bet they are scared!"

3. The teacher facilitated children's responding.

*Consider a situation in which the teacher asks one child to figure out how many 1 more than 3 is.*

One teacher who does not facilitate children's responding says to a child who does not answer, "Someone else can answer." Once another child gave the correct answer the teacher moves on to the next task.

A teacher who does facilitate children's responding says, "Can you show me 3 to get started?" The child says "four." The teacher asks, "Can you teach us how you did that?" After the child explains, the teacher asks, "Did anybody do it a different way?"

---

SOURCE: COEMET.

1994), which uses small-group games and active experiences with different models of number, led to substantial improvement in children's knowledge of number. Children in the program were better able to employ reasonable problem-solving strategies and solve arithmetic problems even more difficult than those in the program. (Core Knowledge includes a mathematics sequence developed by Sharon Griffin based on this work.)

Program children also passed five far-transfer tests that were hypothesized to depend on similar cognitive structures (e.g., balance beam, time, money). The foundation these children received supported their learning of new, more complex mathematics through Grade 1. In a 3-year longitudinal study in which children received consistent experiences from kindergarten through the primary grades, children gained and surpassed both a second low-income group and a mixed-income group that showed a higher initial level of performance and attended a magnet school with an enriched mathematics curriculum. The children also compared favorably with high-income groups from China and Japan (Case, Griffin, and Kelly, 1999). On a more limited scale, a study of 8 classrooms with 112 children found that a 6-week focused mathematics intervention was successful in improving Head Start children's mathematical skills as well as their interest in mathematics (Arnold et al., 2002). Teachers in experimental classrooms were provided with a choice of math-relevant activities to use during circle time, with small groups, and during routines and transitions, while the control classrooms did typical activities. Experimental group children scored significantly higher on the Test of Early Mathematics Ability (TEMA-2) and also reported that they enjoyed mathematics more than the control children. Teachers, too, reported that they increased their knowledge and enjoyment in implementing mathematics activities. Notably, boys showed substantial gains compared with girls, and African American and Puerto Rican children gained more than white children. Like other mathematics interventions, this study includes several variables, making it impossible to determine which particular teaching and learning experiences make the most difference to children. At the very least, the study indicates once again that more intentional teaching of mathematics leads to better mathematics outcomes.

## PRINCIPLES TO GUIDE MATHEMATICS CURRICULUM AND PEDAGOGY

Based on an extensive review of research on the current state of early mathematics education and effective practices, we present a set of principles to guide early childhood mathematics curriculum and instruction. Research points specifically to the following key indicators of an effective mathematics program at the preschool level (e.g., Clarke et al., 2002; Clements and Sarama, 2007b, 2008a; Thomson et al., 2005; Wood and Frid, 2005):

- Uses research to specify a comprehensive set of cognitive concepts, processes, and teaching-learning paths to design developmentally sequenced activities and help teachers collect data by observation and interaction with children and use those data to modify planning and teaching strategies. Tasks are sequenced, but teachers need to adapt for particular students' conceptual development rather than rigidly following a prescribed curriculum.
- Emphasizes mathematization of children's experiences, including redescribing (i.e., with more specific and often mathematical language), reorganizing, abstracting, generalizing, reflecting on, and giving language to what is first understood on an intuitive, informal level (premathematical foundations).
- Builds an awareness of the need for direct, formal development of children's concepts in mathematics together with an instructional focus on mathematics. This includes explicit plans for mathematics as a separate area of the program and ability to plan based on teaching-learning paths.
- Uses a variety of instructional methods, such as a combination of small groups, the whole group, play, routines and transitions, and computer activities. Uses teachable moments as they occur—in general, has the ability to make connections between mathematical ideas, between activities, between mathematics and other subjects, and everyday life.
- Uses an "assisted performance" approach to instruction that supports problem solving and inquiry processes in mathematics activities. Uses a variety of question types to encourage children to explain their thinking and to listen attentively to individual children and understand their level of thinking along mathematical teaching-learning paths.
- Engages and focuses children's thinking through introductions and activities. Draws out key mathematical ideas at the conclusion of an activity or period of study and helps children consolidate and connect their knowledge.
- Across the program, teachers show an interest in mathematics and have high but realistic expectations and clear goals and an ability to communicate these clearly. Engages and cultivates children's interests and motivation to learn mathematics.
- Uses classroom-based formative assessment to make adjustments to teachers' instructional practices so that they better understand children's learning needs and facilitate their mathematical development.

## SUMMARY

Young children in early childhood classrooms do not spend much time engaged in mathematics content. Time spent on mathematics increases somewhat in kindergarten. The time that is spent engaged in mathematics is typically of low instructional quality (La Paro et al., 2008) and, more often than not, is conducted as a part of whole-class activities or embedded in center time or free play. Early childhood teachers rarely teach mathematics in small groups. They report that they are much more likely to use embedded mathematical strategies or do the calendar, which they consider to be teaching mathematics, rather than provide experiences with a primary focus on mathematics in which they scaffold children's progress along important mathematics teaching-learning paths. Formative assessment has considerable potential to provide teachers with meaningful methods for assessing children's mathematical knowledge and improving their instruction to meet children's needs.

On a more optimistic note, the early childhood education field is actively working to improve the teaching of mathematics. The National Association for the Education of Young Children and the National Council of Teachers of Mathematics (2002) issued a joint position statement calling for more and better mathematics curriculum and teaching in early childhood programs. Head Start has launched a new mathematics professional development initiative. In addition, the reauthorization of Head Start calls for research-based curriculum and practices. The time is right to enhance young children's mathematics experiences not only to improve school readiness, but also to lay a foundation for lifelong understanding and enjoyment of mathematics. The challenges as well as the advances in research and policies aimed at improving young children's mathematics learning speak to the need for extensive professional development around young children's mathematics—the focus of the next chapter.

## REFERENCES AND BIBLIOGRAPHY

Archibald, S., and Goetz, M. (2008). *A Professional Development Framework for Pre-Kindergarten Education.* Paper commissioned by the Committee for Early Childhood Mathematics, Mathematics Science Education Board, Center for Education, Division of Behavioral and Sciences and Education, National Research Council, Washington, DC.

Arnold, D.H., Fischer, P.H., Doctoroff, G.L., and Dobbs, J., (2002). Accelerating math development in Head Start classrooms. *Journal of Educational Psychology, 94*(4), 762-770.

Askew, M., Brown, M., Rhodes, V., Johnson, D., and Wiliam, D. (1997, September). *Effective Teachers of Numeracy.* Paper presented at the British Educational Research Association Annual Conference (September 11-14, University of York). Available: http://www.leeds.ac.uk/educol/documents/000000385.htm [accessed July 2008].

Aubrey, C. (1997). Children's early learning of number in school and out. In I. Thompson (Ed.), *Teaching and Learning Early Numbers* (pp. 20-29). Philadelphia, PA: Open University Press.

Aydogan, C., Plummer, C., Kang, S.J., Bilbrey, C., Farran, D.C., and Lipsey, M.W. (2005). *An Investigation of Prekindergarten Curricula: Influences on Classroom Characteristics and Child Engagement.* Paper presented at the National Association for the Education of Young Children.

Barnett, W.S., Yarosz, D.J., Thomas, J., and Hornbeck, A. (2006). *Educational Effectiveness of a Vygotskian Approach to Preschool Education: A Randomized Trial.* Rutgers, NJ: National Institute for Early Education Research. Available: http://www.plan4preschool.org/documents/vygotskian.pdf [accessed August 2008].

Barnett, W.S., Jung, K., Yarosz, D.J., Thomas, J., Hornbeck, A., Stechuk, R., and Burns, S. (2008). Educational effects of the tools of the mind curriculum: A randomized trial. *Early Childhood Research Quarterly*, *23*(3), 299-313.

Baroody, A.J. (1987). *Children's Mathematical Thinking: A Developmental Framework for Preschool, Primary, and Special Education Teachers.* New York: Teachers College Press.

Black, P., and Wiliam, D. (1998a). Inside the black box: Raising standards through classroom assessment. *Phi Delta Kappan*, *80*(2), 139-148.

Black, P., and Wiliam, D. (1998b). Assessment and classroom learning. *Assessment in Education: Principles, Policy, and Practice*, *5*(1), 7-74.

Black, P., and Wiliam, D. (2004). The formative purpose: Assessment must first promote learning. In W. Wilson (Ed.), *Towards Coherence Between Classroom Assessment and Accountability. 103rd Yearbook of the National Society for the Study of Education, Part 2* (pp. 20-50). Chicago, IL: National Society for the Study of Education.

Blair, C. (2002). School readiness: Integrating cognition and emotion in a neurobiological conceptualization of children's functioning at school entry. *American Psychologist*, *57*, 2, 111-127.

Blair, C., and Razza, R.A. (2007). Relating effortful control, executive function, and false belief understanding to emerging math and literacy ability in kindergarten. *Child Development*, *78*, 647-663.

Bodrova, E., and Leong, D. (2007). *Tools of the Mind: The Vygotskian Approach to Early Childhood Education* (2nd ed). New York: Merrill/Prentice Hall.

Boehm, A.E., and Weinberg, R.A. (1997). *The Classroom Observer: Developing Observation Skills in Early Childhood Settings* (3d ed.). New York: Teachers College Press.

Bredekamp, S. (2004). Standards for preschool and kindergarten mathematics education. In D.H. Clements, J. Sarama, and A.-M. DiBiase (Eds.), *Engaging Young Children in Mathematics: Standards for Early Childhood Mathematics Education* (pp. 77-82). Mahwah, NJ: Erlbaum.

Bronson, M.B. (2000). *Self-regulation in Early Childhood: Nature and Nurture.* New York: The Guilford Press.

Brosnan, M.J. (1998). Spatial ability in children's play with Lego blocks. *Perceptual and Motor Skills*, *87*, 19-28.

Brown, M., Blondel, E., Simon, S., and Black, P. (1995). Progression in measuring. *Research Papers in Education*, *10*(2), 143-170, 177-179.

Burchinal, M., Howes, C., Pianta, R., Bryant, D., Early, D., Clifford, R., and Barbarin, O. (2008). Predicting child outcomes at the end of kindergarten from the quality of prekindergarten teacher-child interactions and instruction. *Applied Developmental Science*, *12*(3), 140-153.

Caldera, Y.M., Culp, A.M., O'Brien, M., Truglio, R.T., Alvarez, M., and Huston, A.C. (1999). Children's play preferences, construction play with blocks, and visual-spatial skills: Are they related? *International Journal of Behavioral Development*, *23*, 855-872.

Campbell, P.F., and Silver, E.A. (1999). *Teaching and Learning Mathematics in Poor Communities.* Reston, VA: National Council of Teachers of Mathematics.

Carpenter, T.P., Fennema, E., Peterson, P.L., and Carey, D.A. (1988). Teachers' pedagogical content knowledge of students' problem solving in elementary arithmetic. *Journal for Research in Mathematics Education*, *19*, 385-401.

Carpenter, T.P., Franke, M.L., Jacobs, V., Fennema, E., and Empson, S.B. (1998). A longitudinal study of invention and understanding in children's multidigit addition and subtraction. *Journal for Research in Mathematics Education, 29*, 3-20.

Carpenter, T.P., Fennema, E., Franke, M.L., Empson, S.B., and Levi, L.W. (1999). *Children's Mathematics: Cognitively Guided Instruction.* Portsmouth, NH: Heinemann.

Case, R., and Okamoto, Y. (1996). The role of central conceptual structures in the development of children's thought. *Monographs of the Society for Research in Child Development, 61*(Serial No. 246, Nos. 1-2).

Case, R., Griffin, S., and Kelly, W.M. (1999). Socieconomic gradients in mathematical ability and their responsiveness to intervention during early childhood. In D.P. Keating and C. Hertzman (Eds.), *Developmental Health and the Wealth of Nations* (pp. 125-149). New York: Guilford.

Casey, B., Kersh, J.E., and Young, J.M. (2004). Storytelling sagas: An effective medium for teaching early childhood mathematics. *Early Childhood Research Quarterly, 19*(10), 167-172.

Casey, B., Andrews, N., Schindler, H., Kersh, J.E., Samper, A., and Copley, J. (2008). The development of spatial skills through interventions involving block building activities. *Cognition and Instruction, 26*(3), 269-309.

Catts, H.W., Fey, M.E., Tomblin, J.B., and Zhang, Z. (2002). A longitudinal investigation of reading outcomes in children with language impairments. *Journal of Speech, Language, and Hearing Research, 45*, 1142-1157.

Chi, M.T.H., Leeuw, N.D., Chiu, M.-H., and LaVancher, C. (1994). Eliciting self-explanations improves understanding. *Cognitive Science, 18*, 439-477.

Clarke, B.A. (2004). A shape is not defined by its shape: Developing young children's geometric understanding. *Journal of Australian Research in Early Childhood Education, 11*(2), 110-127.

Clarke, B.A., Clarke, D.M., and Horne, M. (2006). A longitudinal study of mental computation strategies. In J. Novotná, H. Moraová, M. Krátká, and N. Stehlíková (Eds). *Proceedings of the 30th Conference of the International Group for Psychology of Mathematics Education* (vol. 2, pp. 329-336). Prague: PME.

Clarke, D.M., Cheeseman, J., Gervasoni, A., Gronn, D., Horne, M., McDonough, A., et al. (2001). Understanding, assessing, and developing young children's mathematical thinking: Research as powerful tool for professional growth. In J. Bobis, B. Perry, and M. Mitchelmore (Eds.), *Proceedings of the 24th Annual Conference of the Mathematics Education Research Group of Australasia* (vol. 1, pp. 9-26). Sydney, Australia: MERGA. Available: http://dlibrary.acu.edu.au/maths_educ/dougclarke/Clarke%20MERGA%20KEYNOTE%202001.pdf [accessed July 2008].

Clarke, D.M., Cheeseman, J., Gervasoni, A., Gronn, D., Horne, M., McDonough, A., Montgomery, P., Roche, A., Sullivan, P., Clarke, B., and Rowley, G. (2002). *Early Numeracy Research Project Final Report.* Melbourne: Australian Catholic University.

Clements, D.H. (2003). Teaching and learning geometry. In J. Kilpatrick, W.G. Martin, and D. Schifter (Eds.), *A Research Companion to Principles and Standards for School Mathematics* (pp. 151-178). Reston, VA: National Council of Teachers of Mathematics.

Clements, D.H. (2004). Geometric and spatial thinking in early childhood education. In D.H. Clements, J. Sarama, and A.-M. DiBiase (Eds.), *Engaging Young Children in Mathematics: Standards for Early Childhood Mathematics Education* (pp. 267-297). Mahwah, NJ: Erlbaum.

Clements, D.H. (2007). Curriculum research: Toward a framework for "research-based curricula." *Journal for Research in Mathematics Education, 38*, 35-70.

Clements, D.H., and Battista, M.T. (1991). Developing effective software. In E. Kelly and R. Lesh (Ed.), *Handbook of Innovative Research Design in Mathematics and Education.* Englewood Cliffs, NJ: Erlbaum.

Clements, D.H., and Battista, M.T. (1994). Computer environments for learning geometry. *Journal of Educational Computing Research, 10*(2), 173-197.

Clements, P., and Lewis, A.E. (2009). *The Effectiveness of the Big Math for Little Kids Curriculum: Does It Make a Difference?* Paper presented at the American Educational Research Association Annual Meeting, April, San Diego, CA.

Clements, D.H., and McMillen, S. (1996). Rethinking "concrete" manipulatives. *Teaching Children Mathematics, 2*(5), 270-279.

Clements, D.H., and Sarama, J. (2003). Young children and technology: What does the research say? *Young Children, 58*(6), 34-40.

Clements, D.H., and Sarama, J. (2004). Building blocks for early childhood mathematics. *Early Childhood Research Quarterly, 19,* 181-189. Available: http://www.gse.buffalo.edu/RP/PDFs/BB_ECRQ.pdf [accessed July 2008].

Clements, D.H., and Sarama, J. (2005). Young children and technology: What's appropriate? In W. Masalski and P.C. Elliott (Eds.), *Technology-supported Mathematics Learning Environments: 67th Yearbook* (pp. 51-73). Reston, VA: National Council of Teachers of Mathematics.

Clements, D.H., and Sarama, J. (2007a). Early childhood mathematics learning. In F.K. Lester, Jr. (Ed.), *Second Handbook of Research on Mathematics Teaching and Learning* (pp. 461-555). New York: Information Age.

Clements, D.H., and Sarama, J. (2007b). Effects of a preschool mathematics curriculum: Summative research on the Building Blocks project. *Journal of Research in Mathematics Education, 38*(2), 136-163.

Clements, D.H., and Sarama, J. (2008a). Experimental evaluation of the effects of a research-based preschool mathematics curriculum. *American Educational Research Journal, 45,* 443-494.

Clements, D.H., and Sarama, J. (2008b). Mathematics and technology: Supporting learning for students and teachers. In O.N. Saracho and B. Spodek (Eds.), *Contemporary Perspectives on Science and Technology in Early Childhood Education* (pp. 127-147). Charlotte, NC: Information Age.

Clifford, R.M., Barbarin, O., Chang, F., Early, D., Bryant, D., Howes, C., Burchinal, M. and Pianta, R. (2005). What is prekindergarten? Characteristics of public prekindergarten programs. *Applied Developmental Science, 9*(3), 126-143.

Cobb, P., Wood, T., Yackel, E., Nicholls, J., Wheatley, G., Trigatti, B., and Perlwitz, M. (1991). Assessment of a problem-centered second grade mathematics project. *Journal for Research in Mathematics, 22,* 3-29.

Cohen, D.H., Stern, V., and Balaban, N. (1997). *Observing and Recording the Behavior of Young Children* (4th ed.). New York: Teachers College Press.

Connor, C.M., Son, S., and Hindman, A.H. (2005). Teacher qualifications, classroom practices, family characteristics, and preschool experience: Complex effects on first graders' vocabulary and early reading outcomes. *Journal of School Psychology, 43*(4), 343-375.

Copley, J.V., Jones, C., and Dighe, J. (2007). *Math: The Creative Curriculum® Approach.* Washington, DC: Teaching Strategies.

Copple, C., and Bredekamp, S. (2006). *Basics of Developmentally Appropriate Practice: An Introduction for Teachers of Children 3 to 6.* Washington, DC: National Association for the Education of Young Children.

Copple, C., and Bredekamp, S. (2009). *Developmentally Appropriate Practice in Early Childhood Programs Serving Children from Birth Through Age 8.* Washington, DC: National Association for the Education of Young Children.

Davis, E.A., and Miyake, N. (2004). Explorations of scaffolding in complex classroom systems. *Journal of the Learning Sciences, 13*(3), 265-272.

Denham, S.A., and Weissberg, R.P. (2004). Social-emotional learning in early childhood: What we know and where to go from here. In E. Chesebrough, P. King, T.P. Gullotta, and M. Bloom (Eds.), *A Blueprint for the Promotion of Prosocial Behavior in Early Childhood* (pp. 13-50). New York: Kluwer Academic.

Diamond, A., Barnett, S., Thomas, J., and Munro, S. (2007). Preschool program improves cognitive control. *Science*, *318*, 1387-1388.

Dickinson, D., and Smith, M.W. (1993). Long-term effects of preschool teachers' book readings on low-income children's vocabulary and story comprehension. *Reading Research Quarterly*, *29*(2), 104-122.

Dickinson, D., and Tabors, P. (2001). *Beginning Literacy with Language: Young Children Learning at Home and School.* Baltimore, MD: Paul H. Brookes.

diSessa, A.A. (2007). An interactional analysis of clinical interviewing. *Cognition and Instruction*, *25*(4), 523-565.

Dodge, D.T., Colker, L., and Heroman, C. (2002). *The Creative Curriculum® for Preschool* (4th ed.). Washington, DC: Teaching Strategies.

Early, D.M., Barbarin, O., Bryant, D., Burchinal, M., Chang, F., Clifford, R., et al. (2005). *Pre-kindergarten in Eleven States: NCEDL's Multi-state Study of Pre-Kindergarten and Study of State-wide Early Education Programs (SWEEP).* Chapel Hill: University of North Carolina. Available: http://www.fpg.unc.edu/NCEDL/pdfs/SWEEP_MS_summary_final.pdf [accessed August 2008].

Edwards, C., Gandini, L., and Forman, G. (Eds.) (1998). *The Hundred Languages of Children: The Reggio Emilia Approach—Advanced Reflections* (2nd ed.) Greenwich, CT: Ablex.

Emmer, E.T., and Stough, L. (2001). Classroom management: A critical part of educational psychology, with implications for teacher education. *Educational Psychologist*, *36*(2), 103-112.

Epstein, A.S. (2007). *The Intentional Teacher: Choosing the Best Strategies for Young Children's Learning.* Washington, DC: National Association for the Education of Young Children.

Epstein, A.S., Schweinhart, L.J., and McAdoo, L. (1996). *Models of Early Childhood Education.* Ypsilanti, MI: High/Scope Educational Research Foundation.

Farran, D.C., Lipsey, M., Watson, B., and Hurley, S. (2007). *Balance of Content Emphasis and Child Content Engagement in an Early Reading First Program.* Paper presented at the American Educational Research Association.

Fennema, E., Carpenter, T., Franke, M., Levi, L., Jacobs, V., and Empson, S. (1996). A longitudinal study of learning to use children's thinking in mathematics instruction. *Journal for Research in Mathematics Learning*, *27*(4), 403-434.

Fisch, S.M. (2008). *The Role of Educational Media in Preschool Mathematics Education.* Paper commissioned by the Committee for Early Childhood Mathematics, Mathematics Science Education Board, Center for Education, Division of Behavioral and Sciences and Education, National Research Council, Washington, DC.

Flavell, J.H., Green, F.L., and Flavell, E.R. (1995). Young children's knowledge about thinking. *Monographs of the Society for Research in Child Development*, *60*(Serial No. 243, No. 1).

Foegen, A., Jiban, C., and Deno, S. (2007). Progress monitoring measures in mathematics: A review of the literature. *Journal of Special Education*, *41*(2), 121-139.

Forman, G.E. (1982). A search for the origins of equivalence concepts through a microanalysis of block play. In G.E. Forman (Ed.), *Action and Thought* (pp. 97-135). New York: Academic Press.

Frede, E., Jung, K., Barnett, W.S., Lamy, C.E., and Figueras, A. (2007). *The Abbott Preschool Program Longitudinal Effects Study (APPLES).* Rutgers, NJ: National Institute for Early Education Research.

French, L., and Song, M. (1998). Developmentally appropriate teacher-directed approaches: Images from Korean kindergartens. *Journal of Curriculum Studies*, *39*, 409-430.

Fuchs, L.S., Fuchs, D., Karns, K., Hamlett, C.L., and Katzaroff, M. (1999). Mathematics performance assessment in the classroom: Effects on teacher planning and student problem solving. *American Educational Research Journal, 36*(3), 609-646.

Fujiki, M., Brinton, B., and Clarke, D. (2002). Emotion regulation in children with specific language impairment. *Language, Speech, and Hearing Services in Schools, 33*, 102-111.

Fuson, K.C. (1988). *Children's Counting and Concept of Number.* New York: Springer-Verlag.

Fuson, K.C., and Murata. A. (2007). Integrating NRC principles and the NCTM process standards to form a class learning path model that individualizes within whole-class activities. *National Journal of Math Education Leadership, 19*(1), 72-91.

Fuson, K.C., Smith, S.T., and Lo Cicero, A. (1997). Supporting Latino first graders' ten-structured thinking in urban classrooms. *Journal for Research in Mathematics Education, 28*, 738-760.

Fuson, K., Carroll, W.M., and Drueck, J.V. (2000). Achievement results for second and third graders using the standards-based curriculum, everyday mathematics. *Journal for Research in Mathematics Education, 31*(3), 277-295.

Gamel-McCormick, M., and Amsden, D. (2002). *Investing in Better Outcomes: The Delaware Early Childhood Longitudinal Study.* Dover: Delaware Interagency Resource Management Committee and the Department of Education.

Gerhardt, C. (1973). *Hypersurfaces of Prescribed Mean Curvature over Obstacles, Math.* Available: http://www.math.uni-heidelberg.de/studinfo/gerhardt/dissertation-MZ133.pdf [accessed August 2008].

Gersten, R., Chard, D., Jayanthi, M., Baker, S., Morpy, S.K., and Flojo, J.R. (in press). *Teaching Mathematics to Students with Learning Disabilities: A Meta-analysis of the Intervention Research.* Portsmouth, NH: RMC Research Corporation, Center on Instruction.

Ginsburg, H.P. (1997). *Entering the Child's Mind: The Clinical Interview in Psychological Research and Practice.* New York: Cambridge University Press.

Ginsburg, H.P. (2006). Mathematical play and playful mathematics: A guide for early education. In D. Singer, R.M. Golinkoff, and K. Hirsh-Pasek (Eds.), *Play = Learning: How Play Motivates and Enhances Children's Cognitive and Social-Emotional Growth* (pp. 145-165). New York: Oxford University Press.

Ginsburg, H.P., and Amit, M. (2008). What is teaching mathematics to young children? A theoretical perspective and case study. *Journal of Applied Developmental Psychology, 29*(4), 274-285.

Ginsburg, H.P., and Baroody, A.J. (2003). *The Test of Early Mathematics Ability* (3rd ed.). Austin, TX: Pro Ed.

Ginsburg, H.P., and Russell, R.L. (1981). Social class and racial influences on early mathematical thinking. *Monographs of the Society for Research in Child Development, 46*(6, Serial No. 193).

Ginsburg, H.P., Greenes, C., and Balfanz, R. (2003). *Big Math for Little Kids.* Parsippany, NJ: Dale Seymour.

Ginsburg, H.P., Lee, J., and Boyd, J.S. (2008). Mathematics education for young children: What it is and how to promote it. *Social Policy Report Giving Child and Youth Development Knowledge Away, 22*(1). Available: http://www.srcd.org/index.php?option=com_contentandtask=viewandid=232andItemid=1 [accessed August 2008].

Greabell, L.C. (1978). The effect of stimuli input on the acquisition of introductory geometry concepts by elementary school children. *School Science and Mathematics, 78*(4), 320-326.

Greenberg, M.T., Weissberg, R.P., and O'Brien, M.U. (2003). Enhancing school-based prevention and youth development through coordinated social, emotional, and academic learning. *American Psychologist, 58*(6-7), 466-474.

Gregory, K.M., Kim, A.S., and Whiren, A. (2003). The effect of verbal scaffolding on the complexity of preschool children's block constructions. In D.E. Lytle (Ed.), *Play and Educational Theory and Practice: Play and Culture Studies* (pp. 117-134). Westport, CT: Praeger.

Griffin, S. (2004). Number worlds: A research-based mathematics program for young children. In D.H. Clements, J. Sarama, and A.-M. DiBiase (Eds.), *Engaging Young Children in Mathematics: Standards for Early Childhood Mathematics Education* (pp. 325-342). Mahwah, NJ: Erlbaum.

Griffin, S. (2007). *SRA Number Worlds: A Prevention/Intervention Math Program. Assessment Level A.* Columbus, OH: SRA/McGraw-Hill.

Griffin, S., Case, R. and Siegler, R.S. (1994). Rightstart: Providing the central conceptual prerequisites for first formal learning of arithmetic to students at risk for school failure. In K. McGilly (Ed.), *Classroom Lessons: Integrating Cognitive Theory and Classroom Practice* (pp. 25-40). Cambridge, MA: MIT Press.

Griffin, S., Case, R., and Capodilupo, A. (1995). Teaching for understanding: The importance of the central conceptual structures in the elementary mathematics curriculum. In A. McKeough, J. Lupart, and A. Marini (Eds.), *Teaching for Transfer: Fostering Generalization in Learning* (pp. 121-151). Mahwah, NJ: Erlbaum.

Grupe, L.A., and Bray, N.W. (1999). *What Role Do Manipulatives Play in Kindergartners' Accuracy and Strategy Use When Solving Simple Addition Problems?* Albuquerque, NM: Society for Research in Child Development.

Guarino, C.M., Hamilton, L.S., Lockwood, J.R., and Rathbun, A.H. (2006). *Teacher Qualifications, Instructional Practices, and Reading and Mathematics Gains of Kindergartners.* NCES# 2006-031. Washington, DC: National Center for Education Statistics, U.S. Department of Education.

Hamre, B.K., and Pianta, R.C. (2001). Early teacher-child relationships and the trajectory of children's school outcomes through eighth grade. *Child Development*, 72(2), 625-638.

Hamre, B.K., and Pianta, R.C. (2005). Can instructional and emotional support in the first grade classroom make a difference for children at risk of school failure? *Child Development*, 76(5), 949-967.

Hamre, B.K., and Pianta, R.C. (2007). Learning opportunities in preschool and early elementary classrooms. In R.C. Pianta, M.J. Cox, and K. Snow (Eds.), *School Readiness and the Transition to School* (pp. 49-84). Baltimore, MD: Paul H. Brookes.

Hamre, B.K., Downer, J.T., Kilday, C.R., and McGuire, P. (2008a). *Effective Teaching Practices for Early Childhood Mathematics.* Paper commissioned by the Committee for Early Childhood Mathematics, Mathematics Science Education Board, Center for Education, Division of Behavioral and Sciences and Education, National Research Council, Washington, DC.

Hamre, B.K., Mashburn, A.J., Pianta, R.C., and Downer, J. (2008b). *Validation of a 3-Factor Model for Classroom Quality Across Preschool to Fifth Grade.* Manuscript submitted for publication.

Hannula, M.M. (2005). *Spontaneous Focusing on Numerosity in the Development of Early Mathematical Skills.* Turku, Finland: University of Turku.

Harms, T., Clifford, R.M., and Cryer, C. (1998) *Early Childhood Environment Rating Scale-Revised.* New York: Teachers College Press.

Hart, B., and Risley, T.R. (1995). *Meaningful Differences in the Everyday Experience of Young American Children.* Baltimore, MD: Paul H. Brookes.

Hart, B., and Risley, T.R. (1999). *The Social World of Children: Learning to Talk.* Baltimore, MD: Paul H. Brookes.

Head Start Bureau. (1998). *Head Start Program Performance Standards.* Washington, DC: Administration for Children and Families.

Helm, J.H., and Katz, L. (2000). *Young Investigators: The Project Approach in the Early Years.* New York: Teachers College Press.

Heritage, M., Kim, J., and Vendlinski, T. (2008). *From Evidence to Action: A Seamless Process in Formative Assessment?* Presentation at the American Educational Research Association Annual Meeting, March 24-28, New York. Available: http://www.cse.ucla.edu/products/overheads/AERA2008/heritage_assessment.ppt [accessed July 2008].

Hirsch, E.S. (1996). *The Block Book* (3rd ed.). Washington, DC: National Association for the Education of Young Children.

Hohmann, M., and Weikart, D. (2002). *Educating Young Children: Active Learning Practices for Preschool and Child Care Programs.* Ypsilanti, MI: High/Scope Press.

Holton, D., Ahmed, A., Williams, H., and Hill, C. (2001). On the importance of mathematical play. *International Journal of Mathematical Education in Science and Technology, 32*, 401-415.

Hong, H. (1996). Effects of mathematics learning through children's literature on math achievement and dispositional outcomes. *Early Childhood Research Quarterly, 11*, 477-494.

Howes, C., Burchinal, M., Pianta, R., Bryant, D., Early, D., Clifford, R., and Barbarin, O. (2008). Ready to learn? Children's pre-academic achievement in pre-kindergarten programs. *Early Childhood Research Quarterly, 23*(1), 27-50.

Hughes, M. (1981). Can preschool children add and subtract? *Educational Psychology, 1*, 207-219.

Hyson, M. (2008). *Preparing Teachers to Promote Young Children's Mathematical Competence.* Paper commissioned by the Committee for Early Childhood Mathematics, Mathematics Science Education Board, Center for Education, Division of Behavioral and Sciences and Education, National Research Council, Washington, DC.

Johnson-Gentile, K., Clements, D.H., and Battista, M.T. (1994). The effects of computer and noncomputer environments on students' conceptualizations of geometric motions. *Journal of Educational Computing Research, 11*(2), 121-140.

Jones, E., and Nimmo, J. (1994). *Emergent Curriculum.* Washington, DC: National Association for the Education of Young Children.

Jordan, N.C., Huttenlocher, J., and Levine, S.C. (1992). Differential calculation abilities in young children from middle- and low-income families. *Developmental Psychology, 28*, 644-653.

Jordan, N.C., Hanich, L.B., and Uberti, H.Z. (2003). Mathematical thinking and learning difficulties. In A.J. Baroody and A. Dowker (Eds.), *The Development of Arithmetic Concepts and Skills: Constructing Adaptive Expertise* (pp. 359-383). Mahwah, NJ: Erlbaum.

Kamii, C., Miyakawa, Y., and Kato, Y. (2004). The development of logico-mathematical knowledge in a block-building activity at ages 1-4. *Journal of Research in Childhood Education, 19*, 13-26.

Karweit, N. and Wasik, B. (1996). The effects of story reading programs on literacy and language development of disadvantaged preschoolers. *Journal of Education for Students Placed At-Risk, 4*, 319-348.

Katz, L.G., and Chard, S.C. (1989). *Engaging Children's Minds: The Project Approach.* Norwood, NJ: Ablex.

Kersh, J., Casey, B., and Young, J.M. (2008). Research on spatial skills and block building in girls and boys: The relationship to later mathematics learning. In B. Spodek and O.N. Saracho (Eds.), *Mathematics, Science, and Technology in Early Childhood Education* (pp. 233-252). Charlotte, NC: Information Age.

Klein, A., and Starkey, P. (2004). Fostering preschool children's mathematical knowledge: Findings from the Berkeley math readiness project. In D.H. Clements, J. Sarama, and A.-M. DiBiase (Eds.), *Engaging Young Children in Mathematics: Standards for Early Childhood Mathematics Education* (pp. 343-360). Mahwah, NJ: Erlbaum.

Klein, A., Starkey, P., and Wakeley, A. (1999). *Enhancing Pre-Kindergarten Children's Readiness for School Mathematics.* Paper presented at the American Educational Research Association. Montreal, Canada.

Klein, A., Starkey, P., and Ramirez, A.B. (2002). *Pre-K Mathematics Curriculum.* Glenview, IL: Scott Foresman.

Klibanoff, R.S., Levine, S.C., Huttenlocher, J., Vasilyeva, M., and Hedges, L.V. (2006). Preschool children's mathematical knowledge: The effect of teacher 'math talk'. *Developmental Psychology, 42*(1), 59-69.

Kontos, S. (1999). Preschool teachers' talk, roles, and activity settings during free play. *Early Childhood Research Quarterly, 14*(3), 363-382.

Kuhn, D. (2000). Metacognitive development. *Current Directions in Psychological Science, 9*(5), 178-181.

Kuhn, D. (2005). *Education for Thinking.* Cambridge, MA: Harvard University Press.

Kühne, C., van den Heuvel-Panhulzen, M., and Ensor, P. (2005). Learning and teaching early number: Teachers' perceptions. In H.L. Chick and J.L. Vincent (Eds.), *Proceedings of the 29th Conference of the International Group for the Psychology of Mathematics Education* (vol. 3, pp. 217-224). Melbourne: PME. Available: http://www.emis.de/proceedings/PME29/PME29RRPapers/PME29Vol3KuhneEtAl.pdf [accessed July 2008].

La Paro, K.M., Hamre, B.K., LoCasale, J., Pianta, R.C., et al. (2008). *Pre-K and Kindergarten Classrooms: Observational Evidence for the Need to Increase Quality of Children's Learning Opportunities in Early Education Classrooms.* Manuscript submitted for publication.

Lee, J.S., and Ginsburg, H.P. (2007). Preschool teachers' beliefs about appropriate early literacy and mathematics education for low- and middle-socioeconomic status children. *Early Education and Development, 18*(1), 111-143.

Limon, M. (2001). On the cognitive conflict as an instructional strategy for conceptual change: A critical appraisal. *Learning and Instruction, 11*(4-5), 357-380.

Lonigan, C.J., and Whitehurst, G.J. (1998). Relative efficacy of parent and teacher involvement in a shared-reading intervention for preschool children from low-income backgrounds. *Early Childhood Research Quarterly, 13*(2), 263-290.

MacDonald, M. (2007). Toward formative assessment: The use of pedagogical documentation in early elementary classrooms. *Early Childhood Research Quarterly, 22,* 232-242.

Magnuson, K.A., Meyers, M.K., Rathbun, A., and West, J. (2004). Inequality in preschool education and school readiness. *American Educational Research Journal, 41,* 115-157.

Martin, T., Lukong, A., and Reaves, R. (2007). The role of manipulatives in arithmetic and geometry tasks. *Journal of Education and Human Development, 1,* 1. Available: http://www.scientificjournals.org/journals2007/articles/1073.htm [accessed August 2008].

Mashburn, A.J., Pianta, R., Hamre, B.K., Downer, J.T., Barbarin, O., Bryant, D., Burchinal, M., Clifford, R., Early, D., and Howes, C. (2008). Measures of classroom quality in prekindergarten and children's development of academic, language, and social skills. *Child Development, 79*(3), 732-749.

Mayer, R.E. (2002). Rote versus meaningful learning. *Theory into Practice, 41,* 226-233.

Morrow, L.M. (1988). Young children's responses to one-to-one reading in school settings. *Reading Research Quarterly, 23,* 89-107.

National Association for the Education of Young Children. (1997). *Developmentally Appropriate Practice in Early Childhood Programs.* S. Bredekamp and C. Copple (Eds.). Washington, DC: Author. Available: http://www.naeyc.org/about/positions/pdf/PSDAP98.pdf [accessed August 2008].

National Association for the Education of Young Children. (2007). *Developmentally Appropriate Practice in Early Childhood Programs Serving Children from Birth Through Age 8.* Draft position statement. Available: http://www.naeyc.org/about/positions/pdf/draftdap0208.pdf [accessed August 2008].

National Association for the Education of Young Children and National Council of Teachers of Mathematics. (2002). *Early Childhood Mathematics: Promoting Good Beginnings.* A joint position statement of the National Association for the Education of Young Children and the National Council of Teachers of Mathematics. Available: http://www.naeyc.org/about/positions/pdf/psmath.pdf [accessed August 2008].

National Center for Early Development and Learning Pre-Kindergarten Study. (2005). *Early Developments*, 9(1), spring issue. Available: http://www.fpg.unc.edu/~ncedl/PDFs/ED9_1.pdf [accessed August 2008].

National Council of Teachers of Mathematics. (2000). *Principles and Standards for School Mathematics.* Reston, VA: Author.

National Council of Teachers of Mathematics. (2006). *Curriculum Focal Points.* Reston, VA: Author.

National Early Childhood Accountability Task Force. (2007). *Taking Stock: Assessing and Improving Early Childhood Learning and Program Quality.* Washington, DC: Pew Charitable Trusts. Available: http://www.policyforchildren.org/pdf/Task_Force_Report.pdf [accessed August 2008].

National Mathematics Advisory Panel. (2008). *Foundations for Success: The Final Report of the National Mathematics Advisory Panel.* Washington, DC: U. S. Department of Education. Available: http://www.ed.gov/about/bdscomm/list/mathpanel/report/final-report.pdf [accessed August 2008].

National Research Council. (1999). *How People Learn: Brain, Mind, Experience, and School.* Committee on Developments in the Science of Learning. J.D. Bransford, A.L. Brown, and R.R. Cocking (Eds.). Commission on Behavioral and Social Sciences and Education. Washington, DC: National Academy Press.

National Research Council. (2001a). *Adding It Up: Helping Children Learn Mathematics.* Mathematics Learning Study Committee. J. Kilpatrick, J. Swafford, and B. Findell (Eds.). Center for Education, Division of Behavioral and Social Sciences and Education. Washington, DC: National Academy Press.

National Research Council. (2001b). *Eager to Learn: Educating Our Preschoolers.* Committee on Early Childhood Pedagogy. B.T. Bowman, M.S. Donovan, and M.S. Burns (Eds.). Commission on Behavioral and Social Sciences and Education. Washington, DC: National Academy Press.

National Research Council. (2008). *Assessing Accomplished Teaching: Advanced-Level Certification Programs.* Committee on Evaluation of Teacher Certification by the National Board for Professional Teaching Standards. M.D. Hakel, J.A. Koenig, and S.W. Elliott (Eds.). Board on Testing and Assessment, Center for Education. Division of Behavioral and Social Sciences and Education. Washington, DC: The National Academies Press.

Palincsar, A.S., and Brown, A.L. (1984). Reciprocal teaching of comprehension-fostering and comprehension-monitoring activities. *Cognition Instruct., 1*, 117-175.

Peterson, P.L., Carpenter, T.P., and Fennema, E. (1989). Teachers' knowledge of students' knowledge in mathematics problem solving: Correlational and case analyses. *Journal of Educational Psychology, 81*(4), 558-569.

Piaget, J. (1955). *The Language and Thought of the Child.* Cleveland, OH: World.

Piaget, J. (1976a). *The Child's Conception of the World.* (J. Tomlinson and A. Tomlinson, Trans.). Totowa, NJ: Littlefield, Adams.

Piaget, J. (1976b). *The Grasp of Consciousness: Action and Concept in the Young Child.* (S. Wedgwood, Trans.). Cambridge, MA: Harvard University Press.

Piaget, J. (1985). *The Equilibration of Cognitive Structures.* (T. Brown and K J. Thampy, Trans.). Chicago, IL: The University of Chicago Press.

Piaget, J., and Inhelder, B. (1967). *The Child's Conception of Space.* (F.J. Langdon and J.L. Lunzer, Trans.). New York: W.W. Norton.

Piaget, J., and Inhelder, B. (1969). *The Psychology of the Child.* (H. Weaver, Trans.). New York: Basic Books.

Pianta, R.C., Steinberg, M.S., and Rollins, K.B. (1995). The first two years of school: Teacher-child relationships and deflections in children's classroom adjustment. *Development and Psychopathology*, *7*, 295-312.

Pianta, R.C., Howes, C., Burchinal, M., Bryant, D., Clifford, R., Early, C., and Barbarin, O. (2005). Features of pre-kindergarten programs, classrooms, and teachers: Do they predict observed classroom quality and child-teacher interactions? *Applied Developmental Science*, *9*(3), 144-159.

Pianta, R.C., La Paro, K., and Hamre, B.K. (2007). *Classroom Assessment Scoring System™ (CLASS™)*. Baltimore, MD: Paul H. Brookes.

Pianta, R.C., Belsky, J., Houts, R., Morrison, F., and NICHD ECCRN. (2007). Opportunities to learn in America's elementary classrooms. *Science*, *315*, 1795-1796. Available: http://www.sciencemag.org/cgi/content/abstract/315/5820/1795?ijkey=09d80c0aad2b21db100d5ad6115fa1d36666bcdfandkeytype2=tf_ipsecsha [accessed August 2008].

Pianta, R.C., La Paro, K., and Hamre, B.K. (2008). *Classroom Assessment Scoring System*. Baltimore, MD: Paul H. Brookes.

Poag, C.K., Cohen, R., and Weatherford, D.L. (1983). Spatial representations of young children: The role of self-versus adult-directed movement and viewing. *Journal of Experimental Child Psychology*, *35*, 172-179.

Preschool Curriculum Evaluation Research Consortium. (2008). *Effects of Preschool Curriculum Programs on School Readiness*. NCER 2008-2009. Washington, DC: National Center for Education Research, Institute of Education Sciences, U.S. Department of Education.

Prigge, G.R. (1978). The differential effects of the use of manipulative aids on the learning of geometric concepts by school children. *School Science and Mathematics*, *78*(4), 320-326.

Ramey, C.T., and Ramey, S.L. (1998). Early intervention and early experience. *American Psychologist*, *53*, 109-120.

Raver, C.C. (2004). Placing emotional self-regulation in sociocultural and socioeconomic contexts. *Child Development*, *75*(2), 346-353.

Reggio Children. (1997). *Shoe and Meter: Children and Measurement, First Approaches to the Discovery, Function, and Use of Measurement*. Reggio Emilia, Italy: Author.

Resnick, L.B. (1989). Developing mathematical knowledge. *American Psychologist*, *44*, 162-169.

Resnick, L.B. (1992). From protoquantities to operators: Building mathematical competence on a foundation of everyday knowledge. In G. Leinhardt, R. Putnam, and R.A. Hattrup (Eds.), *Analysis of Arithmetic for Mathematics Teaching* (pp. 373-429). Hillsdale, NJ: Erlbaum.

Reys, B.J., Chval, K.B., and Switzer, J. (2008). *Mathematics Standards for Kindergarten: Summary of State-Level Attention and Focus*. Paper commissioned by the Committee for Early Childhood Mathematics, Mathematics Science Education Board, Center for Education, Division of Behavioral and Sciences and Education, National Research Council, Washington, DC.

Rieser, J.J., Garing, A.E., and Young, M.F. (1994). Imagery, action, and young children's spatial orientation: It's not being there that counts, It's what one has in mind. *Child Development*, *65*, 1262-1278.

Rimm-Kaufman, S.E., Early, D.M., and Cox, M.J. (2002). Early behavioral attributes and teachers' sensitivity as predictors of competent behavior in the kindergarten classroom. *Journal of Applied Developmental Psychology*, *23*(4), 451-470.

Ritchie, S., Howes, C., Kraft-Sayre, M., and Weiser, B. (2001). *Emerging Academics Snapshot*. Unpublished, University of California at Los Angeles.

Romberg, T.A., Carpenter, T.P., and Dremock, F. (2005). *Understanding Mathematics and Science Matters*. Mahwah, NJ: Erlbaum.

Sarama, J. (2002). Listening to teachers: Planning for professional development. *Teaching Children Mathematics*, *9*, 36-39.

Sarama, J., and Clements, D.H. (2002a). Design of microworlds in mathematics and science education. *Journal of Educational Computing Research*, *27*(1 & 2), 1-6.

Sarama, J., and Clements, D.H. (2002b). Learning and teaching with computers in early childhood education. In O.N. Saracho and B. Spodek (Eds.), *Contemporary Perspectives on Science and Technology in Early Childhood Education* (pp. 171-219). Greenwich, CT: Information Age.

Sarama, J., and Clements, D.H. (2006). Mathematics, young students, and computers: Software, teaching strategies and professional development. *The Mathematics Educator*, *9*(2), 112-134.

Sarama, J., and Clements, D.H. (2009). *Early Childhood Mathematics Education Research: Learning Trajectories for Young Children*. New York: Routledge.

Sarama, J., and DiBiase, A.-M. (2004). The professional developmental development challenge in preschool mathematics. In D.H. Clements, J. Sarama, and A.-M. DiBiase (Eds.) *Engaging Children in Mathematics: Standards for Early Childhood Mathematics Education* (pp. 415-446). Mahwah, NJ: Erlbaum.

Sarama, J., Clements, D.H., and Vukelic, E.B. (1996). The role of a computer manipulative in fostering specific psychological/mathematical processes. In E. Jakubowski, D. Watkins, and H. Biske (Eds.), *Proceedings of the 18th Annual Meeting of the North America Chapter of the International Group for the Psychology of Mathematics Education*. Columbus, OH: ERIC Clearinghouse for Science, Mathematics, and Environmental Education.

Sarama, J., Clements, D.H., Starkey, P., Klein, A., and Wakeley, A. (2008). Scaling up the implementation of a pre-kindergarten mathematics curriculum: Teaching for understanding with trajectories and technologies. *Journal of Research on Educational Effectiveness*, *1*, 89-119.

Schickedanz, J.A. (2008). *Increasing the Power of Instruction: Integration of Language, Literacy, and Math Across the Preschool Day*. Washington, DC: National Association for the Education of Young Children.

Schweinhart, L. (2007, November). *The High/Scope Model and Mathematics*. PowerPoint presentation at the 2nd Meeting of the Committee on Early Childhood Mathematics, National Academies, Washington, DC. Available: http://www.nationalacademies.org/cfe/Schweinhart%20Presentation.pdf [accessed August 2008].

Scott, L.F., and Neufeld, H. (1976). Concrete instruction in elementary school mathematics: Pictorial vs. manipulative. *School Science and Mathematics*, *76*, 68-72.

Scott-Little, C. (2008). *Mathematics Content Addressed in State-Level Early Learning Standards*. Paper commissioned by the Committee for Early Childhood Mathematics, Mathematics Science Education Board, Center for Education, Division of Behavioral and Sciences and Education, National Research Council, Washington, DC.

Scott-Little, C., Lesko, J., Martella, J. and Milburn, P. (2007). Early learning standards: Results from a national survey to document trends in state-level policies and practices. *Early Childhood Research in Practice*, *9*(1). Available: http://ecrp.uiuc.edu/v9n1/little.html [accessed July 2008].

Seo, K.-H. (2003). What children's play tells us about TEACHING mathematics. *Young Children*, *58*(1), 28-34.

Seo, K.-H., and Ginsburg, H.P. (2003). "You've got to carefully read the math sentence...": Classroom context and children's interpretations of the equals sign. In A.J. Baroody and A. Dowker (Eds.), *The Development of Arithmetic Concepts and Skills: Recent Research and Theory* (pp. 161-187). Mahwah, NJ: Erlbaum.

Seo, K.-H., and Ginsburg, H.P. (2004). What is developmentally appropriate in early childhood mathematics education? In D.H. Clements, J. Sarama, and A.M. DiBiase (Eds.), *Engaging Children in Mathematics: Standards for Early Childhood Mathematics Education* (pp. 91-104). Mahwah, NJ: Erlbaum.

Serbin, L.A., and Connor, J.M. (1979). Sex-typing of children's play preferences and patterns of cognitive performance. *The Journal of Genetic Psychology, 134*, 315-316.

Siegler, R.S., and Ramani, G.B. (in press). Playing board games promotes low-income children's numerical development. *Developmental Science.*

Silver, R.B., Measelle, J., Essex, M., and Armstrong, J.M. (2005). Trajectories of externalizing behavior problems in the classroom: Contributions of child characteristics, family characteristics, and the teacher-child relationship during the school transition. *Journal of School Psychology, 43*, 39-60.

Simon, M. (1995). Reconstructing mathematics pedagogy from a constructivist perspective. *Journal for Research in Mathematics Education, 26*, 114-145.

Skibbe, L., Behnke, M., and Justice, L.M. (2004). Parental scaffolding of children's phonological awareness skills: Interactions between mothers and their preschoolers with language difficulties. *Communication Disorders Quarterly, 25*(4), 189-203.

Smith, C.L., Wiser, M., Anderson, C.W., and Krajcik, J., (2006). Implications of research on children's learning for standards and assessment: A proposed learning progression for matter and the atomic molecular theory. *Measurement: Interdisciplinary Research and Perspectives, 4*(1 & 2), 1-98.

Sophian, C. (2002). Learning about what fits: Preschool children's reasoning about effects of object size. *Journal for Research in Mathematics Education, 33*, 290-302.

Sophian, C. (2004). Mathematics for the future: Developing a Head Start curriculum to support mathematics learning. *Early Childhood Research Quarterly, 19*(1), 59-81.

Sowell, E. (1989). Effects of manipulative materials in mathematics instruction. *Journal for Research in Mathematics Education, 20*, 498-505.

Sprafkin, C., Serbin, L.A., Denier, C., and Connor, J.M. (1983). Gender-differentiated play: Cognitive consequences and early interventions. In M.B. Liss (Ed.), *Social and Cognitive Skills: Gender Roles and Children's Play*. New York: Academic Press.

Starkey, P., Klein, A., and Wakeley, P. (2004). Enhancing young children's mathematical knowledge through a pre-kindergarten mathematics intervention. *Early Childhood Research Quarterly, 19*, 99-120.

Starkey, P., Klein, A., Sarama, J., and Clements, D.H. (2006). *Preschool Curriculum Evaluation Research*. Paper presented at the American Educational Research Association.

Steffe, L.P., and Wiegel, H.G. (1994). Cognitive play and mathematical learning in computer microworlds. *Journal of Research in Childhood Education, 8*(2), 117-131.

Stevenson, H.W., and McBee, G. (1958). The learning of object and pattern discriminations by children. *Journal of Comparative and Physiological Psychology, 51*(6), 752-754.

Stiles, J., and Stern, C. (2001). Developmental change in spatial cognitive processing: Complexity effects and block construction performance in preschool children. *Journal of Cognition and Development, 2*, 157-187.

Taylor, B.M., Pearson, P.D., Peterson, D.S., and Rodriguez, M.C. (2003). Reading growth in high-poverty classrooms: The influence of teacher practices that encourage cognitive engagement in literacy learning. *The Elementary School Journal, 104*, 3-28.

Teaching Strategies, Inc. (2001). *Creative Curriculum®*. Available: http://www.creativecurriculum.net/index.cfm [accessed February 2008].

Thomas, B. (1982). *An Abstract of Kindergarten Teachers' Elicitation and Utilization of Children's Prior Knowledge in the Teaching of Shape Concepts*. Unpublished manuscript, School of Education, Health, Nursing, and Arts Professions, New York University.

Thomas, G., and Ward, J. (2001). *An Evaluation of the Count Me in Too Pilot Project*. Wellington, New Zealand: Ministry of Education.

Thomson, S., Rowe, K., Underwood, C., and Peck, R. (2005). *Numeracy in the Early Years: Project Good Start*. Camberwell, Victoria, Australia: Australian Council for Educational Research.

U.S. Department of Health and Human Services, Administration for Children and Families, Office of Planning, Research, and Evaluation. (2005). *Head Start Impact Study: First-year Findings*. Available: http://www.acf.hhs.gov/programs/opre/hs/faces/index.html [accessed August 2008].

U.S. Department of Health and Human Services, Administration for Children and Families, Office of Planning, Research, and Evaluation. (2006). *Head Start Family and Child Experiences Survey (FACES 2000) Technical Report*. Available: http://www.acf.hhs.gov/programs/opre/hs/faces/index.html [accessed August 2008].

Veenman, M.V.J., Kok, R., and Blöte, A.W. (2005). The relation between intellectual and metacognitive skills in early adolescence. *Instructional Science, 33*(3), 193-211.

Vygotsky, L.S. (1978). *Mind in Society: The Development of Higher Psychological Processes*. Cambridge, MA: Harvard University Press.

Vygotsky, L.S. (1986). *Thought and Language*. (A. Kozulin, Trans.). Cambridge, MA: MIT Press.

Vygotsky, L.S. (1991). Genesis of the higher mental functions. In P. Light, S. Sheldon, and M. Woodhead (Eds.), *Learning to Think* (pp. 32-41). Florence, KY: Taylor and Francis/Routledge.

Wharton-McDonald, R., Pressley, M., and Hampston, J.M. (1998). Literacy instruction in nine first-grade classrooms: Teacher characteristics and student achievement. *Elementary School Journal, 99*(2), 101-128.

Wiltz, N.W., and Klein, E.L. (2001). What do you do in child care? Children's perceptions of high and low quality classrooms. *Early Childhood Research Quarterly, 16*(2), 209-236.

Wolfgang, C.H., Stannard, L.L., and Jones, I. (2001). Block play performance among preschoolers as a predictor of later school achievement in mathematics. *Journal of Research in Childhood Education, 15*, 173-180.

Wood, K., and Frid, S. (2005). Early childhood numeracy in a multiage setting. *Mathematics Education Research Journal, 16*(3), 80-99. Available: http://www.merga.net.au/documents/MERJ_16_3_Wood.pdf [accessed August 2008].

Wright, R.J. (1994). A study of the numerical development of 5-year-olds and 6-year-olds. *Educational Studies in Mathematics, 26*, 25-44.

Wright, R.J. (2003). A mathematics recovery: Program of intervention in early number learning. *Australian Journal of Learning Disabilities, 8*(4), 6-11.

Wright, R.J., Martland, J., Stafford, A.K., and Stanger, G. (2002). *Teaching Number: Advancing Children's Skills and Strategies*. London: Paul Chapman/Sage.

Young-Loveridge, J.M. (2004). Effects on early numeracy of a program using number books and games. *Early Childhood Research Quarterly, 19*, 82-98.

Zins, J.E., Bloodworth, M.R., Weissberg, R.P., and Walberg, H. (2004). The scientific base linking social and emotional learning to school success. In J.E. Zins, R.P. Weissberg, M.C. Wang, and H.J. Walberg (Eds.), *Building Academic Success on Social and Emotional Learning: What Does the Research Say?* New York: Teachers College Press.

# 8

# The Early Childhood Workforce and Its Professional Development

It is often said that the quality of any institution is based on the quality of its personnel. This is especially true of the array of institutions and programs that serve young children. The adults—early childhood teachers—who directly support the academic/intellectual, social, emotional, and physical development of preschoolers in the United States are pivotal to children's short-term development and their long-term outcomes. Early childhood teachers are an essential ingredient in achieving the intentions of this report, notably improved attention to and outcomes in early childhood mathematics. For these reasons, we address the early childhood workforce and their professional development.

Terminology regarding the early childhood workforce is often used inconsistently (Kagan, Kauerz, and Tarrant, 2008). In this discussion, the following terms are used:

- Early childhood education (ECE) teachers or the ECE teaching workforce includes all personnel whose primary role is to provide direct instructional services for young children. Included in this category are lead teachers, assistant teachers, aides, and family child care (FCC) providers.
- ECE workforce includes those who carry out both instructional and noninstructional roles in early childhood education settings. Thus, the term *workforce* is an inclusive one that embraces teachers, others who work in early childhood education settings and whose primary responsibility is not instructional (e.g., administrators), and indi-

viduals who work in settings that support early childhood education (e.g., resource and referral coordinators).

In this chapter, we begin by discussing the nature of the current early childhood workforce. We first present information on this workforce in general, discussing characteristics about the teachers themselves, including age, gender, ethnicity, educational experience, and background and key variables that influence their work, including compensation, turnover, work settings, and beliefs. We then turn to a more specific discussion of the early childhood workforce from a mathematical perspective. In the second section, we discuss the nature of the professional development of the workforce, first addressing the professional development of early childhood teachers in general and then turning to mathematics-specific professional development.

## BACKGROUND ON THE WORKFORCE

### Demographic Characteristics

Over 50 percent of U.S. families with children under the age of 5 rely on nonparental care (Chernoff et al., 2007), and thus the ECE workforce is responsible for the care and education of large numbers of the nation's young children. The early childhood workforce is fairly large, comprising 2.3 million individuals (Burton et al., 2002) and dispersed: About 24 percent work in centers, 28 percent in family child care, and 48 percent in informal family, friend, and neighbor (FFN) settings (Burton et al., 2002). It is important to note that although most early childhood care providers work in FFN settings the majority of children attend center-based programs in which the child-to-teacher ratio is higher (Burton et al., 2002). The focus of this section is on teachers in center-based and FCC settings.

According to national averages, the ECE teaching workforce is mainly comprised of white women in their late 30s and 40s (Saluja, Early, and Clifford, 2002); however, race/ethnicity varies across state and program type (see Table 8-1 for a breakdown of early childhood educators by race/ethnicity). For example, the Head Start and home-based early child care teaching workforce is more ethnically balanced than the prekindergarten workforce (Early et al., 2005; Hart and Schumacher, 2005). In addition, in certain parts of the country, for example, Alameda County, California, the early childhood education and care workforce is more ethnically diverse. Three-quarters of the family child care centers there are staffed by women of color (Whitebook and Bellm, 2004). Also, in the population as a whole, there are increasingly more children who speak English as a second language (as cited in Hart and Schumacher, 2005), and thus there is a need for

**TABLE 8-1** Early Childhood Educators by Race/Ethnicity (percentage)

| | Race/Ethnicity | | | | |
|---|---|---|---|---|---|
| Program Type | White | Black | Latino | Asian | Other |
| Prekindergarten | 64 | 13 | 15 | 2 | 8 |
| Head Start | 36 | 28 | 24 | 2 | — |
| Family child care | 20 | 27 | 26 | 23 | — |

NOTE: Family child care from Layzer and Goodson (2006); Head Start from Hart and Schumacher (2005); prekindergarten by Early et al. (2005). Prekindergarten refers to school or center-based programs that serve 4-year-olds, have an explicit purpose of improving school readiness, and are funded fully or partially by the state.
SOURCE: Kagan et al. (2008).

a more linguistically and ethnically/racially diverse ECE workforce (Howes, James, and Ritchie, 2003).

### Educational Experience and Background

ECE teachers are a diverse group of individuals, with some having formal education and holding degrees from institutions of higher education or community colleges and others receiving credentials of competence offered by the profession. Some have only very limited training that is delivered on the job. Not surprisingly, the amount of formal education and credentials varies by program type; prekindergarten programs generally have the highest percentage of teachers with degrees, while home-based or FCC providers have the lowest levels of formal education (Kagan et al., 2008). Table 8-2 shows the breakdown of percentages by program type. The specific nature of these variations and their relationship to teaching quality and effectiveness are elaborated in the section on the professional development of the workforce.

### Compensation

Compensation, defined as a combination of annual salary or hourly wages and benefits (e.g., health insurance, paid vacation, sick leave, retirement plan), is quite low for some segments of the early childhood workforce. In the United States, the average annual salary for preschool teachers, one group of early childhood educators, is $25,800; for child care workers including FCC providers, it is $19,670 (Bureau of Labor Statistics, 2007); and for Head Start teachers, it is $24,608 (Hamm, 2006). Distinctions exist in the salaries of individuals according to the settings in which they work.

A national survey conducted by the Bureau of Labor Statistics (BLS)

**TABLE 8-2** Level of Formal Education and Training of Early Childhood Education and Care Workforce (percentage)

| | Level of Education and/or Training | | | | |
|---|---|---|---|---|---|
| Program Type | High School or Less | Associate's Degree/Some College | B.A. or More | Child Development Associate | State License or Endorsement |
| Prekindergarten | 13 | 14 | 73 | 23 | 57 |
| Head Start | 31 | 33 | 36 | 22 | N/A |
| Center-based | 30 | 41 | 30 | 18 | 44 |
| Home-based (FCC) | 56 | 32 | 11 | 3 | 7 |

NOTE: Prekindergarten data from Gilliam and Marchesseault (2005); Head Start data from Hamm (2006); center-based data (includes teachers and directors) and home-based data on formal education are from Herzenberg, Price, and Bradley (2005), center-based and family child care data on credentials from Saluja, Early, and Clifford (2002).
SOURCE: Kagan et al. (2008).

characterizes the field in terms of two categories: child care workers and preschool teachers. Child care workers are adults who primarily perform such duties as feeding, dressing, and overseeing the play of children, and preschool teachers provide a more educational experience for the children in their care. Using these definitions, child care workers were near the bottom of the compensation ladder, earning more than only 22 of the 820 occupations that were assessed by BLS in 2004—their earned incomes were within 5 percent of short-order cooks and parking lot attendants and considerably less than preschool teachers (Center for the Child Care Workforce, 2006).

While there is little dispute regarding the wide salary differences that exist among early childhood teachers, most observers suggest that compensation differs according to the particular type of program and its attendant required credentials. For example, preschool teachers who work in settings in which teacher certification is required command higher salaries and compensation packages than teachers who work in settings in which lower levels or no certification is required. Setting and its attendant requirements are not the only variable that influences compensation; it also varies by geographic region, with early childhood educators in southern states receiving the lowest levels of compensation (Center for the Child Care Workforce, 2006).

In addition to low wages, many ECE teachers do not receive health insurance benefits from their employers. Specifically, 28 percent of center-based early childhood educators received health insurance benefits from their employer between 2002 and 2004, and 21 percent of ECE teachers reported that they had no health insurance during this time (Herzenberg,

Price, and Bradley, 2005).[1] Lack of health insurance is a significant issue; it may influence early childhood educators' interactions at work, their overall financial status, and thus their ability to remain in the field over time, fueling heavy personnel turnover rates.

### Stability and Turnover

The turnover of early childhood teachers is quite high in some settings. A longitudinal study in California by Whitebook and colleagues (2001) found that 76 percent of the teachers employed by centers in 1996 and 82 percent of teachers employed by centers in 1994 had left these jobs by 2000 (Whitebook et al., 2001). Such high turnover rates have often been associated with low compensation (Whitebook and Sakai, 2003). For example, Whitebook and colleagues (2001) found that early childhood educators receiving higher than average wages were more likely to remain in their jobs, and those who left the field were more likely to go to higher paying jobs. Wage levels are often directly associated with the program type or sector in which the individual is employed.

One national study showed that, on average, center-based teachers were in their current programs for 6.8 years, teachers in programs in public schools and religious settings were working in their programs for 7.8 years, and teachers in for-profit centers were in their programs for 5.6 years (Saluja, Early, and Clifford, 2002). Confirming these data, a five-state study found that publicly operated prekindergarten programs were found to have lower turnover rates than privately operated programs (Bellm et al., 2002). On average, publicly operated prekindergarten programs offered higher wages than privately operated programs (Gilliam and Marchesseault, 2005), which may be an explanation for the difference in turnover. Moreover, when ECE teachers are compared with K-12 teachers, the salaries for K-12 teachers are significantly higher (Kagan et al., 2008) and turnover is lower (Provasnik and Dorfman, 2005).

Teacher turnover is relevant for all students, and it is particularly important for young children because of the impact on their development and learning. High levels of unpredictable turnover have been linked to poorer developmental outcomes for children, as well as to lower quality service (Helburn, 1995; Howes and Hamilton, 1993; Howes, Phillips, and Whitebook, 1992; Phillips et al., 2001; Whitebook, Sakai, and Howes, 1997, as cited in Kagan et al., 2008).

[1] Although health insurance data were not collected for the remaining 51 percent of early childhood teachers, some probably received health insurance through a spouse when a spouse was present and had health coverage, purchased it privately, or purchased it through Medicaid (Mark Price, personal communication, January 12, 2009).

For example, one study, *The Cost, Quality and Child Outcomes in Child Care Centers* (Cost, Quality, and Child Outcomes Study Team, 1995), found that higher quality programs, in which children demonstrated more advanced language and premathematical skills, were associated with lower turnover rates. Furthermore, the children showed better nonacademic outcomes than did children in high turnover programs. The children had more positive self-concepts, better relations with their teachers, and demonstrated more advanced social behavior and more positive attitudes toward child care situations. The effects of program quality are obvious for children of all socioeconomic backgrounds, but children from low-income backgrounds are especially influenced by the quality (or lack thereof) of their child care (Helburn, 1995). Finally, turnover is important in early childhood settings because many ECE teachers who leave the field are replaced by individuals with less training and experience; thus, turnover has long-term effects on teacher and program quality.

While high turnover is often associated with instability and poorer outcomes for children, it is important to note that turnover is not always a negative factor (Kagan et al., 2008; Whitebook and Sakai, 2003). It may be beneficial when individuals who enter the early childhood education field and find that it is a poor fit for their skills or occupational goals leave (Whitebook and Sakai, 2003). Also, many studies do not distinguish between job turnover, which is defined as the rate at which teachers leave programs to take new positions in the early childhood education field, and occupational turnover, which is defined as the rate at which teachers leave programs to retire or enter a new field of work (Kagan et al., 2008). Clearly, more data are needed on turnover in the early childhood field.

## The Work Environment

In any industry, the environment in which one works is likely to influence one's on-the-job attitude and performance. Work environment is defined as the physical setting, the reward system, clarity about expectations and roles, agency in decision making, supervisor support, and communication (Hatch, 2006; Stremmel, Benson, and Powell, 1993; Whitebook, Howes, and Phillips, 1990). While the measures of work environment vary for different studies, the research shows that the work environment of early childhood educators plays a role in teachers' quality and effectiveness (Kagan et al., 2008). For example, the Child Care Services Association (2003) found that 22 percent of preschool teachers throughout North Carolina planned to leave the field within three years, yet only half as many teachers who worked in supportive environments reported having the same plans. The supports that were presumably related to more positive work environments include: (1) orientation, (2) written job descriptions, (3) written personnel policies, (4) paid education and training expenses, (5) paid breaks, (6) compensatory time for training, and (7) paid preparation/planning time (Child Care Services Association, 2003). Not surprisingly, teachers were more likely to stay in their positions when they understood the responsibilities of their position and the expectations that their supervisors and colleagues had of them, and there were improvements in compensation.

Interestingly, improvements in the work environment have also been related to better psychological functioning, as defined by less emotional exhaustion (Stremmel, Benson, and Powell, 1993). Teachers are required to interact closely with children (Kagan et al., 2008); however, those who show lower levels of emotional well-being are less likely to spend time engaged with children (Hamre and Pianta, 2004). Children who have teachers who are less engaged may have fewer opportunities to learn from teacher-guided situations.

The supervision and leadership that are provided to ECE teachers also make a difference in the quality of the work environment and subsequently in teachers' quality and effectiveness (Kagan et al., 2008). Supervisors must have the management skills and leadership abilities necessary to support early childhood educators. Moreover, they must support teaching staff, but they also need support to continue to develop positive management styles and leadership abilities for themselves. Research by Jorde-Bloom and Sheerer (1992) suggests that professional development programs for supervisory staff improve the overall workplace climate and classroom quality. Fostering these skills in the supervisory staff has the potential to positively impact children's learning through classroom quality and workplace climate.

## Teachers' Beliefs About Early Childhood Education

Like the variables discussed above, early childhood educators' beliefs and values are important to understand. Teachers' beliefs and values about teaching and learning not only shape classroom practices (Fang, 1996; Kagan, 1992; Stipek et al., 2001), but also serve as a filter through which meaning is derived. As such, values and beliefs have a powerful influence on educational change and innovation. Attempting changes in pedagogy without considering teachers' pedagogical beliefs and values about education may lead to resistance in implementation of a new practice if teachers do not agree with the underlying educational value (Lee and Ginsburg, 2007b; Ryan, 2004). Thus, any effort to change educators' classroom practices must include consideration of how those teachers view their roles, the children they teach, and the purpose of the setting in which their interactions take place.

Historically, the field of early childhood education has placed great emphasis on supporting children's social and emotional development, with somewhat less of an emphasis on academic learning as an outcome of experiences in ECE settings (Kowalski, Pretti-Frontczak, and Johnson, 2001). Academic subjects were believed to be less important at this age because young children should investigate and explore their interests so that they develop a love of learning (Lee, 2006). However, in the past decade, there has been a groundswell of focus on academic learning as a legitimate, desirable, and appropriate outcome of preschool enrollment (particularly in publicly funded programs, such as Head Start or state-funded prekindergarten). This movement, challenging teachers' conventional beliefs, has created pressure on early childhood education systems and personnel to address academic achievement more focally and intentionally.

Preschool programs that provide children with social, emotional, physical, and academic learning opportunities are ideal learning environments. Educating the "whole child," including social and emotional development, and providing preschool children with opportunities to engage in developmentally appropriate mathematics[2] is essential to children's immediate and later school success (Duncan et al., 2007; National Association for the Education of Young Children and National Council of Teachers of Mathematics, 2002; National Mathematics Advisory Panel, 2008). It is important to note, in this regard, that the third edition of the National Association for the Education of Young Children's (NAEYC) (2009) guidelines for developmentally appropriate practice emphasize that pre-academic and cognitive skills, including those in mathematics, are essential to developmentally appropriate instruction.

Teachers' educational goals and pedagogical beliefs are also influenced by the backgrounds and characteristics of the children themselves. For example, socioeconomic status (SES) has been found to be related to ECE teachers' instructional practices (Lee and Ginsburg, 2007a, 2007b; Stipek and Byler, 1997). Children from low-SES backgrounds are often behind their more affluent peers in mathematics achievement as early as kindergarten (Clements, Sarama, and Gerber, 2005; Denton and West, 2002; Griffin and Case, 1997; Jordan, Huttenlocher, and Levine, 1994; Lee and Burkam, 2002; National Research Council, 2001b; Saxe, Guberman, and Gearhart, 1987; Starkey and Klein, 1992, 2008; Stipek and Ryan, 1997), and awareness of this disparity may influence teachers' educational goals, beliefs, and instructional practices with children from economically disadvantaged backgrounds. Children coming from low-SES homes, although increasingly enrolled in and benefiting from early childhood education, also require more intensive and appropriate educational interventions in

---

[2]Developmentally appropriate mathematics includes a child-centered and positive non-evaluative mathematics environment, developmentally appropriate mathematics activities and manipulatives, and authentic mathematics assessment (as cited in Lee, 2005).

order to perform at levels consistent with their more advantaged and skilled peers (Hamre and Pianta, 2005). In short, less advantaged children need programs that actually accelerate learning if they are to enter school not behind at the start. However, preschool and kindergarten teachers of low-SES children rate memorizing facts and rote tasks (procedural knowledge) as more important educational goals than problem solving and tasks involving reasoning (conceptual knowledge), and they tend to agree with a more basic skills teaching orientation than teachers of middle-SES children (Stipek and Byler, 1997).

## THE EARLY CHILDHOOD WORKFORCE AND MATHEMATICS

The teaching of mathematics has been considered a part of the early childhood educators' portfolio, along with many other developmental and disciplinary domains (e.g., social and emotional development, physical development, literacy, social studies) that they must address. To understand how the early childhood workforce currently views and addresses mathematics, we examine early childhood teachers' beliefs about mathematics, their mathematics knowledge, and how these beliefs and knowledge actually impact what they do in the classroom.

### Teachers' Values and Beliefs About Mathematics Education in Early Childhood

Generally, early childhood teachers believe that social-emotional and physical development are more important to young children's development and learning than academic activities, including mathematics (Ginsburg et al., 2006a; Lin, Lawrence, and Gorrell, 2003; Piotrkowski, Botsko, and Matthews, 2001). In a recent review of the research, Ginsburg and colleagues (2008) found that preschool teachers report social-emotional development, literacy, and then mathematics—in that order—as important educational goals for young children to achieve.

A second set of beliefs focuses on the nature of mathematics instruction. Early childhood educators generally believe that mathematics education should focus on numeracy and arithmetic through some direct instruction (Lee and Ginsburg, 2007b). They also tend to believe that young children should engage in games and other activities in which mathematics learning is fun and involves interesting toys or materials in small groups and that mathematics learning should not be highly demanding, nor should it be pushed on young children before they are "ready" (Lee and Ginsburg, 2007b).

Finally, a third set of beliefs regarding instructional practice is driven by children's characteristics, particularly SES. Research examining ECE teachers' beliefs about instructional practices as a function of SES is a nascent area; however, recent studies shed light on how this characteristic shapes beliefs about teaching practices. For example, one study showed that early childhood teachers of children from low-SES backgrounds believed that mathematics instruction was an excellent way of preparing children for kindergarten and that children should engage in mathematics activities, even if they initially showed little or no interest (Lee and Ginsburg, 2007b). Conversely, teachers of middle-SES prekindergarten children were more likely to state that, instead of having an academic focus, prekindergarten education should be child-centered and child-initiated and encourage children's social-emotional development (Lee, 2006; Lee and Ginsburg, 2007b). In large part, this belief was in response to the notion that middle-SES parents put significant academic pressure on their children at home (Lee and Ginsburg, 2007b). It should be noted that, while SES-related differences were found in both early childhood educators' beliefs about instructional practices and their educational goals, the field of early childhood education tends to stress social-emotional development rather than academic subjects.

There are multiple reasons that early childhood teachers may not be inclined to focus on mathematics. One explanation is related to ECE policies that put a premium on early literacy at the expense of other subject areas (which is discussed later in this chapter). Another reason stems from the education and training many ECE teachers receive, which has historically placed more emphasis on social-emotional development. Specifically, some researchers suggest that this focus on social-emotional development is rooted in misconceptions or limited knowledge of the young children's developmental capacities. For example, early childhood educators' beliefs that young children are too cognitively immature for mathematics learning may be based on Piagetian theory, which states that young children in the preoperational stage (ages 2 to 6) are not likely to use or understand abstract ideas to make sense of their experiences (Ginsburg, Pappas, and Seo, 2001; Lee and Ginsburg, 2007b). However, Gelman and Gallistel (1986) found that young children do think abstractly in regard to counting objects (e.g., the abstraction principle: any discrete object can be counted, from stones to unicorns). Heuvel-Panhuizen (1990) found that early childhood educators significantly underestimated 6-year-olds' mathematical capability. Specifically, teachers, counselors, and teacher trainers held significantly lower expectations for children's knowledge of symbols, the counting sequence, and adding and subtracting than what child outcomes showed (Heuvel-Panhuizen, 1990).

Others suggest that such beliefs may rest on mistaken assumptions that young children are neither interested in, nor capable of, learning mathematics. In fact, young children from birth to age 5 have informal mathematics knowledge (Clements and Sarama, 2007b; Ginsburg et al., 2006b) and, given developmentally appropriate experiences, enjoy mathematics learning (Gelman, 1980; Irwin and Burgham, 1992). This informal knowledge includes the ideas of more and less, shape, space, pattern, as well as number and operations, and several other important areas (Gelman, 2000).

Moreover, some researchers suggest that teachers' fundamental knowledge about mathematics and mathematics instruction may be limited. For example, most teachers in the United States believe that mathematics is a static body of knowledge that mainly involves manipulating rules and procedures. From this point of view, the main objective in mathematics is to learn about discrete knowledge and arrive at the correct answer (Ball, 1991). Little thought is given to mathematics as a problem-solving process; rather, the outcome (i.e., getting the correct answer) is seen as the most important part of learning mathematics (Thompson, 1992). This belief is reflected clearly in early education instruction that is rote and feedback processes that focus solely on right and wrong answers (Pianta et al., 2005). Traditionally, early childhood educators have been taught that mathematics is a subject that requires the use of instructional practices that are developmentally inappropriate for young children (Balfanz, 1999). In short, it is often the case that preschool teachers believe the content of meaningful mathematics is too difficult for themselves as well as for their students.

### The Impact of Teachers' Beliefs and Knowledge on Instruction

Given these beliefs and knowledge, we examine how early childhood teachers beliefs and understandings about mathematics impact mathematics instruction. Early childhood educators' beliefs are clearly associated with their teaching practices (Charlesworth et al., 1991, 1993; Pianta et al., 2005; Stipek and Byler, 1997; Stipek et al., 2001). Pianta and colleagues (2005), for example, in their multistate study, found that, even after adjusting for teachers' experience or degree status and program factors, such as teacher-student ratio or full-day/part-day classes, prekindergarten teachers' beliefs about children were the factor most related to global classroom quality as measured by the Early Childhood Environmental Rating Scale-Revised (ECERS-R) and the Classroom Assessment Scoring System (CLASS, which reported on two dimensions, instructional climate and emotional climate).

What instructional practices are teachers engaged in? Not only is emphasis on social and emotional development in early childhood settings a belief, but also it is borne out in reality. Pianta and La Paro (2003), characterizing findings from standardized observations in more than a thousand early education settings, note that many early childhood classrooms are socially positive yet instructionally passive. Generally speaking and not surprisingly, preschool teachers spend less instructional time on mathematics than they do on literacy (Clements and Sarama, 2007b; Early et al.,

2005; Layzer, Goodson, and Moss, 1993), a finding not much different from what is observed in the early elementary grades (National Institute of Child Health and Human Development Network Early Child Care Research Network, 2002, 2005; and see Chapter 7 of this report for further discussion of instruction).

Early childhood educators' pedagogical beliefs direct and constrain their instructional practices, which subsequently shape children's academic and social environments. When addressed, early childhood mathematics is usually constrained to basic ideas in number and operations, such as 1-to-1 correspondence, simple addition and subtraction, and number symbols or numerals (Lee and Ginsburg, 2007b). Geometry and measurement are noted less frequently (Clements, 2004). In addition to rote memorization and basic skills, such as memorizing the first 10 or so counting words, young children are capable of understanding more sophisticated mathematical concepts, such as cardinality. The content of young children's mathematics can be both deep and broad, and, when provided with engaging and developmentally appropriate mathematics activities, their mathematics knowledge flourishes. Yet these research findings are largely not represented in practice.

## PROFESSIONAL DEVELOPMENT OF THE WORKFORCE

The professional development of early childhood teachers is nuanced and complicated. We begin our discussion with an overview of professional development, looking at the nature of quality professional development and the context for the delivery of professional development, both in-service and pre-service. We address the impact of professional development on teachers' performance generally. We then turn to a discussion of the professional development for teaching mathematics to young children, addressing the need for mathematics preparation; mathematics content and teacher preparation; efforts at in-service mathematics support, including the outcomes of such support; and efforts at pre-service preparation for teachers in mathematics.

To aid the discussion, we define key terms as follows:

- Professional development: an umbrella term that refers to both formal education and training.
- Formal education: refers to the amount of credit-bearing coursework a teacher has completed at an accredited institution, including two- or four-year colleges and universities.
- Training: refers to educational activities that take place outside the formal education process. Such efforts may include coaching, mentoring, and workshops.

- Pre-service education: refers to the formal education and training that one receives prior to having formal responsibility for a group of children.
- In-service education: refers to the formal education and training that one may receive while having formal responsibility for a group of children.
- Credentialing: refers to the process of demonstrating and receiving formal recognition from an organization for achieving a predefined level of expertise in education.

### The Nature and Quality of Successful Professional Development Efforts

An examination of the literature from the fields of elementary education, early childhood education, and early childhood mathematics education reveals some common principles that characterize high-quality professional development experiences. Research indicates that professional development efforts are most successful when they are focused on producing long-lasting change, longer in duration, focused on content knowledge rather than teaching strategies alone, involve active learning, and are part of a coherent set of professional development experiences (Birman et al., 2000). According to Clements (2004, p. 65), six themes related to professional development emerge from reviews of the research:

1. Professional development should be standards-based, ongoing, and embedded in the job (i.e., practical, concrete, immediate, gradually connecting research and theory).
2. Teachers must have time to learn and work with colleagues, especially a consistent group.
3. Teachers should be provided with stable, high-quality sources of professional development that includes observation, experimentation, and mentoring, with plenty of time for reflection.
4. Professional development experiences should be grounded in a sound theoretical and philosophical base and structured as a coherent and systematic program.
5. Professional development experiences should respond to each individual's background, experiences, and current context or role.
6. Professional development experiences should address mathematics knowledge as well as mathematics education. It should be grounded in particular curriculum materials that focus on children's mathematical thinking and learning, including learning trajectories.

These principles pertain to professional development of all types, including pre-service education and in-service professional development, because they reflect sound practices in adult learning, as well as data on the practices that ultimately lead to improved outcomes in the classroom. While their application may be tailored to a particular cohort or setting, these principles should guide development of personnel preparation programs in early childhood mathematics. The following section describes the overall context of professional development as it pertains to the early childhood workforce.

## The Context for the Delivery of Professional Development

The professional development of early childhood and elementary school teachers happens both prior to teachers' assuming classroom responsibilities through pre-service training and while they are teaching through in-service training. Unlike the professional development of most elementary school teachers, which occurs formally prior to their becoming teachers, many early childhood educators receive the majority of their professional development while they are already working. Moreover, for most elementary school teachers, there is a common entry floor into the profession, typically consisting of the achievement of a B.A. or B.S. degree and the successful completion of the Praxis exams. No such common entry floor for early educators exists. In fact, the range of entry-level requirements for early educators varies from the holding of a health clearance certificate and being 18 years of age to meeting requirements equivalent to those for elementary school teachers.

Although efforts are under way to elevate the quality and consistency of entry-level requirements and professional development opportunities for early educators, abundant variations of requirements and professional development delivery mechanisms exist. Moreover, there is considerable variation in what is required of, and offered to, early educators as professional development, depending on the program sponsor and funding stream or the state or locality in which the early educator practices her work. Complicating this picture, new public policies, some at the federal level but mostly at the state level, mean that early educator teacher and professional development requirements are in constant flux. In this section we elaborate on the unique sociopolitical context in which professional development for early educators exists.

On one hand, the news is quite promising. There is a broad consensus emerging that the professional development of the early childhood workforce is a priority (Kagan et al., 2008). Increasingly, policy makers and the public are recognizing the importance of early experiences on children's brain development, success in school, and general well-being (Center on the Developing Child at Harvard University, 2007; Martinez-Beck and Zaslow, 2006; National Research Council, 2000, 2001a). In addition, increasing attention has been given to closing the achievement gap between children from diverse economic and racial/ethnic backgrounds that has been documented prior to the start of school (Clements, Sarama, and Gerber, 2005; Starkey and Klein, 2008). Mounting evidence of the central role that teachers play in supporting children's development and learning through relationships and teaching interactions in general has added to a sense of urgency to improve the quality of professional development (National Research Council, 2001b).

To that end, a number of federal efforts have supported professional development. The Head Start Program, continuing its historical commitment to professional development, has expanded these efforts by calling for higher professional requirements for its teachers. Good Start, Grow Smart, a presidential initiative launched during the Bush administration, specifically charges all states with developing plans to offer education and training to preschool and child care personnel to receive Child Care Development Fund dollars. In addition, Title II of the No Child Left Behind Act provides competitive grants for the creation of training and educational opportunities for early educators through the Early Childhood Educator Professional Development Program.

At the state level, qualifications for teachers are being increased, as are support and incentives for teachers to seek additional professional development (Tout, Zaslow, and Berry, 2006). The creation of professional development systems and quality rating systems are now abundant nationally and are driving reform in pre-service and in-service education for early educators (Kagan et al., 2008). These changes and initiatives are occurring in a broader climate of increased accountability and standards in education (Kagan et al., 2008), further underscoring the need to provide the early childhood workforce with the knowledge and skills they will need to meet standards for early mathematics learning.

*Access.* Not only have mandates for degrees expanded, but access to higher education has also expanded in many states. Scholarship programs, such as the Teacher Education Assistance for College and Higher Education Grant Program, online degree programs at both the associate and baccalaureate levels, better opportunities for working professionals to link or articulate their community-based training, Child Development Associate (CDA) programs, and other degree programs are all having an influence on the ability of early childhood educators to enter the higher education system and to convert their prior professional development into academic credit.

*The landscape of early childhood teacher education programs in general.* An overview of the general landscape of early childhood teacher education provides a context for considering how ECE teachers are, and might be, prepared for their responsibilities in the domain of mathematics. According to estimates based on data collected in 2004, approximately

1,350 institutions of higher education offer some kind of degree program in early childhood education (Maxwell, Lim, and Early, 2006). Of these, roughly 44 percent offer a bachelor's and/or graduate degree and 56 percent offer an associate's degree, with some institutions offering both. Graduation rates in these programs produce at least 40,000 early childhood teachers per year.

***Associate degree programs.*** There are more than 750 early childhood associate degree programs in the United States (Maxwell, Lim, and Early, 2006). Most are located in community colleges, although some are under the umbrella of a university. In the early childhood degree program (sometimes called child development), a major influence on course offerings is whether the focus is on transfer to local baccalaureate programs in early childhood or elementary education (transfer programs) or whether students are primarily being prepared for work in child care, Head Start, and other settings immediately upon graduation (terminal programs). Although national organizations discourage classifying associate programs as transfer or terminal, in reality many still fall into these categories. Programs primarily aimed at transfer often have very few courses in early childhood curriculum and methods, aiming mainly at giving students a general education foundation with transfer potential. Programs with greater emphasis on immediate career opportunities include many more child development/ECE courses and field experiences.

***Bachelor's degree programs.*** Like associate degree programs, bachelor's degree programs that prepare future early childhood educators are diverse. Some of this diversity derives from state teacher certification categories, which for most programs serve to define the scope of their efforts. For example, some states define early childhood for licensure as birth to age 8; others birth to age 5; others ages 3 to 8; others preschool to Grade 2, and so on.

Programs' identities and the organizational features of the different higher education institutions in which these programs are situated also play a role in creating program diversity. For example, baccalaureate-level early childhood departments or programs may be part of a school or college of education, or the program may be in a different college entirely—for example, a college of human development or a child and family studies department. These institutional arrangements, along with state requirements, may influence what is expected of students in all areas, including mathematics.

On the other hand, despite these promising developments, the overall early childhood educator professional development context is hampered by intransigent workforce challenges. First, given the salary and compensation limitations of the field, those who have achieved professional degrees and teacher certification are often not attracted to early education. In an effort to remedy this situation, some new programs are compensating qualified early education teachers at rates comparable to elementary school teachers. Second, the rampant turnover rate in the field cannot be denied, and departing early educators are being replaced with individuals who are less qualified, making the need for professional development even more important. Third, there are serious questions regarding the quality of the professional development content itself. There are barely a handful of certifications for individuals who provide early childhood mentoring, coaching, or professional development. The few states that do have such credentials have remarkably low bars for those who deliver in-service professional development. Compounding these contextual challenges, there are few consistent delivery mechanisms, except institutions of higher education, that deliver high-quality early educator professional development. Finally, for those wishing to avail themselves of professional development experiences, either out of desire or mandate, there are serious issues of quality of educational opportunity and inequity in access to training. As this review suggests, the context for the professional development of early educators is complex.

## The Impact of General Professional Development on Teacher Quality and Effectiveness

What is the role of a teacher's education in her teaching? Several studies have found that the level and nature of early educators' formal education is related to the overall quality of their teaching (e.g., Barnett, 2003; Tout, Zaslow, and Berry, 2006; Whitebook, 2003). Teachers with higher levels of formal education have also been linked to higher quality programs and more positive teacher-child interactions (Howes, 1997; Tout, Zaslou, and Berry, 2006). However, more recent, multistate studies have found that the evidence on formal education and its link to teacher effectiveness is questionable (Early et al., 2006, 2007), with teacher knowledge, attitudes, and specific teaching practices more predictive of child outcomes. While Early and colleagues (2007) did not find a significant relationship between teachers' level of education and young children's academic outcomes, they suggest that their findings should not dissuade early childhood educators from pursuing postsecondary education. Early and colleagues (2007) did not examine the course content or rigor of early childhood education programs, which may be related to teachers' knowledge, skills, and behaviors. Thus, available data do not provide a comprehensive investigation of the host of variables that are likely to be related to teacher quality or effectiveness (Early et al., 2007; Kagan et al., 2008).

***Questions about degrees and child outcomes.*** Much attention has been focused on several recent studies that have renewed the controversy over the value of degrees as guarantees of quality in early childhood teaching or of positive child outcomes (Early et al., 2006, 2007). Although the results need to be interpreted in light of the limited measures available and other constraints (as discussed earlier in this chapter), these studies call into question the assumption that having a degree—especially an early childhood degree—must produce better developmental and learning outcomes for children. An important next step is to look carefully at the quality of early childhood degree programs (Hyson, Tomlinson, and Morris, 2008).

Another challenge in discerning the relationship between formal education and teacher outcomes is definitional in nature. Kagan et al. (2008) note that, often in the literature, the term "teacher quality" refers to the positive actions and behaviors of teachers, particularly with regard to their interactions with young children. To distinguish this definition from studies that focus on actual child outcomes, Kagan et al. (2008) use the term "teacher effectiveness" to refer to the impact of teachers' actions and behaviors on the accomplishments of the children they teach (Kagan et al., 2008). Given these distinctions, there is some evidence of a relationship between teacher effectiveness and formal education for FCC providers. Clarke-Stewart and colleagues (2002) found children in the care of providers who had not attended college scored lower on cognitive tests than children in the care of providers who had attended college. One explanation for these findings is that FCC homes usually have only one adult present to care for children, and this adult has a significant amount of influence on children's learning and development. Center-based settings, in contrast, have many adults with whom children interact and thus no single teacher will have as much influence on them. To gain a clearer understanding of teacher quality and effectiveness, it will be important to examine teacher preparation and support in preparation programs (Early et al., 2007; Kagan et al., 2008).

Although some early childhood educators receive a formal education to prepare to work with young children, others obtain preparation through general training. It is important to note that training can take place prior to their entering the classroom, but it often occurs after teachers have begun teaching. General training, defined as educational activities that take place outside the formal education system (Kagan et al., 2008), has also been found to impact teacher quality and the quality of classroom environments (Ghazvini and Mullis, 2002; Honig and Hirallal, 1998; Tout, Zaslow, and Berry, 2006). For example, Honig and Hirallal (1998) found that training, independent of education and experience, had a large impact on the quality of services that teachers provided (e.g., positive language interactions, greater support for concept learning). In addition to research linking training to teacher quality, one study suggests that training is linked to teacher effectiveness. Burchinal and colleagues (2002) found that teachers' attendance in workshops predicted global quality and children's receptive language.

In addition to the research examining the relationship between general training and teacher quality, several studies have shown that overall program quality improves when early childhood teachers have specialized training or education in child development (Blau, 2000; Phillips et al., 2001; Tout and Zaslow, 2004; Tout, Zaslow, and Berry, 2006). Furthermore, specialized formal education, defined by an emphasis on child development and early childhood education, has also been linked to improvements in teacher quality—specifically, that teachers who had more child development education were more sensitive, less harsh, and more responsive to children (Howes, 1997).

Separate studies have been conducted on FCC settings and the impact of training. Generally, training for FCC providers has shown similar trends to those found for center-based providers. That is, this training is related to higher scores on measures of global environmental classroom quality (Burchinal et al., 2002; Clarke-Stewart et al., 2002; Norris, 2001). Furthermore, providers who received more training were more likely to offer a variety of activities and toys for children, balance their time indoors and outdoors, and actively interact with them (Norris, 2001). Training was also linked to teacher effectiveness in FCC settings. Specifically, children in the care of individuals who had participated in training in the past year scored higher on cognitive tests (Clarke-Stewart et al., 2002).

Overall, these findings indicate that formal education and training generally have a positive impact on teacher quality and effectiveness. However, the studies on which these conclusions are based are largely correlational, preventing the ability to draw conclusions about a causal relationship between training and/or formal education and teacher quality and effectiveness. Furthermore, questions regarding the impact of certain types of training, hourly requirements for training, or specific formats or content are essentially not addressed (Tout, Zaslow, and Berry, 2006). Despite these limitations, the data indicate that, in general, teacher quality and effectiveness are measurably better when teachers have higher levels of education and training, which in turns lends support for using these pre-service and in-service preparation systems as a means for improving practices and outcomes related to early childhood mathematics.

## Professional Development and Mathematics Education for Young Children

The Joint Position Statement of the NAEYC and the National Council of Teachers of Mathematics (NCTM) on Early Childhood Mathematics

(2002) names five critical areas of knowledge that early childhood teachers must have to be effective in teaching mathematics to young children: (1) knowledge of the mathematical content that they will be teaching, (2) knowledge of children's learning and development, (3) knowledge of effective mathematics pedagogy, (4) knowledge of effective means for assessing children's development and learning, and (5) knowledge of the resources and tools available for teaching early childhood mathematics. In addition to acquiring these areas of knowledge, teachers also need to have a positive attitude toward mathematics (National Association for the Education of Young Children and National Council of Teachers of Mathematics, 2002), believe that young children are competent mathematics learners, and believe that mathematics is appropriate in the early childhood classroom (Ginsburg et al., 2006a; Lee and Ginsburg, 2007b). Themes related to the need for, and the nature of, such preparation are discussed in the following sections.

Early childhood educators need preparation in mathematics for several reasons. Unlike their elementary school counterparts, most early childhood teachers, including those with degrees in early childhood education, have received no prior preparation in teaching mathematics (Copple, 2004; Ginsburg et al., 2006b) Therefore, virtually all early childhood teachers need professional development to build their knowledge and skills around mathematics. This is especially important in light of the recent attention that researchers, funding agencies, major early childhood professional organizations, and policy makers are focusing on targeting improved mathematics outcomes in early childhood, particularly for children from low-income backgrounds (National Association for the Education of Young Children and National Council of Teachers of Mathematics, 2002; National Mathematics Advisory Panel, 2008). As stated by Copple (2004):

> Practically all teachers need to know more about mathematics—the nature of the beast—and how to work with children in mathematics. They need to know much more about what mathematics young children are interested in and capable of doing; many vastly underestimate the range of young children's interests and the extent of their capabilities. (pp. 86-87)

### *Mathematics Content and Early Childhood Teacher Preparation*

A good deal of the research in early childhood mathematics has focused on the content that is necessary to be taught in teacher preparation programs, including both in-service and pre-service programs. That is, this research has focused on (1) mathematics knowledge, (2) mathematics beliefs, and (3) children's mathematical development and curricula to support it.

***Mathematics knowledge.*** Virtually no empirical research exists directly examining teachers' mathematics knowledge (Ginsburg and Ertle, 2008;

National Mathematics Advisory Panel, 2008). However, Ginsburg and Ertle (2008) provide several key reasons that professional development should target teachers' mathematics knowledge. First, teachers need to understand the mathematics that children are learning and how they may be thinking. According to Ginsburg and Ertle (2008), "to understand . . . students' mathematical thinking and then build on it in a way that encourages continued enjoyment of the subject, the teacher must therefore understand the mathematics that the thinking involves" (p. 55).

Second, teachers will be more effective implementers of mathematics curricula, as recommended by NCTM and NAEYC, if they understand the mathematics well themselves. At the pre-service level in particular, this means that teachers may need coursework related to deeply understanding the important mathematical concepts of early childhood rather than simply general mathematics courses that might be appropriate for college students, such as calculus.

Third, teachers can take advantage of teachable moments in mathematics only if they carefully observe, accurately interpret, plan, and implement appropriate activities to further learning, all of which require deep mathematics knowledge. Given that, until recently, teachers may not have had to teach mathematics in early childhood settings, that few have received professional development in early childhood mathematics education, and that many early childhood educators have limited professional preparation in general, researchers and professional organizations have recommended that professional development address teachers' knowledge of mathematics (National Association for the Education of Young Children and National Council of Teachers of Mathematics, 2002).

***Mathematics beliefs.*** As noted earlier, teachers have quite strong beliefs about mathematics, with many feeling it lacks key significance in early childhood programs. Ginsburg and colleagues (2006a), in describing efforts to provide training to teachers using the curriculum, Big Math for Little Kids, stress the importance of directly addressing the emotionally charged beliefs that teachers may have around mathematics. In fact, many early childhood teachers report they are uncomfortable with mathematics (Copley, 1999) and identify it as their weakest subject (Schram et al., 1988). In the prekindergarten settings in which the Ginsburg et al. (2006b) study took place, there appeared to be more resistance to mathematics than is typically found in kindergarten and elementary school, in which mathematics has long been expected to be taught.

***Children's mathematical development and curriculum.*** Naturally, professional development in early childhood mathematics includes helping teachers learn about children's developmental progression in various areas of mathematics, the specific learning experiences they can plan, and the teaching strategies, materials, and supportive environment they can provide to promote mathematical development. A study with California elementary school teachers showed that those who received professional development in which teachers worked directly with curriculum materials associated with NCTM standards were more likely to report reform-oriented teaching practices in mathematics. Furthermore, results suggested that a professional development curriculum that overlaps with the curriculum of students improves instructional practices and student outcomes (Cohen and Hill, 2000).

In early childhood mathematics, few studies exist demonstrating the causal effects of professional development on children's outcomes. Nevertheless, two programs of research in early childhood mathematics have demonstrated a causal link between the delivery of professional development to implement a mathematics curriculum and positive child outcomes (Clements and Sarama, 2007a, 2008; Sarama et al., 2008). This research demonstrates the effectiveness of curriculum-based professional development methods at the early childhood level, which complements and extends the existing data on effective approaches at the elementary level (Cohen and Hill, 2000; Sarama and DiBiase, 2004). Because experimental research is quite limited in this area, no studies comparing alternative approaches to professional development (i.e., curriculum-based versus non-curriculum-based) have been conducted. However, there is a strong rationale for the use of a mathematics curriculum to provide young children with carefully sequenced mathematical experiences in the classroom. Thus, although additional research would broaden understanding of the best means for providing professional development in early childhood mathematics, the current curriculum-based research provides evidence to support the link between curriculum and professional development (Clements and Sarama, 2007a, 2008; Sarama et al., 2008).

### *In-Service Mathematics Support Efforts*

Research on early childhood mathematics has largely been focused on understanding children's mathematical development and the types of experiences that facilitate this learning. This work has also led to the development of an array of early childhood mathematics curricula. However, little research has been done to date on the best methods to prepare educators to support children's mathematical development or how to best provide training on mathematical curriculum implementation. As a result, questions about how to effectively scale up efforts to meet the needs of the early childhood workforce, as described in this chapter, have not yet been adequately addressed. The data that do exist can provide an example of effective practices and are presented below.

Research using the Technology-enhanced, Research-based, Instruction, Assessment, and professional Development (TRIAD) model (Sarama et al., 2008) provides the clearest evidence from the early childhood mathematics literature regarding specifically tested approaches to providing professional development to diverse groups of teachers from various types of programs serving diverse groups of children. TRIAD is a model for developing and scaling up a research-based curriculum. It is during the latter phases of this process that the focus of the research shifts from curriculum development and efficacy testing to the specific testing of the best methods for training and implementation, at first on a small scale and then to larger and more diverse populations (Clements, 2007). TRIAD is focused on successful change of classroom practices around mathematics for the long term. In that spirit, the professional development of teachers is just one component of the overall change process, and teachers are only one of the key players involved. Successful change requires the support not only of teachers, but also of administrators, parents, and children themselves (Clements, 2007).

Evaluations of the TRIAD model have proven it to be effective in improving the quality of the mathematical environment and child outcomes (Clements and Sarama, 2008; Sarama et al., 2008). For example, in one study, mathematics outcomes of children participating in the experimental group demonstrated significant gains over children in the control group (effect size, 1.07, Cohen's *d*) and comparison classrooms (effect size, .47, Cohen's *d*) (Clements and Sarama, 2008). Another TRIAD-based in-service training experiment provided evidence that teachers in the experimental group reported doing more mathematics in the classroom, rating mathematics as more important than did control teachers, and feeling more prepared to teach mathematics.

Key components of the in-service professional development as demonstrated by the TRIAD studies are (1) training is job-specific and tied directly to the use of a curriculum; (2) the training is extensive and ongoing, including an initial training at the outset of the school year, with follow-up sessions; (3) teachers are supported through onsite coaching once per month, aimed at helping with curriculum implementation and discussion of any problems or concerns that teachers have regarding its use; and (4) teachers have opportunities for hands-on practice, discussion, and collaboration with others, as well as for reflection on their practice. In-person coaching is the primary resource for teachers, in contrast with the combination of coaching and web media support offered through Building Blocks.

Two early childhood mathematics curricula, which include in-service professional development, that have been rigorously evaluated are SRA Real Math Building Blocks (Clements and Sarama, 2008) and Pre-K Mathematics (Starkey, Klein, and Wakeley, 2004). An intervention that combined elements of these two curricula has also been tested through experimental research (Sarama et al., 2008). Each is a research-based curriculum that has been evaluated using randomized control-group designs, and both curricula have met the What Works Clearinghouse criteria for inclusion, demonstrating their effectiveness in meaningfully improving child outcomes in mathematics (What Works Clearinghouse, 2007).

The documentation provided to programs adopting Building Blocks details elements of the training and support offered to teachers using the TRIAD model (Clements and Sarama, 2008; Sarama et al., 2008). Building Blocks training and support, which has been demonstrated to be effective through research, consists of three elements over the course of one school year: (1) 34 hours of focused group training, (2) 16 hours of in-class coaching and mentoring, and (3) electronic communications, including the use of an interactive project website (Clements and Sarama, 2008).

Understanding mathematical learning trajectories (which are called teaching-learning paths in this book) is a particular focus of the training, as a part of helping teachers learn the "conceptual storyline" (Clements and Sarama, 2008). In addition, trained coaches provide teachers with regular coaching and mentoring as well as individualized feedback and address any concerns or problems with implementation. The Building Blocks Learning Trajectory web application provides best practice exemplars, video-based illustration of children's mathematical thinking and development, and resources for lesson planning. Finally, teachers receive resources for documenting student progress. Thus, training is fairly extensive, ongoing, hands-on, specific, job-embedded, and tied to curriculum. Furthermore, training is provided by highly qualified trainers, and distance learning facilitates reaching participants in multiple locations. The documented gains in outcomes for teachers, classrooms, and children confirmed the efficacy of this approach to professional development (Clements and Sarama, 2008).

In sum, the research from these examples indicates that professional development in mathematics in early childhood settings is most successful when it is a component of an overall change process that is supported by all key players. They demonstrate that, although teachers can make highly significant improvements in children's mathematics outcomes, learning the knowledge and skills needed to do so requires an ongoing effort with support to achieve this success. Frequently, the number of contact hours in professional development that produces success is substantially greater than typically offered by curriculum publishers, an issue that should be addressed. Mentoring or coaching also appears to play an important role in helping teachers to solve problems as they learn to apply new knowledge and skills, as well as helping to sustain the change process over time. Evidence also shows that providing teachers with knowledge of mathematics and children's mathematical thinking and development, as well as how to apply this knowledge through the use of a particular curriculum, is highly effective at the early childhood level. These early efforts to bring professional development efforts to scale also indicate that technology may play an important role in overcoming logistical barriers to delivering high-quality training to a large, diverse workforce.

### *Outcomes of Mathematics In-Service Preparation in Elementary Education*

To date, there is not much research examining the relationship between in-service preparation and the effectiveness of mathematics teaching for preschool age children. However, one way to examine how formal in-service preparation in mathematics impacts the teaching of mathematics is to investigate the relationship between such preparation and K-12 mathematics outcomes. Research on the K-12 system has found effects between teacher content preparation and teacher effectiveness. For example, Monk (1994) found a positive relationship between mathematics and science secondary teachers who received content-specific preparation and their students' mathematics and science achievement. It should also be noted that the effects of content-specific preparation faded over time, suggesting that professional development opportunities throughout teachers' careers are necessary. It seems, then, that early childhood educators must have a deep knowledge of mathematics as it applies to young children and must have their learning periodically reinforced.

Research on mathematics preparation at the early elementary level also provides some useful implications for early childhood education, because the research is particularly focused on professional development itself, rather than on training as a component of curriculum implementation. A recent review of how professional development affects student achievement at the K-12 level examined over 1,300 research studies and identified only 9 that met the evidence criteria of the What Works Clearinghouse (Yoon et al., 2007). Five of the nine studies targeted mathematics outcomes, either solely or in combination with targeting outcomes in other learning domains. Studies that demonstrated effects on mathematics had an average effect size of 0.57 in mathematics outcomes, evidence of a significant impact on student mathematics learning outcomes. Together, they averaged slightly more than 53 contact hours of training over a period of four months to one year, which is substantially more hours than the typical elementary school teacher would have available for professional development (Yoon et al., 2007) or in which they would typically participate (Birman et al., 2007, as cited in Yoon et al., 2007). Across all nine studies, 14 contact hours or more produced gains in various other domains of student achievement, such as literacy, indicating that mathematics-focused efforts were more sustained or intensive (or both) than those targeting other domains.

Sarama and DiBiase (2004) described the effectiveness of several research-based professional development models for elementary school teachers in mathematics. The authors discuss three models in particular: Teaching to the Big Ideas (TBI), Cognitively Guided Instruction (CGI), and Project IMPACT. While these programs have a number of features, one key cross-cutting element is their emphasis on understanding children's mathematical thinking. There are a number of differences between early childhood and elementary school settings, such as expectations and beliefs about mathematics education and the educational levels of teachers, which make generalizations between them problematic. However, understanding how professional development can effectively help teachers understand the developmental progressions in children's mathematical thinking has important implications for professional development at the early childhood level. According to Sarama and DiBiase (2004), "starting with theory and research is not as effective as starting with practice, and then integrating theory and research into reflections on this practice" (p. 427). This emphasis on helping teachers to understand children's mathematical thinking can inform professional development efforts at the early childhood level, above and beyond adopting and learning a curriculum.

*Pre-Service Teacher Preparation in Mathematics*

The examples of effective in-service professional development indicate the depth and breadth of preparation that all teachers need to address children's mathematics learning effectively, including those who pursue pre-service education. Specifically, teachers need preparation that (1) considers their beliefs about mathematics; (2) provides them with knowledge about mathematics, about children's mathematical development, and how to apply it in the classroom (mathematics education); and (3) affords them opportunities to practice these skills in a classroom setting. However, to date, most college and universities offer little by way of training teachers to effectively teach early childhood mathematics (Ginsburg et al., 2004, 2006a). Furthermore, many of today's early childhood educators completed their university training or general training when mathematics was deemphasized for young children's learning (Early et al., 2007). Thus, many early childhood educators, even the most qualified, degreed teachers, are not sufficiently well prepared to teach young children about mathematics.

To date, there are few if any empirical data sets that examine effective practices in pre-service preparation of early childhood teachers in mathematics. We consider data about the range of existing approaches to providing preparation in mathematics based on a preliminary review, which was conducted for this report, of recent college program submissions for accreditation with the National Council for Accreditation of Teacher Education (NCATE), at both the associate's and bachelor's degree levels.

In addition, we discuss the ways in which the pre-service teacher education could be affected by changes in other related systems. Clearly, more research is needed to determine the effects and the quality of early childhood pre-service mathematics preparation. The following section addresses: (1) issues affecting pre-service preparation for early childhood teachers, (2) the landscape of early childhood teacher education programs in general, (3) the ways in which these programs can address the needs of teachers to be prepared to promote young children's mathematical development, and (4) the ways in which other related credentialing systems can support the needed changes at the pre-service level for adequately preparing teachers in early childhood mathematics.

***Issues affecting pre-service preparation for early childhood teachers.*** Before focusing on the role of mathematics in pre-service teacher preparation, we examine some more general and potentially relevant trends and issues that affect early childhood educators' pre-service preparation. These trends include degree requirements, the academic content in teacher education courses, and assessment of the effectiveness of teacher preparation programs.

*Degree requirements.* Policy makers at the federal and state levels continue to increase their requirements for early childhood educators to possess degrees—and, increasingly, the baccalaureate degree. Thus, one might expect an ever-higher percentage of early childhood educators to pass through the higher education system, creating more opportunities to enhance their mathematical competence through that system.

*Academic content.* State and federal governments have placed greater emphasis on academic content in teacher education. This is reflected in some states' requirements for all education students to have an academic major and in states' limiting the number of credits that can be taken in more applied areas, such as pedagogy. This trend potentially expands opportunities to enhance mathematics content for future early childhood educators, but it may also limit students' opportunities to apply their content knowledge through field experiences and related pedagogical coursework. A related trend, prompted by concerns about the achievement gap in children's literacy skills, has been an increase in state and institutional requirements in the areas of literacy and reading. The potential for competition among literacy, mathematics, and other content areas creates dilemmas for the design of early childhood teacher preparation programs.

*Assessing competence.* There is a growing tendency—spurred to a great extent by NCATE—to focus less on counting time for seatwork assignments and more on assessment of future teachers' competence (including their effects on children's learning), when judging whether a teacher preparation program is effective. This emphasis is posing new challenges for programs as they consider how to conduct standards-based, valid assessments in key areas.

### *Preparing Teachers to Promote Young Children's Mathematics Development*

No systematic national evaluation has been conducted to date of the nature and amount of preparation specifically in mathematics that these degree programs offer. However, a preliminary review of the NCATE submissions of both bachelor's and associate's degree programs conducted for this study indicates that programs currently address mathematics in a number of ways that involve required coursework and field experiences (Hyson, Tomlinson, and Morris, 2008).

***Coursework.*** The coursework that degree programs offer to prepare teachers to teach mathematics at the early childhood level may consist of general mathematics courses, courses on how to teach mathematics, or mathematics education. Pre-service teacher preparation programs have addressed this in a number of ways. Generally, if an early childhood mathematics course is offered, it often focuses on "math methods" (Ginsburg et al., 2006a). Some programs have general education mathematics requirements, either solely or in combination with course requirements in mathematics education. Associate's and bachelor's degree programs may require one or more general mathematics course, such as college algebra, while others offer students the choice of selecting a course in mathematics or in science as part of their degree requirements.

For mathematics education coursework, both associate's and bachelor's degree programs use a range of approaches, such as requiring one or more courses in teaching early childhood mathematics, embedding mathematics education in a general early childhood curriculum course, or combining mathematics and science education. Some offer mathematics education courses focused only on elementary mathematics. This broad range of approaches indicates that there is considerable variability in the depth and breadth of teachers' knowledge, exposure, and experiences in mathematics teaching, even among teachers with degrees, who represent the most qualified in their field.

Overall, the evidence shows that some programs offer in-depth, high-quality early mathematics education, and some programs provide almost no preparation. Pre-service programs should review their coursework in early childhood mathematics to ensure that they are preparing teachers to teach and support their students as effectively as possible. This involves preparing teachers in the following areas:

- **Mathematics.** A deep understanding of the mathematical concepts discussed in Chapter 2 and children's mathematical development as discussed in Chapters 5 and 6 is necessary for teachers to know what and how to teach mathematics effectively to young children.
- **Curriculum.** Teachers need to learn about the curriculum available to them for teaching mathematics to young children. They also need to study the different pedagogical arguments underlying different curriculum in order to be able to make informed choices when they have their own classrooms (see Chapter 7).
- **Assessment.** Programs need to prepare teachers to effectively assess young children's mathematical skills and thinking. Furthermore, teachers should be trained to use assessments to inform and improve on their instructional practices (see Chapter 7).
- **Beliefs.** Pre-service programs should provide teachers with an opportunity to discuss and explore their attitudes and beliefs about mathematics and the effects of those beliefs on their teaching.

***Faculty.*** Some programs, particularly those at the associate's level that rely heavily on adjunct faculty, may face challenges with having personnel qualified to teach early childhood mathematics courses. Because many teacher educators may have been prepared at a time when mathematics was deemphasized for young children, these personnel themselves may require some support to be adequately knowledgeable and prepared to teach the content. Alternatively, programs may take advantage of distance learning and web-based courses offered by mathematics educators at other universities and programs to fill gaps in the mathematics preparation of their students.

***Field experiences.*** Some programs require specific field experiences in mathematics associated with mathematics education coursework, others include it as one component of many in a general student teaching experience or simply do not require any practical mathematics teaching experience at all. Research is clear that effective approaches to professional development in early childhood mathematics require opportunities to practice and use new knowledge and skills and to receive meaningful feedback.

***Role of credentialing systems in preparing teachers in early childhood mathematics.*** To ensure that future degreed teachers have the knowledge and skills that they need to promote early childhood mathematics in the classroom, providers of pre-service preparation programs are likely to need to make changes to their offerings and requirements in early childhood mathematics. While some programs may initiate these changes on their own, in reality four key systems have a great deal of influence over the content and experiences of pre-service education programs in early childhood education. They should be updated to reflect current knowledge in early childhood mathematics, along the lines presented in this report. These systems include: state certification and licensure requirements, Praxis exams, NAEYC standards and other credentialing systems outside of states.

Currently, 48 states have arrangements such that they will give at least initial licensure to a teacher who has graduated from an NCATE-accredited institution, in a program that has been recognized by the appropriate national specialty professional association, such as NAEYC (Margie Crutchfield, NCATE, personal communication, April 2, 2008) rather than specifying particular coursework or credits. However, programs with both NCATE and NAEYC accreditation account for less than one third of all early childhood bachelor's programs (Maxwell, Lim, and Early, 2006).

The Praxis exams, which are used in NCATE's national accreditation/recognition of early childhood programs, include multiple-choice tests of students' basic skills (Praxis I) and tests of their competence in a specific teaching area (Praxis II). These exams serve as gatekeepers at various stages of students' progress through the pre-service program and entry into the profession.

The NAEYC standards are reportedly are used by faculty to guide design and improvement of associate's and bachelor's degree programs (Hyson, Tomlinson, and Lutton, 2007). Also, programs participating in NAEYC's national recognition and accreditation systems are likely to focus on the NAEYC standards. However, while mathematics is explicitly part of the standards (in Standard 4: Teaching and Learning), the current system for national recognition and accreditation does not require pre-service programs to specifically document their graduates competence in math, nor are the actual learning opportunities offered in mathematics explicitly evaluated.

Finally, the Child Development Associate (CDA) and the National Board for Professional Teaching Standards (NBPTS) certification are two credentialing systems that operate outside of state teacher licensure systems. They are important because much of the early childhood workforce obtains or extends their professional development through them. The CDA is obtained through a combination of fieldwork, coursework, and other reading, writing, and conferencing requirements and is the most frequently required qualification for child care center directors (National Child Care Information Center, 2005). A review of the key materials used in CDA training and assessment conducted for this report revealed a need for additional mathematics-related resources to increase the ability of advisers and instructors to support CDA candidates' understanding of and engagement in early childhood mathematics.

The NBPTS uses a rigorous review process to certify "accomplished teachers" in 26 fields, including the early childhood generalist category, which covers teachers with bachelor's degrees who educate and care for children ages 3 to 9. Candidates provide the national board with four portfolio entries that document teaching competence and accomplishments outside the classroom, and demonstrate their content knowledge in a set of "assessment center exercises" specific to their certificate area. NBPTS requires that early childhood candidates include a videotaped mathematics-related instructional sequence in their portfolios (with detailed justification and self-analysis) and that one of two challenging assessment center exercises be in the domain of mathematics. Recent research has linked national board certification with improved child outcomes (National Research Council, 2008).

***Summary of issues related to pre-service teacher preparation in mathematics.*** Early childhood educators who pursue pre-service education prior to their entry into the workforce participate in a range of types of associate's and bachelor's degree programs. These programs, in turn, address mathematics education preparation in a variety of ways, ranging from requiring general mathematics courses or specific mathematics coursework and fieldwork (or both), to combining mathematics with other disciplines, to hardly addressing it at all. While no data on the effects of pre-service mathematics programs on later teaching and outcomes exist, data from effective in-service preparation indicate the content and types of experiences in early childhood mathematics that lead to positive outcomes—specifically, to be prepared to teach mathematics to young children, teachers need knowledge of mathematics, mathematical development, effective pedagogy, including the use of curriculum, and assessment, as well as opportunities to use this knowledge in early childhood classrooms. In addition, beliefs that may hinder the acquisition and application of this knowledge should be addressed. The influence of systems, including licensure requirements, Praxis exams, NAEYC standards, and credentialing systems, is important to consider. These systems are potential levers for increasing the focus on mathematics in early childhood professional development.

## SUMMARY

The nature of the early childhood workforce is important to understand as perhaps one of the most critical contextual factors to improving the mathematical development of young children. As one of the primary vehicles through which children learn mathematics, teachers exert enormous influence. Yet in preparing teachers to take on this challenge, it is critical to face the realities of the workforce—namely that teachers present with a wide range of educational backgrounds, compensation, and work settings but tend to share beliefs and values that are generally less supportive of mathematics in the early childhood classroom than social-emotional development. Compounding the challenge, these teachers, despite their diverse qualifications, have typically received little, if any, preparation to teach early childhood mathematics.

Research on the effective delivery of mathematics-specific professional development is fairly new and there continues to be a need for more work in this area. Research indicates that professional development efforts at all levels are most effective when they address teachers' own mathematics knowledge, beliefs about mathematics, knowledge of children's mathematical thinking and development as well as mathematics pedagogy, knowledge of appropriate mathematical assessment practices, and knowledge of resources for supporting mathematics in their classrooms. Of these, a focus on understanding children's developmental progression in mathematics tied to specific activities through a curriculum is the most salient feature of effective professional development in mathematics.

Effective approaches to in-service professional development in mathematics are ongoing, grounded in theory, tied to a curriculum, job-embedded, at least partially onsite, delivered by a knowledgeable and prepared trainer, supported by administrators, and accompanied by supports for teachers during implementation through mentors, coaches, and technology, meaningful feedback, time for hands-on practice and reflection, and opportunities to work and solve problems collaboratively with other teachers and trainers. Professional development in mathematics may require extensive contact hours and a sustained effort. Furthermore, professional development is but one component of successful teacher/program change. This requires collaboration from administrators, teachers, parents, and children, as well as those from the outside helping to bring about change.

While few data are available regarding effective approaches to pre-service education in early childhood mathematics, the range of approaches to providing this preparation that currently exists demonstrates that many program graduates leave with minimal preparation to teach early childhood mathematics. To prepare early childhood educators at the pre-service level, programs need to require coursework and fieldwork in mathematics, focusing on the content areas described in this report that all teachers need in this domain. To support these changes in programs, teacher educators will require support. Furthermore, licensure and credentialing systems, assessments of teacher competence, and professional and state standards should reflect greater emphasis on mathematics.

Although more data are available at the in-service level than at the pre-service level, even the available studies represent relatively small-scale efforts, presenting considerable logistical challenges to meeting the needs of the field. While data indicate that the use of technology, such as interactive websites and distance learning, is effective in reaching large numbers of teachers in early childhood programs, both at the in-service and pre-service levels, more research and creative solutions will be needed for scale-up efforts.

This chapter describes the importance of the early childhood workforce in promoting children's mathematical development. The next chapter presents the committee's conclusions and recommendations to improve the teaching and learning of early childhood mathematics.

## REFERENCES AND BIBLIOGRAPHY

Balfanz, R. (1999). Why do we teach young children so little mathematics? Some historical considerations. In J.V. Copley (Ed.), *Mathematics in the Early Years* (pp. 3-10). Reston, VA: National Council of Teachers of Mathematics.

Ball, D.L. (1991). Research on teaching: Making subject matter knowledge part of the equation. In J.E. Brophy (Ed.), *Advances in Research On Teaching* (vol. 2, pp. 1-48). Greenwich, CT: JAI Press.

Barnett, W.S. (2003). Better teachers, better preschools: Student achievement linked with teacher qualifications. *Preschool Policy Matters, 2*. New Brunswick, NJ: National Institute for Early Education Research.

Bellm, D., Burton, A., Whitebook, M., Broatch, L., and Young, M. (2002). *Inside the Pre-K Classroom: A Study of Staffing and Stability in State-Funded Prekindergarten Programs.* Washington, DC: Center for the Child Care Workforce.

Birman, B.F., Desimone, L., Porter, A.C., and Garet, M.S. (2000). Designing professional development that works. *Educational Leadership*, May, 28-33.

Birman, B., LeFloch, K.C., Klekotka, A., Ludwig, M., Taylor, J., Walters, K., Wayne, A., and Yoon, K.S. (2007). *State and Local Implementation of the No Child Left Behind Act, Volume II—Teacher Quality Under NCLB, Interim Report.* Washington, DC: U. S. Department of Education, Office of Planning, Evaluation, and Policy Development, Policy and Program Studies Service.

Blau, D.M. (2000). The production of quality in child-care centers: Another look. *Applied Developmental Science, 4*(3), 136-148.

Burchinal, M.R., Cryer, D., Clifford, R.M., and Howes, C. (2002). Caregiver training and classroom quality in child care centers. *Applied Developmental Science, 6*, 2-11.

Burton, A., Whitebook, M., Young, M., Bellm, D., Wayne, C., and Brandon, R.N. (2002). *Estimating the Size and Components of the U.S. Child Care Workforce and Caregiving Population: Key Findings from the Child Care Workforce Estimate.* Preliminary report. Washington, DC and Seattle, WA: Center for the Child Care Workforce and Human Services Policy Center.

Center for the Child Care Workforce. (2006). *Low Salaries for Staff, High Costs to Children.* Washington, DC: Author.

Center on the Developing Child at Harvard University. (2007). *The Science of Early Childhood Development: Closing the Gap Between What We Know and What We Do*. Cambridge, MA: Author.

Charlesworth, R., Hart, C.H., Burts, D., and Hernandez, S. (1991). Kindergarten teachers' beliefs and practices. *Early Development and Care, 70*, 17-35.

Charlesworth, R., Hart, C.H., Burts, D., Thomasson, R.H., Mosley, J., and Fleege, P.O. (1993). Measuring the developmental appropriateness of kindergarten teachers' beliefs and practices. *Early Childhood Research Quarterly, 8*, 255-276.

Chernoff, J.J., Flanagan, K.D., McPhee, C., and Park, J. (2007). *Preschool: First Findings from the Preschool Follow-Up of the Early Childhood Longitudinal Study, Birth Cohort (ECLS-B).* NCES #2008-025. Washington, DC: National Center for Education Statistics.

Child Care Services Association. (2003). *Working in Child Care in North Carolina: The North Carolina Child Care Workforce Survey.* Chapel Hill, NC: Author.

Clarke-Stewart, K.A., Vandell, D.L., Burchinal, M., O'Brien, M., and McCartney, K. (2002). Do regulable features of child-care homes affect children's development? *Early Childhood Research Quarterly, 17*(1), 52-86.

Clements, D.H. (2004). Major themes and recommendations. In. D.H. Clements, J. Sarama, and A.-M. DiBiase (Eds.), *Engaging Young Children in Mathematics: Standards for Early Childhood Mathematics Education* (pp. 7-72). Mahwah, NJ: Erlbaum.

Clements, D.H. (2007). Curriculum research: Toward a framework for "research-based curricula." *Journal for Research in Mathematics Education, 38,* 35-70.

Clements, D.H., and Sarama, J. (2007a). Effects of a preschool math curriculum: Summative research on the building blocks project. *Journal of Research in Mathematics Education, 38,* 136-163.

Clements, D.H., and Sarama, J. (2007b). Early childhood mathematics learning. In F.K. Lester (Ed.), *Second Handbook of Research on Mathematics Teaching and Learning* (pp. 461-555). New York: Information Age.

Clements, D.H., and Sarama, J. (2008). Experimental evaluation of a research-based preschool mathematics curriculum. *American Educational Research Journal, 45,* 443-494.

Clements, D.H., Sarama, J., and Gerber, S. (2005, April). *Mathematics Knowledge of Entering Preschoolers.* Paper presented at the Annual Meeting of the American Educational Research Association, Montreal, Canada.

Cohen, D.K., and Hill, H.C. (2000). Instructional policy and classroom performance: The mathematics reform in California. *Teachers College Record, 102*(2), 294-343.

Copley, J.V. (1999). (Ed.). *Mathematics in the Early Years.* Reston, VA: National Council of Teachers of Mathematics.

Copley, J.V. (2004). The early childhood collaborative: A professional development model to communicate and implement the standards. In D.H. Clements, J. Sarama, and A.-M. DiBiase (Eds.), *Engaging Young Children in Mathematics: Standards for Early Childhood Mathematics Education* (pp. 401-414). Mahwah, NJ: Erlbaum.

Copple, C.E. (2004). Mathematics curriculum in the early childhood context. In. D.H. Clements, J. Sarama, and A.-M. DiBiase (Eds.) *Engaging Young Children in Mathematics: Standards for Early Childhood Mathematics Education* (pp. 83-87). Mahwah, NJ: Erlbaum.

Cost, Quality, and Child Outcomes Study Team. (1995). *Cost, Quality, and Child Outcomes in Child Care Centers Public Report.* Denver: Economics Department, University of Colorado.

Denton, K., and West, J. (2002). *Children's Reading and Mathematics Achievement in Kindergarten and First Grade.* NCES #2002-125. Washington, DC: National Center for Education Statistics.

Duncan, G.J., Claessens, A., Huston, A.C., Pagani, L.S., Engel, M., Sexton, H., et al. (2007). School readiness and later achievement. *Developmental Psychology, 43,* 1428-1446.

Early, D.M., Barbarin, O., Bryant, D., Burchinal, M.R., Chang, F., and Clifford, R.M. (2005). *Pre-Kindergarten in Eleven States: NCEDL's Multi-state Study of Prekindergarten and Study of State-wide Early Education Programs (SWEEP), Preliminary Descriptive Report.* Chapel Hill: University of North Carolina.

Early, D.M., Bryant, D.M., Pianta, R.C., Clifford, R.M., Burchinal, M.R., Ritchie, S., et al. (2006). Are teachers' education, major, and credentials related to classroom quality and children's academic gains in pre-kindergarten? *Early Childhood Research Quarterly*, *21*(2), 174-195.

Early, D.M. Maxwell, K.L., Burchinal, M., Alva, S., Bender, R.H., Bryan, D., et al. (2007). Teachers' education, classroom quality, and young children's academic skills: Results from seven studies of preschool programs. *Child Development*, *78*(2), 558-580.

Fang, Z. (1996). A review of the research on teacher beliefs and practices. *Educational Research*, *38*(1), 47-65.

Gelman, R. (1980). What young children know about numbers. *Educational Psychologist*, *15*, 54-68.

Gelman, R. (2000). The epigenesis of mathematical thinking. *Journal of Applied Developmental Psychology*, *21*, 27-37.

Gelman, R., and Gallistel, C.R. (1986). *The Child's Understanding of Numbers*. Cambridge, MA: Harvard University Press.

Ghazvini, A., and Mullis, R.L. (2002). Center-based care for young children: Examining predictors of quality. *Journal of Genetic Psychology*, *163*(1), 112-125.

Gilliam, W.S., and Marchesseault, C.M. (2005). *From Capitols to Classrooms, Policies to Practice: State-Funded Prekindergarten at the Classroom Level, Part 1: Who's Teaching Our Youngest Students? Teacher Education and Training, Experience, Compensation and Benefits, and Assistant Teachers*. New Haven, CT: Yale University, Yale Child Study Center.

Ginsburg, H.P., and Ertle, B. (2008). Knowing the mathematics in early childhood mathematics. In O.N. Saracho and B. Spodek (Eds.), *Contemporary Perspectives on Mathematics in Early Childhood Education* (pp. 45-66). Charlotte, NC: Information Age.

Ginsburg, H.P., Pappas, S. and Seo, K.-H. (2001). Everyday mathematical knowledge: Asking young children what is developmentally appropriate. In S.L. Golbeck (Ed.), *Psychological Perspectives on Early Childhood Education: Reframing Dilemmas in Research and Practice* (pp. 181-219). Mahwah, NJ: Erlbaum.

Ginsburg, H.P., Jang, S., Preston, M., Appel, A., and VanEsselstyn, D. (2004). Learning to think about early childhood mathematics education: A course. In C. Greenes and J. Tsankova (Eds.), *Challenging Young Children Mathematically* (pp. 40-56). Boston, MA: Houghton Mifflin.

Ginsburg, H.P., Kaplan, R.G., Cannon, J., Cordero, M.I., Eisenband, J.G., Galanter, M., and Morgenlander, M. (2006a). Helping early childhood educators to teach mathematics. In M. Zaslow and I. Martinez-Beck (Eds.), *Critical Issues in Early Childhood Professional Development* (pp. 171-202). Baltimore, MD: Paul H. Brookes.

Ginsburg, H.P., Cannon, J., Eisenband, J.G., and Pappas, S. (2006b). Mathematical thinking and learning. In K. McCartney and D. Phillips (Eds.), *Handbook of Early Child Development* (pp. 208-229). Oxford, England: Blackwell.

Ginsburg, H.P., Lee, J.S., and Boyd, J.S. (2008). Mathematics education for young children: What it is and how to promote it. *Social Policy Report*, *XXII*(I), 3-23.

Griffin, S., and Case, R. (1997). Re-thinking the primary school math curriculum: An approach based on cognitive science. *Issues in Education*, *3*, 1-49.

Hamm, K. (2006). *More Than Meets the Eye: Head Start Programs, Participants, Families, and Staff in 2005*. Head Start series, brief no. 8. Washington, DC: Center for Law and Social Policy.

Hamre, B.K., and Pianta, R.C. (2004). Self-reported depression in nonfamilial caregivers: Prevalence and associations with caregiver behavior in child-care settings. *Early Childhood Research Quarterly*, *19*, 297-318.

Hamre, B.K., and Pianta, R.C. (2005). Can instructional and emotional support in the first-grade classroom make a difference for children at risk of school failure? *Child Development, 76*, 949-967.

Hart, K., and Schumacher, R. (2005). *Making the Case: Improving Head Start Teacher Qualifications Requires Increased Investment.* Head Start series, paper no. 1. Washington, DC: Center for Law and Social Policy.

Hatch, L. (2006). *Labor Turnover in the Child-Care Industry: Exit or Voice? Preliminary Findings.* University of Massachusetts, Amherst, MA.

Helburn, S. (1995). Cost, quality, and child outcomes in child care centers: Key findings and recommendations. *Young Children, 50*, 40-44.

Herzenberg, S., Price, M., and Bradley, D. (2005). *Losing Ground in Early Childhood Education: Declining Workforce Qualifications in an Expanding Industry, 1979-2004.* Washington, DC: Economic Policy Institute.

Heuvel-Panhuizen, M.V.D. (1990). Realistic arithmetic/mathematics instruction and tests. In K.P.E. Gravemeijer, M. van den Heuvel, and L. Streefland (Eds.), *Contexts Free Productions Tests and Geometry in Realistic Mathematics Education* (pp. 53-78). Utrecht, The Netherlands: OW&OC.

Honig, A.S., and Hirallal, A. (1998). *Which Counts More for Excellence in Child Care Staff: Years in Service, Education Level, or ECE Coursework?* Paper presented at the Annual Quality Infant/Toddler Caregiving Workshop, Syracuse, NY, June 15-19.

Howes, C.E. (1997). Children's experiences in center-based child care as a function of teacher background and adult:child ratio. *Merrill-Palmer Quarterly, 43*, 404-425.

Howes, C.E., and Hamilton, C.E. (1993). The changing experience of child care: Changes in teachers and in teacher-child relationships and children's social competence with peers. *Early Childhood Research Quarterly, 8*, 15-32.

Howes, C.E., Phillips, D.A., and Whitebook, M. (1992). Teacher characteristics and effective teaching in child care: Findings from the National Child Care Staffing Study. *Child and Youth Care Forum, 21*(6), 399-414.

Howes, C.E., James, J., and Ritchie, S. (2003). Pathways to effective teaching. *Early Childhood Research Quarterly, 18*(1), 104-120.

Hyson, M., Tomlinson, H.B., and Lutton, A. (2007, March). *Quality of Early Childhood Teacher Preparation: A Moderating Variable Between Teachers' Education and Child Outcomes?* Paper presented at the Biennial Meeting of the Society for Research in Child Development, Boston, MA.

Hyson, M., Tomlinson, H.B., and Morris, C. (2008, March). *Does Quality of Early Childhood Teacher Preparation Moderate the Relationship Between Teachers' Education and Children's Outcomes?* Paper presented at American Educational Research Association Annual Meeting, New York, NY.

Irwin, K., and Burgham, D. (1992). Big numbers and small children. *New Zealand Mathematics Magazine, 29*, 9-19.

Jordan, N.C., Huttenlocher, L., and Levine, S.C. (1994). Assessing early arithmetic abilities: Effects of verbal and nonverbal response types on the calculation performance of middle- and low-income children. *Learning and Individual Differences, 6*, 413-432.

Jorde-Bloom, P., and Sheerer, M. (1992). The effect of leadership training on child care program quality. *Early Childhood Research Quarterly, 7*(4), 579-594.

Kagan, D.M. (1992). Implications of research on teacher belief. *Educational Psychologist, 27*(1), 65-90.

Kagan, S.L., Kauerz, K., and Tarrant, K. (2008). *The Early Care and Education Teaching Workforce at the Fulcrum: An Agenda for Reform.* New York: Teachers College Press.

Klein, A., and Starkey, P. (1988). Universals in the development of early arithmetic cognition. *New Directions for Child Development, 41*, 5-26.

Kowalski, K., Pretti-Frontczak, K., and Johnson, L. (2001). Preschool teachers' beliefs concerning the importance of various developmental skills and abilities. *Journal of Research in Childhood Education, 16*, 5-14.

Layzer, J.I., and Goodson, B.D. (2006). *National Study of Child Care for Low-Income Families Care in the Home: A Description of Family Child Care and the Experiences of the Families and Children Who Use It, Wave 1 Report.* Washington, DC: Administration for Children and Families.

Layzer, J.L., Goodson, B.D., and Moss, M. (1993). *Life in Preschool: Observational Study of Early Childhood Programs for Disadvantaged Four-Year-Olds* (vol. I). Cambridge, MA: Abt Associates.

Lee, J. (2005). Correlations between kindergarten teachers' attitudes toward mathematics and teaching practice. *Journal of Early Childhood Teacher Education, 25*, 173-184.

Lee, J.S. (2006). Preschool teachers' shared beliefs about appropriate pedagogy for 4-year-olds. *Early Childhood Education Journal, 33*(6), 433-441.

Lee, J.S., and Ginsburg, H.P. (2007a). Preschool teachers' beliefs about appropriate early literacy and mathematics education for low- and middle-socioeconomic status children. *Early Education and Development, 18*(1), 111-143.

Lee, J.S., and Ginsburg, H.P. (2007b). What is appropriate mathematics education for four-year-olds? Pre-kindergarten teachers' beliefs. *Journal of Early Childhood Research, 5*(1), 2-31.

Lee, V.E., and Burkam, D.T. (2002). *Inequality at the Starting Gate: Social Background Differences in Achievement as Children Begin School.* Washington, DC: Economic Policy Institute.

Lin, H.-L., Lawrence, F.R., and Gorrell, J. (2003). Kindergarten teachers' views of children's readiness for school. *Early Childhood Research Quarterly, 18*(2), 225-237.

Martinez-Beck, I., and Zaslow, M. (2006). Introduction: The context for critical issues in early childhood professional development. In M. Zaslow and I. Martinez-Beck (Eds.), *Critical Issues in Early Childhood Professional Development.* Baltimore, MD: Paul H. Brookes.

Maxwell, K.L., Lim, C-I., and Early, D.M. (2006). *Early Childhood Teacher Preparation Programs in the United States: National Report.* Chapel Hill: University of North Carolina, FPG Child Development Institute.

Monk, D. (1994). Subject area preparation of secondary mathematics and science teachers and student achievement. *Economics of Education Review, 13*(2), 125-145.

National Association for the Education of Young Children and National Council of Teachers of Mathematics. (2002). *Position Statement, Early Childhood Mathematics: Promoting Good Beginnings.* Washington, DC: Author.

National Child Care Information Center. (2005). *Center Child Care Licensing Requirements: Minimum Early Childhood Education Preservice Qualifications, Administrative, and Annual Ongoing Training Hours for Directors.* Washington, DC: Author. Available: http://www.nccic.org/pubs/cclicensingreq/cclr-directors.html [accessed July 2009].

National Institute of Child Health and Human Development Network Early Child Care Research Network. (2002). Early child care and children's development prior to school entry: Results from the NICHD study of early child care. *American Educational Research Journal, 39*, 133-164.

National Institute of Child Health and Human Development Network Early Child Care Research Network. (2005). Duration and developmental timing of poverty and children's cognitive and social development from birth to third grade. *Child Development, 76*(4), 795-810.

National Mathematics Advisory Panel. (2008). *Foundations for Success: The Final Report of the National Mathematics Advisory Panel.* Washington, DC: U.S. Department of Education. Available: http://www.ed.gov/about/bdscomm/list/mathpanel/report/final-report.pdf [accessed August 2008].

National Research Council. (2001a). *Eager to Learn: Educating our Preschoolers.* B. Bowman, M.S. Donovan, and M.S. Burns (Eds.). Washington, DC: National Academy Press.

National Research Council. (2001b). *Adding It Up: Helping Children Learn Mathematics.* J. Kilpatrick, J. Swafford, and B. Findell (Eds.). Mathematics Learning Study Committee, Center for Education. Division of Behavioral and Social Sciences and Education. Washington, DC: National Academy Press.

National Research Council. (2008). *Assessing Accomplished Teaching: Advanced-Level Certification Programs.* Committee on Evaluation of Teacher Certification by the National Board for Professional Teaching Standards. M.D. Hakel, J.A. Koenig, and S.W. Elliott (Eds.). Board on Testing and Assessment, Center for Education. Division of Behavioral and Social Sciences and Education. Washington, DC: The National Academies Press.

National Research Council and Institute of Medicine. (2000). *From Neurons to Neighborhoods: The Science of Early Childhood Development.* Committee on Integrating the Science of Early Childhood Development. J.P. Shonkoff and D.A. Phillips (Eds.) Board on Children, Youth, and Families. Commission on Behavioral and Social Sciences and Education. Washington, DC: National Academy Press.

Norris, D.J. (2001). Quality of care offered by providers with differential patterns of workshop participation. *Child and Youth Care Forum, 30*(2), 111-121.

Phillips, D., Mekos, D., Scarr, S., McCartney, K., and Abbott-Shim, M. (2001). Within and beyond the classroom door: Assessing quality in child care centers. *Early Childhood Research Quarterly, 15*(4), 475-496.

Pianta, R.C., and La Paro, K. (2003). Improving early school success. *Educational Leadership, 60*(7), 24-29.

Pianta, R.C., Howes, C., Burchinal, M., Bryant, D., Clifford, R.M., Early, D.M., and Barbarin, O. (2005). Features of pre-kindergarten programs, classrooms, and teachers: Prediction of observed classroom quality and teacher-child interactions. *Applied Developmental Science, 9*(3), 144-159.

Piotrkowski, C.S., Botsko, M., and Matthews, E. (2001). Parents' and teachers' beliefs about children's school readiness in a high-need community. *Early Childhood Research Quarterly, 15*(4), 537-558.

Provasnik, S., and Dorfman, S. (2005). *Mobility in The Teacher Workforce: Findings from the Condition of Education, 2005.* Washington, DC: U.S. Department of Education, National Center for Education Statistics.

Ryan, S. (2004). Message in a model: Teachers' responses to a court-ordered mandate for curriculum reform. *Educational Policy, 18*(5), 661-685.

Saluja, G., Early, D.M., and Clifford, R.M. (2002). Demographic characteristics of early childhood teachers and structural elements of early care and education in the United States. *Early Childhood Research and Practice, 4.* Available: http://ecrp.uiuc.edu/v4n1/saluja.html [accessed January 2007].

Sarama, J., and DiBiase, A.-M. (2004). The professional development challenge in preschool mathematics. In D.H. Clements, J. Sarama, and A.-M. DiBiase (Eds.), *Engaging Young Children in Mathematics: Standards for Early Childhood Mathematics Education* (pp. 415-446). Mahwah, NJ: Erlbaum.

Sarama, J., Clements, D.H., Starkey, P., Klein, A., and Wakeley, A. (2008). Scaling up the implementation of a pre-kindergarten mathematics curriculum: Teaching for understanding with trajectories and technologies. *Journal of Research on Educational Effectiveness, 1*, 89-119.

Saxe, G.B., Guberman, S.R., and Gearhart, M. (1987). Social processes in early number development. *Monographs of the Society for Research in Child Development*, *52*(2, Serial No. 216).

Schram, P., Wilcox, S.K., Lapan, G., and Lanier, P. (1988). Changing preservice teachers beliefs about mathematics education. In C.A. Mahers, G.A. Goldin, and R.B. Davis (Eds.), *Proceedings of PMENA 11* (vol. I, pp. 296-302). New Brunswick, NY: Rutgers University.

Starkey, P., and Klein, A. (1992). Economic and cultural influence on early mathematical development. In F.L. Parker, R. Robinson, S. Sombrano, C. Piotrowski, J. Hagen, S. Randolph, and A. Baker (Eds.), *New Directions in Child and Family Research: Shaping Head Start in the 90's* (pp. 4-40). New York: National Council of Jewish Women.

Starkey, P., and Klein, A. (2008). Sociocultural influences on young children's mathematical knowledge. In O.N. Saracho and B. Spodek (Eds), *Contemporary Perspectives on Mathematics in Early Childhood Education* (pp. 253-276). Charlotte, NC: Information Age.

Starkey, P., Klein, A., and Wakeley, A. (2004). Enhancing young children's mathematical knowledge through a pre-kindergarten mathematics intervention. *Early Childhood Research Quarterly*, *19*, 99-120.

Stipek, D.J., and Byler, P. (1997). Early childhood teachers: Do they practice what they preach? *Early Childhood Research Quarterly*, *12*, 305-325.

Stipek, D.J., and Ryan, R.H. (1997). Economically disadvantaged preschoolers: Ready to learn but further to go. *Developmental Psychology*, *33*(4), 711-723.

Stipek, D.J., Givvin, K.B., Salmon, J.M., and MacGyvers, V.L. (2001). Teachers' beliefs and practices related to mathematics instruction. *Teaching and Teacher Education*, *17*, 213-226.

Stremmel, A.J., Benson, M.J., and Powell, D.R. (1993). Communication, satisfaction, and emotional exhaustion among child care center staff: Directors, teachers, and assistant teachers. *Early Childhood Research Quarterly*, *8*(2), 221-233.

Thompson, A. (1992). Teachers' beliefs and conceptions: A synthesis of the research. In D. Grouws (Ed.), *Handbook of Research in Mathematics Teaching and Learning* (pp. 127-146). New York: MacMillan.

Tout, K., and Zaslow, M. (2004). *Tiered Reimbursement in Minnesota Child Care Settings: A Report of the Minnesota Child Care Policy Research Partnership*. Washington, DC: Child Trends.

Tout, K., Zaslow, M., and Berry, D. (2006). Quality and qualifications: Links between professional development and quality in early care and education settings. In M. Zaslow and I. Martinez-Beck (Eds.), *Critical Issues in Early Childhood Professional Development* (pp. 77-110). Baltimore, MD: Paul H. Brookes.

What Works Clearinghouse. (2007). *SRA Real Math Building Blocks Pre-K*. Available: http://ies.ed.gov/ncee/wwc/reports/early_ed/sra_prek/ [accessed July 2009].

Whitebook, M. (2003). *Early Education Quality, Higher Teacher Qualifications for Better Learning Environments: A Review of the Literature*. Berkeley: University of California, Center for the Study of Child Care Employment.

Whitebook, M., and Bellm, D. (2004). *Lessons from CARES and Other Early Care and Education Workforce Initiatives in California, 1999-2004: A Review of Evaluations Completed by Fall 2004*. Berkeley: University of California, Center for the Study of Child Care Employment.

Whitebook, M., and Sakai, L. (2003). Turnover begets turnover: An examination of job and occupational instability among child care center staff. *Early Childhood Research Quarterly*, *18*, 273-293.

Whitebook, M., Howes, C., and Phillips, D. (1990). *Who Cares? Child Care Teachers and the Quality of Care in America. The National Child Care Staffing Study*. Washington, DC: Child Care Employee Project.

Whitebook, M., Sakai, L. and Howes, C. (1997). *NAEYC Accreditation as a Strategy for Improving Child Care Quality: An Assessment by the National Center for the Early Childhood Workforce, Final Report.* Washington, DC: National Center for the Early Childhood Work Force.

Whitebook, M., Sakai, L., Gerber, E., and Howes, C. (2001). *Then and Now: Changes in Child Care Staffing, 1994-2000: Technical Report.* Washington, DC: National Center for the Early Childhood Work Force.

Yoon, K.S., Duncan, T., Lee, S.W.-Y., Scarloss, B., and Shapley, K. (2007). *Reviewing the Evidence on How Teacher Professional Development Affects Student Achievement.* Issues and Answers, REL #2007-No. 33. Washington, DC: U.S. Department of Education, Institute of Education Sciences, National Center for Education Evaluation and Regional Assistance, Regional Educational Laboratory Southwest. Available: http://ies.ed.gov/ncee/edlabs [accessed July 2009].

# Part IV

# Future Directions for Policy, Practice, and Research

# 9

# Conclusions and Recommendations

Over the past several decades there has been an increased focus on the importance of the preschool period—between ages 3 and 5—in providing children with the opportunities they need to get off to a successful start in formal schooling. Many policy makers are now intent on implementing universal public preschool because of the mounting evidence that high-quality preschool can help ameliorate inequities in educational opportunity and begin to address achievement gaps. The importance of supporting literacy in these early childhood settings is widely accepted, but little attention is given to mathematics. However, research on children's capacity to learn mathematics, when combined with evidence that early success in mathematics is linked to later success in both mathematics and reading, makes it clear that basic literacy consists of both reading *and* mathematics. Improvements in early childhood mathematics education can provide young children with the foundational educational resources that are critical for school success. Furthermore, the increasing importance of science and technology in everyday life and for success in many careers highlights the need for a strong foundation in mathematics.

Historically, mathematics has been viewed by many as unimportant to or developmentally inappropriate for young children's learning experiences. However, the research synthesized in this report makes it clear that these beliefs are unfounded. In the course of normal development, young children develop key mathematical ideas and skills that include counting; adding and subtracting; finding which is more (or less); working with shapes by moving, combining, and comparing them to learn some of their properties; experiencing and labeling spatial terms (e.g., above, below);

and understanding length measurement as the number of length units that makes the total; as well as representing and communicating mathematics understanding to others.

Relying on a comprehensive review of the research, this report lays out the critical areas that should be the focus of young children's early mathematics education, explores the extent to which they are currently incorporated into early childhood settings, and identifies the changes needed to improve the quality of mathematics experiences for young children. The committee describes these critical areas of mathematics in terms of teaching-learning paths that can be used to promote optimal learning. Such a path describes the skills and knowledge that are foundational to later learning and lays out a likely sequence of the steps toward greater competence. One can look closely along the path to gauge what children will be able to do next and to design instructional activities that will help them move along the path. The notion of such teaching-learning paths is a framing assumption for the conclusions and recommendations of this report.

To ensure that all children enter elementary school with the mathematical foundation they need for success, the committee recommends a major national initiative in early childhood mathematics. The success of such an initiative requires that parents, early childhood teachers, policy makers, and communities reconceptualize the way they think about and understand young children's mathematics. The early childhood education system (e.g., workforce, early childhood programs, and policies) will need to work coherently together toward this goal. Furthermore, families and communities must also adopt this goal if they are serious about improving children's mathematics education.

In this chapter, the committee summarizes the major conclusions of the report organized around the chapters, articulates the key recommendations that flow from these conclusions, and lays out an agenda for future research.

## CHILDREN'S COMPETENCE AND POTENTIAL TO LEARN MATHEMATICS

The committee's review of developmental research with infants and toddlers demonstrates that the knowledge and competencies relevant to mathematics are present from early in life. As early as infancy, babies are curious about their world and are able to think about it in mathematical ways. Preverbal number knowledge is shared by humans from diverse cultural backgrounds as well as by other species. For example, by 10 months of age, young infants can distinguish a set of two items from a set of three items, and over time they are able to distinguish the number of items in sets with larger numbers. Building on this foundation, young children continue to expand their knowledge and competence and enjoy their early informal experiences with mathematics, such as spontaneously counting toys, excitedly asking who has more, or pointing out shapes.

**Conclusion 1: Young children have the capacity and interest to learn meaningful mathematics. Learning such mathematics enriches their current intellectual and social experiences and lays the foundation for later learning.**

Knowledge and competencies acquired through everyday experiences provide a starting point for mathematics learning. Infants' and toddlers' natural curiosity initially sparks their interest in understanding the world from a mathematical perspective, and the adults and communities that educate and care for them also provide experiences that serve as the basis for further mathematics learning. Children's everyday environments are rich with mathematics learning opportunities, for example, using relational words, such as more than/less than, and counting and sorting objects by shape or size. These foundational, everyday mathematics experiences can be built on to move children further along in their understanding of mathematical concepts.

**Conclusion 2: Children learn mathematics, in part, through everyday experiences in the home and the larger environment beginning in the first year of life.**

Children need rich mathematical interactions and guidance, both at home and school to be well prepared for the challenges they will meet in formal schooling. Parents, other caregivers, and teachers can play a fundamental role in the organization of learning experiences that support mathematics because they can expose children to mathematically rich environments and engage them in mathematics activities. For example, parents and caregivers can teach children to see and name small quantities, count, and point out shapes in the world, "Here are *two* crackers. You have *one* in each hand. These crackers are *square*."

One important way that young children's mathematics learning can be enhanced is through adult support and instruction that is connected to and extends their preexisting mathematics knowledge. For example, a situation in which a young child insists on having "more" teddy bears than his playmate provides an opportunity for the adult to engage the child with a mathematical question (e.g., who has more and how can you find out?). In this instance, the adult can use several key mathematical ideas to help the child understand who has more bears, such as using the number word list to count, 1-to-1 counting correspondence, cardinality (i.e., knowing the total number of items in the set), and comparing the number of bears in the two sets. These kinds of mathematics learning opportunities help children learn to *mathematize* or engage in processes that involve focusing on the mathematical aspects of an everyday situation, learn to represent and elaborate a model of the situation, and use that model to solve problems.

**Conclusion 3: Children need adult support and instruction to build and extend their early knowledge and learn to focus on and elaborate the mathematical aspects of everyday situations—*to mathematize.***

The committee was keenly aware of the influence that developmental and contextual variations have on children's learning opportunities and the quality of their educational environments both inside and outside the classroom. Understanding individual differences in children's development—for example, in executive function or in opportunities to learn about mathematics in their everyday environments—is fundamental to supporting the development of competence in mathematics. Although all children need extensive exposure to mathematics, there is a wide range of individual variation across all domains of learning. This affects the kinds of learning experiences and instruction that individual children need. The need to support early childhood mathematics education in ways that are appropriate for diverse learners and contexts is a theme throughout the committee's discussion of early childhood mathematics.

**Conclusion 4: Due to individual variation, which is related to a combination of previous experiences, opportunities to learn, and innate ability, some children need more extensive support in mathematics than others.**

It is important to understand the sources of observed differences in children's competence and not confuse one source of individual variation for another. For example, low performance might be attributed to a deficit in a child's ability to learn mathematics, when it actually results from other factors, such as that child's lack of opportunities to learn mathematics or difficulties stemming from linguistic and cultural barriers between teacher and child.

Opportunities to explore the mathematics of everyday life differ depending on children's background, including their socioeconomic status (SES) and cultural group. Mathematics knowledge and skills vary within and between cultural groups due to a variety of factors, including language and relative emphasis placed on mathematics. Cultural, linguistic, and socioeconomic factors interact in complex ways that are difficult to tease apart.

The committee was particularly concerned about mathematics teaching and learning for children from low socioeconomic backgrounds because of the particular challenges they face that can have an impact on their knowledge and competence in mathematics. For example, they may be more likely to attend schools with fewer resources and have less support for mathematics at home. Thus, although children with very low and high mathematics knowledge and competence are found across all SES groups, those with low SES will need particular attention. Importantly, providing young children with high-quality mathematics instruction can help to ameliorate systematic inequities in educational outcomes and later career opportunities.

**Conclusion 5: Young children in lower socioeconomic groups enter school, on average, with less mathematics knowledge and skill than their higher socioeconomic status peers. Formal schooling has not been successful in closing this gap for low socioeconomic status children.**

In addition to needing instructional support in mathematics, evidence indicates that young children also need to be supported in their social-emotional development as an integral part of their education. Specifically, during the early education years, children develop general competencies and approaches to learning that include their capacity to regulate their emotions and behavior, to focus their attention, and to communicate effectively with others. In turn, mathematics learning can help to promote the development of these general competencies.

**Conclusion 6: All learning, including learning mathematics, is facilitated when young children also are developing skills to regulate their own learning, which includes regulating emotions and behavior, focusing their attention, and communicating effectively with others.**

## FOUNDATIONAL AND ACHIEVABLE MATHEMATICS FOR YOUNG CHILDREN

On the basis of research evidence about children's knowledge and competence during the early childhood years, as well as on the established consensus of the early childhood mathematics community (see, for example, the NCTM Curriculum Focal Points), the committee identified two areas of mathematics on which to focus: (1) number, including whole number, operations, and relations, and (2) geometry, spatial thinking, and measurement. In each of these areas, the committee offers guidance about the teaching-learning paths based on what is known from developmental and classroom-based research. Each child's progression along these mathematics teaching-learning paths is a function of his or her own level of development as well as opportunities and experiences, including instruction. The teaching-learning paths can provide the basis for curriculum and can be used by teachers to assess where each child is along the path.

Although it is true that young children are more competent in mathematics than many early childhood teachers, parents, and the general public believe, there are limits to what they can do in mathematics. The committee kept this in mind throughout the study process, and thus the teaching-learning paths presented in this report are both foundational and achievable.

*The first content area is number, including whole number, operations, and relations.* Working with number (e.g., learning to count) is the primary goal of many early childhood programs; however, when given the opportunity, children are capable of demonstrating competence in more sophisticated mathematics activities related to whole number, operations, and relations. For example, cardinality—knowing how many are in a set—is a key part of children's number learning. Relations and operations are extensions of understanding number. The relations core consists of such skills as constructing the relations more than, less than, and equal to. The operations core includes addition and subtraction.

*The second major content area is geometry, spatial thinking, and measurement.* Children's foundational mathematics involves geometry or learning about space and shapes in two and three dimensions (e.g., learning to recognize shapes in many different orientations, sizes, and shapes). A fundamental understanding of shape begins with experiences in which children are shown varied examples and nonexamples and understand attributes of shapes that are mathematically relevant as well as those (e.g., orientation, size) that are not. As children progress along the teaching-learning path, they need opportunities to discuss and describe shapes, and, on the basis of these experiences, they gain abilities to combine shapes into pictures and eventually learn to take apart and put together shapes to create new shapes. Young children also need instructional activities involving spatial orientation and spatial visualization. For example, they can use mental representations of their environment and, on the basis of the representation, model relationships between objects in their environment. Importantly, children's knowledge of measurement helps them connect number and geometry because measurement involves covering space and quantifying this coverage. Later, children can compare lengths by measuring objects with manipulable units, such as centimeter cubes.

Number is particularly important to later success in school mathematics, as number and related concepts make up the majority of mathematics content covered in later grades. However, it is important to point out that concepts related to number (and relations and operations) can also be explored through geometry and measurement. In addition, geometry and measurement provide rich contexts in which children can deepen their mathematical reasoning abilities.

**Conclusion 7: Two broad mathematical content areas are particularly important as a focus for mathematics instruction in the early years: (1) number (which includes whole number, operations, and relations) and (2) geometry, spatial thinking, and measurement.**

In the context of these core content areas, young children should engage in both general and specific thinking processes that underpin all levels of mathematics. These include the general processes of representing, problem solving, reasoning, connecting, and communicating, as well as the more specific processes of unitizing, decomposing and composing, relating and ordering, looking for patterns and structures, and organizing and classifying information. In other words, children should learn to mathematize their world: focusing on the mathematical aspects of an everyday situation, learning to represent and elaborate the quantitative and spatial aspects of a situation to create a mathematical model of the situation, and using that model to solve problems.

**Conclusion 8: In the context of each of these content areas, young children should engage in both general and specific mathematical thinking processes as described above and in Chapter 2.**

## THE EARLY CHILDHOOD EDUCATION SYSTEM

The early childhood education "delivery system," which educates and cares for children before kindergarten entry, has a great deal of diversity and is best characterized as a loosely sewn-together patchwork of different kinds of programs and providers that vary widely in the extent to which they articulate and act on their educational missions or are explicitly designed to provide education services. Program types range from friends and relatives who care for children in the home through informal arrangements, to large centers staffed by teachers offering a structured curriculum.

This diversity in the early childhood education system characterizes the education and care arrangements of young children in the United States today. About 40 percent of young children spend their day in a home-based setting, either with a parent or some other caregiving adult (this percentage includes children in home-based relative and nonrelative care as well as children who do not have any regular early education and care arrangements), and about 60 percent are in some kind of center-based care (this includes children in center-based non-Head Start and Head Start settings).

Depending on the type of setting, different regulations regarding educational standards or expectations may be in place, which in turn influence the nature and quality of young children's learning experiences from setting to setting. Increasingly, policy makers are focused on how to provide high-quality preschool education for more children, especially to those whose families cannot afford to pay for it. A number of states are moving toward state-funded preschool education to provide early education and care for these children.

Across all settings, there is a need to increase the amount and quality of time devoted to mathematics. Formal settings with an educational agenda represent the greatest opportunity for implementing a coherent, sequenced set of learning experiences in mathematics. For this reason, the committee focused attention on the kind of curriculum and instruction that can be implemented in centers and preschools. The committee gave more limited attention to how to increase support for mathematics in informal settings. These approaches are discussed in the section "Beyond the Education System."

## Curriculum and Instruction

Having laid out a vision for optimal teaching-learning paths in early childhood mathematics, the committee turned to the evidence base related to curriculum and instruction. The committee first examined the extent to which the content and learning experiences embodied in the teaching-learning paths are represented in current curricula and preschool classrooms. Next, the committee explored what is known about effective mathematics instruction for young children and what might need to be done to improve existing practice. The committee looked for evidence to address two sets of questions: What is known about how much mathematics instruction is available currently to children in preschool settings and of what quality? What is known about the best methods of instruction and effective curriculum to teach mathematics to young children? Although few systematic data exist, the committee was able to identify some useful sources. We conducted original analyses of the standards documents pertaining to early childhood for 49 states and those pertaining to kindergarten for the 10 states with the largest student populations. On the basis of these analyses, the committee concludes:

**Conclusion 9: Current state standards for early childhood do not, on average, include much mathematics. When mathematics is included, there is a pattern of wide variation among states in the content that is covered.**

Although standards represent broad guidance from the states regarding appropriate content for early childhood settings, they do not provide a window on what actually occurs in classrooms. For the latter, the committee examined data from a large-scale study of instruction in state-funded preschools drawn from 11 states as well as several, small-scale studies of curriculum. The results show that when mathematics activities are incorporated into early childhood classrooms, they are often presented as part of an integrated or embedded curriculum, in which the teaching of mathematics is secondary to other learning goals. This kind of integration occurs when, for example, a storybook has some mathematical content but is not designed to bring mathematics to the forefront, a teacher counts or does simple arithmetic during snack time, or points out the mathematical ideas children might encounter during play with blocks. However, data suggest that heavy reliance on integrated or embedded mathematics activities may contribute to too little time being spent on mathematics in early childhood classrooms. Furthermore, the time that is spent may be on activities in which the integrity and depth of the mathematics is questionable. Few of the existing comprehensive early childhood curriculum approaches provide enough focused mathematics instruction for children to progress along the teaching-learning paths recommended by the committee.

> **Conclusion 10: Most early childhood programs spend little focused time on mathematics, and most of it is of low instructional quality. Many opportunities are therefore missed for learning mathematics over the course of the preschool day.**

Evidence examined by the committee suggests that instructional time focused on mathematics is potentially more effective than embedded mathematics. Emerging evidence from a few studies of rigorous mathematics curricula show that children who experience focused mathematics activities in which mathematics teaching is the major goal have higher gains in mathematics and report enjoying mathematics more than those who do not. Furthermore, these studies indicate that a planned, sequenced curriculum can support young children's mathematical development in a sensitive and responsive manner. Supplemental opportunities to use mathematics during mathematical play, sociodramatic play, and with concrete materials (e.g., blocks, puzzles, manipulatives, interactive computer software) can provide children with the opportunity to "practice" mathematics in a meaningful and engaging context.

> **Conclusion 11: Children's mathematics learning can be improved if they experience a planned, sequenced curriculum that uses the research-based teaching-learning paths described in this report, as well as integrated mathematics experiences (e.g., mathematics in the context of a storybook) that extend mathematical thinking through play, exploration, creative activities, and practice.**

Effective mathematics curricula use a variety of instructional approaches, such as a combination of individual, small-group, and whole-group activities focused on mathematics that move children along the research-based teaching-learning paths described in this report. Furthermore, in all these contexts, intentional teaching enhances the mathematics learning of young children. Intentional teaching varies from teacher-guided activities to responsive feedback that builds on and extends the child's understanding. It is also important to engage children in *math talk*—discussion between adults and children that focuses on mathematics concepts, such as how many objects are in a set or how to arrive at an answer—as this facilitates their mathematical development by increasing the connections they make between mathematics concepts, words, and ideas. It should be noted that the committee does not endorse any specific model or curriculum; rather we hope to convey that the research-based principles described in this report should guide choices about development of early childhood mathematics curriculum and instruction.

**Conclusion 12: Effective early mathematics curricula use a variety of instructional approaches and incorporate intentional teaching.**

Evidence also indicates that instruction is more effective when it can build on information about the child's current level of understanding. Such responsive instruction can be accomplished when teachers know how to use formative assessment to guide instruction. Formative assessment is an important component of what teachers need to know to effectively guide children along the mathematics teaching-learning paths.

**Conclusion 13: Formative assessment provides teachers with information about children's current knowledge and skills to guide instruction and is an important element of effective mathematics teaching.**

Evidence from studies of early childhood education indicates that any approach to curriculum and pedagogy is more effective if undertaken in the context of a positive learning environment. Positive relationships between children and their teachers are a key aspect of high-quality early childhood education. In this kind of classroom, children are provided with a safe and nurturing environment that promotes learning and positive interactions between teachers and peers.

**Conclusion 14: Successful mathematics learning requires a positive learning environment that fully engages children and promotes their enthusiasm for learning.**

## Workforce and Professional Development

The early childhood workforce—those who serve both instructional and noninstructional roles in early childhood settings—is central to supporting the academic, social, emotional, and physical development of young children. This workforce consists of people who serve in a variety of roles, are located in a variety of settings, and have a wide range of education and training backgrounds. About 24 percent of early childhood workers are in center-based settings, 28 percent are in regulated home-based settings, and about 48 percent work in informal care arrangements outside both of these systems. Although the majority of early childhood professionals work in informal care settings, the majority of children are in center-based settings. Even in a single setting, individuals fill different roles, such as lead teacher, assistant teacher, classroom aide, or program administrator. Level and type of training can vary by both role and setting. For example, family child-care providers may have little or no specific training in early childhood education, a teachers' assistant may have some formal coursework, and center-based lead teachers may have a 4-year college degree (or even a graduate degree) with specialization in early childhood.

This diversity of roles and educational backgrounds creates challenges for addressing the workforce needs related to supporting early childhood mathematics. Individuals in different roles are likely to need different kinds of knowledge and training to support children's mathematics. Depending on level of education, there are also likely to be differences in individuals' knowledge of mathematics, of children's development in mathematics, and of how to support mathematics learning.

In addition, the field of early childhood has historically placed great emphasis on teaching its workforce to support children's social and emotional development, placing less attention on cognitive development and academic domains. Indeed, academic activities, such as mathematics learning, can be a context in which social-emotional development flourishes. In large part, the heavy emphasis on social-emotional development in early childhood is based on misinterpretations of cognitive development theories; that is, the notion of young children engaging in more abstract thinking, such as mathematics, was believed to be at odds with the development and learning of preschool-age children. Research on early childhood mathematics has disproved this notion, but the idea is still pervasive in the field and continues to be a challenge in moving from research to practice.

**Conclusion 15: Many in the early childhood workforce are not aware of what young children are capable of in mathematics and may not recognize their potential to learn mathematics.**

Professional development, which typically provides training to those already in the workforce, can be a vital mechanism for providing teachers with new or updated skills and knowledge that they need and for reaching those in the workforce who have little or no formal training. Based on studies at the K-12 level, effective approaches to in-service professional development in mathematics are ongoing, grounded in theory, tied to a curriculum, job-embedded, and delivered at least partially onsite by a knowledgeable trainer who allows teachers time for reflection. The committee reviewed emerging data from studies conducted in early childhood settings that support these findings. These studies indicate that professional development focused on understanding children's developmental progression in mathematics in the context of a research-based curricular sequence can improve teachers' instructional effectiveness. An effort to provide professional development to teachers is one important component of successfully improving instruction, but sustainable change will also require collaboration from administrators, teachers, and parents.

**Conclusion 16: In-service education of teachers and other staff to support mathematics teaching and learning is essential to effective implementation of early childhood mathematics education. Useful professional development will require a sustained effort that involves helping teachers to (a) understand the necessary mathematics, the crucial teaching-learning paths, and principles of intentional teaching and curriculum and (b) learn how to implement a curriculum.**

Evidence reviewed by the committee about the formal preparation of early childhood educators (courses taken as part of an associate or undergraduate degree) indicates that there are few opportunities to learn about children's development in mathematics or how to teach early childhood mathematics. To better prepare early childhood educators in mathematics, additional courses and additional materials in existing courses that cover children's development in mathematics and mathematics pedagogy are needed. Furthermore, licensure and credentialing systems exert a great deal of influence over the content and experience of pre-service education programs in early childhood, and few incorporate mathematics requirements.

**Conclusion 17: Pre-service preparation of early childhood educators typically includes few opportunities to learn about children's mathematical development or how to support it. Licensure and certification requirements for credentialing teachers and programs are both potential leverage points for increasing the amount of attention given to supporting mathematics.**

In addition to the challenges already outlined regarding the diverse training and settings of the workforce, attracting and retaining qualified individuals to work in early childhood is difficult due to poor compensation, lack of benefits, and high turnover rates in the field. This situation presents an additional challenge to designing pre-service and in-service experiences that can improve early childhood educators' knowledge of how to support young children's learning in mathematics.

> **Conclusion 18: Improving the training and knowledge requirements for early childhood teachers will present significant challenges unless existing issues of recruitment, compensation, benefits, and high turnover are also addressed.**

## BEYOND THE EDUCATION SYSTEM

A significant number (about 40 percent) of children do not attend centers but instead are educated and cared for by a parent, relative, or another adult in homes. Parents or other caregivers serve as children's first teachers; evidence reviewed by the committee indicates that they can play a key role in shaping children's early mathematics learning through such activities as encouraging play with blocks and other manipulatives, teaching number words, playing counting and board games, sorting, classifying, writing, and viewing educational television programs while talking with children about what they are watching. Math talk has been shown to be a particularly effective way for adults to support the development of mathematical ideas. In fact, math talk beginning as early as infancy is related to children's mathematics knowledge at preschool entry. In addition, informal learning environments, such as libraries, museums, and community centers, have the potential to be resources that parents and caregivers can use to engage children in mathematics activities.

> **Conclusion 19: Families can enhance the development of mathematical knowledge and skills as they set expectations and provide stimulating environments.**

Evidence indicates, however, that low-SES families are less likely than families from higher socioeconomic groups to engage in the kind of practices that promote language and mathematics competence. Although many types of educational programs have been designed to promote the use of these practices with low-SES parents, there is little evidence about the qualities that make such efforts successful. Educational programs for parents based on models that place parents in the traditional role of students learning from "experts" have difficulty sustaining family participation long enough to be successful.

**Conclusion 20: Educational programs for parents have the potential to enhance the mathematical experiences provided by parents; however, there is little evidence about how to design such programs to make them effective.**

The resources available to parents and other caregivers as well as those available through informal educational environments (e.g., libraries, museums, community centers) can also be an effective mechanism for supporting children's mathematics learning. Educational television programming and software, for example, can teach children about mathematics. The committee reviewed research on software and educational programs, as well as models of community-based programs that promote mathematics, and concludes:

**Conclusion 21: Given appropriate mathematical content and adult support, the media (e.g., television, computer software) as well as community-based learning opportunities (e.g., museums, libraries, community centers) can engage and educate young children in mathematics. Such resources can provide additional mathematics learning opportunities for young children, especially those who may not have access to high-quality early education programs.**

## RECOMMENDATIONS

As the committee's conclusions make clear, there is much work to be done to provide young children with the learning opportunities in mathematics that they need. Thus, the committee thinks it is critically important to begin an intensive national effort to enhance opportunities to learn mathematics in early childhood settings to ensure that all children enter school with the mathematical foundations they need for academic success. The research-based principles and mathematics teaching-learning paths described in this report can also reduce the disparity in educational outcomes between children from low-SES backgrounds and their higher SES peers.

The research to date about how young children learn key concepts in mathematics has clear implications for practice, yet these findings are not widely known or implemented by early childhood educators or even those who teach early childhood educators. This report has focused on synthesizing and translating this evidence base into a usable form that can be used to guide a national effort. Thus the committee recommends:

**Recommendation 1: A coordinated national early childhood mathematics initiative should be put in place to improve mathematics teaching and learning for all children ages 3 to 6.**

A number of specific recommendations for action follow from this overarching recommendation. The specific steps and the individuals or organizations that must be involved in enacting them are outlined below.

**Recommendation 2: Mathematics experiences in early childhood settings should concentrate on (1) number (which includes whole number, operations, and relations) and (2) geometry, spatial relations, and measurement, with more mathematics learning time devoted to number than to the other topics. The mathematical process goals should be integrated in these content areas. Children should understand the concepts and learn the skills exemplified in the teaching-learning paths described in this report.**

In both content areas, sufficient time should be devoted to instruction to allow children to become proficient with the concepts and skills outlined in the teaching-learning paths. In addition, the general and specific mathematical process goals (see Chapter 2) must be integrated with the content in order to allow children to make connections between mathematical ideas and deepen their mathematical reasoning abilities. This new content focus will require that everyone involved rethink how they view and understand the mathematics that is learned in early childhood. Early childhood learning goals, programs, curricula, and professional development will need to be informed by and adapted to the research-based teaching-learning paths laid out in this report. The committee therefore recommends:

**Recommendation 3: All early childhood programs should provide high-quality mathematics curricula and instruction as described in this report.**

Early childhood programs will each need to implement a thoughtfully planned curriculum that includes a sequence of teacher-guided mathematics activities as well as child-focused, teacher-supported experiences. Such curricula must be based on models of instruction that are appropriate for young children and support their emotional and social development as well as their cognitive development. As noted previously, effective mathematics curricula use a variety of instructional approaches and should incorporate opportunities for children to extend their mathematical thinking through play, exploration, creative activities, and practice.

Programs will need to review, revise, and align their existing standards, professional development, curriculum, and materials to achieve the teaching-learning paths for early childhood mathematics education presented in this report. It is especially important that children living in poverty receive such high-quality experiences so that they start first grade on a par with children from more advantaged backgrounds. This means that implementation of our recommendations by programs serving economically disadvantaged children, such as Head Start and publicly funded early childhood programs, is particularly urgent.

To make the recommended changes, early childhood programs will need explicit policy directives to do so. To encourage this, the committee recommends:

**Recommendation 4: States should develop or revise their early childhood learning standards or guidelines to reflect the teaching-learning paths described in this report.**

Given the fresh knowledge and perspectives this report affords, it is important that states review their early learning and development standards and guidelines to ensure that they reflect an appropriate emphasis on early mathematics. To that end, we call for all states to examine their early learning and development guidelines, first, to determine that sufficient emphasis is given to the importance of mathematics for young children's development and, second, to ensure that the mathematics content focuses on (1) number (including whole number, operations, and relations) and (2) geometry, spatial thinking, and measurement.

**Recommendation 5: Curriculum developers and publishers should base their materials on the principles and teaching-learning paths described in this report.**

Teachers and early childhood programs need appropriate materials in order to support children's mathematical development and learning. Curriculum developers and publishers who produce materials for curriculum, instruction, and assessment should revise and update them so that they reflect the principles articulated in this report.

The success of this overall effort will need to focus on reaching both the existing early childhood workforce and pre-service educators to provide them with skills and knowledge they need to teach mathematics. Thus, we make several recommendations related to teachers and the workforce.

**Recommendation 6: An essential component of a coordinated national early childhood mathematics initiative is the provision of professional development to early childhood in-service teachers that helps them**

**(a) to understand the necessary mathematics, the crucial teaching-learning paths, and principles of intentional teaching and curriculum and (b) to learn how to implement a curriculum.**

Applying teachers' theoretical knowledge to a curriculum with a strong mathematics component provides them with the opportunity to get feedback and reflect on the instructional practices that they will actually be implementing in the classroom. Professional development should also focus on teachers' beliefs about children's mathematics, the activities and resources in the classroom that can promote children's mathematical development, and their knowledge of curriculum-linked assessment practices. All of these important areas should be included in professional development delivered by a highly qualified teacher educator.

To implement high-quality mathematics instruction, the committee also recommends that early childhood educators be taught to use a range of effective instructional strategies in a variety of formats, including whole-group, pair/small-group, and individual work; exploration and practice; and play and focused activities.

Serious efforts to improve the preparation of early childhood teachers will need to include the state licensure/certification, accreditation and recognition, and credentialing systems that assess teachers' competence and program quality. The early childhood mathematics described in this report should be reflected in the core components of these systems and programs.

**Recommendation 7: Coursework and practicum requirements for early childhood educators should be changed to reflect an increased emphasis on children's mathematics as described in the report. These changes should also be made and enforced by early childhood organizations that oversee credentialing, accreditation, and recognition of teacher professional development programs.**

The committee also recognizes the need to go beyond the formal early childhood education system to reach families and communities—both of which have a strong impact on young children's learning. An important component of reaching all children will need to include strategies aimed at children who are in other settings, such as homes or family child care.

**Recommendation 8: Early childhood education partnerships should be formed between family and community programs so that they are equipped to work together in promoting children's mathematics.**

For example, family education and support programs, such as the Head Start Family and Community Partnerships Program, should include information that provides guidance to families and communities as to why they should and how they can help children develop key mathematical ideas and skills. Furthermore, professionals working with families should be given training focused on early mathematics knowledge and skills, as well as have access to programs and resources on home-based mathematics activities. To this end, there is a need for development of more resources that can support mathematics in informal settings and through media and technology.

> **Recommendation 9: There is a need for increased informal programming, curricular resources, software, and other media that can be used to support young children's mathematics learning in such settings as homes, community centers, libraries, and museums.**

## FUTURE RESEARCH

In its work, the committee conducted a comprehensive review of the existing evidence related to mathematics development and learning in early childhood. As noted, we have determined that the evidence base is robust enough to guide a major national initiative in early mathematics. Yet gaps remain in the knowledge base about children's mathematics education. We think it is critical that the research base continue to advance in a number of key areas outlined below.

*Implications for English language learners.* Increasingly, early childhood classrooms serve significant numbers of children whose first language is not English; these children will be held to the same expectations for future achievement as children whose home language is English. To date, little published research has investigated the teaching and learning of mathematics with preschool age children who are simultaneously learning English. The committee recommends research be conducted that can help identify the best methods of enhancing the mathematical learning of young children who speak a first language other than English.

*Research on the role of teachers in providing effective instruction.* In recent years, researchers have made progress in understanding the process of teaching mathematics at the elementary school level. This research stresses the role of teachers' knowledge and skill including their knowledge of mathematics, their understanding of children's mathematical thinking and learning and their pedagogical content knowledge (i.e., their knowledge of how to structure the classroom and curriculum and to engage children in activities so that the mathematics is accessible). However, there has been much less attention to similar issues in early childhood settings. Research is needed to determine the extent to which the findings from research in the higher grades apply to mathematics instruction in early childhood and what might be unique to early childhood.

*Evaluation of curricula.* In the course of our review of early childhood mathematics, it became clear that many of the available curricula have not been rigorously evaluated for effectiveness. High-quality curriculum research is needed that tracks the effectiveness of curricula during implementation, using the theories and instructional models that were originally used to guide development of the curriculum. This research must also consider how diversity in children's backgrounds and across learning environments influences implementation and effectiveness. To achieve these goals, the committee recommends that curriculum research and development move through phases: from early reviews of relevant research to the creation of learning materials to help children along the teaching-learning paths in this report, to cycles of baseline evaluation, and finally to confirmatory evaluation using rigorous designs, with all phases integrating quantitative and qualitative methodologies. Research of this type will help ensure that early childhood programs can make informed, evidence-based choices among curricula.

*Effective teacher preparation.* Much of the recent research on the preparation of early childhood educators has focused on whether the bachelor's degree is an effective marker for teachers' competency. While this line of inquiry has been helpful in identifying some of teachers' skills that are related to positive child learning outcomes, research in the field needs to move beyond the B.A./non-B.A. distinction. The committee recommends that research on the effectiveness of early childhood teachers focus on the content and quality of teacher education programs rather than on whether or not teachers have a bachelor's degree.

*Parental involvement.* It is unclear why families from low SES backgrounds often do not participate in educational activities and what can be done to promote their involvement in these programs. The committee therefore recommends the conduct of better descriptive studies that examine what parents understand about supporting their children's mathematics learning and how to promote parents involvement in these efforts. Furthermore, if parents do have knowledge about how to support their children's mathematical development but are not putting this knowledge into practice, it is important that research examine the impediments that stand in the way of their actively promoting early childhood mathematics.

*Interventions for children with mathematics learning disabilities.* Exploration of learning difficulties or disabilities in mathematics is a nascent area of research that needs expansion. Further exploration is needed to better understand what early number competencies are predictive of future success in mathematics. Such research can help identify children at risk for learning difficulties or disabilities in mathematics during the preschool years, develop targeted interventions for such children, and test their effectiveness.

# Appendix A

# Glossary

**Accumulator mechanism** refers to the nonverbal counting mechanism of infants that generates mental magnitudes for sets by adding a fixed magnitude for each unit that is enumerated. This system is inherently inexact, and its inexactness increases with increasing number. It provides an approximate numerical representation that does not preserve any representation of the items. Hence, it does not provide a way to distinguish successive numbers, such as 10 and 11.

**Additive comparison** situations are those in which two quantities are compared to find out how much more or how much less one is than the other.

**Analog magnitude system** refers to approximate representations of large numbers beginning with toddler and preschool-age children.

**Attribute blocks** refer to collections of blocks in which attributes (e.g., color, shape, size, thickness) are systematically varied so that children can sort them in multiple ways.

**Cardinality** refers to the number of items in the set.

**Change plus/change minus** situations refer to addition and subtraction situations in which there are three quantitative steps over time, a start quantity, a change, and a result. Change plus situations can be formulated with an equation of the form start quantity + change quantity = result quantity. Change minus situations can be formulated with an equation of the form start quantity – change quantity = result quantity.

**Child-guided experiences** refer to experiences in which children acquire knowledge and skills through their own exploration and through interactions with objects and with peers.

**Composing/decomposing** refers to putting together and taking apart and applies to numbers as well as to geometry and measurement. For example, 10 ones are composed to form one group of 10 and 6 can be decomposed into 5 + 1. Two identical right triangles can be composed to form a rectangle, and a hexagon can be decomposed into six triangles. Measurement itself requires viewing the attribute to be measured as composed of units.

**Computational fluency** refers to accurate, efficient, and flexible computation with basic operations.

**Credentialing** refers to the process of demonstrating and receiving formal recognition from an organization for achieving a pre-defined level of expertise in education.

**Direct instruction** refers to situations in which teachers give information or present content directly to children.

**Early childhood education (ECE) teachers** refer to all personnel whose primary role is to provide direct instructional services for young children. Included in this category are lead teachers, assistant teachers, aides, and family child care providers.

**ECE teaching workforce** refers to those who carry out both instructional and noninstructional roles in ECE settings. The term is an inclusive one that embraces teachers, others who work in the ECE settings and whose primary responsibility is not instructional (e.g., administrators), and individuals who work in settings that support ECE (e.g., resource and referral coordinators).

**Encouragement and affirmation** refers to feedback that relates to teachers' abilities to motivate children to sustain their efforts and engagement.

**Explicit instruction** refers to all of a teachers' instructional actions and interactions that are not unplanned or incidental.

**Feedback loops** refer to sustained exchanges between a teacher and child (or group of children) that leads the child to a better or deeper understanding of a particular idea.

**Finding a pattern** refers to looking for structures and organizing and classifying information. It is a mathematical process used throughout mathematics.

**Focused curriculum (primary mathematics)** refers to a curriculum that is designed and has the primary goal to teach mathematics with meaningful connections to children's interest and prior knowledge.

**Formal education** refers to the amount of credit-bearing coursework a teacher has completed at an accredited institution, including two- or four-year colleges and universities.

**Formative assessment** refers to the process of gaining insight into children's learning and thinking in the classroom and of using that information to guide instruction. It entails the use of several methods—observation, task, and flexible interview—that help the teacher develop ideas about children's thinking and learning and about teaching methods that can help them learn. Formative assessment is often inseparable from teaching and usually not distinctly identified as assessment, but formative assessment can also be used in a deliberate and organized format.

**Geometry** refers to the study of shapes and space, including flat, two-dimensional space as well as three-dimensional space.

**In-service education** refers to the formal education and training that one may receive while having formal responsibility for a group of children.

**Instruction/pedagogy** refers to **intentional teaching.**

**Instructional feedback** refers to a response where the teacher provides students with specific information about the content or process of learning and provides the opportunity to practice and master knowledge and skill.

**Instructional supports** refer to concept development, quality of feedback, and language modeling.

**Integration** refers to the blending together of two or more content areas in one activity or learning experience with the purpose of making content meaningful and accessible but also allowing more content to be covered during the instructional period.

**Intentional teaching** refers to holding a clear learning target as a goal and adapting teaching to the content and type of learning experience for the individual child, along with the use of formative assessment to determine the child's development in relation to the goal.

**Language modeling** refers to a practice by adults when they converse with children, ask open-ended questions, repeat or extend children's responses, and use a variety of words, including more advanced language and building on words the children already know.

**Manipulatives** refer to concrete objects—including blocks, geometric shapes, and items for counting—to support children's mathematical thinking.

**Mathematics teaching-learning path** refers to the significant steps in learning a particular mathematical topic with each new step building on the earlier steps. Teaching-learning paths are often referred to as learning trajectories, a term that emphasizes the sequential and direct route from one skill level to the next. The sources of a teaching-learning path are: (1) the subject matter being taught—what skills and knowledge provide the foundation for later learning, and (2) what is achievable/understandable for children at a certain age given their prior knowledge. Teaching-learning paths also provide a basis for targeting the curriculum, assessing children's progress along the path, and adapting their instruction to help children make continued progress.

**Mathematizing** refers to reinventing, redescribing, reorganizing, quantifying, structuring, abstracting, and generalizing concepts and situations first understood on an intuitive and informal level in the context of everyday activity into mathematical terms. This process allows children to create models of situations using mathematical objects or actions and their relationships to solve problems, including the use of increasingly abstract representations.

**Measurement** refers to the process of determining the size of an object with respect to a chosen attribute (such as length, area, or volume) and a chosen unit of measure (such as an inch, a square foot, or a gallon).

**Morphological marker** refers to the word element that signifies quantity, such as whether the word is singular or plural. For example, the *s* on the end of dog*s*, which indicates that the word is plural, is the morphological marker. The term **quantifier morphology** is used interchangeably with morphological marker.

**Number competencies** refer equally to both the knowledge and skills concerning number and operations that can be taught and learned.

**Number sense** refers to the interconnected knowledge of numbers and operations. It is a combination of early preverbal number sense and the increasingly important influence of experience and instruction.

**Numeral** refers to the symbol used to represent a number.

**Numerosity** refers to the quantity of a set.

**Object file system** refers to the representation of each object in a set comprised of very small numbers, but no representation of set size. For this form of representation, the objects in a small set are in 1-to-1 correspondence with each mental symbol. Thus, a set of three items is represented as "this" "this" "this" rather than "a set of three things."

**One-to-one (1-to-1) correspondence** refers to correspondence between two collections if every member of each collection is paired with exactly one member of the other collection and no members of either collection is unpaired or is paired with more than one member.

**Place value** refers to the meaning of a digit in a written number as determined by its placement within the number.
**Pre-service education** refers to the formal education and training that one receives prior to having formal responsibility for a group of children.
**Primary mathematics/focused mathematics time** refers to a dedicated instructional time focused on mathematics as the primary goal.
**Professional development** is an umbrella term including both formal education and training.
**Prompting thought processes** refers to a particular feedback strategy for mathematics instruction that asks students to explain their thinking or actions.
**Providing information** refers to clarifying incorrect answers or providing very specific information about the correct answer.
**Put together** situations refer to addition/subtraction situations in which two quantities are put together to make a third quantity.

**Relating and ordering** refers to mathematical processes of comparing and placing in order.
**Relating parts and wholes level** refers to a level of thinking that occurs when children combine pattern block shapes to make composites that they recognize as new shapes and to fill puzzles, with growing intentionality and anticipation.

**Scaffolding** refers to an instructional strategy in which the teacher provides information and assistance that allow children to perform at a higher level than they might be able to do on their own. It extends knowledge rather than verifying prior or existing knowledge.
**Secondary (embedded) mathematics** refers to a form of integration through which teaching and exposure to mathematics content is an ancillary activity. One or more subjects other than mathematics, such as literacy or science, are the primary goals of the activity.
**Spatial orientation** refers to knowing where one is and how to get around in the world. Children have cognitive systems that are based on their own position and their movements through space, as well as external references. They can learn to represent spatial relations and movement through space using both of these systems, eventually mathematizing their knowledge.
**Spatial visualization/imagery** refers to the process that occurs when there is understanding and performing imagined movements of two-dimensional and three-dimensional objects. To do this requires creating a mental image and manipulating it, showing the close relationship between these two cognitive abilities.

**Subitizing** is the process of recognizing and naming the number of objects in a set.

**Conceptual subitizing** refers to using pattern recognition to quickly determine the number of objects in a set, such as seeing 2 things and 2 things and knowing this makes 4 things in all.

**Perceptual subitizing** refers to instantly recognizing and naming the number of objects in a set.

**Superposition** is the act of placing one item on top of another.

**Take apart** situations refer to addition/subtraction situations in which a total quantity is taken apart to make two quantities (which do not have to be equal). These situations generally have several solutions. For example: Joey has 5 marbles to put in his 2 pockets. How many can he put in his left pocket and how many in his right pocket?

**Tangram** is a puzzle consisting of seven flat shapes, called *tans*, which are put together in different ways to form distinct geometric shapes.

**Teacher effectiveness** refers to the impact of teachers' actions and behaviors on the accomplishments and/or learning outcomes of the children they teach.

**Teacher-guided instruction** refers to teachers' planning and implementing experiences in which they provide explicit information, model or demonstrate skills, and use other teaching strategies in which they take the lead.

**Teacher-initiated learning experiences** refer to classroom experiences that are determined by the teacher's goals and direction, but ideally also reflect children's active engagement.

**Teacher quality** refers to the positive actions and behaviors of teachers, particularly with regard to their interactions with young children.

**Thinking about parts level** refers to a level of thinking that occurs when preschoolers can place shapes contiguously to form pictures in which several shapes play a single role (e.g., a leg might be created from three contiguous squares) but use trial and error and do not anticipate creation of new geometric shapes.

**Training** refers to the educational activities that take place outside of the formal education process. Such efforts may include coaching, mentoring, or workshops.

**Unitizing** refers to finding or creating a mathematical unit as it occurs in numerical, geometric, and spatial contexts.

**Virtual manipulatives** refer to manipulatives accessed through learning software and composed of digital "objects" that resemble physical objects and can be manipulated, usually with a mouse, in the same ways as their authentic counterparts. Virtual versions of concrete manipulatives typically used in mathematics education include base 10 blocks, Cuisenaire rods, and tangrams. Many available virtual manipulatives are paired with structured activities or suggestions to aid implementation in the classroom.

**Visual/holistic level** refers to a level of thinking that occurs when children have formed schemes, or mental "patterns," for these shape categories. It refers to the ability of preschoolers to learn to recognize a wide variety of shapes, including shapes that are different sizes and are presented at different orientations. They also learn to name common three-dimensional shapes informally and with mathematical names ("ball"/sphere, "box" or rectangular prism, "rectangular block" or "triangular block," "can"/cylinder). They name and describe these shapes, first using their own descriptions and increasingly adopting mathematical language.

# Appendix B

# Concepts of Measurement

At least eight concepts form the foundation of children's understanding of length measurement. These concepts include understanding of the attribute, conservation, transitivity, equal partitioning, iteration of a standard unit, accumulation of distance, origin, and relation to number.

*Understanding of the attribute* of length includes understanding that lengths span fixed distances ("Euclidean" rather than "topological" conceptions in the Piagetian formulation).

*Conservation* of length includes understanding that lengths span fixed distances and the understanding that as an object is moved, its length does not change. For example, if children are shown two equal length rods aligned, they usually agree that they are the same length. If one is moved to project beyond the other, children 4½ to 6 years often state that the projecting rod is longer (at either end; some maintain, "both are longer"; the literature is replete with different interpretations of these data, but certainly children's notion of "length" is not mathematically accurate). At 5 to 7 years, many children hesitate or vacillate; beyond that, they quickly answer correctly. Conservation of length develops as the child learns to measure (Inhelder, Sinclair, and Bovet, 1974).

*Transitivity* is the understanding that if the length of object X is equal to (or greater/less than) the length of object Y and object Y is the same length as (or greater/less than) object Z, then object X is the same length as (or greater/less than) object Z. A child with this understanding can use an object as a referent by which to compare the heights or lengths of other objects.

*Equal partitioning* is the mental activity of slicing up an object into the same-sized units. This idea is not obvious to children. It involves mentally seeing the object as something that can be partitioned (or cut up) before even physically measuring. Asking children what the hash marks on a ruler mean can reveal how they understand partitioning of length (Clements and Barrett, 1996; Lehrer, 2003). Some children, for instance, may understand "five" as a hash mark, not as a space that is cut into five equal-sized units. As children come to understand that units can also be partitioned, they come to grips with the idea that length is continuous (e.g., any unit can itself be further partitioned).

*Units and unit iteration.* Unit iteration requires the ability to think of the length of a small unit, such as a block as part of the length of the object being measured, and to place the smaller block repeatedly along the length of the larger object (Kamii and Clark, 1997; Steffe, 1991), tiling the length without gaps or overlaps, and counting these iterations. Such tiling, or space filling, is implied by partitioning, but that is not well established for young children, who also must see the need for equal partitioning and thus the use of identical units.

*Accumulation of distance and additivity.* Accumulation of distance is the understanding that as one iterates a unit along the length of an object and count the iteration, the number words signify the space covered by all units counted up to that point (Petitto, 1990). Piaget, Inhelder, and Szeminska (1960) characterized children's measuring activity as an accumulation of distance when the result of iterating forms nesting relationships to each other. That is, the space covered by three units is nested in or contained in the space covered by four units. Additivity is the related notion that length can be decomposed and composed, so that the total distance between two points is equivalent to the sum of the distances of any arbitrary set of segments that subdivide the line segment connecting those points. This is, of course, closely related to the same concepts in composition in arithmetic, with the added complexities of the continuous nature of measurement.

*Origin* is the notion that any point on a ratio scale can be used as the origin. Young children often begin a measurement with "1" instead of zero. Because measures of Euclidean space are invariant under translation (the distance between 45 and 50 is the same as that between 100 and 105), any point can serve as the origin.

*Relation between number and measurement.* Children must reorganize their understanding of the items they are counting to measure continuous units. They make measurement judgments based on counting ideas, often based on experiences counting discrete objects. For example, Inhelder, Sinclair, and Bovet (1974) showed children two rows of matches, in which the rows were the same length but each row was comprised of a different number of matches as shown in Figure B-1. Although, from the adult perspective, the lengths of the rows are the same, many children argued that

**FIGURE B-1** Relationship between number and measurement.

the row with 6 matches was longer because it had more matches. Thus, in measurement, there are situations that differ from the discrete cardinal situations. For example, when measuring with a ruler, the order-irrelevance principle does not apply and every element (e.g., each unit on a ruler) should not necessarily be counted (Fuson and Hall, 1982).

### Concepts of Area Measurement

Understanding of area measurement involves learning and coordinating many ideas (Clements and Stephan, 2004). Most of these ideas, such as transitivity, the relation between number and measurement, and unit iteration, operate in area measurement in a manner similar to length measurement. Two additional foundational concepts will be briefly described.

*Understanding of the attribute of area* involves giving a quantitative meaning to the amount of bounded two-dimensional surfaces.

*Equal partitioning* is the mental act of cutting two-dimensional space into parts, with equal partitioning requiring parts of equal area (usually congruent).

*Spatial structuring.* Children need to *structure an array* to understand area as truly two-dimensional. Spatial structuring is the mental operation of constructing an organization or form for an object or set of objects in space, a form of abstraction, the process of selecting, coordinating, unifying, and registering in memory a set of mental objects and actions. Based on Piaget and Inhelder's (1967) original formulation of coordinating dimensions, spatial structuring takes previously abstracted items as content and integrates them to form new structures. It creates stable patterns of mental actions that an individual uses to link sensory experiences, rather than the sensory input of the experiences themselves. Such spatial structuring precedes meaningful mathematical use of the structures, such as determining area or volume (Battista and Clements, 1996; Battista et al., 1998; Outhred and Mitchelmore, 1992). That is, children can be taught to multiply linear dimensions, but conceptual development demands this build on multiplicative thinking, which can develop first based on, for example, their thinking about a number of square units in a row times the number of rows (Nunes, Light, and Mason, 1993; note that children were less successful using rulers than square tiles).

## REFERENCES

Battista, M.T., and Clements, D.H. (1996). Students' understanding of three-dimensional rectangular arrays of cubes. *Journal for Research in Mathematics Education, 27*, 258-292.

Battista, M.T., Clements, D.H., Arnoff, J., Battista, K., and Borrow, C.V.A. (1998). Students' spatial structuring of 2D arrays of squares. *Journal for Research in Mathematics Education, 29*, 503-532.

Clements, D.H., and Barrett, J. (1996). Representing, connecting and restructuring knowledge: A micro-genetic analysis of a child's learning in an open-ended task involving perimeter, paths and polygons. In E. Jakubowski, D. Watkins, and H. Biske (Eds.), *Proceedings of the 18th Annual Meeting of the North America Chapter of the International Group for the Psychology of Mathematics Education* (vol. 1, pp. 211-216). Columbus, OH: ERIC Clearinghouse for Science, Mathematics, and Environmental Education.

Clements, D.H., and Stephan, M. (2004). Measurement in preK-2 mathematics. In D.H. Clements, J. Sarama, and A.-M. DiBiase (Eds.), *Engaging Young Children in Mathematics: Standards for Early Childhood Mathematics Education* (pp. 299-317). Mahwah, NJ: Erlbaum.

Fuson, K.C., and Hall, J.W. (1982). The acquisition of early number word meanings: A conceptual analysis and review. In H.P. Ginsburg (Ed.), *Children's Mathematical Thinking* (pp. 49-107). New York: Academic Press.

Inhelder, B., Sinclair, H., and Bovet, M. (1974). *Learning and the Development of Cognition.* Cambridge, MA: Harvard University Press.

Kamii, C., and Clark, F.B. (1997). Measurement of length: The need for a better approach to teaching. *School Science and Mathematics, 97*, 116-121.

Lehrer, R. (2003). Developing understanding of measurement. In J. Kilpatrick, W.G. Martin, and D. Schifter (Eds.), *A Research Companion to Principles and Standards for School Mathematics* (pp. 179-192). Reston, VA: National Council of Teachers of Mathematics.

Nunes, T., Light, P., and Mason, J.H. (1993). Tools for thought: The measurement of length and area. *Learning and Instruction, 3*, 39-54.

Outhred, L.N., and Mitchelmore, M.C. (1992). Representation of area: A pictorial perspective. In W. Geeslin and K. Graham (Eds.), *Proceedings of the Sixteenth Psychology in Mathematics Education Conference* (vol. II, pp. 194-201). Durham, NH: Program Committee of the Sixteenth Psychology in Mathematics Education Conference.

Petitto, A.L. (1990). Development of number line and measurement concepts. *Cognition and Instruction, 7*, 55-78.

Piaget, J., and Inhelder, B. (1967). *The Child's Conception of Space.* (F.J. Langdon and J.L. Lunzer, Trans.). New York: W.W. Norton.

Piaget, J., Inhelder, B., and Szeminska, A. (1960). *The Child's Conception of Geometry.* London, England: Routledge and Kegan Paul.

Steffe, L.P. (1991). Operations that generate quantity. *Learning and Individual Differences, 3*, 61-82.

# Appendix C

# Biographical Sketches of Committee Members and Staff

**Christopher T. Cross** (*Chair*) is chairman of Cross & Joftus, LLC, an education policy consulting firm. He has been a senior fellow with the Center for Education Policy and a distinguished senior fellow with the Education Commission of the States. He also serves as a consultant to the Broad Foundation and the C.S. Mott Foundation and is on the board of directors of TeachFirst. From 1994 to 2002 he served as president and chief executive officer of the Council for Basic Education. Previously he served as director of the education initiative of the Business Roundtable and as assistant secretary for educational research and improvement in the U.S. Department of Education. He chaired the National Assessment of Title I Independent Review Panel on Evaluation for the U.S. Department of Education in 1995-2001 and the National Research Council Panel on Minority Representation in Special Education in 1997-2002 and was a member of the International Education and Foreign Language project in 2006-2007. He has written extensively in the education and public policy areas and has been published in numerous scholarly and technical publications. He has a B.A. from Whittier College and an M.A. in government from California State University, Los Angeles.

**Oscar Barbarin** is the L. Richardson and Emily Preyer bicentennial distinguished professor for strengthening families in the School of Social Work and a fellow of the Frank Porter Graham Child Development Institute at the University of North Carolina, Chapel Hill. His work has focused on understanding the roles that families play in preschool child competence, including the links between home and school, the early learning needs of

African American children and families, early childhood mental health, ethnic and gender-based achievement gaps, and the factors associated with and outcomes of preschool quality. He conducted a longitudinal study of child development in South Africa after the end of apartheid and authored *Mandela's Children: Child Development in Post-Apartheid South Africa*. Currently, he is leading studies targeting the academic needs of boys of color and their families. He recently organized and led the International Conference: Developmental Science and Early Schooling, sponsored by the Society for Research in Child Development, the Frank Porter Graham Child Development Center, and the Foundation for Child Development, which involved presentations and discussion of issues of translating research into practice. He has a B.A. from St. Joseph's Seminary College, an M.A. in counseling psychology from New York University, and M.S. and Ph.D. degrees in psychology from Rutgers University.

**Sybilla Beckmann** is professor of mathematics at the University of Georgia. Her mathematics research is focused on algebra/group theory, arithmetic geometry/algebraic number theory, commutative algebra/algebraic geometry, and tilings of the plane. She recently completed the second edition of *Mathematics for Elementary Teachers*, along with an activities guide and an instructor resource guide. Her recent work has focused on professional development of pre-service and in-service mathematics teachers, including preparing mathematicians to teach mathematics content to teachers and directly leading professional development workshops with teachers of mathematics. She was a member of the Curriculum Focal Points writing team conducted by the National Council of Teachers of Mathematics. In addition, she was a member of an expert panel on mathematics teacher preparation for the National Research Council Committee on Teacher Preparation. She also taught a daily class of sixth grade mathematics during the 2004-2005 school year. She has a Sc.B. in mathematics from Brown University and a Ph.D. in mathematics from the University of Pennsylvania.

**Sue Bredekamp** is director of research for the Council for Early Childhood Professional Recognition in Washington, DC. In her current role, she develops resources related to the administration of the Child Development Associate National Credentialing System. Previously, during her tenure at the National Association for the Education of Young Children, she developed the accreditation system for early childhood programs and coauthored the initial and revised edition of *Developmentally Appropriate Practice in Early Childhood Programs*. Throughout her career, she has focused on promoting the professional development of the early childhood workforce and developing standards for practice, also serving as a consultant to numerous programs and initiatives. She has a B.A. in English, an M.A. in early childhood education, and a Ph.D. in curriculum and instruction with concentrations in early childhood education and human development from the University of Maryland.

**Douglas H. Clements** is professor in the Department of Learning and Instruction at the State University of New York at Buffalo. He has led a number of initiatives aimed at identifying the key standards for early childhood mathematics, including participating in the writing group of the National Council of Teachers of Mathematics' *Curriculum Focal Points* to specify what mathematics should be taught at each grade level. In addition, he led a joint initiative between the National Association for the Education of Young Children and the National Council of Teachers of Mathematics to produce a joint position statement on the mathematics education of young children. He is also a member of the National Mathematics Advisory Panel created by President George W. Bush. His research and publications have focused on early childhood mathematics development, particularly children's development of geometry skills and the use of computers in mathematics education. He has also coauthored a number of curriculum products based on his Curriculum Research Framework, including a preschool curriculum, *Building Blocks*, which includes print, manipulatives, and the *Building Blocks* software, as well as extensions of that software up through the grades. He has a B.A. in sociology, an M.Ed. in elementary and remedial education, and a Ph.D. in elementary education from the State University of New York at Buffalo. He also has permanent certification to teach in the State of New York at the nursery, kindergarten, and first through sixth grade levels.

**Karen C. Fuson** is professor emerita at the School of Education and Social Policy at Northwestern University. Her recent work has focused on the continued development and revisions of *Children's Math Worlds*, a research-based program for students in kindergarten through fifth grade developed over 10 years in a wide range of classrooms and now published as *Math Expressions*. This research focused on developing a research-based coherent sequence of supportive representations and classroom structures through extensive classroom-based research and using analysis of curricula and strategies from a variety of countries. Through the years Fuson has devoted particular attention to the teaching of mathematical understandings and skills from age 2 to 8 and has also done extended research concerning the mathematics learning of Latino and urban children. She has studied and published widely on children's development of number concepts and arithmetic operations, word problem solving, as well as on mathematics education pedagogy. At the National Research Council, she was a member of the Mathematics Learning Study Committee. She has a B.A. in mathematics from Oberlin College and an M.A.T. in mathematics education and a Ph.D. in teacher education with emphases in mathematics and psychology from the University of Chicago.

**Yolanda Garcia** is director of the E3 Institute Advancing Excellence in Early Education at WestEd in San Jose, California. In this role, she supervises the Compensation and Retention Encourages Stability Program as well as other efforts to improve local early education in a variety of settings and program types through professional development, recruitment, and financial incentives. In addition, she is engaged in research to determine the impact of such programs on child outcomes. Her other research interests have focused on preschool English language learners and language development. Previously she served for 20 years as director of the Children's Services Department of the Office of Education of Santa Clara, California, overseeing services for more than 3,000 children in Head Start, state preschool, and other child care programs. She has served as a fellow in the U.S. Department of Health and Human Services and a senior program officer for the Charles Mott Foundation, focusing on strategies for grant programs on early education and family support. She was a member of the Head Start Quality and Improvement Panel and the National Research Council's Committee on Integrating the Science of Early Childhood Development. She has an M.A. in education administration from San Jose State University and an M.S. in social services administration with an emphasis in child welfare and public policy from the University of Chicago.

**Herbert Ginsburg** is the Jacob H. Schiff Foundation professor of psychology and education at Teachers' College, Columbia University. He is also professor in the Department of Mathematics Education and a Fulbright senior specialist. His research interests have focused on intellectual development and education, especially among poor and minority children, development of mathematical thinking, mathematics education and assessment, and the professional development of teachers. His current research involves evaluating *Big Math for Little Kids*, an early childhood mathematics curriculum he coauthored; examining the use of web-based video vignettes as a professional development tool; and studying computer-guided mathematics assessments for children. He is the author of numerous books, chapters, articles, and reviews, as well as several mathematics textbooks. He is a codeveloper of the Test of Early Mathematics Ability. He has a B.A. in social relations from Harvard University and M.S. and Ph.D. degrees in developmental psychology from the University of North Carolina, Chapel Hill.

**Nancy C. Jordan** is professor of education at the University of Delaware. Since 1998 she has been principal investigator of a federally funded project on children's mathematics difficulties and disabilities. She is the author or coauthor of many articles in mathematics learning difficulties and most recently has published articles in *Child Development*, the *Journal of Learning Disabilities*, *Developmental Science*, and the *Journal of Educational Psychology*. Her work focuses on early prediction and prevention of mathematics difficulties and connections between mathematics and reading difficulties. She has a B.A. from the University of Iowa (phi beta kappa), an M.A. from Northwestern University, and a Ph.D. in education from Harvard University. She completed a postdoctoral fellowship at the University of Chicago. Before beginning her doctoral studies, she taught elementary school children with special needs. She also taught and did clinical work in the Center for Development and Learning at the University of North Carolina, Chapel Hill.

**Sharon Lynn Kagan** is the Marx professor of early childhood and family policy, codirector of the National Center for Children and Families; and associate dean for policy and director of the Office of Policy and Research at Teachers College, Columbia University. She has examined the effects of policies and institutions on the development of children from birth to age 8 and their families, with particular interest in low-income children; private-public collaboration in service delivery; and standards, professional development, organizational change, and family support. Currently, she is working with UNICEF on the development, validation, and implementation of early learning standards in 40 countries. She is chair of the National Task Force on Early Childhood Accountability, coauthor of a recent book on the early childhood teaching workforce, director of the Policy Matters Project, and a consultant to states, foundations, and political leaders on early childhood pedagogy and practice. She was president of the National Association for the Education of Young Children and of Family Support America and chaired the National Education Goals Panel work on readiness. She has been a member of national panels on Head Start and Chapter I and was a member of the Committee on Early Childhood Pedagogy at the National Research Council. Early in her career, she was a Head Start teacher and director. She is the recipient of the Conant award from the Education Commission of the States, the Distinguished Services award from the Council of Chief State School Officers, and the McGraw Hill prize. She has a B.A. in English with a teaching certificate from the University of Michigan, an M.A. from Johns Hopkins University, and an Ed.D. in curriculum and teaching from Columbia University.

**Susan C. Levine** is professor of psychology and chair of the Developmental Psychology Program at the University of Chicago. She has studied early mathematical and cognitive development beginning in infancy, focusing most recently on the role of mathematical language and gesture inputs by parents and teachers. She is coauthor of *Quantitative Development Infancy and Early Childhood*. Her work has focused on basic cognitive developmental research to understand the nature of mathematical development in such areas as early numerical development, measurement, mental rotation, and proportional and spatial reasoning. In addition, she has examined the effects of brain injury and stroke on brain and cognitive development. She has a B.S. from Simmons College and a Ph.D. in psychology from the Massachusetts Institute of Technology.

**Kevin Miller** is professor and cochair of the Combined Program in Education and Psychology at the University of Michigan, where he is also professor in the Educational Studies and Psychology Departments, the Center for Human Growth and Development, and the Center for Chinese Studies. He has conducted extensive cross-cultural research between China and the United States in the areas of cognitive and mathematical development, specifically examining the role of culture, linguistics, and classroom practices in contributing to children's learning. More recently, he has been studying how video representations of teaching and learning can be used in understanding the relations between teaching and learning and improving the preparation of prospective teachers. He is chair of the Mathematics Education Review Panel for the Institute of Education Sciences at the U.S. Department of Education and a member of the Mathematical Sciences Education Board at the National Research Council. He has a B.A. in psychology from Haverford College and a Ph.D. in child and school psychology from the University of Minnesota.

**Robert C. Pianta** is the Novartis US Foundation professor of education and dean of the Curry School of Education at the University of Virginia, as well as professor in the Department of Psychology. He also serves as director of the National Center for Research in Early Childhood Education and the Center for Advanced Study of Teaching and Learning. His work has focused on the predictors of child outcomes and school readiness, particularly adult-child relationships, and the transition to kindergarten. His recent work has focused on better understanding the nature of teacher-child interactions, classroom quality, and child competence, through standardized observational assessment. He has also conducted research on professional development, at both the pre-service and in-service levels. He has recently begun work to develop a preschool mathematics curriculum, incorporating a web-based teacher support component. He has a B.S. and an M.A. in special education from the University of Connecticut and a Ph.D. in psychology from the University of Minnesota. He began his career as a special education teacher.

**Heidi Schweingruber** (*Senior Program Director*) is the deputy director of the Board on Science Education at the National Research Council. She codirected the study that produced the report *Taking Science to School: Learning and Teaching Science in Grades K-8* (2007) and served as research associate on the study that produced *America's Lab Report: Investigations in High School Science* (2005). She is currently directing a congressionally mandated review of precollege education programs at the National Aeronautics and Space Administration. Previously she worked as a senior research associate at the Institute of Education Sciences in the U.S. Department of Education, where she served as a program officer for the preschool curriculum evaluation program and for a grant program in mathematics education. She was also a liaison to the Department of Education's Mathematics and Science Initiative and an adviser to the Early Reading First Program. Previously, she was the director of research for the Rice University School Mathematics Project, an outreach program in K-12 mathematics education, and she taught in the psychology and education departments at Rice University. She has a Ph.D. in psychology (developmental) and anthropology and a certificate in culture and cognition from the University of Michigan.

**Taniesha A. Woods** (*Study Director*) is a senior program officer in the Center for Education and the Board on Children, Youth, and Families at the National Research Council and the Institute of Medicine. Her research interests include the examination of children's educational and social outcomes in an ecological systems framework. Her recent work investigates how school reform, particularly professional development, can improve the educational outcomes of children of color and those from low-income backgrounds. Previously she was a Society for Research in Child Development and American Association for the Advancement of Science congressional fellow assigned to the U.S. Senate Health, Education, Labor, and Pensions Committee and the Children and Families Subcommittee in the office of Senator Christopher Dodd, specializing in K-12 and postsecondary education issues. She has a B.A. in psychology and African and African American studies from the University of Oklahoma and a Ph.D. in developmental psychology, with a formal concentration in quantitative psychology, from the University of North Carolina, Chapel Hill.

# Index

## A

## B



## C

## D

## E



## F

## H



## I



## K



## L

## M

## N

## O



## P

## Q

## R



## S

## T